THE
DYNAMICS
OF MASS
COMMUNICATION

10TH EDITION

THE
DYNAMICS
OF MASS
COMMUNICATION
Media in the Digital Age

Joseph R. Dominick
University of Georgia, Athens

McGraw-Hill
Higher Education

Boston   Burr Ridge, IL   Dubuque, IA   New York   San Francisco   St. Louis
Bangkok   Bogotá   Caracas   Kuala Lumpur   Lisbon   London   Madrid   Mexico City
Milan   Montreal   New Delhi   Santiago   Seoul   Singapore   Sydney   Taipei   Toronto

THE DYNAMICS OF MASS COMMUNICATION: MEDIA IN THE DIGITAL AGE
Published by McGraw-Hill, a business unit of The McGraw-Hill Companies, Inc., 1221 Avenue of the Americas, New York, NY 10020. Copyright © 2009 by The McGraw-Hill Companies, Inc. All rights reserved. No part of this publication may be reproduced or distributed in any form or by any means, or stored in a database or retrieval system, without the prior written consent of The McGraw-Hill Companies, Inc., including, but not limited to, any network or other electronic storage or transmission, or broadcast for distance learning.

Some ancillaries, including electronic and print components, may not be available to customers outside the United States.

1 2 3 4 5 6 7 8 9 0 WCK/WCK 0 9 8

ISBN: 978-0-07-337883-1
MHID: 0-07-337883-6

Vice president and editor-in-chief: *Michael Ryan*
Publisher: *Frank Mortimer*
Sponsoring editor: *Suzanne Earth*
Development editor: *Phil Butcher*
Editorial coordinator: *Erika Lake*
Marketing manager: *Leslie Oberhuber*
Media project manager: *Ron Nelms*
Senior production editor: *Mel Valentín*
Production assistant: *Rachel J. Castillo*

Manuscript editor: *Thomas Briggs*
Art director: *Jeanne M. Schreiber*
Senior designer: *Preston Thomas*
Cover designer: *Preston Thomas*
Interior designer: *Amanda Kavanagh*
Design coordinator: *Margarite Reynolds*
Art editor: *Sonia Brown*
Photo research manager: *Brian Pecko*
Senior production supervisor: *Tandra Jorgensen*

The text was set in 10/12 Palatino by ICC Macmillan Inc., and printed on acid-free 45# New Era Matte by Quebecor-World.

Cover image: © Tim Robberts/Stone/Getty Images

Because this page cannot legibly accommodate all acknowledgements for copyrighted material, credits appear at the end of the book, and constitute an extension of this copyright page.

Library of Congress Cataloging-in-Publication Data

Dominick, Joseph R.
   Dynamics of mass communication : media in the digital age / Joseph Dominick. — 10th ed.
      p. cm.
   Includes index.
   ISBN-13: 978-0-07-337883-1 (alk. paper)
   ISBN-10: 0-07-337883-6 (alk. paper)
   1. Mass media. I. Title.
P90.D59 2009
302.23—dc22

2007051525

www.mhhe.com

>> For Meaghan and for Carole

>> About the Author

Joseph R. Dominick received his undergraduate degree from University of Illinois and his Ph.D. from Michigan State University in 1970. He taught for four years at Queens College of the City University of New York before going to the College of Journalism and Mass Communication at the University of Georgia where, from 1980 to 1985, he served as head of the Radio-TV-Film Sequence. Dr. Dominick is the author of three books in addition to *The Dynamics of Mass Communication* and has published more than 40 articles in scholarly journals. From 1976 to 1980, Dr. Dominick served as editor of the *Journal of Broadcasting*. He has received research grants from the National Association of Broadcasters and from the American Broadcasting Company and has consulted for such organizations as the Robert Wood Johnson Foundation and the American Chemical Society.

>> Brief Contents

>> Contents

> PART III   Specific Media Professions 297

> PART IV   Regulation of the
                 Mass Media   357

Chapter 16
Formal Controls: Laws, Rules,
Regulations   358

>> Boxed Features

Media Talk

Need a good discussion starter? These boxes refer to segments on the accompanying DVD that introduce important issues in mass communication.

Media Tour

Get a firsthand look at how various media operate and hear media professional discuss significant concerns in their fields. These boxes are also keyed to the accompanying DVD.

Social Issues

New developments in mass communication raise new concerns. These boxes explore how the media operate in a social context.

Soundbyte

These brief boxes illustrate the unusual, the ironic, and the offbeat things that sometimes occur in the media world.

>> Preface

I think I have seen the future of the mass media.

First, they will be everywhere. Entertainment and information will show up on what the industry calls multiple platforms: big screens (home TVs), medium screens (computers), and small screens (cell phones and PDAs). Newspapers and magazines will be on the Web and on cell phones. Video and audio will be available in cars, offices, homes, and airplanes and on jogging trails. "Everything everywhere" is the phrase currently being tossed around by media execs.

Second, we're going to be in control. Digital video recorders (like TiVo) and video-on-demand let us watch TV when we want to (and, if we choose, skip the commercials). News aggregators, such as Google, give us a choice of dozens of different news sources. We can download only the tracks we want to hear from iTunes. We can advertise our extra stuff in the newspaper classifieds or on sites like Craig's List, or sell it ourselves on eBay. Don't want to go out to a movie? Download it and watch it when you want.

Third, we're going to be part of them. When the first edition of *Dynamics of Mass Communication* was published (way back in 1982), professional reporters and photographers brought me the news, experts wrote the editorials, advertising practitioners made the ads, TV producers and directors made the TV shows, Hollywood advertised and promoted the motion pictures, and record companies produced the music. Now my friends and neighbors are doing all that. I can watch news clips shot by "citizen journalists," read opinions posted by the blogger down the street, watch TV shows on YouTube made by the kid next door, and download music from new bands on Facebook and MySpace. It's all part of Web 2.0, the new participatory and interactive Internet.

Fourth, the Internet will continue to disrupt everything. Indeed, this new edition might have been titled *The Disruption of Mass Communication*. Newspapers and magazines will carry on their quest to find new business models that incorporate the Web. TV networks and motion picture companies will face competition from a slew of new broadband video channels. Advertising will continue to move to the Internet, as will much of public relations. Web radio will make additional inroads on conventional radio. The sound recording industry will be totally reinvented. E-books may eventually remodel the book publishing industry.

Finally, they're all coming together. The word "convergence" has been rattling around for a while now, but in the past few years it has taken on a new urgency. Many newspapers and magazines have merged their traditional print and online divisions. Most newspapers feature video on their Web sites, and some are even presenting a newscast on a broadband channel. Television networks are posting show episodes on their Web sites and on YouTube. With Apple's iPhone you can connect to the Internet, take pictures, listen to music, check stocks, watch videos, view photos, and even call people. The computer and the TV will eventually merge into an all-purpose information utility.

Well, that's what I think is going to happen. Of course, right now some 14-year-old in a basement somewhere might be inventing something that changes things in ways that I literally can't think of. Nonetheless, the above themes are the ones that are emphasized in this 10th edition of *The Dynamics of Mass Communication*.

In that connection, once again events have shown that I was unusually prescient back in the early 1980s to include the word "dynamics" in the book's title. The media world has never been more dynamic than it is now, and I reiterate what I wrote in the preface for the 9th edition: It's important for today's students to know something about the new media environment that will confront them when they graduate, no matter what their career direction.

Speaking of careers, as most instructors will attest, the introductory media course attracts two types of students. One type is interested in following a professional career in some form of media. This student wants to know the nuts-and-bolts of the mass media—how they are organized, how they work, who does what, and what career possibilities are out there. The second type of student will probably never pursue a mass communication career but will become a member of the audience and consume a great deal of media content. These students are more interested in analyzing and understanding how the media operate and what impact they have on society. To use an overworked expression, they want to become "media literate."

The original goal of the first edition of *Dynamics* was to present an up-to-date, detailed, and comprehensive look at the contemporary media scene that would be of benefit to aspiring media professionals and at the same time provide a useful foundation of media knowledge for those who will end up in other careers. As has been the case nine times before, it is hoped that this new edition still fulfills that goal.

NEW TO THE 10TH EDITION

Prior users will note that two chapters rather than one are now devoted to television. This change was made because there is so much more television these days: YouTube, broadband channels, downloadable video, hundreds of cable and satellite networks, and so on. Accordingly, Chapter 10 is devoted to traditional broadcast television while Chapter 11 looks at cable, satellite, and Internet TV.

Further, the new material in the 10th edition amplifies the main themes discussed above while also exploring other significant developments. Some examples:

- **Multiple platforms.** Chapter 1 gives a general introduction to this trend while Chapter 3 discusses how content providers are making their products more available to cell phones and PDAs. Moreover, Chapter 4 examines how newspapers are emphasizing their Web editions and providing content to cell phone users. Similarly, Chapters 5 and 6 discuss the same trend in the magazine and book publishing industries while Chapter 8 illustrates how iPods, iTunes, and iPhones are making music more accessible. Of course, television is the best example of the move to multiple platforms, and Chapters 10 and 11 describe the efforts of TV programmers to package their shows for iPods, PCs, and broadband channels.

- **User-generated content.** The amazing success of YouTube is discussed in the new Chapter 11. Chapter 12 examines the social networking trend and the blog phenomenon while Chapter 13 looks at the growing trend of citizen journalists. Some of the legal problems of video-sharing sites are considered in Chapter 16. Web 2.0 is explained in Chapter 1 and Chapter 12. All of the chapters in Part II and Part III now have sections explaining how user-generated content is becoming important in the various media and media professions.

- **Convergence.** Chapter 1 introduces the various ways this term has been used and gives examples of each. Chapter 4 looks at the converged print and online newsroom, and Chapter 13 elaborates on the trend toward converged journalists. Chapter 11 discusses how Internet TV is bringing together the computer and the TV set.

- **Disruption.** Chapters 4–11 all detail the unsettling effect that the Internet has had on traditional media. Newspaper and magazine readers are migrating to the Web; traditional radio stations compete with Web radio; the business model in the sound recording industry has been forever changed; and TV networks and Hollywood studios are experimenting with Web delivery of TV shows and movies.

- **Issues in media performance.** Chapter 2 explores the use of social networking sites during the shootings at Virginia Tech. In that connection Chapter 17 probes the ethical problems faced by NBC News after receiving video and print materials from the shooter. Chapter 15 notes the move in advertising from traditional to new, hard-to-measure media and some of the problems encountered along the way. Chapter 16 probes the new government interest in regulating obscenity and violence, as well as looking at the concept of network neutrality and its impact on the future of the Internet. Chapter 14 delves into the use of Web 2.0 by public relations practitioners. Finally, Chapter 11 examines the growing popularity and potential of Internet TV.

Every chapter has been updated to reflect the many media-related developments since the last edition. In addition, all tables now contain the latest statistical information available.

BOX SCORE

As in past editions, the boxed inserts in each chapter provide background material or extended coverage of topics mentioned in the text and raise issues for discussion and consideration. The 10th edition includes 93 new or revised boxed inserts.

The boxes are grouped into several categories. The "Media Talk" boxes refer students to segments on the accompanying CD that introduce important issues in mass communication. Instructors can use these as discussion starters. The "Media Tour" boxes introduce clips on the CD that look at how various media operate and feature media professionals discussing significant concerns in their field. Instructors can use these segments as a general introduction to selected media chapters.

The "Social Issues" boxes highlight matters of social concern that have generated some controversy. Some examples are the social responsibilities of video game creators, the feminization of public relations, and how fraudulent clicks are hurting advertisers on the Internet.

As the name suggests, "Ethical Issues" boxes raise questions about the proper way to act in difficult circumstances. For instance, what is the appropriate way to cover war violence, how much work should be expected of converged journalists, and how much truth should be expected in a personal memoir?

"Critical/Cultural Issues" boxes illustrate how this perspective can be used to further our understanding of mass communication. Examples include the cultural influence of department stores on early radio, an analysis of the reality TV series *The Bachelor,* and a critical examination of the empirical evidence for technological determinism.

The "Media Probe" boxes take an in-depth look at subjects that have significance for the various media. Some examples include the generation gap in the use of digital media, the Internet hype surrounding the movie *Snakes on a Plane,* and the rebirth of the TV antenna.

The "Decision Maker" boxes profile individuals who have made some of the important decisions that have had an impact on the development of the media. Examples include Al Neuharth, Catherine Hughes, Steven Spielberg, and Ted Turner.

And, as before, "Soundbytes" are brief boxes that highlight some of the strange, ironic, offbeat, and extraordinary events that occur in the media.

CONTINUITY

Other than the new Chapter 11, the organization of the book has not changed from the 9th edition. Part I, "The Nature and History of Mass Communication," presents the intellectual context for the rest of the book. Chapter 1 compares and contrasts mass communication with other types of interpersonal communication. Chapter 2 introduces two perspectives commonly used to understand and explore the operations of the media: functional analysis and the critical/cultural approach. Chapter 3 takes a macro-analytic approach and traces the general history of media from the development of language to the cell phone explosion.

Part II, "Media," represents the core of the book. Chapters 4–11 examine each of the major media. The organization of each of the chapters follows a similar pattern. I start with a brief history from the media's beginnings to how it is coping with the digital age. This is followed by a section on the how the medium is becoming more mobile, how it has been affected by user-generated content, what the defining characteristics of each medium is, as well as a discussion of industry structure.

I have continued to emphasize media economics. Since the major mass media in the United States are commercially supported, it is valuable for students to appreciate where the money comes from, how it is spent, and what consequences arise from the control of the mass media by large organizations. This is even more important today as many media industries, facing traditional revenue streams that are drying up, are searching for ways to make their online efforts profitable.

Part III, "Specific Media Professions," examines three specific professions closely associated with the mass media: news reporting, public relations, and advertising. Similar to the approach used in Part II, each chapter begins with a brief history, examines the structure of that particular profession, discusses key issues in the field, and ends with a consideration of career prospects.

Part IV, "Regulation of the Mass Media," examines both the formal and informal controls that influence the media. These are complicated areas, and I have tried to make the information as accessible as possible.

The concluding Part V, "Impact," continues to emphasize the social effects of the mass media. Chapter 17, "International Mass Communication," stresses the global influence of the mass media. Chapter 18, "The Social Effects of Mass Communication," looks at the impact media have on individuals and the larger society. Some introductory texts give the impression that the effects of the media are unknown or simply matters of opinion. Granted, there may be some disagreement, but thanks to an increasing amount of research in the field, there is much that we do know. Moreover, as informed members of our society, we should have some basic knowledge of the effects of the media on our society and across the globe.

Finally, once again, I have tried to keep the writing style informal and accessible and have chosen examples whenever possible from popular culture that I hope all students are familiar with. Technical terms are boldfaced and defined in the glossary. The book also contains a number of diagrams, charts, and tables that I hope aid understanding.

SUPPORTING MATERIALS

These include the DVD, the Online Learning Center, and the Instructor's CD with test bank and slides.

ACKNOWLEDGMENTS

First, a big thanks to all those instructors who used previous editions of *Dynamics of Mass Communication* and were kind enough to suggest improvements. Several colleagues deserve special mention: Professors Kevin Williams, Scott Shamp, and Noah Arcenaux provided boxed inserts as did future-professor Paul Hillier. Professor Michael Castengera's e-newsletter, "Message from Michael," was a valuable resource, and I urge everybody to subscribe to it. Special thanks to model Aimee Douglass, photographer Carole Dominick, and researcher Meaghan Dominick.

Once again I appreciate the sedulous efforts of all the reviewers who offered suggestions for the 10th edition:

Frank A. Aycock, Appalachian State University

Donald G. Godfrey, Arizona State University

Gregory C. Lisby, Georgia State University

Robert M. Ogles, Purdue University

Zengjun Peng, St. Cloud State University

David H. Serlin, University of California at San Diego

Julie Weishar, Parkland College

And, of course, a big thanks to everybody at McGraw-Hill for their help on publishing yet another edition: to Phil Butcher, who chose to complicate a perfectly good retirement by working on this revision; to fellow Cub fan Suzanne Earth for directing the project; to Mel Valentín for handling all of the myriad details needed to get the book into print; to Tandra Jorgensen for her great handling of production issues; to

Brian Pecko for once again finding those great photos; to Emma Ghiselli for screen captures and fine-tuning the art program; to Leslie Oberhuber for her marketing efforts; to Preston Thomas for the design of the 10th edition; and to Ron Nelms for his work on the Web site for the book.

I would also like to thank Professor Rebecca Ann Lind, of the University of Illinois at Chicago, for her superb work developing the content for the Web site to accompany the 10th edition.

In closing, I hope that the 10th edition helps students (and faculty) understand the fast-changing world of mass communication a little better.

JD
Athens, Ga.

Your Guided Tour

CHAPTER 3

CHAPTER 3   HISTORICAL AND CULTURAL CONTEXT

This modern-day storyteller keeps alive the oral culture of our ancestors and introduces another generation to the art of verbal communications.

The historical and cultural contexts of media are important because history tends to be cyclical. This fact has been apparent for centuries. Many ancient civilizations relied on storytellers to hand down the history and culture of their society so that they might learn from the past. The same is true for modern society: Knowing what happened many years ago might help us understand what is going on now. For example, when radio first started in the 1910s and 1920s, its future was uncertain. Many thought radio would compete with the telephone and telegraph as a means of sending messages from point to point, while others saw radio's future in aviation, providing beacons for aircraft.

The first organization to recognize radio's importance was the military; the U.S. Navy led the way during World War I. After the war, as interest in the new medium increased, a totally new function emerged. Radio was used to broadcast information and entertainment to a mass audience. Many individuals and organizations scrambled to make use of this new means of communication: the telephone company, newspapers, businesses, and even universities. None had any clear idea how radio broadcasting would pay for itself. Eventually radio became a commercial medium, dominated by big business, that in fewer than 10 years reached an audience of 50 million. Radio changed America's news and entertainment habits and became a medium whose influence on popular culture is still being felt.

Compare radio's development with that of the Internet, which was started by the Department of Defense to improve military communication. When first developed, the Internet was envisioned as a means of point-to-point communication. It gained popularity through the efforts of scientists and amateur computer enthusiasts. When the World Wide Web and newsgroups offered a place where anyone could post messages and reach a large potential audience, businesses, educational organizations, government agencies, and individuals all scrambled to stake out a site. Everybody is currently trying to figure out how to make Web sites profitable. Will the Web eventually become primarily a commercial medium dominated by big business? (We're already seeing signs of this.) Will it change the way we get our news and entertainment? (Probably.) What sort of cultural impact will it have? (This may take a while to determine.) History may help us answer these questions.

You have probably heard the old joke about the guy who was annoyed because he couldn't see the forest because of all the trees, or couldn't see the blizzard because of all the snow, or couldn't see the city because of all the tall buildings (you probably get the idea by now). Well, sometimes it can be hard to see history because of all the names, places, dates, and events. Consequently, this chapter steps back and takes a broad view of media history, emphasizing major events and general trends. It also provides additional background information by examining communication in the days before mass communication developed.

Specifically, this chapter discusses eight milestones in the development of human communication: language, writing, printing, telegraph and telephone, photography and motion pictures, radio and television, digital media, and mobile media (see Figure 3-1). This overview of the historical and cultural context of mass communication will supplement and make more meaningful the specific histories of the various media presented in Parts II and III of this book.

Chapter-Opening Previews

Chapter objectives and vignettes draw students in and help them concentrate on the important points of each chapter.

Media Tour — Inside *Vibe*

Select the magazine media tour (DVD, Track 1) on the DVD that accompanies this text. The first part provides a look at the magazine's operations, and the second part features the staff discussing a wide range of issues.

The original strategy was for *VIBE* to be another *Rolling Stone* but with different music. *VIBE*'s timing was good: Hip-hop, one of the primary music styles covered in the magazine, was just gaining popularity among both African American and white youths. As a results, the magazine was successful in attracting readers. Its circulation grew from about 100,000 in the early

1990s to 800,000 in 2002.

1. How does the business side of a magazine influence the editorial side?
2. What kind of companies might advertise in *VIBE*?
3. How do cultural trends play into the success of a magazine such as *VIBE*?
4. If you were the publisher of *Rolling Stone*, *VIBE*'s biggest competitor, how would you respond to *VIBE*'s success? How, if at all, would you change your magazine?

Media Tours

Keyed to the companion DVD, these boxes offer focus questions for viewing video tours of different media companies.

Media Talk

Also keyed to the companion DVD, these margin notes offer focus questions for viewing NBC News videos related to chapter topics.

MEDIA TALK

"Deep Throat" and Confidential Sources

DVD, Track 36, 7:36 minutes

Bob Woodward and Carl Bernstein were two young *Washington Post* reporters who used a confidential source to report the Watergate story that eventually led to the resignation of President Richard Nixon. In this clip they discuss their role in the story and the importance of confidential sources. Should reporters have special privileges when it comes to gathering the news? Could the Watergate story have been reported without a confidential source? How many other big stories have been broken with the aid of a confidential source?

Ethical Issues · Covering a War

On October 18, 2006, the CNN program *Anderson Cooper 360* aired video footage of insurgent sniper attacks on U.S. soldiers in Iraq. The video was shot by the insurgents and included audio of the insurgents selecting their targets and praising Allah as they escaped. CNN edited the tapes so that they did not show the actual impact of the shots.

CNN's decision to air the tapes set off another round in the ethical debate over the proper way to cover a war. Critics quickly pointed out that these tapes could cause suffering and anguish for those who have had loved ones killed in the Iraq conflict. In addition, some charged that by airing the tapes CNN was giving a public relations boost to the enemy and might even encourage more sniper attacks. Several bloggers pointed out that the footage was shown only weeks before an important midterm election and accused CNN of using these tapes to influence the results. Some even criticized CNN for not showing the impact of the shots and for sanitizing the gory effects of war.

CNN's decision to air the tape was the subject of a long post in Anderson Cooper's 360 blog by David Doss, the program's executive producer. Doss acknowledged that the footage would be disturbing and that it might prove beneficial to the insurgents in their recruiting efforts. Despite this, he argued, the tape met CNN's criteria for newsworthiness. American deaths in October, 2006, had shown a significant increase, and many of them were due to sniper attacks. The tapes were a vivid reminder of the horrors of war. He also noted that CNN had tried to put the piece in context by interviewing military experts and that the network had aired a warning to viewers before showing the tape. Doss concluded that it was always CNN's goal to present "the unvarnished truth."

Doss's explanations did little to quiet the controversy. A number of bloggers noted that there were times when CNN had no problems shying away from the unvarnished truth. The network refrained from showing people leaping from the World Trade Center during the 9/11 terrorists attacks, nor did it show some of the atrocities during the regime of Saddam Hussein for fear of losing access to stories from Iraq. Others questioned whether it was necessary to show graphic video in order to remind people that war is horrible. As one blogger put it, "It serves no purpose. . . . Do you really need to see some kid get shot to be informed [that war is horrible]?"

The role that economics played in this controversy is unknown. At the time that this story aired, rival Fox had more than 1.5 times the prime-time audience of CNN. Airing a sensational exclusive story would undoubtedly reduce that margin. One would hope, however, that such considerations would not enter into the journalism decision-making process.

Ethical Issues

These boxes challenge students to think critically about ethical issues specific to mass communications industries.

Social Issues · Diversity in Television

Social Issues

New developments in mass communication raise new concerns. These boxes explore how the mass media operate in a social context.

Kweisi Mfume, president of the NAACP, speaking at his organization's national convention, criticized the four major TV networks for the lack of diversity in the new shows planned for the 1999–2000 season. He noted that none of the 26 series had a minority person in a leading or starring role. Mfume's criticism marked another chapter in the continuing controversy over the portrayals of minorities in prime time.

During the early years of TV, African American performers were difficult to find. And when they did appear, it was usually in a menial or subservient role. In 1965, however, a young Bill Cosby costarred with Robert Culp in *I Spy* and paved the way for more substantial roles for African American performers. By the 1970s several shows that featured black casts appeared in prime time—most were situation comedies, such as *The Jeffersons.* The number of African American performers increased slowly but steadily during the 1980s. For most of the 1990s, the proportion of black characters seen in prime-time TV was about the same as the percentage of African Americans in the general population. This increase, however, was due in part to the emergence of UPN and WB, two networks that targeted several of their series to African American viewers.

The apparent lack of diversity in the 1999–2000 season was especially troubling to Mfume. The NAACP noted that minorities were hard to find behind the camera as well. Of all the writers who worked on TV sitcoms and dramas, only 6 percent were black. FCC data show that minorities own about 2.8 percent of all broadcast stations.

Mfume threatened a boycott of the networks and their sponsors unless something was done. The networks responded by adding some minority characters to the casts of existing shows. CBS aired *City of Angels,* a drama set in an inner-city hospital, that featured a predominantly black cast and creative team. The networks also planned to increase minority hiring and to appoint executives in charge of their diversity efforts. These moves apparently satisfied Mfume, who called off plans for the boycott.

The 2000–2001 TV season did not spark similar protests. In addition to *City of Angels,* there were several new series with African Americans in major roles, such as *Boston Public.* The situation behind the camera and in minority ownership, however, was unchanged. Things improved a bit in the 2002 season when there were 43 series featuring multiethnic characters. Back in 1995, there were only 13 such shows on the air.

The diversity issues surfaced again in 2003, but this time the focus was on cable. Members of the Congressional Black Caucus sent a letter to the cable TV industry asking for more minority-themed programs and more minority-owned cable networks. It resurfaced when the NAACP noted that none of the situation comedies scheduled by the major networks for the 2006 season starred an African American actor or actress.

Why should the networks present a diverse view of society? Many would argue that the networks have a social obligation to present an accurate view of society so that members of minority groups do not feel marginalized or disenfranchised from society. Others would suggest that TV should present role models for all groups. These high-minded reasons aside, it also makes economic sense for the networks to present a diverse menu of programs. The 2000 census showed that minorities constitute more than 35 percent of the U.S. population, and their buying power is increasing each year. Presenting shows that appeal to these groups is simply good business.

Further, some critics suggest that paying large amounts of attention to the way the broadcast networks portray minorities overlooks the gains minorities have made in cable. For instance, Black Entertainment Television draws a significant audience. Two Spanish-language networks, Galavision and Univision, are aimed at Hispanics.

Finally, consider the opinion of commentator Earl Ofari Hutchinson, who suggests that prime-time TV is not worth fighting for. He charges that the networks have oversaturated the airways with silly sitcoms and action shows designed to appeal to young, affluent whites. These types of programs, he argues, have no relevance for African Americans, who should focus their attention elsewhere. In a similar vein Cynthia Tucker, the African American editor of the editorial page of the *Atlanta Constitution,* suggests that the NAACP is misplacing its efforts by concentrating on network TV programs. Instead, she argues, the organization should encourage young African Americans to stop watching TV. "Let prime-time TV keep its bland cast of characters," says Tucker. "There are plenty of good books in which black youngsters can find themselves reflected."[1]

---

[1] Quoted in Richard Breyer, "Color TV," *Word and I,* March 2000, 84.

Decision Makers

Profiles of people who have had a significant impact on contemporary mass media.

Decision Makers Judy McGrath

For many of you reading this, Judy McGrath would seem to have the ultimate dream job: She is the president of the MTV Networks Music Group and is responsible for MTV, MTV2, VH1, CMT, and all of the company's digital media services. Under her direction MTV has grown from a small niche cable network to an international brand that symbolizes a unique attitude and lifestyle.

Always a music fan, McGrath first tried to get a job writing for *Rolling Stone*. When her efforts proved unsuccessful, she turned to writing advertising copy and then went to work for *Mademoiselle* and *Glamour*. In 1981 she heard about a new cable channel launched by Warner Entertainment that would be devoted to rock music. Despite the fact that she could not even get the channel on her home TV, McGrath joined the newly created MTV as a copywriter and on-air promotion person. (She was one of the ones responsible for using all the space film footage to promote the channel.) To the surprise of many people, MTV was successful in attracting 16- to 24-year-olds, an audience coveted by advertisers. MTV became part of the huge Viacom conglomerate, and McGrath quickly moved up the ranks to creative director, executive vice president, and eventually chair and chief executive at MTV Networks. Under her direction MTV expanded all over the world.

When the music video novelty began to wear off in the mid-1980s and ratings started to sag, McGrath introduced programs that became popular culture icons: *Beavis and Butt-Head, The Real World, The MTV Music Awards, MTV Unplugged,* and *Total Request Live.* She also introduced political coverage to MTV and was instrumental in the development of the 1992 *Choose or Lose* get-out-the-vote campaign. More recently, McGrath has led MTV into other media: movies, books, and the Internet.

What does she see in MTV's future? Since a high proportion of MTV viewers are also Web surfers and spend a good deal of time on MTV.com, look for more integration of the music on MTV and MTV2 with the Web site. MTV.com will be used to highlight some of the artists or genres featured on the cable channels. In addition, plans are underway for more international expansion, particularly in Asia. Finally, it is likely McGrath will continue to provide special programming that deals with important social issues, such as the 17 hours the channel devoted to hate crimes. And, of course, there will always be music videos.

Media Probes

Additional illustrations, examples, and background to chapter topics.

Media Probe Hype on a Plane

In 1999 *The Blair Witch Project*, a low-budget, independently produced horror/suspense movie starring unknowns, surprised Hollywood by racking up $140 million in box office sales. The movie's success was attributed in large part to a marketing campaign that used the then relatively new Internet to generate interest (or "buzz," as it's known in the trade) about the film. *The Blair Witch Project* skillfully used online sites to make people wonder if the movie was actually a true story. By the time the movie appeared, it had a ready-made audience waiting to see it.

Hollywood executives thought that this new form of online promotion would revolutionize movie marketing. Generate a strong buzz on the Internet, and the studio's marketing job would be done for them. The Internet was a new path to movie profits.

In the post-*Witch* years the Internet proved to be a valuable, if not revolutionary, marketing tool for motion pictures. But nothing ever approached the *Blair Witch* phenomenon—nothing, that is, until the 2006 thriller *Snakes on a Plane* (or *SoaP,* as it was quickly dubbed by its online fans).

Once news got out that New Line Cinema was interested in making a movie with *SoaP*'s wonderfully succinct and evocative title, the Internet community responded with an enthusiasm not seen since *Blair Witch.* Bloggers and other movie fans created slogans, designed T-shirts, created parodies, and even suggested dialogue for the finished film (some online suggestions for dialogue were, in fact, written into the film). With anticipation this high, how could *SoaP* not be a blockbuster?

Well, it wasn't. The film opened with a disappointing take of $15.2 million, far from blockbuster status. After 3 weeks *SoaP* had made only a little more than $30 million worldwide and was well on it way to slithering into the video store where, it was hoped, it would do better. (The production/distribution/marketing costs of the film were probably around $50 million, meaning *SoaP* might eventually turn a profit, but it will be far less than *Blair Witch*.)

How come *Blair Witch* was so successful while *SoaP* flopped? Analysts suggested several reasons. First, the Internet was just gaining popularity in 1999, and for most it was still a novelty. Seven years later, audiences were aware that marketers were using the net as a promotional tool and so may have been more likely to be skeptical of the latest hype. Second, by the time the film came out, perhaps people had had their fill of all of the hoopla. Or perhaps the Internet-savvy crowd who originally touted the film simply downloaded it from BitTorrent or some other site and avoided the theater altogether.

Whatever the reason, Hollywood still can't figure out the Internet. Maybe it's not the great marketing tool that everybody thought it was.

Critical/Cultural Issues

These boxes illustrate the critical/cultural studies approach to mass communication in action.

CRITICAL / CULTURAL ISSUES

The Meaning of Media

Cell phones, laptops, and PDAs belong to that broad class of devices known as *mobile information devices*. It's possible, however, that lumping these devices under one umbrella label may obscure differences in the way audience members perceive their functions. Communication scholars point out that communication technologies may be socially constructed in different ways by their users.

In an article in the June 2003 issue of *Critical Studies in Mass Communication*, Paul Leonardi argues that culture plays a major role in how media are perceived. Leonardi conducted focus groups (structured group interviews guided by a moderator) among Latinos living in the United States. He asked participants to discuss how cell phones, computers, and the Internet were perceived in Latino culture.

His results were somewhat surprising. Latino culture places a high value on consistent and close interpersonal contact, and the cell phone was seen as consistent with that value. Focus group participants revealed that the cell phone was an important tool for communication and was becoming a necessity for daily life. More than 90 percent of respondents had used a cell phone. Almost all of those who didn't currently own a cell phone planned to buy one within a year. Respondents recognized the utility of the cell phone in an emergency and the fact that cell phones represent an alternative way of reaching someone when the land lines are busy. Cell phones had become so ingrained in their daily lives that some participants mentioned that their children used cell phones to call them from another room in the house to ask what was being prepared for dinner. In short, the cell phone fit nicely with cultural values.

On the other hand, computers and the Internet were not such a good fit. Only 40 percent of the respondents had used a computer, and even fewer (27 percent) had ever used the Internet. Respondents appeared to think of computers and the Internet in same way, treating them as similar. They did not see the Internet as a communication medium. Instead, the Latinos in these focus groups perceived it as a tool with which to find information. The use of e-mail, chat rooms, and message boards as communication channels was seldom mentioned. Although computers were perceived as useful devices, they were also seen as inhibiting interpersonal communication among family members and friends. Surfing the Internet was perceived as a solitary activity that isolated people from each other. In short, respondents felt that computers and the Internet did not keep people connected. As a result, interpersonal values were jeopardized by these technologies.

Language also played a role in participants' preference for the cell phone over the computer. Spanish-language cell phones are readily available; Spanish-language computer platforms are harder to find. In addition, only a small portion of Internet content is in Spanish. This posed a cultural problem for Latinos. In order to access the Internet, it was necessary to forgo the use of one's native language.

Although many of the respondents said that they planned to purchase a computer in the near future, their stated reasons for buying a computer had nothing to do with the computer's communication potential. Instead, the Latinos in Leonardi's study recognized that those who didn't have a computer would be in an inferior position to those in mainstream U.S. culture.

Leonardi's findings highlight that Latinos living in the United States do not view these information devices as homogeneous. Instead, they have distinct perceptions based on how cell phones, computers, and the Internet relate to their cultural values regarding communication. As Leonardi sums up: "[T]he communication goals of a particular group of users always play a crucial role in their uses and perceptions of technology. If we forget this, we may blindly adopt technologies because we believe they are a sign of progress without making sure they help us progress."

Full Range of Chapter Review Material

Clear, concise chapter summaries, key terms lists, and review questions provide students with essential study materials.

THE CABLE/SATELLITE AND INTERNET INDUSTRIES

The cable/satellite industry is relatively small, employing about 90,000 people, far fewer than the number who work in traditional broadcasting. Nonetheless, the career outlook appears more positive in this area than in some of the traditional media that we have discussed. There are hundreds of cable/satellite networks now in operation and probably more to come. The industry will need more people in production, performance, publicity, marketing, and community relations.

As with the broadcast industry, newcomers should not be afraid to start at the bottom and work their way up the organization. Likewise, your first job in this area may not last long. Be prepared to move on to other opportunities as they become available.

Moreover, the explosion of broadband channels has opened up new career opportunities, especially for those with a creative bent (see the boxed insert "Breaking into TV Has Never Been Easier"). Finally, the online video surge has produced a number of jobs that didn't exist a few years ago. After all, somebody has to decide what videos to feature on the site's home page; somebody has to sell advertising; somebody has to make sure the system works correctly; and so on.

MAIN POINTS

- Cable TV began in the 1950s as a way of bringing TV signals to places that could not otherwise receive them.
- Cable TV reached maturity by the turn of the century and was facing competition from DBS satellite systems.
- The Telecommunications Act of 1996 permitted cable and telephone companies to compete with one another.
- Internet TV developed in the late 1990s and became more popular with the growth of broadband.
- Cable and satellite systems are structured differently from those of conventional TV.

- Cable television is dominated by large multiple system operators. Two companies, DirecTV and the Dish Network, are the leading DBS providers.
- Internet video can be categorized by source (professional or amateur) and content (original or repurposed).
- User-generated video, such as those on YouTube, has become extremely popular.
- Internet video sites make money by charging a fee for their content or by selling advertising.
- Nielsen provides rating data for cable/satellite networks. Ratings for online video sharing sites are provided by companies that measure Internet usage.

QUESTIONS FOR REVIEW

1. What are the defining features of cable/satellite TV? Of Internet TV?
2. Who are the major owners of cable and DBS systems?
3. How does cable/satellite programming compare to traditional broadcast network programming?
4. Trace the structure of a cable system from head end to home.
5. How can online video sites make money?

QUESTIONS FOR CRITICAL THINKING

1. How, if at all, will VOD change the cable TV industry?
2. Have you ever posted a video online? Why? Have you ever looked at online videos? Why?
3. Google paid $1.65 billion for YouTube. Do you think Google will get its money back?
4. Why do you think many presidential candidates opted to make their announcements using online video as opposed to a press conference?

KEY TERMS

multiple system operators (MSOs) (p. 259)
direct-broadcast satellites (DBS) (p. 259)
voice-over-Internet protocol (VOIP) (p. 259)

Internet TV (p. 260)
buffering (p. 260)
podcast (p. 260)
head end (p. 263)
distribution system (p. 263)
house drop (p. 263)

carriage fee (p. 265)
video-on-demand (VOD) (p. 265)
geosynchronous satellite (p. 266)
encrypted (p. 266)
microcasting (p. 270)

INTERNET RESOURCES

Online Learning Center

At the Online Learning Center home page, www.mhhe.com/dominick10, select Student Center and then Chapter 11.

1. Use the Learning Objectives, Chapter Outline, Main Points, and Time Line sections to review this chapter.
2. Test your knowledge of the chapter using the multiple choice, crossword puzzle, and flashcard features of the site.
3. Expand your knowledge of concepts and topics discussed in the chapter by going to Suggestions for Further Reading and Internet Exercises.

Surfing the Internet

http://wedcast.istreamplanet.com/lwc/whitechapel.asp
The Little White Wedding Chapel in Las Vegas has live and on-demand videos of their weddings.

www.blinx.tv
Example of a video-sharing site that mixes professional and amateur content.

www.historychannel.com
Has more about history than it does about the cable network, but contains good examples of streaming video and interactivity.

www.multichannel.com
Multichannel News is the leading trade publication covering cable, satellite, and wireless companies.

www.ncta.com
Web site of the National Cable Television Association. Contains information about the latest issues facing the industry.

Springboards for Discussion and Research

Critical thinking questions based on the text and Internet resources engage students with issues affecting them as consumers and future professionals.

THE DYNAMICS OF
Mass Communication
Media in the Digital Age
Tenth Edition
Joseph R. Dominick

Information Center

Overview
Feature Summary
New to this Edition
Supplements
Table of Contents
Book Preface
About the Author
Sample Chapter

Online **LearningCenter**

Student Edition
Instructor Edition

Dynamics of Mass Communication: Media in the Digital Age, 10/e

Joseph R. Dominick, University of Georgia

ISBN: 0073378836
Copyright year: 2009

Well-known for its balanced approach to media industries and professions, *Dynamics of Mass Communication* offers a lively, thorough, and objective introduction for mass communication majors and nonmajors alike. This new edition embraces the digital age and brings students up-to-date on the latest developments in mass communication, including iPods, blogs, broadband TV channels, user-generated content such as YouTube, social networking sites, and Web 2.0.

To obtain an instructor login for this Online Learning Center, ask your local sales representative. If you're an instructor thinking about adopting this textbook, request a free copy for review.

©2009 McGraw-Hill Higher Education
Any use is subject to the Terms of Use and Privacy Policy.
McGraw-Hill Higher Education is one of the many fine businesses of The McGraw-Hill Companies.

Online Learning Center, www.mhhe.com/dominick10

This book-specific Web site features practice tests, media timelines, learning objectives, chapter main points, key terms and timelines, suggestions for further reading, and an online glossary. For the instructor, the password-protected area of the Web site offers a teaching guide, detailed chapter summaries, and PowerPoint slides.

Media World DVDs

Packaged with the book, the DVD features videos and study tools that enhance the text.

The MediaWorld DVD contains six exclusive Media Tour videos that provide an inside look at the day-to-day operations and issues facing real media organizations.

The MediaWorld DVD includes 29 Media Talk videos from the NBC News archives. In these segments, media experts give their opinions on matters of current debate and controversy.

PART I

THE NATURE AND HISTORY OF MASS COMMUNICATION

CHAPTER 1

COMMUNICATION: MASS AND OTHER FORMS

This chapter will prepare you to

- recognize the elements of the communication process

- understand the different types of communication settings

- identify the function of gatekeepers

- describe how the Internet has changed mass communication

- explain the various types of mass media convergence

- understand the implications of the trend toward audience segmentation

In addition to all of its other destruction, Hurricane Katrina illustrated the vulnerability of modern mass media.

We live in a golden age of communication. Modern communication technology keeps everybody connected 24/7 and makes information immediately available anytime and anywhere. Need to get in touch with someone? Use a cell phone or a PDA, or send an e-mail or instant message or even a fax. Need to find out what's going on in the world? Read a newspaper or magazine, or tune in a TV or radio newscast, or check out a news site on the Web on your computer or cell phone. Most of us simply take modern communication technology as a given. We are so used to sending messages when we want and receiving information when we want that we never give it a second thought.

Except when it doesn't work.

Hurricane Katrina slammed into the Gulf Coast near New Orleans around 6:10 A.M. local time on August 29, 2005. Later that day, several levees holding back the waters of Lake Pontchartrain gave way, and much of New Orleans was flooded. By the time it was over, the death toll from Katrina in New Orleans and the Gulf Coast was more than 1,800. Total damage was in the neighborhood of $80 billion. Another major casualty of the storm was the modern communication system that we take for granted. In short, New Orleans and Gulf Coast residents were pummeled back to an age in which modern communication technology didn't exist.

One of Katrina's first victims was the phone system. Cell phones proved especially vulnerable. High winds knocked down towers, but the biggest problem was the lack of electrical power. Although cell phones could connect to a local tower, communication from one tower to another was carried underground via wires or fiber optics, a process that requires electricity. When the generators went down and the backups ran out of fuel, the cell phone system was virtually useless.

Wired phones were also hard hit. Poles blew down, and water flooded underground lines and computerized routing equipment. Bell South estimated that more the 1.75 million phone lines lost service. The few lines that still operated were overwhelmed by the volume of calls.

The Internet didn't fare much better. As power failed, computers shut down. Laptops lasted a little while longer, but their batteries eventually failed. Internet traffic was down by more than 90 percent in New Orleans the day after the storm. In the rest of the Gulf Coast area, Internet traffic was so slight that it couldn't be measured. A few people lucky enough to find places where emergency power was available and where they could connect to the Internet started blogs that gave eyewitness accounts of Katrina's impact. Desperate for any shred of information, evacuees and other people nationwide turned to these blogs for details about storm damage and the status of friends and relatives.

The traditional media also fell victim to Katrina. More than a quarter-million homes in New Orleans lost cable service as power failed, lines blew down, and distribution equipment flooded. Those with cable modems also lost their Internet connection. Only one New Orleans radio station was able to stay on the air, thanks to an emergency studio that happened to be on dry ground. People with battery-powered radios were able to get some information, at least until the batteries ran out. In a desperate effort to stay informed, one New Orleans resident ripped out the radio and battery from her partially submerged auto and took them to her roof as she waited for help.

Television stations shared a similar fate. All were knocked off the air and forced to move to safer ground. Several were able to begin broadcasting again, but without power few people in the affected areas were able to get any information from their reports.

Publishing a newspaper proved nearly impossible. Louisiana's largest paper, the *Times-Picayune,* saw its printing plant submerged in water. While a skeleton crew remained in New Orleans city, most of the staff set up shop in Baton Rouge. The *Times-Picayune* did manage to publish an online edition, but once again, the lack of power meant that few people in the hardest-hit areas were able to see it. The Web site was valuable, however, to out-of-towners seeking news about the disaster.

As a result, the people who most needed information about the hurricane were those who were least likely to get it. And when information is in short supply, rumors spread rapidly. TV and radio stations reported cars being hijacked at gunpoint, babies being murdered in the Superdome, and snipers shooting at rescue helicopters. None of these proved true.

Katrina also highlighted communication problems among emergency responders. Incompatible radio equipment meant that the National Guard, police, and government agencies couldn't talk to one another. The many downed radio towers further limited the available channels, which quickly became overloaded with messages. The Federal Emergency Management Association tried to alleviate the problem by providing satellite phones, but these were complicated to operate and had a short battery life. In rural areas rescue personnel had to depend on old-fashioned ham radio operators to relay their messages.

People were forced to stand on rooftops and hold signs that they hoped passing rescue helicopters would see. The emergency personnel in the copters wrote replies on paper, put them in bottles, and dropped them to the people below. Evacuees spray-painted messages that they were OK on the plywood boards that covered windows and doors. The police and the National Guard were reduced to using foot messengers to communicate with one another.

In the case of New Orleans and the Gulf Coast, it took a major hurricane to immobilize modern technology and disrupt communication. In other cases it takes far less. Communication between people is a fragile thing, made even more fragile when technology is involved. The following examples are not as tragic as those that occurred with Katrina, but they are still illustrative:

- In Arizona an officer in a county sheriff's department pushed the wrong key while sending e-mail and sent a report on terrorist activity that was stamped "Do NOT release to the public or media" to all the media in the southern part of the state.

- A million Honda owners' manuals listed a phone number that was supposed to direct callers to a government hotline. Regrettably, the number on the manual was prefaced with an 800 prefix rather than an 888, and callers were connected to a sex talk line.

- In Georgia the e-mail spam filter for the Cobb County school system blocked the lowest bid for new telephone services. The county wound up spending an extra $250,000 by going with another company whose bid was higher.

- A computer error at the company that published the alumni directory for the University of New Hampshire mistakenly listed 500 very much alive alumni as dead.

- The National Weather Service was conducting an internal test of its tsunami warning system when somebody punched the wrong button and the warning message was broadcast on TV and radio stations along the Oregon coast. Hotels and high schools were in the middle of evacuating before the mistake was discovered.

- An Oregon man was surprised when a group of police and search-and-rescue personnel knocked on his apartment door. It seems his new flat-screen TV set was emitting an international distress signal that was picked up by a satellite and relayed to local officials.

- In Sweden a TV anchor for a news channel was embarrassed while doing a live report when one of the monitors in the background was tuned to a wrong channel and started playing a porn movie.

- About 240,000 subscribers to the *Boston Globe* and *Worcester Telegram and Gazette* were shocked to find that a computer error caused their names and credit card numbers to be printed on the back of the paper used to wrap newspaper bundles.

- In Canada a bank mistakenly sent hundreds of faxes containing confidential information about its customers to a junkyard operator in West Virginia.

Despite their apparent lack of similarity, these examples share certain elements common to human communication. They serve as a springboard for an examination of the differences between mass and other forms of communication.

THE COMMUNICATION PROCESS

Figure 1-1 depicts the communication process. We will refer to this figure as we examine the process more fully.

▲ Encoding: Transmitting the Message

To begin with, the **source** initiates the process by having a thought or an idea that he or she wishes to transmit to some other entity. Naturally, sources differ in their communication skills ("Garçon, I will have the Boeuf Haché Grillé au Charbon de Bois" versus "Gimmeaburger"). The source may or may not have knowledge about the receiver of the message. As I write these lines, I have only a general notion about the kinds of people who will read them, and I have no idea what you'll be doing while you're reading them (that's probably for the best). Sources can be single individuals, groups, or even organizations.

Encoding refers to the activities that a source goes through to translate thoughts and ideas into a form that may be perceived by the senses. When you have something to say, your brain and your tongue work together (usually) to form words and spoken sentences.

FIGURE 1-1 Elements of the Communication Process

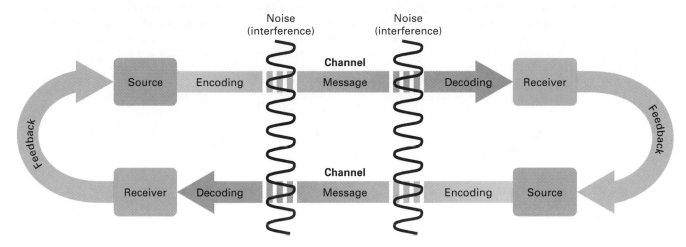

When you write a letter, your brain and your fingers cooperate to produce patterns of ink or some other substance that can be seen on paper. Encoding in a communication setting can take place one or more times. In a face-to-face conversation, the speaker encodes thoughts into words. Over the telephone, this phase is repeated, but the phone subsequently encodes sound waves into electrical energy.

The **message** is the actual physical product that the source encodes. When you talk, your speech is the message. When you write a letter home, what you put on the paper is the message. When a television network presents *Lost* or *24*, the programs are the message. Human beings usually have a large number of messages at their disposal that they can choose to send, ranging from the simple but effective "No!" to something as complicated as Darwin's *On the Origin of Species*. Messages can be directed at one specific individual ("Dude!") or at millions (*People* magazine). Messages can be cheap to produce (the spoken word) or very expensive (this book). Some messages are more under the control of the receiver than others. For example, think about how hard or easy it is for you to break off communication (1) in a face-to-face conversation with another person, (2) during a telephone call, and (3) while watching a TV commercial.

Channels are the ways the message travels to the receiver. Sound waves carry spoken words; light waves carry visual messages. Air currents can serve as olfactory channels, carrying messages to our noses—messages that are subtle but nonetheless significant. What kind of message do you get from someone who reeks of Chanel No. 5? Of Brut? Of garlic? Touch is also a channel (such as braille). Some messages use more than one channel to travel to the receiver. For example, radio signals travel by electromagnetic radiation until they are transformed by receiving sets into sound waves that travel through the air to our ears.

▲ Decoding: Receiving the Message

The **decoding** process is the opposite of the encoding process. It consists of activities that translate or interpret physical messages into a form that has eventual meaning for a receiver. As you read these lines, you are decoding a message. If you are playing the radio while decoding these lines, you are decoding two messages simultaneously—one aural, one visual. Both humans and machines can be thought of as decoders. The radio is a decoder; so is a DVD playback unit; so is the telephone (one end encodes and the other end decodes); so is a film projector.

A single communication event can involve many stages of decoding. A reporter attends a city council meeting and takes notes on a laptop (decoding), and then writes a story and sends it to an editor who reads (decoding) and edits it. Eventually, it is published and read by an audience (decoding). What we said earlier about encoding also applies to decoding: Some people are better at it than others. Many of you will not be able to decode "¿Dónde está el baño?"; others will. Some people are able to read 1,500 words a minute; others struggle along at 200.

The **receiver** is the target of the message—its ultimate goal. The receiver can be a single person, a group, an institution, or even a large, anonymous collection of people. The receivers of the message can be determined by the source, as in a telephone call, or they can self-select themselves into the audience, as with the audience for a TV show. It should also be clear that in some situations the source and receiver can be in each other's immediate presence, while in other situations they can be separated by both space and time.

▲ Feedback

Now let us examine the bottom half of Figure 1-1. This portion of the figure represents the potential for **feedback** to occur. Feedback refers to those responses of the receiver that shape and alter the subsequent messages of the source. Feedback represents a reversal of the flow of communication. The original source becomes the receiver; the original receiver becomes the new source. Feedback is useful to the source because it allows the source to answer the question "How am I doing?" Feedback is important to the receiver because it allows the receiver to attempt to change some element in the communication process. Communication scholars have traditionally identified two different kinds of feedback—positive and negative. In general terms, positive feedback from the receiver usually encourages the communication behavior in progress; negative feedback usually attempts to change the communication or even to terminate it.

Carrie Underwood's "Before He Cheats" contains several examples of negative feedback.

Consider the following telephone call:

"Bambi?"

"Yes."

"This is Harold. I sit in front of you in econ class."

"Are you the one who keeps scratching your head with a pencil?"

"Gee, I never noticed it. I guess I do it unconsciously. Say, I was wondering if you would like to have coffee with me sometime after class."

"Are you kidding?"

Click.

This is *negative* feedback—the original receiver terminated the message. Here is another conversation:

"Bambi, this is Rod."

"Oh, hi, Rod. Has your leg healed up from the last game yet?"

"Yeah."

"How are your classes going?"

"I can't get econ."

"I'll be over in 20 minutes to give you some help. OK?"

"OK."

Click.

This is *positive* feedback—the original receiver encouraged the communication.

Feedback can be immediate or delayed. Immediate feedback occurs when the reactions of the receiver are directly perceived by the source. A speech maker who hears the audience boo and hiss while he or she is talking is getting immediate feedback. On the other hand, suppose you just listened to the latest CD by a popular group and decided it wasn't very good. To communicate that evaluation to the source, you would first have to identify the company that distributed the CD and find a mailing address, phone number, e-mail address, or Web site address. You would then have to send your feedback via the appropriate channel. If you got your message through to the company, it would still have to be passed on to the group, a process that might take several days or even longer.

▲ Noise

The final factor we will consider is **noise.** Communication scholars define *noise* as anything that interferes with the delivery of the message. A little noise might pass unnoticed, while too much noise might prevent the message from reaching its destination. There are at least three different types of noise: semantic, mechanical, and environmental.

Semantic noise occurs when different people have different meanings for different words and phrases or when the arrangement of words confuses the meaning. If you ask a New Yorker for a "soda" and expect to receive something that has ice cream in it, you'll be disappointed. The New Yorker will give you a bottle of what is called "pop" in the Midwest. An advertising copywriter penned the following slogan for a cough syrup company: "Try our cough syrup. You will never get any better." An article in a college newspaper included the following: "A panel of representatives from the sports world met to discuss performance-enhancing drug use at the Journalism School last night."

Noise can also be mechanical. This type of noise occurs when there is a problem with a machine that is being used to assist communication. A TV set with a snowy picture, a pen running out of ink, and a static-filled radio are all examples of mechanical noise.

A third form of noise can be called environmental. This type refers to sources of noise that are external to the communication process but that nonetheless interfere with it. Some environmental noise might be out of the communicator's control—the noise at a restaurant, for example, where the communicator is trying to hold a conversation. Some environmental noise might be introduced by the source or the receiver; for example, you might try to talk to somebody who keeps drumming her or his fingers on the table.

As noise increases, message fidelity (how closely the message that is sent resembles the message that is received) goes down. Clearly, feedback is important in reducing the effects of noise. The greater the potential for immediate feedback—that is, the more interplay between source and receiver—the greater the chance that noise will be overcome.

COMMUNICATION SETTINGS

▲ Interpersonal Communication

Having considered the key elements in the communication process, we next examine three common communication settings, or situations, and explore how these elements vary from setting to setting. The first and perhaps the most common situation is **interpersonal communication**, in which one person (or group) is interacting with another person (or group) without the aid of a mechanical device. The source and receiver in this form of communication are within each other's physical presence. Talking to your roommate, participating in a class discussion, and conversing with your professor after class are all examples of interpersonal communication.

The source in this communication setting can be one or more individuals, as can the receiver. Encoding is usually a one-step process as the source transforms thoughts into speech and/or gestures. A variety of channels are available for use. The receiver can see, hear, and perhaps even smell and touch the source. Messages are relatively difficult for the receiver to terminate and are produced at little expense. In addition, interpersonal messages can be private ("Whassup?") or public (a proclamation that the end of the world is near from a person standing on a street corner). Messages can also be pinpointed to their specific targets. For example, you might ask the following of your English professor: "Excuse me, Dr. Iamb, but I was wondering if you had finished perusing my term paper?" The very same message directed at your roommate might be put another way: "Hey, Space Cadet! Aren't you done with my paper yet?" Decoding is also a one-step process performed by those receivers who can perceive the message. Feedback is immediate and makes use of visual and auditory channels. Noise can be either semantic or environmental. Interpersonal communication is far from simple, but it represents the least complicated setting.

▲ Machine-Assisted Interpersonal Communication

Machine-assisted interpersonal communication (or technology-assisted communication) combines characteristics of both the interpersonal and mass communication situations. The growth of the Internet and the World Wide Web has further blurred the boundaries between these two types of communication. This section focuses on those situations that are closer to the interpersonal setting. The next section examines how the computer and the Internet have redefined many of the features of mass communication.

In the machine-assisted setting, one or more people are communicating by means of a mechanical device (or devices) with one or more receivers. One of the important characteristics of machine-assisted interpersonal communication is that it allows the source and receiver to be separated by both time and space. The machine can give a message permanence by storing it on paper, disk, or some other material. The machine can also extend

Microsoft's Bill Gates uses machine-assisted communication to get his point across at the annual meeting of the World Economic Forum. *(Raymond Reuter/Sygma)*

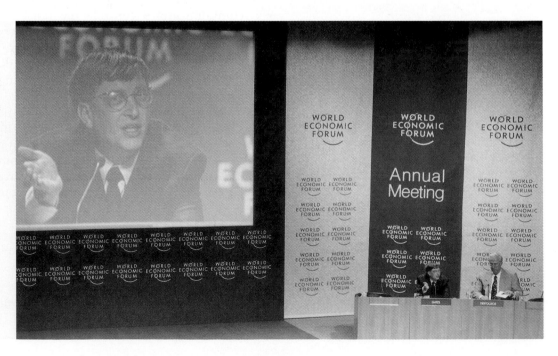

the range of the message by amplifying it and/or transmitting it over large distances. The telephone, for example, allows two people to converse even though they are hundreds, even thousands, of miles apart. A letter can be reread several years after it was written and communicate anew.

A tremendous variety of modern communication falls into this category. Here are some diverse examples of machine-assisted communication:

- E-mail allows people to send messages across the country in a matter of seconds.
- People get money from automatic teller machines by inserting a magnetic card and following the machine's instructions.
- An American inventor has developed a video-equipped tombstone that houses a computer with a microchip that enables it to show a video message prerecorded by the grave's occupant.
- In Berlin the trash bins play a recorded thank-you message every time someone throws rubbish into them.

The source in the machine-assisted setting can be a single person (as in the e-mail example) or a group of people (as in the trash bin example) who may know the receiver (e-mail) or not have firsthand knowledge of the receiver (the automatic teller example).

Encoding in this setting can be complicated or simple, but there must be at least two distinct stages. The first occurs when the source translates his or her thoughts into words or symbols. The second occurs when one or more machines encode the message for transmission or storage. When you speak on the telephone, for example, you choose and pronounce your words (stage 1), and a machine converts them into electrical impulses (stage 2).

Channels are more restricted in the machine-assisted setting. Whereas interpersonal communication can make use of several channels simultaneously, machine-assisted settings generally rely on only one or two. E-mail, for instance, relies on sight; a phone call uses electrical energy and sound waves.

Messages vary widely in machine-assisted communication. They can be tailor-made for the receiver (such as e-mail) or limited to a small number of predetermined messages that cannot be altered once they are encoded (the automatic teller can't comment on your new haircut). Messages in this setting can be private or public and relatively cheap to produce.

Decoding can go through one or more stages, similar to the encoding process. Reading a letter requires only one stage, but reading e-mail requires two: one for the computer to decode electrical energy into patterns of light and dark, and another for your eyes to decode the written symbols.

The receiver in this setting can be a single person, a small group, or a large group. Receivers can be in sight of the source or out of view. They can be selected by the source (as with a phone call) or self-select themselves into the audience (as when taking a pamphlet from somebody on the street).

Feedback can be immediate or delayed. A band playing at a concert will hear the audience applaud following a song. A band that provides streaming audio of a new song on its Web site might have to wait for days to see if people liked it. In many situations feedback is limited to one channel, as in a phone conversation. In some situations feedback can be difficult if not impossible. If the automatic teller gives you a message that says, "Insufficient funds," you cannot tell it, "I just made a deposit this morning. Look it up."

Noise in the machine-assisted setting can be semantic and environmental as in interpersonal communication, but it can also be mechanical. Interference with the message might be due in part to difficulties with the machine involved.

In the future, machine-assisted communication will become more important. New mobile media, such as cell phones, personal digital assistants, and laptop computers, will become more and more popular and continue to expand the scope and impact of personal communication (see Chapter 3). The Internet may come to function more as an aid to interpersonal communication than as a mass medium (see Chapter 12). Finally, the differences between machine-assisted communication and mass communication will continue to blur.

▲ Mass Communication

The third major communication setting is the one that we will be most interested in. The differences between machine-assisted interpersonal communication and mass communication are not that clear. **Mass communication** refers to the process by which a complex organization with the aid of one or more machines produces and transmits public messages that are directed at large, heterogeneous, and scattered audiences. There are, of course, situations that will fall into a gray area. How large does the audience have to be? How scattered? How heterogeneous? How complex must the organization be? For example, suppose a billboard is constructed on a busy street in a small town. Obviously, this would qualify as machine-assisted communication (a machine was used to print the billboard), but is this better defined as mass communication? An automatic letter-writing device can write thousands of similar letters. Is this mass communication? There are no correct answers to these questions. The dividing line between machine-assisted interpersonal communication and mass communication is not a distinct one.

The line is even less distinct when the Internet and the Web are considered. Take an e-mail message, for example. It can be addressed to one person, much like machine-assisted interpersonal communication, or it can go to thousands, a situation closer to mass communication. Or take the case of a chat room where one person might be communicating with dozens of others. If two people want more privacy, they can move to a "private" room, a situation that resembles machine-assisted interpersonal communication. On the other hand, feedback in the chat room is limited, a feature of mass communication. The usual clues from personal appearance, facial expressions, tone of voice, and gestures are not present.

Source   Until the advent of the Internet and the Web, the source in the traditional mass communication situation was typically a group of individuals who acted in predetermined roles in an organizational setting. In other words, mass communication was the end product of more than one person's efforts. For example, think about how a newspaper is put together. Reporters gather news; writers draft editorials; a cartoonist draws an editorial cartoon; the advertising department lays out ads; editors lay out all these elements on a sample page; technicians transfer this page to a master; other technicians print the final paper; the finished copies are given to the delivery staff; and, of course, behind all this is a publisher who has the money to pay for a building, presses, staff, trucks, paper, ink, and so on. This institutional nature of mass communication has several consequences that we will consider later in this book.

The advent of Internet-based mass communication changes this situation. Thanks to the World Wide Web, one person can become a mass communicator. The full implications of this change may take some time to become clear.

For both traditional and Internet-based mass communication, the source usually has little detailed information about its particular audience. The author of a Web site has little detailed information about individuals who visit the site. Traditional mass media may have collective data, but these are typically expressed as gross audience characteristics. The newspaper editor, for example, may know that 40 percent of the readers are between 25 and 40 years old and that 30 percent earn between $20,000 and $50,000, but the editor has no idea about the individual tastes, preferences, quirks, or identities of these people. They are an anonymous group, known only by summary statistics.

Encoding/Sending   Encoding in mass communication is always a multistage process. Suppose a film producer has an idea. He or she explains it to a screenwriter. The writer goes off and produces a script. The script goes to a director, who translates it for the camera. Cinematographers capture the scenes on film. The raw film goes to an editor, who splices together the final version. The film is copied and sent to theaters, where a projector displays it on the screen, where the audience watches it. How many examples of encoding can you find in that oversimplified version of moviemaking?

Mass communication channels are characterized by the imposition of at least one, and usually more than one, machine in the process of sending the message. These machines

E-mail is fast and environmentally friendly; it uses no paper, and vehicles burn no gasoline delivering the message. It is no wonder, then, that American businesses send billions of e-mail messages every year.

translate the message from one channel to another. Television makes use of complicated devices that transform light energy into electrical energy and back again. Radio does the same with sound energy. Unlike interpersonal communication, in which many channels are available, mass communication is usually restricted to one or two.

Decoding/Receiving Messages in mass communication are public. Anyone who can afford the cost of a newspaper or a CD player or a TV set can receive the message. Additionally, the same message is sent to all receivers. In a sense, mass communication is addressed "to whom it may concern." Of all the various settings, message termination is easiest in mass communication. The TV set goes dark at the flick of a switch; an automatic timer can turn off the radio; the newspaper is quickly put aside. There is little the source can do to prevent these sudden terminations other than bullying the audience ("Don't touch that dial!") or trying to stay interesting at all times ("We'll be back after these important messages").

Mass communication typically involves multiple decoding before the message is received. The CD player decodes patterns of light waves into sound waves for our hearing mechanism. The TV receiver decodes both sight and sound transmissions.

Receiver One of the prime distinguishing characteristics of mass communication is the audience. First, the mass communication audience is a large one, sometimes numbering in the millions of people. Second, the audience is also heterogeneous; that is, it is made up of dissimilar groups who may differ in age, intelligence, political beliefs, ethnic backgrounds, and so on. Even in situations where the mass communication audience is well defined, heterogeneity is still present. (For example, consider the publication *Turkey Grower's Monthly*. At first glance, the audience for this publication might appear to be rather homogeneous, but upon closer examination we might discover that members differ in intelligence, social class, income, age, political party, education, place of residence, and so on.) Third, the audience is spread out over a wide geographic area; source and receiver are not in each other's immediate physical presence. The large size of the audience and its geographic separation both contribute to a fourth distinguishing factor: The audience members are anonymous to

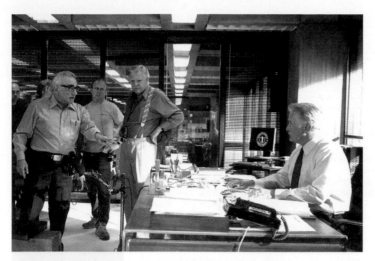

Encoding at the movies. Director Martin Scorcese directs Martin Sheen in a scene from *The Departed*. A motion picture goes through several stages of encoding before it gets to the audience: concept, story, script, filming, and editing.

one another. The person watching the *CBS Evening News* is unaware of the several million others in the audience. Lastly, in keeping with the idea of a public message, the audience in mass communication is self-defined. The receiver chooses which film to see, which paper to read, which Web site to visit, and which program to watch. If the receiver chooses not to attend to the message, the message is not received. Consequently, the various mass communication sources spend a great deal of time and effort to get your attention so that you will include yourself in the audience.

Feedback   Feedback is another area where there are differences between interpersonal and mass communication. The message flow in mass communication is typically one-way, and feedback, in many instances, is more difficult than in the interpersonal setting. This situation, however, is rapidly changing because of the Internet. Newspapers often include e-mail addresses of reporters to encourage reader feedback. Producers of TV shows scan Web sites and blogs to glean the latest reaction to their episodes. Systematic, large-scale feedback conducted by media research companies, such as the Audit Bureau of Circulations for newspapers and MRI for magazines, tends to be more delayed, but there are exceptions. Nielsen Media Research, for example, provides overnight ratings for network TV shows.

Noise   Finally, noise in the mass communication setting can be semantic, environmental, or mechanical. In fact, since there may be more than one machine involved in the process, mechanical noise can be compounded (as when watching a scratchy copy of an old film on a snowy TV set).

Table 1-1 summarizes some of the differences among the three communication settings that we have talked about.

TABLE 1-1

Differences in Communication Settings

Element		Settings		
		Interpersonal	Machine-Assisted Interpersonal	Mass
	Source	Single person; has knowledge of receiver	Single person or group; has great deal of knowledge or no knowledge of receiver	Organizations or single person; has little knowledge of receivers
	Encoding	Single stage	Single or multiple stage	Multiple stages
	Message	Private or public; cheap; hard to terminate; altered to fit receivers	Private or public; low to moderate expense; relatively easy to terminate; can be altered to fit receivers in some situations	Public; can be expensive; easily terminated; same message sent to everybody
	Channel	Potential for many; no machines interposed	Restricted to one or two; at least one machine interposed	Restricted to one or two; usually more than one machine interposed
	Decoding	Single stage	Single or multiple stage	Multiple stages
	Receiver	One or relatively small number; in physical presence of source; selected by source	One person or small or large group; within or outside physical presence of source; selected by source or self-defined	Large numbers; out of physical presence of source; self-selected
	Feedback	Plentiful; immediate	Somewhat limited; immediate or delayed	Highly limited; usually delayed
	Noise	Semantic; environmental	Semantic; environmental; mechanical	Semantic; environmental; mechanical

▲ Defining Mass Media

In the broadest sense of the word, a *medium* is the channel through which a message travels from the source to the receiver ("medium" is singular; "media" is plural). Thus in our discussion we have pointed to sound and light waves as media of communication. When we talk about mass communication, we also need channels to carry the message. **Mass media** are the channels used for mass communication. Our definition of a mass medium will include not only the mechanical devices that transmit and sometimes store the message (TV cameras, radio microphones, printing presses) but also the institutions that use these machines to transmit messages. When we talk about the mass media of television, radio, newspapers, magazines, sound recording, and film, we will be referring to the people, policies, organizations, and technologies that go into producing and distributing mass communication. A **media vehicle** is a single component of the mass media, such as a newspaper, radio station, TV network, or magazine.

In this book we will examine eight different mass media: radio, television, film, books, sound recordings, newspapers, magazines, and the Internet. Of course, these eight are not the only mass media that exist. Billboards, comic books, posters, direct mail, matchbooks, and buttons are some other kinds of mass media one could choose to examine. The eight types of media we have chosen, however, have the largest audiences, employ the most people, and have the greatest impact. They are also the ones with which most of us are most familiar.

CHARACTERISTICS OF TRADITIONAL MASS MEDIA ORGANIZATIONS

Since a large portion of this book will examine the institutions that are in the business of mass communication, it will be to our advantage to consider some common characteristics that typify mass communicators. This task has been made more complicated by the emergence of the computer and the Internet as communications media. Internet mass communication is distinctly different from the traditional forms of mass communication. We will first explore the salient characteristics of traditional mass communicators and then examine how communication on the Internet has blurred the established definition of mass communication sources. Here are the five traditional defining features:

1. Mass communication is produced by complex and formal organizations.
2. Mass communication organizations have multiple gatekeepers.
3. Mass communication organizations need a great deal of money to operate.
4. Mass communication organizations exist to make a profit.
5. Mass communication organizations are highly competitive.

Getting past the gatekeepers in network television is difficult. ABC's hit series *Desperate Housewives* was first turned down by HBO, CBS, NBC, Fox, Showtime, and Lifetime.

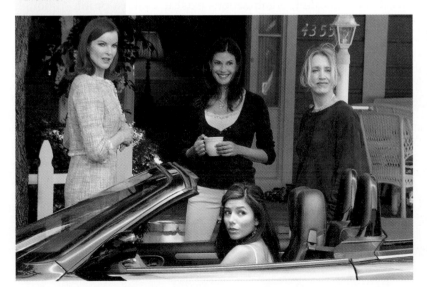

▲ Formal Organizational Structure

Publishing a newspaper or operating a TV station requires control of money, management of personnel, coordination of activities, and application of authority. Accomplishing all these tasks requires a well-defined organizational structure characterized by specialization, division of labor, and focused areas of responsibility. Consequently, traditional mass communication is the product of a bureaucracy. As in most bureaucracies, decision making takes place at several levels of management, and channels of communication within the organization are formalized. Thus, many of the decisions about what gets included in a newspaper or in a TV program, for instance, are made by committees or groups. Further, decisions are made by several individuals in ascending levels of the bureaucracy, and communication follows predetermined and predictable patterns within the organization. This results in end products that seldom resemble the original idea of the creator.

▲ Many Gatekeepers

Another important factor that characterizes the traditional mass communicator is the presence of multiple **gatekeepers.** A gatekeeper is any person (or group) who has control over what material eventually reaches the public. Some gatekeepers are more obvious than others, such as the editor of a newspaper or the news director at a TV station. Others are less visible. To illustrate, in the newsroom an assignment editor decides whether to send a reporter to cover a certain event. The reporter then decides if anything about the event is worth reporting. An editor may subsequently shorten the story, if submitted, or delete it altogether. Obviously, gatekeepers abound in mass communication. The more complex the organization, the more gatekeepers that will be found.

▲ Large Operating Expenses

It costs a lot of money to start a mass communication organization and to keep it running. A private investor group bought the Spanish-language TV company Univision for $13.6 billion. Another private group offered $18.7 billion for radio giant Clear Channel. Rupert Murdoch's News Corporation bought Dow Jones & Company, publisher of the *Wall Street Journal*, for $5 billion.

Once the organization is in operation, expenses are also sizable. In the early 2000s it cost approximately $4–5 million annually to run a small daily newspaper (one with a circulation of about 35,000–40,000). A radio station in a medium-sized urban market might spend upward of $700,000 annually in operating expenses. A TV station in one of the top 10 markets might need more than $10 million per year to keep going. Only those organizations that have the money to institute and maintain these levels of support are able to produce mass communication.

Media economics have contributed to another trend that made itself evident by the end of the 20th century: consolidation of ownership. Companies that have strong financial resources are the likeliest to survive high operating expenses and are better able to compete in the marketplace. Consequently, by 2007 a number of global media giants had emerged to dominate the field. Table 1-2 lists these "megamedia" companies; these names will turn up frequently in succeeding chapters.

▲ Competition for Profits

In the United States mass communication organizations exist to make a profit. Although there are some exceptions (the Public Broadcasting Service, for example), most newspapers, magazines, record companies, and TV and radio stations strive to produce a profit for their owners and stockholders. And while radio and TV stations are licensed to serve

TABLE 1-2 Global Media Giants	Company (home country)	2005 Revenue (in billion U.S. dollars)*
	Time Warner (United States)	$43.6
	Walt Disney Co. (United States)	34.3
	Sony** (Japan)	34.1
	News Corp. (United States)	25.7
	Vivendi (France)	23.8
	Comcast (United States)	22.3
	Bertelsmann (Germany)	21.2

*To give some perspective to these data, General Motors' revenue for the same period was $193 billion; General Electric's was $150 billion.
**Includes only revenue from media divisions.

The rather ungraceful, tongue-twisting word **disintermediation** refers to the process whereby access to a product or a service is given directly to the consumer, thus eliminating the intermediary, or "middleman," who might typically supply the product or service. The Internet and the World Wide Web have created a ubiquitous and easily accessible network through which buyers and sellers make direct contact. The Internet has already provided several examples of disintermediation: Travelers bypass travel agents and book airline tickets directly online; traders bypass brokers and purchase stocks directly online; consumers bypass salespeople and buy insurance online. (Some businesses have more to fear from disintermediation than others. For example, it's unlikely that consumers will bypass restaurants because of the Internet.)

Disintermediation is of obvious concern to mass media organizations. Those media that can easily be distributed over the Internet are the first to feel its effects. Take sound recording, for example: An artist can use the Web to distribute a CD directly to consumers; the recording company, distributor, and retailer are no longer needed in the process. Or consider book publishing: An author can put a book directly on a Web site for readers to download, thereby bypassing publishing companies and bookstores altogether.

Other mass communication organizations that do not have the immediate fears of the recording and publishing industries still have to face the implications of this phenomenon. For example, audience members can listen to radio on the Web; local stations are no longer necessary. Before long, movie fans will be able to download current full-length films onto DVDs. Will motion picture theaters become obsolete? The chapters in Parts II and III of this book will have more to say about disintermediation and its impact on the various media.

the public interest, and newspapers commonly assume a watchdog role on behalf of their readers, if they do not make money, they go out of business. The consumer is the ultimate source of this profit. When you buy a CD or a movie ticket, part of the price includes the profit. Newspapers, TV, magazines, and radio earn most of their profits by selling their audiences to advertisers. The cost of advertising, in turn, is passed on by the manufacturers to the consumer. The economics of mass communication is an important topic, and we will explore it later in this book.

Since the audience is the source of profits, mass communication organizations compete with one another to attract an audience. This should come as no surprise to anyone who has ever watched television or passed a magazine stand. The major TV networks compete with one another for ratings, spending millions of dollars each year to promote the new fall season. Radio stations compete with other stations that have similar formats. Record companies spend large sums promoting their records, hoping to outsell their competitors. Daily newspapers compete with weeklies and with radio and television. Motion picture companies gamble millions on films to compete successfully. This fierce competition has several consequences, and we will return to this topic time and again.

THE INTERNET AND MASS COMMUNICATION

The emergence of the Internet has created a new channel for machine-assisted and mass communication. (Chapter 11 offers a more detailed look at the Internet.) As we have seen, e-mail and chat rooms are examples of machine-assisted communication via the Internet. The World Wide Web brings the Internet into the realm of mass communication and reverses the traditional pattern of one-to-many communication. Web sites offer everybody the *chance* to become mass communicators; mass communication is never guaranteed, but the potential is there.

This situation is possible because the Internet brings down the cost of mass communication to a level at which almost anybody can afford it. A single individual can create and maintain a Web site for a relatively small sum. The affordability of this channel can make anybody an electronic publisher with access to a potential audience of millions, thus creating a whole new type of mass communicator.

These new Web communicators represent exceptions to the five characteristics of mass communication sources listed on page 13. First, Web sites can be produced by single individuals; there is no need for a large staff. Second, many Web sites bypass gatekeepers, a

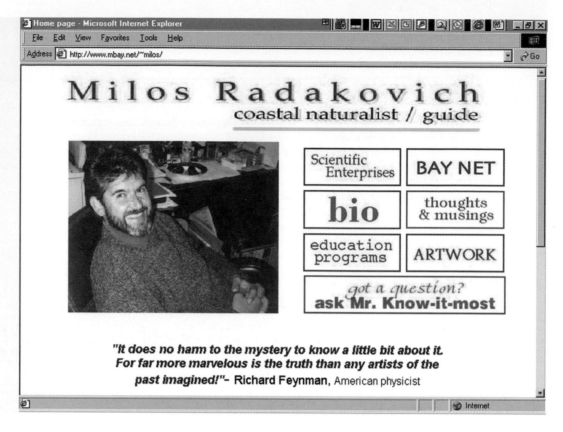

The World Wide Web has changed the nature of mass communication: Anybody can imitate Milos Radakovich and become a mass communicator. Yahoo! has a listing of more than 20,000 personal pages such as this one.

circumstance that has both positive and negative consequences. (On the one hand, individuals have the freedom to post whatever they want to without fear that somebody will censor or alter the content. On the other hand, there's no guarantee that what is made available will be accurate or worthwhile. Rumors, conspiracy theories, and truly tasteless content abound on the Internet. There are no editors to sort out the credible from the bizarre or to distinguish merit from trash.) Third, as already noted, start-up and operating costs for Web sites are not typically high. Fourth, although many companies have started Web sites to make a profit, many others have no such motivation. Some Web sites apparently exist to serve the public or to gain attention and prestige for their owners. Fifth, competition for an audience may be typical of many commercially sponsored Web sites, but there are many others for which competition is not a factor.

Note that just because the Internet gives everybody the chance to become a mass communicator doesn't mean that everybody who puts up a Web site is automatically engaging in mass communication. If nobody visits the Web site, no mass communication takes place. The fact that Uncle Harold publishes a Web page does not necessarily mean that Uncle Harold is on the same level as Time Warner as a mass communicator. True, both Uncle Harold and Time Warner face the same challenges—creating Web content that people want to see, persuading them to visit the site, and convincing them to return—but Time Warner has far more resources with which to meet the challenges. In short, the potential to be a mass communicator exists for everybody, but actually becoming one is difficult.

In addition, the Internet seems to be evolving into more of an interpersonal than a mass medium. There are, of course, many Web sites that fit the criteria of traditional mass communication (CNN.com, ESPN.com, usatoday.com), but consider the operations that have been most successful on the Internet (blogs, eBay, Facebook and MySpace, e-mail, Skype and other Napster-like file sharing programs). All of them are examples not so much of mass communication as of machine-assisted interpersonal communication involving targeted communications between single individuals (such as writing on "the wall" in Facebook) or among small groups of people (such as the common interest groups on Facebook).

In addition, none of these endeavors was started by a big media company (although big media bought in when these sites became successful).

Many media professionals have predicted that traditional media content (TV, movies, sound recording, newspapers, and magazines) will eventually morph into digital form and be distributed via the Internet, making the Net the single most important channel of mass communication. We are already seeing the beginnings of this trend with iTunes and TV networks making their programs available on their Web sites and movie companies testing new ways to deliver movies to home computers. There are dangers, however, associated with this development. If we come to depend too much on the Internet, what happens if a natural disaster (such as Katrina) or human-made calamity (such as a terrorist attack) disables the system? Will we be thrust into the situation faced by the Katrina victims?

Whatever its ultimate use, the Internet has prompted mass communication scholars (and textbook writers) to rethink conventional definitions and categories of mass communication. This new channel has also necessitated fresh models to describe the mass communication process, a topic that we will turn to next.

MODELS FOR STUDYING MASS COMMUNICATION

The traditional model of mass communication was a "one-to-many" model. It suggested that information from the environment (both news and entertainment) is filtered through a mass media organization (newspaper, TV network, movie studio) where it is decoded, interpreted, selected, and finally encoded into a message that is reproduced many times over and distributed through the appropriate channel. For example, newspaper reporters cover events and encode stories that are evaluated by editors (gatekeepers) to see if they should make it into that day's edition of the paper.

Once through the gate, the paper is reproduced and physically distributed to readers. The readers, the receivers of the message, decode and interpret the message. Some audience behavior, (buying a product, watching a TV show, subscribing to a magazine) is monitored by the media organization and is used as feedback to help shape future messages. Under the traditional model there is little direct interaction between sources and receivers.

Figure 1-2 is a rough attempt to represent Internet communication, a new arrangement that makes possible several different levels of communication: one source communicating with one receiver (e-mail), one source communicating with many receivers (CNN.com), a few sources communicating with a few receivers (chat rooms, blogs), and many sources communicating with many receivers (eBay).

Note that in this simplified model content is provided not only by organizations but also by individuals. In this circumstance there are no organizational gatekeepers. A single individual performs the decoding, interpreting, and encoding functions. Also note that Figure 1-2 is not a one-way model. Communication doesn't proceed from left to right but flows inward. The traditional mass communicator no longer necessarily initiates the process. Instead, it is possible for the receiver to choose the time and manner of the interaction. Suppose you want to find out what happened in a game involving your favorite baseball team that went into extra innings and finished late at night. With the traditional media you have to wait for a newspaper to be published or for your favorite TV station, cable network, or radio station to report the score. With the Internet you can visit a sports news Web site and find the information immediately. Furthermore, if you want to know more, you can visit your team's Web site for more details and check message boards for the reactions of others to the outcome. In short, the audience member has more control of the process.

Another area of contrast between the traditional and Internet models is that the messages that flow to each receiver are not identical. For example, you have many different choices about what you can use as your starting page when you access the Internet. In addition, it's possible to customize the information you receive. Excite, for example, offers many different configurations that allow you to choose specific sports scores, news

FIGURE 1-2

Internet Mass
Communication Model

headlines, stock market reports, weather forecasts, and entertainment news. Each receiver can customize the information that he or she receives. Some writers have characterized the traditional mass communication model as a "push" model (the sender pushes the information to the receiver), whereas the Internet model is a "pull" model (the receiver pulls only the information that he or she wants).

Finally, Figure 1-2 shows that both individuals and organizations are linked through a computer-mediated environment. This makes interaction and feedback much easier. The online magazine Slate.com, for example, has a site titled "Enter the Fray," where readers can comment on stories in the magazine. This environment allows people and organizations to be linked in unprecedented ways, in totally new forms of interaction. The auction site eBay joins buyers and sellers all over the world. The newsgroup humanities.classics brings together people who were probably never aware of one another and lets them talk about Descartes and Wagner. The Internet links producers and customers and makes e-commerce possible (see Chapter 11). All in all, the new model, incomplete as it might be, suggests a new way of conceptualizing communication in the age of the Internet.

MODERN MASS MEDIA: EMERGING TRENDS

As media continue to evolve, several trends are already apparent: (1) audience segmentation, (2) convergence, (3) increased audience control, (4) multiple platforms, (5) user-generated content, and (6) mobile media. We will present a brief discussion of each term below, and subsequent chapters will point out additional examples.

▲ Audience Segmentation: The End of Mass Communication As We Know It?

Media audiences are becoming less "mass" and more selective. For example, in the 1930s nearly everybody tuned their radios to *Amos 'n' Andy*. Today the top-rated radio station in a major market is lucky if it captures 10 percent of the audience. In the 1950s *I Love Lucy* was a top-rated TV show with about 50 percent of viewers tuning in. In the 1980s *The Cosby Show* was number one with about a 33 percent share, and in 2007, top-rated *CSI* got about 13 percent.

About three out of every four adults read a newspaper in the 1960s; today that's down to about one out of two. *Reader's Digest* had a circulation of 18 million in 1976; today it's down to around 10 million.

All of these numbers illustrate the segmentation or fractionalization of the mass audience. What are some of the reasons for this change? First, for many in today's audience, time has become a scarce commodity, with much of it devoted to commuting, working, and child rearing. All of this means less available time for media, and when audience members do spend time with the media, they tend to look for content geared to their special interests.

Second, there are more media today to choose from: From just three TV networks in the 1950s to hundreds of cable and satellite channels, as well as DVDs, video games, and YouTube; from single-screen movie theaters to 18-screen multiplexes and movies on demand; and from a dozen or so local radio stations to hundreds of channels on satellite radio. Finally, advertisers have turned from mass to target marketing, paying a premium to reach those people most likely to buy their product or service. The ultimate consequence of all these factors is that the audience for any single media vehicle is reduced.

Does all this mean that *mass communication* is no longer a meaningful term? Should this book be titled *The Dynamics of Segmented Communication?* Well, not quite yet. First, the definition of *mass communication* given earlier still applies. Complex organizations still use machines to transmit public messages aimed at large, heterogeneous, and scattered audiences. Audiences are still large (even a flop TV show can reach 4 million households), scattered, and heterogeneous enough to justify using the term *mass communication*. Second, the channels of mass communication are unchanged, although there are more and more mass media using these channels: about 13,000 radio stations today compared with half that number a couple of decades ago, more than 3,000 new magazines in the past decade, hundreds of TV stations, and so on. The messages sent by these mass media through the channels of mass communication have become more specialized. Magazines, newspapers, radio, TV, and Web sites are aiming their content at more defined audience niches, in part to meet the demands of advertisers and in part because it's more cost-efficient. Consequently, it's harder for any one media vehicle to reach a large number of audience members. Nonetheless, the potential is still there for the right message in the right medium to transcend the limits of specialized content and to attract a mass audience in the broadest sense of the term. This happened, for example, with *Titanic*, the coverage of the 9/11 attacks, *American Idol*, and Super Bowl XLI. Obviously, although the content of the media has become more specialized, the potential for reaching a mass audience still exists.

▲ Convergence

The dictionary defines *convergence* as the process of coming together or uniting in a common interest or focus. Convergence is not a new idea (some past examples are sporks, clock radios, and brunch), but the word has enjoyed renewed popularity in recent years and has become the centerpiece in discussions about future trends in mass communication. It is a difficult term to discuss, however, because it has been used to refer to several different processes.

At one level it refers to **corporate convergence.** This trend started in the 1980s with synergy. Companies that were content providers, such as movie studios and record labels, acquired distribution channels such as cable TV. As digital technologies emerged, synergy turned into convergence, a vision of one company delivering every service imaginable.

The long tail theory was popularized by Chris Anderson of *Wired Magazine*. To understand its implications, take a look at the accompanying figure. Those readers who have taken an economics course will recognize it as a basic demand curve. Sales are measured on the vertical axis, and products on the horizontal. The part of the curve to the left of the dotted line represents products that are big sellers; the part of the curve to the right of the dotted line (the tail of the curve) represents all those products that sell only a little.

The Long Tail

Traditionally, media companies concentrated on the left part of the curve—the blockbuster movies, the platinum albums, the best-selling books. However, as Anderson points out, the new technologies, particularly the Internet, have made it easier for audience members to find niche products, items that a relatively small number of people demand.

For example, a traditional brick-and-mortar music store is limited by physical size and shelf space. Accordingly, it only stocks those CDs that are likely to sell in large numbers (the left part of the curve). CDs that only a few people want to buy aren't profitable; their shelf space is better occupied by more copies of a (potential) hit. With online merchants, however, physical space is not a problem. They can stock many thousands of titles (Amazon.com's virtual inventory consists of nearly 4 million books) and let customers browse their offerings online. If items are stored digitally, the cost of storing

huge numbers is practically nothing. The iTunes inventory, for example, can theoretically run into the millions of songs, and there might be only a small demand for each of them. This means that the right side of the curve is theoretically infinite. Anderson suggests that merchants such as iTunes, Amazon .com, and Netflix can make just as much money (if not more) from sales on the right side of the curve as they can from the left. In short, rather than selling one song to a million people, iTunes can sell a million different songs to one person each.

Interestingly, this revenue distribution is already taking shape. Amazon.com has reported that less popular books already make up about 25 percent of its sales. Rhapsody, the online music company, makes 40 percent of its revenue from songs that wouldn't be stocked at Target or Wal-Mart.

The social and cultural implications of this trend are still unclear. On the one hand, there is more choice and more diversity available for audience members. Whereas the music-buying public was once restricted to what was on the shelves of the major retailers, now there is music to be downloaded to fit every conceivable taste and niche. When only three TV networks existed, entertainment had to be crafted to fit the lowest common denominator. As cable, satellite, and the Internet emerged as alternate channels of video, producers created programs that appealed to smaller groups, such as travel fans and devotees of courtroom drama. On the downside there may be the problem of having too much choice. How does a consumer decide which one of a 100,000 movies to view? Will the browsing take more time than the actual viewing. There is also the problem of the loss of a common culture, something that everybody shares and can relate to and talk about. If everybody is wrapped up in his or her niche, there may be little left that draws us together.

(For more information on long tail theory, see Chris Anderson's book *The Long Tail: Why the Future of Business Is Selling Less of More*. As of 2007 its sales ranking on Amazon .com was 289 out of nearly 4 million books. That puts it firmly in the left side of the curve.)

The early years of the new century saw several attempts at corporate convergence, but most were unsuccessful. For example, the merger between "old" media Time Warner and "new" media AOL didn't fulfill expectations. In France the convergence between "new" media company Vivendi and "old" media Universal Studios and Universal Music failed. In 2005 Viacom "de-converged," spinning off "old" media CBS, Infinity Radio, and a publishing house into a separate company while keeping "new" media MTV networks and a home video company.

Will corporate convergence reemerge when most Americans are connected to the Internet via broadband? Maybe, but for now the trend in corporate circles seems more toward divergence than convergence.

Another type of convergence is **operational convergence.** This occurs when owners of several media properties in one market combine their separate operations into a single effort. For example, in Florida, TV station WFLA, the *Tampa Tribune*, and TBO.com operate a converged news department. In Lawrence, Kansas, convergence occurred when the Lawrence *Journal-World* combined the news reporting functions of the paper, the paper's Web site, and its local cable news channel. All in all, an estimated 50 examples of this kind of convergence are currently under way. And if cross-media ownership rules are relaxed, this trend may accelerate.

The advantages of this type of convergence are obvious. It saves money because, rather than hiring a separate news staff for each medium, an operation can have the same reporters produce stories for the paper, Web site, and TV station. In addition, each medium can promote its partners. For instance, the TV newscast can encourage readers to visit the Web site or the print newspaper.

There are, of course, disadvantages as well. Reporters require additional training to master various media. This has generated some controversies among print reporters who are not eager to become "backpack journalists" (see Chapter 12) and carry around video cameras and audio recorders as part of their reporting tools. Further, many critics worry that converged operations mean fewer independent and diverse forms of journalism. Some conclude that, although operational convergence may be good for the media companies, it may not be good for consumers. In any case, the jury is still out on the merits of operational convergence.

Finally, what may be the most important type of convergence is **device convergence,** combining the functions of two or three devices into one mechanism. Apple's new iPhone, for example, is a phone, an MP3 player, and a camera, and it can connect to the Internet. Apple has also announced a device that will allow consumers to download movies to their computers and display them on their big-screen TVs. The latest model video game platforms can also play DVDs. Some cell phones incorporate navigation systems. Experts predict that eventually the home PC will converge with the TV set in one information appliance that will include e-mail, phone, Internet, DVD playback, and TV functions. Of course, the fact that the functions of more than one device can be combined doesn't mean that consumers will buy it. (There probably isn't much demand, for example, for a combination cell phone/electric razor.) In addition, there is always the danger that convergence will result in a piece of equipment that is too complex for consumers to operate.

Device convergence is manifesting itself in yet another way. All media seem to be converging on the Internet as a major channel of distribution. Newspapers and magazines have online editions. Music downloads are fast replacing CDs as the preferred delivery method. TV networks are making their episodes available for downloading as well as starting their own broadband channels. Movies and even books are also available in digital download forms.

▲ Increased Audience Control
The following is from the March 28, 2005, edition of the trade journal *Advertising Age:* "[We are] in an era in which the consumer controls his or her media. From the Internet to the

Apple iPod to digital radio to a dizzying array of mobile devices, technology has handed the public the power to choose the exact nature of their entertainment" (p. 20). And, as the writer might have added, the power to choose their information.

Audience members are more in charge of what they want to see and/or hear and when they want to do it. Let's take television as an example. For many years viewers had to watch programs broadcast by local stations and the major networks according to the media's schedule. However, recent technological advances have given more power to the consumer. The VCR allowed time shifting, or recording a program to be viewed at a more convenient time. Remote controls made it easier for viewers to select what they wanted to watch. Cable and satellite channels offered hundreds of new viewing opportunities. Home video gave individuals the chance to make their own videos. In the past few years, digital video recorders (DVRs) such as TiVo have made time shifting easier and more efficient. Viewers can pause live TV, fast-forward through commercials, and store up to 80 hours of programming. Many cable companies now offer video on demand, enabling viewers to select content that they can watch at their convenience. In short, power has shifted from the source to the receiver.

The same trend is apparent in news. For many decades most Americans were dependent on the news provided by their local newspaper or TV network. Today audience members can choose from 24-hour cable news networks, Internet sites such as CNN.com that are devoted to news, and sites such as Google News that aggregate news from many different sources. If an audience member is not content with the traditional news outlets, she or he can read one of the hundreds of blogs that discuss news events.

Until recently, consumers were forced to buy recorded music packaged according to the wishes of industry executives. If an audience member wanted to buy just one or two songs by an artist, he or she was out of luck. The consumer had to buy an entire album. The success of Napster and other filesharing programs clearly demonstrated that individuals were not satisfied with that arrangement. The music industry was slow to respond, but now consumers can download individual tracks from iTunes and other online sources.

Before the Internet consumers with something to sell had to rely on the local newspaper's classified ad section. Now they can create their own ads on eBay or Craigslist. Similarly, employers once had to depend on the "Help Wanted" section of the paper. Now, however, they can scan the résumés of hundreds of potential employees on Monster.com.

Subsequent chapters will contain other examples of this trend, but by now the point is probably clear: The audience is gaining more control over the mass communication process.

▲ Multiple Platforms

"Everything. Everywhere": This has been the mantra at many media companies as they try to adapt to the changing world of media technology. The strategy is to make content available to consumers using a number of delivery methods to a number of receiving devices (or multiple platforms in the industry jargon).

Music videos may be the best illustration of this trend. For many years music video fans had to be content watching videos on MTV, VH1, Fuse, or one of the other cable/satellite networks. Then Yahoo! Music and other Web sites began streaming music videos. In 2005 consumers watched 4 billion clips on the Yahoo! site. Recording companies realized that consumers were watching more videos on their computer screens than on their TV screens. Apple's video iPod and cell phones opened up other possibilities. Today music videos still run on traditional TV screens, but the record labels have also struck deals with Apple and phone companies, such as Verizon, to take advantage of the new screens.

Television companies have also moved in this direction. NBC, for example, made entire episodes of *The Office* available for downloading on iTunes the day after their network broadcast. In addition, the network started a broadband comedy channel and another Internet site called NBCFirstLook.com, which will premiere new shows before their broadcast dates. Fox produced a cell phone version of its hit show *24*. CNN created CNNtoGo, a service that delivers news stories to cell phones. In short, the networks are trying to make their content available on as many screens as possible.

Other media are also taking advantage of multiple platforms. Almost all major newspapers and magazines have Web sites for their digital versions that usually include video clips. The *Atlanta Journal-Constitution* and the *Seattle Post-Intelligencer*, like many other newspapers, deliver news to PDAs (such as a Blackberry) and to cell phones. Entertainment and news can be heard on a traditional radio set, a satellite receiver, or a computer and downloaded to an iPod.

We may not be quite there yet, but having everything available everywhere may not be that far in the future.

▲ User-Generated Content

Like you, I was greatly honored to be chosen as *Time* magazine's 2006 Person of the Year. As you are probably aware by now, *Time* honored all of us who created content for the Web. From blogs to YouTube, from podcasts to Facebook, we were the founders and framers of the "new digital democracy." (But, to tell the truth, you probably deserved the honor more than I did. I never posted a video; I never blogged or podcasted. I just managed to produce a rather lame Facebook site. Most of the readers of this book probably did much more. And you have a chance to show just how good you are—see the boxed insert "Generate Some Content, Users.")

User-generated content (UGC) or peer production has been the most celebrated trend over the past few years. The evidence is everywhere. Here are just a few examples: YouTube (recently acquired by Google for $1.65 billion), MySpace, (recently acquired by News Corp for $580 million), and Flickr (acquired by Yahoo! for about $30 million), Wikipedia (not yet acquired), as well as 40 million bloggers.

This trend, so far at least, has shown no signs of slowing down. In San Francisco one TV station actually fired its news staff and now depends totally on items submitted by viewers. Even the Associated Press has an agreement with a Web site that lets "citizen journalists" contribute content. As this book went to press, there were about 80 of these "citizen" sites, ranging from Al Gore's Current.tv to Ourlittle.net, a site that lets residents in small towns post news about their neighborhoods.

Much of the popularity of UGC is due to user-friendly technology. Digital cameras have dropped in price, and video- and picture-sharing sites such as YouTube and Flickr have made it easy for audience members to upload their content. A person with just a minimum of technical skills can use a blogging program such as Movable Type or WordPress and be posting online in a matter of minutes. Creating content at FaceBook or a MySpace page is ridiculously simple. A report by research firm

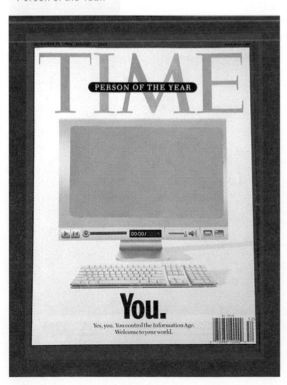

Time recognized the growing trend toward user-generated content when it named the interactive, uploading, web-savvy audience (that would be you, readers) its 2006 Person of the Year.

IDC estimates that by 2010, 70 percent of the world's digital data will be created by individuals not corporations.

The move to UGC is one characteristic of what Web gurus call Web 2.0. What is Web 2.0? Here is the definition as provided (appropriately enough) by the user-generated Wikipedia: ". . . a phrase . . . that refers to a perceived or proposed second generation of web-based services such as social networking sites, wikis, [and] communication tools." In short, the new Web 2.0 encourages sharing and collaboration.

Whereas the old Web 1.0 was about companies, Web 2.0 is about communities. Whereas Web 1.0 was about pages, Web 2.0 is about people. Whereas Web 1.0 was about downloading, Web 2.0 is about uploading.

Of course, Web 2.0 and UCG might merely be a passing fad and might disappear as soon as the novelty wears off. Nonetheless, in subsequent chapters we will show how Web 2.0 and UGC are changing traditional media.

▲ Mobile Media

Much of modern mass communication involves people looking at screens. For the past couple of decades, the two main screens have been the TV screen and the computer screen. Now a parade of small screens has joined the lineup: the screen on a cell phone, personal digital assistant (PDA), iPod, or laptop computer. The emergence of the small screen has encouraged the emergence of the final trend: Mass media have become increasingly mobile.

The examples of this trend are everywhere. TV networks, magazines, and newspapers can send their content to phones, PDAs, and laptops. Many cell phones and PDAs can access the Internet. Laptops can connect to the Internet without wires. Consumers can subscribe to services that send TV shows to their cell phones. Newer models can double as MP3 players. In Japan individuals can download entire novels to their phones.

The movies have become mobile as well. A person can download a movie to a laptop computer or play one on a portable DVD unit. The new Sony portable Play Station can even show movies. Apple's iPod contains enough memory for thousands of songs and a screen that can display photographs and video. The iPod has spawned podcasting, which lets people take prerecorded audio programs with them. As suggested earlier, mobile media are another manifestation of the "anywhere" characteristic of multiple platforms.

The implications of this trend are of such great consequence that it is included in Chapter 3 as one of the significant milestones in the development of communication. In addition, the chapters in Part II of this book contain a section that details how each element of the mass media is becoming more mobile.

MAIN POINTS

- The elements in the communication process are a source, encoding process, message, channel, decoding process, receiver, feedback, and noise.

- The three types of noise are semantic, environmental, and mechanical.

- The three main settings for communication are interpersonal, machine-assisted interpersonal, and mass communication.

- Each element in the communication process may vary according to setting.

- *Mass communication* refers to the process by which a complex organization, with the aid of one or more machines, produces public messages that are aimed at large, heterogeneous, and scattered audiences.

- Traditionally, a mass communicator was identified by its formal organization, gatekeepers, expensive operating costs, profit motive, and competitiveness. The Internet has created exceptions to these characteristics.

- New models have been developed to illustrate Internet mass communication.

- Communication content has become more specialized in the past 40 years, but the channels of mass communication still have the potential to reach vast audiences.

- Six trends that characterize modern mass communication are audience segmentation, convergence, user-generated content, increased audience control, multiple platform, and more mobility.

QUESTIONS FOR REVIEW

1. What are the main elements in the communication process?

2. What are the three types of noise?

3. Compare and contrast interpersonal communication with machine-assisted interpersonal communication.

4. How has the Internet changed the characteristics of the sources of mass communication?

5. What is the difference between a "push" and a "pull" model of mass communication?

QUESTIONS FOR CRITICAL THINKING

1. What's the most embarrassing communication breakdown that's happened to you? Analyze why it happened. Was it due to semantic noise? Environmental noise? Mechanical noise?

2. Keep a media diary for a day. Tabulate how much of your time is spent in interpersonal, machine-assisted interpersonal, or mass communication. What conclusions can you draw?

3. What are some of the shortcomings of the communication model in Figure 1-2? Are there some elements that are missing?

4. Can you find additional examples of the six trends that characterize modern mass media? Are there some media that will be less affected by these trends? Do you think these trends are positive or negative developments?

KEY TERMS

source (p. 4)
encoding (p. 4)
message (p. 5)
channels (p. 5)
decoding (p. 5)
receiver (p. 6)
feedback (p. 6)

noise (p. 7)
interpersonal communication (p. 8)
machine-assisted interpersonal communication (p. 8)
mass communication (p. 10)
mass media (p. 13)
media vehicle (p. 13)

gatekeepers (p. 14)
disintermediation (p. 15)
corporate convergence (p. 19)
operational convergence (p. 20)
device convergence (p. 21)

INTERNET RESOURCES

Online Learning Center

At the Online Learning Center home page, www.mhhe.com/dominick10, *select* Student Center *and then* Chapter 1.

1. Use the Learning Objectives, Chapter Outline, Main Points, and Time Line sections to review this chapter.

2. Test your knowledge of the chapter using the multiple choice, crossword puzzle, and flashcard features of the site.

3. Expand your knowledge of concepts and topics discussed in the chapter by going to Suggestions for Further Reading and Internet Exercises.

Surfing the Internet

Listed here are sites that deal with interpersonal and mass communication.

www.aber.ac.uk/media/Documents/Short/trans.html
A thorough and lucid review and critique of the transmission model of communication. Contrast this model with Figure 1-2.

www.mymissourian.com
As the site's slogan indicates ("Grassroots Journalism by Mid-Missourians"), a good example of user-generated content.

http://dcc.syr.edu
The latest research on and experiments about convergence, sponsored by the Convergence Center at Syracuse University.

www.mobilemedia.com
The Web site of a company that is at the leading edge of the mobile media business.

CHAPTER 2

PERSPECTIVES ON MASS COMMUNICATION

This chapter will prepare you to

- understand the differences between the functional approach and the critical/cultural approach to studying mass communications

- explain the value of each approach in the analysis of the mass communication process

- describe the five functions mass media perform for society

- explain uses-and-gratifications analysis

- recognize the dysfunctions of mass communication

- understand the concepts of *meaning, hegemony,* and *ideology*

Sanjaya made it to the top seven on *American Idol*. The programs and its contestants have been the focus of analysis by professionals, critics and mass media researchers.

People study mass communication for a variety of reasons. Scholars study it to better comprehend the process and to develop theories that explain and predict how the media operate. Critics study it to offer insights about its influence and to suggest improvements. Media consumers study it to become media literate, to be able to understand the elements involved in the mass communication process, and to analyze and critically evaluate information presented in the mass media. Those in the media industry study it in order to increase their operating efficiency and maximize their profits when they sell news and information products to the general public.

No matter what the reason for study, it is helpful to use a **paradigm** (a model or pattern used to analyze something) to guide the way we think about the mass communication process. A paradigm is useful for several reasons:

- It provides us with a consistent perspective from which to examine mass communication.

- It generates concepts that are helpful in understanding media behavior.

- It helps us identify what is or is not important in the process.

There are many paradigms that we could use to study mass communication. This chapter will introduce two that provide different ways of looking at media and society. The **functional approach** emphasizes the way that audiences use mass communication and the benefits people receive from media consumption. A second paradigm, which many have labeled the **critical/cultural approach,** examines the underlying power relationships in media exposure and stresses the many meanings and interpretations that audience members find in media content. (Chapter 19 introduces a third model, the empirical paradigm, an approach that has been commonly used to investigate the social effects of the mass media.)

A recent example highlights the difference between these two approaches. The Fox reality series *American Idol* started its sixth season in 2007. *Idol* has been a ratings powerhouse throughout its existence, and its 2007 premier drew an estimated 37 million people.

Everybody is probably familiar with the format of the show. Hosted by Ryan Seacrest, the show starts off with a series of auditions of hopeful amateurs in several cities across the United States. The finalists eventually appear before a panel of judges consisting of regulars Paula Abdul, Randy Jackson, and Simon Cowell and an occasional guest celebrity. The judges rate the performances, and the television audience is also encouraged to vote via phoning in or text messages. After a long elimination process, one performer is crowned the next American idol.

A functional analyst would want to know several things. First, why do people audition for the show, especially those who have little or no singing talent? What makes individuals a good or poor judge of their own talent? Second, why do people watch this show? Do they get some sense of superiority by watching Simon Cowell put down would-be stars? What makes them identify with some contestants and not with others? Does voting give them a sense of participation in the program?

A critical/cultural researcher would be interested in other questions. This researcher would observe that in addition to how will the contestants sing, the judges also comment on their appearance and personal background. Does *American Idol* make judging people more socially acceptable? Moreover, when someone is judged, he or she is evaluated just like any other commodity. Some of the desirable qualities possessed by contestants might be white teeth, attractive hair, a good complexion, and a slender build—all of which advertised merchandise can help people achieve. Are people choosing the winner based on criteria determined by marketers? Finally, note that the program allows audience members to vote as often as they wish. This is not necessarily a sign of egalitarianism on the part of the program's producers. Every vote rings up more calling fees and text message fees for the program and the phone company. A critical analyst would analyze this and other subtle methods by which the program encourages capitalism.

All in all, this event could serve as the springboard for many disparate avenues of inquiry. This chapter will first examine functional analysis and then look at the critical/cultural approach.

FUNCTIONAL ANALYSIS

In its simplest form the functional approach holds that something is best understood by examining how it is used. In mass communication this means examining the use that audiences make of their interactions with the media.

By way of introduction, here are some actual responses given by college students to three questions:

1. Why do you watch TV?
   - I like to watch when there's nothing else to do.
   - I like to vegetate sometimes.
   - I don't like eating alone.
   - It's easier to do than jog.
   - Television keeps me informed and entertained and it beats the hell out of studying.
   - It makes up for the newspaper I fail to read.
   - I watch TV to be entertained. Also, if the TV is on, my girlfriend's mother thinks we're watching it.

2. Why do you go to movies?
   - Because movies take you to La-La Land, a fantasy place.
   - Movies are a good place to take a date.
   - To escape the everyday doldrums of life.
   - My boyfriend works at a movie theater and I get in for free.
   - I need an escape and movies are more socially positive than drugs.
   - I like to sit in the dark with sticky shoes.
   - I like the popcorn and the Jordan Almonds.
   - Movies are a fantastic way to be entertained while with a geek-me-out date.

3. Why do you use Facebook?
   - I use Facebook because it is a good way to keep in touch with people I otherwise wouldn't see. (It also lets me see how cute people are, if I was drunk when I met them.)
   - I use Facebook because I have no life and I'm compulsive about who my ex-boyfriends are conversing with.
   - I use Facebook because it gives me a way to put off studying.
   - I like to see the incriminating photos that people put up there.

Responses such as these, varied though they are, have led to several generalizations about the functions that media have for a society and for its individual members. This section will focus on cataloging and describing those functions.

▲ The Role of Mass Communication in Society

Perhaps the best way to appreciate the role that mass communication plays in our society is to imagine what it would be like if, all of a sudden, the whole system never existed. How would we find out what was on sale at the local supermarket? How would we know Paris Hilton's current love interest? (Would there *be* a Paris Hilton?) How could we find out what was happening in the Middle East? How could we avoid the traffic jams during rush hour? How would we spend our evenings? Obviously, the mass media are a pervasive part of our lives. Just how pervasive might become clear if we charted the various functions the media perform for us. Before we do this, however, we need to realize that different media have different primary uses. Not many people, for example, listen to CDs to find out the latest news or read the newspaper while driving their cars. Moreover, different groups of people use the same mass media content for different reasons. History professors, for example, might read articles in scholarly journals in order to keep up with their profession. Others who pursue history as a hobby might read the same journals in order to relax and be diverted from their normal routine.

One more qualification needs to be mentioned before we begin examining the functions and uses of mass communication. It is possible to conduct this analysis on at least two levels. On the one hand, we could take the perspective of a sociologist and look through a wide-angle lens to consider the functions performed by the mass media for the entire society (this approach is sometimes called **macroanalysis**). This viewpoint focuses on the apparent intention of the mass communicator and emphasizes the manifest purpose inherent in the media content. On the other hand, we could look through a close-up lens at the individual receivers of the content, the audience, and ask them to report on how they use mass media (this approach is called **microanalysis**). Sometimes the end results of these two methods are similar in that the consumer uses the content in the way that the source intended. Sometimes they are not similar, and the consumer uses the media in a way not anticipated by the mass communicator—a phenomenon noted by both the functional and critical/cultural paradigms. Let's begin our analysis by using the wide-angle lens.

▲ Functions of Mass Communication for Society

For a society to exist, certain communication needs must be met. These needs existed long before Gutenberg bolted together his printing press and Morse started sending dots and dashes. Primitive tribes had sentinels who scanned the environment and reported dangers. Councils of elders interpreted facts and made decisions. Tribal meetings were used to transmit these decisions to the rest of the group. Storytellers and jesters entertained the group. As society became larger and more complex, these jobs grew too big to be handled by single individuals. Throughout the following discussion we will examine the consequences of performing these communication functions by means of mass as opposed to interpersonal communication. Furthermore, there may be instances in which these consequences are undesirable from the point of view of the welfare of the society. These harmful or negative consequences are called **dysfunctions.** We will consider some of these as well. Lastly, these functions are not mutually exclusive, one example might illustrate several different categories.

Surveillance   **Surveillance** refers to what we popularly call the news and information role of the media. The media have taken the place of sentinels and lookouts. The output of the thousands of media journalists in this country is impressive. The four major television networks provide about 600 hours of regularly scheduled news programs, and CNN, Fox, and MSN provide similar services. Web sites such as CNN.com update news continuously, and many big-city radio stations broadcast nothing but news. News magazines reach nearly 9 million people, and approximately 1,500 daily newspapers and 7,000 weeklies also spread the news. The size of the news audience is equally impressive. On any given day about 60 million Americans are exposed to mass-communicated news.

This public-service campaign is an example of the warning function of the media.

The surveillance function can be divided further into two main types. Warning, or **beware surveillance,** occurs when the media inform us about threats from terrorism, hurricanes or volcanoes, depressed economic conditions, increasing inflation, or military attack. These warnings can be about immediate threats (a television station interrupts programming to broadcast a tornado warning), or they can be about long-term or chronic threats (a newspaper runs a series about air pollution or unemployment). There is, however, much information that is not particularly threatening to society that people might like to know about. **Instrumental surveillance** has to do with the transmission of information that is useful and helpful in everyday life. News about films playing at the local theaters, stock market prices, new products, fashion ideas, recipes, and teen fads are examples of instrumental surveillance.

Note also that not all examples of surveillance occur in what we traditionally label the news media. *People* magazine and *Reader's Digest* perform a surveillance function (most of it instrumental). Smaller, more specialized publications such as technical journals also perform the job of surveillance. In fact, the surveillance function can be found in content that is primarily meant to entertain. HBO's *Sex and the City* performed a surveillance function for fashions and designer footwear.

What are some of the consequences of relying on the mass media to perform this surveillance function? In the first place, news travels much faster, especially since the advent of the electronic media. It took months for the news of the end of the War of 1812 to travel across the Atlantic. In contrast, more than 90 percent of the U.S. population knew about the terrorist attacks of September 11, 2001, within 2 hours of the events. The initial air strikes in Operation Iraqi Freedom were reported on television minutes after they happened. Speed sometimes leads to problems, however; inaccuracies and distortions travel just as fast as truthful statements. In 2006, for example, the media erroneously reported that 12 men had survived a coal mine disaster in West Virginia when in fact only one survived.

The second consequence is a bit more subtle. In prehistoric times, if war broke out, it was fairly simple for people to find out about it: A stranger would appear and belt you with a club. The world of early men and women was small and easily surveyed. All of it was within the range of their eyesight, and seldom did it extend over the next hill. Today, thanks to the mass media, there are no more hills. Our world now extends well beyond our eyesight, and we can no longer observe all of it directly. The media relay news from environments beyond our immediate senses, news that we cannot easily verify.

Much of what we know about the world is machine-processed, hand-me-down information. News is prescreened for us by a complex arrangement of reporters and editors, and our conception of reality is based on this second-generation information, whose authenticity we do not usually question. For example, human beings have allegedly walked on the moon. Millions saw it—on TV. Not many saw it in person. Instead, we took the word of the TV networks that what we were seeing was fact, not fiction. However, some people feel that television staged the whole thing somewhere in Arizona as part of a massive, government-inspired publicity stunt. The same phenomenon occurred in 2004 with the rovers landing on Mars; as some people thought the pictures received from Mars were fakes. The point is this: In today's world, with its sophisticated system of mass communication, we are highly dependent on others for news. Consequently, we have to put a certain amount of trust in the media that do our surveillance. This trust, called **credibility,** is an important factor in determining which news medium people find the most believable. We will discuss the concept at length in Chapter 13.

The widespread use of the Internet to transmit news does not change this basic idea. The stories posted on cnn.com or other news-oriented Web sites have been screened by several reporters and editors. Other Web sites that deal with news, such as the Drudge Report or the many blogs that have recently appeared, may not have a layer of editors, a circumstance that may affect the sites' credibility. Information that is spread through e-mail and by lesser-known Web sites may be especially suspect. In the aftermath of the 9/11 attacks, many people opened their e-mail to find a picture of a tourist atop the World Trade Center with an approaching plane in the background. The picture was later exposed as a hoax, but many people were fooled into believing it. Whether the news is filtered or unfiltered, we still have to decide how much faith we invest in the media that provide it.

On the dysfunctional side, media surveillance can create unnecessary anxiety. In 2004 the media began reporting on an impending epidemic of bird flu that could kill anywhere from 5 million to 150 million people worldwide. As of early 2007, the epidemic had yet to materialize. (Of course, if an epidemic eventually occurs, this is a really bad example.)

The fact that certain individuals or issues receive media attention means that they achieve a certain amount of prominence. Sociologists call this process **status conferral.** At the basis of this phenomenon is a rather circular belief that audiences seem to endorse: If you *really* matter, you will be at the focus of mass media attention, and if you are the focus of media attention, then you *really* matter. Knowing this fact, many individuals and groups go to extreme measures to get media coverage for themselves and their causes so that this status conferral effect will occur. Parades, demonstrations, publicity stunts, and outlandish behavior are commonly employed to capture airtime or column inches.

Interpretation   Closely allied with the surveillance function is the interpretation function. The mass media do not supply just facts and data. They also provide information on the ultimate meaning and significance of events. One form of interpretation is so obvious that many people overlook it. Not everything that happens in the world on any given day can be included in the newspaper or in a TV or radio newscast. Media organizations select those events that are to be given time or space and decide how much prominence they are to be given. Stories that ultimately make it into the paper, on the newscast, or on a media organization's Web site have been judged by the various gatekeepers involved to be more important than those that did not make it.

Another example of this function can be found on the editorial pages of a newspaper. Interpretation, comment, and opinion are provided for the reader as an added perspective on the news stories carried on other pages. A newspaper might endorse one candidate for public office over another, thereby indicating that, at least in the paper's opinion, the available information indicates that this individual is more qualified than the other.

Interpretation is not confined to editorials. Articles that analyze the causes of an event or that discuss the implications of government policy are also examples of the interpretation function. Why is the price of gasoline going up? What impact will a prolonged dry spell have on food prices? Radio and television also carry programs or segments of programs that fall under this heading. An editorial by the manager of the local TV or radio station is an example, as are TV documentaries. When the president broadcasts a major political address, network correspondents usually appear afterward to tell us what the president "really said." After the 2006 midterm elections, experts offered their opinions about the causes and consequences of the many victories by Democrats. In 2007 authorities on global warming offered their ideas about how to address the problem.

Interpretation can take various forms. Editorial cartoons, which originated in 1754, may be the most popular form. Other examples are less obvious but no less important. Critics are employed by the various media to rate motion pictures, plays, books, and records. Restaurants, cars, buildings, and even religious services are reviewed by some newspapers and magazines. One entire magazine, *Consumer Reports*, is devoted to analysis and evaluation of a wide range of general products. Political "spin doctors" try to frame the way media cover news events in a way that is positive for their clients. Many blogs interpret news events in line with their own political philosophy.

The interpretation function can also be found in media content that at first glance might appear to be purely entertainment. The comic strip *Dilbert* and TV shows such as *The Office* reflect a certain viewpoint about corporate America. *Martha Stewart Living* sends a message about what constitutes the "good life."

What are the consequences of the mass media's performing this function? First, the audience is exposed to a large number of points of view, probably far more than they could come in contact with through personal channels. Because of this, a person (with some effort) can evaluate all sides of an issue before arriving at an opinion. Additionally, the media make available to the individual a wide range of expertise that he or she might not have access to through interpersonal communication. Should we change the funding structure of Social Security? Thanks to the media, a person can read or hear the views of various economists, political scientists, politicians, and several hundred bloggers.

There are, however, certain dysfunctions that might occur. First, there is no guarantee that interpretations by experts are accurate and valid. In late 2005, for example, the media carried a report issued by the National Association of Realtors that analyzed sales trends and predicted that median new home prices would rise about 7 percent in 2006. Unfortunately for sellers, they barely went up. Second, there is the danger that an individual may, in the long run, come to rely too heavily on the views carried in the media and lose her or his critical ability. Accepting without question the views of the *New York Times* or Rush Limbaugh may be easier than forming individual opinions, but it might lead to the dysfunctional situation of audience passivity and of people allowing others to think for them.

Linkage   The mass media are able to join different elements of society that are not directly connected. For example, mass advertising attempts to link the needs of buyers with the products of sellers. Legislators in Washington may try to keep in touch with constituents'

Steven Colbert offers his own, often offbeat, interpretations of current events.

feelings by reading their hometown papers. Voters, in turn, learn about the doings of their elected officials through newspapers, television, radio, and Web sites. Telethons that raise money for the treatment of certain diseases are another example of this **linkage** function. The needs of those suffering from the disease are matched with the desires of others who wish to see the problem eliminated.

Another type of linkage occurs when geographically separated groups that share a common interest are joined by the media. Publicity about the sickness known as Gulf War syndrome linked those who claimed to be suffering from the disease, enabling them to form a coalition that eventually prompted government hearings on the issue. The Comcast Cable Company offers a service called "Dating on Demand" that allows subscribers to watch 5-minute video profiles of potential dates. If a person sees someone interesting, he or she can contact the individual for a rendezvous.

The best examples of linkage, however, are on the Internet (see the insert "Accustomed to Your Face(book)"). The online auction site eBay lets a person who wants to sell a bronze cremation urn link up with potential buyers across the world. WebMD offers subscribers various "communities" where they can discuss their problems with others who have similar maladies. Craigslist.org lets users find jobs, roommates, dog walkers, and motorcycles for sale. Match.com boasts that it "gets singles connected to the millions of romantic possibilities out there, and often, to one very special someone." After a person finds that special someone, she or he can check out thenest.com, a blog where newlyweds share their experiences about the ups and downs of married life.

The linkage function is present in other media as well. The magazine *Gambling Times* allows a person interested in games of chance to be linked to others with a similar interest. Cell phones link parents with children. Sports talk radio joins people with a common interest in athletics.

The media can also create totally new groups by linking members of society with similar interests, a process known as audience building. An example of this phenomenon occurred in 2003–2004 when TV sparked a poker craze that swept the country. The Travel Channel's *World Poker Tour* drew an audience of more than 1.2 million viewers. ESPN's *World Series of Poker* had about the same level of viewership. Dozens of online poker sites sprang up, and many local bars began weekly poker nights.

On the other hand, this linkage function may have harmful consequences. In 2006 it was estimated that there were more than 300 "hate" sites on the Internet. Terrorists can use these sites to spread hate propaganda and to recruit new members. Some Web sites provide password-protected online discussion groups in which veteran terrorists can persuade new members to join their cause.

Transmission of Values   The transmission of values is a subtle but nonetheless important function of the mass media. It has also been called the **socialization** function. *Socialization* refers to the ways an individual comes to adopt the behavior and values of a group. The mass media portray our society, and by watching, listening, and reading, we learn how people are supposed to act and what values are important. Consider the images of an important but familiar concept as portrayed in the media: motherhood. The next time you watch television or thumb through a magazine, pay close attention to the way

There are no more dramatic examples of the linkage and audience-building function than the social networking sites, such as MySpace and Facebook, that have recently become popular on the Web. Of the two, Facebook is probably better known to the readers of this book since it targets college students.

Facebook was started in 2004 by Mark Zuckerberg, then a sophomore at Harvard. It became instantly popular. In March 2005 the site had about 4 million unique visitors; by March 2006 that number had zoomed to nearly 13 million. About 7 million people at more than 2000 universities have their faces (or at least a text profile) on Facebook, and the number continues to grow.

The commercial potential of Facebook and MySpace has not been overlooked by the business community. The sites are gaining members while most traditional media are losing audience. They attract a young demographic that is particularly appealing to advertisers. It should come as no surprise, then, that MySpace was purchased by Rupert Murdoch's News Corp. for $580 million. (Facebook turned down an offer of $750 million, hoping for more.)

Facebookers don't seem to care too much about the business doings—they're too busy learning how to maneuver around the site. First, they have to learn a new vocabulary. As most of you already know, a "poke" is a way to get somebody's attention without actually sending a written message. The "pulse" is a list of what movies, books, and music are popular. "Tags" link photos to members' profiles. The "wall" is a place where friends post messages and have conversations. There are also rules of etiquette: Post a picture that actually looks like you; poke people before you ask them to be your boyfriend or girlfriend; and respond to messages in a timely manner.

Facebook obviously has many educational uses. Students studying *Beowulf* can chat about the deeper meanings of the text. Those who were absent from class can get notes and a general updating from classmates. News about what professor to avoid is quickly shared. The biggest use, however, is social. One survey found that 60 percent of students log on to chat, send messages to friends and maybe even flirt with the cute guy or girl in their psych class.

There is, however, a dark side to all of this. Some students seemed to ignore the fact that the Internet is public. Anybody with an account can view your profile. Some underage students discovered this the hard way when they posted photos of themselves drinking alcohol and were disciplined by their universities. Others posted provocative photos of themselves and their class schedules, making it easy for potential stalkers to target them. Some colleges are examining ways to regulate speech on the site after discovering that some members were posting derogatory, demeaning, and inflammatory messages. Facebook recently tightened its security measures so that members had greater control over who sees what.

There's also the chance that what's on Facebook or MySpace now might have implications for the future. Employers have been known to check out the Facebook or MySpace profiles of job candidates to get clues to their personality and habits. Those students who contemplate a career in politics might find those racy party pictures they posted on Facebook coming back to haunt them.

Finally, Facebook is addictive. Members check into the site often and can easily spend large chunks of time on the site. It's easy to see how Facebook activity might wind up displacing studying or sleep. Too much linkage may be bad for you.

Will Facebook last, or is it simply another one of those dot-com sites that are hugely popular until some other hot spot takes its place? Some social networks sites, such as Yahoo!'s GeoCities, have already lost popularity, and college students tend to be a rather fickle audience. On the other hand, college students form a tight community and share a similar culture. They are also at a time in their lives when self-discovery and self-definition are paramount, and both processes are easier to get through with a little help from friends. But friends are hard to find in a new environment—unless you're on Facebook, where you can link up with far more people than you could in person.

---

mothers and children are presented. Mass media mommies are usually clean, pretty, cheerful, and affectionate. Ivory Snow laundry detergent typically adorns the packages of its products with a wholesome-looking mother and healthy child smiling out across grocery aisles. (Incidentally, the company was embarrassed back in the 1980s when one of their clean-cut, all-American types went on to star in X-rated films.) The Clairol company sponsored an ad campaign that featured the "Clairol Mother," an attractive and glamorous female who never let raising a child interfere with maintaining her hair. When they interact with their children, media mothers tend to be positive, warm, and caring.[1] Consider these media mommies drawn from TV: Marge Simpson, Lorelei Gilmore (*The Gilmore Girls*), Rochelle Rock (*Everybody Hates Chris*), Cheryl (*According to Jim*), and Lynette Scavo (*Desperate Housewives*). All are understanding, reasonable, friendly, and devoted to their children.

---

[1] OK, Mrs. Costanza, George's mother on *Seinfeld*, might be an exception.

Started in 1995 by Craig Newmark, craigslist.org gets about 3 billion page views per month.

These examples show that the media portray motherhood and child rearing as activities that have a positive value for society. Individuals who are exposed to these portrayals are likely to grow up and accept this value. Thus, a social value is transmitted from one generation to another.

Mass Media and Socialization   Sometimes the media consciously try to instill values and behavior in the audience. Many newspapers report whether accident victims were wearing seat belts at the time of impact. In 1989, for instance, TV writers voluntarily agreed to portray alcohol usage more responsibly in their programs and to include references to designated drivers whenever possible. The next time you watch current TV shows, see if you can find anyone smoking a cigarette. The health concerns regarding smoking have prompted it to virtually disappear from prime-time TV.

There are probably countless other examples of values and behavior that are, in part at least, socialized through the media. Let us examine some of the consequences of having the mass media serve as agents of socialization. At one level value transmission via the mass media helps stabilize society. Common values and experiences are passed down to all members, thereby creating common bonds among them. On the other hand, values and cultural information are selected by large organizations that may encourage the status quo. For example, the "baby industry" in this country is a multimillion-dollar one. This industry advertises heavily in the media; it is not surprising, then, that motherhood is depicted in such an attractive light. To show mothers as harried, exhausted, overworked, and frazzled would not help maintain this profitable arrangement.

Mass media can also transmit values by enforcing social norms. In 2006 *Seinfeld* alum Michael Richards unleashed a racist and profane tirade while performing at a comedy club. The episode was captured on a cell phone and was widely publicized by the media. Richards apologized profusely for the incident, but many experts suggested that it may have irreparably damaged his career. A few months later, radio "shock jock" Don Imus made racially insensitive comments on his radio program. The resulting outrage, carried prominently in the mass media, eventually resulted in his firing.

Not every attempt by the media to enforce social norms is successful. In an effort to combat binge drinking by college students, several campuses launched media campaigns designed to show that excessive alcohol consumption was not as widespread or normal as many students might think. The idea behind the campaign was to show college students that most of their peers drink only moderately or less, thus reducing pressure on them to drink to excess. A report released in 2003, however, found no drop in student binge drinking on university campuses that used a social norms media campaign in their prevention efforts.

TV and Socialization   Of all the mass media, television probably has the greatest potential for socialization. By the time an individual is 18, he or she will have spent more time watching television than in any other single activity except sleep. A prime-time program that is popular with young people might draw an audience of 6 million 6- to 11-year-olds. Because of this wide exposure, several writers have warned of possible dysfunctions that might occur if television is the most important channel of socialization. For instance, since so many TV programs contain violence, it has been feared that young people who watch many such programs might be socialized into accepting violence as a legitimate method of problem solving. In one survey among grade schoolers, heavy TV viewers were more likely than light TV viewers to agree with this statement: "It's almost always all right to hit someone if you are mad at him or her." Another possibility is that the pervasiveness of television violence will encourage fearfulness about the "real world." One study, for example, found that children who were heavy TV viewers were more fearful of going out at night than were light TV viewers. We will discuss this topic at greater length in Chapter 19.

Finally, it has been argued that for many years the image of minority groups transmitted from one generation to the next by the mass media reflects the stereotypes held by those in power: white, Anglo-Saxon, Protestant males. As a result, Native Americans and black Americans endured many years during which Native Americans were seen as savages who murdered civilized whites, and blacks were depicted in menial and subordinate roles. These stereotypes were slow to change, partly because it took a long time for members of these minority groups to influence the workings of large media organizations.

Entertainment   Another obvious media function is that of entertainment. Two of the media examined in this book, motion pictures and sound recordings, are devoted primarily to entertainment. Even though most of a newspaper focuses on the events of the day, comics, puzzles, horoscopes, games, advice, gossip, humor, and general entertainment features usually account for around 12 percent of the content. (If we considered sports news as entertainment, that would add another 14 percent to this figure.) Television is primarily devoted to entertainment, with about three-quarters of a typical broadcast day falling into this category. The entertainment content of radio varies widely according to station format. Some stations may program 100 percent news, while others may schedule almost none. In like manner some magazines may have little entertainment content (*Forbes*), while others are almost entirely devoted to it (*National Lampoon*). Even those magazines that are concerned primarily with news—*Time* and *Newsweek*, for example—usually mix some entertainment features with their usual reporting.

The scope of mass media entertainment is awesome. By 2007 approximately 47 million people in the United States had paid to see *Pirates of the Caribbean: Dead Man's Chest*. About 90 million people watched the 2007 Super Bowl. The comic strip *Doonesbury* is read by more than 15 million people per day. More than 11 million people bought copies of *Harry Potter and the Deathly Hallows*. Carrie Underwood's album *Some Hearts* sold 5 million copies. In a typical month about 3 million people read (or at least look at) *Playboy*.

The importance of the entertainment function of mass media has grown as Americans have accumulated more leisure time. The workweek has decreased from about 72 hours at the turn of the 20th century to the current 40 hours.

The emergence of mobile media (discussed in more detail in Chapter 3) has also amplified the entertainment function of the media. Specially equipped vehicles let children watch DVDs as they go on family trips. Travelers in airport terminals can play games on their cell phones or watch movies on their laptops while they wait. Commuters can play video games on handheld devices while they travel.

Troubadours, storytellers, court jesters, and magicians fulfilled the entertainment function in the centuries before the media. What are the consequences of having this task now taken over by mass communication? Clearly, the media can make entertainment available to a large number of people at relatively little cost. On the other hand, entertainment that is carried by the mass media must appeal to a mass audience. The ultimate result of this state of affairs is that media content is designed to appeal to the lowest common denominator of taste. More programs that resemble *Survivor* and *Jerry Springer* will find their way to TV than will opera performances. Newsstands are filled with more imitators of *Playboy* than imitators of *Saturday Review*. We are more apt to see sequels such as *Star Trek VIII, Wes Craven's New Nightmare,* and *Lethal Weapon VII* than we are to see *Much Ado About Nothing II* and *More King Lear*. Rock stations outnumber classical stations 20 to 1.

One other consequence of the widespread use of media for entertainment is that it is now quite easy to sit back and let others entertain you. Instead of playing baseball, people might simply watch it on TV. Instead of learning to play the guitar, an adolescent might decide to listen to a tape of someone else playing the guitar. Critics have charged that the mass media will turn Americans into a nation of watchers and listeners instead of doers.

▲ How People Use the Mass Media

It is probably clear by now that statements made about the functions of mass communication in society could be paralleled by statements about how the media function at the level of the individual. Consequently, we will now focus on how the individual uses mass communication (in other words, we are moving from macro-to microanalysis). At the individual level the functional approach is given the general name of the **uses-and-gratifications model.** In its simplest form the uses-and-gratifications model posits that audience members have certain needs or drives that are satisfied by using both nonmedia and media sources. This discussion will be concerned more with media-related sources of satisfaction. The actual needs satisfied by the media are called media gratifications. Our knowledge of these uses and gratifications typically comes from surveys that ask people questions about how they use the media (much like the questions at the beginning of this chapter). Several researchers have classified the various uses and gratifications into a four-category system: (1) cognition; (2) diversion; (3) social utility; and (4) withdrawal.

Cognition   Cognition is simply the act of coming to know something. When a person uses a mass medium to obtain information about something, he or she is using the medium in a cognitive way. Clearly, the individual's cognitive use of a medium is directly parallel to the surveillance function at the macroanalytical level. At the individual level researchers have noted that two different types of cognitive functions are performed. One has to do

An examination of the shootings at Virginia Tech in 2007 reveals two developments in the way we now operate during times of crisis. First, many of the functions normally served by traditional media are shifting to the Internet. Second, those people who are part of the crisis are taking an active role in reporting news about the crisis. In the Internet age everybody is a potential journalist.

Surveillance is one of the major functions performed by the media. When news breaks, most people hear about it from television or radio. In the case of the Virginia Tech tragedy, the Internet was the first source of information for a large number of people. Those who were not near a TV set or radio found out about the killings from one of the many news-oriented Web sites, such as CNN or MSNBC.

For many college students the social networking site Facebook supplemented the traditional media as a news source. While the mainstream media were limited to reporting the official information released by the school and the police, students were using the Web to get the word out faster. Shortly after the shooting started, students were posting eyewitness accounts on their Facebook pages. One reported hearing sirens blaring and then the faint sound of gunshots from across campus. Another reported the story of his girlfriend who narrowly missed an encounter with the gunman. Some sites even listed the names of some of the victims before there was official confirmation.

The traditional media also discovered Facebook and other social networking sites. Correspondents scanned students' pages and tried to contact those who had posted compelling entries. One student posting on LiveJournal received requests for an interview from MTV, ABC News, and the *Boston Herald*. Some blog entries were broadcast on national television.

The Facebook site also vividly illustrated the function of audience building, the linking together of members of society with similar interests. More than 500 support groups were formed to commemorate the tragedy and pay tribute to those who perished. One group, called "A Tribute to Those Who Passed at the Virginia Tech Shooting," had more than 350,000 members. The linkage function was also demonstrated by a Facebook group called "I'm OK at VT," where students posted their condition and whereabouts. Parents and friends searching for information about a particular student could use Facebook to link up with the individual.

The emotional release function was apparent in the comments that appeared in many student blogs. Some vented their anger about gun control laws or the apparent lack of timely warnings about the situation. Others expressed their grief. Still others vented their anger at the gunman.

The Internet is not immune from the dysfunctions that go along with mass communication, however. The lack of a gatekeeper meant that some questionable content appeared online. Some students, for example, started sleuthing around Facebook, MySpace, and various student blogs to see if they could identify the gunman. Some soon found a Facebook page with photos of an Asian male holding several guns who had recently broken up with his girlfriend. Although the young man had no connection with the crime, he received numerous death threats and menacing phone calls. His ordeal finally ended when police announced that the actual gunman was dead. Moreover, posting the names of those who were thought to have been killed raises serious issues. In the first place, those who publicize the names before official confirmation might get them wrong, causing great anguish. Second, it seems cruel to post the names of the deceased before the families have been informed.

In any case, the tragic events at Virginia Tech suggest that when a catastrophe occurs, both reporters and those directly involved in the event will turn to the Internet to help get the news out.

---

[1]Prepared with the assistance of Meaghan E. Dominick.

Shock jock Don Imus violated a social norm when he made a racist comment while on the air. The resulting firestorm of criticism led to his dismissal. (As of late 2007, Imus was reportedly planning a return to radio.)

with using the media to keep up with current events, while the other has to do with using the media to learn about things in general or things that relate to a person's general curiosity.

Several surveys have found that many people give the following reasons for using the media:

- I want to keep up with what the government is doing.
- I want to understand what is going on in the world.
- I want to know what political leaders are doing.

These reasons constitute the current-events type of cognitive gratification. At the same time, many people also report the following reasons for using mass media:

- I want to learn how to do things I've never done before.
- I want to satisfy my curiosity.

- The media make me want to learn more about things.
- The media give me ideas.

These statements illustrate the second type of cognition—using the media to satisfy a desire for general knowledge.

Diversion   Another basic need of human beings is for diversion. Diversion can take many forms. Some of the forms identified by researchers are (1) stimulation, or seeking relief from boredom or the routine activities of everyday life, (2) relaxation, or escape from the pressures and problems of day-to-day existence, and (3) emotional release of pent-up emotions and energy. Let us look at each of these gratifications in more detail.

S O U N D B Y T E

What . . . No Metallica?

Researchers who study the diversion function of the mass media focus on the process by which people seek rewarding media content. No less important is the opposite process: avoiding those forms of entertainment people cannot stand. For example, an Illinois high school teacher was looking for a way to cut down on the number of students who were kept after school as punishment. He started playing Frank Sinatra albums during detention. School behavior improved dramatically.

Stimulation   Seeking emotional or intellectual stimulation seems to be an inherent motivation in human beings. Psychologists have labeled these activities "ludic behaviors"— play, recreation, and other forms of activity that seem to be performed to maintain a minimum level of intellectual activity. Many people report that they watch, read, or listen simply to pass the time. The media have taken advantage of this need to avoid boredom in many creative ways. Airlines provide audio and video entertainment during long flights. Supermarkets have grocery carts with video screens that display the latest bargains. Restaurants and coffeehouses have computers on their tables to allow customers to surf before they sup. Special magazines are distributed only to doctors' waiting rooms. And advertisements can be found on walls and the backs of stall doors in rest rooms.

Relaxation   Too much stimulation, however, is undesirable. Psychological experiments have indicated that human beings are negatively affected by sensory overload, in which too much information and stimulation are present in the environment. When faced with sensory overload, people tend to seek relief. The media are one source of this relief. Watching *American Idol* or reading *People* magazine represents a pleasant diversion from the frustrations and problems of everyday life. The choice of material used for relaxation might not always be apparent from surface content. Some people relax by reading articles about Civil War history; others read about astronomy or electronics. Still others might relax by listening to classical music. The content is not the defining factor, since virtually any media material might be used for relaxation by some audience members.

Emotional Release   The final manifestation of the diversion function is the most complex. On the one hand, the use of the media for emotional release is fairly obvious. For instance, the horror movie has had a long history of popularity in America. Starting with *Dracula* and *Frankenstein* and continuing through *The Creature from the Black Lagoon*, *Them*, and *The Thing* right up to *Nightmare on Elm Street*, *Friday the 13th*, *The Ring*, and *Scream*, people have sat in dark theaters and screamed their lungs out. Tearjerkers have also drawn crowds. *Broken Blossoms*, *Since You Went Away*, *The Best Years of Our Lives*, *Terms of Endearment*, *Dying Young*, *Titanic*, and *The Notebook* have prompted thousands, perhaps millions, to cry their eyes out.

On the other hand, emotional release can take more subtle forms. One of the big attractions of soap operas, for example, seems to be that many viewers are comforted by seeing that some people (even fictional people) have troubles greater than their own. Other individuals identify with media heroes and participate vicariously in their triumphs. Such a process evidently enables these people to vent some of the frustrations connected with their everyday lives.

Strawberries with Sugar is a popular teenage soap opera that is carried on Portuguese television. In a recent episode a life-threatening virus threatened a school, causing dizziness, breathing problems, and itching among the characters. A few days after the episode aired, hundreds of Portuguese schoolchildren reported having similar symptoms and stayed home from school. Several schools, thinking that they were facing a real epidemic, closed their doors. Strangely, no adults or preschoolers were afflicted, only schoolchildren.

An example of the media causing mass hysteria? Probably not. More likely, it illustrates the use of the mass media for avoidance. School officials noted that the health complaints surfaced at about the same time that the schools were having their final exams.

Emotional release was probably one of the first functions to be attributed to media content. Aristotle, in his *Poetics,* talked about the phenomenon of **catharsis** (a release of pent-up emotion or energy) occurring as a function of viewing tragic plays. In fact, the catharsis theory has surfaced many times since then, usually in connection with the portrayals of TV violence. Chapter 19 contains a discussion of research that has dealt expressly with the catharsis notion.

Social Utility   Psychologists have also identified a set of social integrative needs, including our need to strengthen our contact with family, friends, and others in society. The social integrative need seems to spring from the individual's need to affiliate with others. The media function that addresses this need is called **social utility,** and this usage can take several forms. Have you ever talked with a friend about a TV program? Have you ever discussed a current movie or the latest song you downloaded? If so, then you are using the media as **conversational currency.** The media provide a common ground for social conversations, and many people use things that they have read, seen, or heard as topics for discussion with others. There is a certain social usefulness in having a large repository of things to talk about so that, no matter where you are, you can strike up a conversation and be fairly sure that the person you are talking to is familiar with the subject. ("What did you think of the Super Bowl?" "How did you like *Little Miss Sunshine*?")

Social utility is apparent in other instances as well. Going to the movies is probably the most common dating behavior among adolescents. The motion picture theater represents a place where it is socially acceptable to sit next to your date in a dark room without parental supervision. In fact, many times the actual film is of secondary importance; the social event of going out has the most appeal.

Other people report that they use the media, particularly television and radio, as a means to overcome loneliness. The TV set represents a voice in the house for people who might otherwise be alone. Radio keeps people company in their cars. In fact, some viewers might go so far as to develop feelings of kinship and friendship with media characters. This phenomenon is called a **parasocial relationship,** and there is some evidence that it actually occurs. For example, one study that examined parasocial relationships between the audience and TV newscasters found that more than half the people surveyed agreed with the statement "The newscasters are almost like friends you see every day."

Withdrawal   At times, people use the mass media to create a barrier between themselves and other people or activities. For example, the media help people avoid certain chores, as children are quick to learn. This hypothetical exchange might be familiar:

"It's your turn to let the dog out."

"I can't. I want to finish watching this program. You do it."

In this case attending to mass media content was defined as a socially appropriate behavior that should not be interrupted. In this manner other tasks might be put off or avoided entirely.

Many people turn to the media for breaking news events such as the protests over NFL star Michael Vick's dog-fighting activities.

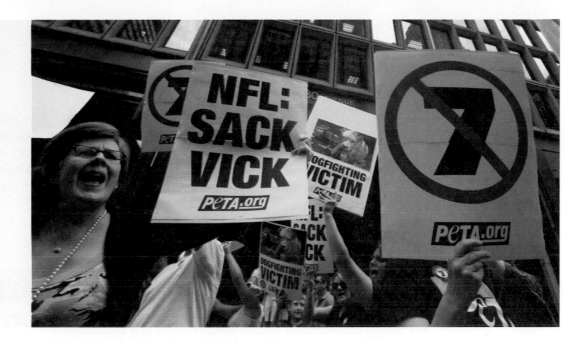

People also use the media to create a buffer zone between themselves and others. When you are riding a bus or sitting in a public place and do not want to be disturbed, you bury your head in a book, magazine, or newspaper. If you are on an airplane, you might pop in your iPod ear buds and tune everybody out. Television can perform this same function at home by isolating adults from children ("Don't disturb Daddy; he's watching the game") or children from adults ("Don't bother me now; go into the other room and watch *Sesame Street*").

Content and Context   In closing, we should emphasize that it is not only media content that determines audience usage but also the social context within which the media exposure occurs. For example, soap operas, situation comedies, and movie magazines all contain material that audiences can use for escape purposes. People going to a movie, however, might value the opportunity to socialize more than they value any aspect of the film itself. Here, the social context is the deciding factor.

It is also important to note that the functional approach makes several assumptions:

- Audiences take an active role in their interaction with various media. That is, the needs of each individual provide motivation that channels that individual's media use.
- The mass media compete with other sources of satisfaction. Relaxation, for example, can also be achieved by taking a nap or having a couple of drinks, and social utility needs can be satisfied by joining a club or playing touch football.
- The uses-and-gratifications approach assumes that people are aware of their own needs and are able to verbalize them. This approach relies heavily on surveys based on the actual responses of audience members. Thus, the research technique assumes that people's responses are valid indicators of their motives.

A great deal of additional research needs to be done in connection with the uses-and-gratifications approach. In particular, more work is needed in defining and categorizing media-related needs or drives and in relating those needs to media usage. Nonetheless, the current approach provides a valuable way to examine the complex interaction between the various media and their audiences.

CRITICAL/CULTURAL STUDIES

The functional approach relies on empirical methods common to the social sciences. Researchers who use this approach ask people questions and tabulate the results or enumerate characteristics of media content. In contrast, critical/cultural researchers use a more qualitative and humanities-oriented approach. This perspective takes a macroanalytic outlook and examines such concepts as ideology, culture, politics, and social structure as they relate to the role of media in society. Some background on this school of thought may be helpful.

▲ A Brief History

Most scholars suggest that the origins of the critical/cultural model can be traced to the Frankfurt School during the 1930s and 1940s. The Frankfurt School was a group of intellectuals committed to the analytical ideas of Karl Marx. (Keep in mind that we are discussing Marxism as a philosophical system and an analytical tool. Marxism as a political and economic system has fallen on hard times of late.) In simplified terms the core of this Marxist approach was that the best way to understand how a society worked was to examine who controlled the means of production that met the basic needs of the population for food and shelter. Marx noted that many Western countries had adopted a system of industrial capitalism in which mass production created wealth for the capitalists—the ones who owned the factories where the goods were produced. Mass production ensured that the basic needs of a society were met, but at a cost: tension between the haves (the wealthy) and the have-nots (the workers who labored in all those factories). In other words, the capitalist system exploited the working class and guaranteed their domination by the wealthy. Because capitalists were interested in creating more capital (or wealth), they had a vested interest in ensuring that the system stayed in place. Marx suggested that life would be better for all if some other, more equitable system of sharing wealth were in place.

The members of the Frankfurt School extended Marxist analysis into the cultural life of a society. They noted that, just as big firms controlled the production of economic goods, other big companies controlled the production of cultural goods. The radio industry, motion picture studios, newspaper and magazine publishers, and later the television business all adopted the capitalist model of production. According to the Frankfurt School, the culture industry exploited the masses just as capitalists did. They published and broadcast products based on standardized formulas that appealed to the mass audience and at the same time glorified and promoted the capitalist culture. For example, during the Depression of the 1930s, Hollywood did not make films that advocated a different economic or political system. Instead, the studios churned out glitzy musicals and comedies that portrayed common people who get a break and make it big despite bad economic times. The television sitcoms of the 1950s showed well-off families content with their lives in the suburbs: Ozzie and Harriet never agitated for a new economic system.

Much of the writing of members of the Frankfurt School was designed to show the exploitative character of mass culture and the way the culture industry helped destroy individuality by promoting the social dominance of large corporations. The object of the critical theory espoused by these writers was resistance to this mass culture and exploitation. The media were so powerful and pervasive, however, that critical resistance to these forces was nearly impossible. The media continued to reinforce the status quo.

The viewpoint of the Frankfurt School was criticized for being pessimistic and gloomy and for underestimating the power of the audience. Nonetheless, this perspective caused

Moviegoers can find emotional release by laughing at the antics of Will Ferrell and Jon Heder in *Blades of Glory*.

many to analyze the impact of the media industries on the political and economic life of society and to use interdisciplinary theories and methods in their investigations.

The next important stage in the development of the critical/cultural approach took place in Great Britain during the late 1950s and early 1960s. Scholars at the Centre for Contemporary Cultural Studies at Birmingham University noted that members of the British working class used the products of mass culture to define their own identities through the way they dressed, the music they listened to, the hairstyles they favored, and so forth. The audience did not seem to be manipulated by the media, as the Frankfurt School argued; instead, the relationship was more complicated. Audience members took the products of mass culture, redefined their meaning, and created new definitions of their self-image.

This emphasis on meaning was reinforced by studies of film and television. A theory developed by British film critics suggested that cinematic techniques (camera angle, editing, imagery) subtly but effectively impose on the audience the meanings preferred by the filmmaker.

This theory was later amended to acknowledge that, although films and TV shows could try to impose their preferred meanings on people, audience members were free to resist and come up with their own meanings. For example, although the dominant theme in a documentary about efforts to control pollution might be how hard industry is trying to control the problem, some in the audience might see the program as nothing more than an empty marketing gesture by big companies.

Important to the cultural studies group were the values that were represented in the content. Again drawing from Marx, the group noted that the values of the ruling class became the dominant values that were depicted in mass media and other cultural products. Marx analyzed dominant values in economic terms, but the cultural studies scholars extended the perspective to class, race, and, with the growth of feminist studies, gender. In Britain, and later in the United States, the dominant values that were represented were those of white, upper-class, Western males. The media worked to maintain those values by presenting versions of reality on TV and films that represented this situation as normal and natural, as the way things should be.

During the Depression most Hollywood films refrained from making social or political statements about the hard times. Instead, films like *My Man Godfrey*, shown here, suggested that things were fine and that, with a little luck, everyone could afford the good life portrayed in the film.

The audience, however, was not passive. The dominant values may have been encoded in complex and subtle ways (much critical/cultural research is aimed at describing and analyzing these subtle depictions), but viewers can supply their own meanings to the content (much critical/cultural research tries to catalogue how various audience members interpret content in different ways). One of the classic studies examined how the audience made sense of a British TV program, *Nationwide*. One group of viewers seemed to accept the dominant message of the program that British society was harmonious and egalitarian; another group "negotiated" their own, somewhat different interpretation; and a third group, young blacks who were not part of the mainstream, rejected it altogether.

The critical/cultural approach gained prominence in the United States during the 1970s and 1980s and was adopted by communication researchers and scholars engaged in feminist studies. Like Marxist analysis, feminist analysis saw inequalities in the way that wealth and power were distributed in society. Marx, however, argued that this inequality stemmed from industrial capitalism; feminist scholars suggested that it stemmed from male domination of women in society (sometimes referred to as *patriarchy*). Feminist critics examined how the media and other forms of culture contributed to the oppression of women. Advertising, for example, might suggest that the proper (or natural) place for a woman is in the home or that looking good is the preferred way for women to achieve success.

Not all critical/cultural scholars, however, emphasize power relationships. James Carey, for example, contended that researchers should study how communication creates, maintains, or modifies a culture. He argued that it is valuable to look upon communication as a ritual—how it draws people together and how it represents a sharing of beliefs. Someone interested in the ritual role of mass communication, for instance, might examine the cultural meanings of men gathering to watch *Monday Night Football* and how this rite illustrates the social bonds that help maintain society. Other critical/cultural scholars have examined how cultural myths are embodied in mass communication. A myth is an expressive story that celebrates a society's common themes, heroes, and origins. Studying the way popular media programs utilize the collective myths of a culture might help us understand their success. *Star Trek*, for example, has spawned a cult following, four TV series, and at least a half-dozen movie sequels. A mythic analysis of the TV show suggests that it draws upon a myth deeply rooted in American history—the myth of the frontier where a wagon train heads hopefully into uncharted and potentially dangerous territory in search of better horizons. Note that the *Star Trek* prologue describes space as "the final frontier," the *Enterprise* takes the place of the wagon train, Klingons take the place of hostile Indians, and Kirk becomes the wagon master while Spock serves as trusty sidekick.

As is probably obvious by now, the critical/cultural perspective is multidimensional and encompasses a wide variety of topics and analytic methods. It is difficult to summarize the important notions of such an eclectic approach, but the ones listed next have general relevance.

▲ Key Concepts

Like most other specialized ways of examining the audience, the critical/cultural approach has developed its own specialized vocabulary. We will examine some of the key terms.

Cultural studies, naturally enough, broaden the study of mass communication to encompass the notion of **culture.** Culture is a complex concept that refers to the common values, beliefs, social practices, rules, and assumptions that bind a group of people together. Hence, it is possible to identify a street culture or an Asian American culture or even a college student culture.

Culture is studied through the practices and texts of everyday life. A **text** is simply the object of analysis. Texts are broadly defined: They can be traditional media content such as TV programs, films, ads, and books, or they can be things that do not fit into the traditional category, such as shopping malls, T-shirts, dolls, video games, and beaches.

Texts have **meaning,** the interpretations that audience members take away with them from the text. In fact, texts have many meanings; they are **polysemic.** Different members of the audience will have different interpretations of the same text. Some may interpret it the way the source intended; others may provide their own unique meanings.

Ideology is contained in texts. Broadly, an ideology is a specific set of ideas or beliefs, particularly regarding social and political subjects. Mass communication messages and other objects of popular culture have ideology embedded in them. Sometimes the ideology is easy to see. Commercials, for example, illustrate the belief that consumption is good for you and for society. Other times the ideology is subtler and harder to detect.

Hegemony has to do with power relationships and dominance. In the United States, for example, those who own the channels of mass communication possess cultural hegemony over the rest of us. Groups with political and economic power extend their influence over those groups who are powerless or at the margins of society. Hegemony, however, is not based on force. It depends on the dominated group's accepting its position as natural and normal and believing that the status quo is in its best interest. Media rules, regulations, and portrayals all help the dominant class present the status quo as customary and desirable. Hegemony creates the positions of the superior and the inferior. This division is unstable and continuously being negotiated through interpretations of meaning.

A couple of examples will illustrate how these concepts are used in the critical/cultural approach. One critical/cultural study used the long-running TV show *60 Minutes* as its text. The analysis found predictable themes and formulas in the program. One common type of *60 Minutes* segment can be interpreted as the classic American detective story. Somebody, maybe a business that is ripping off consumers, is committing a crime. The *60 Minutes* reporters have to hunt down clues and gather information. They may sneak in a hidden camera to catch the wrongdoers in the act. The reporters become the heroes; the business people are the villains. The story is eventually resolved, and those who were committing the bad deeds are exposed or brought to justice.

This seems to be a meritorious service to the public. But upon closer inspection, this kind of *60 Minutes* story seems to be reinforcing the hegemony of the dominant class. Note that these stories go after companies or businesses that have violated some basic values of American capitalism: "Thou shalt not cheat the customer" and "thou shalt not promise more than thou canst deliver." The stories never question the basic ideology that

CRITICAL/CULTURAL ISSUES

PE Teachers in the Movies

Over the past 15 years many local school boards have cut physical education (PE) programs. In 2005 it was estimated that only about 1 in 4 students in the United States attended a daily physical education class. At the same time, teenage obesity has become a serious problem. In 2002 about 15 percent of children and teens were considered overweight, a 300 percent increase from 1980.

Is it possible that the deemphasis of PE programs could somehow be linked to the way that PE is portrayed in popular culture? A study in a 2003 issue of *Sports, Education and Society,* by Bryan McCullick, Don Belcher, Brent Hardin, and Marie Hardin, provided relevant information on this question by examining recent media portrayals of PE instructors.

The authors noted that popular culture can be meaningful in shaping how students and others view their relationship to education and educational programs. The article used a conceptual framework called *symbolic convergence theory,* which suggests that mass media provide stories with overarching themes that are shared by most members of a culture. These themes become part of the audience's notion of reality and can be more powerful than the "real thing." With this as a foundation, the researchers set out to find if there were common themes in the way PE instructors are depicted in the motion picture medium.

The authors identified 18 movies from 1990 to 2000 that portrayed physical education teachers. They included many that will probably be familiar to readers of this text: *Clueless, Mr. Holland's Opus, The Faculty, Scary Movie, Never Been Kissed,* and *Whatever It Takes.* The next step was to view the videotape of each movie and to identify common themes and representations.

Several themes emerged. First, PE teachers were seldom shown teaching. Instead, they were on the sidelines "cheering, chiding or deriding the students for lack of ability or machismo. The message is clear: teachers might be found in the classroom but not in the gymnasium."

Second, PE teachers were bullies. In several of the films, they enjoyed humiliating and verbally and physically embarrassing their students. In *Never Been Kissed* the main character becomes fatigued while running and drags herself to the teacher and asks for a drink of water. The teacher responds with "What do I look like, a waitress?" and threatens the student that if she doesn't finish running she will fail PE. In another movie the PE teacher repeatedly hits a male student with a baseball. Similar scenes occur throughout the film, and each time the teacher verbally abuses the student by calling him a girl.

Finally, there was a vast difference in how male and female PE teachers were depicted. Female teachers were portrayed as lesbians. In *Clueless* the main character describes her PE teacher as "in the grand tradition of PE teachers, same-sex oriented." In *Scary Movie* the teacher, Miss Mann, is a female with heavy facial hair and broad shoulders. On the other hand, male PE instructors were portrayed as sex-obsessed heterosexuals. In *Mr. Holland's Opus,* for example, the PE teacher continually talks to the main characters about sex.

The authors speculate about some of the possible consequences these stereotypes might have. The connection between physical education and sexuality might stop both males and females from entering the field because they might want to avoid what they might perceive as the negative connotations that go with the profession. Negative portrayals of PE might also reinforce an unfavorable image that school boards and school officials might have of the topic. As the authors put it: "If school administrators voted for the elimination of physical education after viewing . . . *Clueless, Sidekicks,* and *Never Been Kissed,* they could hardly be blamed."

The researchers acknowledge that their study provides no evidence of a causal link between their findings and the attitudes of audience members toward physical education. They argue, however, that their study provides students, educators, and administrators with information that might help them design strategies to combat these stereotypes and to help PE professionals develop more positive approaches for their chosen vocation.

capitalism is good for you. Instead, they imply that life would be fine if we could just expose all those companies that do not play by the rules of free enterprise and bring them back into the fold. Further, note how the program stands up for the "little person." The reporters are our friends and champions. Everything is fine with the system, and CBS can continue to make money selling ads in a top-rated program. It is easy for viewers to come away with an interpretation that simply reinforces the economic and social hegemony of the powerful.

A second example concerns arcade video games as a text. These games are typically played by a relatively powerless segment of society—younger teenagers. Nonetheless, these players can find a meaning in the games that lets them resist, for a rather short time, forms of social control, allowing them to form their own cultural identity. The arcade games, for instance, reverse the traditional relationship between machine and machine operator. In industry the two work together to produce some commodity; in the arcade the player plays against the machine. The idea is to consume, not to produce.

Playing arcade games is regarded by some with a certain amount of disapproval; some games are violent, and others have mature themes. There is also the view that game playing is a waste of time, and this disapproval on the part of *non*players probably plays a role in the games' attraction for those who *do* play. In addition, the joystick or steering wheel offers the player a direct means to control his or her environment, something that may not be possible in much of everyday life. These factors may account for the continuing popularity of this type of entertainment. Nonetheless, a closer look suggests that, although video games allow the player some freedom of cultural interpretation, the games still work to reinforce the dominant ideology—the social values contained in the games are the common ones in society. Thus, arcade players get a chance to blow away monsters, aliens, drug runners, thugs, and other assorted bad guys; there is no opportunity to show disfavor with the prevailing social norms. And, of course, many of those quarters from the arcade go back to the video game companies, which maintain their economic hegemony and make more games that teens can play to make them feel as though they are resisting the dominant ideology while they are actually supporting it.

This book presents a series of boxed inserts that illustrate the critical/cultural approach and demonstrate the range and diversity of critical/cultural topics. For example, see the boxed insert "PE Teachers in the Movies" in this chapter; in Chapter 5 you will find a critical/cultural analysis of teen magazine Web sites.

Some friction exists between those who choose the traditional effects or functional approaches and those who adopt the critical/cultural approach. This discord seems unnecessary since these various paradigms ask different questions about media and society and use different tools to look for answers. In addition, each approach can learn from the others. No technique is somehow better than the rest. All are useful in the quest to understand the complicated relationships between mass communication and its audience.

MAIN POINTS

- Functional analysis holds that something is best understood by examining how it is used.
- At the macro level of analysis, mass media perform five functions for society: surveillance, interpretation, linkage, transmission of values, and diversion. Dysfunctions are harmful or negative consequences of these functions.
- At the micro level of analysis, the functional approach is called *uses-and-gratifications analysis.*
- The media perform the following functions for the individual: cognition, diversion, social utility, and withdrawal.

- The critical/cultural approach has its roots in Marxist philosophy, which emphasized class differences as a cause of conflict in a society.
- The critical/cultural approach suggests that media content helps perpetuate a system that keeps the dominant class in power. It also notes that people can find different meanings in the same message.
- The key concepts in the critical approach are text, meaning, hegemony, and ideology.
- Although they are different approaches, both functional and critical/cultural studies can be valuable tools for the analysis of the mass communication process.

QUESTIONS FOR REVIEW

1. What is the difference between macroanalysis and microanalysis?

2. What is a dysfunction? What are some examples?

3. What is status conferral? How does it work?

4. What is meant by the uses-and-gratifications approach? What are its assumptions?

5. What are the key terms in the critical/cultural approach?

QUESTIONS FOR CRITICAL THINKING

1. Compare and contrast the functional and the critical/cultural approaches. How does each view the audience? How does each view the media?

2. Compare your own reasons for watching TV and going to the movies with those that appear at the beginning of the chapter. Are there any similarities?

3. Can you find any more current examples of status conferral? Linkage? Media dysfunctions?

4. As mentioned in the text, one of the assumptions of the uses-and-gratifications approach is that people can verbalize their needs. Suppose this assumption is false. Is the uses-and-gratifications approach still useful?

5. Review the boxed insert "PE Teachers in the Movies," an example of the critical/cultural approach. Are movie portrayals of teachers in general more positive than the portrayal of PE teachers? Why does Hollywood continue to perpetuate these stereotypes? Is it related to profits?

KEY TERMS

paradigm (p. 27)
functional approach (p. 27)
critical/cultural approach (p. 27)
macroanalysis (p. 29)
microanalysis (p. 29)
dysfunctions (p. 29)
surveillance (p. 29)
beware surveillance (p. 30)

instrumental surveillance (p. 30)
credibility (p. 30)
status conferral (p. 31)
linkage (p. 33)
socialization (p. 33)
uses-and-gratifications model (p. 37)
catharsis (p. 40)
social utility (p. 40)

conversational currency (p. 40)
parasocial relationship (p. 40)
culture (p. 45)
text (p. 45)
meaning (p. 45)
polysemic (p. 45)
ideology (p. 45)
hegemony (p. 45)

INTERNET RESOURCES

Online Learning Center

At the Online Learning Center home page, www.mhhe.com/dominick10, *select* Student Center *and then* Chapter 2.

1. Use the Learning Objectives, Chapter Outline, Main Points, and Time Line sections to review this chapter.

2. Test your knowledge of the chapter using the multiple choice, crossword puzzle, and flashcard features of the site.

3. Expand your knowledge of concepts and topics discussed in the chapter by going to Suggestions for Further Reading and Internet Exercises.

Surfing the Internet

The following are useful sites that are related to the material in this chapter. In addition, scan some of the newsgroups on the Net to see some of the special-interest topics that bring people together.

http://eserver.org
Page contains links to works using the critical/cultural approach in many disciplines.

www.aber.ac.uk/media/sections/gen08.html
Site containing links to articles that discuss the uses-and-gratifications approach.

www.aejmc.net/ccs
Home of the Critical and Cultural Studies division of the Association for Education in Journalism and Mass Communication.

www.uky.edu/~drlane/capstone/mass/uses.htm
A discussion of the various approaches and models used to analyze the role of media in society.

CHAPTER 3

HISTORICAL AND CULTURAL CONTEXT

This chapter will prepare you to:

- describe the major events and general trends in media history

- recognize the milestones in the development of human communication

- understand the role that these advances played in prompting significant changes in our culture and society

- learn that the emergence of new communications advances changes but does not make extinct those communications that came before

- understand that each advance in communication increases our power to convey and record information

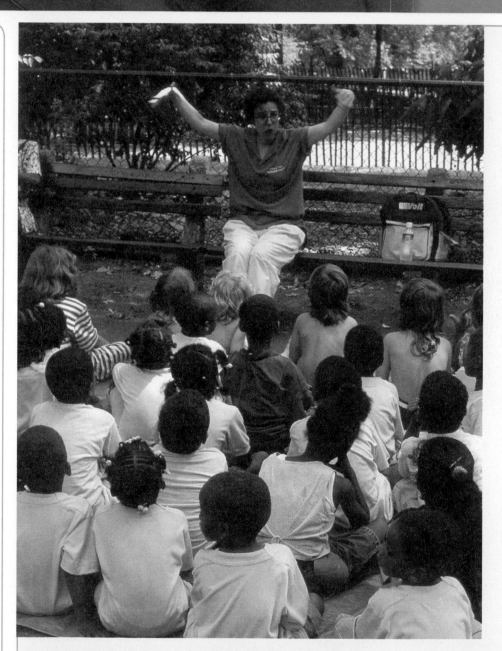

This modern-day storyteller keeps alive the oral culture of our ancestors and introduces another generation to the art of verbal communications.

The historical and cultural contexts of media are important because history tends to be cyclical. This fact has been apparent for centuries. Many ancient civilizations relied on storytellers to hand down the history and culture of their society so that they might learn from the past. The same is true for modern society: Knowing what happened many years ago might help us understand what is going on now. For example, when radio first started in the 1910s and 1920s, its future was uncertain. Many thought radio would compete with the telephone and telegraph as a means of sending messages from point to point, while others saw radio's future in aviation, providing beacons for aircraft.

The first organization to recognize radio's importance was the military; the U.S. Navy led the way during World War I. After the war, as interest in the new medium increased, a totally new function emerged. Radio was used to broadcast information and entertainment to a mass audience. Many individuals and organizations scrambled to make use of this new means of communication: the telephone company, newspapers, businesses, and even universities. None had any clear idea how radio broadcasting would pay for itself. Eventually radio became a commercial medium, dominated by big business, that in fewer than 10 years reached an audience of 50 million. Radio changed America's news and entertainment habits and became a medium whose influence on popular culture is still being felt.

Compare radio's development with that of the Internet, which was started by the Department of Defense to improve military communication. When first developed, the Internet was envisioned as a means of point-to-point communication. It gained popularity through the efforts of scientists and amateur computer enthusiasts. When the World Wide Web and newsgroups offered a place where anyone could post messages and reach a large potential audience, businesses, educational organizations, government agencies, and individuals all scrambled to stake out a site. Everybody is currently trying to figure out how to make Web sites profitable. Will the Web eventually become primarily a commercial medium dominated by big business? (We're already seeing signs of this.) Will it change the way we get our news and entertainment? (Probably.) What sort of cultural impact will it have? (This may take a while to determine.) History may help us answer these questions.

You have probably heard the old joke about the guy who was annoyed because he couldn't see the forest because of all the trees, or couldn't see the blizzard because of all the snow, or couldn't see the city because of all the tall buildings (you probably get the idea by now). Well, sometimes it can be hard to see history because of all the names, places, dates, and events. Consequently, this chapter steps back and takes a broad view of media history, emphasizing major events and general trends. It also provides additional background information by examining communication in the days before mass communication developed.

Specifically, this chapter discusses eight milestones in the development of human communication: language, writing, printing, telegraph and telephone, photography and motion pictures, radio and television, digital media, and mobile media (see Figure 3-1). This overview of the historical and cultural context of mass communication will supplement and make more meaningful the specific histories of the various media presented in Parts II and III of this book.

FIGURE 3-1   Media Time Line

LANGUAGE

Our prehuman ancestors must have had some means of communication, probably nonverbal—maybe using gestures and body movements—and then eventually developed verbal communication using a spoken language. But why? Why didn't humans continue to depend on nonverbal communication and use their mouths merely for eating and breathing? Such a scenario is certainly possible. Hearing- and speech-impaired people do this. What made spoken language superior? The truth is, we're not sure. Several theories have been advanced to explain the phenomenon. One theory notes that sign language is not very effective in the dark. If prehistoric humans were to be successful while hunting or moving about at night, they had to work out other means of communicating. Charles Darwin argued that language superseded gesture because language left both hands free to work with tools or handle weapons. Whatever the reason, early humans talked rather than gestured. *When* they started talking is another question that is hard to answer. Some scholars think the inception of verbal communication dates back hundreds of thousands of years; others suggest it developed around 40,000 B.C.

How exactly did language develop? Again, nobody knows for sure. There are some picturesque theories (see the Soundbyte "You Don't Say"), but none seems entirely adequate. What is fairly certain is that language was a tremendous factor in the advance of early civilization. For example, hunting became more efficient since directions could be given to coordinate the hunt (directions to a better place to camp could be reported to others in the tribe). Further, a more defined social power structure emerged, as the strong could issue commands to the weak. Instructions for making tools or utensils could be passed on to others. Language helped develop conceptual thinking and provided a means to manipulate ideas, transmit culture, and deal with abstractions. The birth of language marked a major development in the history of the human race.

Our ancestors developed an oral culture—one that depended upon language and the spoken word. Such a society (several examples still exist today) is tremendously dependent on memory. Much of the history, beliefs, and folklore of the culture is transmitted by individuals who memorize large amounts of information and recite it to those in the next generation who, in turn, pass it on to their offspring. This has several implications. Because there is a limit to what a person can remember, the growth of knowledge and information in such a society is slow. Further, there is the risk that an advance or break-through will not be remembered well enough to be transmitted. The Incas, for example, apparently made great strides in architecture that were lost because the oral tradition was too fragile to preserve them.

As humans developed further, so expanded the variety of food-gathering means: Farm-ing reduced the need to roam over large territories to seek food. Instead, small agricultural villages developed. As more and more people settled in villages and towns, it became harder to rely on the oral tradition to fulfill communication needs. Efficient farming need-ed a means to keep track of when to plant crops. It was also helpful to have records of who owned the domesticated animals that were part of the village. As the village's popula-tion grew, it was useful to monitor what belonged to each family. This need to keep more detailed, permanent, and accessible records was probably the impetus behind the next great communications revolution—writing.

WRITING

Two problems had to be solved before a system of writing was invented: (1) Decide what symbols were to be used to represent spoken sounds or ideas, and (2) select the surface on which to write the symbols.

▲ Sign Writing Versus Phonetic Writing

The first problem was solved in two ways. One early symbol system might be called *sign writing,* in which each symbol was based on a picture that resembled the thing it stood for. Thus, a circle with wavy lines radiating from it might stand for the sun, while a series of wavy lines stacked on top of each other might stand for water. One early form of this style of writing developed in Sumeria (present-day Iraq) about 3500 B.C. A second, more familiar example developed in Egypt a few hundred years later and came to be known as *hiero-glyphics.* The most durable form of sign writing blossomed in China about 2000–1500 B.C. This method required learning thousands of different pictographs that represented various objects and actions.

The second type of writing system was based more on sound than signs. A group of letters, called an **alphabet,** was used to symbolize each of the sounds that make up words. The Phoenicians are generally credited with having developed the alphabet being used to write this sentence. The Phoenicians were sea traders, and their invention gradually spread across the Mediterranean to Greece, where a standard alphabet of 24 letters was constructed. The epic poems of Homer were put into written form about 800 B.C. Later, the Romans modified the Greek alphabet into the 26 letters that are now standard in English. The alphabet was a more efficient way of writing than the pictographs used by the Egyp-tians and Chinese. For example, a computer keyboard with 47 keys can easily write any sentence in English complete with numbers and all punctuation marks. To do the same in the Chinese pictograph system would require about 9,000 keys. Eventually, even the picto-graphs used by the Egyptians evolved into an alphabet based on sounds.

▲ Clay Versus Paper

The problem of selecting a writing surface was solved in various ways. The Sumerians used soft clay tablets and a wedge-shaped tool to record their pictographs. Clay was inexpensive and durable (many of the Sumerian clay tablets still exist today). On the other hand, tablets were not very transportable, and it was difficult to make fine lines and delicate markings in clay. The Egyptians made papyrus from a plant that grew in the Nile region. Strips of papyrus were woven together, soaked, and pounded into a flat surface that was polished with a rock until smooth. Hieroglyphics were painted or

Early forms of picture writing such as this were developed in Sumeria and Egypt about 5,000 years ago.

scratched on the papyrus with a brush or a pen. The Greeks wrote on parchment, made from treated animal hides. Parchment was more durable than papyrus but much more expensive to manufacture. Sheets of parchment or papyrus could be stitched together into long scrolls. It was the Chinese who developed the writing surface that was to become the standard—paper. Mixtures of rags, tree bark, and other fibrous materials were soaked in tubs, pounded with mallets, pressed into sheets, and left to dry in the sun. The resulting paper had many advantages: It was lightweight, cheap, and easy to write on. Moreover, sheets of paper could be stacked and bound together, producing what we today would recognize as a book. The Chinese were making paper by about A.D. 100, but it took nearly another thousand years before paper became widely used in Europe.

▲ The Social Impact of Writing

The arrival of writing carried with it several consequences for early society. In the first place, it created a new division in society. Before the written word, almost everybody had about the same degree of communication skills if they could speak and hear. But not everybody could read and write. Those who could had access to information not available to the rest of the population. And, as is usually the case, with greater access to information comes greater access to power. This power was concentrated in the rulers and the scribes who served those in power. In Egypt, for example, only privileged children, who would later become priests or government scribes for the pharaohs, were taught to read and write.

Second, writing helped make possible the creation of empires. Writing made organization easier. Tax collection records could be kept more efficiently, as could the accounts of payments. An army could be established and paid regularly. Written orders to commanders simplified administration. Writing helped develop trade and increased a country's treasury. Although it is difficult to say what role writing played in its development, it is probably no coincidence that the first Egyptian dynasty under Menes (the ruler who united upper and lower Egypt and established a capital at Memphis) came into being about the same time as the Egyptians were developing their hieroglyphics. Additionally, writing helped establish and maintain both the Greek and the Roman empires. Note that this is not to say that writing *caused* empires to develop; other political, economic, and social conditions had to be present as well. But it is probably safe to say that writing made it *easier* for these empires to come about.

A third, more subtle effect had to do with the nature of knowledge itself. For the first time, it was possible to preserve and nourish a permanent body of knowledge. Before the written word, the transmission of knowledge from one generation to the next was hampered by the limits of human memory and distortion. Knowledge that was written down, however, could be stored. The Greeks established the Great Library at Alexandria around 311 B.C., which eventually contained about a half-million scrolls. Scholars from all over the Greek world came to Alexandria to use the library and to further increase the store of knowledge.

Finally, writing made it possible to develop a consistent and enduring code of laws. Before the written word, legal decisions were made by local judges representing the particular village or community where they were located. There was no general, overarching,

The growth of international travel and global marketing has started a trend back toward pictographic communication, a method that cuts across languages. Airports all over the world, for example, have adopted a common pictograph system with symbols that denote baggage claim, rest rooms, ground transportation, and the like. Many products also use pictographs to convey information. See if you can identify what the following pictographs represent. (Answers are below.)

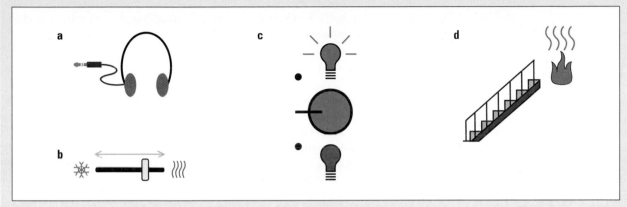

(a) headphone plug; (b) defroster in car; (c) power switch; (d) fire escape.

impersonal body of law on which decisions were based. With writing, law became tangible in the establishment of codes that transcended locale and individual circumstances. The first great legal document in history, the Code of Hammurabi, was written in Sumeria around 2000 B.C.

▲ Writing in the Middle Ages

The Roman Empire came to an end around the sixth century and was followed by the feudal period in Europe. By this time books were becoming more numerous but were far from common. Early books were copied by hand by scribes, a long and laborious process. As Christianity spread through Europe, bookmaking became centered in monasteries, where monks, working on parchment, would carefully copy and illustrate the most important religious books of the period. Sometimes the original was garbled in the process since spelling varied widely from place to place, and many authors used abbreviations known only to them. The resulting volumes were treated as works of art and were closely guarded; some were even chained to keep them from being taken from the monastery. Another problem with many of the early books was that, once written, they disappeared in the monastery's library because there was no system for others to locate them. Books were placed on the shelf in the order in which they were acquired by the library. There was no filing according to subject or author. Scholars had to depend on the librarian's memory to find anything. (Umberto Eco's 1980 novel *The Name of the Rose* provides a fascinating description of a medieval library.)

As trade increased throughout medieval Europe, the demand for information grew. Merchants needed to keep track of financial transactions and to document the various currencies in circulation. The idea of a university probably originated in India and North Africa and eventually spread to Europe. The University of Paris was founded around 1150, and Oxford began holding classes in the same century. As the feudal system gave way to strong, centralized monarchies, governments needed more information to help collect taxes and defend their borders. Lawyers needed to record the outcomes of legal cases. All this demand helped move the process of bookmaking away from the monastery and into lay society. Writing shops, or *scriptoria*, opened all across the continent. The copying business was helped by the widespread introduction of paper, which had finally made its way into Europe from China. Books copied on paper were cheaper than books on parchment, but they were still expensive. If you wanted a copy of a book in the early 14th century, for example, you would have to hire a scribe; negotiate a price; decide on the ink color, binding, and illustrations; and then wait, maybe as long as a year, for the book to be produced.

Demand for books still outran supply, however, and there were not enough scribes to handle all the work. Consequently, the scribes were able to charge even higher fees, and books became even more a medium of the elite. Economic and social progress seemed to have hit a roadblock.

This problem was solved around 1450 with the invention of the printing press and movable type, the third of our communication milestones.

PRINTING

The invention of printing is actually a story of many inventions. One of these was the development of paper by the Chinese. China was also responsible for the development of block printing—character outlines were carved out of a block of wood, and the raised parts were inked and pressed against a piece of paper. The oldest surviving block-printed book was published in 868. The Chinese also perfected a system of movable type, using first clay and later blocks of wood for individual characters. The Koreans were experimenting with movable metal type by the beginning of the 15th century.

The next major invention occurred in Germany, where Johann Gutenberg is generally credited with developing a printing press that used movable metal type. Gutenberg published his famous Bible around 1453, and his new printing method quickly spread across Europe. Only 30 years after Gutenberg's Bible appeared, there were printing presses in more than 110 towns in western Europe alone. The total increase in the number of books available in Europe is impossible to calculate, but it is probably safe to say that by 1500 there were hundreds of times more books available than in 1450. As books proliferated, their cost went down. Although still expensive, books were no longer the exclusive possession of the very rich. The printed book could now be afforded by those who were simply relatively prosperous.

The consequences of the printing revolution are so far-reaching and extensive that it is impossible to discuss all of them. Most scholars seem to agree, however, on the most significant results.

Johann Gutenberg was a wine connoisseur as well as a metallurgist. His design for the printing press was borrowed from a similar device used in wine making.

▲ Effects of the Gutenberg Revolution

The printing press facilitated the development of vernacular (everyday) languages across the European continent. Most of the pre–printing press, hand-lettered books had been written in Latin—the language of the Catholic Church and of higher education. Reading these works therefore required the knowledge of a second language, which restricted potential readership to the educated elite. Many early printers, however, recognized that a broader market for their books would be available if they were published in French, German, or English. Many printers also felt closer ties to their home country than to the church, further encouraging the printing of books in native languages. This trend had other consequences. Bodies of information now became more accessible to more people, further encouraging the growth of literacy, and, in turn, prompting more books to be published. Finally, the use of the vernacular probably helped pave the way for the nationalism that swept Europe in succeeding centuries.

The printing press played a role in the religious upheaval that swept Europe in the 16th century. Before the press, those clerics who disagreed with the doctrines and policies of the church had limited channels for expression. Handwritten copies of their views were few, had limited circulation, and could easily be censored or confiscated by authorities. The situation was forever changed after Gutenberg. Theologian and religious reformer Martin Luther's writings were translated from Latin into the vernacular, printed as pamphlets, and distributed all over Europe. It has been estimated that it took only a month for his famous Ninety-five Theses (the ones he nailed to the church door in Wittenberg, Germany) to be diffused across Europe. One of his later pamphlets sold 4,000 copies in a month. Despite efforts by the church to confiscate and burn Luther's writings, the Reformation movement continued. In addition, the printing of the Bible in the vernacular meant that individuals now had direct access to the core of their religious belief system. The Bible could be read directly and interpreted individually; there was no need for clerical intervention. This increased access to information further weakened the power of the Catholic Church and helped the spread of Protestantism.

Moreover, the arrival of printing speeded up the publication of scientific research. Although it would still be considered agonizingly slow in the era of e-mail and the Internet, printing a book of scientific findings took far less time than it did when manuscripts were handwritten. Printing also ensured that identical texts would be read by scientists in different countries and helped them build on the work of others. Galileo and Newton made their contributions to science in the 17th century, after advances in 16th-century printing.

The printing press even helped exploration. The travels of the Vikings are little known, due in part to the fact that they explored during a time when it was difficult to record and publicize their exploits. Columbus visited America after printing developed, and his deeds were widely known in Europe a year after his return. Printed accounts of the discoveries of early explorers found a ready audience among those eager to find wealth and/or bring religion to the New World. Many early developers published glowing (and sometimes overly optimistic) accounts of life in the new lands, hoping to promote investments and help business. The journeys of the early voyagers were helped by printed books that contained navigational and geographic information about the Americas.

Further, the printing press had a profound effect on the growth of scholarship and knowledge. Whereas access to handwritten textbooks was difficult, university students now had printed texts. (Think how hard it would be to take this course if everybody in the class had to share just one textbook.) As the number of books increased, so did the number of students who studied at a university. Literacy increased further. Interest in the classical works of Greece and Rome was revived as they appeared in printed books that were read by many. Books based on the scholarship of other countries appeared. The advances in mathematics made by the Indians, Muslims, and Arabs were disseminated. Without the printing press the Renaissance of the 16th century might not have occurred.

Finally, the printing press led to the dissemination of what we would today call *news*. As will be discussed in Chapter 4, newspapers sprang up in Europe at the beginning of the 17th century. These early publications were primarily concerned with foreign news. It wasn't long, however, before these papers focused on domestic news as well. This development did not sit well with some monarchies, and government attempts to suppress or censor news content were not unusual. It took until the end of the 17th century to establish the notion of a press free of government control (more on this topic in Chapter 4). The early newspapers made government and political leaders more visible to the public and helped create a climate for political change in both Europe and America.

▲ Technology and Cultural Change

Before leaving this topic, we should note that it is easy to ascribe too much significance to the printing press, to assume that the printing press was the prime mover behind all the effects mentioned. Such a view is called **technological determinism**—the belief that technology drives historical change. A more moderate position suggests that technology functions with various social, economic, and cultural forces to help bring about change. Printing did not cause the Reformation, but it probably helped it occur. And vernacular languages were growing in importance before Gutenberg, but his invention certainly helped them along. In any case, the birth of printing marks the beginning of what we have defined as *mass communication,* and it is certainly a momentous event in Western history.

The next centuries brought further refinements to printing. A metal press was developed by the late 1790s; steam power to drive the press was added shortly thereafter. Advances in printing technology helped usher in the penny press, a truly mass newspaper (see Chapter 4). A better grade of paper made from wood pulp came into use in the 1880s, about the same time as the Linotype machine, a device that could compose and justify a whole line of metal type. Photoengraving brought better visuals to the paper in the 1890s, as did the development of halftone photography a few decades later. Hot-metal type gave way to photocomposition and offset printing in the 1970s and 1980s, and the computer ushered in an age of relatively cheap desktop printing a few years later. Printing has changed a great deal over the years, but its consequences are still very much with us.

The next two communication milestones occurred during what many have called the age of invention and discovery, the period roughly encompassing the 17th–19th centuries. The reasons behind the many achievements of this period are several. The great explorations of previous centuries had brought different cultures together, and scholars were able to share ideas and concepts. Further, there was a change in the way people generated knowledge itself. The traditional authority of the Catholic Church was eroding, and intellectuals looked less to faith and revelation as a source of knowledge and more toward reason and observation. Philosophers such as Bacon, Descartes, and Locke argued for systematic research based on what the senses could perceive. In addition, scientific societies in Italy, France, and Great Britain helped advance the frontiers of knowledge. And, as already mentioned, the printing press helped distribute news of current discoveries to all, prompting others to achieve new breakthroughs. Whatever the reasons, these three centuries saw such advances as Galileo's use of the telescope and notion of a heliocentric solar system, the theory of blood circulating through the body, Newton's theory of gravitation, the roots of modern chemistry, the utilization of electricity, and the discovery of microscopic bacteria. Inventions came along at a dizzying rate: the steam engine, the locomotive, the plow, the internal combustion engine, the automobile, the sewing machine, the dynamo, and a host of others. Not surprisingly, the field of communication also saw major developments, as the next two milestones demonstrate.

CONQUERING SPACE AND TIME: THE TELEGRAPH AND TELEPHONE

It is appropriate that we spend some time discussing the telegraph and telephone, two related technologies that presaged many of the features of today's media world. For instance, the telegraph harnessed electricity; it demonstrated the technology that would eventually be used in radio. It was also the first medium to use digital communication (dots and dashes). The telephone, with its interconnected network of wires and switchboards, introduced the same concept now at the core of the Internet: Everybody was linked to everybody else.

▲ Development of the Telegraph

It is difficult for people raised in an age of cell phones, cable TV, fax machines, e-mail, and the Internet to appreciate the tremendous excitement that greeted the development of the telegraph. Before the appearance of the telegraph in the early 19th century, messages could

travel only as fast as the fastest form of transportation (with some minor exceptions). A messenger on horseback would clop along at around 15–20 miles per hour. A train carrying sacks of mail could travel about 30 miles per hour. The fastest form of message transportation was the carrier pigeon, which could cover more than 35 miles per hour. Then along came the telegraph, which sent messages traveling over wires at the almost unbelievable speed of 186,000 miles per second, the speed of light itself. No wonder that, when it first appeared, the telegraph was described as the great "annihilator of time and space." It was the first device that made possible instantaneous point-to-point communication at huge distances. It was also the forerunner of what we today might call, to use an overworked cliché, the *information superhighway.*

The technology necessary for the telegraph dates back to the discovery of electricity. Many early inventors realized that electricity could be used to send messages simply by varying the time the current was on and off. Experiments with early versions of the telegraph (*telegraph* comes from Greek words meaning "to write at a distance") were performed in the late 1700s. By the 1830s and 1840s, workable telegraph systems had been developed in England and the United States.

Samuel Morse was the principal force behind the creation of the telegraph in America. His device consisted of a sending key, a wire, and a receiver that made marks on a paper tape in concert with changes in the electrical current. Later versions did away with the paper tape and let the operator read messages by listening to the clicks made by the receiver. To simplify message transmission, Morse developed a code consisting of dots and dashes that is still in use today.

Morse demonstrated his device in the late 1830s and eventually received a grant from the government to continue his work. He constructed a line between Baltimore and Washington, D.C., and opened the nation's first telegraph service with the famous message "What hath God wrought?"

▲ The Cultural Impact of the Telegraph

Public reaction to the new machine was a combination of awe and amazement. The telegraph wires that swayed between poles were called *lightning lines.* The early telegraph offices set out chairs so that spectators could watch as messages came in from distant cities. Some people refused to believe that the new invention worked until they traveled to the source of the telegraphic message and verified it with the sender. Some were afraid that all that electricity flowing around above them posed a danger to their health, and they refused to walk under the wires.

Despite these fears the telegraph grew quickly, and lightning lines soon criss-crossed the nation. By 1850 almost every town on the expanding Western frontier could communicate with every other city. Maine could talk to Texas at the speed of light. By 1866 a cable had been laid underneath the Atlantic Ocean, linking Europe and America. Four years later, the overland wires and undersea cable carried more than 30 million telegraphic messages (telegrams).

The telegraph was changing communication at about the same time another invention was changing transportation—the railroad. Interestingly, the telegraph wires generally followed the railroad tracks, and stationmasters were often the first telegraphers. The telegraph made it possible to keep track of train locations and coordinate the complex job of shipping goods to various parts of the country—particularly to the West. The telegraph helped the train bring settlers to the frontier and played a role in the country's westward expansion.

The conduct of war was also changed by the telegraph. Troops could be mobilized quickly and moved, usually by railroad, in response to tactical and strategic developments. The significance of the telegraph for the military was demonstrated many times during the Civil War.

Morse's invention had an impact on commerce as well. It sped up communication between buyers and sellers, reported transactions, and organized deliveries. Instant communication brought about standard prices in the commodity markets. Before the telegraph the price of corn varied with local market conditions and might be several dollars cheaper in, say, Chicago than in St. Louis. After the telegraph connected all markets, local variations were evened out.

Further, as we will discuss in more detail in Chapter 4, the telegraph greatly enhanced newspapers' ability to transmit news. Information from distant places had previously taken weeks to reach the newspaper office. With the telegraph and Atlantic cable, even news from Europe could make the next day's edition. Newspaper publishers were quick to recognize the potential of this new device and used it heavily. Many incorporated the word "Telegraph" into their name. The telegraph also helped the formation of news agencies, or *wire services* as they were also called. The Associated Press made great use of the expanding telegraphic service to supply news to its customers. Finally, the telegraph changed the style of reporting. Because the early telegraph companies charged by the word, news stories became shorter. Rather than wordy, reflective, and interpretive reports, scoops, breaking news, and the bare facts began to characterize news reports.

▲ Government and Media

The telegraph also set the precedent for the relationship between the government and large media companies. In many other countries, since the telegraph was used to deliver messages, it seemed an extension of the post office, and the government agency that assumed responsibility for the postal service also administered the telegraph. However, this model was not followed in the United States. Although some in the government endorsed a federal takeover of the telegraph system, the prevailing sentiment was in favor of private, commercial development. By the end of the 19th century, telegraphic communication was dominated by one company, Western Union. As we will see in later chapters, other mass media—motion pictures, radio, television—were also developed as private rather than government enterprises and were dominated by one or a few large companies.

▲ A Change in Perspective

Another consequence of the telegraph was subtler and harder to describe. In some ways the telegraph changed the way people thought about their country and the world. By erasing the constraints of space, the telegraph had the potential to function as an instant linkage device (see Chapter 2) that tied people together. Morse wrote how the telegraph would make a neighborhood of the whole country. A Philadelphia newspaper, shortly after the successful demonstration of the device, wrote that the telegraph destroyed the notion of "elsewhere" and made everywhere "here." The paper declared that the telegraph would "make the whole land one being." An article in a magazine of the period was even more expansive: The telegraph "binds together by a vital cord all nations of the earth." It may not be too much of an overstatement to contend that the telegraph introduced the notion of a global village that was to be popularized a century later by Marshall McLuhan. It created a sense of unity among Americans and encouraged them to think in national and international terms.

Alexander Graham Bell demonstrates a version of his telephone for representatives of the business community. Bell and his colleagues eventually received 30 patents for telephone-related inventions.

In the camera obscura a small opening containing a lens produces an inverted and reversed image of an object. Many artists used the camera obscura to help them draw precise images of people, landscapes, and buildings.

The telegraph was joined by a companion invention, the telephone. Like the Morse invention the telephone conquered time and space and had the added advantage of requiring no special skills, such as Morse code, for its use. It transmitted the human voice from point to point. There was some confusion over the precise role the telephone would play in society, but the notion of linking phone users by wires and the development of the switchboard eventually made it possible to connect one place with many others. This arrangement helped the telephone become a fixture in businesses and homes across the nation. The telephone made private communication easier to achieve. It was now possible for people to converse away from the watchful eyes of parents, bosses, and other authority figures. Finally, like the telegraph industry the telephone industry would be dominated by a large corporation, AT&T, which would eventually gain control of Western Union.

In sum, the telegraph and the telephone enabled people to communicate over vast distances in what we now call *real time* and had a far-reaching impact on the political, economic, and social development of the United States and the rest of the world. We will discuss this impact in detail throughout the book. In many ways it is still making itself felt today.

CAPTURING THE IMAGE: PHOTOGRAPHY AND MOTION PICTURES

The telegraph and the telephone drew upon advances in the science of electricity. The next communication advance we will examine could not have occurred without advances in the field of chemistry.

▲ Early Technological Development

Two things are required to permanently store an image. First, there must be a way to focus the image on a surface. Second, the surface must be permanently altered as a result of exposure to the image. The first requirement was fulfilled in the 16th century with the creation of the camera obscura, a dark chamber with a pinhole in one wall. The light rays that entered the chamber through the small hole projected an image on the opposite wall. The second requirement took longer to achieve. In the 1830s two Frenchmen, Joseph Niepce and Louis Daguerre, experimented with various substances that changed upon exposure to light rays. Silver iodide provided the best results, and Daguerre sold this discovery to the French government. An English scientist, William Fox Talbot, working at about the same time as Daguerre, refined the process by capturing his images on paper in the form of negatives, permitting copies to be made. Other advances quickly followed, including the

Mathew Brady's famous 1864 photo of a war-weary Abraham Lincoln. Part of this portrait was later used on the 5-dollar bill.

use of flexible celluloid film. George Eastman's company introduced the Kodak box camera in the 1890s with the slogan "You press a button. We do the rest." The Kodak was designed for the mass market. Amateur photographers simply loaded a roll of film in the camera, aimed the camera, pressed the button, and then sent the film off to Kodak to be developed and printed.

There were several long-range consequences of these technological advances. Early photos (called *daguerreotypes*) required long exposure times, making them particularly suitable for portraits, for which the subject could remain still. These early portraits provided a way to preserve and humanize history. Our images of George Washington, for example, are from paintings that show him in an idealized manner, usually in noble poses making him appear distinguished and powerful. Our images of Abraham Lincoln, however, come from the many photographs that were taken of him during his term in office. The early photos, taken around 1860, showed him in flattering poses. The later photos, taken after years of war, showed a man grown visibly older, with lines creasing his forehead and tired eyes.

▲ Photorealism and Mathew Brady

The Civil War was the first American war to be photographed extensively. Before the camera the public's view of war was probably shaped mostly by paintings and etchings that showed magnificent cavalry charges and brave soldiers vanquishing the enemy, not the horror and carnage of actual combat. Mathew Brady persuaded the U.S. government to give him access to the battlefield. (Brady apparently thought the government would cover the costs of his venture, but his expectations were never met, and many of his photos were lost.) Because early photography was not able to capture action scenes, Brady was limited to photographing scenes of the aftermath of a battle. These images, however, were powerful enough. In 1862 Brady's colleagues photographed the battleground at Antietam just two days after the battle and before all the dead had been buried. The resulting photographs were the first to show the actual horrors of war. When the photos went on view in a New York gallery, they caused a sensation. The carnage of battle was revealed to all. As Oliver Wendell Holmes remarked, "Let him who wishes to know what war is like look at this series of illustrations." A hundred years later, other communication advances would bring scenes of horror from the Vietnam War directly into American living rooms.

Photography had an impact on art. Now that a means had been developed to preserve realistic images, artists were free to experiment and develop different ways of portraying the world. Again, although it is hard to say how much of a role photography played in influencing painting, the impressionist, postimpressionist, and cubist schools of painting came to prominence at about this same time. At the other end of the spectrum, photography itself became a fine art, as virtuosos such as Alfred Steiglitz, Margaret Bourke-White, and Edward Steichen created masterpieces of graphic reproduction.

▲ Photography's Influence on Mass Culture

One did not have to be an artist, however, to take pictures—everybody could and did. Advances in film and camera technology put cameras in the hands of the masses. Ordinary people took photos of significant people, objects, and events: marriages, new babies, new cars, pets, vacations, family reunions, proms, and so on. Photo albums quickly became a part of each family's library. Photography enabled each generation to make a permanent record of its personal history.

Advances in the printing process, such as halftone photography, also made it possible for photographs to be published in magazines and newspapers. By the beginning of the 20th century, dozens of illustrated dailies and weeklies were being published in the United States. This development created a new profession—**photojournalism**—and changed America's conception of news. Photojournalism reached new popularity in the 1920s when the pace of life increased, and many innovations cropped up that promised to save time for the consumer—lunch counters for fast meals, express trains, washing machines, vacuum cleaners, and so forth. When it came to news reporting, the biggest time-saver was the photograph. Readers could look at photos much more quickly than they could read the long text of a story. As a consequence, printed columns decreased and space devoted to pictures increased, helping popularize the tabloids and picture magazines such as *Life* (see Chapter 5).

Photojournalism had subtler effects as well. First, it changed the definition of *news* itself. Increasingly, news became that which could be shown. Accidents, natural disasters, demonstrations, and riots were natural photo opportunities. This visual bias in news reporting remains a topic of concern even today. Second, as photo historian Vicki Goldberg put it, photography created "a communal reservoir of images." Certain historic events were fixed forever in the minds of the public by their photos: the fiery crash of the *Hindenburg*, the young girl screaming over the body of a dead student at Kent State, the smoking remains of the World Trade Center, the toppling of the statue of Saddam Hussein in Baghdad. All of these images have been etched permanently on the national consciousness.

Modern cell phone cameras have made photographers of everybody, and that, in turn, has raised privacy issues. Cell phones with cameras are banned in many locker rooms and health spas. Nearly every state has a law governing photographic voyeurism. Compounding the problem are the many Internet sites that showcase user-generated content, such as Flickr, Fotolog, and Phanfare. Unsuspecting people might be shocked to find that photos taken without their knowledge or permission all of a sudden show up on the Internet.

▲ Pictures in Motion

The technology behind photography led to the development of another way to capture an image. The goal behind *this* new milestone, however, was to capture an image in motion. Chapter 9 details the early history of the motion picture medium and traces how it evolved from a series of toys into a giant entertainment industry. It is significant that this new medium evolved while three significant trends were occurring in the United States. The first was industrialization. In the Industrial Revolution, which began in the early 19th century and continued into the 20th, production and manufacturing both increased significantly. Along with industrialization came the second trend, urbanization, as people moved into the cities to be near the plants and factories where they could find jobs. In the United States one-fourth of all Americans lived in an urban area by 1914. The third trend was immigration. About 25 million people immigrated to the United States between 1871 and 1914, and most of them wound up in cities where they went to work in manufacturing plants.

The culmination of these trends was the creation of a huge audience that was drawn to the new medium of motion pictures. The first movie houses sprang up in the cities. They were called *nickelodeons*, storefronts that had been turned into makeshift theaters, with uncomfortable benches or folding chairs for the audience, a tinkling piano, and poor ventilation. Nonetheless, nickelodeons were big hits among the newly arrived immigrants. By 1910 there were more than 10,000 of these nickelodeons around the country, and film exhibitors and filmmakers quickly recognized that there was a market for filmed entertainment. The motion picture business had started. Film eventually moved to plusher theaters and tried to appeal to the middle class, but it left its mark on the immigrant population. Many learned the customs and culture of their new country from nickelodeons.

▲ Motion Pictures and American Culture

The long-range impact of the motion picture lay mainly in the areas of entertainment and culture. As the demand grew for feature-length films, only very large companies were able to come up with the money needed to pay production costs. As will be noted in

Edwin S. Porter's *The Great Train Robbery* was the first American film to tell a story. This classic Western was actually shot in New Jersey.

Chapter 9, these large companies came to dominate the production, distribution, and exhibition of movies. Today's film industry is controlled by global conglomerates that still follow many of the patterns established in the 1920s.

Movies forever altered America's leisure time. Vaudeville soon died out. Going to the movies became an important social activity for the young. Saturday afternoons that once were spent going to parks and friends' houses were now spent inside a darkened theater.

The movies became a major cultural institution. Photography and the mass-appeal newspaper had made it easier for people to recognize and follow the fortunes of their favorite celebrities, but motion pictures raised this process to a new level. Hollywood produced cultural icons, the movie stars. The popularity of motion pictures was based on their appeal to all social classes. Unlike serious drama, opera, and ballet, which appealed to the elite, movies attracted the masses. The movies helped bring about the notion of a popular culture, a phenomenon whose benefits and liabilities are still being debated.

In 1915 American poet Vachel Lindsay published *The Art of the Moving Picture,* which signaled the beginnings of a new popular art form. Lindsay's book was the first of many serious attempts to develop a theory of film. Although a popular entertainment form that blended business and art, film soon became a topic worth serious study, a trend still with us today as evidenced by the many universities that teach film as part of their curricula.

In the early 1930s the Payne Fund sponsored a series of studies on the possible harmful effects of attending motion pictures. This was the first of many studies that tried to establish just what impact film and, later, broadcasting have on society (see Chapter 19 for more details). The Payne Fund studies were significant because they marked the first time the public had decided that a medium, in this case motion pictures, had an effect on society and was deserving of serious examination.

Finally, although film played its most prominent role as a medium of entertainment, it is important to note that it had an influence on journalism as well. Started around 1910, newsreels appeared weekly or semiweekly and pictured the major events of the period. The big movie studios eventually controlled the production of newsreels. They standardized the content of the 10-minute reels so that audiences could expect to see something from Europe, some national news, some sports, a feature or two, and perhaps a human-interest story. The newsreels were discontinued in the 1950s and 1960s as pictorial journalism moved to television. These early news films, however, influenced many of the conventions and expectations of broadcast news reporting.

NEWS AND ENTERTAINMENT AT HOME: RADIO AND TELEVISION BROADCASTING

Radio, the first medium that brought live entertainment into the home, would not have been possible without advances in physics. The discovery of electromagnetic waves caught the attention of many scientists, who looked for ways to use this new discovery to send messages. Advances in wire telephony in the United States made it possible to send voice and music over the air and prompted AT&T to fund a massive research program in the area. Radio development, however, was stymied by patent problems. Had it not been for World War I, radio's development might have taken far longer. The war had a couple of

Mathew Brady's decision to photograph dead soldiers on the Antietam battlefield started a controversy that persists even today: What is the proper way to cover the carnage caused by a war? Is it fitting to show dead American soldiers on the nightly newscast or in the newspaper? How about dead enemy soldiers or civilian casualties?

For many years the U.S. government forbade the photographing of dead U.S. soldiers for fear that it would demoralize the home front. Franklin Roosevelt reversed that policy during World War II when he felt that those at home had become too complacent and too removed from the realities of combat. Accordingly, in 1943 *Life* magazine published a photograph of the sand-covered bodies of three unidentifiable U.S. soldiers on an invasion beach in New Guinea. A short time later, John Huston's classic documentary film *The Battle of San Pietro* contained scenes of actual combat and resulting casualties. Decades later, during the Vietnam conflict, filmed scenes of wounded and dead GIs found their way onto the network news.

Operation Iraqi Freedom reopened the controversy. Since many reporters were embedded with combat troops, battlefield coverage was sometimes shown live or shortly after it occurred. For the most part the reporting on the part of the U.S. media was restrained. This led some observers to charge that the media were sanitizing the war and avoiding its harsh realities. On the other hand, when *USA Today* published a front-page photo of the bodies of two dead Iraqis, the paper received dozens of letters and more than a hundred phone calls criticizing the newspaper for its lack of judgment and accusing it of being antiwar.

Media professionals expressed different viewpoints concerning their responsibilities in time of war. Quoted in the *Washington Post*, ABC's Ted Koppel argued in favor of showing dead bodies: "One thing you cannot do is leave people with the impression that war is not a terrible thing." CNN's Walter Rodgers apparently felt the same way. During a live broadcast from outside Baghdad, Rogers showed the body of a dead Iraqi soldier next to a burned-out personnel carrier. Said Rodgers in a story in *Newsday*, "You ought to show even more than taste allows so no one has any illusions how terrible carnage and war are."

But does the audience really need to see grisly scenes to be reminded of the horrors of war? Doesn't everybody already know that war is horrible? Steve Capus, an NBC news producer, contended that a newscast should communicate the reality of war without wallowing in death or injury. News anchor Charles Gibson went further: "Any time you show dead bodies, it is simply disrespectful."

John Szarkowski, former director of photography at the Museum of Modern Art, offers another perspective. He argues that editors and reporters should not show every bloody scene they come across. After a while people become inured to the violence in the images, and each successive scene has less power than the one before it.

In sum, this debate will go on as long as reporters cover wars, and journalists will continue to struggle with their ethical obligations to their profession and to the audience.

major consequences for radio's development. The U.S. Navy solved the legal problem by asserting control over all patents that made possible major advances in technology. Further, a large number of soldiers went into the Signal Corps, where they learned the fundamentals of the new medium. When they came back from the war, these men kept interest alive in radio, helping popularize many amateur radio clubs, and provided the basis for a ready-made audience for early broadcasting.

▲ Radio Broadcasting

The shift from using radio as a point-to-point communication device (like the telegraph) to using it as a point-to-many broadcasting medium caught many by surprise. Thanks to the popularity of early radio stations, broadcasting became a national craze, and by the early 1920s the stage was set for the emergence of another mass communication milestone. Radio was the first mass medium that brought sports, music, talk, and news into the living room.

In addition to World War I, other historical circumstances influenced radio's development. It is easy to overlook today, but when radio first started out, there was no system in place that permitted it to support itself. Many radio stations went on the air simply for the novelty of it, with little thought as to how to fund their operations. Significantly, modern radio emerged in the Roaring Twenties, when economic conditions were vigorous, consumer goods were easily available, stocks were soaring, and many people in the business world were accumulating fortunes. In the midst of this climate, it was easy for radio broadcasting to turn to commercials for its economic base. Accepting advertising brought quick profits and was in tune with the business-is-good philosophy of the times. Business was so good, in fact, that the federal government generally kept out of it. Radio, however, needed government intervention. Overlapping signals from too many radio stations broadcasting on too few frequencies was a serious problem. In 1927 Congress created a Federal Radio Commission (FRC), whose main task was to regulate the technical side of the medium. Unlike the situation in some European countries, the FRC and its successor, the Federal Communications Commission, took a generally light-handed approach to regulation and favored the fortunes of commercial broadcasters.

It was also the era when newspaper chains and many other businesses were consolidating their operations. The development of radio networks fit nicely into this model, and it was not long before national programming was supplied by two, and later three, national radio networks. Further, tabloid newspapers were capturing readers, and Hollywood films were booming. These trends were to have an impact on the future of radio programming. In concert with its evolution as an advertising medium, radio moved toward mass-appeal programming that provided an audience of consumers for those who bought commercial time on the new medium.

Ironically, the Depression of the 1930s, which did some financial damage to radio, also helped its programming. Many performers from vaudeville, the recording industry, and the theater, rendered unemployed by the Depression, took their talents to radio, particularly network radio. As a result, the level of professionalism and the caliber of entertainment improved, and the networks solidified their grasp on the industry. By 1937 almost every powerful radio station in the country was a network affiliate. News broadcasting came of age about this same time, and radio soon became a more important source of news than the newspaper.

▲ The Cultural Impact of Radio

In terms of the long-term impact of this medium, several elements stand out. First, and most obviously, radio helped popularize different kinds of music. One of the early radio stations with a powerful signal was WSM in Nashville, which carried broadcasts of *The Grand Old Opry,* a program that introduced country music to many thousands. Broadcasts of black rhythm-and-blues music crossed the race barrier and gained listeners among whites. In more recent years radio helped popularize rock and roll, reggae, and rap.

Radio made its own contributions to the popular culture. Although early programs recycled many vaudeville acts, genres original to the medium soon developed. One of these was the soap opera, whose familiar formula later made the transition into television. In 1940 soaps accounted for more than 60 percent of all network daytime programming. Entertainment series aimed at children introduced youngsters to *Jack Armstrong—The All-American Boy* and *Captain Midnight.* The significance of these programs may be less in their style or content and more in the fact that they signaled the radio broadcasters' attitude that children were a viable market and that it was acceptable to send advertising their way. Situation comedies such as *Amos 'n' Andy* and action-adventure programs such as *Gangbusters* were other formats that persisted into television.

After a somewhat shaky start, radio news came of age in the 1930s and 1940s. Audiences tuned to the new medium for live coverage of the events leading up to World War II. Listeners could hear live the voices of world leaders, such as Adolf Hitler and British prime minister Neville Chamberlain. Commentators would then provide what in a more modern era would be called *instant analyses* of what was said. Radio personalized the news: Unlike newspapers, where a byline might be the only thing that identified a reporter, radio news had commentators and reporters with names, distinctive vocal styles, and personalities. A list of famous radio news personnel of the period includes H. V. Kaltenborn, Edward R. Murrow, and Lowell Thomas. These individuals became celebrities and introduced a new component into journalism—the reporter as star. This trend would also carry over into television as network anchors and reporters were able to command multimillion-dollar salaries, just like movie stars and sports heroes.

Finally, like the movies, radio changed the way Americans spent their free time. Radio was the prime source of entertainment and news. Families would faithfully gather around the radio set in the evenings to listen to the latest episodes of their favorite programs. By the 1940s household radio listening time averaged more than 4 hours per day, most of it in the early evening hours. A new phrase emerged to describe this period of peak listening activity. It was called *prime time,* another concept that passed over to TV.

▲ Television Broadcasting

Television, as will be discussed in Chapters 10 and 11, also had its beginnings in the 1920s and 1930s, and, as was the case with radio, a war interrupted its development. World War II halted the growth of TV as a mass medium. Early transmitting stations went off the air during the war, and TV receivers were no longer manufactured. The technology behind TV, however, received a substantial boost from the war effort, as new discoveries in the field of radar were translated into an improved TV broadcast system.

Also, like radio, television became popular during an age of relative prosperity. After a period of postwar retooling, American industry began churning out consumer goods. The self-denial of the war years gave way to a fulfillment of long-repressed desires, as Americans bought new cars, dishwashers, barbecue grills, and air conditioners. But the TV set was the most sought-after appliance. Television swept the country during the 1950s. It took the telephone about 80 years to reach 85 percent of the country's homes, and the automobile did it in 49 years. Television did it in 10. Approximately 10 million homes had TV in 1950; by 1959 that number had more than quadrupled. While new, labor-saving appliances increased leisure time, more often than not that leisure time was spent watching TV. Household furniture had to be rearranged to accommodate the TV set in the living room.

▲ The Cultural Impact of TV

Television grew up surrounded by other dramatic social trends and events. Americans were moving into the suburbs, and commuting thus became a ritual. Women were beginning to enter the workforce in greater numbers. The 1960s saw the emergence of the civil rights movement, the escalation of the war in Vietnam, and the growth of the counterculture. Television brought these happenings into the nation's living rooms.

Today, television is in 99 percent of all households, and the set is on about 8 hours every day. In an astoundingly short period, TV replaced radio as the country's most important entertainment and information medium and became a major cultural and social force. In fact, television probably has not been with us long enough for us to see all of its ultimate consequences. Some, however, are fairly obvious. Television has become a major consumer of time. Sleeping and working account for the most time in a person's day, but TV watching ranks third. Television also has transformed politics. Political conventions are staged for TV; candidates hire TV consultants; millions are spent on TV commercials; candidates debate on TV; and so on. TV has exerted a standardizing influence on society as well. Clothing, hairstyles, language, and attitudes seen on TV pervade the nation and, for that matter, the rest of the world. Further, television news became the most important and believable source of information. And, like the motion picture, television created a whole new slate of stars and celebrities. It has also been suggested that television has become an important source of socialization among children and that TV programs inspire antisocial and other undesirable behavior. (Chapter 19 reviews the evidence for these assertions.)

Although the telegraph was the first to be called the "great annihilator of time and space," television might be a better candidate for that title. Audiences have seen TV pictures live from Baghdad, Earth's orbit, the moon, and Mars (well, as live as they can be from a place so far away). In fact, today's TV viewer expects to see live reports of breaking stories, no matter where they are; no place seems far away anymore.

The cultural influence of television is sometimes subtle. Shows such as cable network TLC's *Trading Spaces* revived interest in home remodeling and interior design.

Photography was credited with creating a reservoir of communal experience. Television, however, has widened and deepened that reservoir. For example, televised images of President Kennedy's funeral, the *Apollo 11* moon landing, the *Challenger* explosion, and the planes striking the World Trade Center have all been indelibly impressed upon the national consciousness.

THE DIGITAL REVOLUTION

In his book *Being Digital,* Nicholas Negroponte, director of MIT's Media Laboratory, summed up the digital revolution as the difference between atoms and bits. Traditionally, the mass media delivered information in the form of atoms: Books, newspapers, magazines, CDs, and DVDs are material products that have weight and size and are physically distributed. Negroponte maintains that this is rapidly changing: "The slow human handling of most information in the form of [recorded music], books, magazines, newspapers, and videocassettes is about to become the instantaneous transfer of electronic data that move at the speed of light." In short, atoms will give way to bits.

As an example, consider the difference between e-mail and traditional paper mail. In the traditional system a letter must be placed in an envelope with a postage stamp and given to the U.S. Postal Service, whose employees sort it, transport it, and deliver it a few days later to its recipient. E-mail needs no paper, no postage, and no delivery by postal carriers. It is a series of bits of information that travels electronically and is delivered in seconds rather than days. With e-mail the same message can be copied a thousand times and sent to a thousand different people much more quickly and cheaply than with paper mail.

At the risk of oversimplifying a rather complicated topic, we can describe **digital technology** as a system that encodes information—sound, text, data, graphics, video—into a series of on-and-off pulses that are usually denoted as zeros and ones. Once digitized, the information can be duplicated easily and transported at extremely low costs.

As will be discussed in Chapter 12, the computer was the first device to use the digital system to process information. The innovation quickly spread to other media. Digital technology makes possible the special effects now common in motion pictures and television, as well as digital audio, digital video, digital photography, and digital equivalents of newspapers, magazines, and books.

The development of the Internet meant that computers could send digital information to all parts of the globe. All of a sudden, a new distribution medium was available that permanently changed the media environment. In short, digital technology and the Internet triggered a revolution in the way information is stored and transmitted. As a result, the traditional mass communication media found themselves in uncharted waters and had to figure out how to cope with this drastic development. Newspapers, for example, used to exist only on paper (atoms). Now they exist in both paper and digital form (bits). Big recording companies used to distribute music on tape or on disk (atoms). Napster and

All the communication milestones discussed in this chapter changed the way information was stored or transmitted. Starting with the printing press, they all expanded the scope of human communication by making it possible for people to share information with other people in other places or at other times. This achievement prompted a rather optimistic attitude toward the social benefits of the media. For example, the telegraph was viewed as a force for morality, understanding, and peace. Both radio and TV were touted as means of bringing education, high culture, and refinement to the masses. Cable TV was supposed to bring new forms of entertainment to minority groups and open the way for two-way TV that would aid the democratic process by making possible electronic polling. None of these things has yet come to pass. Nonetheless, the Internet, with its ability to connect everybody to everybody, is currently being touted as an information revolution that will affect society as deeply as the printing press. Whether this will happen is a matter of debate, but for now it might be useful to ask if new communication technologies automatically carry with them social benefits. Have they been liberating or constrictive?

A number of social critics have pointed out that new communication media expand the potential for freedom of expression and have greatly enlarged the scope of human culture. The cost of sending messages over long distances has dramatically decreased. Thanks to the telegraph, telephone, and Internet, people can do business, socialize, and argue with people all over the world. The new media have made information available to all. And, if information is power, the new media will empower more individuals. New means of communication make it easier for democracy to function. Film, radio, and TV have opened up new art forms and patterns of entertainment.

Others suggest a different interpretation. The new communication media have spurred the growth of large conglomerates whose main goal is profit, not cultural enrichment. Further, new communication media create an overload of information, some of it overpowering and pervasive, such as commercials, junk e-mail, and telemarketing. The information made available by the new technologies may be neither interesting nor useful nor profound, and it may interfere with people's attempts to identify the truly significant.

Moreover, although technological advances—such as the telegraph, telephone, and Internet—have expanded the scope of communication, is any of the communication worthwhile? Check out any chat room or Facebook page, and you will probably find that much of the communication consists of greetings, good-byes, flirting, and "how-are-you's." Newsgroups exchange recipes, talk about sports, review cigar brands, and discuss other information that most could live without. How much real dialogue actually occurs? Is it possible to have a meaningful conversation with people whom you can't see and who may not even be who they say they are? The new media have done little to promote political participation. Voter turnout in the United States continues to decline, and political apathy continues to increase. Most people would rather stay at home and watch TV than go to a political forum. Further, many critics would argue that the new media have provided little that is new and fresh in the arts and entertainment. Expanded TV channels have brought us more of the same.

In sum, advances in communication media have the potential for both positive and negative consequences.

---

other music-sharing sites proved that individuals could download music files (bits) from other individuals on the Internet, totally bypassing the recording companies. The chapters in Parts II and III of this book discuss how the media are adapting to the digital age.

The digital revolution, of course, has had profound impact not only on the mass media but also on other institutions. It has, for example, transformed business. Even companies that deal in atoms rather than bits have found that they have to devise whole new marketing and distribution schemes to capitalize on the new digital age. It is not possible (yet) to have a tennis racket physically delivered over the Internet, but you can go online, search the various sporting goods sites for bargains, and order one that appeals to you. The Postal Service or a package delivery company, however, still has to deliver the racket (atoms) to you. The importance of this new form of buying and selling has added a new noun, *e-commerce*, to our vocabulary.

Of course, for most people reading this book, the digital revolution is no longer a revolution—it's their life. Access to powerful information processing and storage tools is no longer earthshaking; it's taken for granted. Today's college students do most of their research online, store their music and photos digitally, communicate via instant messages and e-mail, make their travel arrangements through the Web, and entertain themselves with video games, digital TV, streaming video, iPods, and DVDs.

The aftermath of this revolution, as has been mentioned previously, has been the empowerment of the individual audience member. Fledgling writers no longer need a publisher; they can create a blog, discussed in Chapter 12. New bands can bypass music companies and make their music available online. People with items to sell no longer have to pay a newspaper to run classified ads; they can find buyers for free on the Internet. Traditional news media no longer have monopolies over information. Many pictures of the 2004 South

Almost everybody knows that Alexander Graham Bell was the inventor of the wired telephone, but not too many people know about Martin Cooper, the person generally given credit for inventing the cell phone. Cooper received a degree in electrical engineering, and after a stint in the Navy, he went to work for the Motorola Company in 1954. During his early years at Motorola, Cooper worked on developing portable communication devices. In 1967 he perfected a portable handheld police radio.

Motorola then gave Cooper the task of leading its research into cellular communication technology. At the time Motorola was in a heated competition with rival Bell Labs to come up with a workable system. While the scientists at Bell worked to develop a bulky car phone, Cooper convinced Motorola to develop a personal phone, one small enough and light enough for people to carry around. After several years of experimentation, Motorola was ready to unveil its invention to the public. In April 1973, on his way to a press conference in New York City, Cooper decided to give the phone one last test. Standing outside a New York hotel, Cooper pulled out his prototype cell phone, which looked like a white brick with a number pad and an antenna. To the amazement of passersby, Cooper dialed a number and began talking out loud into his phone, thus making the first private personal cell phone call. Who was at the other end of Cooper's call? His rival at Bell Labs. Cooper can't remember his first words, but they were probably something like "Guess what? We did it." He does remember that there was a long period of embarrassed silence at the other end.

As of this writing, Cooper, now in his seventies, is still active in cellular technology. He is chairman of a company that is trying to improve wireless access to the Internet.

Asian tsunami were taken by tourists with digital cameras and shared over the Internet. All in all, the digital age has made technology accessible and cheap so that information may be obtained and shared.

The potential social and cultural implications of the digital age are considerable.

First, the notion of community may have to be rethought. In the past people developed friendships based on local geography. But the digital world of the Internet makes possible virtual communities based on shared needs and interests rather than locale. African Americans, for example, no matter where they live, who visit Web sites such as NetNoir, BlackVoices, and BlackPlanet can make friends, discuss relevant issues, and connect to African American culture and lifestyles.

Second, as mentioned in Chapter 1, digital technology has made it possible for everyone to be a mass communicator. This, in turn, is having a huge impact on how people are getting news, opinion and entertainment. The trend toward user-generated content is one manifestation of this. In a typical month about 20 million people visit YouTube to watch videos posted by other people—that's a bigger audience than most hit prime-time TV shows attract. And YouTube is not the only video-sharing site. At last count there were more than 60 similar Web sites. It would appear that we are all trying to entertain each other.

The number is hard to pin down, but there are probably more than 6 million blogs on the Internet. The Pew Internet and American Life Project estimated that a new blog is created every 6 seconds. Bloggers have become citizen journalists, reporting live from the scene of major news events such as the Katrina disaster mentioned in Chapter 1. They have also influenced debates on such topics as Social Security reform and party politics. Many blogs, such as Power Line and The Daily Kos, have become powerful editorial voices.

Third, consider what the digital age might mean for politics. A huge amount of political information—party platforms, candidates' positions, text of speeches—is available in digital form on the Web. A Pew Foundation survey found that the number of Americans who got campaign information online doubled from the 2000 to the 2004 elections. Ideally, this should result in a better-informed electorate. The confusion and bitterness surrounding the results of the 2000 presidential election in Florida prompted many to call for a system of online voting. Indeed, the Internet raises the possibility of true direct democracy. Our current representative democracy was conceived in part as a solution to the practical problem that all the people could not be physically present in one place to debate and vote. The Internet now makes it possible for computer owners to debate and cast a ballot at home. Do we still need representatives? Should we institute "digital democracy"?

The impact of the digital revolution on the economy cannot be overstated. In the United States around 90 million people buy something online every year. In 2006 it was estimated

CRITICAL / CULTURAL ISSUES

The Meaning of Media

Cell phones, laptops, and PDAs belong to that broad class of devices known as *mobile information devices*. It's possible, however, that lumping these devices under one umbrella label may obscure differences in the way audience members perceive their functions. Communication scholars point out that communication technologies may be socially constructed in different ways by their users.

In an article in the June 2003 issue of *Critical Studies in Mass Communication*, Paul Leonardi argues that culture plays a major role in how media are perceived. Leonardi conducted focus groups (structured group interviews guided by a moderator) among Latinos living in the United States. He asked participants to discuss how cell phones, computers, and the Internet were perceived in Latino culture.

His results were somewhat surprising. Latino culture places a high value on consistent and close interpersonal contact, and the cell phone was seen as consistent with that value. Focus group participants revealed that the cell phone was an important tool for communication and was becoming a necessity for daily life. More than 90 percent of respondents had used a cell phone. Almost all of those who didn't currently own a cell phone planned to buy one within a year. Respondents recognized the utility of the cell phone in an emergency and the fact that cell phones represent an alternative way of reaching someone when the land lines are busy. Cell phones had become so ingrained in their daily lives that some participants mentioned that their children used cell phones to call them from another room in the house to ask what was being prepared for dinner. In short, the cell phone fit nicely with cultural values.

On the other hand, computers and the Internet were not such a good fit. Only 40 percent of the respondents had used a computer, and even fewer (27 percent) had ever used the Internet. Respondents appeared to think of computers and the Internet in same way, treating them as similar. They did not see the Internet as a communication medium. Instead, the Latinos in these focus groups perceived it as a tool with which to find information. The use of e-mail, chat rooms, and message boards as communication channels was seldom mentioned. Although computers were perceived as useful devices, they were also seen as inhibiting interpersonal communication among family members and friends. Surfing the Internet was perceived as a solitary activity that isolated people from each other. In short, respondents felt that computers and the Internet did not keep people connected. As a result, interpersonal values were jeopardized by these technologies.

Language also played a role in participants' preference for the cell phone over the computer. Spanish-language cell phones are readily available; Spanish-language computer platforms are harder to find. In addition, only a small portion of Internet content is in Spanish. This posed a cultural problem for Latinos. In order to access the Internet, it was necessary to forgo the use of one's native language.

Although many of the respondents said that they planned to purchase a computer in the near future, their stated reasons for buying a computer had nothing to do with the computer's communication potential. Instead, the Latinos in Leonardi's study recognized that those who didn't have a computer would be in an inferior position to those in mainstream U.S. culture.

Leonardi's findings highlight that Latinos living in the United States do not view these information devices as homogeneous. Instead, they have distinct perceptions based on how cell phones, computers, and the Internet relate to their cultural values regarding communication. As Leonardi sums up: "[T]he communication goals of a particular group of users always play a crucial role in their uses and perceptions of technology. If we forget this, we may blindly adopt technologies because we believe they are a sign of progress without making sure they help us progress."

SOUNDBYTE

Where Did I Leave That Thing?

One of the problems associated with portable, handheld media is that they are easy to lose. A survey of cab companies in Chicago found that in just one year about 85,000 cell phones, 21,000 PDAs, and 4,000 laptops were accidentally left behind when their owners got out of cabs. Luckily, about 90 percent of the passengers were reunited with their lost gear thanks to considerate cab drivers who tracked down the owners.

that e-commerce sales totaled $100 billion, up 44 percent from 2004. About $1 out of every $8 spent in the United States is spent online. Experts estimate that the Internet has created more than 6 million jobs.

Americans are already living in digital homes. They talk on digital telephones, play digital video games, watch digital TV, save programs on digital video recorders such as TiVo, rent digital video disks (DVDs), listen to digital music, take pictures with digital still and video cameras, and interconnect home computers via digital networks. The digital world touches everyone's life every day.

Finally, the arts have entered the digital age. There's a Digital Art Museum online that exhibits the work of leading artists. There are many other Web sites that feature digital artwork. Musicians, sculptors, and graphic artists have also embraced digital technology.

On the downside, now that the digital age has torn down the barriers to accessing and producing information, there is a whole lot of it. Enter "digital revolution" into a Google search, and you'll get about a half-million hits. The information is organized into not what you think is relevant but what the search engine thinks is relevant. Consequently, the results of the search seem chaotic, and you may have to scroll through several pages before you find something that is even remotely connected to what you are looking for. The digital revolution has resulted in an information glut. As scholar Neil Postman describes it in a recent article in the *Harvard International Journal of Press/Politics*, "Like the sorcerer's apprentice, we are awash in information without even a broom to help us get rid of it. Information comes indiscriminately, directed at no one in particular, in enormous volume, at high speeds, severed from import and meaning."

Finally, there is the problem known as the "digital divide." In the United States, although the gap shows signs of narrowing, families making more than $50,000 per year are more than twice as likely to have Internet access compared to those earning $30,000 or less. And whereas about 69 percent of the population of North America is connected to the Internet, in Africa it is about 3.5 percent. In the future those who have access to information will also have more access to power than those who do not. Will this digital divide translate into more serious social, economic, and political divisions?

MOBILE MEDIA

Sometimes it's hard to see a milestone when you're in the middle of it, but the signs are getting hard to miss. Walk around campus or on a busy main street, and see how many people are talking on cell phones or sending e-mails on their personal digital assistants (PDAs). Check out any airport waiting lounge, and see how many people are laboring over laptop computers. What you see are indications that the next wave of communication technology is breaking over us.

The number of cell phone users in the United States topped 219 million in 2006. More than 60 million carry around laptops, and another 15 million use PDAs. All of these devices share common characteristics:

- They depend on wireless technology.
- They are portable, making it possible for people to access information from anywhere. The new portable media are the best illustration of one of the major themes of this book: increased media mobility.
- They are interconnected, making it possible for people to hook into the Internet or the worldwide phone network.
- They are blurring the distinction between mass and interpersonal communication.

Before the cell phone and PDA, two screens dominated American lives: the TV screen and the computer screen. Cell phones and PDAs have become the third screen—a screen that has the potential to drastically transform traditional media and American culture. Let's first take a look at how mobile media are serving some of the traditional media functions discussed in Chapter 2.

We'll start with surveillance. Radio and TV stations have been providing traffic reports for decades, but now subscribers to a company called Traffic411 can hear the latest information tailor made for their particular commute over their cell phone. Sports fans can receive scores, standings, and the latest news about games in progress over their phones and PDAs if they subscribe to ESPN wireless. Several services offer the latest stock prices to their phone customers. Need to check ski conditions before heading out to the slopes? Motorola offers an Internet-ready cell phone that allows you to stay informed.

The newest generation of cell phones lets users take still pictures or video clips and post them on the Web in seconds. Imagine millions of Americans walking around with video-equipped cell phones. When breaking news occurs, people in the area can take video and still photos before the media even arrives on the scene. The most striking images of the 2004 Asian tsunami were taken by tourists, and many photos were placed directly on the Web. The news was transmitted without a traditional reporter or news organization. A cell phone video of Saddam Hussein's execution made its way onto the Web. In the future we might all be reporters.

Entertainment is firmly entrenched on the small screen. Almost all cell phones come with preloaded video games. New-generation phones are equipped with MP3 players so that subscribers can download and listen to music over their phones. Some companies are providing entertainment content specifically for the small screen. As part of the "Everything. Everywhere" trend discussed in Chapter 1, entertainment companies are supplying their content to mobile phones and laptops. Time Warner, for example, offers Mobile Access, a program that lets Time Warner Cable subscribers watch live TV on their phones. AT&T mobile subscribers can download segments of *Saturday Night Live*. The most memorable moments of *The Office* are also available thanks to a deal between NBC and mobile game provider I-Play. Fox produced a spin-off program from its popular *24* expressly designed for cell phones. And there are several Web sites, including iTunes, where audience members can download full versions of movies to their laptops. Some experts predict that the mobile entertainment market might top $27 billion annually by decade's end.

Turning now to linkage, it's obvious that being connected to millions of other people all over the world makes everyday life easier. What was once considered wasted time can now be used productively. Laptops enable people to read documents, send e-mail, prepare reports, and analyze data while waiting for a plane or even sitting on the plane itself. Businesspeople trapped in a traffic jam can make calls and stay in touch with the office through their cell phones and PDAs. A special use of the linkage function is achieving safety and security. A *Consumer Reports* survey found that security was the number-one reason people buy cell phones. Cell phone users can report accidents and other emergencies in seconds, no matter where they occur. More than 30 percent of all 911 calls come from a cell phone.

If you're late, you can call or send a message over your PDA alerting those at your destination. If you're lost, you can call for directions. If you're buying groceries for dinner, you can check to see if people want fish or chicken. There are many other examples, but the words of one 17-year-old pretty well sum it up: "With my cell phone I can order pizza from anywhere." This use vividly illustrates how wireless portable media are serving the linkage function of communication; thanks to the Internet and the cell phone network, everybody can be linked to everybody.

The new mobile media have already transformed American culture. Society has had to develop a new set of rules regarding cell phone etiquette. The LetsTalk.com Web site summarizes the most obvious ones: Turn off the phone in the movie theater, don't shout, pay attention when walking, and so on.

The cell phone has taken on symbolic properties. Users customize their phone's appearance and ring tones to reflect their own individuality and/or status. Having the latest, thinnest model with all the bells and whistles has become "cool." Cnet.com has a test on its Web site to match a person with the phone that is best suited to his or her personality (sample personality types: "busy executive," "gear head," "weekend warrior").

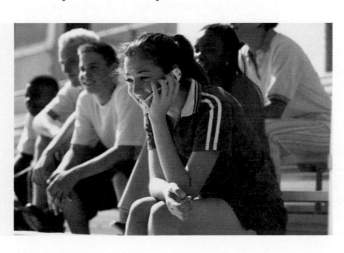

The cell phone is now the primary mode of socializing for teenagers. More than half of teens in the United States have their own phone.

Family life has been forever altered because of cell phones. About 75 percent of all teenagers now have access to a cell phone, and more than 50 percent own one. The increasing number of teens with cell phones is due in part to parents who want their children to be prepared in the case of an emergency or who want to check up on them when they are out of the house. In a family in which parents are on the go

The Walt Disney Company has taken the concept of mobile parenting one step further with the introduction of a wireless service that allows parents to control how kids use their cell phones and gives them the ability to track their kid's (or at least their phone's) location.

The devices contain controls that permit parents to set limits on how much time their kids can spend on the phone and to regulate what numbers they can call at various times of the day. During school hours, for example, kids could be blocked from calling all but emergency numbers. Moreover, the phones can be equipped with a Global Positioning System that lets parents use the Internet to locate their child's phone on a map.

Finally, family members can use the system to send priority text messages to one another. The people at Disney, aware that parents are not as savvy as kids when it comes to text messaging, have built in a simplified menu so that parents can press one button to send such messages as "Where R U?"

because both hold jobs and children have to get to soccer or gymnastics or band practice, the cell phone provides a way for parents to monitor offspring by phone rather than in person. This new phenomenon is called **mobile parenting.**

Cell phones have even changed our culture's conception of time, a phenomenon called **time softening.** You've probably experienced this scenario several times. You're supposed to meet a friend at a restaurant at eight. A few minutes after eight, your friend calls you on your cell phone and says he's in his car only a couple of miles away and should be there in 10 minutes. If you're in contact, can you really be late?

Time softening also occurs when two people don't set a firm time for a meeting. Rather than saying, "I'll meet you at seven," PDA and cell phone users often say, "I'll call you when I'm leaving the office, and we'll set something up." The time-softening effect is an example of how wireless media, like traditional media, can have a socialization function. In this case they have changed the value that society has traditionally placed on punctuality.

Of course, like most revolutions mobile media have a downside. Most importantly. driving and talking on a cell phone don't mix. A study done at Harvard in 2002 suggested that cell phone use while driving might be linked to as many as 2,600 traffic deaths a year. Another study concluded that drivers on cell phones contribute to as many as 1.5 million accidents a year. It's no surprise, then, to find that as of 2004, legislatures in 35 states were considering laws to limit cell phone usage while driving.

Camera-equipped cell phones have also raised privacy issues. Celebrities have to put up with star-obsessed fans (dubbed the "snaparazzi") taking their photos while they are eating, shopping, or walking down the street and posting them on the Web. In New York City several restaurants, clubs, and gyms frequented by celebrities have banned cell phones.

For every person who appreciates the convenience of a cell phone, there's another person who wishes that they would just shut up. Most professors are not amused by cell phones ringing during lectures. People eating at restaurants find their dining experience marred by people at other tables chatting loudly into their phones. Commuters relaxing or reading on trains and buses are disturbed by the loud conversations of cell phone users. A conversation with someone who owns a PDA is always subject to frequent interruptions as e-mail appears. Some people have become fed up. "Cell phone rage" has been blamed for several altercations.

Finally, wireless mobile media can be expensive. The Motorola Razr 3 camera phone retails for nearly $400. A new Blackberry PDA goes for around $300. If it turns out that only the rich can afford these devices, then the digital divide between rich and poor will only increase.

CONCLUDING OBSERVATIONS: THE IMPACT OF NEW MEDIA

In 1839 the director of the Paris Observatory, François Arago, was speaking to the French Parliament about a new technology that was then sweeping Europe: the daguerreotype, the ancestor of the modern photograph (see page 62). Many critics were hostile to the new technique because they feared it would have a harmful effect on French society by destroying the livelihood of thousands of French portrait painters and perhaps even put an end to the art of painting itself.

CRITICAL / CULTURAL ISSUES

Cell Phones, Religion, and Culture

Professor Heidi Campbell has studied the cultural implications of the widespread adoption of the cell phone[1]. She points out that the cell phone is more than a phone. It is a means of individual expression (personal ring tones, wallpaper, phone covers) as well as a tool for business, creating a social network of employees and clients. In fact, the cell phone has the potential for generating unexpected cultural impact.

The impact of the cell phone has spread to religion. Campbell argues that religious groups are using the cell phone to incorporate religious practices into society's new on-the-go lifestyle. For example, religious groups in many countries offer daily Bible text messages. Pope Benedict XVI sent out an inspirational text message to subscribers just a few days after his elevation. Catholics in the Philippines can receive the "Mobile Way of the Cross," and the "Mobile Rosary" on their cell phones. Muslims can buy a special phone that reminds them of prayer times and a digital compass that indicates the direction of Mecca. A British youth group uses cell phones to create a national prayer chain. All members receive a text message at specific times encouraging them to pray.

Of course, new technologies and religious culture do not always mesh smoothly. Muslims have criticized those who send text messages during Ramadan rather than making traditional personal visits. Hindus objected to an image of a Hindu god talking on a cell phone.

As Campbell points out, religious groups are receptive to those aspects of new technology that support their traditions but tend to resist those advances that cause friction with the traditional culture and beliefs. This process is a dynamic one, and often a new technology is shaped by a culture in order to fit in. Campbell presents a prime example of this process by analyzing the reactions of one ultra-orthodox religious group to the cell phone.

The average Israeli spends about 450 minutes per month talking on a cell phone, one of the highest rates in the world. Not all segments of Israeli society, however, have taken to the device. Ultra-orthodox Jews belong to a community that rejects modernity and its secular values. The cell phone is seen as a device that could be harmful to this community because it could easily deliver materialistic content to its users. At the same time, however, ultra-orthodox Jews note that the cell phone could possess certain benefits for the community.

What grew out of this tension is the "kosher phone," a specially designed handset that preserves the phones calling function but disabled text messaging, Internet access, video, and voice mail applications. The kosher phone emerged after long negotiations between cell phone manufacturers and a council of rabbis. The council also drafted guidelines about how the technology would be used.

As Campbell concludes, if a technology with questionable features is deemed valuable to a community, a "culturing process" takes place. This culturing process may involve changes in both the culture of a community and the technology itself. In short, culture can influence both the form and function of any new technology.

[1]See Heidi Campbell, "Texting the Faith: Religious Users and Cell Phone Culture," in A. Kavoori and N. Arceneaux (eds.), *The Cell Phone Reader* (New York: Peter Lang, 2006).

In defending the daguerreotype, Arago maintained that these fears were shortsighted. He voiced what we can call Arago's rule of technology: The greatest potential impact of a new invention is not how it changes or replaces old things but how it generates things that are entirely new. Arago's rule certainly held true for photography. It may have put a few portrait painters out of work, but more importantly, it led to the development of mechanically reproduced images, photojournalism, and the motion picture—developments that helped usher in the age of mass communication, something that the members of the 1839 French Parliament could not even have imagined.

One lesson we can learn from these milestones in the development of human communication is that, as Arago realized, it is impossible to predict the ultimate use of a new medium. When the telegraph was invented, many people thought it would have a profound effect on the world order. Since nations were linked by the telegraph and could send instant messages to one another, it was predicted that misunderstandings would cease, prejudices would vanish, and peace would reign. Things did not quite go in that direction. Alexander Graham Bell suggested that the telephone be used as a means of communication among the various rooms of a house or that phones be sold only in pairs, linking just two specific points, such as a person's office and home. The phonograph was first used to record business dictation.

When radio first started, most thought it would be used as a substitute for telegraph or telephone communication. All of these inventions became mass communication media that their creators never envisioned. We may be at the same point with the digital and wireless mobile milestones. We can see some of their possibilities, but their ultimate evolution is impossible for us to predict. Arago's rule may be validated all over again.

It appears that the emergence of a new communications technology changes *but does not make extinct* those advances that came before it. The telegraph and the telephone did not kill the printed word; nor did film, radio, TV, and the Internet. Television did not make radio extinct, but it did cause a major change in the way the medium was used. Likewise, the computer, the Internet, and mobile media will probably not cause any of the traditional media to evaporate, but they will probably change the way we use these "old" media.

Figure 3-1 (see page 52) is a time line that displays when each of the eight milestones occurred. A quick examination of the figure makes clear that the pace of communication innovations has accelerated. It took humans dozens of centuries to get from language to writing. The jump from writing to printing took about 5,000 years. The telegraph and telephone cropped up only 300 years later, followed quickly by photography and motion pictures. Radio was invented only a few years after that, as was TV. The computer followed on the heels of television. In fact, a person born in 1908 and who lived a hundred years (an accomplishment becoming increasingly more common) would have lived through several milestones: radio/TV, computers, and mobile wireless media. Each advance in communication increases our power to convey and record information, and each has played a role in prompting significant changes in our culture and society. It is becoming difficult to digest fully the impact of one communication medium before another comes on the scene.

MAIN POINTS

- Eight milestones in the evolution of human communication are language, writing, printing, telegraphy and telephony, photography and motion pictures, radio and television, digital media, and wireless handheld media.

- Language led to the development of an oral culture in which information was passed on by word of mouth from one generation to another.

- The invention of an alphabet and the development of a usable surface made writing possible. Writing created a social division in society. Those who could read and write had access to more information than those who could not.

- Writing helped create and maintain empires as well as make storehouses of information, such as libraries, possible.

- Printing made information available to a larger audience. It helped the development of vernacular languages, aided the Protestant Reformation, and contributed to the spread and accumulation of knowledge.

- The telegraph and telephone were the first media to use electricity to communicate. They marked the first time the message could be separated from the messenger.

The telegraph helped the railroads move west and permitted the newspapers to publish more timely news. The telephone linked people together in the first instance of a communication network.

- Photography provided a way to preserve history, had an impact on art, and brought better visuals to newspapers and magazines. Motion pictures helped socialize a generation of immigrants and became an important part of American culture.

- Radio and TV broadcasting brought news and entertainment into the home, transformed leisure time, and pioneered a new, immediate kind of reporting. Television has an impact on free time, politics, socialization, culture, and many other areas as well.

- The digital revolution changed the way information was stored and transmitted and made e-commerce possible.

- The next communication milestone is the move to mobile media.

- In general, it is difficult to predict the ultimate shape of a new medium. New media change but do not replace older media. The pace of media inventions has accelerated in recent years.

QUESTIONS FOR REVIEW

1. What is the difference between writing based on signs and writing based on an alphabet?

2. Why was the telegraph labeled "the great annihilator of time and space"?

3. What exactly is the "communal reservoir of images" created by photojournalism? Can you think of other examples of images that are forever fixed by photographs?

4. What digits are used in digital technology? Why could the telegraph be considered the first digital device?

QUESTIONS FOR CRITICAL THINKING

1. Printing was known in China for a long time before Gutenberg appeared. Why wasn't there a social revolution in China as there was in Europe when printing appeared?

2. Suppose Henry David Thoreau (see page 58) were alive today. What do you think he would say about the Internet?

3. Many people would argue that, of all the communication media discussed in this chapter, television has had the greatest impact on society. Do you agree?

4. When the Internet was first developing, the term *information superhighway* appeared frequently in news stories about it. Now that the Internet has been around for a while, news stories rarely contain that term. Why is this so?

5. Do you own a PDA or cell phone? If so, how have they changed your life?

6. Consider the boxed insert "Cell Phones, Religion, and Culture." Can you think of other technological devices that have been subjected to a "culturing" process? How does the "kosher phone" relate to the concept of a community? Who should decide what features of a new technology are introduced to a particular culture?

KEY TERMS

alphabet (p. 53)
technological determinism (p. 57)

photojournalism (p. 63)
digital technology (p. 68)

mobile parenting (p. 74)
time softening (p. 74)

INTERNET RESOURCES

Online Learning Center

At the Online Learning Center home page, www.mhhe.com/dominick10, *select* Student Center *and then* Chapter 3.

1. Use the Learning Objectives, Chapter Outline, Main Points, and Time Line sections to review this chapter.

2. Test your knowledge of the chapter using the multiple choice, crossword puzzle, and flashcard features of the site.

3. Expand your knowledge of concepts and topics discussed in the chapter by going to Suggestions for Further Reading and Internet Exercises.

Surfing the Internet

Here are some sites that provide information on media history. Some of the sites mentioned in Chapters 4–11 are also of relevance here.

www3.iath.virginia.edu/abell/homepage.html
Home page of Alexander Graham Bell. Reconstructs Bell's path to the invention of the telephone.

http://mediahistory.umn.edu
The best all-around site for media history. Contains an extensive time line, other net links, book reviews, articles, archives, chat boards, and pages on the history of specific media.

www.archive.org
Home of the Wayback Machine. Surf the Web the way it used to be.

www.cln.org/themes/history_film.html
Provides links to many sites that contain information about film history.

www.gutenbergdigital.de
Gutenberg's Bible on the Web.

http://inventors.about.com/library/inventors/bltelegraph.htm
Page devoted to Samuel Morse and telegraphy. Contains diagrams of early telegraphs and relevant links.

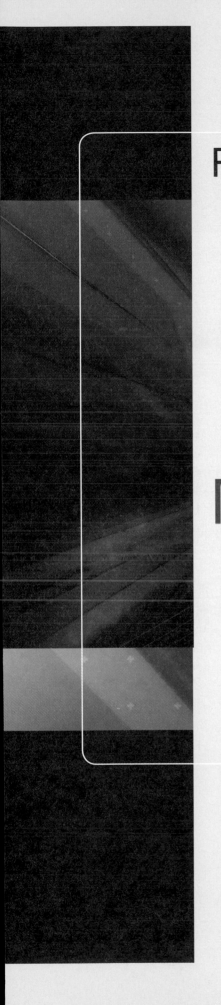

PART II

MEDIA

CHAPTER 4

NEWSPAPERS

This chapter will prepare you to:

- describe the challenges newspapers face in today's digital age

- recognize the conditions that had to exist before a mass press could come into existence

- understand the significance of the penny press

- explain the features that define both online and print versions of newspapers

- recognize the convergence of online and print newspapers

- understand the function of the Audit Bureau of Circulations (ABC)

- identify the various methods newspapers are using to gain readership

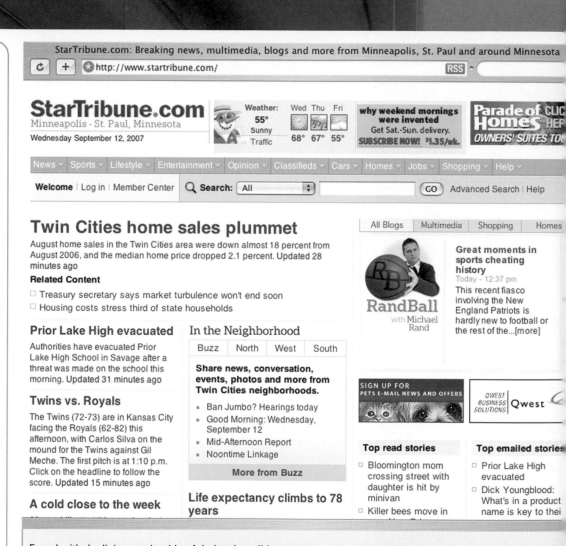

Faced with declining readership of their print editions, many newspapers are hoping that income from their Web sites will compensate for lost revenue.

All in all, the early 2000s have not been good years for the newspaper industry. Take the case of the Knight Ridder chain of papers. In 2005 Knight Ridder was the second-largest newspaper publisher in the United States, with papers in 28 markets. The next year Knight Ridder got out of the newspaper business.

Faced with declining circulation and uncertain advertising revenue, and under pressure from major stockholders, Knight Ridder was put up for sale. At first it appeared that nobody wanted the company. Nearly three dozen potential buyers were approached, but only one made a serious offer. In the end Knight Ridder was purchased by a much smaller newspaper chain, the McClatchy Company, at what experts termed a bargain price. The McClatchy Company, in turn, sold off 12 of the papers it acquired from Knight Ridder. (McClatchy also sold one paper it originally owned, the *Minneapolis Star Tribune,* taking a more than $600 million loss.)

The Knight Ridder saga is an indication of the state of the industry. Nationwide, newspaper circulation has been declining for 20 years, down another 3 percent from 2005 to 2006 alone. Many papers have slashed their payrolls. Newspaper audiences keep getting older (average age about 55), and young people are moving from newspapers to online sources for their news. Classified ad sites on the Internet have also bled off newspaper revenue.

The recording industry (see Chapter 8) was the first to see its business model drastically affected by the shift from atoms to bits (see Chapter 3), and now the newspaper industry seems next in line. Many in the industry are betting that the future of the industry lies not with paper (atoms) but with Web sites (bits). This chapter looks at the history, economics, structure, and future of this industry as it wrestles with the challenges of the digital age.

A BRIEF HISTORY

▲ Journalism in Early America

Before we get to the details, it might be helpful to identify some general features of newspapers in early America:

- There were few papers.
- Printers and postmasters did most of the early publishing.
- News was not as timely as it is today.
- The idea of a free press was not endorsed by colonial governments.

In 1690 Boston printer Benjamin Harris published the first American newspaper, *Publick Occurrences both Foreign and Domestick.* One of the items in the paper alleged an affair between the king of France and his son's wife. This news story infuriated the Puritan officials of the colony, and they shut down the paper after one issue. The notion of a free press had yet to surface in America; most colonists believed that a paper had to have royal consent to be published.

Fourteen years later, John Campbell, the local Boston postmaster, put out the *Boston News Letter.* Published with royal permission, the paper was dull and lackluster, with many news stories simply reprinted from European papers. Campbell's paper had only about 300 subscribers and never made a profit.

A few years later, another Boston paper, the *New England Courant*, came on the scene. It was published by James Franklin, Ben's older brother, without government permission. Eventually, the elder Franklin's paper got him into trouble with the local authorities, and he was thrown into prison. Ben took over, and the paper prospered under his leadership. Ben eventually moved on to Philadelphia, where he started the *Pennsylvania Gazette,* which boasted such innovations as more legible type, headlines, and a cleaner layout.

Ben Franklin retired from a successful publishing career at the age of 42. During his career: he had started several papers, published one of America's first magazines, run the first editorial cartoon, proved that advertising copy could sell merchandise, and, perhaps most importantly, demonstrated that journalism could be an honorable profession.

▲ The Beginnings of Revolution

Tensions between the colonies and the Crown were rising during Franklin's tenure as publisher, and this controversy sparked the development of the early American press. One example

Benjamin Franklin became the publisher of the *Pennsylvania Gazette* in 1729, when he was 24 years old. The paper became the most successful colonial newspaper, and Franklin the best-known colonial journalist and publisher.

of this tension was the trial of John Peter Zenger. Zenger published a paper openly critical of the British governor of New York. The governor threw Zenger into jail and charged him with criminal libel. Zenger's lawyer argued that no American jury should feel bound by laws formed in England, and Zenger was acquitted, striking a symbolic blow for press freedom.

Newspapers grew in numbers during the Revolutionary War, and most were partisan, siding with the colonies or with the Crown. This period marked the beginnings of the **political press,** which openly supported a particular party, faction, or cause.

In 1776, when the Continental Congress adopted the Declaration of Independence, the text of the document was published in the *Pennsylvania Evening Post* on July 6. The next year the Continental Congress

FREEDOM'S JOURNAL.

"RIGHTEOUSNESS EXALTETH A NATION."

BY JNO. B. RUSSWURM.   NEW-YORK, FRIDAY, MARCH 14, 1828.   VOL. I.—NO. I.I.

THE COLORED AMERICAN.

SAMUEL E. CORNISH, } Editor.   New-York, Saturday, May 13, 1837.   PHILIP A. BELL, } Proprietor.

Two early examples of the black press: *Freedom's Journal* was started in 1827 by John Russwurm, the first black person to graduate from a college in the United States, and by Samuel Cornish. Cornish later edited the *Colored American,* a paper that had subscribers from Maine to Michigan.

authorized Mary Katherine Goddard, publisher of the *Maryland Journal,* to print the first official copies of the Declaration with the names of the signers attached. Under Goddard's direction the *Journal* became one of the leading colonial papers during the war. Goddard was one of about 30 women who printed or published colonial newspapers.

▲ The Political Press: 1790–1833

The politicization of newspapers did not end with America's victory in the Revolutionary War. Instead, partisan leanings of the press were transferred into another arena—the debate over the powers of the federal government. The participants in this controversy included some of the best political thinkers of the time: Alexander Hamilton, James Madison, Thomas Jefferson, and John Jay. Newspapers were quick to take sides in this debate, and their pages were filled with Federalist or anti-Federalist propaganda. Heated political debate gave way to name-calling and quarreling between these two groups, and the content of many newspapers became colored by inflammatory language.

At the vortex of this debate between Federalists and anti-Federalists was the Constitution of the United States. Although the original document made no mention of the right of a free press, the Bill of Rights did contain such a provision. The **First Amendment** held that "Congress shall make no law . . . abridging the freedom of speech, or of the press." Thus, the idea of a free press, which had emerged during the Revolutionary period, became part of the law of the new nation when Congress ratified this amendment in 1791.

Newspapers grew with the country in the first 20 years of the 19th century. The daily newspaper began in 1783 and developed slowly. By 1800, however, most large cities had at least one daily paper, and by 1820 there were 24 dailies, 66 semi- or triweeklies, and 422 weeklies. These newspapers were read primarily by the upper socioeconomic classes; early readers had to be literate and possess money to spend on subscriptions (about $10 per year or 6 cents per issue—a large sum when you consider that during those years 5 cents could buy a pint of whiskey). The content was typified by commercial and business news, political and congressional debates, speeches, acts of state legislatures, and official messages.

Politics was still the main focus of many of the nation's papers, and several papers sent correspondents to Washington to report political news. James Gordon Bennett, whom we will meet again later, covered Washington for a New York paper. The first woman to achieve recognition as a political journalist was Anne Royall, who published two papers in Washington between 1831 and 1854. Royall was a crusader for free speech and state's rights, and she campaigned against graft and corruption.

During this period several newspapers were formed in response to the needs and interests of minority groups. *Freedom's Journal,* the first of over 40 black newspapers published before 1860, was founded in the late 1820s by the Reverend Samuel Cornish and John Russwurm. Written and edited by blacks, the paper championed the cause of black people by dealing with the serious problems arising from slavery and by carrying news of foreign countries such as Haiti and Sierra Leone that appealed to its black audience.

At about the same time, in 1828, another minority group, the Cherokee Nation, published the *Cherokee Phoenix,* written in both Cherokee and English. When the Cherokees were evicted from their home in Georgia and forcibly resettled in Oklahoma, a new paper, the *Cherokee Advocate,* was started and continued to operate until 1906. The *Advocate* was revived in the 1970s and now publishes a monthly edition.

▲ Birth of the Mass Newspaper

Several conditions had to exist before a mass press could come into existence:

- A printing press had to be invented that would produce copies quickly and cheaply.
- Enough people had to know how to read to support such a press.
- A mass audience had to be present.

In 1830 the U.S. manufacturing firm R. Hoe and Company built a steam-powered press that could produce 4,000 copies per hour. This and subsequent steam-powered presses that were even faster made it possible to print an extremely cheap newspaper that everybody could afford.

The second element that led to the growth of the mass newspaper was the increased level of literacy in the population. The first statewide public school system was established during the 1830s. The increased emphasis on education led to a concomitant growth of literacy as many people in the middle and lower socioeconomic groups acquired reading skills.

The final element was subtler and harder to explain. The mass press appeared during an era that historians call the age of Jacksonian democracy, an age in which ordinary people were first recognized as a political and economic force. Property requirements for voting had died out. Every state but one chose presidential electors by popular vote. In addition, this period was marked by the rise of an urban middle class. The trend toward democratization of business and politics fostered the creation of a mass audience responsive to a mass press.

▲ The Penny Press

Development of the Penny Press   Benjamin Day was only 22 years old when he launched the mass-appeal *New York Sun* in 1833. Day's idea was to sell his daily paper for a penny (a significant price reduction from the 6 cents a copy for other big-city dailies). Moreover, the *Sun* contained local news, particularly those items that featured sex, violence, and human-interest stories. Conspicuously absent were stodgy political debates. Day's gamble paid off as the *Sun* attracted readers, and the **penny press** was launched.

Others imitated the *Sun's* success. The colorful James Gordon Bennett launched the *New York Herald* in 1835, which was an even more rapid success than the *Sun*. The *Herald* introduced a financial page, a sports page, and an aggressive editorial policy that emphasized reform.

Front page of the *New York Sun:* Benjamin Day's reliance on advertising for revenue is illustrated by the several columns of classified ads appearing on the front page.

Another important pioneer was Horace Greeley. His *New York Tribune* appeared in 1841 and soon ranked third behind the *Herald* and *Sun* in circulation. Greeley used his editorial pages for crusades and causes. He opposed capital punishment and gambling and favored trade unions and westward expansion.

Greeley also supported women's rights. In 1845 he hired Margaret Fuller as literary critic for the *Tribune*. In addition to providing commentary on the fine arts, Fuller wrote articles about the hard lot of prostitutes, women prisoners, and the insane. Greeley's decision to hire Fuller is typical of his publishing philosophy: Like Fuller he never talked down to the mass audience but rather attracted readers by appealing to their intellect more than to their emotions.

The last of the major newspapers of the penny-press era that we will consider began in 1851 and, at this writing, is still publishing. The *New York Times*, edited by Henry Raymond, promised to be less sensational than the *Sun* or the *Herald* and less impassioned than Greeley's *Tribune*. The paper soon established a reputation for objective and reasoned journalism.

All these publishers had one thing in common: As soon as their penny papers were successful, they doubled the price.

Significance of the Penny Press   At this point, we should consider the major changes in journalism that were prompted by the success of the mass press during the period from 1833 to 1860. We can identify several key changes:

- The basis of economic support for newspapers
- The pattern of newspaper distribution
- The definition of what constituted news
- The techniques of news collection

Prior to the penny press, most of a newspaper's economic support came from subscription revenue. The large circulation of the penny papers made advertisers realize that they could reach a large segment of potential buyers by purchasing space. Moreover, the readership of the popular papers cut across political party and social class lines, thereby assuring advertisers a broad-based audience. As a result, advertisers were greatly attracted to this new medium, and the mass newspapers relied significantly more on advertising revenues than did their predecessors.

Older papers were distributed primarily through the mail; the penny press, although relying somewhat on subscriptions, also made use of street sales. Vendors would buy a hundred copies for 67 cents and sell them for 1 cent each. Soon it became common to hear newsboys hawking papers on street corners in the larger cities. Since these papers had to compete with one another in the open marketplace of the street, editors went out of their way to find original and exclusive news that would give their paper an edge.

The penny press also redefined the concept of news, hiring people to go out and look for news. Reporters were assigned to special beats: police, financial, sports, and religion, to name a few. Foreign correspondents were also popular. And newspapers changed their emphasis from the affairs of the commercial elite to the social life of the rising middle classes.

This shift meant that news became more of a commodity, something that had value. And, like many commodities, fresh news was more valuable than stale news. Any scheme that would get the news into the paper faster was tried. Stories were sent by carrier pigeon, Pony Express, railroads, and steamships. The Mexican War of 1846 made rapid news transmission especially desirable, and many newspapers first used the telegraph to carry news about this conflict. All in all, the penny papers increased the importance of speed in news collection.

▲ Newspapers as Big Business

A new reporting technique emerged during the Civil War as telegraphic dispatches from the war zones were transformed into headlines. Because telegraph lines sometimes failed, the opening paragraphs of the story contained the most important facts. If the line failed during transmission of a story, at least the most important part would get through. Thus, the "inverted pyramid" style of reporting was developed.

After the war, from about 1870 to 1900, the total U.S. population doubled, and the urban population tripled. Newspapers grew even faster than the population; the number of dailies quadrupled, and circulation showed a fivefold increase. As a result, newspapers became a big business, and some big-city papers were making more than $1 million a year in profits by the mid-1890s. The thriving newspaper business also attracted several powerful and outspoken individuals who had a profound influence on American journalism. We will consider three: Pulitzer, Scripps, and Hearst.

Joseph Pulitzer came to the United States from Hungary and eventually settled in St. Louis. After a string of unsuccessful jobs, he found he had a talent for journalism and turned the *St. Louis Post-Dispatch* into a success. In 1883, he bought the *New York World.* In a little more than three years, Pulitzer increased the paper's circulation from 15,000 to 250,000.

What was Pulitzer's formula for success? Pulitzer stressed accuracy. He also introduced practices that appealed to advertisers: more advertising space and ads priced on the basis of circulation. Moreover, he aimed his paper at the large population of immigrants then living in New York by stressing simple writing and many illustrations. Pulitzer also reintroduced the sensationalized news format of the penny press, as the *World's* pages carried stories about crime, violence, and tragedy. Finally, Pulitzer endorsed the notion that a paper should promote the welfare of its readers, particularly the underprivileged. Although Pulitzer did not originate the idea, he certainly put it into practice. The paper crusaded against unsanitary living conditions, corrupt politicians, and big business, all topics that gained Pulitzer many supporters among the working class.

Attempts to reach a working-class audience were not confined to the East. In the Midwest E. W. Scripps started papers in Cleveland and Cincinnati, both growing industrial cities with large populations of factory workers. The Scripps papers featured concisely edited news, human-interest stories, editorial independence, and frequent crusades for the working class. Scripps pioneered the idea of a newspaper chain. By 1911 he owned 18 papers.

Perhaps the best-known of these three newspaper giants, thanks to the film *Citizen Kane,* is William Randolph Hearst. While Pulitzer was succeeding in New York and Scripps was acquiring papers in the Midwest, the 24-year-old Hearst was given control of the *San Francisco Examiner,* thanks to the generosity of his wealthy father. Hearst went after readers by appealing to their emotions. Fires, murders, and stories about love and hate were given splashy coverage. Hearst banked heavily on sensationalism to raise his readership level. His strategy worked: The *Examiner* shot to the number-one position.

William Randolph Hearst, the successful publisher of the *San Francisco Examiner* and later the *New York Journal,* employed sensationalism (yellow journalism) to win the circulation wars of the late 1800s. He created a major publishing empire consisting of a chain of newspapers, a wire service, and four syndicates.

▲ Yellow Journalism

Hearst, like Pulitzer before him, then invaded the big league—New York City. In 1895 he bought the *New York Journal.* Soon, Pulitzer and Hearst were engaged in a fierce circulation battle as each paper attempted to outsensationalize the other. As one press critic put it, the duel between these two spread "death, dishonor and disaster" all over page one. Sex, murder, self-promotion, and human-interest stories filled the two papers. This type of reporting became known as **yellow journalism,** and whatever its faults, it sold newspapers.

The battle between Pulitzer and Hearst reached its climax with the Spanish-American War in 1898. In fact, many historians have argued that the newspapers were an important factor in shaping public opinion in favor of hostilities. When the battleship *Maine* was blown up in Havana harbor, the *Journal* offered a $50,000 reward for the arrest of the guilty parties. Circulation promptly jumped over the 1 million mark. War was finally declared in April, and the *World* and the *Journal* pulled out all the stops. Hearst chartered a steamer and equipped it with printing presses. He also brought down his yacht and sailed with the U.S. fleet in the Battle of Santiago. The *Journal* put out 40 extras in a single day.

Although the period of yellow journalism was not the proudest moment in the history of the American newspaper, some positive features did emerge from it. First, it brought enthusiasm, energy, and verve to the practice of journalism, along with aggressive investigative reporting. Second, it brought wide exposure to prominent authors and led to some fine examples of contemporary writing. Stephen Crane, Frank Norris, Dorothy Dix, and Mark Twain all wrote for newspapers during this period (1880–1905). Further, yellow journalism helped popularize the use of layout and display devices—banner headlines, pictures, color printing—that would go on to characterize modern journalism.

▲ The Early 20th Century

From 1900 to 1920, consolidation characterized the newspaper business. Although circulation and profits went up, the number of daily newspapers decreased, and the number of cities with competing newspapers dropped by 60 percent. What happened?

First, the cost of new technology—Linotype machines, high-speed presses—proved too much for many marginal papers. Second, advertisers showed a preference for the paper with the largest circulation in the market. Smaller-circulation papers saw their revenues shrink to the point at which they could no longer compete. Third, consolidation had increased profits in the railroad, grocery, and hotel businesses, and newspaper publishers decided it could do the same for them. Consequently, newspaper chains—companies that owned several papers—grew quickly. By 1933 six chains—Hearst, Scripps-Howard, Patterson-McCormack, Block, Ridder, and Gannett—controlled 81 dailies with a combined circulation of more than 9 million, about one-fourth of all daily circulation.

Appearing with the consolidation trend and enjoying a short but lively reign was **jazz journalism.** At the end of World War I, the United States enjoyed a decade of prosperity known as the Roaring Twenties. The radio, Hollywood, the airplane, Prohibition, and Al Capone all captured national attention. The papers that best exemplify jazz journalism all sprang up in New York between 1919 and 1924. All were characterized by two features: (1) They were **tabloids,** printed on a page that was about one-half the size of a normal newspaper page; and (2) they were richly illustrated with photographs.

The *New York Daily News* debuted first. After a slow start, by 1924 the *News* had caught on. Its tabloid size was easy for people to handle while riding buses and subways; it abounded with photos and cartoons; and the writing style was simple and short. The biggest content innovation of the *News,* and the most noticeable, was the lavish use of pictures. The entire front page was frequently given over to one or two pictures, and a two-page photo spread was included on the inside.

▲ The Impact of the Great Depression

The Depression had huge social and economic impact on newspapers and magazines. During the 1930s total daily newspaper circulation increased by about 2 million; the total population increased by 9 million. The total income of the newspaper industry, however, dropped about 20 percent in this decade. Marginally profitable papers were unable to stay in business, and approximately 66 dailies went under.

Although worsening economic conditions were one cause of the newspaper's decline, more important was the emergence of radio as a competitor for national advertising dollars. From 1935 to 1940, newspapers' share of national advertising revenues dropped from 45 to 39 percent, while radio's share jumped from 6 to more than 10 percent. By 1940, however, thanks to increased revenue from local advertisers, newspaper revenues had rebounded. Nevertheless, the economic picture was not rosy, and the number of daily papers declined to 1,744, an all-time low, in 1945.

When Lyndon Johnson signed the Civil Rights Act of 1964, he invited leaders of the civil rights movement to join him in the Oval Office. Only one woman was among the group that witnessed the historic moment—Ethel L. Payne, an African American journalist who had reported on civil rights issues for more than a decade.

Payne was the granddaughter of slaves. She originally wanted to become a lawyer but was denied admission to law school because of her race. In 1948 she went to Japan to work with African American troops who were stationed there. Two years later Payne showed excerpts from her personal journal about the problems of black soldiers to a reporter for the *Chicago Defender* who was visiting Japan. Her stories became a series in the newspaper and launched Payne on a journalism career.

Based in Chicago, Payne won awards for her coverage of problems in the African American community. She went to Washington in the mid-1950s to cover the beginnings of the civil rights movement. She wrote stories analyzing the historic *Brown* v. *Board of Education* Supreme Court decision. Payne made her presence felt at White House press conferences when she asked President Dwight Eisenhower pointed questions about the lack of progress on civil rights during his administration.

In 1956 Payne covered the arrest of Rosa Parks in Montgomery, Alabama, and the subsequent bus boycott. She reported the big stories of the civil rights movement, including the efforts to integrate the University of Alabama; the violence in Little Rock, Arkansas; the confrontation at Selma, Alabama; and the march on Washington in 1965. She was one of the first reporters to interview Dr. Martin Luther King Jr.

In 1966 she traveled to Vietnam to cover African American troops, who were involved in much of the fighting. She later accompanied Secretary of State Henry Kissinger on a six-nation tour of Africa. In 1978, at age 67, she ended her career with the *Chicago Defender* to write a syndicated column. Seven years later she became a leader in the effort to free South Africa leader Nelson Mandela.

Ethel Payne died in 1991. The *Washington Post* published a tribute to her on its editorial page. It praised her for being fair, straightforward, and independent, an assessment probably shared by her millions of readers.

▲ Postwar Newspapers

After World War II economic forces continued to shape the American newspaper. Some trends of the postwar period were created by advances in print and electronic technology, but others had begun even before the war. For example, the postwar economy forced the newspaper industry to move even further in the direction of contraction and consolidation. Although newspaper circulation rose from approximately 48 million in 1945 to about 62 million in 1970, the number of dailies stayed about the same. There was actually a circulation loss in cities with populations of more than a million, and several big-city papers went out of business. Moreover, the number of cities with competing dailies dropped from 117 to 37 between 1945 and 1970. This meant that about 98 percent of American cities had no competing papers.

In 1945, 60 chains controlled about 42 percent of the total daily newspaper circulation. By 1970 approximately 157 chains accounted for 60 percent of total circulation. Why had the number of chains continued to grow? One factor was the sharp rise in costs of paper and labor. Newspapers were becoming more expensive to print. The large chains were in a position to share expenses and to use their presses and labor more efficiently. For instance, several papers could share the services of feature writers, columnists, photographers, and compositors, thus holding down costs.

The consolidation trend was present across media, as several media conglomerates controlled newspapers, magazines, and radio and TV stations. Black newspapers were also caught up in the trend toward concentration. In 1956 the *Chicago Defender* changed from a weekly to a daily, and its owner, John Sengstacke, started a group of nine black papers, including the Pittsburgh *Courier* and the Michigan *Chronicle.*

Another continuing trend was the competition among media for advertising dollars. The total amount of advertising revenue spent on all media nearly tripled between 1945 and 1970. Although the total spent on newspapers did not increase at quite this pace, the amount spent on television increased by more than threefold. The rising TV industry cut significantly into the print media's national advertising revenue.

▲ Contemporary Developments

The biggest development of the 1980s was the birth of *USA Today.* Following are some of the innovations sparked by this paper:

- Splashy graphics and color

- Short, easy-to-read stories
- Many graphs, charts, and tables
- Factoids (a *factoid* is a list of boiled-down facts—much like this list)

Many newspapers across the country incorporated these changes into their editions.

Throughout the 1990s and into the new century, the newspaper industry wrestled with the problems of decreasing circulation, increasing competition from the Web, and rapid shifts in social and market conditions. As will be detailed later, print newspaper circulation has been declining more or less steadily since the 1970s, with younger readers tailing off the most. Although most newspapers continued to be profitable in 2007, the downturn in circulation and the aging readership are ominous signs for the future. Indeed, the situation has gotten to the point at which many in the industry are reexamining the basic business model that has sustained the industry since the 18th century.

Modern newspapers have to compete for audience attention with online news sources, blogs, iPods, cell phones, podcasts, and video games as well as with TV and radio and other traditional media competitors. Moreover, the competition for advertising dollars continues to heat up. In the past newspapers could count on a fairly steady income from classified ads: the want ads, autos for sale, job opportunities, and so on. Today, Web sites such as craigslist.com, monster.com, and autotrader.com have siphoned off a significant chunk of this income.

American society is also changing. The number of single-parent households is increasing, as is the ethnic population. People are moving more often, and commuting time is getting longer. All of these factors affect newspaper readership.

Newspapers also face a different market. Big retailers, such as Wal-Mart, have squeezed out many local retailers, the ones most likely to buy newspaper ads. Wal-Mart, in contrast, does little newspaper advertising. To make matters worse, many advertisers have turned away from newspaper display ads to online ads because they find online ads more efficient. Google, for example, gives advertisers a "pay per click" result that lets them see exactly how many people paid attention to the ad. There is also a "pay per transaction" arrangement in which the advertisers pay only if there is a sale. Print ads in the newspaper cannot offer this.

Rather than end on this gloomy note, it should be mentioned that newspapers have struggled with changing business and social conditions since they were first published. Newspapers adjusted to the rise of mass society and to the increasing numbers of immigrants coming to the United States. Although their circulation numbers plummeted, they also survived the increased competition from radio and television. They will probably survive again but not without significant change. The newspaper 5–10 years in the future may look very different from the newspaper of today.

NEWSPAPERS IN THE DIGITAL AGE

The newspaper industry is still experimenting to find the best way to incorporate an online presence in the traditional print edition.

▲ Online Newspapers

Online papers have certain advantages over traditional newspapers:

- Printed newspapers are limited by the **newshole,** the amount of news that can be printed in one edition. Online papers have no such limitations. The full text of lengthy speeches, transcripts of interviews, and extensive tables and graphs can be accommodated easily.
- Online papers can be updated continuously; there are no edition deadlines.
- Online papers are interactive. E-mail addresses, bulletin boards, and chat rooms allow readers to provide quick feedback to the paper. Many have searchable archives and links to other sites.

MEDIA TALK

Jayson Blair and the New York Times

DVD, Track 26, 6:48 minutes

One of the scandals that have hurt the credibility of newspapers involved *New York Times* reporter Jayson Blair. Watch this clip in which Blair talks about his misdeeds and the reason behind his behavior. Do you believe he is sincere in regretting his actions? What more should Blair do in order to make up for his transgressions? What steps should journalists and editors take to ensure accurate reporting? What can consumers do to make sure they are getting the truth?

A blog, as defined by Webster's, is a "Web site that contains an online personal journal with reflections, comments, and often hyperlinks provided by the writer." Blogs exist in a part of cyberspace called the *blogosphere.*

Blogs are a fairly recent phenomenon. There were only a couple dozen in 1999, but their number grew quickly thanks to the development of automated publishing systems that made it easy for anybody to start one. Recent estimates put the total number of blogs on the Web somewhere between 20 to 30 million. A new blogger joins the crowd every couple of minutes or so. About 10 million people read blogs every day.

To be candid, most of the blogs are of interest only to their creators and friends. Critics call them "soapboxes for the self-absorbed," an "electronic vanity press," or "a self-aggrandizing fad." Despite their faults blogs have already had a significant effect on journalism and may become even more important in the future.

The power of blogs was demonstrated in 2003 when Senate Majority Leader Trent Lott made a racially insensitive remark. The mainstream media reported the statement, but most then let the story drop. Bloggers, however, kept the story alive, and eventually, the major media followed the bloggers' lead. The story regained national prominence, and Lott was forced to step down. Blogs also played a major role in the controversy surrounding the use of apparently forged documents by CBS's *Sixty Minutes II* during the 2004 election campaign (see Chapter 12 for the full story). Blogs were criticized for leaking early election day exit poll results that erroneously predicted a John Kerry win.

Blogs are another illustration of one of the major themes in this book: The audience is exerting greater control over media content. Reporter and cyber columnist Dan Gillmor compared traditional journalism to a lecture: Reporters told you what they thought was important, and the audience listened or tuned out. With blogs journalism is more like a conversation, with the audience taking an active role. Rather than the traditional top-down model, blogging represents bottom-up journalism. Anybody with access to the Internet becomes a reporter and commentator. When a news event occurs, the audience is no longer limited to the news distributed by huge media conglomerates. As Gillmor sums it up, blogs add something to the journalistic mix that was missing—the voice of the readership.

Along with their potential, however, blogs present new problems. How much credibility can you put into a blogger's report? The election day mix-up suggests that skepticism is always warranted. The information is unfiltered, unedited, and not checked for accuracy. (A mistake might eventually be caught by other bloggers, but that might take a long time.) Bloggers' self-interest may show through in how they "spin" or color the facts. Further, are bloggers bound by the same ethical rules as journalists? At a recent conference a speaker asked that his remarks remain off the record. Reporters in the audience honored his request, but several bloggers didn't. In the blog era will anything be off the record?

Blogs have also raised knotty legal problems. Can a newspaper be held liable for something defamatory (see Chapter 16) that appears in a reporter's blog? Most legal experts counsel that newspapers should treat material published in a blog the same as if it were published in the paper. This means, of course, that an editor has to screen the blog before it gets posted, and that, in turn, takes away from the blog's immediacy and spontaneity. It also raises questions about who actually owns the blog—the reporter/blogger or the newspaper.

What about the reporter who blogs from home, maybe on a topic totally removed from his or her job as a newspaper reporter? This situation is complicated. In some cases the newspaper is unlikely to be held accountable for problems caused by the blogger. If the blogger, however, has achieved notoriety because of his or her work for the newspaper, then it might be a different story. All in all, there are many questions yet to be worked out concerning the role blogs will play in newspaper journalism.

(Check out www.daypop.com/blogrank for links to the most popular blogs.)

- Online papers can provide photos and video and audio clips to accompany news stories and advertisements. Some even offer social networking possibilities.
- Online papers can feature user-generated content.

In 1994 about 20 daily papers had Web sites. By 2007 it was rare for a paper not to have one.

During the early years of the Internet, online newspaper sites were slow to innovate. There was a fear that the Web site would steal readers from the print version. Thus, many of them simply took their print stories and placed them online, updating them only once a day. Some even withheld stories until they were published in the print edition. Newspapers, however, now realize that if they want to compete with other news sites such as CNN and CBS News, their Web sites have to do more.

A 2005 survey of the top 100 newspaper sites found that newspapers were exploring new ways to connect with readers. About 80 percent of the sites contained blogs, and most of those let readers post comments, another example of user-generated content. (Newspaper blogs can also pose problems—see the boxed insert "Blogging It.") Papers were not as eager, however, to let readers add comments at the end of news stories; only 19 percent had this feature. This low number might be due to the increased time demands that come with

More than 140 newspapers publish replica editions of the paper, or, as they are sometimes called, *e-editions*.

monitoring comments, or it may simply reflect the fact that reporters and editors don't want readers criticizing their efforts.

Video is big. More than 60 of the top 100 Web sites offered video clips. Some of these clips were from the Associated Press video service, while others were original productions by the newspaper's staff or video submitted by readers. The leader in this category, the *New York Times*, created more than a half-million pieces of video for its Web site in 2005.

Podcasting was not as popular. Only one-third of the top 100 employed podcasting, and most of these sites were created by the larger papers.

In sum, these findings suggest that papers are reaching out to online readers using all the channels at their disposal.

▲ Replica Editions

A replica edition of a newspaper is not the same as an online edition. The online edition looks different from the print edition; the online paper has no page numbers, its pages are not divided into columns, it has no top or bottom, the text is printed in a different font from the print version, and it does not contain the same ads as the print version. On the other hand, a replica edition offers the same content as the printed newspaper but in a format that can be read on a computer screen.

Replica editions have both good and bad points. Consumers reading the print edition can judge the importance of a story by the size of the headlines and photographs and the placement of articles—clues that are typically absent in the online version. Replica editions are also cheap to produce. The conversion to the digital production of a print newspaper means that virtual pages are already assembled on computer screens. Thus, they can be assembled into replica editions with little added effort. Replica editions can also carry links to advertisers' Web sites and are easily archived. Finally, replica editions are even more attractive now that the Audit Bureau of Circulations (see below) counts readership of replica editions as part of the newspaper's circulation totals.

On the other hand, replica editions may not be updated as often as online editions, resulting in some news stories that might be stale. Further, there is considerable clicking and scrolling involved in reading a replica, which some users might find annoying and time-consuming.

As of middecade, more than 140 papers were publishing replica editions with a combined circulation of nearly a half-million. These numbers are relatively small, but in an industry in which circulation is falling, every bit helps.

▲ Mobile Media

Newspapers traditionally have been delivered to a place—a person's home or office. In the digital age newspapers are increasingly delivered to a person, thanks to the growing availability of wireless connections to the Internet and the increasing popularity of various handheld information devices: cell phones, personal digital assistants (PDAs), and laptops. About two of three Americans, for example, owns a cell phone (for more on wireless handheld media, see Chapter 3). These devices are becoming new delivery channels for newspapers. The *Wall Street Journal*, for example, offers a mobile edition to subscribers over their cell phones. *USA Today* provides news over cell phones and PDAs to more than 100,000 customers. The newspaper even delivers video clips to some subscribers with special digital assistants.

The *Palm Beach Post* is a good illustration of how a local newspaper is using multiple mobile platforms to reach consumers. Subscribers can get breaking news and weather information e-mailed to their laptops or PDAs. Consumers with an Internet-enabled cell phone can log onto the *Post's* Web site and read the online edition. Those with iPods can download podcasts of the week's most interesting stories, as well as downloading the paper's database of local bars and restaurants. Many papers have similar arrangements.

Other companies also recognize the potential of news delivered via cell phone or PDA. MobiTV works with cell phone companies to offer several news channels, including CNN and ABC, on its service. And MSNBC offers subscribers the ability to receive news via cell phone, PDA, or podcast.

The advertising and marketing potential of this channel is significant since ads delivered via mobile media reach people near the point of purchase. Checking sports scores on your PDA? While you're at it, why not purchase tickets to a game? In addition, many young people are heavy users of cell phones and PDAs. This is the same group that has turned away from traditional print newspapers. Handheld media offer publishers one way of reaching this segment of the audience.

In sum, look for newspapers to be designed for multiple digital platforms, not just paper. As *New York Times* publisher Arthur Sulzberger Jr. put it, "Newspapers cannot be defined by the second word—paper. They've got to be defined by the first—news."

▲ User-Generated Content

Newspapers are joining the user-generated movement. The Tribune Company, a long-time member of the "old" media, recently hired a video-sharing company to manage user-generated videos on the company's 50 newspaper Web sites. The Gannett Company introduced a concept called "crowdsourcing" to bring readers into the news-gathering process. The publisher of the *Denver Post* and the *Rocky Mountain News* have created YourHub.com, a series of local Web sites that feature user-generated content accessible from the newspaper's home page. Several papers have sponsored Saturday workshops for readers who want to know more about reporting. Even smaller papers, such as *Bluffton Today* in South Carolina, have started community blogs and sites where readers can post pictures.

Relying on citizen journalists, of course, carries some risk. The credibility and objectivity of the average citizen reporter may be suspect. It is difficult to know if citizen journalists are pursuing some personal agenda or how knowledgeable they are. The citizen who writes a story about a new school board policy might have children directly affected by the policy. The citizen journalist who calls *Talladega Nights* the best comedy film he ever saw may have seen only three comedy films in his life. There's no way of knowing.

DEFINING FEATURES OF NEWSPAPERS

The online and print editions of the newspaper share some defining features. First, the newspaper is made up of diverse content. Newspapers contain international, national, and local news. In addition, they feature editorials, letters to the editor, movie listings, horoscopes, comics, sports, film reviews, recipes, advice columns, classified ads, and a host of other material. Their range of content is extensive.

Second, newspapers are conveniently packaged. Both the print and online versions are organized according to content. There are sections devoted to general news, financial news, sports, and entertainment. In addition, each story contains a headline that makes it easy for readers to decide if they want to peruse the rest of the story.

Third, newspapers are local. Reporters cover meetings of the local school board, the city council, and the zoning commission. They cover the local police station and tell about the newest store openings in the local mall. Sports sections cover the hometown Little League and high school teams. Local people with merchandise to sell use the classified ads. Newspapers are the only medium with the resources to report all the neighborhood activities in a community.

Fourth, more than any other medium, the newspaper serves as a historical record. One writer described newspaper journalism as "the first draft of history." The typical paper contains a record of daily events, some profound, some not so profound, that influence our lives. If a person wants to get a sense of what life was like in the 1940s, for example, he or she can flip through some old issues of the paper and see what events were on people's minds, what movies they were seeing, and what products were being advertised.

Fifth, newspapers perform the watchdog role in our society. They monitor the workings of government and private industry for misdeeds and wrongdoings. They alert the public to possible threats and new trends.

Finally, newspapers are timely. News is not useful if it is stale. Recognizing this fact, the largest-circulation newspapers in the United States publish daily and online editions that can break news any time of the day. Getting the news out fast has always been one of the characteristics of the newspaper business.

ORGANIZATION OF THE NEWSPAPER INDUSTRY

This section will first examine the organization of the traditional ink-and-paper newspaper industry and then consider the online versions. The print newspapers that are published in this country are many and varied. They range from the *Wall Street Journal*, a nationally oriented financial daily, to the *Daily Journal of Commerce*, a small financial paper published in Portland, Oregon; from the *National Enquirer* to the *Daily Lobo*, the college newspaper of the University of New Mexico; from the million-plus-circulation *New York Times* to the 6,000-circulation Gallipolis *Daily Tribune* in Ohio. Obviously, there are many ways to categorize an industry as diverse as this one. For our purposes we will group papers by frequency of publication (dailies and weeklies), by market size (national, large, medium, small), and by their appeal to specialized groups. Table 4-1 shows the top 10 newspapers by circulation and the percentage change in circulation between 2005 and 2006.

TABLE 4-1

Top 10 Newspaper Circulation

Note: With few exceptions newspaper circulation has seen a slow but steady decline.

Paper	2006 Circulation (million)	2005 Circulation (million)	Percent Change
USA Today	2.27	2.30	−1.3
Wall Street Journal	2.04	2.08	−1.9
New York Times	1.09	1.13	−3.5
Los Angeles Times	0.78	0.84	−7.0
New York Post	0.70	0.67	+4.0
New York Daily News	0.69	0.68	+1.0
Washington Post	0.66	0.68	−3.0
Chicago Tribune	0.58	0.58	0
Houston Chronicle	0.51	0.53	−4.0
Newsday	0.41	0.43	−5.0

▲ Print Dailies

To be considered a daily, a newspaper has to appear at least five times a week. In 2006 there were 1,456 dailies, down slightly from 2000 (see Figure 4-1), and about 6,700 weeklies. Whether a daily or a weekly, the chief concern of a newspaper is its **circulation,** the number of copies delivered to newsstands and vending machines and to subscribers. Weekday morning circulation has increased and Sunday circulation has stayed about the same in the past 20 years. Evening circulation, however, has shown a major decrease. As a result, total daily newspaper circulation has declined to approximately 53 million, a figure that dropped steadily between 1965 and 2005 (see Figure 4-2). At the same time, the population of the United States has been growing. Consequently, the ratio of newspapers per household has declined. To illustrate: In 1960, 111 newspapers were sold per 100 households; in 2006, about 50 newspapers were sold per 100 households. This circulation crunch has not hit all papers with equal force, and this becomes evident when we divide daily newspapers into market groups.

National Newspapers Only a handful of papers fall into this category. These are publications whose content is geared not for one particular city or region but for the entire country. These papers typically use satellites to transmit images and information to regional printing plants where the papers are assembled and distributed. The newest addition to this category, with a circulation of about 2.3 million, is the Gannett publication *USA Today,* started in 1982. The paper's use of color and graphics and focus on such topics as sports and weather had a significant impact on other newspapers. Other papers with a national edition are the *New York Times, Wall Street Journal*, and *Christian Science Monitor*.

Large Metropolitan Dailies Although big-city populations have increased since 1986, the circulation of newspapers in cities with populations of more than 500,000 decreased by nearly 18 percent in the same period. The past few years have also seen the demise of

FIGURE 4-1

Number of Daily Newspapers in the United States, 1910–2006

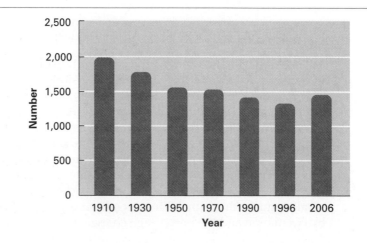

FIGURE 4-2

Daily Newspaper
Circulation, 1980–2005

Daily newspaper circulation (millions)

several big-city papers including the *Indianapolis News* and the *Dallas Times-Herald*. Why the drop in big-city circulation? There are several reasons including migration to the suburbs, transient populations, and increased competition from other media.

Medium-Sized Dailies   Although communities (100,000–500,000 in size) are home to only 12 percent of all newspapers, they account for about 33 percent of circulation. Although circulation in this area is up about 28 percent from 1986, it has recently tailed off, dropping 11 percent from 1996 to 2006.

Small-Town Dailies   This category of newspapers has suffered the most from circulation losses. Since 1986 newspapers in towns whose population numbers 50,000 or less have lost about half of their circulation. Many of these papers faced increased competition from weekly newspapers and free neighborhood newsletters.

▲ Print Weeklies

The number of weekly newspapers in the United States has remained fairly stable at about 6,700 over the past 10 years. The circulation of weeklies, however, increased from 29 million in 1970 to more than 45 million in 2005. Despite this increase in circulation, the rising costs of printing and distribution have made weekly publishers more cost-conscious.

S O U N D B Y T E

Honey, I Shrunk the Paper

"All the News That's Fit to Print" has been the slogan of the *New York Times* for more than a hundred years. As of 2008, however, the *Times* may have a harder time fitting in all the news because the paper is shrinking—literally. The old *Times* was 54 inches wide; the new, narrower edition will be only 48 inches. The change will mean a loss of about 5 percent of the paper's newshole, but the *Times* announced that it will make up for some of the loss by adding pages.

Other major papers including *USA Today* and the *Washington Post* have also opted for the leaner look. The reason behind all the trimming? Money: The slimmer *Times* will save about $40 million a year.

▲ Recapturing Readers

No matter what their size or frequency of publication, all print newspapers face the task of maintaining their loyal readers while attracting new ones. Newspaper executives are aware that spending time with the daily paper is no longer the habit it once was. What are some of the things that newspapers are doing to attract readers?

- They are using more color. Readers generally like color, and papers are using it liberally. Even the gray and proper *New York Times* and the conservative *Wall Street Journal* have introduced color to their pages.

- They are changing their writing and editing style. Stories are shorter and are accompanied by summary decks under the headline or have story-related information in sidebars on either side of the story. Some papers run highlighted synopses within long stories.

Al Neuharth got into the newspaper business when he was 11 years old, delivering the *Minneapolis Tribune*. At 13 he had a part-time job in the composing room of a local weekly.

After serving in the military, he took a job as a reporter for a paper in South Dakota and later moved to the *Miami Herald*. Neuharth moved up rapidly through the ranks and eventually entered management. In 1960 he was appointed an assistant executive editor of the *Detroit Free Press*. His achievements there brought him to the attention of executives of the Gannett Company, who persuaded him to leave Detroit to manage two of Gannett's papers in New York. Neuharth's success there earned him a promotion to the position of chief of Gannett's operations in Florida. By 1970 Neuharth had become CEO of the company.

His emphasis was on the bottom line. During his tenure Gannett's annual revenue increased from $200 million to $3.1 billion. Neuharth continued the strategies of his predecessors by acquiring small-and medium-market dailies that enjoyed monopoly status in their markets and keeping costs down while raising ad rates. Strung by criticism that his papers emphasized profit at the expense of journalism, Neuharth strengthened the editorial operations of Gannett papers

Al Neuharth, the man responsible for making Gannett the nation's biggest newspaper company.

and by 1980 many had won awards for excellence in reporting.

Neuharth's biggest gamble came in the early 1980s when he decided to use a network of communication satellites and regional printing plants to produce *USA Today*, a national general-interest newspaper. The new paper was greeted with derision by critics, who dismissed it as a "McPaper" that served up flavorless "fast-food" journalism. *USA Today* was an immediate hit with readers, however, and quickly garnered more than a million readers. Advertisers took a little longer to get on board, but the paper eventually turned a profit.

Now most experts agree that, after more than 20 years on the newsstands, *USA Today* has had a significant impact on the industry. Most newspapers have incorporated color, splashy page makeup, more charts and graphics, and shorter, more tightly written stories.

Neuharth retired in 1989 to become chair of the Freedom Foundation, an organization dedicated to furthering the cause of a free press in society. He also continues to write a syndicated newspaper column. The *Washington Journalism Review* named him the most influential person of the 1980s in print media.

- They are changing the content of the paper. Many papers have become less dependent on lengthy stories dealing with local government. Appearing with more frequency are features dealing with lifestyles, fashions, and entertainment and articles usually described as "news you can use" (e.g., "How to Find the Perfect Babysitter," "Best Open-Late Restaurants," and "Managing Your Money").
- In big cities they are giving away free tabloids to younger readers.

Will these efforts pay off? So far the results have not been encouraging. A glance at Table 4-1 reveals that only two of the top 10 daily newspapers gained circulation from 2005 to 2006. There are even more troubling signs. Market research has suggested that although young people like news, they don't really care for paper. They don't want to thumb through the pages of a newspaper, and they don't want copies of old papers cluttering up their houses. On the plus side young adults are more positive about reading the news online. They like its speed and convenience and the fact that when they read news Web sites at the office, it looks like they're doing research, not goofing off. As is probably apparent by now, traditional newspapers face many challenges when it comes to recapturing younger adults.

▲ Special-Service and Minority Newspapers

Special-service newspapers are those aimed at several well-defined audience segments. There are, for example, many newspapers published specifically for the African American

Editors and reporters at work in the newsroom.

The best known member of the Spanish language press is *El Diario* published in New York city. The paper has a circulation of more than 50,000.

community. The African American press in this country has a long history, dating back to 1827. Most early papers were started to oppose discrimination and to help gain equal rights and opportunities. The African American press reached its circulation peak in the 1960s when approximately 275 papers had a circulation of about 4 million. Since that time the African American press has seen a significant decline in both numbers of papers and circulation.

In 2005 approximately 200 African American papers were publishing in 35 states and the District of Columbia. Papers such as the *Chicago Defender* and the *Philadelphia Tribune* are leading voices in their communities.

Hispanics are the fastest-growing minority group in America, and the Spanish-language press has grown with them. According to the National Hispanic Media Directory, the number of daily Spanish-language newspapers grew from 14 in 1990 to more than 40 in 2007, while the number of weeklies increased from 152 to nearly 320. Some of the prominent Hispanic newspapers include *El Diario* in New York and *La Opinion* in Los Angeles. Like newspapers in general, the Hispanic press is trying to boost its readership.

There are many other ethnic newspaper publishers in the United States. Twelve cities have at least one Chinese-language newspaper, and eight cities have papers targeted to Polish Americans.

Another special type of newspaper is exemplified by the college press. Although numbers are hard to pin down, as of 2005 there were about 1,500 college papers published at four-year institutions, with a total circulation of more than 6 million. College newspapers are big business; consequently, more and more papers are hiring nonstudent professionals to manage their operations. Two of the largest college papers in terms of circulation are the University of Minnesota's *Minnesota Daily* and Michigan State University's *State News,* both with circulations of approximately 30,000. College newspapers get high readership scores. A 2005 survey found that 71 percent of college students read at least one issue of their college newspaper in the past week. The comparable number for the mainstream press was 41 percent.

▲ Organization of Online Newspapers

One way to organize online newspaper sites is the ease with which a reader can gain access: paid, registration, or free.

Paid Access   Most early online versions were free, and publishers hoped that the Web version would drive subscribers to the print version. When this did not happen, newspapers had to search for ways to make their online ventures profitable. One of the earliest business models was the pay-for-access approach, whereby consumers paid a fee to access the online edition. This model has worked for a small number of papers, including the *Wall Street Journal.* The *Journal,* for example, offers a subscription to its online version for $99 a year, or $49 if the user also subscribes to the print version. As of 2007, only about two dozen papers had adopted this model.

Registration Access   A second arrangement is the registration model, whereby readers have to provide some personal information to gain access to the full site. Publishers then sell this information to advertisers. Travelocity, for example, would be interested in the e-mail addresses of people who marked "travel" as an interest during their registration. Additionally, salespeople for the online site could use this data to show potential advertisers that they were reaching their target audiences by purchasing ads on the online newspaper's site.

Results from the registration model have been mixed. There are Web sites that provide user names and passwords to get past the registration screen. As of 2006 only 23 of the top 100 U.S. newspapers required registration. A few newspapers, such as the *Houston Chronicle* and the *Toronto Star,* have abandoned the registration model and gone back to free access. Moreover, it is difficult to know how accurate the registration data provided by readers are or how many people are scared off by the registration process. Nonetheless, some newspapers have more than a million registered users.

Free Access   The most common model allows readers to access the site without a paid subscription or a registration. These sites support themselves by selling advertising or merchandise or by starting social networking sites. The *New York Post* and the *Chicago Sun-Times,* for example, follow this model.

NEWSPAPER OWNERSHIP

The most significant facts about newspaper ownership are the following:

- Concentration of ownership is increasing as large group owners acquire more papers.
- There has been a decrease in the number of cities with competing papers.

The biggest newspaper group is the Gannett Company with 90 dailies and a combined circulation of about 7.3 million. Other newspaper chains that own dailies with a combined circulation of more than 2 million are Advance Publications, the Tribune Company, and the New York Times Company (see Table 4-2).

▲ The Decline of Competition

Concentration of ownership is not a new trend in the newspaper business. What is new, however, is the dominance of the industry by big group owners. The 21 largest group owners account for 68 percent of all daily newspaper circulation.

TABLE 4-2	Name	Number of Papers Owned	Top Paper
Biggest Newspaper Groups, 2005, by revenue	Gannett Company	90	*USA Today*
	Tribune Co.*	11	*Chicago Tribune*
	New York Times Co.	18	*New York Times*
	McClatchy Co.	32	*Miami Herald*
	Advance Publications	25	*Cleveland Plain Dealer*

*As of late 2007, the Tribune Co. was in the process of being acquired by real-estate investor Sam Zell.

Coupled with the growth of group ownership is the decline of newspaper competition within individual markets. Back in 1923, more than 500 cities had two or more competing daily papers, including 100 that had three or more. By 2006 there were only about a dozen cities that had independent competing newspapers. In some cities competition was kept alive only through a **joint-operating agreement (JOA).** A JOA is formed, under approval by the Justice Department, to maintain two newspapers in a city when otherwise one would go out of business. Functions of the two papers—circulation, advertising, and production—are combined to save money. Only the editorial staffs remain separate and competitive. JOAs exist between papers in Cincinnati, Tucson, and Birmingham, to name a few.

▲ The Pros and Cons of Group Ownership

The pros and cons of group ownership and decreasing competition have been widely debated by newspaper executives and press critics. Critics maintain that fewer competing papers means a loss in the diversity of opinions available to the audience. They also claim that top management in group operations places profits above quality. A newspaper owned by a chain, say these critics, would likely avoid local controversy in its pages to avoid offending advertisers. It has also been charged that chain newspapers are usually under the direction of absentee owners, who may have little knowledge of or concern for local community interests.

On the other hand, those who favor newspaper groups argue that group owners can accomplish certain things that smaller owners cannot. For example, a large group owner can afford to have correspondents and news bureaus in Washington, D.C., and in important foreign cities—an arrangement too expensive for a small owner to maintain. The chains are also better able to afford the latest technology. Finally, chains have the resources to provide for more elaborate training and public service programs than those provided by individually owned papers. The validity of each of these arguments depends in great measure on the particular group owner involved. Many group-owned papers are doing excellent jobs; others may not rate so highly.

PRODUCING THE PRINT AND ONLINE NEWSPAPER

▲ Departments and Staff

The departmental structure and staffing of a newspaper vary with its size. At the most general level, all papers are divided into three departments: (1) business, (2) production, and (3) news-editorial. The business department is in charge of selling advertising space in both the print and online editions and building the paper's circulation and Web site traffic. As the title implies, the production department handles the physical and electronic tasks necessary to get the news printed on paper and available on the Web site.

The most complex department is news-editorial. Note that these two functions—news and editorial—are kept separate in both the online and print versions. The editorial pages contain opinion, while the news pages contain objective reporting.

In the past, newspapers maintained separate departments for the print and online versions. At some papers the online staff was on a different floor or even in a different building. The current trend, however, is toward merging the two. *USA Today* and the *New York Times,* for example, combined their digital and print newsrooms in 2005. The *Atlanta Journal Constitution* reorganized its newsroom in 2007, putting its print and digital editions on equal footing. Note that this trend is an example of the operational convergence mentioned in Chapter 1.

The merged newsroom is typically directed by a managing editor who oversees and coordinates the day-to-day operations of the department. A city editor supervises local coverage, assigns reporters to beats (such as city hall, police, and health), and directs general-assignment reporters to handle a variety of stories. A wire editor edits international and national news from the Associated Press and other major news services. Most newspapers also have one or more people who are responsible for preparing the editorial pages.

▲ Prepublication Routine

Operational convergence is evident in the way the print and online editions are prepared. The traditional print newsroom had one deadline when all stories had to be ready. The modern converged newsroom is a 24/7 operation in which news on the paper's Web site is updated continuously.

There are two basic sources for news: local reporting and wire services. Early in the day the wire editor scans the outputs from the wire services and flags possible stories for the print and online editions. At the same time, the city editor is assigning reporters to various stories that will appear in print and online, and the managing editor is gauging the available space, the newshole, that can be devoted to news in that day's print edition. The greater the number of print ads, the greater the number of pages that can be printed, and the larger the newshole. The online edition, of course, has no such limitations.

Convergence is also showing up at the individual level. As the day progresses, reporters file stories for both the print and online editions. Many reporters also shoot and edit video for the Web site or record audio for a podcast. Since the Web version is continuously updated, some online stories may be rewritten several times. But this isn't all that is expected of the 21st-century newspaper reporter. She or he may be expected to write a blog, participate in chat rooms, and respond to reader e-mail. (These new duties have caused some problems; see the insert "What's the Appropriate Job Description for a Converged Reporter?")

Editors for the print edition edit stories and design page makeup. Photos and graphics are added, and the finished pages are sent to a composing room. Eventually, the pages make their way to the press room, where they are printed and bundled together for delivery.

The above paragraph, of course, does not apply to the online version. Web editors post and update stories when needed. They also decide what photos and video and audio clips will accompany the day's stories. When everything is in order, the story and related graphics are posted to the Web site. There is no need for a composing room, printing press, paper, or delivery truck.

THE ECONOMICS OF NEWSPAPER PUBLISHING

As mentioned in the chapter opener, the business model that has sustained the newspaper industry for the past few centuries is changing. A print newspaper has two sources of revenue: (1) advertising, which provides about 80 percent of total revenue, and (2) circulation, money from subscriptions and single-copy sales, which provides the rest. These two sources are related, of course—the higher the circulation, the more a paper can charge for advertising.

The economic health of the newspaper industry is still good. Newspaper profit margins were above the average for most U.S. businesses, though profits were buoyed by cutting expenses rather than increasing revenue. Starting in the 1990s and continuing into the new millennium, staff sizes have been reduced, paper sizes narrowed, circulation areas compacted, and new production techniques introduced, all in an effort to cut costs.

Costs, however, can be reduced only so much, and there are ominous signs that revenue growth will be hard to come by in the future, making the long-term economic outlook for newspapers somewhat gloomy. First, newspapers face increased competition for advertising dollars from cable TV, billboards, direct mail, and Web sites. Newspapers' share of the total amount of money spent on advertising was 29 percent in the late 1970s. By 2007 that number had slipped to about 17 percent. Second, the number of people who regularly read a newspaper has been dropping steadily for more than 25 years.

A 2006 survey disclosed that newspapers were hit the hardest when advertisers redirected their money from traditional to new media. First, about half of the respondents reported spending less on newspapers and more on the Internet. Second, the number of people who read the paper has been dropping, and the drop is most pronounced among young people, the exact audience that newspapers are trying desperately to reach. Finally, for many years most newspapers enjoyed a monopoly in their market when it came to classified ads, one of the newspaper industry's important revenue streams (see below). Having a monopoly, of course, means that a company has great control over the price of its product or service. The emergence of eBay, Craigslist, and monster.com, however, changed that situation. Why pay money to a newspaper to advertise something for sale when you can do it for free on Craigslist or other Web sites? In addition, online classified sites are more current and easily searched. The loss of classified ad revenue presents a serious problem for newspapers.

On the bright side the newspaper industry highlights the fact that online readership is up and, for many papers, more than offsets the loss of print readers. The *Los Angeles Times*, for instance, has a print circulation well under a million, but its Web site averaged about 4 million unique visitors per month in 2006. The problem with this is that the increased online readership has yet to translate into enough advertising dollars to offset the print losses. People look at fewer pages online. They also spend less total time with the online edition—only a few minutes per day compared to the half-hour per day that print readers spend with the paper. These facts make online audiences less valuable to advertisers. Consequently, online revenues still make up only a small part of a newspaper's total revenue. At Gannett, for example, through the first part of 2006, online ad revenue accounted for only 6 percent of the company's income.

Newspaper executives, of course, are aware of this situation and are exploring ways to increase online revenue. In 2007 several newspaper companies announced a deal with Internet giant Yahoo! to share content and advertising. The industry is also exploring ways to generate income from search engine advertising. It will be a few years, however, before we know whether this strategy was successful.

▲ Advertising Revenue

For the print version, advertising revenue comes from four separate sources: (1) local retail advertising, (2) classified ads, (3) national advertising, and (4) prepaid inserts. Local retail advertising is purchased by stores and service establishments. Department stores, supermarkets, auto dealers, and discount stores are the businesses that buy large amounts of space. Classified advertising, which is bought by local businesses and individuals, is generally run in a special section in the back of the newspaper. Buyers and sellers purchase classified ads for a wide range of products and services. National advertising originates with manufacturers of products that need to reach a national market on a mass basis. The majority of these ads are for automobiles, food, airlines, and Web-based companies. Prepaid inserts, or preprints, are advertising supplements put together by national, regional, and local businesses that are inserted into the copies of the paper. Companies such as Sears and Best Buy frequently use preprints. The paper charges the advertiser for the distribution of the preprints.

Local retail ads account for the most advertising revenue, about 46 percent. Classified ads rank next, accounting for about 33 percent in 2005. This figure is down from about 40 percent in 2000, probably due to the competition from Web sites such as Monster.com that carry classified ads. The remaining 21 percent of revenue comes from preprints and national ads.

The online version of the paper sells banner and display advertising. Usually, ad sales are bundled—advertisers buy a combination print and online ad. As a result it's difficult to tell what portion of ad income is attributable to the print or online versions. Online the advertising tends to be local, and a significant amount comes from the classifieds. If the online paper uses the registration version, it can also sell e-mail lists to advertisers wishing to target a particular audience.

▲ Circulation Revenue

Circulation revenue includes all the receipts from selling papers to consumers. The newspaper, however, does not receive the total price paid by a reader for a copy of the paper because of the many distribution systems employed to get the newspaper to the consumer. The most common method is for the paper to sell copies to a distributor at wholesale prices, usually about 25 percent less than the retail price. Other methods include hiring full-time employees as carriers and billing subscribers in advance. These methods show promise, but they also increase the cost of distribution.

One closely studied factor in determining circulation revenue is the effect of increased subscription and single-copy prices. In 1970, 89 percent of newspapers were priced at 10 cents a copy. In 2006 none cost less than 25 cents, and most cost 50 cents or more. Sunday papers have shown similar increases. In 1970 the typical price was 25 cents; by 2005 it was more than $1.50 or more. The rising price of newspapers has probably had a negative impact on circulation revenue. Several papers have noted a decrease in subscriptions among older, fixed-income residents following a price increase.

Those online papers that charge a subscription fee generate money directly from circulation. For the others circulation usually does not directly bring in revenue, but the more circulation, the higher the ad rates. In addition, many newspapers offer paid access to their back issues.

▲ General Expenses

The costs of running a newspaper can be viewed in several ways. One common method is to divide the costs by function:

- News and editorial costs
- Expenses involved in selling local, national, and classified ads
- Mechanical costs, including composition and production
- Printing costs, such as newsprint (the paper), ink, and the cost of running the press

- Circulation and distribution costs
- General administrative costs, such as secretarial and clerical services and the cost of soliciting for subscriptions

Some of these costs are variable. For example, printing costs increase as the number of printed copies increases. Distribution costs also increase with circulation size. Other costs are fixed. For example, the expense of sending a reporter to the airport to cover a visiting dignitary is about the same for a paper with a circulation of 10,000 as for one with a circulation of 100,000. This means that the cost of running a newspaper depends somewhat on the size of the paper. For a small paper (circulation about 25,000), general administrative costs rank first, accounting for about one-third of all expenses. The cost of newsprint and ink ranks second, followed by mechanical costs. In the case of a big-city daily (circulation of 200,000 or more), newsprint and ink costs rank first, followed by administrative expenses and mechanical costs. On average, newsprint accounts for about 25–30 cents of every dollar spent by a paper.

For the online paper, production and distribution costs are minimal. Salaries make up the bulk of expenditures, followed by software, hardware, and server space.

Newspapers are turning to automation to save money. These robot paper movers work for the *Rocky Mountain News*.

FEEDBACK FOR NEWSPAPERS

▲ The Audit Bureau of Circulations

The best-known feedback system for newspapers is that connected with the **Audit Bureau of Circulations (ABC).** During the early 1900s, with the growth of mass advertising, some publishers began inflating the number of readers in order to attract more revenue from advertisers. In an effort to check this deceptive practice, advertisers and publishers joined to form the ABC in 1914. The organization's purpose was to establish ground rules for counting circulation, to make sure that the rules were enforced, and to provide verified reports of circulation data. The ABC audits about three-fourths of all print media in the United States and Canada—about 2,600 publications.

The ABC functions in the following manner: Publishers keep detailed records of circulation data. Twice a year, publishers file a circulation statement with the ABC, which the ABC in turn disseminates to its clients. Once a year, the ABC audits publications to verify that the figures that have been reported are accurate. An ABC representative visits the publication and is free to examine records and files.

Circulation scandals in 2004 prompted the ABC to reexamine its methods (see the insert "Numbers Game"). The organization announced that more field auditors would be hired and the ABC staff would survey subscribers and newsstand operators to confirm that customers were actually paying for the copies that the newspaper reported as sold. The ABC also promised stiff punishment for any newspapers that deliberately faked their numbers. The scandals also triggered an investigation by the Securities and Exchange Commission to see if such activity was harmful to those who hold newspaper stock.

Those publishers who want feedback on their online audience size can subscribe to Nielsen/NetRatings (see Chapter 12). The company releases monthly reports on the number of unique visitors to various popular Web sites. If more detailed information is needed, executives can examine the traffic reports for their individual Web sites to determine what online stories generated the most clicks.

Many of you have probably heard about the scandals at Enron, Worldcom, and HealthSouth, but it's doubtful that you've heard much about the newspaper circulation scandals mentioned in the text. Despite the fact that the deception had been going on for years and that it may cost hundreds of millions for some newspapers to repay advertisers who were defrauded, media coverage of this affair was generally muted, and much of it was confined to the business press. This is unfortunate because the whole episode raises a serious ethical question about the business of journalism.

First, some background: Newspapers charge advertisers on the basis of their circulation. The bigger the circulation, the more they can charge. Circulation is counted by taking the number of papers printed on a given day and subtracting the number returned (unsold). One way to boost circulation is to print a lot of copies and have few returned. Several papers went out of their way to make sure that was the case. At *Newsday,* for example, the paper created a program in which hawkers sold the paper on the streets. The hawkers were told to dump any unsold papers in the trash. Newsstand operators also were given twice the number of papers they requested and told to destroy the rest. Further, hundreds of papers were given away as free samples and counted as paid circulation. The paper was even delivered to people who hadn't subscribed, and subscribers who tried to cancel their subscriptions were ignored. Finally, dead people were kept on the subscription lists. At the *Chicago Sun-Times,* the paper took in money for recycling newsprint and then spent the money to buy copies of the paper to distribute free in schools, therefore paying itself to buy its own papers to hype circulation figures. All in all, the *Sun-Times* inflated figures by as much as 50,000 per day; *Newsday,* by as much as 40,000.

After the wrongdoings were exposed, the *Sun-Times* set aside more than $25 million to compensate advertisers who had bought ads whose prices were based on the bogus figures; *Newsday* set aside $35 million. The ultimate costs might be much higher since there were about a dozen class action lawsuits filed against the papers.

How were the papers able to get away with this? Doesn't the text mention that the Audit Bureau of Circulations (ABC)

monitors circulation figures? Yes, it does, but apparently not closely enough. The "circulation irregularities," as they are called in the business, were not uncovered by the ABC. They were uncovered by the papers during internal audits. In sum, this whole episode raises ethical questions about the proper relationship between the industry and the group that's supposed to watch over it.

In the electronic media A. C. Nielsen and Arbitron, both independent organizations, collect ratings data. Broadcasters and cablecasters have relatively little influence over their procedures. On the other hand, the ABC is funded by dues from its members, and many of its executives come from the publishing industry. Over the years the ABC has bent some of its rules in response to industry pressure. Before 2001 newspapers could count as circulation only copies of the paper that sold for at least 50 percent of purchase price. Then the rules were changed to allow papers to count as paid circulation copies that were discounted 75 percent. As a result newspapers increased their bulk sales to airlines, hotels, hospitals, and other places where papers were generally given away, sometimes to people who did not want them. The ABC also allowed newspapers to count as circulation papers given to employees (that's about 5,000 copies a day at *Newsday*) and to exclude many days when sales were low from counting toward circulation. All of these measures allowed newspapers to keep their circulation numbers higher. Given the flexibility of the rules, it's easy to see how the pressure to build circulation led to some ethically questionable or downright fraudulent techniques to keep numbers high.

The scandals prompted the ABC to reassess its close ties to publishers. The organization issued an open letter to media buyers and publishers stating that the ABC believed that those papers that broke the rules were not representative of the publishing industry. Nevertheless, the letter went on to endorse the ABC's tougher counting rules and its intention to increase its punishments for those publications that break the rules. The future will tell if these measures restore advertisers' faith in the ABC's numbers.

▲ Newspaper Audiences

As of 2005 approximately 53 million copies of morning and evening papers, either purchased at the newsstand or delivered to the doorstep, found their way into American homes every weekday. Daily newspaper circulation, in absolute terms, has decreased since 1970, as a glance at Table 4-3 shows. The population, however, has been increasing. To reflect this fact and to provide additional perspective, the final column of the table presents the ratio of daily circulation to the total adult population of the United States (expressed in thousands). As can be seen, daily newspaper circulation is not keeping pace with the overall growth of the population.

The percentage of adults reading one or more papers every day has declined from about 80 percent in the early 1960s to about 50 percent in 2006. The most pronounced decline has occurred in the 18–29 and 30–44 age groups and among those who have not attended college. The overall drop in daily circulation has been most noticeable in urban areas.

TABLE 4-3

Daily and Weekly
Newspaper Circulation

Source: Compiled by
author.

Year	All Daily Papers	All Weekly Papers	Daily Circulation per 1,000 Adults
1960	58,882,000	21,328,000	475
1970	62,108,000	29,423,000	428
1980	62,201,840	40,970,000	360
1990	62,327,962	56,181,047	329
2000	55,772,847	47,990,892	287
2005	53,345,043	49,541,617	245

Why the overall decline? Some have attributed it to the increased mobility of Americans, the increase in single-person households, more expensive subscription and per-copy prices, a general decline in the literacy of young people, and competition from other media.

Print newspapers are losing readers to online media. In 1995 about 4 percent of the U.S. population went online at least once a week to get their news. By 2006 the figure was more than 30 percent. A recent survey by the Pew Research Center found that one in seven Internet users have reduced the amount of time they spend with daily newspapers. The key demographic group that reads most of its news online is young adults—the same group that reads print papers the least. When people go online for news, however, they do not necessarily go to online newspapers. Many visit portals such as Excite or Yahoo!; some go to search engines such as Google; others check CNN.com or a TV network news Web site.

THE NEWSPAPER INDUSTRY

The newspaper industry is a big employer. In 2006 newspaper employment exceeded 370,000 people. And more women are entering careers in journalism—the 2006 workforce was about 50 percent female.

The newspaper business has historically been one of the lowest-paying media industries. A 2005 survey by the University of Georgia found that entry-level reporters for print newspapers were making around $29,000.

▲ Entry-Level Positions

A person seeking an entry-level job as a reporter has the best chance of landing a job at a small daily paper or weekly. Starting out at a small paper gives a newcomer experience in several areas of newspaper work, since the division of labor at these papers is less clear. A reporter might also take photographs, edit wire copy, and write headlines. One possible way to break into the profession is to secure a summer job or an internship. Additionally, some people break into the profession as proofreaders, rewrite persons, or researchers.

No matter what sort of entry-level job a person is seeking, one thing is certain: He or she will have to be a "converged" journalist. Knowing how to write a story for a print newspaper is no longer enough. Tomorrow's reporters will also have to know how to write for the Web—that is, to take, store, and retrieve digital photos; to shoot, edit, and post video; to blog; and to create podcasts.

Other entry-level jobs can be found on the business side of the paper. Students who are interested in this type of work should have a background in business, advertising, and economics, along with a knowledge of mass communication. Since advertising is such an important source of newspaper revenue, most newspapers will gladly accept a newcomer who wishes to work in the sales department.

▲ Upward Mobility

A person who is seeking an entry-level position in newspapers should consider where the job might lead and how long it will take to get there. In the case of a reporter, upward mobility can come in one of two ways. A reporter can advance by becoming skilled in

Select the newspaper media tour (DVD, Track 2) on the DVD that accompanies this text. This video reveals the daily operations of The Record, *a newspaper based in New Jersey.* The Record *and its sister publication,* The Herald News, *have a combined daily circulation of more than 175,000. The first segment describes how the editorial team gathers and reports news and outlines the functions of the advertising, circulation, and publishing departments. The rest of the clip features a discussion of some of the key issues currently facing newspapers.*

The Record

The Record is one of those newspapers that doesn't have the name of a local town, city, or region in its title. It was originally called *The Bergen Record,* but the publisher evidently felt that putting the name of the paper's home county in the title might

make it seem foreign to some subscribers who lived in other areas. Located just west of New York City, *The Record* serves readers in many communities across northern New Jersey.

1. What is the prevailing form of public criticism for newspapers? How do the reporters and editors defend themselves?

2. When covering a disaster, what ethical questions do reporters need to keep in mind?

3. What medium poses the greatest threat to newspapers today? How could this same technology help newspapers survive in the future?

4. What types of degrees should an aspiring journalist consider? Why?

editing and move up to the position of copyeditor or perhaps state editor, regional editor, or wire editor. The ultimate goal for this person would be the city editor's or managing editor's slot. Other reporters might not wish to take on the additional administrative and desk work that goes with a managerial position. If that is the case, then career advancement consists of moving on to larger-circulation papers in big cities or to increased specialization in one field of reporting.

On the business side the route for advancement in the advertising department usually leads from the classifieds to the national advertising division. This department works with manufacturers of nationally distributed products and services and plans display advertising for these companies. Those who begin in the circulation department can eventually rise to the position of circulation manager. Ultimately, the top job that can be reached, short of publisher, is that of business manager, the person in charge of the entire business side of the paper.

MAIN POINTS

- Newspapers in colonial America were published with permission of the local government. A free press did not appear until after the Revolution.

- The mass newspaper arrived in the 1830s with the publication of Benjamin Day's *New York Sun,* the first of the penny-press papers.

- The era of yellow journalism featured sensationalism, crusades, and human-interest reporting and introduced more attractive newspaper designs.

- Many newspapers were merged or folded during the early 1900s, as tabloid papers became popular. The trend toward consolidation would continue into the years following World War II.

- There are four types of daily papers: national newspapers, large metro dailies, suburban dailies, and small-town dailies. Other major types of papers are weeklies, special-service newspapers, and minority newspapers.

- Almost all papers now have online versions.

- Newspaper ownership is characterized by large group owners and declining competition.

- Newspapers are reexamining their business model and converging their print and online operations.

- Newspaper audiences are measured by the Audit Bureau of Circulations. Newspaper readership has declined for the past several decades, but online readership is growing.

QUESTIONS FOR REVIEW

1. Trace the changes in the definition of *news* from the 1600s to the 2000s.
2. What are the defining characteristics of newspapers?
3. What are some of the advantages the traditional ink-and-paper newspaper has over the online version?

What are some of the advantages the online version has over the print version?

4. What are the main revenue sources for print newspapers? For online?

QUESTIONS FOR CRITICAL THINKING

1. Why don't young people read newspapers? What, if anything, could newspapers do to recapture this audience segment?
2. Has the growth of newspaper group owners helped or hurt the newspaper industry? Has it helped or hurt society?
3. Should newspapers be allowed to own broadcast stations in their markets? Why or why not?
4. Will the online version eventually replace the print version of a newspaper? Why or why not?
5. What will the newspaper industry look like in 10 years?

KEY TERMS

political press (p. 82)
First Amendment (p. 83)
penny press (p. 84)
yellow journalism (p. 86)

jazz journalism (p. 87)
tabloids (p. 87)
newshole (p. 89)
circulation (p. 94)

joint-operating agreement (JOA) (p. 98)
Audit Bureau of Circulations (ABC) (p. 103)

INTERNET RESOURCES

Online Learning Center

At the Online Learning Center home page, www.mhhe.com/dominick10, *select* Student Center *and then* Chapter 4.

1. Use the Learning Objectives, Chapter Outline, Main Points, and Time Line sections to review this chapter.
2. Test your knowledge of the chapter using the multiple choice, crossword puzzle, and flashcard features of the site.
3. Expand your knowledge of concepts and topics discussed in the chapter by going to *Suggestions for Further Reading* and *Internet Exercises*.

Surfing the Internet

The following are examples of sites that deal with the newspaper industry. All listings were current as of late 2007.

http://atlanta.creativeloafing.com
Creative Loafing Online for Atlanta, a guide to the arts, culture, and entertainment. A good illustration of the nontraditional weekly press.

www.decaturdailydemocrat.com
A good example of a slick online paper published by a small-town daily.

www.naa.org
Site of the Newspaper Association of America, a major industry trade organization. Contains information on newspaper circulation, public policy, and diversity, as well as links to the organization's *presstime* magazine. A hot-link feature allows visitors to see a list of newspapers online in a chosen state.

www.ojr.org
The *Online Journalism Review,* published by the University of Southern California, the best single source for the latest information on Internet journalism.

www.theonion.com
Looks like an authentic online paper but is actually satirical.

www.usatoday.com
Colorful site of the national daily *USA Today.* Note the emphasis on video, photos, and blogging.

CHAPTER 5

MAGAZINES

This chapter will prepare you to:

- discuss the characteristics of magazines

- understand how the magazine industry is divided

- understand the function of Mediamark Research Inc. (MRI)

- appreciate the efforts of magazine publishers to incorporate the Internet into their business model

- identify the five main magazine content categories

- describe the departments that produce magazines

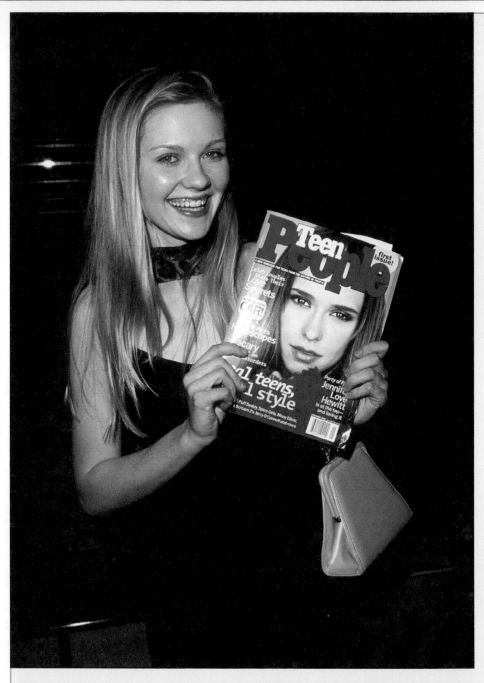

Teen People had high hopes when it debuted in 1998 (Kirsten Dunst is holding the first copy), but the magazine couldn't cope with increased competition from online teen sites.

When it first launched back in 1998, *Teen People* took the then revolutionary step of launching a Web site (teenpeople.com) along with its print edition. By any measure the early years of the magazine were a great success. Publisher Time Inc. reported that *Teen People* had a circulation of 1.6 million in 2001, and it was the leader in the teen magazine category. The American Society of Magazine Editors gave it a general excellence award in that same year.

Then things got complicated. Teenagers started migrating to the Internet for their celebrity news. They spent less time reading print magazines and more time visiting social networking sites such as MySpace and talking to friends on their ever-handy cell phones. Advertisers followed the crowd.

Teen People watched its advertising decline, down nearly 5 percent in 2005 and nearly 15 percent in the first half of 2006. Despite staying near the top of the teen magazine category in circulation in 2005, the decline in advertising revenue meant that the title was losing nearly $5 million annually. Faced with these facts, the executives at Time Inc. decided to fold *Teen People*. The Web site survived for a few months but was eventually folded in with People.com. (*Teen People* was not the only casualty in the teen magazine category. Hachette, publisher of *Elle Girl*, also dropped the print version but kept the Web site.)

The saga of *Teen People* says a lot about the modern magazine industry. First, magazines publishers depend heavily on advertising to stay in business. High circulation figures don't necessarily mean high profit margins. Second, as with the newspaper business discussed in Chapter 4, the Internet is having a dramatic impact on the traditional business model of magazine publishing. The Internet is drawing readers away from paper copies of magazines. Teens in particular are growing more technologically savvy, so it is not surprising that magazines that cater to this group would be the first to feel the Internet's impact. Finally, many publishers are betting that the future lies with more cost-effective online versions and with new distribution models that take advantage of the Internet and mobile media.

This chapter will explore the history, structure, and organization of this industry as it enters a transitional period.

A BRIEF HISTORY

▲ The Colonial Period

In colonial times *magazine* meant "warehouse" or "depository," a place where various types of provisions were stored under one roof. The first magazines printed in America were patterned after this model; they were to be storehouses of varied literary materials gathered from books, pamphlets, and newspapers and bound together under one cover.

It was Ben Franklin who first announced plans to start a magazine in the Colonies. Unfortunately for him, a competitor named Andrew Bradford got wind of his idea and beat Franklin to the punch. Bradford's *American Magazine* was published a few days before Franklin's *General Magazine* in 1741. The two publications carried political and economic articles aimed at an intelligent audience.

Both Franklin's and Bradford's magazines were ambitious ventures in that they were designed for readers in all 13 colonies and deliberately tried to influence public opinion; both quickly folded because of financial problems. The next significant attempt at magazine publishing occurred in Philadelphia when another Bradford (this one named William) started the *American Magazine and Monthly Chronicle* in 1757. This publication also contained the usual blend of political and economic articles mixed with a little humor; it was well edited and able to support itself for a year.

As America's political relations with England deteriorated, magazines, like newspapers, assumed a significant political role. Thomas Paine, who in his rousing pamphlet *Common Sense* argued for separation from England, became editor of the *Pennsylvania Magazine.* This publication strongly supported the Revolution and was a significant political force during the early days of the war. It became an early casualty of the conflict, however, and closed down in 1776.

All these early magazines were aimed at a specialized audience—one that was educated, literate, and primarily urban. Their overall impact was to encourage literary and artistic expression and to unify the colonies during America's struggle for independence from England.

▲ After the Revolution

Magazines popular during the late 18th and early 19th centuries contained a mix of political and topical articles directed primarily at an educated elite. The birth of the modern newsmagazine can be traced back to this period. *Niles Weekly Register,* which reported current events of the time, was read throughout the country.

Politics was also reflected in other magazines of the period. One of the most influential was the *Port Folio,* edited by the colorful nonconformist Joseph Dennie. Dennie's intended audience was a select one; he wished to reach "Men of Affluence, Men of Liberality, and Men of Letters." Although the major thrust of the paper was political, Dennie interspersed travelogues, theater reviews, satirical essays, and even jokes.

▲ The Penny-Press Era

While the penny press was opening up new markets for newspapers (see Chapter 4), magazine publishers were also expanding their appeal and coverage. The *Knickerbocker, Graham's Magazine,* and the *Saturday Evening Post,* all established between 1820 and 1840, were written not so much for the intelligentsia as for the generally literate middle classes. By 1842 *Graham's,* under the direction of Edgar Allan Poe, had a circulation of 40,000. The growing social and economic importance of women was illustrated by the birth of *Godey's Lady's Book* in 1830 and *Peterson's* in 1842. These two magazines offered articles on fashion, morals, diets, and health, and printed elaborate, hand-colored engravings in their pages. *Godey's,* under the editorship of Sara Hale, was a pioneer for women's rights and was the first magazine to campaign for wider recognition of women writers (see the boxed insert "Sara Josepha Buell Hale").

In 1850 *Harper's Monthly* was started as a magazine that would present material that had already appeared in other sources (rather like the *Reader's Digest,* except that the articles were reprinted in full). *Harper's* also included elaborate woodcut illustrations along

Sara Josepha Buell Hale was responsible for having Thanksgiving declared an annual holiday and was the author of the popular nursery rhyme "Mary Had a Little Lamb." She was also one of the women who left a lasting impression on 19th-century American journalism.

Sara Josepha Buell married David Hale, a New Hampshire lawyer, who encouraged her to write articles and poems for local magazines. By the time she was 38, she had published 17 poems, many magazine articles, two short stories, a literary review, and a novel.

Her literary accomplishments brought her to the attention of Louis Godey, publisher of *Godey's Lady's Book*, who offered her the position of editor. She brought to the magazine an intimate editor-reader relationship that proved so popular that the magazine had a circulation of 150,000 by 1860, a remarkable figure for the time.

Sara Hale not only edited *Godey's Lady's Book* but also wrote about half of every issue. In addition, she found time to champion women's rights and was influential in persuading Matthew Vassar to start the college that still bears his name.

She spent 40 years editing the magazine and finally retired at age 89. Thanks to her efforts, *Godey's Lady's Book* is credited with being the best women's magazine of the period.

This political cartoon, titled "Under the Thumb," was created by Thomas Nast and appeared in *Harper's Weekly* during the summer of 1871.

with its articles in double-sized issues. *Harper's Weekly* was instituted seven years later and was to become famous for its illustrations of the Civil War. In 1863 this magazine began publishing reproductions of Mathew Brady's war photographs.

The most famous example of the crusading approach of the penny press was the *Harper's Weekly* campaign against the corrupt political administration in New York in 1870. Under the control of William "Boss" Tweed, a group of unscrupulous politicians managed to bilk the city out of approximately $200 million. The editorial cartoons of Thomas Nast were credited with helping to bring down this ring.

▲ The Magazine Boom

In 1860 there were approximately 260 magazines published in the United States; by 1900 there were 1,800. Why the surge? The primary factors were more available money, better printing techniques that lowered prices, and especially the Postal Act of 1879, which gave magazines special mailing rates. It became possible to aim for a national market on a mass scale, and several magazines set out to do just that.

The most successful of the magazines seeking a mass market was *Ladies' Home Journal*, founded by Cyrus Curtis in 1881. The first issue, eight pages long, contained an illustrated short story, an article on growing flowers, fashion notes, child care advice, needlework hints, and recipes. Curtis was the first to recognize the potential for national advertising in the magazine industry.

The general crusading spirit of the press spilled over onto the pages of leading magazines of the late 1800s and early 1900s. Theodore Roosevelt dubbed the magazines that embraced this reform movement **muckrakers**. Corrupt practices in big business was the first issue to activate the muckrackers' zeal. *McClure's* ran an exposé of Standard Oil Company by Ida M. Tarbell. Although it carried the innocuous title "History of the Standard Oil Company," the article was filled with dynamite, for it revealed bribery, fraud, unfair business practices, and violence. Shocking stories on political corruption in big cities and another series on crooked practices in the railroad industry followed Tarbell's

Time magazine celebrated its 75th birthday in 1998. Henry Luce, its creator, was only 24 years old when he published this first issue. (The person on the cover is Joseph Cannon, long-time speaker of the House of Representatives.)

initial effort. Other magazines joined in. *Cosmopolitan* published "The Treason of the Senate" in 1906 and followed up with attacks on the International Harvester Company. By 1912 the trend toward crusades and exposés had spent itself. Many of the problems uncovered by the muckrakers had been remedied. Most importantly, the public had grown tired of the crusades, and magazines had to search for other ways to attract readers.

▲ Between the Wars

Shifting economic conditions and changing lifestyles in the decades following World War I also influenced magazine development. Three distinct types evolved in the years between World War I and World War II: (1) the digest, (2) the newsmagazine, and (3) the pictorial magazine.

The finest example of the digest genre, *Reader's Digest,* appeared in 1922. Although this magazine reprinted articles that had appeared elsewhere, it first condensed and edited the material so that it could be read by people in a hurry.

The idea of a newsmagazine was not new—examples could be found in the 19th century. *Time,* however, borrowed little from its predecessors. From its beginning in 1923, *Time* based its format on an original concept: the distillation and compartmentalization of news under various departments. Other innovations included the use of the narrative style to report news stories; group journalism produced by the pooling of the efforts of reporters, writers, and editors into anonymous articles; the institution of a large research department;

The beginning of life for *Life:* The magazine's first cover was shot by famous photographer Margaret Bourke-White.

and a brash, punchy, jargonish writing style. The magazine grew slowly, but by 1930 it was turning a substantial profit. Two imitators, *Newsweek* and *U.S. News,* appeared in 1933.

In the mid-1930s two magazines, *Life* and *Look,* revived the tradition of the pictorial weekly originated by *Harper's* and *Leslie's. Life* was launched in 1936 and had almost a quarter-million subscribers before it even had a name. It featured public figures caught in unguarded moments, photo essays, occasional glamour shots, and articles on the arts. In this format *Life* would live for 36 years (it would reappear in the late 1970s in a totally different format). *Look* hit the newsstands in 1937, just a few months behind *Life. Look* lacked the current-affairs emphasis of its forerunner and concentrated more on personalities and features. Over the years it evolved into a family-oriented magazine. *Look* expired in 1972.

Hispanics are the largest minority group in the United States, numbering about 40 million. They are also becoming an economic force whose combined buying power will reach $1 trillion in 2008. Naturally, magazine publishers are taking notice of this market, but they are discovering that reaching Hispanic readers is a challenging task.

The number of Hispanic titles grew from 58 in 1996 to about 116 in 2006, but, given the size and growth rate of the Hispanic population, experts point out that the market is still underdeveloped. Advertising has also lagged. The number of ad pages in Hispanic magazines was basically unchanged from 2005 to 2006, and several magazines have folded, including *Shape en Espanol, Fuego,* and *Christina la Revista* (named after a Hispanic talk-show hostess).

Why haven't Hispanic magazines done better? First, the Hispanic community is made up of groups of smaller communities, such as Mexican, Cuban, Puerto Rican, and South American. It's difficult to find a magazine that will appeal to all groups.

Second, there is the language issue. There are many readers who speak only Spanish and prefer a Spanish-language magazine. Then there are those Hispanics who have lived in the United States for many years and have been educated in U.S. schools. They generally prefer to read in English. Finally, there are those who are bilingual, speaking Spanish at home but English everywhere else. They may prefer to read a magazine in either language. An advertiser who wants to reach a large segment of this market must spend money to construct and place English and Spanish versions of the ad. Many advertisers have decided to avoid this problem altogether and simply advertise on television. Figures from 2006 indicate that Hispanic magazines received only 2 percent of total Hispanic media spending while TV grabbed 64 percent.

Publishers, however, have not given up trying to attract this rapidly growing group of readers. *People en Espanol,* one of the leading Spanish-language publications, does continuous market research into readers' content preferences, demographics, and purchasing behavior. The magazine has also been helped by the growing number of Hispanic celebrities— Shakira, Eva Longoria, America Ferrera—who can be profiled. *Latina,* another successful title, sponsors tours and special events where copies of the magazine are given away.

Hispanic publishers are also paying more attention to magazine-related Web sites. *People en Espanol* embellishes its "100 Most Influential Hispanics" feature with additional content on its Web site. *Latina* recently set up its own social networking site.

Despite these innovations advertisers are still unenthusiastic about devoting more ad dollars to magazines. Hispanic magazine publishers, just like any other publisher, must demonstrate to advertisers the value of reaching this target market before they can be successful.

▲ The Postwar Period

Magazines of the postwar era reflected publishers' firm belief that the one way to become profitable was to specialize. Increased leisure time created a market for sports magazines such as *Field and Stream, Sports Afield, Golf Digest, Popular Boating,* and *Sports Illustrated.* Scientific advances also generated a resurgence of a popularized version of *Scientific American.*

The rapid expansion of urban communities and urban lifestyles gave rise to many specialized publications. Liberalized attitudes toward sex prompted such ventures as *Confidential* (1952) and the trendsetting *Playboy* (1953). During the 1960s the rebirth of an interest in urban culture encouraged the rise of "city" magazines, of which *New York* is probably the best example. For the black press the most significant development in the 1950s was the expansion of black magazines. John Johnson had started *Negro Digest* back in 1942 and used his profits to publish *Ebony,* whose format imitated that of *Life,* in 1945. In the early 1950s he added *Jet,* a weekly newsmagazine, and *Tan.* These were followed later by *Black World* and *Essence.*

▲ Contemporary Magazines

Although other media were bouncing back from the economic downturn that occurred during the first few years of the new century, the magazine industry was slow to recover. Revenue growth was flat from 2004 to 2005, and projections suggested that the next few years would not be much better. Some major magazines, such as *YM, Lifetime, Budget Living,* and the English version of *Premiere,* ceased operations.

Why were magazines struggling? First, they faced marketing problems. Supermarkets and big discount stores, such as Wal-Mart, were becoming more selective about the number of magazines they would display on their shelves. Sweepstakes competitions, such as the

CRITICAL / CULTURAL ISSUES

Teen Magazine Web Sites: What's the Message?

More and more teenage girls are going online, and among their top destinations are the Web sites of teen magazines. Much like their print counterparts, these Web sites contain articles on beauty, fashion, and relationships, but the Web sites offer additional features. They are interactive. Most have chat rooms, bulletin boards, and quizzes with instant feedback. In addition, they are private. Teenage girls looking for information about sexuality, for example, might feel more comfortable looking at this information online rather than reading it in a magazine. Finally, the information on the Internet can remain available indefinitely.

What are the messages that these Web sites are presenting to young women? Feminist theorists suggest that teen magazines may play an important part in teaching young girls about what it means to be feminine. They may emphasize the importance of physical appearance and stress that attracting men is the most important goal for teenage girls. Are teen Web sites doing the same?

This question was the focus of an article by Magdala Labre and Kim Walsh-Childers in the fall 2003 issue of *Mass Communication and Society*. The researchers analyzed the Web sites of *Cosmogirl, Teen People, Seventeen,* and *Teen* and identified the major themes present in the Web sites. One theme was that beauty was a requirement to be successful and to feel good about oneself. The researchers were quick to point out that the beauty presented in these Web sites was not natural beauty but beauty that had to be created. Young girls' body parts were portrayed as problem areas to be fixed. The underlying message seemed to be, "You are not OK as you are." As an illustration the authors pointed to a magazine Web site that offered help for eyebrows; another had an online poll that asked what girls hated most about their hair.

A second theme followed naturally from the first: Beauty is achieved through products. The Web sites offered a wide array of beauty products for those girls who were dissatisfied with the way they looked. Moreover, the sites portrayed the use of these products as the natural and accepted mode of behavior. The *Cosmogirl* site, for example, featured a survey that asked readers to name their favorite beauty products and to say why they love them. Another part of the site asked, "What's in your make-up bag?" The Web site seemed to assume that all its readers had favorite products and that owning a makeup bag was the norm.

A third theme, not unexpectedly, was that the Web sites could help teenage girls find the right products to make them beautiful. The sites took on the role of best friend or big sister, someone who knew about beauty problems and how to solve them. Some of the Web sites had experts, usually identified by just a first name, who offered tips on what to buy. The underlying lesson appeared to be that buying lots of cosmetics is the natural way for a young woman to become beautiful.

The authors conclude that the notion that beauty equals success sends the wrong message. Young women are being taught that they can gain power and happiness by purchasing the right brand of cosmetics, and not through personal achievements. The content of the Web sites also support one of the criticisms frequently voiced by feminist critics: These sites polarize gender roles by promoting the idea that women in society have roles restricted to making their bodies beautiful in order to attract male attention. Finally, the researchers point out that these sites capitalize on teenage girls' insecurities about their bodies to stimulate consumption. By defining beauty as physical perfection and urging the purchase of products to achieve that perfection, these sites (as well as their print counterparts) are creating unrealistic expectations in their young readers. Many young women may spend a good deal of time and money pursuing an ideal that can never be achieved.

one sponsored by Publisher's Clearinghouse, have nearly disappeared because of legal problems, and the national do-not-call list has made it more difficult to recruit subscribers over the phone.

Second, cable TV and the Internet have encroached upon magazines' biggest selling point—attracting a specialized audience. Targeted cable channels, such as the Food Network and Oxygen, offer advertisers an alternative and sometimes more efficient way to reach their audiences. The Internet offers even more precise targeting. Doityourself.com., for example, is a natural place for Lowe's and Home Depot to advertise.

Publishers have been trying several strategies to improve their fortunes. As suggested above, most publishers are strengthening their Web presence in an attempt to offset print advertising shortfalls. Other companies are branching out into ancillary activities, such as sponsoring conferences and trade shows. All are becoming more cost conscious.

Although the weak economic environment has discouraged some from entering the business, the magazine industry continues to be competitive. More than 350 new consumer magazines were launched in 2005, down significantly from prior years, but it still means that more and more magazines are competing for about the same number of readers. Not surprisingly, 60 percent of new magazines don't last a year. In addition, the current trend in magazine publishing is to find a hot topic and quickly launch a magazine to capitalize on it. If the topic cools, so do the magazines devoted to it. Take the low-carb diet craze of 2004. As interest in low carbs faded, so did the readership of magazines such as *LowCarb Energy* and *Low Carb Living.*

Finally, the magazine industry continues to be dominated by a few big companies that publish best-selling magazines. Table 5-1 contains a list of the leading companies as of 2006 (see page 118).

MAGAZINES IN THE DIGITAL AGE

Magazines are still learning how best to use the Internet. In the early days of the Web, many magazines simply took articles from the print edition and posted them online. The main purpose of the online edition was to encourage people to subscribe to the print edition. Today, however, magazine Web sites have become more sophisticated and are treated as equal to their print counterparts. Many online magazines now have their own original content.

For readers a digital version of a magazine has obvious advantages. First, it may be available days before the print version arrives. Second, readers can easily e-mail articles to friends, order products advertised on the Web site, and search back issues. For the publisher the biggest advantage is cost. Producing and distributing an online edition is far cheaper than putting out a print edition.

Almost all major magazines have developed some kind of a Web presence. More than 150 new or revised magazine sites were launched by publishers in 2006 alone, and many featured the latest in Web technology. *Martha Stewart Living*, for example, launched a social community network on its site. *Time Out New York* started its own broadband video channel, while *Food and Wine* added video podcasts. Blogging has also become a popular feature. *TV Guide* has a celebrity blog, and *The New Yorker* features blogs produced by five of its writers.

Publishers are pursuing several strategies to generate revenue from the Web. Several have started advertising-supported, Web-only titles, which cost far less to launch than print titles.

The home page of zinio.com, where you can subscribe to your favorite magazine in digital form.

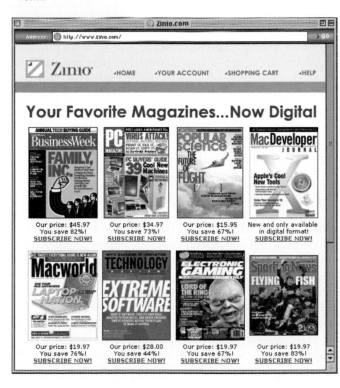

OfficePirates.com, for example, is an effort by Time Inc. to reach young males. Other magazines repackage print content in digital form and offer it for sale. *U.S. News & World Report* charges a fee to access the premium edition of its *America's Best Graduate Schools*. Playboy.com charges a fee to join its CyberClub, which allows subscribers access to its photo archives. Magazines can also sell space on their Web sites for display or banner advertising. In addition, they can use their sites for e-commerce. *Playboy*, for example, sells its branded merchandise at playboystore.com, and publisher Conde Nast has launched Stylefinder.com, where visitors can order stylish clothes. Finally, as always, publishers can use the Web site to help sell the print edition.

▲ Replica Editions

As with newspapers, the print version of many magazines is available digitally in replica form. A replica edition tries to duplicate the paper magazine reading experience as closely as possible. Unlike an online edition, where a reader can choose from a menu of stories and other features created expressly for the Web, a digital replica contains all the stories, graphics, fancy layouts, headlines, ads, and page numbers—and even those annoying little subscription cards—that the reader would find in the print edition. The replica version is displayed one page at a time, and the pages are side by side, just as in the print version.

Several companies offer electronic delivery of replica editions to subscribers. The biggest is Zinio Systems with hundreds of titles available, including *Popular Science, TV Guide,* and *PC World*. Zinio's biggest competitor is Texterity, whose offerings include *Glamour, Allure, Vanity Fair,* and a preview version of *Sports Illustrated's* swimsuit edition.

▲ Mobile Magazines

Magazines, like newspapers, are making their publications available across a variety of mobile platforms. Consumers can now read magazines on their laptops, PDAs, and cell phones, as well as download video and audio podcasts. In the market for a car? *Car and Driver* publishes a version designed for cell phones that lets consumers check reviews, get the latest auto news, and even research prices, all while they are in the auto showroom. Subscribers to Mobile.Maxim.com can access jokes, photos, and even video. In 2007 publishing giant Hearst announced that *Seventeen* and *Cosmo Girl* were going mobile with sites where consumers could find fashion tips and dating advice and download ring tones. Some companies, such as Sendandsee, specialize in creating mobile magazines aimed at cell phone users.

Mobile magazine delivery isn't without problems. For instance, it is unclear how long subscribers will spend with mobile editions, and they may not want long articles sent to their phones. Then there's the problem of payment. Suppose a magazine sends a news alert to a cell phone? Who should pay for the time? The sender, or should it be part of the subscription cost? Despite these problems, look for magazine publishers to continue to find creative ways to use this technology to increase their revenues.

▲ User-Generated Content

Publishers are cautiously experimenting with user production of content. Part of their caution stems from their desire to maintain editorial control over the content on their Web site, and ensure that offensive or distasteful content does not appear. A second concern is the lack of a clear way to turn this content into a revenue generator. Nonetheless, some publishers have come up with ways to use reader-generated content to build their audience base and, if all goes according to plan, enhance their advertising revenue.

Prevention, for example, is a natural place for user-generated content. Readers share stories of their aches, pains, and remedies on the magazine's Web site forum. Visitors to ExecutiveTravel.com can contribute reviews of hotels and share travel tips with their fellow readers. American Express uses a social networking Web site, Wetpaint, where readers of *Travel and Leisure* and *Food and Wine* can share recipes, post opinions about wines, and recommend travel destinations. For those magazines wishing to incorporate more user content, the Prospero Company offers a service to publishers that allows them to set up blogging and community forum sites that can be monitored by a staff member of the magazine.

In sum, given the increased emphasis on Web 2.0 (see Chapter 1), it is likely that user-generated content will figure more prominently in magazines' future.

DEFINING FEATURES OF MAGAZINES

The first defining feature of magazines is that, of all the media discussed in this book, they attract the most specialized audiences. There are publications designed to reach specific demographic groups (*AARP Magazine, Maxim*), specific occupational groups (*Pointe,* the magazine for ballerinas, or *Builder*), specific interest groups (*Cigar Aficionado, American History*), specific political groups (*National Review, Mother Jones*), specific geographic groups (*Southern Living, Arizona Highways*), and a host of other very specific groups (*Latin CEO*).

The second defining feature is magazines' relationship with social, demographic, economic, and social trends. Of all the media, magazines are most in tune with such trends. As consumer and business needs change, some new magazines emerge, some old magazines cease publication, and others fine-tune their content. To illustrate, the Hispanic population in the United States rose more than 10 percent from 2000 to 2004, about four times the increase of the overall U.S. population. Magazine publishers were quick to offer publications aimed at this growing segment of U.S. society. *People en Espanol, Reader's Digest's Selecciones, Shape en Espanol,* and *Healthy Kids en Espanol* were just some of the titles launched in the past few years. To take another example, a poker craze swept the United States in 2004–2005. Magazine publishers were quick to respond with titles such as *All In* and *Bluff.* (Keep in mind that trendiness is a two-edge sword. Should the poker craze fade, so will the magazines.)

The third feature is that, as we have seen, magazines can *influence* social trends. Magazines helped fuel the American Revolution. The muckrakers at the turn of the 20th century prompted social reform. In the 1950s *Playboy* launched the sexual revolution in the United States. In the 1970s *Ms.* helped usher in the women's movement.

Will the digital magazine spell the end of the traditional print edition? As the preceding discussion suggests, probably not. Despite the advances in mobile technology, the print magazine is still the most convenient form to take with you. You can roll it up, or fold it, and it doesn't depend upon a wireless or a WiFi connection. Second, as noted in Chapter 1, audience segmentation is becoming more and more pronounced. Magazines were the first medium to adapt to this changing condition, and they remain well situated for the future.

This is not to say that there won't be changes. Magazines that aim for a large, undifferentiated audience, such as *Reader's Digest,* will have a harder time staying profitable. Some magazines, such as *Elle Girl,* will shift entirely to the Web. Others will go part of the way. *TV Guide* moved its TV schedules to the Web while narrowing the focus of the magazine to appeal to a smaller audience of dedicated TV fans. Finally, the magazine industry may find a totally different business model. One suggestion is the digital newsstand, sort of an iTunes for magazines, where readers can pick and choose the articles they want from one or more magazines and download them to their computers, phones, or PDAs. One thing is clear: The next few years will be challenging ones for magazine publishers.

ORGANIZATION OF THE MAGAZINE INDUSTRY

One of the problems in discussing the magazine industry is deciding what exactly is a magazine. The dictionary defines *magazine* as a "periodical publication, usually with a paper cover, containing miscellaneous articles and often with illustrations or photographs." This definition is broad enough to include *TV Guide,* with a circulation of more than 9 million; *Water Scooter,* a magazine for boating enthusiasts; *Sky,* given away to airline passengers by Delta Airlines; *Successful Farmer,* the magazine of farm management; *Go,* distributed to Goodyear tire dealers; *The Journal of Social Psychology;* and the *Bird Watcher's Digest.* There are around 17,000 magazines published in the United States. Both the number and the diversity of these publications are staggering. For example, *Burrelle's Media Directory,* a directory of advertising rates and other pertinent information about magazines, lists 116 automotive magazines, 68 horse-oriented publications, and 7 periodicals devoted to snowmobiling. There are more than 4,000 magazines sold regularly on newsstands, and the number of new consumer titles continues to rise: more than 600 in 2007. Obviously, classifying the magazine industry into coherent categories is a vexing problem. For our purposes we will employ two organizational schemes. The first classifies print and online magazines into six main content

A glance at any newsstand will illustrate that consumer magazines fall into major general-interest categories such as sports, health, computers, business, and women's interests.

categories: (1) general consumer magazines, (2) business publications, (3) custom magazines, (4) literary reviews and academic journals, (5) newsletters, and (6) public relations magazines. The second scheme divides the magazine industry into the three traditional, functional components of manufacturing: production, distribution, and retailing.

▲ Content Categories

General Consumer Magazines   A consumer magazine is one that can be acquired by anyone, through a subscription or a single-copy purchase or as a free copy. These magazines are generally shelved at the corner newsstand or local bookstore. (Other types of magazines are usually not available to the general public.) These publications are called *consumer magazines* because readers can buy the products and services that are advertised in their pages. One noticeable trend in the content of consumer magazines is, as mentioned, the movement away from broad, general-appeal to more specialized publications. Some of the better-known consumer magazines are *People, Time, Reader's Digest, TV Guide, Sports Illustrated,* and *Woman's Day* (see Table 5-1). Note that consumer magazines can exist in both print and online versions.

Business Publications   Business magazines (also called *trade publications*) serve a particular business, industry, or profession. They are not sold on newsstands, and their readership is limited to those in the profession or business. The products advertised in these publications are generally those that would be purchased by business organizations or professionals rather than by the general public. *Business Publications Rates and Data* lists approximately 4,000 titles of business magazines. Most of these magazines are published

TABLE 5-1	Title	Circulation (millions)	Percent Change from 2003
Top 10 Consumer Magazines, 2006, by Circulation	*AARP The Magazine*	23.1	10
	Readers Digest	10.0	−10
	Better Homes and Gardens	7.6	0
Note: With a couple of exceptions, magazine circulation has been flat.	*National Geographic*	5.1	−23
	Good Housekeeping	4.6	0
	Ladies' Home Journal	4.1	0
	Time	4.1	0
	Family Circle	4.1	0
	Women's Day	4.0	0
	People	3.8	1

An article in a recent issue of *Ski* magazine about a driving tour of Colorado noted that the Land Rover was the preferred vehicle for such a trip. Seven pictures of the vehicle accompanied the article, and the text mentioned that the vehicle's "well-crafted lines lend a rugged but cosmopolitan look." Interestingly, Land Rover just happens to be an advertiser in *Ski*.

A feature article in *Country Living* explains how a reader, with the help of Home Depot's EXPO Design Center, can turn a dreary kitchen into a dazzling workspace. That same issue also carries an eight-page advertising insert from Home Depot.

Coincidence? Maybe, but the above examples might also illustrate a growing trend in magazine publishing whereby the line between advertising and editorial content is increasingly blurred, a trend that has disturbed many journalists.

The reasons for this trend are easy to see. Magazines are having a hard time generating revenue. The growing number of custom magazines, for which advertisers totally control the content, is eating into profits. Moreover, product placement in movies, video games, and TV programs such as *Queer Eye for the Straight Guy* and *The Apprentice* has become common. It is no surprise that advertisers might expect the same treatment from magazines. From the publisher's standpoint, trading editorial mentions for advertising dollars is one way to stimulate the bottom line.

The danger in this trend is that it damages the credibility of the magazine. How can a reader be sure if what's written about a product, service, or company is accurate or if it's simply well-camouflaged advertising? Some magazine professionals respond that the width of the dividing line between content and advertising varies by publication. Using television as an example, they point out that although you might see product placement on *Extreme Makeover Home Edition,* you don't see it on the *ABC Evening News*. Likewise, what is unacceptable for *Time* and *The New Yorker* might be tolerated in some fashion or shopping magazines.

The guidelines of the American Society of Magazine Editors (ASME), the watchdog group for the industry, clearly specify that "the clear distinction between advertising and editorial content is never blurred." Nonetheless, the ASME was reevaluating its policies in light of the "new advertising realities." In that connection a consumer group along with a number of journalism and law professors wrote the ASME asking that the group block further intrusion of commercial messages into magazine articles. The letter asked that the ASME require full disclosure of product placement and clear labeling of advertising inserts that might be mistaken for legitimate articles. The letter concluded, "If magazines become mere tout sheets for products and the interest of those who sell them, then every story will be suspect."

by independent publishing companies that are not connected with the fields they serve. For example, McGraw-Hill and Penton are two private publishing companies that publish business magazines in a variety of areas. Other business publications are put out by professional organizations, which publish them as a service to their members. The degree of specialization of these magazines is seen in the medical field, which has approximately 375 publications serving various medical specializations. Some business publications are called *vertical* because they cover all aspects of one field. For example, *Pulp and Paper* reports on all segments of the paper mill industry. Other publications are called *horizontal* because they deal with a certain business function, no matter in what industry it exists. *Selling,* for example, would be targeted at salespeople in all industries. Leading business magazines include *Computerworld, Oil and Gas Journal,* and *Medical Economics.* Business publishers are also active in supplying databases and computer bulletin board systems to their clients. Like consumer magazines, business publications can exist in print and online.

Custom Magazines   Custom magazines are published by corporations that try to keep existing customers satisfied while attracting new clients. Some are distributed for free at various business locations; others can be purchased at newsstands. Lexus, for example, publishes a magazine that promotes its automobiles, while Hilton publishes *Grand Times,* enticing people to vacation at their resorts.

Custom magazines have been around for a while. Airlines have published them for decades, but in the last few years custom magazines have become more visible primarily because businesses have discovered that they are an effective marketing tool.

Custom magazines present at least two problems for the traditional magazine industry. First, they siphon off advertising dollars from more conventional magazines. If Lexus can target its potential customers with its magazine, it might reduce its advertising buys in *Time, Newsweek,* or other consumer publications. Second, a custom magazine editorial staff may have less independence than a traditional magazine. It would be highly unlikely that a story in Hilton's *Grand Times* would say something negative about the company. Be that as it may, custom magazines likely will be a more important factor in the years to come.

Literary Reviews and Academic Journals   Hundreds of literary reviews and academic journals, generally with circulations under 10,000, are published by nonprofit organizations and funded by universities, foundations, or professional organizations. They may publish four or fewer issues per year, and a large number do not accept advertising. These publications cover the entire range of literary and academic interests, and they include such journals as *The Kenyon Review, Theater Design and Technology, European Urology, Journalism and Mass Communication Quarterly, Poultry and Egg Marketing,* and *The Journal of Japanese Botany.* Some literary reviews and journals have online versions.

Newsletters   When some people hear the word *newsletter,* they think of a club, PTA, or church bulletin filled with helpful hints. Although these newsletters are important to their readers, we are talking about newsletters typically four to eight pages long and usually created by desktop publishing. They are sold by subscription, and in recent years they have become big business. In fact, there is even a *Newsletter on Newsletters,* published for those who edit newsletters. The coverage area of a newsletter may be broad or narrow. It might deal with one particular business or government agency, or it might report on a business function that crosses industry lines. The *Federal Budget Report,* for example, reports on just the president's budget and appropriations. On the other hand, the *Spear Report* covers financial developments that have an impact on many industries.

Newsletters are extremely specialized, with small circulations (typically under 10,000) but high subscription prices. Typical fees are about $200–300 a year, but fees of $600–800 are not unheard of, and some daily newsletters cost as much as $4,000 annually. Some influential newsletters are *Aerospace Daily, Oil Spill Intelligence Report,* and *Drug Enforcement Report.* In the mass communication area, *Media Monitor* cover events in the print and broadcast industries, and *Communication Booknotes* reviews new books about the mass media. Many newsletters are available online, and some can be delivered to PDAs and other mobile devices.

Public Relations Magazines   These are magazines published by a sponsoring company and intended specifically for one of its publics. An internal public relations (PR) magazine is aimed at employees, salespeople, and dealers. An external PR magazine is directed to stockholders, potential customers, and technical service providers.

These publications typically carry little advertising, apart from promotional items for the sponsoring organization. These publications also have their own professional organization, the International Association of Business Communicators. Most PR magazines exist only in print, but some have online counterparts.

▲ Functional Categories

A second useful way of structuring the magazine industry is to divide it by function into the production, distribution, and retail segments.

The Production Function   The production phase of the industry, which consists of approximately 2,000–3,000 publishers, encompasses all the elements necessary to put out a magazine—copy, artwork, photos, titles, layout, printing, and binding. A subsequent section will describe in more detail how a magazine is produced.

The Distribution Function   The distribution phase of the industry handles the job of getting the magazine to the reader. This is not a simple job. In fact, the circulation department at a large magazine may be the most complex in the whole company. As with newspapers, circulation of magazines means the total number of copies that are delivered through subscriptions or bought at the newsstand. There are two main types of circulation. In **paid circulation** readers pay to receive the magazine, either through a subscription or at the newsstand. Paid circulation has two main advantages: (1) Periodicals that use paid circulation qualify

Walk by the men's section of any newsstand in the United States, and you can see the influence that Felix Dennis has had on magazine publishing. You will see titles such as *Maxim, Stuff, FHM,* and *King* with scantily clad women on the covers and articles with titles such as "Get in Bed with Anna Kournikova," "The Girls of Reality TV," "The Ugliest Brawls in Sports History," and "The Best of E-Mail Pranks."

Before Felix Dennis men's magazines in the United States were generally of two types: (1) general-interest magazines such as *Esquire* and *GQ,* and (2) magazines devoted to a single subject: cars, sports, health, nude women, and so on. The prevailing publishing wisdom was that men would not read a magazine that offered self-help advice. *Men's Health* redefined the category in 1986 when it offered service articles akin to those found in women's magazines, but it was Dennis who totally revamped the category by taking the "lad magazine" concept from Great Britain and introducing it in the United States.

At the risk of oversimplifying, the lad magazine's formula consists of sex, sports, beer, gadgets, clothes, and fitness. The unashamedly heterosexual *Maxim,* for example, seems based on the philosophy that the adult American male is simply an overgrown adolescent. A typical issue contains ample doses of sexy models, frat-boy humor, and "man-to-man" advice articles. Unlike *Esquire* and *GQ,* says Dennis, *Maxim* is for the man who likes sex better than he likes socks.

Dennis has been quoted as saying that his one talent is that he knows what people want minutes before they know it themselves, and his past history bears him out. Dennis got into the publishing business in the 1960s when he published an underground magazine in Great Britain. In the 1970s he published magazines based on current fads, such as kung-fu movies, and collectible items from films such as *Star Wars* and *E.T.* In 1985 he published *MacUser* just before Macintosh personal computers became popular. Dennis eventually sold the U.S. edition of the magazine for $25 million, which he used to finance the start of other computer magazines that proved successful, including *Computer Buyer* and *Computer Shopper.* By the mid-1990s Dennis was the fourth largest publisher in the United Kingdom.

In 1995 Dennis launched the British edition of *Maxim.* Once again, he was able to detect a popular trend. *Maxim* became profitable two years after its launch, about twice as fast as most successful magazines. Flushed with success, he launched *Maxim* in the U.S. market. The magazine quickly developed a readership. By 2002 its circulation hovered around the 2.5 million mark, making it the best-selling men's magazine. The magazine has also spun off a line of furniture and hair grooming products.

In the magazine business, however, nothing is certain, and the general decline in circulation has hit the men's category as well. By 2006 *Maxim's* circulation was down to about 2 million, and Dennis was considering selling the magazine.

If he sells, he will have plenty of other things to keep him busy. He publishes a political magazine and is a fan of high-end automobiles. He is also the author of a critically acclaimed book of poetry—not the sort of thing you'd expect from a publisher of a lad's magazine.

for lower, second-class postal rates; and (2) paid circulation provides a revenue source to the publisher in addition to advertising. On the negative side, paid-circulation magazines must undertake expensive promotional campaigns to increase subscriptions or to sell single copies. Paid-circulation magazines have the added expense of collecting subscription payments and keeping records. Most consumer magazines use paid circulation.

The alternative to paid circulation is **controlled circulation**. Controlled-circulation magazines set specific qualifications for those who are to receive the magazine. Magazines that are provided to airline passengers or hotel/motel guests are examples. Controlled circulation has two main advantages: (1) Publications using it can reach all the personnel in a given field, and (2) these publications avoid the costs of promoting subscriptions. On

The tremendous diversity of the magazine industry is illustrated by this magazine display in a bookstore. Magazine publishers compete vigorously for prime space (front row, eye level) in such a display.

the negative side, controlled-circulation magazines gain no revenue from subscriptions and single-copy sales. Further, postage for these publications costs more. Controlled circulation has generally been used by business custom magazines and public relations magazines.

No matter what method is chosen, the circulation of a magazine is an important number. The larger the circulation, the more the magazine can charge for its advertising space.

For a paid-circulation magazine, distributing copies to subscribers is a relatively simple affair. The complicated (and expensive) part of this process is getting subscribers. There are

TABLE 5-2	Rank	Company	Revenue (billions)	Top Magazines
Leading Magazine Publishers, 2005, by Revenue	1	Time Warner	$4.0	*People, Time*
	2	Advance Publications	3.4	*Parade, Vogue*
	3	Hearst Corp.	2.1	*Cosmopolitan, Good Housekeeping*
	4	Meredith Corp.	1.0	*Ladies' Home Journal, Better Homes and Gardens*
	5	Reader's Digest Association	0.9	*Reader's Digest, Taste of Home*

no fewer than 14 methods used by magazines to build subscription lists. They include employing cash-field agencies, which have salespeople make house-to-house calls to sell subscriptions directly to consumers; employing direct-mail agencies; mounting direct-mail campaigns sponsored by the publisher; and, finally, using what are called *blow-in cards*, those annoying little cards that fall out of a magazine as soon as you open it.

Single-copy distribution to newsstands and other retailers is a multistep process. The publisher deals with only one party, the national distributor. Four national distributors work with the nation's publishers. The national distributor handles from a dozen to 50 or more titles. At least once every month, representatives of the magazine sit down with the national distributor and determine the number of magazines to be distributed for an upcoming issue. The national distributor then delivers the magazines to wholesalers who sell magazines and paperback books within specified areas. In any given month a wholesaler might receive 500–1,000 magazines to distribute to dealers.

The particulars of online magazine distribution, of course, are much different. Online magazines and newsletters can be distributed by e-mail or sent to cell phones, with "copies" going only to those who request them, or they can exist on a Web site, where they wait for readers. Whatever the arrangement, online magazines have no need for national distributors or wholesalers.

The late John Johnson was the founder and publishes of *Ebony* and *Jet* magazines.

The Retail Function   The retailer is the last segment of the industry. The best available figures indicate that there are approximately 140,000 retail outlets in the United States. Wal-Mart is the single biggest retailer, accounting for 12 percent of all magazines sales in 2005. Supermarkets accounted for about 46 percent. Supermarket sales have become so important that publishers pay the stores a premium of about $25 per checkout rack to have their titles prominently displayed. When a dealer receives a magazine, he or she agrees to keep the magazine on the display racks for a predetermined length of time (usually a week or a month). At the end of this period, unsold copies are returned to the wholesaler for credit.

MAGAZINE OWNERSHIP

Recent mergers and acquisitions have resulted in a magazine industry dominated by large corporations. Many of the conglomerates (Time Warner, Hearst) have extensive holdings in other media. Table 5-2 contains a ranking of the top consumer magazine publishers by 2005 revenue and lists their well-known titles.

PRODUCING THE MAGAZINE

▲ Departments and Staff

The publisher is the chief executive officer at a magazine. He or she is responsible for budgeting, maintaining a healthy advertising position, keeping circulation high, and making sure the magazine moves in a consistent editorial direction. The publisher oversees four main departments:

1. *Circulation:* This department is responsible for keeping current readers satisfied and attracting new readers.
2. *Advertising and Sales:* As the name suggests, this department is responsible for selling space in the magazine to advertisers.
3. *Production:* This department oversees the actual printing and binding of the magazine.
4. *Editorial:* The head of this department supervises the editorial staff, plans topics for upcoming issues, and helps out with various public relations activities. The managing editor handles the day-to-day operation of the magazine, such as making sure articles are in on time, choosing artwork, and changing layouts.

Some magazines might have an additional department to handle their online operations, but declining revenues have compelled many publications to converge the online and print operations.

▲ The Production Process

Everything moves in cycles. Early magazine publishers were printers as well as writers, but during the 19th century the production function was divorced from the editorial function. Many magazines have now gone full circle: Computers enable writers and editors to set their words into type and make up pages, reuniting the production and editorial functions.

The first step in all magazine production is preliminary planning and idea generation for upcoming issues. Once the overall ideas are set, the next step is to convert the ideas into concrete subjects for articles. At this point preliminary decisions concerning article length, photos, and accompanying artwork are made. Then the managing editor assigns certain articles to staff writers or freelancers.

The next step involves putting together a miniature **dummy,** a plan or blueprint of the pages for the upcoming issue that shows the contents in their proper order. This phase can now be done electronically, thanks to computer programs that allow editors to view 32 pages at a time.

At about this same time, schedules are drawn up to ensure that an article will get to the printer in time to be included in the forthcoming issue. A copy deadline is set—this is the day the writer must hand in the story to the editor. Time is set aside for editing, checking, and verifying all copy. A timetable is also set up for illustrations and artwork.

Articles are written and edited at the computer. Once they are in acceptable form, a computerized typesetter sets the copy in body and display-size type, and the articles are sent to the press or posted on the magazine's Web site.

ECONOMICS

There are four basic sources of magazine revenue: (1) subscriptions, (2) single-copy sales, (3) advertising, and (4) ancillary services such as e-commerce, custom publishing, and database assistance. This section will concentrate on the first three of these.

The magazine industry was facing lean times at mid-decade. After a record-setting year in 2000, total revenue either declined slightly or stayed flat from year to year. According to the trade publication *Folio,* total revenue in 2005 was $32.4 million, up a tiny fraction from 2004.

Time magazine has been running its annual Person of the Year issue for nearly eight decades. *People* hasn't been around as long, but its 50 Most Beautiful People issue attracts a lot of attention. *Esquire* publishes its Women We Love edition, and even the financially oriented *Forbes* gets into the act with its Celebrity 100 list of highly paid entertainers.

But do these special issues actually help sales? The short answer is "Sometimes." Take *People*, for example; its last three 50 Most Beautiful People issues sold about 20 percent more copies than its weekly average. On the other hand, *Forbes'* Celebrity 100 issue sells about the same as a normal issue. *Time* does pretty well with its Person of the Year issue, which nearly doubles the sales of a normal copy of the weekly. The special issue that does the best, however, is *Sports Illustrated's* swimsuit issue, which sells 1000 percent more copies than the average weekly issue.

In addition, there were troubling signs on the horizon. Thanks to deeply discounted subscriptions, single-copy sales continued to fall, down about 20 percent from 2000 to 2005. Moreover, total circulation declined about 4 percent during the same period. A glance at Table 5-1 shows that, of the top 10 consumer magazines, only two increased circulation from 2003 to 2006.

Another significant trend is the growing importance of advertising in the revenue mix. In 1995 advertising accounted for about 56 percent of all revenue, with newsstand sales and subscriptions making up the rest. In 2005 advertising accounted for nearly 70 percent. Magazines usually improve as the general advertising climate improves. Unfortunately for publishers, that trend didn't hold true in the mid-to-late decade. While other media showed significant increases in advertising revenue, the magazine industry lagged behind. Magazines are turning to their online editions to help improve their bottom lines, but so far the impact has not been significant.

The relative importance of subscription impact, single-copy sales, and advertising varies tremendously from magazine to magazine. *Reader's Digest* gets almost all of its money from subscriptions and advertising. On the other hand, *Cosmopolitan* gets only a small proportion from subscriptions and relies mainly on advertising and newsstand sales. To gain some perspective on advertising, in 2006 it cost about $156,000 for a full page ad in *People* and $214,000 for a full page in *Ladies' Home Journal.*

Yet another economic problem for the industry was a shift in the marketing environment. Big retailers such as Wal-Mart and supermarkets want to display only those titles that are best-sellers; cluttering up their shelves with unsold copies hurts their bottom line. As a result it was becoming more difficult for new magazines to find shelf space.

From the perspective of the consumer, it makes sense to subscribe to a magazine rather than to purchase it regularly at the newsstand. From 1996 to 2005, average annual subscription rates actually dropped from about $30 to $26. On the other hand, average cover prices during that same period shot up from $1.71 to about $3.00.

Where does the money go? The typical dollar breaks down approximately as shown in Table 5-3. Two items included in the manufacturing and distribution category of Table 5-3 have increased at the fastest rate: paper and postage.

TABLE 5-3	Expense	Amount
Breakdown of a Consumer Magazine's Dollar	Advertising expenses	$0.08
	Circulation costs	0.31
	Editorial costs	0.10
	Manufacturing and distribution	0.40
	Other costs	0.01
	Administration	0.10

FEEDBACK FOR MAGAZINES

The print magazine industry, like the newspaper industry, depends on the Audit Bureau of Circulations (ABC) for information about who is reading the publication. The ABC audits most consumer magazines and issues a "pink sheet"—so called because its report is printed on pink paper—every June and December. The ABC statement reports the magazine's average paid circulation and its **rate base.** The rate base is the number of buyers guaranteed by the magazine and is also the number that the magazine uses to compute its advertising rates. Other information in the report includes circulation for each issue in the past 6 months, state-by-state circulation data, and a report on 5-year trends.

The ABC circulation figures were called into question in 2003 during a contentious court case between Rosie O'Donnell and Gruner and Jahr, publisher of *Rosie,* that followed the magazine's demise. As the lawsuit went on, the Gruner and Jahr circulation manager admitted that she had inflated the newsstand sales of the magazine to the ABC. It was later revealed that sales numbers for *YM,* another Gruner and Jahr title, had also been overstated. As a result advertisers took a closer look at the circulation figures for all magazines, and the ABC announced plans to institute stricter auditing procedures.

Another company, Business Publication Audit (BPA), specializes in business and trade magazines. It issues reports similar to those of the ABC, with additional information concerning the occupations of readers who receive controlled-circulation publications.

Although it is helpful to know the total circulation figure for a magazine, that number does not tell the whole story. Circulation measures the **primary audience,** those people who subscribe to the magazine or buy it at the newsstand. In addition, there is the **pass-along audience,** those people who pick up a copy at the doctor's office, at work, on the road, and the like. **Mediamark Research Inc. (MRI)** provides data on the total audience for magazines. This company selects a large sample of the magazine-reading public and conducts personal interviews with individuals to get an exposure score for each magazine. The reports issued by MRI are extremely detailed and encompass many volumes. They contain such specific information as the percentage of a particular magazine's readers who make more than $50,000 per year and detailed product use data, such as how many readers used a headache remedy in the past month. A small portion of an MRI report is reproduced in Figure 5-1.

Several companies including the ABC and Nielsen/NetRatings supply feedback about online readership. These reports usually tabulate the "unique visitors" to a Web site in some period of time, usually a month. The number of unique visitors to a magazine Web site may be much larger than its print circulation. *Sports Illustrated,* for example, has a print circulation of about 3 million; in contrast, si.com often receives more than 10 million visitors in a month. *Business Week* has a print circulation just under a million, but businessweek.com typically sees about 6 million visitors a month.

▲ Magazine Audiences

Although data on the audience of a particular magazine are readily available, information about the total audience for magazines is hard to come by, primarily because of the difficulty in defining what qualifies as a magazine. Nonetheless, some figures are available. In 2005, as reported to the ABC, total circulation of the top 589 magazines exceeded 352 million copies. Of these, about 11 percent were bought at the newsstand, while the remaining 89 percent were delivered as part of a subscription. If we examine circulation figures per 1,000 people, as we did with newspapers, we find that magazine circulation exceeded the growth in the adult population during the 1980s and 1990s and into 2006.

FIGURE 5-1   Excerpt from an MRI Report

Copyright © by Mediamark Research Inc.

BASE: FEMALE HOMEMAKERS	% TOTAL U.S. *000	% A *000	ALL B % DOWN	ALL C % ACROSS	ALL D INDEX	TIMES/LAST 7 DAYS HEAVY & MEDIUM 3 OR MORE A *000	B % DOWN	C % ACROSS	D INDEX	LIGHT LESS THAN 3 A *000	B DOWN	C ACROSS	D INDEX
ALL FEMALE HOMEMAKERS	85323	6628	100.0	7.8	100	4397	100.0	5.2	100	2231	100.0	2.6	100
MONEY	2719	*310	4.7	11.4	147	*214	4.9	7.9	153	*95	4.3	3.5	134
MOTOR TREND	499	*18	.3	3.6	46	*2	-	.4	8	*16	.7	3.2	123
MUSCLE & FITNESS	1109	*99	1.5	8.9	115	*86	2.0	7.8	150	*13	.6	1.2	45
NATIONAL ENQUIRER	11898	1134	17.1	9.5	123	770	17.5	6.5	126	*364	16.3	3.1	117
NATIONAL GEOGRAPHIC	12588	692	10.4	5.5	71	*416	9.5	3.3	64	*276	12.4	2.2	84
NATIONAL GEOGRAPHIC TRAVELER	889	*19	.3	2.1	28	*7	.2	.8	15	*13	.6	1.5	56
NATIONAL LAMPOON	*313	*21	.3	-	-	*21	.5	-	-	-	-	-	-
NATURAL HISTORY	662	*76	1.1	11.5	148	*6	.1	.9	18	*70	3.1	10.6	404
NEWSWEEK	8286	637	9.6	7.7	99	*447	10.2	5.4	105	*190	8.5	2.3	88
NEW WOMAN	3214	*206	3.1	6.4	83	*129	2.9	4.0	78	*77	3.5	2.4	92
NEW YORK MAGAZINE	728	*117	1.8	16.1	207	*87	2.0	12.0	232	*30	1.3	4.1	158
NEW YORK TIMES (DAILY)	1355	*67	1.0	4.9	64	*31	.7	2.3	44	*36	1.6	2.7	102
NEW YORK TIMES MAGAZINE	2087	*159	2.4	7.6	98	*116	2.6	5.6	108		1.9	2.1	79
THE NEW YORKER	1189	*81	1.2	6.8	88	*51	1.2	4.3	83	*43	1.3	2.5	96
OMNI	975	*102	1.5	10.5	135	*47	1.1	4.8	94	*30	2.5	5.6	216
1,001 HOME IDEAS	3610	*315	4.8	8.7	112	*290	6.6	8.0	156	*55	1.1	.7	26
ORGANIC GARDENING	1904	*35	.5	1.8	24	*28	.6	1.5	29	*25	.3	.3	12
OUTDOOR LIFE	1864	*121	1.8	6.5	84	*107	2.4	5.7	111	*6 *15	.7	.8	31

Almost everybody does some type of print or online magazine reading. In an average month 85 percent of U.S. adults read at least one copy of a magazine. Most read more. One study reported that adults read or look through an average of 10 magazines per month. About 28 percent read a magazine on an average day, and the typical adult spends about 25 minutes daily reading magazines. As far as demographics are concerned, the typical magazine reader is more educated and usually more affluent than the nonreader. Magazine readers also tend to be joiners. One survey found them far more likely to belong to religious, scientific, and professional organizations than nonreaders.

THE MAGAZINE INDUSTRY

As we move toward the end of the decade, the job outlook for the magazine industry is not optimistic. Many publications are cutting back on staff. Time Inc., for example, cut 300 jobs in 2006 after laying off 600 in the previous year. The one bright spot is online publications. As many print magazines incorporate the Web into the future plans, job opportunities in this area may improve.

▲ Entry-Level Positions

Most jobs in the magazine industry are found at small publications or at business and trade magazines. In the editorial department the most common entry-level job is that of editorial assistant. Editorial assistants do a little bit of everything: proofreading, researching, replying to authors' letters, coordinating production schedules, filing, indexing, cross-referencing, and answering readers' mail.

Another beginning-level position at some magazines is that of researcher. A researcher spends her or his time pulling together assorted facts and data for staff writers or compiling folders and research notes for articles that are in the planning stage. This particular job requires a general education, skill at using the library, and familiarity with reference books and the Internet.

Many newcomers start out as readers. When articles or stories arrive at the magazine, they are assigned to a reader, who studies them, summarizes them for an editor, and even makes recommendations about what to publish. Some beginners become staff writers. The assignment editor gives the staff writers assignments such as preparing a calendar of upcoming events of interest to the readers or editing a section of helpful household hints.

Newcomers in the circulation department are usually found in the subscription fulfillment department, where they update subscription lists, send out renewal notices, and handle complaints. Other beginning-level positions in this department are subscription salesperson and assistant to the subscription director or to the single-copy sales manager. In the advertising department entry-level employees are typically assistants to a staff member. Assistants to an advertising copywriter help prepare copy for leaflets and display cards, compile various reports, and assist in the preparation of direct-mail letters. Assistants to the sales promotion manager compile and verify statistical tables and charts, check promotional materials, handle routine correspondence, and suggest new promotional ideas.

▲ Upward Mobility

Career advancement in the editorial department can follow two different routes. Editorial assistants move up the ladder to become assistant editors, usually assigned to a specific department of the magazine. The next steps are associate editor and then senior editor. From there the person may go on to be managing editor or perhaps even editor in chief.

In the circulation department the next step after an entry-level position is into the subscription director's or single-copy sales manager's slot. Advancement from this position consists of moving into the top management ranks by becoming circulation director. For many the circulation director's job has led to a position as associate publisher or even publisher. In the advertising department upward mobility consists of moving into the position the newcomer was formerly assisting, such as copywriter or sales promotion manager. Another route upward involves joining the magazine's sales staff. Ultimately, the top position to aspire to in the advertising department is that of advertising director, a member of the magazine's top management team. The job of advertising director frequently serves as a springboard to the publisher's position.

MAIN POINTS

- The first American magazines appeared during the middle of the 18th century and were aimed at an educated, urban, and literate audience.

- The audiences for magazines increased during the penny-press era as mass-appeal publications became prominent.

- Better printing techniques and a healthy economy helped launch a magazine boom during the latter part of the 19th century.

- The muckrakers were magazines that published exposés and encouraged reform.

- Magazines began to specialize their content following World War I. Newsmagazines, digests, and picture magazines became popular.

- The magazine industry is turning to the Web to help increase its revenue.

- Magazines are specialized, current, influential, and convenient.

- The magazine industry is dominated by large publishing companies.

- The magazine industry can be divided into the production, distribution, and retail divisions.

- A typical magazine publishing company has several main departments, including circulation, advertising, production, and editorial.

- Magazines get revenues from subscriptions, single-copy sales, and advertising.

- MRI is a company that measures magazine readership.

QUESTIONS FOR REVIEW

1. What are the four defining features of contemporary magazines? Should any other features be added to this list?

2. Why did the general-interest magazines *Look* and *Life* go out of business?

3. How is the magazine industry learning to coexist with the Internet?

4. What are the major departments at a magazine?

QUESTIONS FOR CRITICAL THINKING

1. Are there dangers in having large corporations dominate the magazine publishing industry?

2. *Playboy, Cosmopolitan,* and *Ms.*—three magazines that influenced social trends—all came on the scene before 1980. Are there any more current magazines that have been influential in shaping American culture and society? If not, why not?

3. Is it possible for a magazine to become too specialized? How big does a specialized audience have to be to support a print magazine? A Web-only magazine?

4. Muckraking by magazines never reappeared after its heyday in the early 20th century. Why not?

5. Read the boxed insert "Teen Magazine Web Sites: What's the Message?" (See page 114), and consider the following: Do these Web sites have a responsibility to present a more realistic and well-rounded view of young womanhood? How might the emphasis on beauty and beauty products affect young women who may not be able to afford the "right" cosmetics? Would the same messages be contained in Web sites for magazines targeted at adult women?

KEY TERMS

muckrackers (p. 111)
paid circulation (p. 120)
controlled circulation (p. 121)

dummy (p. 123)
rate base (p. 125)
primary audience (p. 125)

pass-along audience (p. 125)
Mediamark Research Inc. (MRI) (p. 125)

INTERNET RESOURCES

Online Learning Center

At the Online Learning Center home page, www.mhhe.com/dominick10, *select* Student Center *and then* Chapter 5.

1. Use the Learning Objectives, Chapter Outline, Main Points, and Time Line sections to review this chapter.

2. Test your knowledge of the chapter using the multiple choice, crossword puzzle, and flashcard features of the site.

3. Expand your knowledge of concepts and topics discussed in the chapter by going to Suggestions for Further Reading and Internet Exercises.

Surfing the Internet

The following are examples of sites of or related to magazines. All sites were current as of late 2007.

http://money.cnn.com
A cooperative venture between CNN and *Money* magazine, both owned by Time Warner. Note the interactive tool you can use to look up a stock price.

www.people.com
Makes extensive use of photos and video.

www.magazine.org
The site of the major trade association of the industry, the Magazine Publishers of America. Contains statistics, FAQs, press releases, and research reports.

www.zinio.com
Provides digital delivery of magazines. Download the software and a sample issue to see for yourself how this process works.

CHAPTER 6

BOOKS

This chapter will prepare you to:

- understand that books are the oldest form of mass communications

- recognize the factors that led to the commercialization of book publishing

- explain how the digital revolution may change the underlying structure of the book industry

- identify the main parts of the book industry

- understand the economics that support the book industry

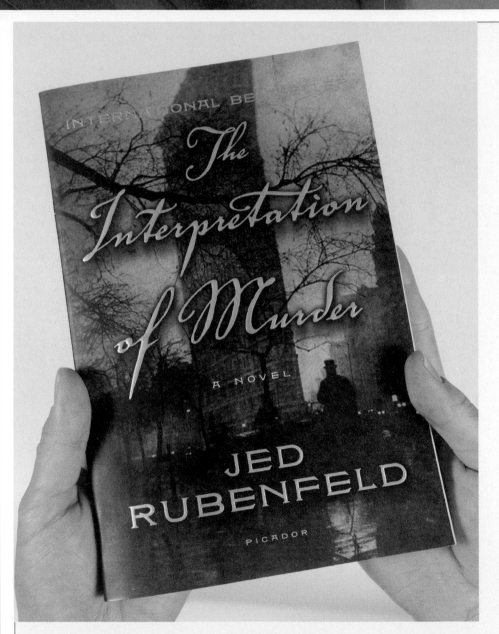

Publisher Henry Holt & Company gambled that *The Interpretation of Murder* would be a blockbuster. It didn't quite turn out that way.

The editor at publishing giant Henry Holt & Company thought that the novel had all the makings of the next *The Da Vinci Code*. It was a well-researched historical thriller with a plot that involved murder, had a sprinkling of sex, and starred Sigmund Freud. The book was *The Interpretation of Murder*, a debut novel by Yale law professor Jed Rubenfeld. If the editor was right, the book would be a bonanza. *The Da Vinci Code* was a huge hit, selling more than 17 million hardcover copies and another 6 million in paperback and spawning a successful motion picture. In publishing, however, nothing is certain, but in order to gain rewards, companies must be willing to take a risk.

Holt decided to gamble on *The Interpretation of Murder*. The company paid an advance of $800,000 for the North American rights to the book, one of the highest it has ever paid. Holt further invested $500,000 in a marketing campaign that included a cover-page ad in *Publisher's Weekly*, the leading trade magazine. About 10,000 preview copies of the book were sent to bookstores and handed out at the annual booksellers' convention. Rubenfield traveled to New York, Boston, and San Francisco to meet with major book store executives.

Early signs suggested that the marketing campaign was paying off. The first published reviews were positive. The American Booksellers Association named the book its pick of the month, a decision that meant the book would be displayed in more than 1,200 independent bookstores across the country. In a sign of optimism, Holt ordered a first printing of 185,000, a huge number for a debut novel.

Then the sales figures started coming in. The book debuted at number 18 on the *New York Times* best-seller list—a good showing but no *Da Vinci Code*. It dropped to number 20 the next week, and then more bad news hit: Rival publisher Simon & Schuster published Diane Setterfield's *The Thirteenth Tale*, another historical novel. Simon & Schuster got a lucky break when executives at Barnes & Noble chose the book for its new program Barnes & Noble Recommends, which focused all of the retailers' promotional might behind a single title. Consequently, *The Thirteenth Tale* opened at number one on the *Times* best-seller list and stayed there for the next week. Meanwhile *The Interpretation of Murder* slid to number 30 and then disappeared. In sum, the book sold less than 20,000 copies, a far cry from what Holt had hoped for. The book did a little better in England, but the gamble had not paid off.

At around the same time, Venezuelan president Hugo Chavez was speaking before the United Nations when he held up a copy of a fairly obscure book by linguist Noam Chomsky, *Hegemony and Survival: America's Quest for Global Dominance*. Sales of Chomsky's book soared, and *Hegemony and Survival* went to the top of Amazon.com's best-seller list. Who published *Hegemony and Survival*? Holt.

The above saga illustrates several key features of the modern book publishing industry. First, and most obviously, there's a lot of uncertainty. Books that look like sure winners can fail, and little-known ones can surprise everybody and succeed.

Second, it's a highly competitive business. If a book doesn't immediately sell, the big bookstores will replace it with a hotter title. There are only a limited number of slots on store display cases, and no retailer wants to devote space to a title that's not moving.

Third, the publishing industry is dominated by big companies. Henry Holt is part of a large German conglomerate. Simon & Schuster is the publishing arm of the media conglomerate CBS Corporation. Critics have complained that these big companies put such an emphasis on profits that they focus on potential blockbusters, such as *The Da Vinci Code*, and ignore other efforts with plenty of artistic but little commercial value. In that sense the book industry is becoming more like Hollywood, where a few movies get the biggest budgets and biggest promotional campaigns.

Fourth, promotion is an important part of the industry. Author tours, media campaigns, in-store displays, and good reviews are all necessary if a book has any chance at success. One of the problems with *The Interpretation of Murder's* promotional campaign was that it might have peaked too early.

The book publishing industry continues to be a major social and economic force in America. Of all the mass media, it has been the one least affected by the digital revolution. But that may be changing. Let us begin our consideration of this industry by taking a brief look at how it evolved.

Many early medieval manuscripts, such as this hymn book, were "illuminated" with colorful drawings and graphics.

A BRIEF HISTORY

Early books were inscribed by hand and lavishly decorated; many were valued as works of art. Until approximately the 12th century, most books in Europe were produced by monks in monasteries. As noted in Chapter 3, all this changed with the invention of movable type that worked with a printing press.

The invention of movable metal type suitable for printing is generally credited to Johann Gutenberg. Trained as a metalworker, Gutenberg developed a way to cast metal type and to encase it in a wooden mold that could then be attached to a printing press. In about 1455 Gutenberg printed his first book—the Bible. First put on sale at the Great Frankfurt Fair, the book cost the equivalent of 3 years of wages for the typical laborer of that time.

Gutenberg's innovations spread quickly throughout Europe. The Protestant Reformation and the writings of Martin Luther spurred the printing of religious books. Printed books appeared in England in 1476. Although book publishing was not considered a socially important force, Henry VIII recognized its potential as a political force and required all printers to obtain government approval before setting up shop.

▲ Colonial America

By the early 17th century, book publishers had followed the early immigrants to North America. In 1640 the Puritans in Cambridge, Massachusetts, printed the *Bay Psalm Book*. About 90,000 other titles were to follow it as book publishing took hold in the American colonies. Early publishers functioned as printers and sometimes as authors. One of the early printer-publishers who went on to fame was Benjamin Franklin. His *Poor Richard's Almanack* sold about 10,000 copies a year. Most book content was religious, such as that in *The Practice of Piety* and *Day of Doom*. Sentimental novels, many of them imported from England, also sold well. As the Revolutionary War approached, many book printers turned out political pamphlets. Thomas Paine's *Common Sense* sold 100,000 copies in just 10 weeks.

▲ The Penny-Press Era

The change in printing technology and the growth of literacy mentioned in Chapter 4 also helped the book publishing industry. Many of the publishing companies still active today can trace their roots to the early 1800s. Many publishers specialized in professional and educational books, while others addressed their efforts to the general public. Book prices declined and authors such as James Fenimore Cooper and Henry Wadsworth Longfellow became popular, as did the works of English authors. Public education and the penny newspaper created a demand for reading materials. The number of public libraries tripled between 1825 and 1850. Book reading became a symbol of education and knowledge.

The novels of Charles Dickens and Walter Scott were best-sellers during this period, as were books by Herman Melville and Henry David Thoreau. Specialized books also appeared. In the late 1840s textbooks were profitable, as were reference, medical, and engineering books. The most significant book of the period, however, was probably Harriet Beecher Stowe's *Uncle Tom's Cabin*, published in 1852. It sold 300,000 copies in its first year and was credited with converting many readers to an antislavery position.

▲ The Paperback Boom

During the Civil War soldiers turned to reading to fill the idle time between campaigns. This created a demand for cheap reading materials, and before long a series of paperbacks priced at 10 cents apiece flooded the market. These "dime novels" included the popular Frank Merriwell and Horatio Alger stories. By 1880 about one-third of all books published in the country were paperbacks, and 15 firms were selling the softbound volumes at prices ranging from 5 cents to 15 cents. Many of the best-selling paperbacks were pirated editions of best-sellers in England and other European countries. By the late 1880s this problem was so bad that a new copyright law was adopted. The effect of this new law, combined with years of cutthroat competition and price cutting, spelled the end of this era of paperback popularity.

▲ The Early 20th Century

The period from 1900 to 1945 saw the commercialization of publishing. Prior to this time, many publishing companies had been family-owned and specialized in publishing one particular kind of book. Publishers had been a close-knit group, and their dealings with one another resembled what might take place in a genteel private club. However, several events altered this situation. First, a new breed of literary agents, concerned with negotiating the best bottom line for their authors, entered the scene. Forced to pay top dollar for the rights to books, the publishing business became more businesslike. Second, many publishing houses expanded into the mass market, publishing popular works of fiction. To compete in the mass marketplace, these publishing houses introduced modern promotion and distribution techniques to the book industry. Third, a depression in the 1890s and a subsequent sluggish economy meant that the book industry was forced to depend more on banks for finance capital. The banks, of course, insisted that the book companies be run with the utmost efficiency, with an eye toward increasing profits. By World War II all these factors combined to make the book industry more commercially oriented.

The content of popular books was highly variable during this period. Outdoor adventures written by such authors as Jack London and Zane Grey were popular at the turn of the century. During the Roaring Twenties light fiction such as *The Sheik* and P. G. Wodehouse's Jeeves stories were best-sellers. Detective fiction by Erle Stanley Gardner (Perry Mason was his hero) and Ellery Queen sold well during the Depression. In 1936 two books broke the 2-million mark in sales: Dale Carnegie's *How to Win Friends and Influence People* and Margaret Mitchell's *Gone with the Wind*.

▲ Postwar Books: Paperbacks and Consolidation

Margaret Mitchell's *Gone with the Wind* was turned down by 25 publishers before Macmillan published it.

Shortly after the end of World War II, new paperbacks published by Bantam, Pocket Books, and New American Library appeared. These books were popular because of their 25-cent price and because new channels of distribution were used to market them. Wire racks filled with paperbacks appeared in train stations, newsstands, drugstores, and tobacco shops. A whole new audience was thus exposed to paperbacks. In 1950 the "quality" paperback appeared. These were serious nonfiction or literary classics that found their prime markets in education.

Moreover, expanded leisure time and more disposable income made book reading a popular means of recreation. In short, the book publishing business looked like a good investment for the future. Consequently, large corporations began acquiring book companies. Between 1958 and 1970, there were 307 mergers or acquisitions of publishing companies. These mergers brought new financial and management resources to the book industry, which helped it stay profitable during the 1970s.

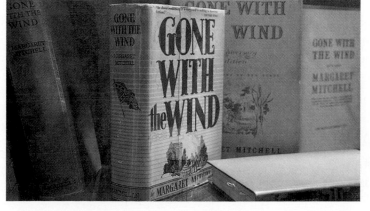

The content of popular books during this period was varied. The first big paperback best-seller following World War II was Dr. Benjamin Spock's *Baby and Child Care.* Other notable paperbacks followed. Mickey Spillane's Mike Hammer was a hard-boiled private eye who appeared in six novels during the 1950s that sold 17 million copies. *Peyton Place,* a novel famous for its racy (for the time) parts, sold 10 million in paperback. All in all, from 1946 to 1970, paperback sales were dominated by light fiction and an occasional how-to book.

▲ The Contemporary Book Industry

The wave of consolidation that began in the 1970s continued into the new century. Bertelsmann acquired Random House, and HarperCollins bought Morrow. Consequently, as of 2005, book publishing was dominated by a few big companies.

The 1990s and early 2000s ushered in major changes in the way books are marketed. Amazon.com was the first major company to offer books for sale online direct to consumers, with no trip to the bookstore necessary. Barnesandnoble.com and bordersstores.com provide similar services. In 2006 online sellers sold more than $2 billion worth of books.

The contemporary book industry has also seen a jump in the number of outlets where books are sold. In addition to chain and independent bookstores, consumers can buy books at mass marketers, such as Wal-Mart, and at grocery stores, hardware stores, cheese shops, and office supply stores. Walk into any Starbucks and you're likely to find books for sale.

Book publishers are also cautiously exploring digital developments. Apple's iTunes has a selection of audiobooks available for downloading, and Sony has recently introduced its e-book Reader and a Web site where books can be downloaded (see below).

The content of books today is remarkably varied. On the fiction side books by Danielle Steel, John Grisham, Nora Roberts, and Stephen King generally go to the top of the best-seller lists. J. K. Rowling's sixth book in the Harry Potter series sold more than 8 million copies in the United States and Britain the first day it was published. The seventh book in the series, *Harry Potter and the Deathly Hallows,* was already a runaway best-seller when it appeared in July 2007.

Books dealing with politics and politicians also remain popular. Presidential candidate Barack Obama's *The Audacity of Hope* was a 2006–2007 best-seller. And diet books are perennial favorites, as are self-help books: Rhonda Byrnes's *The Secret* sold about 3.75 million copies thanks to an endorsement by Oprah Winfrey. All in all, the varied content of the modern book industry reflects the specialized tastes of today's reading public.

BOOKS IN THE DIGITAL AGE

As mentioned at the start of this chapter, although the digital revolution has significantly transformed the way we consume newspapers, magazines, radio, recordings, movies, and television, it has yet to spread to the book industry. Granted, book production has been affected by digital technology (authors submit text in digital form, and publishers set type from these electronic texts), but readers still purchase paper pages bound between a cover (atoms) rather than a digital version (bits).

▲ The E-Book

There have been prior attempts to introduce a digital version of a book, generally referred to as an **e-book**. Around the turn of the century, big publishing companies such as Random House and Time Warner rushed into the e-book business and rushed out just as fast. For one thing there was a problem with the devices. Existing e-book readers were expensive and hard to use and had poor image quality. On top of that, there weren't enough titles in digital form to spur consumers into buying the new technology. One bright spot was big, heavy reference books, which were more convenient in digital form. But overall e-books accounted for less than 1 percent of book industry revenue at mid-decade.

Now, however, the e-book may finally make its mark, thanks to the introduction of the Sony Reader, a device about the same size and weight as a paperback novel that has enough memory to hold 80 average-size books. The Reader uses a new technology, called *e-ink* (see the boxed insert "Electronic Ink"), that creates a sharp page image on a 6-inch screen (measured diagonally) that is viewable even in direct sunlight. Readers can increase the type size for easier viewing and bookmark individual pages. (The Reader also plays MP3 files and displays photos.)

Sony has also created a Web site where readers can purchase and download books to their Reader (sort of like iTunes for books). As of mid-2007 there were about 12,000 titles available on the site (keep in mind, however, that a typical Barnes & Noble or Borders store probably stocks more than five times that number). Digital versions sell for about 20 percent less than print versions.

Will Sony's effort succeed where others have failed? There are reasons for optimism. First, the Reader is easier to use and has better image quality than previous hardware. Second, people, especially young people, are now more accustomed to getting information from handheld devices. They read text messages on their cell phones and get news and weather on their PDAs. Third, there is more digital content available. Sony plans to expand its Web site as it makes deals with more publishing companies.

But there are some problems. The Reader is pricey—about $350. Also, maps and charts don't show up well, and there are occasional line-spacing issues. Finally, the Reader may not work with other content not in the Sony format. In any case, the next few years should give us a clearer reading on the future of the digital book.

Maybe it's the start of a trend. When you walk in the front door of the new library at Valparaiso University in Indiana, you enter a room equipped with a grand piano, black leather couches, and a glass wall. The library also has a café and a technology center with computer-equipped booths where students are encouraged to socialize and converse (no more "Quiet Please" signs and shushing librarians). The building also contains books, but a lot of them are in a vault that students can't enter. Instead, they have to make a request, and the book is retrieved by a robotic arm.

Is this the future? The digital revolution has made huge amounts of information available online at the click of a mouse button. When was the last time you went to a library and actually touched a book? Do students still need big brick-and-mortar book depositories?

Many university libraries are grappling with that last question. At some campuses books are being moved out to make space for more people-friendly areas such as lounges and for computer stations. Marquette University in Wisconsin, for example, recently built a new library but left almost all its books behind in the old building. The bridge connecting the two buildings has a café, couches, big-screen TV, and live music. The Valparaiso library has gas fireplaces and Wi-Fi access throughout the building. In short, libraries are becoming social centers on many campuses.

Students seem to like the change. At Marquette library usage has tripled since it opened its new building. At Valparaiso library traffic increased 433 percent in the first year after the new library opened.

Is there a downside to this trend? What is lost when students do their research online and never need to check out a book? For one thing, not everything is online. Despite the increasing number of books and other sources of information that are being digitized, there is still a huge amount of information that is available only in print form. The new libraries make it more difficult to access this information. In addition, people used to go to libraries in order to have a quiet place to think, concentrate, reflect, and learn. The new libraries make this more difficult; it's hard to ponder around a piano. Finally, this trend toward library as social center seems to assume that the library should cater to technologically hip young people who do their research while sipping lattes and Googling on their laptops. But libraries should serve everybody. The more money spent on couches, pianos, and espresso machines, the less money there is to spend on enlarging collections and subscribing to journals that help encourage research and scholarship.

▲ Printing on Demand

Another possibility thanks to digitalization is **printing on demand**. This publishing method is a little less radical than that of the e-book. In this approach traditional publishers are still part of the mix, but books are printed and distributed differently.

Here's how it works: Publishers create a huge database of books in digital form. A customer goes to a bookstore, browses through a catalogue, and selects a book. A machine in the bookstore then downloads the book and prints it while the customer waits.

The implications of printing on demand are impressive. Traditional book publishers look for books that will sell enough copies (usually a large number) to make a profit. They then print thousands of books, ship them to bookstores, and hope that most of them are not returned as unsold copies. With printing on demand, however, publishers do not have to guess how many books they should print. They simply print one whenever somebody orders it. This eliminates all the production and shipping costs and guarantees that no books will be returned unsold. Eliminating these costs and the guesswork involved in forecasting demand means that publishers can make money on a book that sells only a few hundred copies. This might open up the way for a multitude of special-interest books that would be too expensive to publish with the traditional method.

Printing on demand has yet to make its way into the local bookstore. It was estimated that, as of 2005, printing on demand accounted for less than 1 percent of total book sales. Nonetheless, the technique has gained ground. Much printing on demand takes place between printers and publishers of scientific and medical books.

No one is suggesting that the e-book and printing on demand will ever totally replace the traditional ink-and-paper book. People will still be drawn to the feel and texture of books and the unique experience of reading paper pages bound between covers. Even so, the digital age has already opened up a number of possibilities for the book industry, and even more will become apparent as technology continues to evolve.

▲ Mobile Books

The e-book, of course, is just as portable as a paper-and-ink version. Digital books can be downloaded to a dedicated book reader (such as Sony's) or to other handheld devices, such as a Treo. As cell phone screens become larger and easier to read, they can make the book even more mobile. Japan already has a system whereby consumers can download full-length novels to their cell phones.

▲ User-Generated Content

There have been a few beginning steps in the area of user-generated content as publishers begin to explore its potential and pitfalls. The British division of Penguin Books announced the creation of a wiki-novel, *A Million Penguins,* in 2007. Visitors wound up creating about 400 pages in the first month, but what they produced might charitably be described as disorganized. Random House is planning a user-generated book focusing on business uses of the Internet. Harlequin, the publisher of romance books, launched a Web site where readers could provide their own answers to evocative questions such as "What is love?" The best answers will be published in an e-book.

DEFINING FEATURES OF BOOKS

The sucess of *The Da Vinci Code* notwithstanding, books are the least "mass" of the mass media. It took about 40 years to sell 20 million copies of *Gone with the Wind,* but more than 50 million people watched the movie version in a single evening when it came to television. Even a flop TV show might have 5 million people in its audience, whereas a popular hardcover book might make the best-seller list with 125,000 copies sold. Even a mass-market paperback might sell only about 6 million copies.

Books, however, can have a cultural impact that far outweighs their modest audience size. *Uncle Tom's Cabin* is credited with helping to change a nation's attitude toward slavery. Dr. Spock and his *Baby and Child Care* altered the way parents brought up their children and became the target of critics who blamed him and his methods for the social unrest of the 1960s. Rachel Carson's *Silent Spring* changed the nation's attitudes toward the environment.

Finally, books are the oldest and most enduring of the mass media. Gutenberg printed his first book in the 15th century. Public libraries have been around for hundreds of years. Many individuals have extensive collections of books in their own home libraries. People throw away newspapers and magazines shortly after reading them, but most save their books.

> **S O U N D B Y T E**
>
> **You Really Can't Tell a Book by Its Cover**
>
> The publisher of *Married Lust: The Ten Secrets of Long Lasting Desire* faced a unique marketing dilemma. Market research disclosed that husbands and wives liked the book but were reluctant to buy it because they were afraid their children might read it or they would be embarrassed to read the book in a public place, such as on the beach or on an airplane.
>
> The author came up with a novel solution: a reversible cover. On one side is the legitimate cover. On the other side is a nonembarrassing, kid-proof title: *Modern Tactics in Higher Education.* The publisher agreed that no self-respecting child would ever open a book with that title.

ORGANIZATION OF THE BOOK INDUSTRY

The book publishing industry can be divided into three segments: publishers, distributors, and retailers.

▲ Publishers

The publishing segment consists of the 2,600 or so establishments that transform manuscripts submitted by authors into books that are sought by readers. Every year these companies publish 100,000 to 150,000 new titles. Book publishing is a highly segmented industry. Publishers have developed a classification system for the industry based upon

Sony's E-Book Reader goes anywhere and holds about 80 average-size novels.

the market that is served. The following are the 10 major divisions suggested by the Association of American Publishers:

1. *Trade books:* Titles aimed at the general consumer and sold primarily through bookstores. They can be hardbound or softbound and include works for juveniles and adults. Trade books include hardcover fiction, nonfiction, biographies, cookbooks, and art books.

2. *Religious books:* Includes Bibles, hymnals, prayer books, theology, and other literature of a devotional nature.

3. *Professional books:* Titles aimed at doctors, lawyers, scientists, accountants, business managers, architects, engineers, and all others who need a personal reference library in their work.

4. *Book club and mail order:* These may at first sound more like part of a distribution channel than a division of the publishing segment, but some book clubs publish their own books, and almost all prepare special editions for their members. Mail-order publications consist of books created for the general public and marketed by direct mail. These are different from book clubs because the books are marketed by the publisher, and customers do not incur any membership obligations in an organization.

5. *Mass-market paperbacks:* Softbound volumes on all subjects that achieve their major sales in places other than bookstores. Typically, these are the books sold from racks in supermarkets, newsstands, drugstores, airports, chain stores, and so on.

6. *Elementary and secondary textbooks:* Hard- and softcover books, workbooks, manuals, and other printed materials, all intended for use in the classroom. Logically enough, schools are the primary market for these publishers. (This division is also referred to as *elhi* publishers—from *el*ementary and *hi*gh school.)

7. *Higher education:* Texts and workbooks for the college market.

8. *Audiobooks*: Books released on tape or CD that consist of a person reading the text of a book.

9. *E-books*: As mentioned above, those digital versions available for downloading to computers or special readers.

10. *Other:* These include university presses, reference books, and standardized tests.

Table 6-1 shows the relative importance of each of these segments to the industry. As can be seen, trade, professional, and textbook publishing are the major divisions, accounting for 84 percent of sales.

TABLE 6-1	Division	Percentage of Sales
Sales by Publishing Industry Division, 2005	Trade	31
	Elhi	26
	Higher education	14
	Professional	13
	Book club/mail order	6
	Mass-market paperback	4
	E-books	1
	Audio books	1
	All other	4

FIGURE 6-1

Channels of Book
Distribution

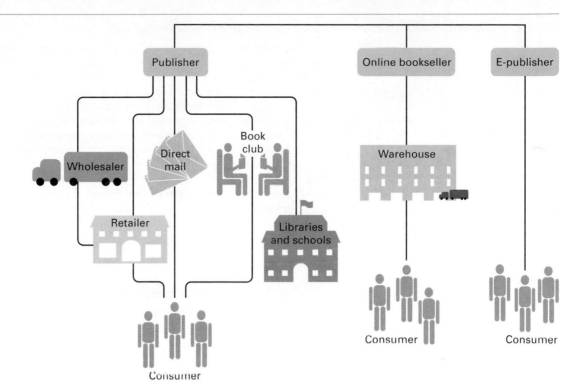

▲ **Distributors**

The Internet has drastically changed the book distribution system. There are now three main channels by which books get to consumers. In the traditional method the publisher usually ships copies of the book to a wholesaler or distributor who, in turn, sends the books to a retail outlet where consumers can buy them. Online booksellers such as Amazon.com use a different approach. The consumer orders a book from the Web site, and the book is shipped from the seller's warehouse directly to the consumer, bypassing the distributor and retail outlet. E-books, of course, go directly from publisher to consumer, bypassing everything in between. Figure 6-1 illustrates these distribution arrangements.

▲ **Retailers**

There are more than 20,000 traditional "brick-and-mortar" bookstores in the United States plus the big online booksellers mentioned earlier. Big chains, such as Barnes & Noble, Borders-Waldenbooks, and Books-A-Million dominate traditional bookselling. In 2005, these firms took in about $9.3 billion in revenue. Amazon.com ranked fourth.

Other retail channels include college bookstores and direct-to-consumer booksellers such as book clubs and mail-order sellers.

OWNERSHIP IN THE BOOK INDUSTRY

The book industry is dominated by large conglomerates with interests in other media. The top five companies as of 2005 were the following:

1. *Pearson Publishing:* A global media company that is the world's largest educational publisher, with imprints such as Scott, Foresman and Prentice-Hall. It also owns the Penguin Group of consumer publishing firms (Penguin, Dutton, and Viking) as well as the *Financial Times* business newspaper. Its Pearson Television produces more than 300 programs worldwide.

2. *Random House:* Part of the Bertelsmann media empire, which includes interests in 600 companies in 53 countries and is engaged in books, music, magazines, TV, and radio.

3. *HarperCollins:* Rupert Murdoch's worldwide communications company, which owns HarperCollins as well as 20th Century Fox, the Fox TV network, and various newspapers and magazines.

4. *Simon & Schuster:* Part of CBS/Viacom, a conglomerate that has TV networks, radio stations and a radio network, cable networks, theme parks, and a TV syndication company.

5. *Time Warner Publishing:* Part of the Time Warner company, the biggest media conglomerate in the world, with an online service, cable systems, magazines, and TV and radio, movie production, and other interests. The publishing group includes Warner Books, Time-Life Books, and Little, Brown.

PRODUCING THE BOOK

▲ Departments and Staff

There are four major departments in a typical publishing company: (1) editorial, (2) production, (3) marketing, and (4) general administration or business.

The editorial department is in charge of dealing with authors; it is responsible for selecting manuscripts and preparing them for publication. Some editors specialize in procuring new manuscripts, and some read manuscripts, write reports on them, and recommend acceptance, revision, or rejection. Other editors work with accepted manuscripts, checking grammar, language, accuracy, and so on.

As its name suggests, the production department oversees the physical design of the book. This department is responsible for type style, composition, paper, printing, and binding.

The marketing department supervises sales, promotions, and publicity. The actual type of marketing depends on the book and its intended audience. Publishers of elhi textbooks sell mainly to school systems. Mass-market paperbacks are sold to retailers who, in turn, sell them to the public. Advertising in trade magazines, television interviews, and reviews in respected publications are common marketing tools.

The business manager at a publishing company is responsible for several functions. One of the most important is accounting. Further, this department prepares budgets and makes long-range financial forecasts. Other responsibilities include dealing with internal personnel policies and supervising the general day-to-day operational needs of the company.

Jeff Bezos was always tinkering with things. When he was 3, he took apart his bed. Eleven years later, he tried to make a hovercraft out of a vacuum cleaner. Sixteen years after that, he tinkered with the way books were sold and totally revolutionized the business by starting Amazon.com.

After growing up in Houston and Miami, Bezos enrolled at Princeton, where he studied computer science and engineering. After a couple of jobs in the financial marketplace, he wound up at a Wall Street investment company. One day in 1993, while doing financial research, he came across a startling statistic: The Internet was growing at a rate of 2,300 percent a year. Bezos recognized the tremendous selling potential of the net and decided to launch an online business. He reasoned that things that are big mail-order sellers should also do well online. Accordingly, he made a list of the top 20 mail-order products and determined that books would be the best item to sell. A virtual bookstore would have the space to list all the millions of books in print; no brick-and-mortar store could do that. Further, book wholesalers had already produced CD-ROMs that listed all available titles. Bezos recognized that the existing book databases could easily be put online.

Bezos's family and friends invested $300,000 in his idea, and Bezos moved to Seattle, the home of many net-savvy programmers who would be needed to get the business online. Seattle was also the home of one of the biggest book wholesalers in the country.

Working out of his garage, Bezos created a Web site that he tested among his friends. It seemed to work well, and Bezos decided to open the site to everybody. But what to call it? He originally wanted to call it Cadabra.com, as in "abracadabra," the magic incantation. When he tried this name out on his lawyer, however, the lawyer thought Bezos said "Cadaver.com" and wanted to know why he would name his site after a dead body. Bezos went back to the drawing board and eventually settled on Amazon.com, after one of the world's longest and most powerful rivers.

The rest, as they say, is Internet history. The company grew quickly. In 1996 Amazon.com had 300 employees. In 2004 it had about 9,000. From a few thousand customers in its first year, it now has more than 20 million in about 150 countries. Sales in 2005 exceeded $8 billion. Its brand name is more recognizable than Burger King or Barbie. Amazon.com has also branched out from books and now sells CDs, toys, electronics, and gifts from its Web site.

Further, Amazon.com is one of the companies that have defined the Internet economy, where growth seems more important than profits. As of 2000, the company had lost more than $1.5 billion. Nonetheless, its stock was selling at $113 a share. Then reality set in. Like many other dot-coms, Amazon was hit hard by a stock slump in mid-2000, and its stock price dropped 76 percent. Despite this precipitous loss investors value Amazon at $15 billion, more than Barnes & Noble, Kmart, and J. C. Penney combined. Bezos has recently slashed costs, and the company posted $359 million in net income in 2005.

No matter how profitable or unprofitable Amazon.com may become, one thing is certain: It has helped make pointing and clicking a significant part of Americans' shopping behavior.

▲ The Publication Process

Editors get their books in three ways: (1) through submissions by agents, (2) as unsolicited books sent in by authors, and (3) as book ideas generated by the editor. Most trade manuscripts are submitted through literary agents. Agents are known quantities and will not generally submit manuscripts that they know are unacceptable to the editor. Unsolicited manuscripts are given an unflattering name in the business: "slush." As they come in, these manuscripts are put in the slush pile and eventually read, if the author is lucky, by an editorial assistant. Most of the time they are rejected with a form letter, but every once in a while an author gets through. For instance, E. D. Baker's *The Frog Princess* has sold well and has been translated into several languages. Editors also generate ideas for books. If an editor has a good idea for a book, he or she will generally talk to one or more agents who will suggest likely candidates for the assignment. This is another good reason writers should have agents. In any case, the author typically submits a proposal consisting of a cover letter, a brief description of the planned book, a list of reasons it should be published, an analysis of the potential market, an outline or a table of contents, and perhaps one or two sample chapters. The proposal usually goes to an acquisitions editor and is evaluated. If the publishing decision is favorable, a contract is signed, and the author begins work in earnest.

Editorial work starts as soon as the author submits chapters to the publisher. Editors look at the overall thrust of the book to make sure it makes sense and achieves its original intent.

Moreover, the mechanics of the book are checked to make sure that the general level of writing is acceptable, that all footnotes are in order, that all necessary permissions to reproduce material from other sources have been obtained, and that all artwork is present. Eventually, both author and editors will produce a manuscript that is mutually satisfactory.

While all this editing is going on, other decisions are being made about scheduling, designing the interior look of the book, and designing the cover. When everything is in order, the book is printed, bound, and sent to the warehouse to await distribution, or it is distributed online.

THE ECONOMICS OF BOOK PUBLISHING

Despite competition from other media and continuing predictions that reading is becoming a lost art, the book industry has shown modest gains over the past few years (see Figure 6-2). According to data from the Association of American Publishers, sales decreased from 2003 to 2004 but bounced back a bit in 2005 when the industry garnered $25.1 billion, an increase of 9.9 percent over 2004. And preliminary figures for 2006 suggested that the total would be nearly unchanged from 2005.

At the consumer level it is obvious that books have become more expensive. In 2007, a hardcover copy of *Harry Potter and the Deathly Hallows* had a list price of $35, while best-selling paperbacks went for $9.99. The high prices have prompted many consumers to buy from discount sellers and the used-book market.

A publisher has two main sources of income: (1) the money that comes from book sales and (2) money from **subsidiary rights** (sales to book clubs, foreign rights, paperback rights, and reprint permissions). Of these two the income from book sales is the most important. It should be noted, however, that the publisher does not get all the money from the sale of a book. The list price is discounted for wholesalers and booksellers. These discounts might amount to 40 percent for many books.

FIGURE 6-2

Book Publishing
Revenue, 1983–2005

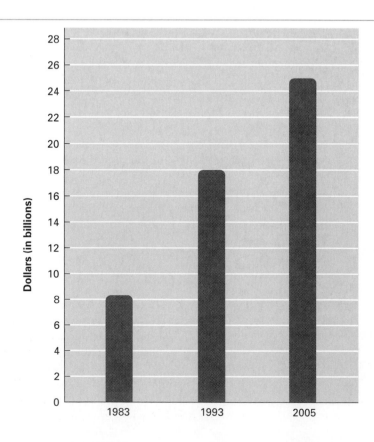

CRITICAL / CULTURAL ISSUES

Labor Versus Management in Journalism Textbooks

As mentioned in Chapter 2, the critical/cultural approach examines texts, broadly defined. In a paper presented at the 2000 convention of the Association for Education in Journalism and Mass Communication, Dr. Jon Bekken took a more literal approach and examined textbooks—in this case, journalism textbooks—to discover if these texts were instilling a professional ideology in their readers.

Bekken notes that studies of the coverage of business conflicts have generally found that the media cover these disputes from a perspective that does not favor labor or labor unions. For example, labor reporting focuses on the inconvenience strikes cause for consumers rather than on the issues that lead to a strike. Wages rather than health and safety are portrayed as the central concern of labor. In addition, there is a trend toward ignoring labor news altogether. Fewer than a dozen newspapers employ even one full-time labor reporter.

Bekken wondered if these attitudes might have been fostered during a reporter's academic training. He was specifically interested in the way organized labor was portrayed in 29 media writing and reporting textbooks. After performing a critical/cultural analysis, he concluded that the texts marginalized labor, making it seem unimportant. For instance, he noted that some textbooks have exercises that ask students to write articles about layoffs or hiring freezes based on press releases or notes from interviews with corporate or government officials. The subtle lesson conveyed in these exercises is that the important perspectives do not include those of labor. Other texts simply make little or no mention of labor or labor unions despite the fact that many newspaper workers belong to the International Typographical Union, and several newspapers have been plagued by labor-management troubles.

Most texts generally gloss over labor problems in the newspaper industry itself. Health risks such as carpal tunnel syndrome, poor working conditions, and inadequate pay are seldom mentioned. The idea that joining a union might help address some of these issues is not discussed.

Bekken chronicles other examples of how labor is almost trivialized. One textbook devotes as many words to covering labor as it does to covering weddings. Another urges reporters to avoid an antibusiness attitude in their stories and to rely on corporate officials, financial analysts, and government regulators as sources for business news. When textbooks do discuss how to cover labor, their emphasis is on covering strikes, violence connected with strikes, or unfair labor practices.

What are some of the results of the way these texts depict labor? As Bekken says,

> Students carry blind spots towards labor inculcated in their academic training into newsrooms across the country. Editors and publishers have slashed the number of labor reporters. . . . Reporters and editors typically do not look to the labor movement for news—rather they wait for strikes, or include labor in discussions of special interest groups said to dominate the political system.

Bekken ends his analysis by noting that in recent decades textbook authors have tried to remove sexist language and pay more attention to cultural sensitivity. Moreover, newer editions of reporting texts have been expanded to cover topics such as religious news and consumer news. Nonetheless, he points out, most journalism textbooks do not do a good job covering that large number of Americans who labor for a living. The fact that many of the students who read these books go on to ignore labor in their own reporting ought not surprise us.

The costs a publisher incurs are many. First, there is the cost of manufacturing the book: printing, typesetting, and paying royalties to the author. These costs are variable and are tied to the number of books printed. For example, paper costs would be more substantial on a book with a press run of 20,000 than on one with a run of 2,000. There are also operating expenses, including editorial, production, marketing, and general administration expenses. Table 6-2 shows a hypothetical operating statement for an adult trade hardcover book published by a typical publishing company. The book has a list price of $20 (all numbers are rounded for convenience), and 10,000 copies were printed. After a year 2,000 copies were unsold and were returned to the publisher for a credit. This means that 8,000 copies were sold. Allowing a 40 percent discount from the list price leaves the publisher with revenues of about $12 per book. Multiplying 8,000 by $12 gives us the gross sales amount: $96,000. From this are subtracted the costs of returns and allowances, leaving a balance of $77,000 in net sales revenue. Manufacturing costs and author royalties amounted to $45,400. This sum is subtracted from the net sales to find the gross margin on sales (the amount that net sales exceeded the cost of sales)—in this case, $31,600. Table 6-2 also assumes that the publisher sold some subsidiary rights (to a book club or a paperback publisher) and received $6,900 in return. So far, the total income from the book is $38,500

TABLE 6-2

Profit-Loss Statement of Trade Hardcover with $20 List Price

Press run	10,000 copies		
Returned	2,000 copies		
Gross sales	8,000 copies	@ $12 per	$96,000
Returns and allowances			(19,000)
Net sales			77,000
Cost of sales			
Manufacturing			27,700
Royalties			17,700
Total cost of sales			45,400
Operating expenses			
Editorial			4,500
Production			1,600
Marketing and fulfillment			18,500
Administration			10,000
Total operating expenses			34,600
Margin of net sales over cost of sales			31,600
Other income			6,900
Net income			3,900

($31,600 + $6,900). Subtracting the total operating expense of $34,600 from $38,500 yields a net income of $3,900.

These figures, of course, would vary for other publishers and for other segments of the book industry. Profit margins typically varied from 2 to 20 percent during the period between 1999 and 2006. Advances and acquisition rights are two of the big expenses in publishing. For example, Random House paid Charles Frazier, author of the best-seller *Cold Mountain*, an $8 million advance for his second novel, *Thirteen Moons*.

FEEDBACK IN BOOK PUBLISHING

The most important form of audience feedback in the book industry is the best-seller lists compiled by newspapers such as the *New York Times* and *USA Today* and the trade publication *Publisher's Weekly*. These organizations use slightly different methods to tabulate a rank ordering of the best-selling books, but all involve collecting data from a sample of the various channels of book distribution—chain bookstores, independent bookstores, newsstands, and price clubs—and then assigning various weights to the numbers to come up with the rankings. Making the best-seller list is important since many bookstores automatically order large numbers of all books that make the list. Consequently, appearing on the list can mean added sales for a book.

In addition to best-seller lists, the industry uses Nielsen BookScan, a service that measures actual sales data from about 6,500 major retailers across the United States, including big chains and independent stores. In a typical week the service tabulates sales figures on more than 300,000 different titles. Companies that subscribe to BookScan can access sales data broken down by region, subject, and format.

▲ Audiences

A recent book industry survey of readers by the National Endowment for the Arts noted that most books are purchased by people over 40 and that book reading is positively related to age and income. It noted

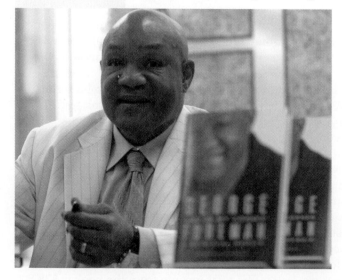

Champion boxer, cook, and author George Foreman signs books on a book tour.

Comedy Central's Steven Colbert introduced the word *truthiness* to the American people during one of his reports. As defined by the *Urban Dictionary*, *truthiness* means the quality of stating concepts that one wishes or believes to be true rather than the facts. Odd as it may seem, truthiness was at the core of one of the most publicized controversies in the book publishing industry in 2006.

At issue was James Frey's *A Million Little Pieces*, a powerful memoir about the author's struggles with addiction, the law, and himself, concluding with his eventual rehabilitation. The book was published in 2003 and became a huge bestseller when Oprah Winfrey chose it as one of her book club selections. Shortly thereafter, thesmokinggun.com reported that it was unable to find any record of Frey's alleged run-ins with the law and subsequent prison time. Faced with these discrepancies, Frey admitted that parts of his memoir were, in fact, based on fiction. For example, Frey wrote that he spent 3 months in jail; the actual police records showed that he spent only a few hours in custody. He also admitted that he lied when he wrote about running over a police officer and undergoing a root canal without Novocain, nor could he produce any records that supported his claims of struggles in rehab.

The reaction to these revelations ran the gamut from condemnation to support. Oprah Winfrey initially supported Frey, claiming that, even with the fabrications, the "underlying message" of the book was still valid. Other literary types sounded a similar theme. They argued that a memoir was based not on what actually happened but on how the author remembered what had happened. It was the "essential message," or the "essence of the experience," or "the larger truth," or the "inner core of the story" that counted, not factual matters.

Readers, however, thought otherwise. Many said they felt betrayed. Even Oprah changed her stance, removed the book from her reading list, and berated the author for his transgressions during an episode of her program. Two readers even filed a lawsuit against the publisher for breach of contract and deceptive advertising for calling the book a work of nonfiction.

What are the ethical implications of this situation? Does the author of a personal memoir have an ethical obligation to his or her readers to inform them that what they are reading might contain some exaggerations or embellishments or even outright fiction? What about the publisher? Should they publish a disclaimer about the accuracy of a memoir? Are they under any ethical obligation to check on the veracity of the information they publish? (Interestingly, courts have held that publishers are not legally bound to check facts, but what is their ethical obligation to their readers and to other memoirists who actually write the truth and whose reputation may be sullied by those who don't?)

In the aftermath of the scandal, several things occurred. Some publishers conceded that they will be looking more closely at some of the more extreme claims made by authors who submit memoirs. James Frey was dropped by his publisher and his contract for additional books was canceled. Plans for a movie based on the book (Brad Pitt and Jennifer Aniston bought the film rights) were put on hold. Despite all of these developments, "truthiness" can still be profitable. Frey's royalties for *A Million Little Pieces* amounted to more than $4 million.

---

that 47 percent of the people surveyed never opened a single book of fiction in the course of a year, down from 57 percent in 1982. Researchers were alarmed to find that the rate of the decline has tripled in the past decade. The number of young adults (18–34) who read fiction showed the steepest drop, nearly 30 percent since 1982. Those most likely to read novels were the ones who watched the least amount of TV.

THE BOOK PUBLISHING INDUSTRY

Book publishing is a small industry; there are only 70,000–75,000 jobs nationwide in the entire business. Consequently, there is a lot of competition for many of the jobs, particularly those on the editorial side.

There are two general areas to pursue in book publishing: editorial and business. Entry-level positions are competitive, and most newcomers typically join a publishing company as editorial assistants. There are numerous clerical tasks to be performed in publishing: answering authors' letters, reading manuscripts, writing reports about manuscripts, checking facts, proofreading, writing catalogue copy, and so on. Editorial assistants do these and countless other tasks.

The next logical step up the career ladder is to become an assistant or associate editor. These individuals work with senior editors in several areas: manuscript acquisition, copyediting, design and production, artwork, and so on. Eventually, this path leads to a position as an editor. After getting the necessary experience, editors are promoted to senior editors, managing editors, or executive editors, positions that carry a good deal of administrative responsibility.

On the business side there are several career paths open. Many people start as sales representatives and sell their company's books to the appropriate customers. Sales and marketing experience are so vital to the well-being of the industry that the path to top management usually begins in the sales department. At many companies presidents and vice presidents are almost always former salespeople with extensive experience in marketing.

It is not always necessary to work for a publishing company to find employment in this area. Many people work as freelance editors, designers, proofreaders, indexers, artists, and photographers. These typically are people who have had some experience and have branched out on their own.

MAIN POINTS

- The book is the oldest form of mass communication. Early books were printed by hand until the invention of movable type and the printing press.
- In early America publishers were also printers. Books became more popular during the 17th and 18th centuries.
- From 1900 to 1945, the book publishing industry became more commercialized. Continuing consolidation has resulted in a modern book industry that is dominated by a few large companies.

- The digital revolution has yet to have a drastic effect on the book industry. E-books and printing on demand have yet to become important parts of the industry. Despite the slow progress of digital content, there are signs that it is moving forward.
- The book industry consists of publishers, distributors, and retailers. The emergence of online booksellers has changed the way books are sold and distributed.
- Despite some ups and downs, book publishing has been profitable during the past few decades.

QUESTIONS FOR REVIEW

1. How has the content of popular books changed from the 17th to the 21st century?
2. What are the defining features of books?
3. What are the main revenue sources for book publishers?
4. What is the difference between a trade book and a mass-market paperback?

QUESTIONS FOR CRITICAL THINKING

1. What would you prefer—a traditional ink-and-paper book (such as this one) or an e-book? Why?
2. Book sales have not increased in the last couple of years. What might be some of the reasons? What impact, if any, do you think the Internet has had on book reading?
3. In the face of an apparent declining readership, why do publishers keep publishing more books?
4. What advantages and disadvantages are connected with a book industry dominated by a few big firms?
5. Read the boxed insert "Labor vs. Management in Journalism Textbooks," on page 143, and then consider the following. To what extent—and why—does it matter whether such texts avoid discussing labor problems in the media industry or carry a promanagement bias? If you are taking a course in writing/reporting, look at the text you are using. Does it marginalize or trivialize labor? What can students do to raise awareness of these issues in class?

KEY TERMS

e-book (p. 135)   printing on demand (p. 136)   subsidiary rights (p. 142)

INTERNET RESOURCES

Online Learning Center

At the Online Learning Center home page, www.mhhe.com/dominick10, *select* Student Center *and then* Chapter 6.

1. Use the Learning Objectives, Chapter Outline, Main Points, and Time Line sections to review this chapter.

2. Test your knowledge of the chapter using the multiple choice, crossword puzzle, and flashcard features of the site.

3. Expand your knowledge of concepts and topics discussed in the chapter by going to Suggestions for Further Reading and Internet Exercises.

Surfing the Internet

Remember, Web sites change all the time; some move, some evaporate, and some transform.

www.bookweb.org
The home page of the American Booksellers Association, the trade group representing independent bookstores. Contains the current best-sellers list.

www.bookwire.com
Takes a look inside the book business. Includes news, features, and links to other related sites.

www.bisg.org
The home page of the Book Industry Study Group. Provides research information about the industry.

www.nea.gov/pub/ReadingAtRisk.pdf
A link to the National Endowment for the Arts survey of literary reading in America.

www.publishersweekly.com
The online version of *Publisher's Weekly*, the leading trade magazine. Includes job listings.

CHAPTER 7

RADIO

This chapter will prepare you to:

- explain how radio broadcasting developed in the 1920s

- recognize how television affected radio

- discuss the defining features of radio

- understand that radio gets programming from local stations, networks, and syndication companies

- explain how the digital age is affecting radio

- appreciate the potential of high-definition radio

- understand how consolidation has affected the radio industry

A new high-def radio receiver. Hundreds of radio stations have gone digital and are broadcasting HD radio signals.

The next era in radio broadcasting can be found in your local Wal-Mart. The mass marketer is selling JVC HD (high-definition) radio receivers at nearly 2,000 of its U.S. stores for about $190.

Radio has been using the same analog technology for about the past 80 years and has been slow to adopt the digital revolution. Now, faced with competition from satellite radio, iPods, and the Internet, the radio industry is looking to HD radio to help it maintain its listening audience. (We will have more to say about the specifics of HD radio in a subsequent section.) Radio broadcasters have committed more than $200 million to promote their new digital HD channels.

HD radio has been available since 2004 but has attracted little attention, primarily because of its high price tag, around $250–300. The deal with Wal-Mart is significant because it marks an effort by the radio industry to introduce HD radio to a mass market, something that has to happen if the new technology is to fulfill the industry's high hopes. For its part Wal-Mart is cautiously optimistic. The chain will see how the new receivers are selling before adding other brands.

If the new HD receivers catch on, it will revolutionize the way the people listen to radio and might even change the fundamental structure of the industry. But we are getting ahead of ourselves. Let's first take a look the development of traditional radio to see how radio got to where it is today.

A BRIEF HISTORY

In 1887 Heinrich Hertz, a German physicist, successfully sent and detected radio waves. Guglielmo Marconi used Hertz's efforts to build a wireless communication device that could send Morse code—dots and dashes—from a transmitter to a receiver. Marconi started a wireless telegraphy company that would play an important part in early radio's development.

Reginald Fessenden and Lee De Forest provided the breakthroughs that would make broadcasting—as opposed to sending dots and dashes—possible. Fessenden, with the help of General Electric (GE), built a high-speed, continuous-wave generator that could broadcast the human voice and music. De Forest invented the vacuum tube, originally called the *audion*, which made it much easier to receive radio signals.

The development of early radio was hampered by legal battles over patent rights to various inventions. When World War I broke out, the U.S. Navy assumed responsibility for all relevant patents, and radio made great technical strides during the war.

▲ The Birth of Commercial Radio

Big Business After the war corporate America recognized the potential of radio. A new company, the Radio Corporation of America (RCA), was formed and acquired the assets of the U.S. division of the Marconi Company. Stock in RCA was held by some of the biggest companies of the period: AT&T, GE, and Westinghouse. Note that these companies thought RCA would be in the wireless telegraphy business. Despite the efforts of Fessenden and De Forest, it was hard to envision that broadcasting news and entertainment to the general public could make money.

Some individuals, however, were more prescient. David Sarnoff, an employee of the Marconi Company who later became head of RCA, suggested that one day this new invention would become a "radio music box." Sarnoff himself would be one of the central figures in the development of this new medium.

A Mass Audience Frank Conrad, an engineer for Westinghouse in Pittsburgh, tinkered with radio as a hobby. He built a radio transmitter in his garage and started broadcasting recorded music, reporting sports scores, and showcasing the musical abilities of his sons. In a short time he had attracted an enthusiastic audience of radio fans. A local department store started selling radio sets so that more people could hear Conrad's programs. Westinghouse built a station so that Conrad's signal would be heard by more people. Westinghouse also built the radio sets and received "free" advertising because of its connection with the station. The station, KDKA, signed on in 1920 and is still on the air, making it the country's oldest station.

KDKA was a success. In response, RCA, GE, and AT&T, along with many other companies and organizations, started radio stations. Radio listening became a national craze. By discovering that an audience existed for broadcast programs intended for the general public, radio found the role it would play for the foreseeable future.

Better Receivers Early radio receivers were not user-friendly. They were powered by an assortment of large, bulky, and sometimes leaky batteries. Tuning required patience, a steady hand, and a knowledge of electronics.

A young boy listens to an early radio set.

CRITICAL / CULTURAL ISSUES

Department Stores and the Early Days of Radio

Contributed by Noah Arceneaux
Assistant Professor of Media Studies, San Diego State University.

In 1922, the year of the famed "broadcasting boom," a few dozen department stores built their own radio stations. These stations were not as numerous as those operated by newspapers or universities, though they warrant a close examination. Radio, as a new technology, could have developed in a number of ways, though department stores promoted the idea that it should be used to deliver nonoffensive entertainment, mixed with advertisements. The success of their stations helped to pave the way for the advertising-supported, commercial system of broadcasting that would eventually dominate the American radio industry.

The fact that department stores were early adopters of radio is not surprising given their prior uses of electrical lighting, elevators, and telephones. Many individuals in the late 19th century, for example, first encountered these technologies inside the stores. These retailers also had a history of developing new forms of promotion, such as full-page, illustrated newspaper advertisements. Stores also organized elaborate promotional events, fashion shows, musical concerts, and parades to impress their customers. When Horne's department store in Pittsburgh promoted Frank Conrad's experimental broadcasts in an advertisement, it was not trying to inspire a national phenomenon. It was simply doing what department stores had done all along.

For their radio programming, stores favored opera, classical, and conservatory music. In an attempt to support the least offensive kinds of content, they avoided radical political views as well as jazz, which was considered vulgar by some elite members of society at the time. Their radio advertisements were not overt, though whenever the announcer identified the station, he would always mention the name of the store (and sometimes the address). In order to maximize the publicity value, the stores presented lectures based on specific types of merchandise, such as shoes or women's clothing. It was hoped that a listener would associate the store with this particular item, an association that might result in a sale.

The balance between commercial advertisements and editorial content is a delicate issue for all forms of media, though many store stations were praised for the high quality of their programming. Most listeners did not object to the indirect advertising, and some of the stations, such as WOR in Newark and WIP in Philadelphia, established national reputations. In the second half of the 1920s, resistance to advertising decreased, and more stations adopted this practice. The number of store stations decreased at this time, as retailers discovered that it was easier to buy airtime on other stations than to establish their own.

Department stores also made a deliberate effort to bring women into the radio audience. The majority of listeners in the early 1920s were male, many of whom had built their own receivers from spare parts. The stores, which catered to female shoppers, sold attractively designed, factory-built receivers intended for the living room. In the midmorning hours, when presumably all the men were at work, the store stations aired cooking, sewing, or fashion programs to entertain housewives. The hosts of these programs were women, while announcers for other kinds of shows were almost exclusively men.

This brief history illustrates a critical/cultural approach to media in that it does not take a dominant system—in this case, commercial broadcasting—to be natural or logical. The goal rather is to explain how this particular system came to be and how it was promoted by specific institutions, such as department stores. The groups that supported the commercial system of broadcasting did not simply impose their vision on a passive public. Listeners enjoyed the programming from the first commercial stations and accepted the indirect approach to advertising. The success of these stations, including the ones from department stores, encouraged other broadcasters to mix advertisements with content. In this regard the commercialization of American radio broadcasting should be understood as a hegemonic process in which coercion mingled with consent.

The ways in which women were incorporated into the radio audience also illustrates a critical/cultural perspective. It may seem a positive development that the early radio industry sought to appeal to women, though we must consider the narrow range of identities offered to women. They could cook, mend clothing, and otherwise look beautiful for their husbands. Similarly, when women presented lectures on the radio, the topics had to be suitably "feminine." This restrictive vision on what it meant to be a woman reveals the patriarchal view that was dominant in the 1920s, a view that is still evident in many contemporary radio and television programs.

(*Note:* Adapted from "Department Stores and the Origins of American Broadcasting, 1910–1931," Ph.D. dissertation, University of Georgia, 2007.)

By 1926, however, set manufacturers had improved their product. New radios ran on household current, could be tuned with just two knobs, had better antennas, and looked like a fashionable piece of furniture. Between 1925 and 1930, 17 million radio sets were sold, and radio was becoming truly a mass medium.

▲ The Commercialization of Radio

One of the curious things about early radio broadcasting was that very little of it was done by broadcasters. The early stations were owned by a polyglot of organizations. WLS in Chicago was owned by Sears, Roebuck (*World's Largest Store*); WGN by the *Chicago Tribune* (*World's Greatest Newspaper*); WSM in Nashville by the National Life and Accident Insurance Company (*We Shield Millions*); and WHB in Kansas City by the Sweeney Automotive and Electrical School.

Early broadcasting was not expensive, and radio station owners figured they got their money's worth through the exposure they received through the station. Before long, however, operating expenses began to pile up, and stations searched for a way to have their stations turn a profit.

Nobody knew quite how to do it. Some felt listeners should send in voluntary contributions; others wanted a tax on radio tubes. It was the phone company that finally came up with a workable plan. AT&T began selling time on WEAF, their flagship station in New York, to anybody who wanted to broadcast a message. The most logical customers for this new service were companies that had things to sell. Thus, in 1922 the Queensboro Realty Company paid $300 for five radio talks that extolled the benefits of living in the country, preferably on a lot bought from Queensboro Realty. Other companies quickly recognized the advertising potential of this new medium and bought time on WEAF and other stations. The problem of financing radio broadcasting was solved—broadcasting would be supported by advertising.

Networks   Linking radio stations into a **network** made good economic sense. Rather than having each individual station pay the costs of producing its own program, it was much cheaper for all stations to share the cost of a single program and broadcast the same show on all stations. Moreover, a linked network of stations gave advertisers the ability to reach a larger audience in a wider geographic area.

The first network was the National Broadcasting Company (NBC), a subsidiary of RCA, set up in 1926. NBC actually started two networks. One consisted of stations originally owned by RCA, and another was made up of stations acquired from AT&T when the phone company decided to get out of the broadcasting business. NBC got a competitor when the Columbia Broadcasting System (CBS) went on the air the next year. William S. Paley, whose career with CBS would last into the 1980s, headed the new network.

Radio receivers in the 1930s no longer required a knowledge of electronics to operate. A family could simply sit back and listen.

The two networks grew quickly. By 1937 NBC had 111 affiliated stations, while CBS had 105. Advertisers were spending more than $27 million annually on network radio. It was obvious that the network-affiliate arrangement would persist for some time to come.

Revenues from advertising permitted the networks to hire big-name entertainers. Jack Benny, Ed Wynn, and George Burns and Gracie Allen were all well-known vaudeville entertainers who successfully made the transition to radio. The most successful program, however, was *Amos 'n' Andy*, a comedy starring Charles Correll and Freeman Gosden, two white comedians working in blackface. Although considered racist today, it was a top-rated show during the late 1920s and early 1930s, and listening to it became a national habit.

"This . . . is London." Edward R. Murrow's famous opening was familiar to millions of Americans who listened to his reports from the British capital during World War II. Murrow went on to a distinguished career in TV journalism.

Government Regulation   The early success of radio broadcasting had unanticipated consequences. As more and more stations went on the air during the 1920s, interference became a tremendous problem, and the government lacked the authority to do anything about it.

Congress finally acted to resolve this situation by passing the **Radio Act of 1927.** This act set up the Federal Radio Commission (FRC), a regulatory body that would issue licenses and try to clean up the chaos that existed. The commission defined the AM broadcast band, standardized channel designations, abolished portable stations, and moved to minimize interference. By 1929 the situation had improved, and the new radio medium was prevented from suffocating in its own growth.

Thus, by the end of the 1920s, the framework for modern radio broadcasting was in place. It would be a commercially supported mass medium dominated by networks and regulated by an agency of the federal government.

▲ The Depression Years and World War II

By most standards radio was not hit as hard by the Depression as were other industries. In fact, the amount of money spent on radio advertising tripled from 1930 to 1935. Profits may not have been as high as they would have been in better economic times, but the radio industry was able to weather the Depression with relatively little hardship.

The FCC   The most significant legal development for radio during the Depression years was the formation of the **Federal Communications Commission (FCC).** President Roosevelt wanted to create a government agency that would consolidate the regulatory functions of the communications industry. In response to the president's demands, Congress passed the **Communications Act of 1934,** which consolidated responsibilities for broadcast and wire regulation under a new seven-member FCC. The expanded commission had increased responsibilities, but the fundamental philosophy underlying the original Radio Act of 1927 remained unchanged.

The Birth of FM   In the mid-1930s Edwin Howard Armstrong, a noted inventor, demonstrated frequency-modulated radio, or FM, to his friend David Sarnoff, head of RCA. At the time, Sarnoff was more interested in promoting the development of television and, despite the technical advantages of FM, was not interested in backing Armstrong's creation. Armstrong tried to develop FM on his own. He set up his own transmitter for demonstrations and by 1940 had sold the rights to manufacture FM receiving sets to several companies. Sarnoff then offered Armstrong $1 million for a license to his invention, but Armstrong, probably still angry over Sarnoff's earlier rejection, refused. FM's further development was interrupted by the start of World War II.

Radio Programs   Depression-era programs reflected a need for diversion and escape. Action-adventure series, such as *The Lone Ranger,* were popular, as were daytime soap operas. Network radio news grew during the 1930s, and live coverage of special events, such as the abdication speech of Edward VIII of England, drew huge numbers of listeners. Broadcasts from Europe on the eve of World War II kept many listeners glued to their radio sets for the latest bulletins. During the war Edward R. Murrow gained fame through his reports from war-torn London.

World War II   Radio did well during the war. The number of dollars spent on radio ads nearly doubled from 1940 to 1945. Helped by a newsprint shortage and an excess-profits tax that encouraged companies to advertise, radio broadcasting outpaced the newspapers as a national advertising vehicle in 1943.

The shape of modern broadcasting would be significantly altered by a court ruling that came in the middle of the war. In 1943 the Supreme Court ruled that NBC must divest itself of one of its two networks. NBC chose to sell the weaker network to Edward Noble, who had made his fortune selling Life Savers candy. Noble renamed his network the American Broadcasting Company (ABC), and by the end of the war, ABC had 195 affiliates and was a full-fledged competitor for the older networks.

▲ Innovation and Change: 1945–1954

The nine-year period following World War II was marked by great changes in both the radio and recording industries, changes that ultimately drove them closer together. The development of television delayed the growth of FM radio, altered the nature of network radio, and forced the radio industry to rely on records as the most important part of a new programming strategy.

The Growth of FM   Despite the fact that FM sounded better than AM, was static free, and could reproduce a wider range of sound frequencies, AM broadcasting had started first, and FM struggled to catch up. FM had the misfortune of beginning its development at the same time as TV. In addition, because of technical considerations, both FM radio and TV are suited for about the same place in the electromagnetic spectrum, and in 1945 the FCC decided to give the rapidly expanding TV service the space formerly occupied by FM. The commission moved FM "upstairs" to the 88- to 108-MHz band (where it is today), thus rendering obsolete about half a million FM radios.

The Emergence of Television   Of course, the biggest change in radio's fortunes came about because of the emergence of television. (Chapter 10 has more to say about the development of TV.) By 1948 it was apparent that TV would take over the mass entertainment function served by network radio. The emergence of TV meant changes in the content, economics, and functions of radio. Although many individuals believe that television cut into the revenues of the radio industry, no such thing happened. In fact, radio revenues rose steadily from 1948 to 1952 and, after a brief drop from 1953 to 1956, continued to rise. The part of the industry upon which TV did have a drastic effect was network radio. The percentage of local stations with network affiliations dropped from 97 percent in 1947 to only 50 percent by 1955. Network revenue dropped by 60 percent in approximately the same period. Faced with this loss, stations relied more heavily on revenue from ads for local businesses. In short, they redistributed the makeup of their revenue dollar. As TV became the new mass medium, local stations cut back on their budgets; relied more heavily on music, talk, and news; and began searching for a formula that would allow them to coexist with television.

Specialized Formats   By 1956 it was obvious that the radio networks would no longer be the potent programming source they had been in the past. In that year radio networks were carrying only about 35 hours of sponsored evening programs each week. Finally, by 1960 all the once-popular evening programs and daytime serials had come to an end. Radio network service was limited primarily to news and short features, usually amounting to no more than 2 or 3 hours of time a day.

Local stations soon adapted to this change. Now that they no longer were tied to the networks for the bulk of their programming, they were free to develop their own personalities. Most did so by adopting a specialized format, a sound that had distinctive appeal to a certain segment of the audience. The most successful experiment occurred in the Midwest, where a station began monitoring the sales of records and sheet music and playing those tunes that were selling the most. Hence, the Top 40 format was born. Featuring a

In the 1950s the DJ became an important figure in radio programming. In fact, many became stars in their own right. DJs sent out glossy pictures of themselves to their fans; they appeared at supermarket openings and record hops; they were the emcees at personal appearances by rock-and-roll groups. As the DJs became more influential, they also began to program their own shows. They picked the records that they would play during their shifts.

Record promoters also recognized the tremendous importance of airplay in the marketing of a hit. The more a record was played on the radio, the more copies it sold. Naturally, record promoters and DJs began to develop close ties. In the beginning the relationship was innocent enough. Promoters would make sure that DJs got the latest releases their companies were offering, and they also put in a good word or two about their companies' products. Competition grew intense, however, and by 1959 about 250 new records were being released every week. Some unscrupulous promoters resorted to more than words to advance their records. At first, they would send DJs an elaborate Christmas gift. If that did not work, some even "hired" the DJ as "creative consultant" and paid him or her a fee every month. Others would cut the DJ in on the action and offer to pay a penny to the DJ for every record sold in the market. Eventually, most promoters stopped these charades and simply passed the DJ an envelope filled with cash in return for airplay of their company's songs. In 1958 and 1959, record distributors reportedly spent over a quarter-million dollars in the larger markets on payola.

The news of this illicit business practice did nothing to help the image of rock and roll or of broadcasting. Section 508 was added to the 1934 Communications Act to stop this practice, but it was not altogether successful. New payola scandals broke out in the industry in the early 1970s. At least one record company was accused of offering drugs to station personnel in return for increased airplay, and some concert promoters were accused of offering monetary bribes. Payola resurfaced in 2000 when 80 program directors at Spanish-language stations were investigated for allegedly taking bribes from Fonovisa Records.

The most recent twist in the payola saga involves independent promoters who charge music labels a fee to promote their records and pay money to radio stations for access to their programmers and playlists. The money involved can be substantial. In large markets the promoters might funnel as much as $300,000 to the stations. Record labels consider this just another promotional cost in getting their songs on radio. This arrangement is perfectly legal since no covert money flows directly from the labels to the stations. Despite its legitimacy the practice has drawn criticism from several sources. *Rolling Stone* labeled it "legal payola," and congressional leaders found the practice troubling. In response Clear Channel and other radio group owners announced in 2003 that they were cutting their ties with independent promoters. But in 2005 Sony BMG was involved in yet another payola scandal.

Most recently, the nation's four largest radio companies agreed to a $10 million deal in payments and other considerations in order to settle a year-long FCC investigation into claims that stations owned by the companies accepted cash and other gifts from music companies in return for playing their releases. Part of the money in the 2007 agreement would go to a fund to be used in training stations to avoid payola.

Only time will tell if this latest development will stop the practice. Payola seems to be one problem that will not disappear.

---

bright, continuous, and upbeat sound, the format was ruled by the **clock hour,** which specified every element of programming. The success of the Top 40 sound encouraged radio stations to experiment with other specialized formats. By 1964 at least a dozen different formats, ranging from country to rock to classical, had sprung up.

▲ Growth and Stabilization: 1955–1990

The number of radio stations continued to grow during these years, from 3,343 in 1955 to more than 7,000 in 1970. More and more stations adopted the Top 40 format, and it very quickly became the format of choice among young listeners—who, as it happened, had a good deal of money to spend on the records they heard played by their favorite disc jockey, or DJ. Since at this time the DJ had control of what songs were played on the air, he or she became the focus of promotional efforts by record companies to gain airplay for their new songs. All too soon this arrangement led to the growth of **payola** (see the boxed insert, "Payola").

The most significant development in radio during the 1970s and 1980s was the emergence of FM. By the early 1960s AM stations were becoming harder to obtain; it was easier to get an FM license. The FCC passed the **nonduplication rule,** which prevented an AM-FM combination from duplicating its AM content on its FM station for more than 50 percent of the time. Faced with this ruling, FM stations developed their own kind of sound (many went to a rock format) that capitalized on FM's better technical qualities. As a result the

FIGURE 7-1

Division of AM and FM
Audiences

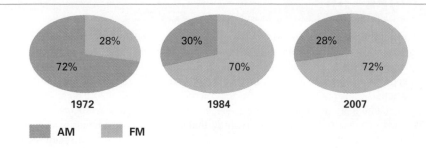

number of FM stations tripled between 1960 and 1970, and profits began to increase. By 1990 FM accounted for about 70 percent of listening time. Many AM stations switched to a news/talk format in order to stop the audience erosion (see Figure 7-1).

A noncommercial radio network, **National Public Radio (NPR),** went on the air in the early 1970s with an 80-station network. Over the next few years its number of affiliates doubled, and by 1980 it was reaching a cumulative audience of more than 5 million people per week. Its most successful programs were its daily news programs *Morning Edition* and *All Things Considered.*

▲ Consolidation and Specialization: 1990–Present

The pivotal event for radio in the 1990s was the passage of the **Telecommunications Act of 1996.** The act was concerned primarily with encouraging competition in the new communication technologies, but the radio industry, through skillful lobbying, was able to include itself in the bill. Only a few sentences in the final version of the act concern radio, but those few sentences had an impact out of proportion to their length. A key provision completely erased the cap on the number of stations a company could own and increased to eight the number of stations a company could own in a single market.

The new law caused an avalanche of buying and selling of radio properties, and some stations were sold several times in a single year. In a typical year before the act, about $2 billion was spent on radio acquisitions and mergers. In 1996 the number hit $14.4 billion. That figure was eclipsed the next year when $15.3 billion was spent. New radio giants sprang up almost overnight. The radio industry became even more consolidated as a few large group owners dominated the industry.

On the programming front, talk became the hottest format on AM radio, thanks to the success of such performers as Rush Limbaugh, Dr. Laura Schlessinger, Tom Joyner, and Sean Hannity. The trend toward format specialization continued on FM as stations recognized that attracting as little as 2–3 percent of the audience was enough to keep them profitable.

A weak economy and the demise of the dot-com companies hurt radio's advertising revenue at the start of the new century. After several years of prosperity, many radio stations cut back on expenses and laid off employees.

The contemporary radio industry is still characterized by consolidation. Consolidation may make good business sense, but it has its downside. Radio has lost its local roots since most stations are owned by big companies headquartered in some other place. Further, local radio news has practically disappeared. The corporate emphasis on the bottom line has increased the number of commercials and promotional announcements that clutter up airtime. It may be that big companies are beginning to appreciate these disadvantages. In 2006 Clear Channel, the largest single owner of radio stations, announced that it was being sold to a group of private investors and put about 450 of its stations up for sale. Experts predict that the next few years may see the consolidation trend reversing itself.

Radio stations are also facing more competition. Satellite radio has drained away listeners. Many people prefer to listen to their favorite music on their iPods rather than a radio station. Internet radio has cut into office listening time. The average amount of time a person spends listening to the radio has decreased steadily since 1994, and listening time of young people has decreased most of all (see the boxed insert "Missing Persons: Teens"). While the rest of the economy was doing well, advertising revenue for radio increased only

1 percent from 2005 to 2006. As mentioned in the chapter opening, the industry is promoting HD radio in order to counteract these trends.

Despite these difficulties the radio industry is still a significant advertising medium. More than 220 million Americans listen to broadcast radio every week, and about 70 percent of people age 12 and older listen to radio every day.

RADIO IN THE DIGITAL AGE

Radio stations were slow to enter the digital age, but there are signs that things are speeding up.

▲ Web Sites

Early radio station Web sites simply streamed the audio from the station's analog broadcast. Current Web sites contain schedules of special events, movie and album reviews, and photos of station personalities, and some have even started social networking options. Stations now use their Web sites to generate additional revenue. Advertisers who buy ads on the radio can also buy space on the Web site.

▲ High-Definition (HD) Radio

Hoping to capitalize on the public's increasing awareness of high-definition television (HDTV), the radio industry is introducing HD radio, a digital service that greatly improves the signal quality of terrestrial radio stations. With HD radio an FM station sounds as good as a CD while an AM station sounds as good as a current FM station and is static free. Moreover, digital signals can be compressed so that a single radio station can broadcast more than one program at a time. For example, a station might program Top 40 on its main analog and digital signal while broadcasting hip-hop and jazz on its digital-only subchannels.

Unlike satellite radio HD radio is free as long as a person has an HD radio receiver. As mentioned in the opening of the chapter, HD radios are becoming available at many stores, with more than 40 models to choose from. Some automakers are offering HD radio as an option in their new models. Those people who choose not to buy a new HD receiver can still listen to the traditional analog signals on their existing radio sets. Of course, if radio does go all-digital, conventional sets will become obsolete.

As of 2007 about 1,200 radio stations were broadcasting a digital signal (that's less than 10 percent of all stations), but more are going digital every month. HD radio has moved slowly because traditional radio has been doing well, and broadcasters see no reason to disrupt a profitable situation. Further, the transition to digital is expensive, and there are still relatively few listeners who can receive the digital signals. Increased competition and sluggish advertising revenue, however, have sped up the process.

There are some problems standing in the way of HD radio's ultimate acceptance. The receivers are expensive, and there's not that much additional programming available. Portable HD receivers are a problem; HD radios consume so much power that battery life would be unacceptably short. Further, so far digital radio has broken no new ground. It simply offers more of the same with better audio quality. Will that be enough to woo listeners from their iPods and satellite services? Most experts predict that if receiver costs continue to decline and if radio

Radio talk show host Sean Hannity. His syndicated program reaches about 12 million people.

The XM portable satellite radio receiver with a built-in digital recorder. A subscriber can record about 5 hours of programming and play it back when convenient.

stations offer more innovative content, the odds are good for HD radio's ultimate success.

▲ Satellite Radio

As this book went to press, two companies provided direct satellite-to-car-radio digital service. XM radio, launched in 2001, offers 170 music and talk channels, most of them commercial free, for a subscription fee of about $13 per month. Sirius launched a similar service in 2002 with 130 digital channels. In 2006 the companies announced plans to merge but faced a lengthy process in getting regulatory approval. As of 2007 XM had about 8 million subscribers while Sirius had about 6 million.

Satellite radio, of course, finds its primary market with commuters. Both XM and Sirius have introduced local channels for major cities that broadcast continuous weather and traffic information. The companies are also expanding beyond the automobile. Both have portable receivers that can be used in the home.

After a high-flying start, satellite radio has come back to Earth. In 2005 XM lost $667 million, and Sirius $863 million. Part of the problem was that both companies spent millions acquiring exclusive programming. For instance, Sirius paid Howard Stern about $100 million a year to move his program to satellite, while XM signed up Oprah Winfrey for $55 million. Both satellite companies have had trouble with "churn," people who don't renew their subscriptions. In addition, the satellite companies have tried to boost subscribership by offering their services free when people buy a new car. BMW, for example, throws in a year's subscription to Sirius. It is unclear how many subscribers will opt to stay with the service once their free time runs out. Some analysts predict that satellite radio may come to resemble HBO, a profitable service but one that appeals to a relatively small consumer base.

▲ Internet Radio

Internet radio stations are of two types: (1) traditional over-the-air broadcasters who also stream their signals on the Internet and (2) Internet-only stations. Together these stations attract about 50 million listeners per week.

Many Internet-only stations offer specialized formats, such as reggae or techno rock. Some stations have formats that would never be heard on traditional radio. For example, one channel currently on the Web features only accordion music while another broadcasts air traffic control transmissions.

Internet stations are trying to attract audiences that are dissatisfied with traditional radio, and there are indications that they are succeeding. Internet radio listening jumped 71 percent from 2005 to 2006. The biggest Internet radio providers are Yahoo!, American Online Radio, and Live365.

The biggest problem facing Internet radio is a financial one. Web stations must pay fees to music performers as well as songwriters and composers (Over-the-air radio does not pay fees to performers.) New regulations in 2007 increased the fees that stations had to pay to performers to .08 cents per song per listener. Although that may not sound like much, it's enough to put some small stations out of business. As this book went to press, Internet station executives were trying to get these fees reduced.

Catherine Hughes, head of Radio One, the nation's largest radio group targeting black listeners, is the first African American woman to head a publicly traded company. Her path to the top was not an easy one.

Hughes started in radio by working in the sales department at Howard University's radio station. Eventually, she became the station manager. She decided to start her own radio station in 1980 by buying WOL-AM in Washington, D.C. At the time she was a single mother with limited financial resources. Bank after bank rejected her loan application. She finally found one bank willing to lend her part of the money she needed, and she secured additional backing from a consortium of financiers who specialized in funding black business enterprises.

The station nearly failed. Hughes had her house and car repossessed and even sold some family heirlooms to pay the bills. She actually moved into the station, sleeping in a sleeping bag and cooking on a hot plate. She saved programming costs by doing her own talk show. Trying desperately to get advertising, she went door-to-door persuading small retailers to spend $10 for a minute of commercial time. Seven years later, the station finally turned a profit.

Hughes next decided that the time was right for expansion. She noted that African American family income was growing along with its buying power. Taking advantage of relaxed federal ownership regulations, Hughes acquired another 11 stations over the next 6 years. When she took her company public in 1999, Radio One's stock price nearly doubled in the first 3 months.

In 2006 Radio One was the seventh largest radio broadcaster in the United States based on its revenue of more than $350 million. The company owns 70 stations in 22 cities and programs five channels on the XM satellite radio service. No more cooking on a hot plate for Catherine Hughes.

▲ Mobile Radio

As noted below, mobility and portability have always been part of the defining features of traditional radio. Now both satellite and Internet radio are becoming more mobile. Both XM and Sirius market car and in-home receivers. Sirius offers a "boom box" model, while XM sells a miniature "My Fi" set, about the size of a deck of cards, with a built-in satellite antenna.

Radio is also showing up on cell phones. Since there are about 2 billion cell phone users worldwide, radio broadcasters are seriously looking at ways to reach this audience. Motorola, for instance, offers iRadio, a service that lets subscribers listen to a preselected lineup of stations on their cell phones. In 2006 Clear Channel revealed plans to stream radio content to Cingular subscribers, and Infinity Radio announced a similar plan in cooperation with Nokia. Market research indicates that about 50 percent of people would like to have radio on their cell phones.

▲ User-Generated Content

The most obvious example of user-generated content is podcasting—recording an audio program and making it available for downloading from a Web site. Many traditional radio broadcasters, such as NPR and the BBC, produce hundreds of podcasts per year, but audience members can also get into the act. Podcast.net lists thousands of available programs ranging from personal rants to teen fashions.

DEFINING FEATURES OF RADIO

Radio is portable. Some radio sets, like the Walkman, are small and personal. Others, like the boom box, are big and public. No matter their size, radio sets are easily transported and go everywhere—the beach, sporting events, jogging trails, the workplace. Car radios provide news and entertainment to commuters on their way to and from work. In fact, it is hard to find a place where radio cannot go.

Radio is supplemental. Most radio listening occurs while we are doing something else—driving, working, studying, falling asleep, waking up, cleaning, and so on. Radio rarely is the prime focus of our attention; it provides an audio background for our activities.

Radio is universal. Virtually every household has at least one working radio. In fact, the average house has about six. Almost every car is equipped with a radio. In an average day about 70 percent of Americans listen to radio.

Radio is selective. Much like the magazine industry (see Chapter 5), the radio industry has become a niche medium. Radio stations choose formats that attract a small, narrowly defined audience that is attractive to advertisers. As mentioned earlier, if a radio broadcaster can find a formula that attracts just 2–3 percent of the audience, odds are that the station will turn a profit.

ORGANIZATION OF THE RADIO INDUSTRY

There are more than a half-billion working radio sets in the United States. That works out to about two radios per person. There are about 13,500 radio stations in operation. Thanks in part to an FCC philosophy that encouraged competition, the number of stations grew from about 6,900 in 1970 to about 13,500 in 2006, an increase of 96 percent. To understand how this rapidly growing business is organized, we will examine it from several perspectives: programming, technology, and format.

▲ Local Stations, Nets, and Syndicators

Local radio stations operate in cities, towns, and villages across the country. Big cities have many stations. New York City has about 90; Los Angeles, about 60. Smaller towns may have only one or two. Whitefish, Montana, for example (population 4,000), has four stations. Programming for these stations is provided by networks (nets) and by program syndication companies. Technically, the distinction between a net and a syndication service is that all stations on a network carry the net program at the same time, while syndicated programming is carried at different times by the stations. In practice, however, much syndicated radio programming is satellite-delivered and carried simultaneously, and many network affiliates record net programming and broadcast it later. To make things even more complicated, the traditional networks also offer syndicated programs. Consequently, the distinction between the two services may no longer be meaningful.

Networks were important programming sources during the earlier years of radio. After the emergence of TV, the importance of radio networks diminished, and they provided only news and public affairs programs to their affiliates.

Network radio staged a mild resurgence during the early part of the century. The leading radio networks were ABC, Westwood One, and Dial Global.

The demand for syndicated shows was still strong in 2007. Rush Limbaugh continued to lead the syndication race while the drive-time shows of Sean Hannity and Tom Joyner also remained popular.

There are about 50 companies that provide syndicated programs of various length. For example, the American Comedy Network offers a library of thousands of comedy bits. The Motor Racing Network supplies coverage of 50 NASCAR races and NASCAR-related features to about 400 stations.

The WYNK humvee on a remote in Baton Rouge, Louisiana. Remotes are an important part of promotion for a local radio station.

▲ AM and FM Stations

Broadcast radio stations are either AM or FM. **AM** stands for *amplitude modulation*, and **FM** stands for *frequency modulation*. As we saw earlier in the chapter, since about 1975 the fortunes of FM radio have been increasing while those of AM stations are on the decline. In 2007, almost three-quarters of listenership went to the FM stations. Keep in mind, however, that some AM stations, particularly those in large markets, are doing quite well. In 2007, AMs were the top-rated stations in Boston (WBZ), St. Louis (KMOX), and Cincinnati (WLW).

All physical factors being equal, radio signals sent by AM travel farther, especially at night, than signals sent by FM. The AM dial on a typical radio set illustrates the precise frequencies in the electromagnetic spectrum where the AM station operates. AM stations are further classified by channels. There are three possible channels: clear, regional, and local. A clear channel is one with a single dominant station that is designed to provide service over a wide area. Typically, these dominant stations have a strong signal because they broadcast with 50,000 watts of power. For example, the 720 spot on the AM dial is a clear channel with WGN, Chicago, the dominant station, operating at 50,000 watts. The 770 position is also a clear channel with WABC, New York, dominant. A regional channel is one shared by many stations that serve fairly large areas. A local channel is designed to be shared by a large number of stations that broadcast only to their local communities.

FM signals do not travel as far as AM, but FM has the advantage of being able to produce better sound qualities than AM. FM radio is also less likely to be affected by outside interference such as thunderstorms. Similar to AM, FM stations are organized in classes. Class C FM stations are the most powerful, operating at 100,000 watts. Class B and Class A stations are less powerful. A glance at the FM radio dial reveals that FM stations operate in a different part of the electromagnetic spectrum than does AM. Figure 7-2 is a simplified diagram of the spectrum showing where AM, FM, and television signals are located.

Much of a radio station's operation is automated. A computer sequences when songs play, when commercials run, and when the DJ talks. Modern radio broadcasting equipment has become so compact that a radio station could easily fit inside the average dorm room (except for the antenna tower).

When radio stations broadcast a digital signal, the old analog transmission is replaced by a series of 0s and 1s that represent various sound frequencies. The digital receiver translates these numbers back into sound waves. Obviously, the AM and FM distinctions do not apply to digital radio.

▲ Station Formats

Perhaps the most meaningful way we can organize radio stations is according to their **format,** a type of consistent programming designed to appeal to a certain segment of the audience. A format gives a station a distinctive personality and attracts a certain kind of audience that advertisers find desirable. In fact, the development of radio after 1960 is

---

FIGURE 7-2   Simplified Diagram of the Electromagnetic Spectrum

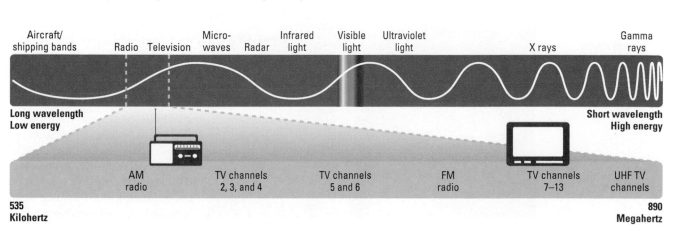

marked by the fine-tuning of existing formats and the creation of new ones that appeal to people in distinct demographic and lifestyle categories. Most modern stations can offer an amazingly precise description of the kind of listener they want their format to attract. An adult contemporary station, for example, might set its sights on men and women, ages 25–45, with college educations, making more than $80,000 a year, who read *Rolling Stone,* drive either a BMW or a Volvo, and go to the mall at least twice a week. In our discussion we will cover three basic categories of radio formats: music, ethnic, and news/talk.

The Music Format   The music format is the largest category and includes many subdivisions and variations. In 2006 the two most listened-to formats were adult contemporary (AC) with about 15 percent of the audience and contemporary hit radio (CHR) with about 11 percent. The main appeal of the AC format is to 25- to 49-year-old females. AC stations play the "hits of the '80s, '90s, and today" with a blend of about 80 percent oldies and 20 percent current tunes. John Mayer, The Fray, and Nickelback are artists that are likely to be heard on AC stations.

CHR (also called Top 40) features a small playlist of hits in a fast rotation. The format does best with the 16–24 age group. Artists whose songs were frequently played on CHR stations in 2007 included Gwen Stefani, Beyonce, and Fall Out Boy.

Other top formats are urban and country. The urban format showcases a large number of African American artists and plays rap, hip-hop, and dance music. The format is aimed at city dwellers but has attracted listeners in rural areas as well. As of 2007, some prominent urban artists were R. Kelly, Kanye West, and Jay-Z.

Country stations, as the name suggests, play hit country-and-western singles and employ DJs who are down-home, friendly, and knowledgeable about country music. The country format has two main divisions: (1) traditional country stations that play mainstream classic, twangy country music and (2) contemporary country stations that play more current artists who might use synthesizers and other modern sounds. A country station's audience still mainly comprises adults ages 35–55.

Black and Ethnic Formats   These formats aim for special audiences that are defined primarily by race and nationality. There are about 175 stations that program for the black audience, and about 260 stations that serve the Hispanic audience. Many of the black and Hispanic stations feature urban contemporary music and run news, features, and special programs of interest to their audiences. In addition, about 60 stations have formats aimed at other ethnic groups: Polish, German, Italian, French, Irish, and Greek.

Format Homogenization   Radio stations sound pretty much alike no matter where you are. Almost all the major music formats are represented in the large and medium markets, and it seems that every market has its morning "zoo crew"; an AC station that specializes in "the classic hits" of the 1980s, 1990s, and today; a modern rock station that calls itself

Hits by artists such as Jay-Z are a mainstay on the playlists of urban contemporary stations.

"Power" or "Z" or "Q" something or other; an easy-listening station with a "warm" format that dedicates love songs at night; and maybe even an AM station that specializes in "golden oldies." Even the DJs sound pretty much the same.

There are several reasons for this trend toward homogenization. The most important is the increasing consolidation in the industry. Big radio companies own stations in all the big markets. What works in one market

It's 11 P.M. Do you know where your radio DJ is?

Thanks to an innovation called *voice tracking,* he or she might be a recorded voice from Los Angeles, Tampa, Norfolk, or Dallas. The concept behind voice tracking is simple enough. A DJ somewhere else records chatter, music introductions, and music recaps. The music itself can be added later. At the local station this recorded content is mixed together with local weather, and traffic updates, promotions, and commercials. Thanks to computers and satellite distribution, the whole process sounds seamless, and most listeners cannot tell the difference.

The reason for the growing popularity of voice tracking is also simple: It saves money. Rather than pay six DJs salaries and benefits, a company can pay one DJ to voice track for six shows in six different markets at a substantially lower cost. Since most of a DJ's shift consists of music, one DJ can voice track a 4-hour shift in about 30 minutes.

The consolidation of the radio industry has added extra impetus to the voice tracking phenomenon. Clear Channel, the largest owner of radio stations, used voice tracking in every one of its 255 markets except New York, where union rules make it too expensive. Currently, most voice-tracked programs occur overnight, at midday, and in the evening; most drive-time shows are still live and local.

Executives at Clear Channel and other companies defended the practice as a way of bringing more professional-sounding programming to local markets. From a purely technical perspective, most would agree that the DJs who do voice tracks are smoother and sound more skilled than most local DJs. The production itself is professional and usually error-free. The companies also tout the greater efficiency and savings of the technique.

Opponents cite the fact that voice tracking has put many local DJs out of work. They also note that the philosophy of localism has always been at the heart of the radio industry. Starting in the 1920s, radio stations were licensed to serve the public interest in a local community. Voice tracking is undesirable because it eliminates local talent and severs ties to the local community.

Perhaps a more pertinent ethical argument against voice tracking is the fact that it is based on deception. The audience is not told that its local DJ taped his or her show in some distant city. In fact, voice-tracking DJs go to great pains to make people believe that they are in fact local. They read local newspapers and Internet sites to learn about local events and drop local references into their chatter ("Don't forget the big rock concert at [insert local name here] on Saturday"); they learn about local traffic hot spots to make their traffic intros sound credible ("How's traffic looking on [insert local name here]? Let's get an updated traffic report"); and they might act as if they had attended a local event ("Wasn't that a great game at [insert local sports venue here]? The crowd was something else").

What do listeners think? Surveys have shown that some feel cheated once they learn that they have been listening to voice tracking and not a live DJ. Others do not seem to care. Many report they listen to hear music and never pay attention to the DJ.

---

is likely to work in another. In addition, it is cheaper to program the same music from market to market. Finally, radio has become so competitive that programming decisions are based on the recommendations of program consultants and on surveys and focus groups. Since the same records are generally tested in all markets and usually score high, the recommendations about what to play are the same from market to market. Not surprisingly, many stations prefer to adopt a "safe" format, one that has worked in other markets, rather than risking a sizable amount of money on a new and untested format.

Voice Tracking   One controversial trend in the industry is the rise of **voice tracking** (see the boxed insert "Voice Tracking in Radio: Is Anybody There?"). Voice tracking makes use of a single DJ who prerecords song intros and extros and chatter for music programs on several different stations. The music is mixed in later, and the total program is delivered by satellite to local stations. The biggest advantage of voice tracking is cost cutting; one DJ can do the work that was previously done by several.

News/Talk Format   This format is becoming more and more popular on the AM band and accounts for 17 percent of all radio listening time. Some stations emphasize the news part of the news/talk format. National, regional, and local news reports are broadcast periodically throughout the day. Sports, traffic, weather, editorials, public affairs programs, and an occasional feature round out the programming day. News stations appeal primarily to a male audience in the 25- to 54-year-old age category.

The talk format attracts listeners in about the same age group. Common types of programs that appear on stations using the talk format are call-in shows, usually hosted by an opinionated and maybe even abrasive host; interview shows; advice shows; and roundtable discussions. News, weather, traffic reports, and other feature material are blended in with these programs. Unlike the music formats, which do not demand their listeners' close attention, the talk format requires that its audience concentrate on the program in order to follow what is being said.

▲ Noncommercial Radio

Many of the early radio stations that went on the air during the 1920s were founded by educational institutions. As the commercial broadcasting system became firmly established, many educational stations were bought by commercial broadcasters, and the fortunes of noncommercial radio dwindled. In 1945, with the coming of FM broadcasting, the FCC set aside several frequencies for educational broadcasting. This action sparked a rebirth of interest in this kind of broadcasting, so that by 2007 there were about 2,400 noncommercial radio stations on the air.

Most noncommercial radio stations are owned by educational institutions or private foundations. Noncommercial radio gets its support from the institutions that own the stations. Ultimately, much of this support comes from tax revenue since taxes support most public educational institutions. Other sources of support are endowments (gifts), grants from foundations or the federal government, and listener donations.

Noncommercial stations are served by National Public Radio (NPR). Founded in 1970, NPR provides program services to about 800 affiliates around the country. Member stations pay a fee based on audience reach and annual budget and receive in return about 50 hours of programming per week. Many of these shows are produced at NPR headquarters; others are produced at NPR stations and distributed by NPR. Probably the best-known NPR programs are *All Things Considered* and *Morning Edition*. About 26 million people listen to NPR every week.

The public radio stations that help support NPR receive financial support from the Corporation for Public Broadcasting (CPB), a private, nonprofit organization funded by Congress. Member stations receive money from the CPB, and those that decide to affiliate with NPR pay some of this money to the network as a fee. NPR also receives grants directly from the CPB. Congress, however, has threatened to cut the CPB's budget, which, in turn, would lead to less money for stations and for NPR. Consequently, many public radio stations have resorted to underwriting, a practice in which the station accepts money from a person or an organization in return for an acknowledgment on the air. In some cases these acknowledgments sound suspiciously like commercials. In contrast, NPR for the most part has resisted the pressure to air these minicommercials. In 1995, however, NPR relented a bit and allowed underwriters to broadcast brief slogans. NPR's financial fortunes were helped in 2003 when Joan Kroc, widow of McDonald's founder Ray Kroc, donated $200 million to the network.

Unlike commercial radio networks, NPR has found a way to generate significant revenue from the digital revolution: The network is one of the biggest podcasters in the world.

Ira Glass is producer and host of NPR's *This American Life.*

Apple's iTunes lists more than 50 NPR shows in its menu, with more than 300 titles available to download. NPR sells sponsorship of these podcasts to advertisers who wish to reach the network's relatively affluent listeners. Podcasts sponsored by the auto maker Acura, for example, have been downloaded more than 25 million times. The success of NPR's podcasts has caused some controversy, however. Local NPR affiliates worry that people will download the

A Sacramento, California, radio station thought it had a great idea: Run a contest with a hard-to-get Nintendo Wii as a prize. Radio contests, of course, are nothing new. Be the 34th caller and win concert tickets. Identify the amount of cash in the jackpot and win the money. Those kinds of promotions are so familiar that nobody notices them any more. What the station was looking for was a new, clever, and maybe slightly outrageous idea that would create a "buzz" for the station and raise ratings.

The station came up with this: "Hold Your Wee for a Wii." Contestants had to drink as much water as possible without going to the bathroom or throwing up. To make the competition even more intense, the contestants had to drink 8 ounces of water every 15 minutes. The 20 contestants all signed a waiver stating that they were aware of the consequences of competing in the contest.

One of the contestants, a 28-year-old mother of three, consumed about 2 gallons of water before she bowed out of the competition. A few hours after the event, the woman was found dead at her home, a victim of water intoxication.

This tragic event raises questions at several levels. As this book went to press, the station was facing a wrongful death lawsuit by the woman's family. Those involved with the promotion were fired. The FCC was also looking into the incident. Putting the legal implications aside for the moment, let's examine the ethical issues raised by this promotion.

First, as will be noted in Chapter 17, one guiding ethical principle states that human beings should not be used as objects or as a means to an end. The station's personnel showed little appreciation for the humanity of the contestants. During the course of the Wii contest, a nurse called the station and warned that consuming too much water can be fatal. One on-air DJ acknowledged that they were aware of the risk, but another DJ chimed in with, "Yeh, but they signed waivers, so we're not responsible. We're OK." Not only did the on-air DJs ignore her warning, but they even joked about it.

Despite what the DJs said about being aware of the risks, they showed a shocking lack of knowledge about the dangers of what they were doing. Just 2 years earlier, a student at a California university died from water intoxication during a fraternity hazing, but the DJs apparently were ignorant of that fact. One DJ said, "The body is 98 percent water so why can't they take as much as they want?" (Water makes up about 50–65 percent of the human body.) Another said, "If they get to the point where they have to throw up, then they are out of the game before they die, so that's good, right?" It seems apparent that the station was exploiting these individuals in an effort to increase their ratings.

Extreme radio promotions are nothing new. The "winner" of one promotion in the 1980s was covered in honey and tossed into a swimming pool filled with paper money. She got to keep all the bills that stuck to her. Another promotion, "Whirl 'til You Hurl," involved a $50,000 prize for the person who could ride the longest time on a roller coaster. The station had to stop the promotion after 10 weeks(!) when it was feared that the 73-year-old roller coaster used for the promotion was becoming unsafe. What is new is the level of outrage involved in the new stunts. One station offered concert tickets to the person who could sit on dry ice (temperature –172 degrees Farenheit) for the longest time. Three contestants wound up in the hospital for 10 weeks recovering from skin grafts. In another famous example a New York radio station ran a contest that rewarded people for having sex in public places (such as St. Patrick's Cathedral). The "winning" couple was arrested.

The usual defense when something like this occurs is that the contestants were adults, were responsible for their own actions, and signed a consent waiver. In order to allow an informed decision to consent, however, there is an ethical obligation to reveal all relevant risks to a person. Did the Sacramento station mention that death might be a result in this case? It is unclear just how much of the risk involved was revealed to the participants. There apparently were no medical personnel present at the contest site, nor was it clear if a physician had read the waiver form and approved it. In any case, it is doubtful that many people would agree to participate if they knew they were risking death over a $250 game system.

The station obviously was guilty of severe ethical lapses but what about the participants? Why would they endure pain and humiliation for such a relatively small reward? Maybe part of the blame lies with our culture. There are television shows (*Fear Factor*) and movies (*Jackass*) that glorify people doing outrageous things—eating cockroaches, swimming in sewage, mowing the lawn while naked. Has the craving for celebrityhood become so overpowering that people will do anything for their 15 minutes of fame? In such a world it's unlikely that outrageous radio promotions will go away.

---

podcasts and not listen to the local station, thus hurting the local station's chances to raise money during on-air fund drives.

The other noncommercial radio network, Public Radio International (PRI), was formerly known as American Public Radio. The Minneapolis organization is a network that acquires and distributes programming from station-based, independent and international producers. Unlike NPR, PRI does not produce any of its programming, but it does finance program production at member stations. A noncommercial station can be an affiliate of both NPR and PRI.

Students who ride the bus to school (and there are millions of them) might have a more entertaining ride if an idea from a Massachusetts company catches on. Bus Radio equips school buses with a special audio connection controlled by the bus driver. The school system pays nothing for the service. In fact, Bus Radio will pay money to the school district based on how many students are exposed to the programs. A flip of the appropriate switch, and students can listen to an hour-long radio program produced especially for their school group: elementary, middle, high. Each hour-long block contains about 44 minutes of music, talk, and interviews. The remaining 16 minutes contain public service announcements ("Stay in your seats while on the bus" "Stay in school"), and . . . commercials. And therein lies the controversy.

Critics maintain that students are a vulnerable audience who lack the sophistication and judgment to recognize the manipulation involved in commercials. In addition, when it comes to riding the school bus, the kids are a captive audience. They must listen to the commercials or be forced to find

a way to block them out. Bus Radio offers to eliminate specific ads if parents object to them. The company also screens the music to make sure no suggestive lyrics or offensive words get by.

The squabble over Bus Radio is another example of a continuing battle between school districts strapped for cash and critics who oppose all commercial activity in schools. The in-school news service, Channel One, prompted much of the controversy several years ago when it started beaming commercials along with its news. Today Channel One reaches about 7 million teens in middle schools and high schools—about 30 percent of all teenagers in the United States.

Maybe the most interesting observation about Bus Radio came from a school bus driver in Massachusetts. He noted that a lot of bus drivers let students listen to commercial FM radio during their rides to and from school and that the music on Bus Radio was a better alternative than some of the stuff they heard from over-the-air broadcasters. He particularly liked Hannah Montana.

OWNERSHIP IN THE RADIO INDUSTRY

As mentioned earlier, the 1996 Telecommunications Act drastically changed the landscape of the radio industry by producing a wave of consolidation that left the industry controlled by a few big media companies. Clear Channel, for example, managed to acquire more than 1,200 radio stations. As of 2007, however, that trend appeared to be changing. Clear Channel sold off hundreds of its stations in preparation for its sale to a group of independent investors. CBS sold more than 15 of it stations, and the Walt Disney Company, parent of ABC, sold its radio network and 22 of its stations. Despite these moves, big group owners such as Cumulus (more than 300 stations) and Entercom (more than 100 stations) still play a major role in the industry.

PRODUCING RADIO PROGRAMS

▲ Departments and Staff

The departmental structure of a radio station varies according to its size. Obviously, a small station with five or six employees has a departmental setup different from that of a large station with a hundred-person staff.

The two top management positions are the general manager and the program director. The manager has the responsibility for planning and carrying out station policy, maintaining contact with the community, and monitoring program content, audience ratings, and sales information. The program director is responsible for the station's sound. He or she supervises the music or other program material that the station broadcasts and also hires and fires announcers and DJs.

The sales department consists of the sales manager and the station's sales force. The news department is responsible for compiling the station's local newscasts and rewriting the wire service reports of national and regional news. The engineering department, under the supervision of the chief engineer, is staffed with technicians responsible for keeping the station on the air and maintaining the equipment.

▲ Putting Together a Program

This section will concentrate on how radio programs are produced for the music, talk, and news formats.

FIGURE 7-3

Format Wheel for a
Contemporary Rock
Station

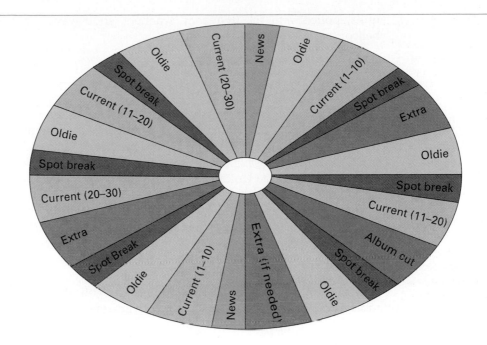

Music Format When the staff of a local station puts together their program, the first step is generally to lay out a **format wheel** (also called a *format clock*), a pie chart of an hour divided into segments representing different program elements. Figure 7-3 is a simplified version of a wheel for a contemporary rock station. (Note that Figure 7-3 is a visual aid, not something you would find at a radio station. All of the sequencing and scheduling represented in Figure 7-3 is handled by computers.)

Note that the music is structured to flow from one segment to another. Album cuts and hits from the past are spread around the wheel. Additional wheels would be constructed for the various parts of the broadcast day (that is, one wheel for morning drive time, another for 10 A.M.–4 P.M., another for evening drive time, and another for 7 P.M. midnight).

Talk Format Most of the content of the talk format is produced by the local station. As is the case with the music format, the makeup of the audience is taken into account. During drive time, talk segments should be relatively short and liberally interspersed with news, weather, and traffic reports. The audience for the 10 A.M.–4 P.M. segment tends to be primarily female, and therefore, topics for discussion reflect the interests of that group. The early-evening audience is generally younger and contains more males.

Producing a talk show requires more equipment than does producing a simple DJ program. Speaker telephones and extra telephone lines are needed, as is a delay system. This device gives the talk show moderator a 7- to 30-second delay period during which he or she can censor what is said by the caller. Another important part of the talk show is the telephone screener. The screener ranks the waiting calls by importance, letting the most interesting callers go first, and filters out crank calls or calls from regulars who contact the station too frequently.

All-News Format The all-news station also works with a programming wheel, similar to that of the music format. Instead of music, however, the news wheel shows the spacing between headlines, weather, news, sports, business reports, and commercials. It also illustrates the **cycle,** the amount of time that elapses before the program order is repeated.

The all-news format is the most difficult to produce. A large staff, consisting of anchorpersons, a managing editor, local reporters, editors, rewrite people, a traffic reporter, and stringers (freelance reporters who are paid per story), is needed. The list of necessary equipment and facilities is also long: radio wire services, sports wire, weather wire, mobile units, police- and fire-frequency scanners, short-wave receivers, and perhaps even a helicopter.

THE ECONOMICS OF RADIO

After several years of impressive revenue growth, radio revenue slumped in 2001. Since that time, radio has recovered somewhat, but annual revenue gains are nowhere near what they were during the 1990s. In 2005, for example, radio took in about $20 billion in advertising revenue, up just 2 percent from 2003. Further, radio's share of the total amount spent on advertising in the United States has been flat, hovering around the 8 percent mark for the past several years.

Most analysts suggest that the next few years will be crucial in determining radio's future. As noted, the industry is facing competition from satellite services, and the "aux" audio input in most new cars lets consumers play their iPods and other MP3 devices over the car radio. The ultimate success of HD radio is still an unknown in the equation. On the bright side, the drive-time audience is growing, and commuting time continues to increase. Programming is cheap (most music comes free courtesy of the recording companies), and radio attracts the niche audiences that advertisers are looking for.

▲ Sources of Revenue

Radio stations earn their money by selling advertising time. The amount that a radio station charges for time is included in its rate card. A typical radio commercial costs several hundred dollars in large cities. The same commercial in a small town might cost only a few dollars.

The radio industry has three sources of income from the sale of commercial time. The first comes from the sale of spots on network programs to national advertisers trying to reach a broad market. The second is the sale of time on local stations to advertisers who wish to reach a specific region (such as, the Northeast) or a specific type of market (such as, rural areas). This is called *national spot advertising*. The third source is advertising purchased by local establishments that want their commercials to be heard only in the immediate community. In 2004 each of these sources represented the following amounts of each dollar of radio revenue:

- Network: $0.05
- National spot: $0.17
- Local: $0.78

As the numbers indicate, the overwhelming amount of revenue in radio came from local commercials.

▲ General Expenses

Expenses in radio are divided into five areas: (1) technical, (2) programming, (3) sales, (4) general administration, and (5) news. Technical expenses include the payroll for the engineering staff and the cost of maintaining and replacing equipment. Program costs cover salaries paid to talent, outlays for tapes and CDs, and music fees paid to the music licensing organizations. Sales costs are made up of the salaries of the sales staff and all the other expenses that go with selling. General administrative expenses include the salaries of all management, secretarial, and clerical personnel; the depreciation of physical facilities; the cost of office supplies; and any interest that is due on loans to the station. News expenses consist of the costs involved in covering local and national stories.

As of 2006, general administration expenses ranked first, accounting for about 40 percent of all expenses. Programming came next, making up about 20 percent of the expense dollar, followed closely by costs associated with sales. News and technical expenses taken together accounted for about 15 percent.

CRITICAL / CULTURAL ISSUES

Radio and the Local Community

The philosophy that guided the development of radio in the United States was based on localism. Radio stations were licensed to serve the public interest of those who could hear their signals. Stations were expected to be integral parts of their local communities and responsive to the needs of local residents. The Federal Radio Commission set aside a number of AM channels that were dedicated to lower-power stations serving a particular town. Over the years other regulations were enacted that favored local ism. To encourage the development of roots in the community, owners were required to hold on to stations for 3 years before they could be sold. Stations had to survey their listeners and ascertain the needs of their community, and then provide programs to address those needs. Caps were placed on the number of stations one company could own to discourage large corporations from becoming out-of-town station owners with little or no ties to the community. In an effort to assure access for many voices, there were further caps on the number of stations that could be owned in one market.

As pointed out by Charles Fairchild in his article "Deterritorializing Radio: Deregulation and the Continued Triumph of the Corporatist Perspective in the USA," which appeared in a 1999 issue of *Media, Culture and Society,* this localist philosophy is not much with us today. His analysis of changes in the radio industry in recent decades is a good example of a critical/cultural investigation that focuses on ideology and power relationships in society.

In essence, Fairchild argues that recent changes have removed the connection between a radio station and its local community. He suggests that there are two dominant ideologies in force that compete as definitions of the *public interest.* One, the statist position, conceives of government as the protector of the public interest and an agency that assures that the broadest number of people benefit from

the medium. The other, the corporatist view, holds that the market is the best determiner of the public interest. The most economically successful service is that which succeeds best in the marketplace. In other words, the public interest is what interests the public.

Fairchild notes that the corporatist view has been the dominant model in recent radio operations. Due in part to an active industry lobby and the economic power wielded by large communications corporations, recent changes have almost erased the notion of local service. Following are just a few of those changes: The 3-year ownership rule has been dropped; the requirements for ascertaining the needs of the community have been minimized; and perhaps most importantly, the cap on the total number of stations that can be owned has been removed, and the limit on the number of stations that can be owned in a market has been raised to eight.

What are the effects of this change in ideology? The radio industry has become consolidated, with big corporations controlling hundreds of stations. Locally owned stations that had deep roots in the community have been gobbled up by big companies whose headquarters are in some faraway city and whose main interest is the bottom line. Consequently, local programming has been reduced in favor of standardized entertainment and news fed from some central location nowhere near the local community. Programming decisions are left to consultants and syndicators who have no local ties whatsoever. Hence, as Fairchild suggests, radio has become "deterritorialized," detached from a community connection.

Fairchild concludes that the corporatist ideology has triumphed: "Local radio stations are the objects of unaccountable control from outside local communities and neither the government nor the public have any levers of power with which they can influence broadcasters to provide access to those voices which cannot gain any serious measure of volume elsewhere."

FEEDBACK FOR RADIO

▲ Ratings and Shares

In the radio industry feedback is provided by ratings conducted by professional research organizations. The major company that measures the radio audience is **Arbitron.** Arbitron surveys radio listening in approximately 280 markets across the United States and reports its results to broadcasters and advertisers.

Within a given market Arbitron chooses people at random from a listing of all telephone numbers in the market. Individuals who agree to participate in Arbitron's survey are sent a pocket-sized diary to record both in-home and out-of-home listening. Participants are instructed to fill in the diary on a day-to-day basis, noting the time spent listening to radio and identifying the station. Approximately 3,000–4,000 of these diaries are mailed in a given market, and Arbitron follows up with several reminder calls to persons in the sample. Nevertheless, less than 50 percent of the diaries are returned in usable form. Figure 7-4 is an example of an Arbitron radio diary. Once the diaries have been returned, Arbitron

FIGURE 7-4

Sample Arbitron Radio
Diary

Source: Arbitron Ratings:
Your Radio Ratings Diary.
Copyright © Arbitron
Ratings Company.
Reprinted by permission.

begins an analysis that typically takes 3–4 weeks. The end product of this process is a ratings book, which is sent to participating stations.

Measurements of radio and television audiences gathered by the diary method are usually expressed in terms of two related concepts: (1) ratings and (2) share of the audience. A **rating** is simply the ratio of listeners of a particular station to all people in the market. Suppose that in a market with 100,000 people, 20,000 listen to radio station KYYY from 9:00 A.M. to 9:15 A.M. The rating of KYYY would be 20,000/100,000, or 20 percent. A **share of the audience** is the ratio of listeners of a particular station to the total number of radio listeners in the market. For example, again suppose that 20,000 people are listening to KYYY from 9:00 A.M. to 9:15 A.M. and that in the total market 80,000 people are listening to the radio during the same period. KYYY's share of the audience would be 20,000/80,000, or 25 percent. Shares of the audience divide the listening audience among all stations in the market. When they are summed, shares should total 100 percent. Ratings books are important to stations because they are used to establish the rates stations will charge advertisers.

In an effort to improve the accuracy of radio ratings, Arbitron and Nielsen Media Research are testing a "peoplemeter" (PPM) for radio. This new device is designed to be clipped to an individual's clothing. Radio stations encode an inaudible, unique signal as part of their broadcasts. The PPM "hears" this signal and records the station and the time spent listening. Such a device requires far less effort on the part of respondents.

Radio stations, however, are not enthusiastic about the new PPM. It is about 50 percent more expensive than traditional paper diary method. Moreover, early tests of the PPM showed reduced levels of listening time when compared to diaries, something that radio stations do not like to see. Consequently, radio stations are searching for alternative ways of measuring the audience.

▲ Radio Audiences

There are almost twice as many radio sets in this country as there are people. As of January 2007, there were more than 575 million radio receivers scattered around the United States, with car radios accounting for about one-third of this number. On a typical day at least three-fourths of all adults will listen to radio, and the average person will listen, or at least have the radio on, for about 3 hours. Most people listen to radio in the early morning when they are getting ready for and driving to work and in the late afternoon when they are driving home. These two "day parts," consisting roughly from 6 A.M. to 10 A.M. and 4 P.M. to 7 P.M., are called *drive time*.

The precise audience makeup for a given station depends on that station's format. Top 40 stations draw an audience composed primarily of 12- to 24-year-olds, with females outnumbering males by about three to two. Modern rock attracts 18- to 34-year-olds, in about equal proportions of men and women. Jazz, classical, alt-country, and all-news formats generally attract an older crowd, with most of their audience coming from the 45-and-over age group. Country music stations seem to have an across-the-board appeal to those over 25. As a person gets older, he or she tends to evolve out of the audience for one format and move on to another.

THE RADIO INDUSTRY

About 110,000 people are employed at radio stations and radio networks. The average station employs about 8 full-time people. Consolidation has made employment prospects less optimistic than in earlier years. Experience is a big plus. How does a newcomer gain experience? One good way is to volunteer to work at your college or university radio station. Try to do as many jobs as possible and learn as much as you can. Another possibility is to arrange for an internship at a local station.

▲ Entry-Level Positions

The best place to break into radio is at a small-market station. Small stations hire people who are versatile. A DJ might have to work in sales. A salesperson might have to write commercial copy and produce radio ads. It would be virtually impossible to get this sort of experience at a large station.

Most employment counselors recommend that a beginner take any job that is offered at a station, even if the job is not exactly what you want to do. Once inside the organization, it is easier for you to move to your preferred area.

The two areas in which most entry-level jobs can be found are the programming and sales departments. Of these two the programming area is the more competitive; many people who enter the radio field want jobs as announcers or DJs. Nonetheless, it is possible to find a job if you are persistent and willing to work unusual hours.

The best chance of landing a beginning job in radio can be found in the sales department. Radio stations, especially those in smaller markets, are usually in need of competent salespeople with a knowledge of and an interest in radio. The worst prospects for landing

171

WKNE

Select the radio media tour (DVD, Track 3) on the DVD that accompanies this text. The first part provides a look at the radio station's operations and its various departments; the second segment features the staff discussing some important issues facing the radio industry.

The story of WKNE is typical of many radio stations in that it has changed hands twice in the last few years. It was acquired in the late 1990s by Tele-Media, a company with interests in cable TV, telephone, and Internet services. In 2003 the station was sold to Saga Communications, the 18th-largest radio group owner in the United States, with 56 stations. WKNE is also typical of many small-market radio

stations. As the clip shows, its personnel often do more than one job, and it faces challenges generating advertising dollars in its market.

1. How is consolidation affecting the daily operations of radio stations? What are the positive effects? What are the negative effects?

2. What area of the radio industry is the most lucrative? Which poses the greatest risk? Why?

3. How has the ratio of music and public affairs (news) programming changed over the years?

4. How has computer technology advanced radio programming?

---

a job are in radio news. Aside from some large-market AM news/talk stations, most stations have drastically cut back their local news staffs.

▲ Upward Mobility

For talent there are two distinct avenues of upward mobility. For DJs it consists of moving up to larger markets and better time slots. The ultimate goal of most DJs is a drive-time shift in one of the top 10 markets. In addition, many DJs progress within a station by moving up to the chief announcer's spot and from there to program director.

The sales department offers the best route for upward mobility. Competent salespeople are given bigger and more profitable accounts to service. Some will move up to the sales manager position, and from there many will progress to general manager.

Remember that radio stations are not the only places of potential employment. Program syndicators hire announcers and those experienced in programming music formats. Companies that produce packaged feature programs need producers, writers, and directors. Satellite radio offers further opportunities.

MAIN POINTS

- Radio started out as point-to-point communication, much like the telephone and telegraph. The notion of broadcasting did not come about until the 1920s.

- The decade of the 1920s was an important one in radio. Big business took control of the industry, receivers improved, commercials were started, networks were formed, and the FRC was set up to regulate radio.

- The coming of TV forced local stations to adopt formats, such as Top 40 or country.

- FM became the dominant form of radio in the 1970s and 1980s. Sparked by a loosening of ownership rules, a wave of consolidation took place in the industry during the 1990s.

- Radio is moving slowly into the digital age. Satellite radio and Internet radio are two digital services that will

compete with traditional radio. Radio stations are introducing high-definition radio.

- Radio programming is provided by local stations, networks, and syndication companies.

- Stations have refined their formats to reach an identifiable audience segment.

- Most radio revenue comes from local advertising. Big companies now dominate large-market radio.

- National Public Radio is the best-known public broadcaster.

- Radio audiences are measured by the Arbitron Company using a diary method. The demographic characteristics of the radio listener vary greatly by station format.

QUESTIONS FOR REVIEW

1. What were the key developments during the 1920s that helped shape modern radio?
2. What impact did the Telecommunications Act of 1996 have on the radio industry?
3. What are the defining features of radio?
4. What is the function of a format wheel?
5. How is radio listening measured?

QUESTIONS FOR CRITICAL THINKING

1. What might have happened if radio had developed during the 1930s—the Depression years—instead of the Roaring Twenties?
2. What formats might radio stations have developed if rock and roll had not come along?
3. The radio industry is more consolidated than ever before. Consolidation may have helped radio's bottom line, but is the listener better served? Why or why not?
4. Listen to the radio stations in your market. Are there audience segments in the market that are not being served?
5. Read the boxed insert "Radio and the Local Community" on page 169, and consider the following: What effect might the Internet have on the amount of local news, information, and other services in a given community? Will the Internet allow access to "those voices which cannot gain any serious measure of volume elsewhere"? Who owns the radio stations in your home town? How do the locally owned stations compare with those that are corporate owned?

KEY TERMS

network (p. 152)
Radio Act of 1927 (p. 153)
Federal Communications Commission
   (FCC) (p. 153)
Communications Act of 1934 (p. 153)
clock hour (p. 155)
payola (p. 155)

nonduplication rule (p. 155)
National Public Radio (NPR) (p. 156)
Telecommunications Act
   of 1996 (p. 156)
AM (p. 160)
FM (p. 160)
format (p. 161)

voice tracking (p. 163)
format wheel (p. 167)
cycle (p. 167)
Arbitron (p. 169)
rating (p. 170)
share of the audience (p. 170)

INTERNET RESOURCES

Online Learning Center

At the Online Learning Center home page, www.mhhe.com/dominick10, *select* Student Center *and then* Chapter 7.

1. Use the Learning Objectives, Chapter Outline, Main Points, and Time Line sections to review this chapter.
2. Test your knowledge of the chapter using the multiple choice, crossword puzzle, and flashcard features of the site.
3. Expand your knowledge of concepts and topics discussed in the chapter by going to Suggestions for Further Reading and Internet Exercises.

Surfing the Internet

Web sites devoted to radio are about as changeable as the medium itself. With luck these will still be functioning.

www.otr.com
A site devoted to radio's Golden Age. Listen to clips from kids' after-school serials, radio dramas, and classic comedy shows.

www.westwoodone.com
Home page of the Westwood One radio networks.

www.entercom.com
Entercom Communications Corporation home page. Click on "markets" to locate all of Entercom's holdings.

www.kisw.com
KISW-FM, a Seattle rock station. Includes streaming media, links to YouTube, and stuff you can buy.

www.npr.org
The home of National Public Radio. Note the links to podcasts.

www.rab.com
Home page of the Radio Advertising Bureau. Filled with useful statistics and facts about radio.

CHAPTER 8

SOUND RECORDING

This chapter will prepare you to:

- understand the development of the recording process

- explain the impact of the Depression and World War II on the industry

- recognize the significance of the CD

- discuss the impact of Napster and its successors

- explain how the digital age is affecting the recording industry

- describe the departments that make up the recording industry

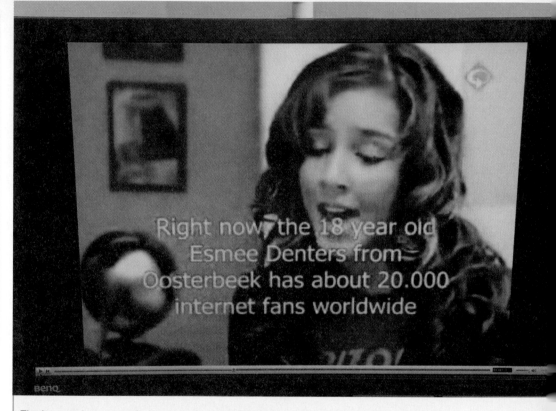

The Internet has created new ways for recording artists to be discovered. Esmee Denters went from a YouTube favorite to opening act for Justin Timberlake.

In the old days BI (before the Internet), if an aspiring artist wanted to pursue a career in the music business, he or she had to work up a repertoire of songs, rent a recording studio, put together a demo tape, ship the tape off to record producers, and hope that the tape didn't wind up in the trash. Not any more.

Case in point: Esmee Denters, an 18-year-old girl living in a small town in the Netherlands, used a karaoke machine and a cheap Web cam to put together a series of clips of her singing hits by Beyonce and Monica that she then posted on YouTube. As of mid-2007, Denters's clips had been streamed some 8 million times. About 20,000 people subscribed to her channel on YouTube, and her MySpace site had about 14,000 friends.

This kind of Internet "buzz" gets the attention of today's recording company executives. One label rep called a hotel in Denters's hometown and asked the clerk for the telephone numbers of the Denters who lived in the town. The rep then called them one-by-one until he found Esmee.

As of this writing, Denters has traveled to the United States, met with numerous recording industry heavyweights, acquired a producer/manager (who has written hits for Jessica Simpson), recorded a demo with Kelly Rowland, and listened to potential TV deals. She recently signed a record contract with a major label.

In the post-Internet age, it's entirely possible for an artist to record and distribute songs without the help of a record company. Recording and production costs have fallen with the advent of digital equipment, and distribution can be done over the Web using firms such as INgrooves. Promotion can also be done online using a number of commercial music networking sites. Of course, such an option involves a good deal of risk for the artist.

For their part the record labels are also a bit cautious about Internet sensations such as Denters. It is unclear how online popularity translates into record sales. Sandi Thom, for example, generated a lot of buzz with her Web casts, but her debut album did poorly in the States.

Whatever the future holds for Denters and the ones who follow her, it's apparent that the Internet makes it possible for contemporary artists to build a substantial fan base with far less cost and labor than was possible before the online world existed. It's also apparent that the Internet brings with it new challenges for both artists and the industry.

Of all the media discussed in this book, the recording industry has been the most affected by the digital revolution. The Internet has transformed the industry's distribution system, its economic base, and its traditional business model. This chapter will examine the history, structure, organization, and economics of this rapidly changing industry.

A BRIEF HISTORY

▲ Early Technologies

Thomas Edison recited "Mary Had a Little Lamb" into a primitive recording machine consisting of a tinfoil-wrapped cylinder, needle, microphone, and crank. It is interesting to speculate what might have happened if Edison had sung the nursery rhyme rather than recited it. Perhaps innovators would have been more aware of the music potential of this new medium, and the history of the recording industry might have been different. As it was, Edison and others thought his **phonograph,** the name he gave his 1877 invention, might best be suited to recording the spoken word. He eventually tried to sell it to the business community as an aid to dictation. At the time the idea of using the phonograph to bring musical entertainment into the home was too wild to imagine.

Edison's phonograph faced new competition when Chinchester Bell and Charles Tainter patented a device called the **graphophone,** in which Edison's foil was replaced by a wax cylinder. In 1887 more competition emerged when Emile Berliner patented a system that used a disk instead of a cylinder. He called his new invention a **gramophone.**

By 1890 three machines that recorded and played back sound were on the market. At about this time big business entered the picture as Jesse Lippincott, who had made a fortune in the glass tumbler business, purchased the business rights to both the phonograph and the graphophone, thus ending a bitter patent fight between the respective inventors. Lippincott had dreams of controlling the office-dictating market, but stenographers rebelled against the new device, and the talking-machine business fell upon hard times. Strangely enough, relief appeared quickly and financial solvency returned, a nickel at a time, thanks to a new idea: using the phonograph to record music instead of the spoken voice.

One of Lippincott's local managers hit upon the idea of putting coin-operated phonographs in the many penny arcades and amusement centers that were springing up all over America. For a nickel you could listen through a pair of stethoscope-like earphones to a cylinder whose 2-minute musical recording had a technical quality that could only be described as awful. Still, these **nickelodeons** were immensely popular, and the demand for "entertainment" cylinders grew. Companies quickly scrambled for a share in the new recording production business.

▲ Rivalry and Growth

The two decades spanning the turn of the 20th century were a time of intense business rivalry in the recording industry. While the two major companies, the Columbia Phonograph Company and Edison's North American Phonograph Company, fought one another, Berliner's United States Gramophone Company perfected the process of recording on flat disks. Ultimately, Columbia recognized the superiority of the disk and attempted to break into the market by selling the zonophone, its own version of the disk player. As for Berliner, along with machinist Eldridge Johnson, he formed the Victor Talking Machine Company, which had as its trademark a picture of a dog peering into the bell of a gramophone and the slogan "His Master's Voice." Thanks to aggressive marketing, this new company was highly successful and in 1906 introduced the Victrola, the first disk player designed to look like a piece of furniture. By 1912 the supremacy of the disk over the cylinder had been established.

On the eve of World War I, record players were commonplace throughout America. A dance craze in 1913 sent

The phonograph is just one of Thomas Edison's inventions. His 1877 model was hand-cranked, and the sound waves were preserved as scratches in tinfoil.

The 100th anniversary of phonograph recording on a flat disk was 1988. This technology was created by Emile Berliner, an immigrant from Germany, who worked as a stock clerk in a clothing store while investigating the intriguing new world of sound amplification and recording. Berliner quickly noted that the cylinders used by Edison had too many disadvantages to be practical. He perfected a way to encode sound on a flat disk that could be easily duplicated by using a master mold, much like pressing waffles in a waffle iron.

His invention was slow to catch on in the United States because of competition from Edison, but it was a success in Europe. Eventually, Berliner introduced to the American market the phonautograph, which he renamed the gramophone. This eventually replaced the cylinder.

In one area Berliner clearly saw the future. He predicted that prominent singers and performers would collect royalties from the sale of his disks. He was wrong on another count, however. He thought that musicians and artists who were unable to appear at a concert would simply send a record to be played on stage instead.

Berliner also developed the prototype of the modern microphone, and both his inventions—the disk and the microphone—came together when electronic recording was perfected during the 1920s. Even the modern CD owes him a debt. Like his original invention the CD stores information in a spiral on a flat, rotating surface.

profits soaring, a trend that was to continue throughout the war. In 1914, 27 million records were manufactured; 107 million were produced in 1919 following the end of the war. The record industry had entered a boom period.

The boom continued when the years after World War I ushered in the Jazz Age, a period named after the spirited, popular music of the Roaring Twenties. **Jazz,** which emerged from the roots of the black experience in America, was spontaneous, individualistic, and sensual. Because of its disdain for convention, jazz was widely denounced as degenerate during its early years (about 30 years later, another spontaneous and sensual musical innovation, rock and roll, would also be denounced).

The good times, however, did not last. In the beginning no one in the record industry regarded radio as a serious threat. Record company executives were sure that the static-filled, raucous noise emanating from radios would never compete with the quality of their recordings. They were wrong.

▲ The Impact of Radio on the Recording Industry

Radio gained popularity in the 1920s, and the recording industry felt the effects. By the end of 1924, the combined sales of players and records had dropped 50 percent from those of the previous year. In the midst of this economic downturn, the recording companies quietly introduced electronic recording, using technology borrowed from their bitter rival, radio. The sound quality of records improved tremendously. But despite this improvement, radio continued to be thought of as the medium for "live" music, and records were dismissed as the medium of "canned" music.

In 1926 the record industry began to market radio-phonograph combinations, an obvious testament to the belief that the two media would coexist. This attitude was also prevalent at the corporate level. In 1927 rumors were flying that the Victor Company would soon merge with the Radio Corporation of America (RCA). Frightened by this prospect, Columbia, Victor's biggest rival, tried to get a head start by merging with the new (and financially troubled) radio network United Independent Broadcasters. All too soon, however, the record company became disillusioned and dissolved the deal. The much-discussed RCA and Victor merger came about in 1929, with the new company dominated by the radio operation.

▲ The Depression Years

The Great Depression of the 1930s dealt a severe economic blow to sound recording. Thomas Edison's record manufacturing company went out of business in 1930. Record sales dropped from $46 million in 1930 to $5.5 million in 1933, and several smaller labels folded. The entire industry was reeling.

During the 1940s the local record shop was the place to hang out with friends and listen to the latest releases.

In the midst of all this gloom, the recording industry was saved once again by the nickel. Coin-operated record players, called *jukeboxes* (the origin of this term is obscure), began appearing in the thousands of bars and cocktail lounges that sprang up after the repeal of Prohibition in 1933. These jukeboxes were immensely popular and quickly spread to diners, drugstores, and restaurants. Starting in 1934, total record sales began to inch upward; by 1939 sales had increased by more than 500 percent.

▲ World War II and After

The record industry did not do well during the war. First, the U.S. government declared shellac—a key ingredient of disks—vital to the national defense, and supplies available for making records dropped drastically. Second, the American Federation of Musicians, fearful of losing jobs because of canned music, went on strike. The strike lasted from 1942 to 1944, and as a result, record sales increased slowly during the war years. However, it was also during the war that Capitol Records embarked on a novel approach to record promotion. The company mailed free records to radio stations, hoping for airplay. This action marked formal recognition of a new industry attitude: Radio could help sell records. This new philosophy would revolutionize the recording industry.

In 1948 Columbia introduced the 33⅓-rpm long-playing record (LP). The new disks could play for 25 minutes a side and were virtually unbreakable. Rather than adopt the Columbia system, RCA Victor introduced its own innovation, the 45-rpm extended-play record. The next few years were described as the "battle of the speeds," as the record-buying public was confronted by a choice among 33⅓, 45, and 78 records. From 1947 to 1949, record sales dropped 25 percent as people waited to see which speed would win. In 1950 RCA conceded and began issuing 33⅓ records. Columbia won only a partial victory, however. The 45 would become the preferred disk for single pop recordings, and the 33⅓ would dominate album

Elvis Aron Presley sold more than 250 million records, starred in 33 movies, and forever changed American popular music.

sales. The 78 became obsolete. There were also changes in record players. High-fidelity sets came on the market in 1954, followed 4 years later by stereophonic record players. Record sales more than doubled during this period.

The mushrooming popularity of television during the 1950s had an impact on both radio and the recording industry. Television took away the big national stars from radio and forced local stations to experiment with new formats in an attempt to keep their audiences. One of the most popular radio formats that emerged was Top 40, a sound that relied on a set playlist based on record sales. The emergence of rock and roll helped the new Top 40 format become popular with a young audience. As we saw in Chapter 7, this young audience had a good deal of money to spend on the records they heard played by their favorite DJs.

▲ The Coming of Rock and Roll

Rock had its roots in black rhythm and blues, commercial white popular music, country and western, and jazz. In July 1955, Bill Haley and the Comets moved into the number-one spot on the charts with "Rock Around the Clock." Less than a year later, another performer who would enjoy a far more substantial career came on the scene. "Heartbreak Hotel," recorded by a then relatively unknown Elvis Presley, would stay at the number-one position for seven straight weeks. It was with Elvis that rock and roll first blossomed. Combining a country-and-western style with the beat and energy of black rhythm-and-blues music, Elvis's records sold millions. He appeared on Ed Sullivan's network TV show (from the waist up—Sullivan thought Elvis's pelvic gyrations too suggestive). Through Elvis rock and roll gained wide recognition, if not respectability.

Presley's success inspired other performers from the country-and-western tradition. Jerry Lee Lewis combined Mississippi boogie-woogie with country music to produce a unique and driving style. His "Whole Lotta Shakin' Going On" sold 6 million copies from 1957 to 1958.

Several rock pioneers came from traditional black rhythm-and-blues music. Perhaps the most exciting (certainly the most energetic) was Richard Penniman, or, as he called himself, Little Richard. Except for a period of 3 months, Little Richard had a record in the Top 100 at all times from 1956 to 1957 (best known are "Long Tall Sally" and "Tutti Frutti"). About the same time, on the South Side of Chicago, Chuck Berry was singing blues in small nightclubs. Discovered by the owner of a Chicago-based record company, Berry was the first artist who paid more than passing attention to the lyrics of rock and roll. His style would later influence many musical groups, including the Beatles.

▲ The Commercialization of Rock

By 1959, through a combination of bizarre events, all the pioneers of rock had disappeared. Elvis had enlisted in the Army. Jerry Lee Lewis had married a 13-year-old girl said to be his cousin and dropped from sight. Little Richard was in the seminary. And Chuck Berry was incarcerated in federal prison. Thus, the way was open for a whole new crop of stars. Economics dictated what this new crop would look and sound like.

Record companies recognized that huge amounts of money could be made from the rock-and-roll phenomenon if it was promoted correctly. Unfortunately, rock and roll had an image problem. In 1959 the record industry was shaken by the payola scandals (see Chapter 7) that, arriving on top of years of bad publicity and criticism of rock and roll as responsible for most of society's ills, threatened rock's profitability. Since rock and roll had too much moneymaking potential to be abandoned, the record companies decided to clean up rock's image.

As the 1960s opened, the new look in rock was characterized by middle-class, white, clean-cut, wholesome performers. Rock stars were young men and women you would not hesitate to bring home and introduce to your parents. On the male side Ricky Nelson, Bobby Vee, Bobby Vinton, Fabian, Paul Anka, Frankie Avalon, and the Four Seasons were popular. There were fewer examples on the female side. Those who had hits included Annette Funicello, Connie Francis, Brenda Lee, and Lesley Gore. All fit the new image of rock and roll. Consequently, the early 1960s saw few musical innovations. In 1963, however, the music changed again.

▲ The British Invasion

Their name was inspired by Buddy Holly and the Crickets, but instead of choosing the entomologically correct "Beetles," the group decided to spell their name "Beatles" (which incorporated the word *beat*). In early 1964 they took the United States by storm. Musically, the Beatles were everything that American rock and roll was not. They were innovative, especially in vocal harmony, and introduced the harmonica as a rock instrument. Ultimately, they would change the shape of the music business and American popular culture. The Beatles had seven number-one records in 1964; they held down the top position for 20 of the 52 weeks that year.

Motown star Diana Ross and Berry Gordy Jr.

Berry Gordy began as an assembly-line worker in Detroit but ended up as the head of one of the largest black-owned businesses in America. Along the way he introduced black performers to a wider audience and permanently shaped the evolution of American popular music.

In 1957 Gordy wrote a hit song for R&B artist Jackie Wilson. While Gordy and Wilson were in the studio working on other projects, a group called the Matadors auditioned for Wilson. Although Wilson was unimpressed with their songs, Gordy noticed the potential of their lead singer, a young man named Smokey Robinson.

Over the next few years, Gordy continued to write and produce songs for a number of black artists. Unsatisfied with the way his songs were handled by the major record labels, Gordy decided to start his own. He took an $800 loan from his family and in 1959 opened what would later become Motown Records. The company released its first single in 1959 and had its first number-one hit 2 years later with the Marvelettes' "Please Mr. Postman."

In its early years Motown appealed primarily to black audiences, but Gordy's strategy was to appeal to both whites and blacks. Motown's advertising slogan was "The Sound of Young America." During the mid-1960s Gordy's company pioneered the Motown sound, which revolutionized the music industry. Artists such as Stevie Wonder, Marvin Gaye, Smokey Robinson, and Diana Ross and the Supremes became popular with both black and white record buyers. A few years later Gordy introduced the Jackson Five, featuring a young Michael Jackson as lead singer.

In 1988 Berry Gordy was inducted into the Rock and Roll Hall of Fame along with the Supremes, Bob Dylan, and the Beatles. That same year, Gordy sold Motown Records to MCA for more than $60 million. He continued, however, to head Motown's record publishing division and its film and television sections. The sound Gordy created will continue to influence the musical tastes of future generations.

Their success paved the way for a veritable British invasion. Most British rock at this time resembled American rock: cheery, commercial, and white. Not surprisingly, some of the first groups that followed the Beatles represented this school (Herman's Hermits, Freddie and the Dreamers, the Dave Clark Five, and Peter and Gordon, to name a few). There was another style of British rock, however, far less cheery, as represented by the Rolling Stones and the Animals. This style was blues-based, rough-hewn, slightly aggressive, and certainly not bouncy and carefree.

American artists were not silent during this influx of British talent. Folk music, as performed by Bob Dylan and Joan Baez, was also popular. It was only a matter of time before folk merged with rock to produce folk rock. Soul music, as recorded on the Motown label, also made its mark during the 1960s.

The Beatles have more gold albums—47—than any other group in the history of sound recording.

▲ Transitions

The late 1960s was a time of cultural transition. Freedom, experimentation, and innovation were encouraged in almost all walks of life, and popular music was no exception. Sparked by the release of the Beatles' *Sgt. Pepper* album, a fractionalization of rock began to take place. Several trends of this period are notable. In 1968 Blood, Sweat and Tears successfully blended jazz, rock,

The 1960s was a decade of change in American music. Compare early-1960s recording star Annette Funicello (shown in her Mouseketeer costume) with late-1960s star Janis Joplin.

and at times even classical music. The Band introduced country rock. The Who recorded a rock opera, *Tommy*. In the midst of all this experimentation, commercial formula music was also healthy. The Monkees, a group put together by ads in the newspaper, sold millions of records. Bubblegum rockers the Archies kept "Sugar, Sugar" at the top of the charts for a month in 1969 (it replaced a song by the Rolling Stones, "Honky Tonk Woman").

Toward the end of the 1960s and the beginning of the 1970s, rock music became part of the counterculture; in many instances it went out of its way to break with the establishment. Musically, many of the songs of this era were characterized by the **heavy metal** sound; amplifiers and electronic equipment began to dominate the stage. The artists also broke sharply with tradition. The pioneers in this style of rock were all vaguely threatening, a trifle unsavory, and definitely not the type you would bring home to the folks.

▲ Industry Trends: 1970s–1990s

The recording industry enjoyed a boom period during the mid-1970s, resulting in large measure from the popularity of disco. A downturn during the early 1980s reversed itself during the second half of that decade thanks to Michael Jackson's *Thriller* album and a few popular movie soundtracks. The 1990s saw the CD replace tape as the preferred playback medium. Record companies were happy about this since the profit margins on CDs were greater than for tape. As a result recording industry revenues showed some fluctuation but generally increased during the 1990s.

▲ The Contemporary Sound Recording Industry

The biggest development in the past decade has been the emergence of portable MP3 players, such as Apple's iPod, and their impact on the industry. By the start of 2007, more than 3 billion songs had been downloaded from Apple's iTunes Web site. This single fact has put the industry on notice that its old business model is outdated. Consumers no longer want to pay $16–17 for a CD with only a couple of songs on it that they like; they would rather purchase songs individually by downloading them to their computers and MP3 players. Thus, there was a slow but steady decline in the number of CDs purchased from 2005 to 2007. Meanwhile, digital downloads have increased significantly. In sum, the industry is moving away from selling shiny discs (atoms) to consumers and embracing the notion that its future is selling music online (bits).

One of the strangest trends in the evolution of popular rock-and-roll music has been a small but persistent genre of records that can only be classified under the somewhat macabre title of "morbid rock." Although its roots probably go back further, it became especially notable in the 1960s. Among the first songs to become a hit was "Teen Angel," the tale of an unfortunate couple whose car stalled on the railroad tracks. Although the young man of the song is smart enough to run like crazy, the young woman goes back to the car to retrieve her sweetheart's high school ring. The train arrives at the same time. End of romance.

Another early example was J. Frank Wilson's "Last Kiss," a tragic tale of a guy and girl out on a date who plow into a disabled car. He survives. She doesn't. End of romance. "Tell Laura I Love Her" told the teary story of a young man who needs money to continue his romance with his girlfriend and so resorts to stock car racing to provide extra income. He totals his car and himself. End of romance. "Patches" concerned the romance between a young woman from the wrong side of the tracks and a middle-class young man. Despondent, the young woman drowns herself in the river. At the end of the song, the young man is contemplating the same thing. Even wholesome Pat Boone got into the act with "Moody River," a song that also told the story of two people who throw themselves into the river and drown.

The trend was less noticeable in the early 1970s, but a song titled "Billy, Don't Be a Hero" enjoyed wide popularity. This song was about a boy who goes off to war, against the wishes of his girlfriend, and gets killed. End of romance. (For those who are true fans of this genre, Rhino Records has collected 10 teen tragedy songs ranging from "Last Kiss" to the little-known but nonetheless moving "The Homecoming Queen's Got a Gun." Incidentally, the back cover of the LP doubles as a tissue dispenser.)

The trend resurfaced in 1999 when Pearl Jam's remake of "Last Kiss" went to number two on the charts. Apparently, morbid rock isn't dead yet.

The downturn in sales has meant problems at the retail level. Tower Records and Musicland both filed for bankruptcy in the mid-2000s. At the same time, competition was increasing in the digital download market. In addition to iTunes, Wal-Mart, MTV, Yahoo!, Virgin, and FYE all started music downloading services.

The industry continues to fight against illegal file sharing, but it is difficult to tell if their efforts are paying off. Lawsuits effectively put the original Napster out of business, and subsequent legal efforts against successors such as Grokster were also successful. The industry also started suing individuals who had illegally downloaded large numbers of songs and were sharing them online (see the boxed insert "The Recording Industry Cracks Down on Campus"). Many people paid cash settlements to the recording companies to settle the lawsuits. In 2006 the head of the Recording Industry Association of America (RIAA) declared that the industry's efforts had "contained" the practice. Data from online measurement services, however, disclosed that illegal file sharing actually increased from 2005 to 2006. Whatever the case, the recording industry is still committed to battling the problem with all the legal methods at its disposal.

Despite best-selling albums by performers such a Fall Out Boy, recording industry revenues are still being hurt by illegal downloading.

On the business front the industry is now more concentrated than ever. The music divisions of Sony and Bertelsmann merged in 2003 to create the second largest recording company in the world. The top four recording companies account for more than 80 percent of all music sales.

The growing concentration of the recording industry had an effect on what music people heard. The quest for a better bottom line puts the emphasis on turning out CDs that sell big numbers. The music that racks up big sales tends to be predictable

It's no secret that much illegal file sharing takes place on college campuses. Most colleges have a lot of bandwidth available, and students have the time and the technological expertise. Every fall the number of people trading files increases significantly.

The recording industry is aware of this practice and has responded with a barrage of lawsuits directed at illegal downloading on campus. In early 2007 the Recording Industry Association of America (RIAA) released a list of the 25 universities that received the most copyright complaints. The RIAA charged that nearly 15,000 students at those universities had participated in illegal file sharing. The penalties for most of these students range from a cease-and-desist order from their university to a semester's suspension. For those students who do the most illegal file sharing, usually making hundreds or even thousands of songs available to others, the penalty can be more severe: The RIAA targets them for a civil lawsuit.

Students identified by the RIAA are contacted by mail and offered a "prelitigation" settlement. In short, the RIAA offers students a chance to pay a smaller amount of money to avoid being sued for a larger amount. There is even a Web site, p2playsuits .com, where students can go to negotiate a deal. Although illegal file sharing should not be condoned, the RIAA's methods are not without controversy. The prelitigation settlement bypasses the legal system and seems to rely on threat and intimidation. Some students have labeled it a form of extortion.

Furthermore, the RIAA does no investigation to determine if the students they are threatening to sue are actually the ones who engaged in illegal activity. In some cases students who were targeted for lawsuits claimed that they had never participated in any file sharing and had no idea why they were being singled out. The RIAA has the resources to sue hundreds and even thousands of people, based only on the IP addresses of their computers, a nine-number sequence in which numbers could easily be transposed. The suit is filed in the city where the student's Internet service provider is based—usually not where the student lives—thus making it difficult for the student to offer a defense.

In short, the student is left with a difficult dilemma: Pay around $3,000–4,000 to settle the threatened lawsuit, or shell out many times that to hire a lawyer and contest the suit in court. And even then there is the possibility of losing and being liable for an even greater amount. College students rarely have the money to fight these lawsuits in court, and many, even the innocent ones, take the less expensive way out.

Will this tactic curtail illegal downloading on campus? It might, but recent history suggests that students will turn to file-sharing systems that are even harder to monitor. On top of that, the lawsuits do not help the recording industry's reputation among students. It may be that the industry is alienating some of its best customers.

and formulaic rather than new and original. Indeed, many observers have blamed the drop in music sales not so much on illegal downloading as on the lack of any new and compelling musical styles.

Figure 8-1 shows a "family tree" of rock and roll, offering one way of looking at the interrelationships among the genre's many subgenres.

SOUND RECORDING IN THE DIGITAL AGE

As we have seen, throughout most of its history, sound recording used the analog technique. Sound waves were first etched into grooves of a vinyl disk or into rearranged particles on a magnetic tape. In both cases the recording industry manufactured and distributed the products (disks or tapes) that consumers purchased. The digital technique changed that by encoding music as pure information, a string of binary numbers, from which music could be recovered. As a result consumers no longer needed to buy the product from the record companies. All they needed were the numbers and their hard drives or blank CDs. This development would not have been a problem for the industry as long as there was no efficient way of getting those numbers to the consumer. The development of the personal computer and the Internet, however, made it easy for consumers to download digital information to their home computers and other portable devices.

As we have already seen, the recording industry was thrust into the digital age before it was fully prepared for the consequences. At first, music executives dismissed downloading from the Internet as something only a few geeks would be interested in. Then came Napster, Kazaa, and their progeny, and the business was forever changed. Never had so much music been available to so many for free. All of a sudden, as recording industry expert John Kennedy put it, the recording industry had to figure out a way to make music easier to buy than to steal. Now, with iPod and iTunes and similar devices and services, it

FIGURE 8-1

The Rock-and-Roll
Family Tree, Circa 2004,
Greatly Simplified and
Somewhat Subjective

If you disagree, draw new
arrows and circles.

Recording industry profits slipped steadily from 2000 to 2003. Most experts concede that part of this decrease (some would say most of it) was due to downloading free music. With only a few exceptions, almost everybody in the recording industry considers downloading songs from file-sharing sites such as Kazaa and eDonkey to be stealing (or "pirating" as the industry calls it). On the other hand, with few exceptions, people who download music feel quite the opposite.

In that connection, every semester I ask my students the following question: Would you go to a store and walk out with a CD without paying for it? Aside from a couple of sarcastic replies, almost all students answer in the negative and concede that taking a CD without paying for it is stealing. I next ask them this: Would you download music from the Internet and share it online without paying for it? Almost everybody answers this in the positive. I then ask them what the difference is between the two situations. Their answers reveal a lot of the complexities involved in developing an ethical stance about file-sharing programs.

Their rationales for their behavior generally fall into these broad categories:

- It's okay to download and share music because the record companies have been overcharging us for CDs and have been exploiting performers for years (just listen to Courtney Love), and the companies deserve it. File sharing is a righteous protest, just another way to "stick it to the Man," a philosophy that was popular during the 1960s.

- It's okay to download and share music because on the Internet all information should be free.

- It's okay to download and share music because I only download stuff that I wouldn't buy anyway, so I'm not really hurting anybody.

Let's look in turn at each of these arguments from an ethical point of view.

Taken to its logical extreme, the first argument suggests that it's okay to steal from any individual company that you think charges too much for its goods or services or somehow mistreats its workers. Would you steal a Buick because you think GM has been pricing its cars too high? Even assuming the premise about exploiting performers is correct (and it should be noted that many of these "exploited" performers have a rather impressive lifestyle), is it okay to steal from companies whose conduct you disapprove of? Suppose some clothing company pays its workers in Thailand only a couple of dollars an hour. Should you steal its goods? Would that make it become less exploitive? This sounds like endorsing the policy that two wrongs actually do make a right. One well-known ethical principle is Kant's Categorical Imperative (see Chapter 17), which states that you should act in the same way that you want others to act toward you. If you ran a business, would you want people who decide they disapprove of your business to steal from you?

The argument that "information should be free" is a common one. At its core is the belief in some sort of entitlement to information, that somehow the existence of the Internet means we have a right to share freely the works of others. In the first place, information doesn't simply appear; somebody has to create it. It would seem more reasonable to argue that the individual who created the information (music, movies, or video) should be the one to decide if it's free. If members of a musical group think that free exposure on the Internet will help them charge more for their concert appearances, they should be able to post their music on file-sharing systems. (Many groups have done this.) On the other hand, if a group decides that it wants people to pay to hear its music, it should have that right. This is the notion behind the legal doctrine of intellectual property. Take an example: Suppose you create a clever new video game and share the software with some friends. Suppose further that Microsoft hears about it and offers you a large sum of money to market the game. In the meantime, however suppose one of your friends, a strong believer in the idea that information should be free, posts your game on the Web, and it becomes so popular that Microsoft decides the market is already saturated and withdraws the offer. Shouldn't you have the right to decide what to do with your creation?

The argument about downloading only stuff that otherwise wouldn't be bought raises an interesting question. In the first place, if you share files, other people who might have otherwise bought the record might download it and not buy it. This would seem to hurt those who created the music. Second, your decision not to buy might have been influenced by the presence of the music for free on the Internet. Who's to say that you might have a different attitude toward the music if it weren't freely available on the net? Maybe you would buy it after all.

Putting aside the various legal arguments about downloading, it would appear that all the common arguments justifying downloads from file-sharing systems don't stand up to an ethical analysis. Indeed, now that legal downloading services are available as an alternative, the common rationalizations seem even weaker. Nonetheless, many students appear to be unfazed and continue to download. They apparently don't believe it's stealing.

Why the ethical disconnect between walking out of store without paying for a CD and downloading a CD without paying? Part of the explanation is the gap between action and consequence. Taking a CD from a store has an immediate and clear effect: The retailer loses the money that he or she paid for the CD. There is a visible victim. Downloading music from the amorphous and impersonal Web separates the act from its harmful consequence. There is no apparent victim. The record companies and the artists who are harmed by downloading are removed and abstract. Would downloading be as popular if the downloader had a clear idea about how his or her act directly affected the artist?

appears as if the industry may have found a way to survive the digital revolution.

▲ The Rise of the iPod

More than 100 million iPods had been sold by the beginning of 2007, and more than a billion songs have been downloaded from iTunes. In addition to introducing a new business model, the iPod brought about other changes. First, it created a new cottage industry. More than 200 accessories can be purchased for the iPod, including nylon carrying cases, external speakers, a remote control, and a mechanical iDog musical companion that moves to the beat of the music. Many new cars carry an "aux" outlet that lets drivers plug their iPods into the car's sound system. Second, the iPod had a cultural impact. Many clubs have iPod nights, when customers plug in their iPods to the sound system and become instant DJs. Then there's iPod jacking, whereby two strangers meet, swap earbuds, and listen to each other's music. Next, of course, there are podcasts, prerecorded programs that people download to their devices. Podcasts didn't exist before the iPod became popular. Finally, the iPod gave birth to a whole new radio format. Drawing upon the fact that iPod owners store a wide range of music on their devices, many FM stations switched to a format called "Jack FM" or "Dave FM" that resembled an iPod set to random shuffle, capitalizing on the unpredictability of what would be played next.

▲ The Decline of the CD

The digital revolution has caused a seismic shift in the way consumers buy and store music. Throughout much of recent history, the recording industry sold collections of songs, called *albums*, in a variety of formats: vinyl records, tape cassettes, and plastic CDs. Typically, consumers found that there were only two or three songs per album that they actually liked, but they were still forced to buy the whole collection. The digital revolution put more power in the hand of consumers, who could now buy and download only those songs that they liked. Needless to say, consumers began abandoning the album format.

Sales of CD albums have been slowly declining since 2000. They dropped another 5 percent from 2005 to 2006. The first quarter of 2007 saw an even sharper falloff as the number of CDs sold dropped 20 percent from the same period a year before. Meanwhile, the number of digital downloads increased an impressive 65 percent from 2005 to 2006. It doesn't take a genius to see that the old way of selling music is on the way out. Unfortunately for record companies, the increased revenue from downloading of individual tracks is not enough to make up for the losses from the decrease in CD album sales.

▲ New Products

The recording industry has developed a symbiotic relationship with the cell phone industry. People like to personalize their ring tones, and the recording companies are eager to help them. Individuals can download snippets of songs from several places on the Web to their cell phones, where they play every time a call comes in. Some of these short segments of music can cost about $2.50 (pretty expensive when you consider that a person can download a whole song from iTunes for 99 cents). In 2006 ring tone sales exceeded $600 million, more than double the 2004 figure. This is still a small percentage of the overall total for the recording industry, but indications are it will continue to grow. *Billboard* magazine now includes a chart of the most popular ring tones.

▲ Mobile Music

The Sony Walkman was the first device that enabled consumers to take their recorded music with them. The iPod continues that tradition, but it is not the only device that makes music portable. Cell phone companies such as Sprint and Verizon also offer services whereby consumers can download songs directly to their MP3-equipped phones.

The wireless providers, however, are at a disadvantage when it comes to pricing. Record labels charge phone companies a higher rate than they charge online services, thus making it more expensive to download a song to the phone. There is another concern about the actual method of getting the songs to the phone. With iTunes and similar services, consumers download a song to their computer and then to their mobile device. Downloading a song to a cell phone is done directly—no computer involved. It is unclear how many subscribers would prefer the direct-to-phone downloads. Nonetheless, with hundreds of millions of cell phones in use across the globe, this is one area that both the recording industry and wireless providers are closely studying.

▲ User-Generated Content

Both the recording industry and aspiring performers realize that user-generated content is becoming more important. Fledgling bands and singers produce their own amateur video and audio for social networking sites, such as MySpace, to generate buzz and, if everything goes well, get noticed by a big record label.

Cingular, another important company in the mobile music business, has a revenue-sharing program that lets amateur artists turn their music into ring tones and offer them for sale through their MySpace pages. Recording companies are even releasing unused music and video clips to sites such as YouTube, where individuals can use them as part of their homemade videos.

Recording artists are making use of this content source as well. The Beastie Boys had fans shoot footage for one of their music videos. Janet Jackson let fans design the cover art for a recent album. Rapper Lil Jon and Yahoo! Music sponsored a contest that asked fans to make videos of themselves dancing to one of his songs. The winning entries were edited together and posted on Yahoo! Music, where they were streamed more than 2 million times.

DEFINING FEATURES OF SOUND RECORDING

Sound recording is a cultural force. Its products help characterize social groups and define movements and trends in American society. Recorded music has been at the center of a great deal of cultural and social controversy. Sound recording helped usher in the Jazz Age during the Roaring Twenties. This new style of music was condemned as corrupting the nation's morals. The same criticisms were heard during the 1950s when rock-and-roll music became the rallying point for a new youth culture. During the 1960s recorded music joined the counterculture, and big record companies (benefiting from the status quo) earned huge profits from selling albums that challenged the status quo. In the 1990s rap music recordings introduced the hip-hop culture to the rest of America. All in all, the sound recording industry has played a major role in shaping modern culture.

S O U N D B Y T E

An Ear for Music?

A Japanese firm announced in 2004 that it had developed a CD made from corn.

Sound recording is also an international enterprise, with recording artists selling their music worldwide. For instance, Ricky Martin's eponymous album sold 14 million copies worldwide and 7 million in the United States. Celine Dion's greatest-hits album sold 5 million in the United States and 9 million internationally. Recording artists also tour all around the globe.

The recording business is a unique blend of business and talent. Recording companies are continually searching for new artists and new sounds that will succeed in the marketplace. The singers and musicians may be the stars, but the recording companies are the star makers. Most hit recordings owe much of their success to the marketing and promotion efforts of their record labels.

ORGANIZATION OF THE RECORDING INDUSTRY

The recording industry consists of the various creative talent and business enterprises that originate, produce, and distribute records to consumers. Rock music accounts for more than 50 percent of the total sales of the record industry; country and rhythm and blues account for another 10 percent each; gospel, jazz, and classical make up the rest. Although this chapter concentrates on rock, remember that the other music styles are also part of the industry. For our purposes we will divide the business into four major segments: (1) talent, (2) production, (3) distribution, and (4) retail.

▲ Talent

The talent segment of the industry consists of all the singers, musicians, songwriters, arrangers, and lyricists who hope to make money by recording and selling their songs. The phrase "hope to make money" is important because far more performers are laboring in virtual obscurity in and around Detroit, Seattle, Nashville, New York, and Los Angeles than are cashing royalty checks from their recordings. Exactly how many people are "out there" hoping to make it big is impossible to pinpoint.

Performers start out as a beginning act. The initial motivation may be simply personal pleasure. Many begin performing during high school. For example, Bob Dylan (then known as Bob Zimmerman) started out with a high school band in Hibbing, Minnesota.

In years past the next step for the novice musician or musical group was to form a traveling act that played anywhere and everywhere to gain experience, a little money, and recognition. Weezer, for example, kicked around southern California for several years, playing in places with names such as Club Dump and Bob's Frolic Room before finding commercial success.

Country group Rascal Flatt's album "Me and My Gang" sold more than 4 million copies.

Although some bands and artists still go this route, many others, such as Esmee Denters, turn to the Internet and post videos on YouTube, Facebook, or MySpace. If the act is good (and lucky), it may be noticed by a talent scout or producer from a major recording label (the record companies keep an eye on the Web and regularly check out anybody who has created an Internet "buzz"). If things go well, the act is signed to a recording contract.

▲ Production

The recording company brings the act to a recording studio, where a large number of songs are recorded. Audio engineers and elaborate sound-mixing facilities are used to get exactly the right sound. Eventually, a single or an album is put together. The company also supplies publicity, advertising, merchandising, and packaging expertise. Promotion, which in the recording industry consists primarily of getting the record played on

FIGURE 8-2

Music Distribution
Channels

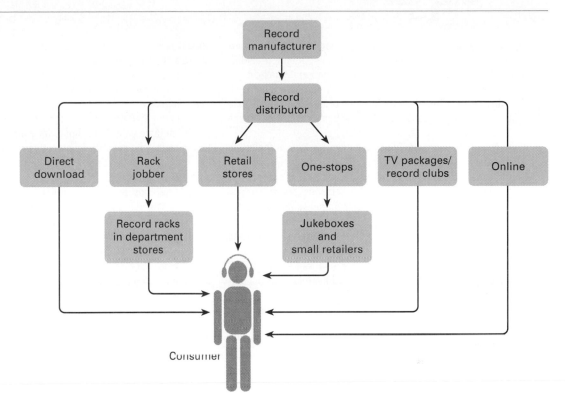

influential radio stations and prominently displayed on iTunes and getting the music video on TV, is also the responsibility of the company. There are dozens of record companies, but a handful dominate the business: Time Warner, Sony BMG, Universal, and EMI.

▲ Distribution

There are six main outlets for music distribution: (1) direct retail, (2) rack jobbers, (3) one-stops, (4) direct consumer sales, (5) online sales, and (6) direct download (see Figure 8-2). Of these six outlets, mass marketers and rack jobbers are most important, accounting for more than 60 percent of all sales.

Direct retail refers to stores that specialize in the sale of CDs, tapes, and related products. Many retail stores are chain operations with several outlets in different parts of the country.

Rack jobbers service the tape and CD racks in variety or large department stores. Wal-Mart and Sears, for example, all have their tape and CD shelves serviced by rack jobbers. The rack jobber chooses the records that are sold in these locations, thus relieving store management of the task of keeping up with the latest Eminem CD and such other tasks as reordering titles and returning unused merchandise.

One-stops purchase records from record companies and resell them to retail stores. For example, a small, independently owned retail store might not qualify for credit from the record companies and so might purchase its records from a one-stop.

TV packagers and record clubs sell directly to the consumer. You have probably seen TV ads for collections of music (*The Best of Heavy Metal, Connie Francis's Greatest Hits, Zamfir and the Pan Flute*). Packagers receive licenses from record manufacturers and use TV advertising to market their products. Record clubs depend more on direct-mail advertising and usually offer an attractive introductory deal ("Six CDs for 99 cents") with the stipulation that consumers buy a certain number of offerings in the next year or so.

Online distribution is direct: The consumer deals directly with an online retailer, such as Amazon.com, and the product is delivered to his or her door.

The mechanics of digital downloading are also relatively simple: A consumer visits one of the many sites that offer downloads for sale, such as iTunes, Napster, eMusic, MSN Music, or Wal-Mart, and selects a single track or album that he or she wishes to download. Most sites now offer a single download for less than a dollar although this price will probably go up. The price to download an album varies depending on how many songs are available to download. Some sites also require a monthly subscription fee. In addition, each site may have certain restrictions on what you can do with the song. Wal-Mart, for example, allows the consumer to download the music to three computers, make 10 burns to a CD, and make unlimited transfers to a portable MP3 player.

▲ Retail

The times are not good for traditional record stores. Competition from online music sites and mass-market stores such as Wal-Mart has made it difficult for many retailers to survive. Wherehouse Music filed for bankruptcy in 2003 followed by Tower Records in 2004. Big retailer HMV closed dozens of stores. Transworld Entertainment (TWE), which operates nearly a thousand FYE, Coconuts, and Strawberries stores, lost millions in 2004. And Tower eventually folded in 2006, as did Musicland.

While the importance of the traditional record stores declined, the importance of mass marketers such as Target and Wal-Mart increased. In 1992, according to the Recording Association of America, 25 percent of all CDs and tapes were purchased at mass merchandise stores. In 2006 that figure rose to 65 percent. Over that same period the percentage sold in traditional record retail stores dropped from 53 to less than 30 percent.

Retailers are aware that if online downloading becomes the preferred way of delivering music to consumers, there will be little need for brick-and-mortar retail stores. Some retailers now stock DVDs, video games, magazines, and electronic equipment as well as gift cards that let people download from iTunes and other sources. In some retail outfits music accounts for less than half of all sales. Moreover, some electronics retailers, including Circuit City and Best Buy, have gotten into the music-downloading business.

OWNERSHIP IN THE RECORDING INDUSTRY

The recording industry is one of the most concentrated of all media industries. As shown in Table 8-1, big companies dominate the business, accounting for more than 85 percent of the market. The four companies that dominate the industry are (1) Universal Music

TABLE 8-1	Company	Major Labels	Top Stars
Top Four Recording Companies, 2007	Universal Music Group	Geffen, Island Def Jam, Motown	U2, Kanye West, Fallout Boy
	Warner Music	Atlantic, Warner Bros., Maverick	James Blunt, Rob Thomas, Madonna
	Sony BMG	Arista, Epic, Jive	Beyonce, Britney Spears, Jessica Simpson
	EMI	Virgin, Capitol, Blue Note	ColdPlay, Keith Urban, KT Tunstall

Group, owned by the French conglomerate Vivendi; (2) Sony BMG, formed in 2004 by a merger between the music divisions of Sony and German conglomerate Bertelsmann; (3) EMI Group, owned by a British firm; and (4) Warner Music, formerly part of the Time Warner empire but now owned by a private investment group.

PRODUCING RECORDS

There are seven departments within a typical recording company:

1. *Artists and Repertoire (A&R):* This department serves as the talent scout for the industry. A&R personnel monitor influential Internet music Web sites and keep an eye on local markets to see who's hot. Once in a while, they might also venture out on the road to check out acts (called *garage bands* in the trade) in the hopes of finding the next superstar.

2. *Sales and Distribution:* As the name suggests, this department sells the company's products and then makes sure the tapes and CDs get to the stores where consumers can buy them.

3. *Advertising and Merchandising:* This division is responsible for planning media ad campaigns and point-of-purchase displays in sales outlets. The efforts of this department are coordinated with those of the promotion department.

4. *Promotion:* This department helps market and promote the company's artists. Although getting a song played on an influential radio station is still an important part of the promotion process, other strategies are effective as well. A song played during a hit TV show (such as the Fray's "How to Save a Life" on *Grey's Anatomy*) can significantly boost sales. Having an Internet presence is also a necessity.

5. *Business:* This department includes lawyers, accountants, market researchers, financial analysts, and secretarial and clerical staffers. It functions in the recording industry the same as in any other business or industry.

6. *Publicity:* This department attempts to get press coverage for new performers and new releases and also has the job of getting new acts and albums reviewed by influential publications such as *Rolling Stone* and *Billboard.*

7. *Artist Development:* The duties of this department include coordinating tour dates, making sure the act has a well-produced concert show, and arranging for TV appearances.

▲ Making a Recording

For a performer or a group to win a recording contract, they first must convince someone in a record company that they have a sound that will sell. Some artists produce a **demo,** a disc that provides a sample of their sound. Others post videos on the Internet and hope that they catch on. Still others bombard the A&R department with e-mails and MP3 attachments or links to music Web sites. These initial efforts don't have to be professional grade, but they do have to highlight the strengths of the performer or group.

If things work out, the performer or group is signed to a contract to produce an album or perhaps just one or two tracks. At that point the act moves into a recording studio to make a master recording.

A sophisticated mixing board such as this one handles as many as 48 separate sound tracks that contain recordings of instruments and vocals. Note the computer monitors. Computer programs remember previous mixing setups, making the process faster and easier.

Resembling something you might see at NASA's mission control center, with banks of modern equipment, blinking lights, and digital readouts, the modern recording studio does multitrack recording. Professional studios have machines capable of recording up to 48 different tracks. This means that different instruments and vocals can be recorded on different sections of a disc. Thus, a piano might be recorded on one track, drums on another, bass on another, lead vocals on another, background vocals on yet another, and so on. So that one track does not leak onto another, the studio is set up with careful placement of microphones and wooden baffles—soundproof barriers that keep the sound of one instrument from spilling over into the mikes recording the other instruments. Once the session starts, the producer makes most of the creative decisions. The producer decides when the performers take a break, when the tune has to be played over because of a bad note, when the music should be played back so the group can hear itself and perhaps make changes in the arrangement, and so on.

The advent of multiple-track recording has revamped the music-making process. Currently, it is not even necessary for band members to record together. The instrumentalists can come in one at a time and "lay down" their tracks, the lead singer or singers can add the vocals later, and everything can be put together at the mixing console.

After the recording session the next step is the mix down, the technically exacting job of mixing down the multiple tracks onto a two-track stereo master. In the mix down each track is equalized; echo, overdubbing, or other special effects are added; and certain passages are scheduled for rerecording. If an album is being produced, each track has to be precisely placed on the stereo spectrum. A track can be placed in the left or right speaker or in the center, where it is heard equally in both speakers. Mixing a 16- or 24-track tape down to 2 tracks can take several days. The job has been made somewhat easier in recent years thanks to computerized mixing boards. After the mix is completed, the master is stored on a disc for possible manufacturing and distribution. At the same time, the promotion department is given a preview of the new release, and the advertising and publicity departments begin their efforts.

THE ECONOMICS OF SOUND RECORDING

We will approach the topic of economics at two levels. First, we will examine the economic structure of the industry as a whole. Next, we will investigate the financial ups and downs of a typical musical group trying to make it in the recording business.

▲ Economic Trends

After enjoying nearly two decades of economic growth, recording industry revenues went into a tailspin that started in 2000 and continued through 2005. Figure 8-3 illustrates the decline. Preliminary reports for 2006 suggested that the decline was continuing. Industry experts are quick to point out that 2000 was the year Napster and other illegal peer-to-peer file-sharing programs became popular.

One bright spot in this gloomy picture was that legal downloading services, such as iTunes, were booming. Consumers purchased more than 580 million digital tracks in 2006,

FIGURE 8-3

Recording Industry
Revenues, 1980–2005

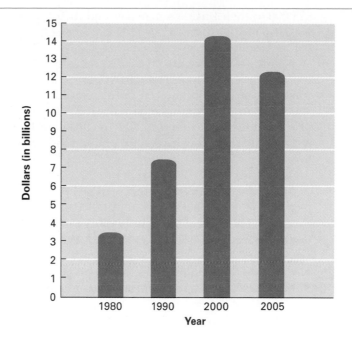

four times as many as in 2004. Nonetheless, downloads accounted for only 11 percent of total industry revenue that year; CD sales made up the rest. The increase in download purchases did not make up for the losses in CD sales. Obviously, the record labels make more money from the sale of a $15 CD than from a 99-cent download.

Table 8-2 shows how the revenue from a $14 CD from a 99-cent digital download is divided.

▲ Rock Performers: The Bottom Line

Most of the people who read this book will not go on to be rock stars. Nonetheless, examining the financial arrangements that surround the production of popular music is useful for all readers as it can tell a lot about the economics of the business.

There are many stories about the fantastic sums of money earned by pop music stars. Some stars do make a lot of money. (R.E.M.'s most recent contract with Time Warner was for $80 million.) Others, however, are not quite so lucky. A new artist or group will receive a royalty rate of about 9–12 percent of the suggested retail price of a CD or cassette. A more established act might negotiate a rate that is a little higher, maybe 15 percent. Really successful performers might get 20 percent or more. Royalty rates on downloads run to about 11 percent. For simplicity, let us say a hypothetical group of four performers is getting a 15 percent royalty rate on CDs and digital album sales and 11 percent on single-track downloads. They also get a $1-million advance from their record company (totally unrealistic for a new group, but this is a best-case scenario). They spend half of the advance to record the album, leaving $500,000. They have to pay $100,000 to their manager and

TABLE 8-2

Where the Recording
Revenue Goes

Source: Based on data
from the Future of Music
Coalition and *Billboard*,
October 29, 2005, p. 14.

Destination	Typical CD ($14 price)	Destination	Downloaded Digital Track (99-cent price)
Record label	$5.04	Record label	$0.50
Retailer	2.52	Artist royalty	0.11
Artist royalty	1.82	Service provider	0.14
Distributor/manufacturer	2.66	Distributor	0.09
Publisher	0.84	Publisher	0.08
Miscellaneous	1.12	Miscellaneous	0.07

$25,000 to their business manager and their lawyer. After $170,000 in taxes, the group has $180,000 to split four ways, or $45,000 a person. And the group has to live on that for a year before the album gets released.

Again, let us take the best-case scenario and say the CD sells 500,000 copies, the digital album is downloaded 200,000 times, and there are a million downloads of single tracks from the album. The group would get about $1 million from sales of the CD, $300,000 from the digital album downloads, and $100,000 from single-track downloads. The band also goes on tour. The record company kicks in $200,000 to cover expenses, recoupable from royalties. A lot of tours lose money, but we'll be optimistic and say this tour makes $100,000 in profit. Total income for the group equals $1.5 million. Sounds good so far.

There are, however, expenses involved. The $1-million advance is recoupable by the record label. The label spends about $300,000 promoting the band; costs are charged against royalties. The record company spends $100,000 making a music video. A typical contract would charge half of that to the band. What's left after about a year of work and all this accounting? No more than $150,000, divided four ways, or $37,500 apiece—before taxes. Not exactly the kind of riches the band was probably dreaming about.

Of course, the band might make a little money from TV appearances, overseas sales, and merchandising. Most artists, however, do not see much money until they have had a couple of back-to-back hits. And even such luck is no guarantee of riches. The group TLC, for example, declared bankruptcy after selling $175 million in CDs.

The truth is that relatively few acts are able to command large sums of money. The riches in the music industry are disproportionately divided, with a small number of artists at the top making most of the money. According to the RIAA, of the 27,000 or so new recordings released every year, only 10 percent are profitable.

FEEDBACK FOR SOUND RECORDING

▲ *Billboard* Charts

Every week disk jockeys, program directors, and record company executives scan the *Billboard* charts, the most important channel of feedback in the sound recording industry (see Figure 8-4).

How is the *Billboard* chart put together? In general, the *Billboard* charts are based on two components: (1) exposure and (2) sales. To measure sales, *Billboard* relies on Nielsen SoundScan, a data-reporting system that keeps track of sales and digital downloads in the United States and Canada. Sales data are collected weekly from about 14,000 retail stores, mass merchandisers, and online outlets.

To measure exposure, *Billboard* uses data from Nielsen Broadcast Data Systems (NBDS). This organization monitors airplay on more than 1,200 radio stations in the United States, Canada, and Puerto Rico that play a variety of formats. NBDS reports that it detects more than 100 million songs every year. For some of its charts—the Hot 100, for example— *Billboard* combines the two measures and winds up with a single index number for each song and rank-orders it accordingly.

Note that another mass medium, radio, plays an important part in the feedback mechanism for sound recording. Radio stations with a music format rely on the *Billboard* charts to determine what songs they should play. Thus, sound recording also functions as a feedback mechanism for radio. This reciprocity is another example of a symbiotic relationship between media (see Chapter 1).

▲ Sound Recording Audiences

Information regarding the audience for sound recording (records, tapes, and CDs) is somewhat difficult to uncover, partially because the recording industry is supported by audience purchases and not by advertising. This means that recording companies concentrate on compiling overall sales figures and that detailed demographic information about the

FIGURE 8-4 Excerpt from a *Billboard* Chart

audience is typically not sought after. True, some record companies have sponsored market research to find out more about their audiences, but the results of these studies are usually not made available to the general public. It has been estimated that more than 90 percent of all households in the country have some means of playing a CD or a downloaded music track. In 2006, this audience bought more than a billion tapes and discs.

In general, those people who have a sound system have paid about $500–800 for their equipment. They listen to discs and downloads about an hour a day.

Record buying is related to age. Older consumers are accounting for more record purchases. In 2006, people over 30 accounted for about 55 percent of the total dollar value spent on prerecorded music, a 25 percent increase from 1988. At the same time, consumer spending by those ages 19 and under declined from 32 percent to 21 percent. The percent of the dollar values of all purchases is currently split about evenly between males and females.

THE RECORDING INDUSTRY

▲ Entry-Level Positions

These are difficult times for the recording industry, and the job outlook for the next few years is not promising. Nevertheless, there are several different career paths for those willing to tolerate a little uncertainty in their future: (1) engineering, (2) creative, and (3) business. We will examine each of these in turn.

Over the past two decades, the technical aspects of sound recording have become tremendously complex. Sometimes it takes two engineers to operate the giant control panel—one to run the machines and the other to do the actual recording. If the engineering side of the industry is of interest to you, you might study at a college that has its own recording studio so that you can become familiar with the equipment. You could also take courses offered by the Recording Institute of America (RIA) in multitrack engineering and sound production.

If your interests lie more in the creative area, and you wish to become a record producer, college courses in mass media, business administration, and music are relevant. You will also need some practical experience in directing a recording session. This can be done by working at a college that has a recording studio or by volunteering your services at a local commercial studio.

If the business side of the profession appeals to you, a college background in business administration and mass media would be most helpful. If you are interested in promotion and sales, you should check whether there is a branch office of a major label or independent distributor located nearby. Your goal should be an entry-level position as a local promotion person or a sales rep in a particular market.

The same advice holds for someone interested in advertising and merchandising. A branch office might be able to start you off at a beginning position from which you can move up to the parent company. Those seeking careers in publicity usually have a college background in journalism or public relations.

It is a little more difficult to provide advice on how to get started in the A&R department. Many A&R people come from the promotion department. Others start off as secretaries or clerks and work their way up within the division. A good ear and a knowledge of what will sell and how to sell it are essential for a career in this area.

▲ Upward Mobility

There are several paths that lead toward advancement in the recording industry. Beginning audio engineers progress to staff engineers and ultimately to senior supervising engineer. Some engineers do cross over and become record producers, but this is rare. Once you have committed yourself to a technical career in the control room, you will generally stay there.

People who start out as producers advance by becoming staff producers with major labels. The next step up would be the position of executive producer. The executive producer in the record business is analogous to the executive producer in motion pictures or TV. Another upward path is to start off with an established label and then go into independent production. Many independent producers go on to form their own labels.

Those who start off in one of the business departments at a recording company advance by moving up the corporate ladder. The most common route to top management has been through either the production or the sales and distribution department.

MAIN POINTS

- Thomas Edison pioneered the development of the phonograph, which was first used as a device to record voice. Emile Berliner perfected the modern technique of recording music in a spiral pattern on a disk. By the end of World War I, record players were found in most American homes.

- The coming of radio and the Depression hurt the development of the recording industry, but the business was able to survive because of the popularity of jukeboxes.

- After World War II the industry grew quickly because of the development of magnetic tape recording and the LP record and, most of all, because radio stations began to play recorded music as part of their formats.

- Rock-and-roll music helped spur record sales and made young people an important part of the market for recorded music.

- File-sharing software and legal digital downloading may transform the basic way the music industry conducts business.

- There are four segments in the recording industry: talent, production, distribution, and retail.

- Four big companies dominate the record business.

- *Billboard* magazine's charts are the most important form of audience feedback for the industry.

- After several years of growth, the recording industry's revenue has declined, due in part to file sharing on the Internet.

QUESTIONS FOR REVIEW

1. Trace the various media that have been used to record sound, from Edison's time to the present.

2. How do legal downloading sites such as iTunes work? Why are they examples of disintermediation?

3. Trace the distribution arrangement in the sound recording business. How many of the distribution channels have you personally used?

4. If the chance of financial success is so small, why do so many people still try to make it in the recording industry?

QUESTIONS FOR CRITICAL THINKING

1. Why did it take the recording industry so long to figure out that radio airplay helped record sales? Will the same be true with file sharing?

2. What are the implications of large corporate ownership in the record business? Are big companies less likely to promote new acts and risky musical styles?

3. What are the ethical implications of downloading and sharing music from services? If you have ever downloaded music, did you feel guilty doing it? Why or why not?

4. What will be the future of the retail record store in the digital era? If you can download music directly to your computer, why go to a store? Do people go to record stores for purposes other than simply buying an album?

KEY TERMS

phonograph (p. 176)
graphophone (p. 176)
gramophone (p. 176)
nickelodeons (p. 176)

jazz (p. 177)
heavy metal (p. 181)
rack jobbers (p. 189)
one-stops (p. 189)

demo (p. 191)
Billboard (p. 194)

INTERNET RESOURCES

Online Learning Center

At the Online Learning Center home page, www.mhhe.com/dominick10, *select* Student Center *and then* Chapter 8.

1. Use the Learning Objectives, Chapter Outline, Main Points, and Time Line sections to review this chapter.

2. Test your knowledge of the chapter using the multiple choice, crossword puzzle, and flashcard features of the site.

3. Expand your knowledge of concepts and topics discussed in the chapter by going to Suggestions for Further Reading and Internet Exercises.

Surfing the Internet

Web sites for the recording industry are just as evanescent as the industry itself. The following were current as this book went to press.

http://kunaki.com
Want to make and market your own CD? Here's a Web site that will help you.

www.billboard.com
Billboard magazine's online version. Contains the latest news about the industry plus recent charts.

www.sonybmg.com
Home page of Sony BMG. Lists all top artists and has links to the company's various labels.

www.apple.com/itunes
If you don't already know how it works, check out the home of Apple's iTunes Music Store.

www.riaa.org
Site of the Recording Industry Association of America. Contains industry data, the latest news, and legal information.

CHAPTER 9

MOTION PICTURES

This chapter will prepare you to:

- explain how the motion picture industry developed

- describe how the studios dominated the industry

- discuss how television affected the film industry and its audience

- understand the implications that digital moviemaking holds for the industry

- explain how the digital age is affecting film

- describe the components of the movie industry and how a motion picture is produced

Apple TV's slogan: "If it's on iTunes, it's on your wide screen TV."

Will history repeat itself? Apple's iPod caused a seismic shift in the music industry. Will Apple do the same to the motion picture industry? In 2007 the company introduced a device that has the potential of becoming an integral part of the evolving digital household: **Apple TV.** Experts have been predicting for years that the computer and TV will eventually converge, but so far that has been slow to happen. Apple TV may speed up the process. To oversimplify, Apple TV wirelessly streams content from a computer to a television set. The device is about 8 inches square and weighs only a couple of pounds, but it contains a 40-GB hard drive that can store up to 50 hours of video, 9,000 songs, 25,000 photos, or a combination of each and is capable of delivering high-definition TV. Used in connection with Apple's iTunes, this means that consumers can download movies to their computer and then enjoy watching them on their big-screen, HD TVs. The advantages for movie fans are obvious—no more driving to the video store or waiting for a movie to arrive by mail. Simply download it from iTunes to your computer and watch it on your TV.

Apple TV is not without problems. It only works with movies available on iTunes. The picture quality leaves something to be desired, and the technology may not work with older TVs. Even so, movie executives are carefully considering what impact devices such as Apple TV will have on their industry.

The motion picture business has always been characterized by risk and uncertainty. The digital revolution promises to raise the uncertainty level even further. This chapter takes a look at the history, structure, and economics of the movie business as Hollywood prepares for the future.

A BRIEF HISTORY

Motion pictures and television are possible because of two quirks of the human perceptual system: the phi phenomenon and persistence of vision. The **phi phenomenon** refers to what happens when we see one light source go out while another one close to the original is illuminated. To our eyes it looks like the light moves from one place to another. In **persistence of vision,** our eyes continue to see an image for a split second after the image has disappeared from view. In the early 19th century, a host of toys that depended on this principle were created in Europe. Bearing fanciful names (the Thaumatrope, the Praxinoscope), these devices made a series of hand-drawn pictures appear to move.

▲ Early American Cinema

The Edison Lab   Before long, some key inventors realized that a series of still photographs on celluloid film could be used with these devices instead of hand drawings. In 1878 a colorful Englishman (later turned American), Edward Muybridge, attempted to settle a $25,000 bet over whether the four feet of a galloping horse ever simultaneously left the ground. He arranged a series of 24 cameras alongside a racetrack to photograph a running horse. Rapidly viewing the series of pictures produced an effect much like that of a motion picture. Muybridge's technique not only settled the bet (the feet did leave the ground simultaneously in certain instances) but also demonstrated, in a backward way, the idea behind motion picture photography. Instead of 24 cameras taking one picture each, what was needed was one camera that would take 24 pictures in rapid order. It was Thomas Edison and his assistant, William Dickson, who finally developed what might have been the first practical motion picture camera and viewing device. Using flexible film, Dickson solved the vexing problem of how to move the film rapidly through the camera by perforating its edge with tiny holes and pulling it along by means of sprockets. In 1889 Dickson perfected a machine called the **Kinetoscope** and even starred in a brief film demonstrating how it worked.

These early efforts in the Edison lab were not directed at projecting movies to large crowds. Edison thought the device could make money by showing brief films to one person at a time for a penny a look. He built a special studio to produce films for this new invention, and by 1894 Kinetoscope parlors were springing up in major cities. However, the long-range commercial potential of this invention was lost on Edison. He reasoned

An early version of the Praxinoscope. Later models would be able to project a moving image onto a large screen for many people to view at once.

Media Probe   Birth of a Controversy

D. W. Griffith's *Birth of a Nation* was made to commemorate the 50th anniversary of the end of the Civil War. The film was based on a novel titled *The Clansman*. In 1906 a stage play based on the novel had caused disturbances in Philadelphia when it opened, but Griffith chose to go ahead with his plans to turn the work into a movie.

The story paints the prewar South as a happy and idyllic place whose serenity is disrupted by the war. At the war's conclusion, Southern whites are shown being victimized by renegade African Americans, northern carpetbaggers, and corrupt politicians. In response whites form the Ku Klux Klan, which exacts vengeance on black people and restores the prewar utopia.

The NAACP objected to the film when it opened on the West Coast. About 40,000 African Americans demonstrated in California. In response the San Francisco city censor (several big cities had film censorship boards in this era) ordered a couple of the film's more controversial scenes cut out. A delegation called on the mayor of New York City to stop the premiere but was rebuffed. When the movie opened in Boston, several brawls broke out outside the theater. Unrest was averted in Chicago when the mayor agreed to seat a black man on the city's film censorship board. Griffith, for his part, never understood the feelings of black people toward the film. He responded to these actions by issuing a pamphlet about free speech.

Birth of a Nation is rarely screened today. Modern audiences find the racial depictions unacceptable. The film is remembered not so much for its content as for its technical achievements and because it served notice that motion pictures could exert a political and social force.

that the real money would be made by selling his peep-show machine. If a large number of people were shown the film at the same time, fewer machines would be needed, so he was not interested in adapting the machine for larger audiences.

Developments in Europe proved Edison wrong as inventors there devised large-screen projection devices. Faced with competition, Edison perfected a projector called the *Vitascope* and unveiled it in New York City in 1896.

Early movies were simple snippets of action—acrobats tumbling, horses running, jugglers juggling, and so on. Eventually, the novelty wore off, and films became less of an attraction.

The Nickelodeons   Public interest was soon rekindled when early filmmakers discovered that movies could be used to tell a story. In France, Alice Guy Blache produced *The Cabbage Fairy,* a 1-minute film about a fairy who produces children in a cabbage patch, and exhibited it at the Paris International Exhibition in 1886. Blache went on to found her own studio in America. Better known is the work of a fellow French filmmaker and magician, Georges Méliès. In 1902 Méliès produced a science fiction film that was the great-great-grandfather of *Star Wars* and *Star Trek;* it was called *A Trip to the Moon.* Méliès, however, did not fully explore the storytelling freedom afforded by film. His films were basically extravagant stage plays photographed by a stationary camera. It was an American, Edwin S. Porter, who in his *Great Train Robbery* first discovered the artistic potential of editing and camera placement. This and other new narrative films were extraordinarily popular with audiences and proved to be financially successful. Almost overnight, 50- to 90-seat theaters, called *nickelettes* or *nickelodeons* because of the 5-cent admission price, sprang up in converted stores throughout the nation.

Nickelodeons depended on audience turnover for their profits. Keeping the audience returning required that films be changed often—sometimes daily—to attract repeat customers. This policy created a tremendous demand for motion pictures, and new production companies were quickly formed. (In these early days films were regarded as just another mass-produced product; hence, early film studios were called *film factories*.) New York and New Jersey served as the bases for these early film companies.

Adolph Zukor and D. W. Griffith   Adolph Zukor decided to copy European filmmakers who were making longer, more expensive films aimed at a middle-class audience. He acquired the four-reel French film *Queen Elizabeth,* starring Sarah Bernhardt, the most famous actress

United Artists (UA) was founded in 1919 by actors Charlie Chaplin, Mary Pickford, and Douglas Fairbanks and director D. W. Griffith. It soon became, as proclaimed by its original slogan, "The company built by the stars," the first movie studio to be owned by the people who actually made the movies. Throughout its early history UA was known for the broad artistic freedom it gave to its filmmakers. Big-name producers such as Howard Hughes, Samuel Goldwyn, Walt Disney, and Darryl Zanuck were just some of the talented people who made films for UA during the 1930s, 1940s, and 1950s.

UA went public in 1957, and 10 years later the company built by the stars became another part of corporate America when UA was purchased by the Transamerica financial services conglomerate. Over the next 12 years UA had some of its biggest successes with films such as *Rocky, One Flew over the Cuckoos Nest,* and *Annie Hall.* In 1980, however, UA bet nearly $50 million on a lavish Western called *Heaven's Gate.* The film tanked and left the company short on cash. Less than a year later, UA was acquired by the film studio MGM.

Over the next 25 years UA drastically cut its film production, releasing only a few films a year. It scored the occasional hit, such as *Rainman* in 1988 and *Capote* in 2005. Nonetheless, the company was still just a shadow of its former self and underwent a number of different owners as parent MGM was bought and sold several times.

In late 2006, however, actor Tom Cruise and his business partner, Paula Wagner, announced that they had become partial owners of a resurrected UA. The new deal allows Cruise and Wagner to make at least four movies a year at an average budget of $50 million, relatively modest by Hollywood standards. In fact, it's doubtful if the new UA can even afford to make a film with Cruise in it. His 2006 film *Mission Impossible III* cost more than $150 million.

Whether the new UA will be successful is still an open question. Nevertheless, once again, UA is a company owned (at least in part) by people who actually make movies.

of the period, and distributed it in the United States at the then-exorbitant price of a dollar a ticket. His experiment was successful, proving that American audiences would pay more and sit still for longer films. Nevertheless, *Queen Elizabeth* remained essentially the filming of a stage play.

It was an American, D. W. Griffith, who eventually took full advantage of the film medium and established film as its own art form. Although controversial and racist in its depictions (see the boxed insert, "Birth of a Controversy"), his brilliant Civil War drama, *Birth of a Nation,* was released in 1915 and became the most expensive American film produced to that date ($110,000). The 3-hour movie, which was shot without a script, introduced history as a film topic. Griffith went on to top *Nation*'s figures with an even bigger epic, *Intolerance,* a piece comprising of four scenarios dealing with life's injustices. The movie was completed in 1916 at a cost of about $2 million (the same film made in the 2000s would easily cost $90–110 million).

In response to the controversy generated by *Birth of a Nation,* two African American brothers, George and Noble Johnson, made films that presented a more realistic and accurate view of African Americans. The first of these, *The Realization of a Negro's Ambition,* demonstrated that there was an African American audience that would support films that spoke to their community. The Johnsons' company, Lincoln Motion Pictures, stayed in operation until the early 1920s, when a lack of capital and an inability to secure bookings at white theaters forced it out of business.

Birth of the MPPC   Events in moviemaking during the decade of 1908–1918 had far-reaching effects on the future shape of the film industry. As the basic economic structure of the film industry developed, the center of filmmaking moved to the West Coast, and independent film producers, having survived attempts by the major studios to stamp them out, became an important force in the industry. The tremendous demand for new pictures brought enormous competition into the field. Small film companies cut corners by using bootlegged equipment (for which they paid no royalty fees) and started making films. Competition quickly reached the cutthroat level; lawsuits were filed with alarming frequency. In an effort to bring order to the business (and to cut down on legal expenses), the leading manufacturers of films and film equipment banded together, pooled their patents, and formed the **Motion Picture Patents Company (MPPC)** to restrict moviemaking to the nine companies that made up the MPPC. Film exhibitors were brought into line by a

$2-per-week tax, which entitled the theaters to use projection equipment patented by the MPPC. Failure to pay this tax meant that the theater owners would no longer be supplied with MPPC-approved films. Eventually, to accommodate the growing industry, a new role, that of film distributor, was created. The film distributor served the function of a wholesaler, acquiring films from the manufacturers and renting them to exhibitors. This three-level structure—production, distribution, and exhibition—is still with us today. The MPPC was quick to take control of film distribution as well.

Instead of squelching competition, the MPPC actually fueled it. Annoyed by the repressive regulations, independent producers began offering films to exhibitors at cheaper rates than MPPC members. Full-length feature films, several reels in length, were imported from Europe. In response the MPPC declared war. "Outlaw" studios were raided and equipment smashed. In an effort to escape the harassment of the MPPC, independent producers fled New York and New Jersey. They were looking for a location with good weather, interesting geography, low business costs, and proximity to a national border so that the independents could avoid the MPPC's subpoenas. Florida proved to be too humid; Cuba was too inconvenient; Texas was too flat. Finally, they found the perfect environment—a rather sleepy suburb of Los Angeles called Hollywood. By 1913 this new home had so encouraged independent filmmaking that the MPPC could no longer contain its growth. And so, by 1917, for all practical purposes, the patents organization had lost its power.

The Star System   The aura of glamour surrounding Hollywood and its stars might not have emerged if the MPPC had not been so stubborn. Whereas the patents company refused to publicize its performers, the independents quickly recognized that fan interest in film actors and actresses could be used to draw crowds away from the movies offered by the MPPC. Carl Laemmle, an independent producer, shrewdly publicized one of his actresses with a poetic name—Florence Lawrence—until she became what we might call the first movie star. As Florence's fame grew, her pictures brought in more money, spurring other independents to create their own stars to keep pace. The two artists who best exemplified the growth of the star system were Mary Pickford and Charlie Chaplin. In 1913 Chaplin was working in movies for $150 a week, a good salary in those days. Just 4 years later he was paid a million dollars for making eight pictures. Mary Pickford, nicknamed "America's Sweetheart," was paid $1,000 per week in 1913. By 1918 she was making $15,000–20,000 per week in addition to earning a cut of up to 50 percent of her films' profits.

In 1919 the star system reached its natural conclusion. Both Chaplin and Pickford joined with other actors and filmmakers to start their own production company—United Artists. The employees now owned the shop. (See the boxed insert "History Repeating Itself?" for an update on UA.)

The star system had other, subtler effects. Once stars became popular, the public demanded to see them in longer movies. However, feature-length films that ran 1–2 hours were more expensive to make. Further, audiences could not be expected to sit for several hours on the wooden benches found in many of the nickelodeons. A need had been created for large, comfortable theaters that could accommodate thousands of patrons and, at the same time, justify higher admission costs. In 1914 the Strand opened in New York. With seats for more than 3,000 people, it occupied a whole city block and had space for an entire symphony orchestra. On the West Coast, Sid Grauman opened his Egyptian Theater (across from the Chinese Theater) in 1922 at a cost of almost a million dollars. His ushers were dressed in Cleopatra costumes. Clearly, the nickel was no longer the symbol of the movies.

Consolidation and Growth   The increased cost of filmmaking made it imperative for producers to make sure that a company's movies were booked into enough big, new theaters to turn a profit. Under this economic pressure the film industry moved in the direction of consolidation. Adolph Zukor, whose company would ultimately become Paramount Pictures, combined the production and distribution functions into one corporate structure.

Charlie Chaplin, one of the first movie superstars created by the Hollywood star system, delighted film audiences throughout the world. This scene is from one of his earlier works, a 1916 short called *One A.M.*

Paramount and its chief rival, Fox, began building their own theaters, and Marcus Loew, owner of a large chain of theaters, purchased his own studio (later to become MGM). Studio owners could exert control over independent exhibitors through another policy known as **block booking.** To receive two or three topflight films from a studio, the theater owner had to agree to show five or six other films of lower quality. Although this policy was not very advantageous to exhibitors, it assured the production companies of steady revenue for their films.

All this was taking place as World War I devastated Europe. When the war ended in 1918, the American film industry was the dominant film force in the world, accounting for upwards of 80 percent of the worldwide market. By the beginning of the 1920s, the major production companies were comfortable and prosperous and enjoyed as firm a lock on the film business as had the old MPPC, which they had replaced only a few years earlier.

▲ The Roaring Twenties

The prosperity boom that followed the war exploded in Hollywood with more force than in other business sectors. Profits were up, and extravagance was the watchword as filmmakers endorsed the principle that the only way to make money was to spend money. Between 1914 and 1924, the cost of a feature film increased 1,500 percent. Salaries, sets, costumes, props, and rights to best-sellers all contributed to the mushrooming costs. Even the lawyer for United Artists was paid $100,000 a year. By 1927 the average film cost about $200,000, and many films easily topped that. *Ben Hur* (1925) was made for a reported $6 million.

Huge salaries created a boomtown atmosphere in Hollywood, and many people—some still quite young—were unprepared to deal with the temptations that came with sudden wealth. Before long, newspapers were reporting stories about orgiastic parties, prostitution, studio call girls, bootleg whiskey, and drugs. Hollywood was dubbed "Sin City." In 1922, within a few short months, comedian Fatty Arbuckle was involved in a rape case, two female stars were implicated in the murder of a prominent director, and popular actor Wallace Reid died while trying to kick his drug addiction. Public reaction to these revelations was predictable: indignation and outrage. By the end of the

Al Jolson in *The Jazz Singer*. This film convinced the industry that audiences wanted to see "talkies," or films with sound, thus ushering in a new era in Hollywood.

year, politicians in 36 states had introduced bills to set up censorship boards for films. The motion picture companies hired a well-respected former postmaster general, Will Hays, to head a new self-regulatory body for the industry. Called the Motion Picture Producers and Distributors Association, this organization was successful in heading off government control, and the basic standards it laid down would be in force for almost four decades.

▲ The Coming of Sound: The Late 1920s

Since optical recording of sound on film had been feasible since 1918, why did Hollywood wait until the late 1920s to introduce sound films? Money.

Business was good during the 1920s, and the major studios did not want to get into costly experimentation with new techniques. Warner Brothers, however, was not as financially sound as the other studios. Since Warner did not own movie theaters in the big cities and could not exhibit all its pictures in the most lucrative markets, the company was willing to try anything to get its films into theaters. In 1927 Warner released *The Jazz Singer*, in which Al Jolson not only sang but spoke from the screen. Within 2 years the silent film, for all practical purposes, was dead.

The novelty of sound gave a boost to the film industry, despite the devastating economic effects of the Depression. In 1929 average weekly movie attendance was 80 million; by 1930 it had reached 90 million—a fact that led many to regard filmmaking as a Depression-proof industry. They were quickly proved wrong as attendance dropped in 1931 and again in 1932. The industry generated several innovations to attract audiences. *Becky Sharp* was filmed in the new Technicolor process in 1935. Theaters also began the practice of showing double features, two feature films on the same bill. Animated cartoons began to draw sizable audiences. All this new activity called for Hollywood to produce even more films—almost 400 per year during the 1930s—to meet the demands of the market. This high production volume was a boon to major studios since they could churn out larger numbers of films more economically. Moreover, the tremendous amount of money needed to convert to sound and the poor financial conditions created by the Depression forced many small companies out of business, leaving eight major studios with a lock on the industry.

▲ The Studio Years: 1930–1950

The 20 years from 1930 to 1950 were the studio years, with MGM, 20th Century Fox, RKO, Warner Brothers, Paramount, Universal, Columbia, and United Artists dominating the industry. These studios created hundreds of acres of back-lot movie sets, constructed elaborate soundstages, and built up showy stables of creative talent, carefully groomed for stardom. Audiences adored and emulated their favorite screen idols, who were presented as larger-than-life gods and goddesses inhabiting a glamorous fantasyland.

Individual studios left their imprint on the films of the period as each studio's products took on a distinct personality. For example, during this period Warner Brothers became best known for its gangster films, 20th Century Fox for its historical and adventure films, and MGM for its lavish, star-studded musicals.

Orson Welles in a scene from the 1941 film *Citizen Kane*. Welles was 25 when he directed, produced, and starred in this film, considered by many critics the best American movie ever made.

The most significant period for motion picture achievement were the years from 1939 to 1941. *Gone with the Wind,* which showcased the new Technicolor film process, was released in 1939. In that same year two other soon-to-become-classics, *The Wizard of Oz* and *Stagecoach* (starring John Wayne in his first major role), were released. Just 2 years later, Orson Welles directed and starred in *Citizen Kane,* which some critics consider the best American film ever made.

The financial backing and diverse holdings of the studio system helped the film industry survive the Depression. Attendance and profits began climbing in 1934 and held steady throughout World War II. During the 1940s going to a movie was just as much a part of American life as watching television is today. In fact, the all-time peak for filmgoing was 1946, when average weekly attendance reached over 90 million. By 1948, however, all this was to change.

Back in 1938, the Justice Department had filed suit against Paramount and the other major film companies, charging that the industry's vertical control of production, distribution, and exhibition constituted restraint of trade and monopolistic practices. The case had been set aside during the war, but by 1948 the courts had ordered the major studios to get rid of at least one of their holdings in these three areas. Most chose to divest themselves of their theater chains. The court also eliminated the block booking system and thus deprived the studios of guaranteed exhibition for all their films. As a result the studios had to cut back on film production and reduce costs.

▲ The Reaction of the Film Industry to TV

When television began building a sizable audience during the late 1940s, it cut into the motion picture industry's profits. The first reaction of the film industry was to fight back. Studios stubbornly refused to advertise their films on TV, and they would not release old films for showing on the newer medium. Many studios wrote clauses into the contracts of their major stars forbidding them to appear on TV. None of their efforts had an appreciable

One of the problems with 3-D movies was the uncomfortable plastic glasses that audience members had to wear to appreciate the three-dimensional effects.

effect on television's growing popularity; more and more Americans bought TV sets, while film attendance slipped.

Hollywood looked for ways to recapture some of its audience from TV. By the early 1950s the film industry thought it had found the answer—technical wizardry. The first technical gimmick was 3-D (three-dimensional film). The audience wore special polarized glasses to perceive the effect and were treated to the illusion of spears, trains, arrows, knives, birds, and even Jane Russell jumping out at them from the film screen. Unfortunately, the glasses gave some people headaches, and the equipment was too expensive for most theater owners to install, and audiences quickly became bored with the novelty. It was soon apparent that 3-D was not the answer. The second technical gimmick concerned screen size. Cinerama, which involved the use of three projectors and curved screens, surrounded the audience with film. Less expensive techniques that enlarged screen size, such as Cinemascope, Panavision, and Vistavision, were ultimately adopted by the industry but did little to stem Hollywood's loss of money.

The attitude of the movie companies toward TV during those early years was a clear example of shortsightedness. What the film companies failed to see was that they could have played a dominant role in TV's evolution. Because the major networks were not eager to supply early TV shows, film companies would have been logical sources for programming. Somewhat belatedly, Hollywood recognized that it was in its best interest to cooperate with television. In the late 1950s the studios began to release their pre-1948 films to TV and to supply programs to the networks. In 1960 post-1948 theatrical films were made available to the smaller TV screens.

By the 1950s, when it became clear that TV would be a formidable competitor, the film industry cast about for new ways to draw audiences back to the theaters. It tried big-budget, spectacle movies, such as *Cleopatra,* as well as films that addressed more adult subjects, such as adultery and homosexuality, that could not be shown on TV.

▲ Realignments: The Film Industry from 1960 to 1990

The 1960s were marked by the waning power of the major studios and by a closer affiliation with their old competitor, television. The continued rise of the independent producer led to a concomitant loss of power by the studios. As major production houses cut back operations, they released many actors, writers, and directors who, naturally enough, formed small, independent production companies. Using the big studios for financing and distribution, these independents and the artists they employed frequently took small salaries in exchange for a percentage of a film's profits. By the mid-1960s roughly 80 percent of all American films were independent productions.

The poor economic climate brought about other changes. Large studios, faced with ever-worsening financial conditions, were absorbed by larger conglomerates. In the early

1970s both the MGM and 20th Century Fox studios were sold to make room for real estate developers.

The late 1960s also saw a change in the regulatory climate that surrounded films. The Supreme Court issued several decisions that loosened controls on content, and filmmakers were quick to take advantage of their new freedom. In 1968 the Motion Picture Association of America (MPAA) liberalized its attitudes toward self-regulation. Whereas the old production code attempted to regulate content, the new system attempted to regulate audiences by instituting a G-PG-R-X labeling system.

The relationship between film and television became even closer in the 1960s, as movies made expressly for TV appeared in the middle of the decade. In 1974 about 180 of these TV movies were shown on network television. In that same year the major film companies distributed only 109 films to theaters.

Film history from 1970 to 1990 was marked by several trends: Revenue went up, as did the budgets of many feature films, and several motion pictures racked up astonishing gross receipts. Foremost among the trends was a reversal of the slump in box office receipts that began in 1946 and finally bottomed out in 1971. With the exception of temporary declines in 1973 and 1976, the general trend has been upward. In 1977 the total box office gross came to about $2.4 billion; by 1981 it had risen to nearly $3 billion, although some of this increase could be attributed to inflation.

With more cash flowing into the box office, more money became available for the budgets of feature films. In fact, films of the late 1970s and early 1980s were reminiscent of the extravaganzas of the 1920s. Perhaps the most interesting film phenomenon of the era was the rise of the blockbuster. From 1900 to 1970 only two films (*The Sound of Music* and *Gone with the Wind*) managed to surpass $50 million in film rentals; between 1970 and 1980, 17 films exceeded this mark (see Table 9-1).

TABLE 9-1

All-Time Box Office Leaders, 2006

The figures are based on film rentals, that is, the money received by film distributors from motion picture theaters. This figure is not the same as box office receipts, nor does it include DVD or videocassette rentals and sales. The table includes only data from the United States and Canada.

Rank	Title	Year	Rental Income (millions)
1	*Titanic*	1997	$601
2	*Star Wars*	1977	461
3	*Shrek 2*	2004	441
4	*E.T.*	1982	435
5	*Star Wars—Phantom Menace*	1999	432
6	*Pirates of the Caribbean—Dead Man's Chest*	2006	423
7	*Spider-Man*	2002	404
8	*Star Wars—Revenge of the Sith*	2005	380
9	*Lord of the Rings—Return of the King*	2003	377
10	*Spider-Man 2*	2004	374

In 1999 *The Blair Witch Project,* a low-budget, independently produced horror/suspense movie starring unknowns, surprised Hollywood by racking up $140 million in box office sales. The movie's success was attributed in large part to a marketing campaign that used the then relatively new Internet to generate interest (or "buzz," as it's known in the trade) about the film. *The Blair Witch Project* skillfully used online sites to make people wonder if the movie was actually a true story. By the time the movie appeared, it had a ready-made audience waiting to see it.

Hollywood executives thought that this new form of online promotion would revolutionize movie marketing. Generate a strong buzz on the Internet, and the studio's marketing job would be done for them. The Internet was a new path to movie profits.

In the post-*Witch* years the Internet proved to be a valuable, if not revolutionary, marketing tool for motion pictures. But nothing ever approached the *Blair Witch* phenomenon—nothing, that is, until the 2006 thriller *Snakes on a Plane* (or *SoaP,* as it was quickly dubbed by its online fans).

Once news got out that New Line Cinema was interested in making a movie with *SoaP*'s wonderfully succinct and evocative title, the Internet community responded with an enthusiasm not seen since *Blair Witch*. Bloggers and other movie fans created slogans, designed T-shirts, created parodies, and even suggested dialogue for the finished film (some online suggestions for dialogue were, in fact, written into the film). With anticipation this high, how could *SoaP* not be a blockbuster?

Well, it wasn't. The film opened with a disappointing take of $15.2 million, far from blockbuster status. After 3 weeks *SoaP* had made only a little more than $30 million worldwide and was well on its way to slithering into the video store where, it was hoped, it would do better. (The production/distribution/marketing costs of the film were probably around $50 million, meaning *SoaP* might eventually turn a profit, but it will be far less than *Blair Witch*.)

How come *Blair Witch* was so successful while *SoaP* flopped? Analysts suggested several reasons. First, the Internet was just gaining popularity in 1999, and for most it was still a novelty. Seven years later, audiences were aware that marketers were using the net as a promotional tool and so may have been more likely to be skeptical of the latest hype. Second, by the time the film came out, perhaps people had had their fill of all of the hoopla. Or perhaps the Internet-savvy crowd who originally touted the film simply downloaded it from BitTorrent or some other site and avoided the theater altogether.

Whatever the reason, Hollywood still can't figure out the Internet. Maybe it's not the great marketing tool that everybody thought it was.

On another front, in 1985 the MPAA instituted a new rating category—PG-13. This category was designed for those films for which parental guidance for children under 13 was recommended. Yet another new category, NC-17, replaced the X rating in 1990.

▲ Contemporary Trends

Piracy and illegal file sharing are nagging problems for the motion picture industry. Making and selling bootlegged copies of movies on DVDs is a global phenomenon. A recent raid in China, for instance, turned up about 1.6 million illegal copies of movies. For the entire year of 2006, law enforcement authorities seized about 81 million counterfeit DVDs.

Moreover, movie executives fear that movies will be traded on the Internet the same way that music files were illegally shared on the original Napster. A bootlegged copy of *Star Wars: Episode III—Revenge of the Sith,* for example, was posted on a file-sharing site only hours after it opened in theaters. Hollywood originally thought that they were safe from this problem because movie files are huge and have long download times. Regrettably for the industry, a new file-sharing program, BitTorrent, speeds up the process and allows individuals to swap big files, such as movies. Hollywood responded to this development much like the recording industry, bringing lawsuits against Web sites that featured the BitTorrent program.

The magnitude of the piracy problem was demonstrated by a study sponsored by the MPAA that calculated movie industry losses to pirates of more than $6 billion in 2005. About 60 percent of that loss was due to pirated DVDs. A visit to the home page of the MPAA reveals that much of it is devoted to catching "movie thieves."

On the financial front box office revenue declined a bit from 2004 to 2005 but bounced back in 2006 to nearly $9.5 billion. On the downside movie admissions continued to decline, down about 6 percent from 2004 to 2006. The increase in revenue has come from higher individual ticket prices. Although the box office is important, sales and rentals of DVDs have become the chief sources of Hollywood's revenue.

The motion picture industry remains dominated by six big companies: Sony/MGM, NBC Universal, Disney, Fox, Warner Brothers, and Paramount. These firms both produce and distribute motion pictures and typically control about 80 percent of the market.

Modern film content continues to be highly varied. The box office champ in 2006 was a film based loosely on an amusement park ride, *Pirates of the Caribbean—Dead Man's Chest*, which took in more than $400 million in the United States. Animated films were also popular. *Cars, Happy Feet,* and *Ice Age: The Meltdown* all ranked in the top 10 at the 2006 box office.

MOTION PICTURES IN THE DIGITAL AGE

The digital revolution is affecting the production, distribution, and exhibition of motion pictures.

▲ Making Digital Movies

Digital moviemaking is already a reality. Many big-budget motion pictures, such as *Superman Returns* and *Miami Vice*, were shot with digital cameras. In *300* only the actors were real; the backgrounds, sets, and locations were all digital creations. In fact, most of the special effects that Hollywood uses are generated digitally.

▲ Digital Distribution to Theaters

Under the current system hundreds of copies of a celluloid film are printed, put into big metal cans, and shipped to theaters across the country. Each of these copies can cost as much $2,000.

Digital distribution is much cheaper. Movies can be sent on disc or electronically by satellite or optical fiber or even the Internet. Along with cutting costs, digital distribution eliminates the scratches, dust, and "gate jitter" that often occur with traditional celluloid film.

The biggest problem with moving to such a system is that most movie theaters are not yet equipped to handle digital distribution or projection. Converting theaters to the new technology will require a significant financial commitment.

▲ Digital Distribution to the Home

Apple TV, as mentioned at the beginning of the chapter, is just one of several methods that capitalizes on digital delivery to the home. AOL, MovieLink, iTunes, and Amazon.com, among others, offer consumers the chance to download movies to their home computers. MovieLink, for example, offers movies for sale for about $15 for new releases and about $10 for older films. Rental fees are around $5. Rental movies have to be viewed within a 24-hour period while purchased movies can be kept and viewed indefinitely. A typical

A scene from *300*. With just a couple exceptions, the entire film was shot indoors against a blue screen, with digital effects added later.

film downloads in 30–90 minutes. The long-range popularity of this delivery technique remains to be seen.

▲ Digital Projection

Once the digital movie gets to the theater, it has to be shown on a special digital projector. Several companies, including Kodak, have developed digital projectors and are working to improve them, but large-scale manufacturing of the devices is still in the future. One of the problems is making sure that the digital projectors match the color and sharpness found in traditional celluloid film. A second problem is cost. Equipping each screen with a digital projection system will cost about $150,000. Theater owners, still recovering from a wave of overexpansion, falling profits, and bankruptcies, are not eager to foot the bill. They argue that the studios and the distributors should pick up the tab since they will be the ones saving the most money. For their part distributors have been reluctant to lead the way. They point out that for several years they will have increased costs because they will have to supply both digital and traditional film versions as the new technology slowly catches on.

These problems have significantly slowed the adoption of digital projection. In mid-2007 only 2,200 out of about 37,000 movie screens were equipped with digital projectors. Things might change, however, thanks to a compromise between theater owners and studios. Announced in 2006, the plan calls for movie studios to pay a fee to theater owners on each digital copy they produce in order to defray the cost of installing digital equipment.

▲ Mobile Movies

Movies are probably the least portable of all media. They were designed to be seen in a large hall on a large screen. Nonetheless, the digital age has opened new possibilities. Portable DVD players that weigh less than 2 pounds and are not much bigger than this book are becoming popular. Many SUVs and vans have video screens installed so that passengers in the back can watch DVDs during a trip. And, as we have already mentioned, there are many services that give subscribers the ability to download movies onto their laptops. On top of that, some entrepreneurs are investigating ways to show films on a cell phone. In Sweden a theatrical movie was prereleased to cell phones before opening in a movie theater. There is even a company that offers pornographic films delivered to a cell phone.

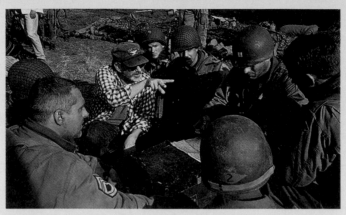

Steven Spielberg started making movies at age 12 using his father's 8mm camera. One of his earliest productions was a horror film starring his three younger sisters. He continued to make his own films during his college days, but he graduated with a degree in English because his grades were too low to get him into film school. One of Spielberg's independently made films caught the attention of

Steven Spielberg directing *Saving Private Ryan.*

an executive at Universal Pictures, who hired the young Spielberg to direct episodes of a TV series. The young director eventually wound up directing a made-for-TV movie, *Duel,* that won much critical acclaim.

On the basis of his success with *Duel,* Spielberg got approval to direct his first theatrical movie, *The Sugarland Express.* Although praised by critics, the movie did poorly at the box office. Nonetheless, the studio gave him a new assignment: directing the movie version of a best-selling novel about a huge shark. The movie, *Jaws,* released in 1975, marked a significant milestone in movie history. It was the first of

the big-budget summer action movies, a strategy that movie studios still follow (consider *Twister, Independence Day,* and *The Patriot*). *Jaws* was also the first of the movie blockbusters, raking in more than $250 million. Hollywood studios quickly adopted a "big budget equals big blockbuster" mentality.

Spielberg also hit upon a formula for making successful pictures that resonated with moviegoers: Take tried-and-true, classic adventure themes, and enhance them with cutting-edge special effects. The *Indiana Jones* trilogy, *Jurassic Park, E.T.,* and *Close Encounters of the Third Kind* are all examples of this formula. Spielberg also tackled more serious themes, as exemplified in *The Color Purple, Schindler's List, Amistad, Saving Private Ryan,* and *Munich.*

In a career that has spanned more than a quarter-century, Spielberg has won two Oscars and numerous other movie awards. Of the top 25 all-time movie hits, 4 were directed by Steven Spielberg.

▲ User-Generated Content

Given the nature of film production, user-generated content is not yet a major part of the medium. Nonetheless, there are a few examples. During the production of *Snakes on a Plane,* New Line Cinema reshot some scenes to incorporate suggestions from fans across the Internet. A British producer in 2007 announced plans to "crowdsource" a major motion picture. That is, individuals who invest about $50 in the project will be able to have a say in all the creative aspects of the movie.

DEFINING FEATURES OF MOTION PICTURES

The most noticeable characteristic of motion pictures is their potential cost. Many big-budget Hollywood movies have production expenses that routinely top the $100-million mark. Tack on another $20 million or so for marketing and distribution, and you're talking real money. No other media product—book, magazine, TV series, CD—costs as much as motion pictures. (Of course, filmmakers sometimes put together films for much less and sometimes make big money—*Little Miss Sunshine,* for example—but these tend to be rare events.)

Partly because commercial moviemaking is so expensive, the industry has become dominated by big conglomerates. As noted earlier, six major companies now control most of the market. These companies have the financial resources to risk $100 million or so on a few dozen films each year in hopes of finding a blockbuster. Making motion pictures tends to be only one of many media interests in which these conglomerates are involved. Some have holdings in TV and the Internet; others own publishing companies and recording companies.

Film has a strong aesthetic dimension. Of all the media discussed in this book, film is the one most often discussed as an art form. My university library lists 110 entries under the heading "motion picture aesthetics." This characteristic introduces a tension in the field because most big-studio films are produced to make a profit rather than to showcase their artistic merit. Many independent filmmakers, however, make films not because of the bottom line but because they find their efforts artistically satisfying. Although this chapter discusses primarily mainstream Hollywood moviemaking, keep in mind that thousands of freelance filmmakers work outside the established corporate structure and produce films of varying length on a myriad of topics.

Going to the movies continues to be a social experience. It is the only medium that facilitates audiences gathering in large groups to be exposed to the same message. And, of course, moviegoing is still a popular dating activity. In fact, the social dimension of movie-going might be the most important one.

ORGANIZATION OF THE FILM INDUSTRY

Although film is an art form, the film industry is in business to make a profit. If an occasional moneymaking film also turns out to have artistic merit, so much the better, but the artistic merit is usually a by-product rather than the main focus. Our analysis of the film industry divides its structure into three areas: (1) production, (2) distribution, and (3) exhibition.

▲ Production

Films are produced by a variety of organizations and individuals. For many years the major studios controlled virtually all production, but independent producers have recently become prevalent. The major studios now finance and distribute many films made by independent companies.

Film studios differ in their arrangements, but a typical setup involves four main departments: (1) film production, (2) distribution, (3) TV production, and (4) administration. The film production department handles all those elements that actually go into the making of a film, including story development, casting, art, makeup, and sets. The distribution department handles sales and contracts for domestic and worldwide duplication and delivery of films to theaters and to home video. As its name suggests, the TV division develops and produces movies and series for first-run and syndicated television. Sales, financial deals, and legal arrangements are the provinces of the administration department.

SOUNDBYTE

This Movie Really Bombed

As part of the promotional campaign for *Mission Impossible III*, Paramount Pictures placed digital music devices in 4,500 news racks scattered across Southern California. When a customer opened the news rack, the device, a red plastic box with wires, played the *Mission Impossible* theme. A great promotional idea, right? What could possibly go wrong?

Well, in some racks the devices fell off and landed on the stack of papers. When a consumer in Santa Clarita, California, opened the rack and saw the box with wires, he thought it was a bomb and called police. Taking no chances, the bomb squad blew up the news rack.

▲ Distribution

The distribution arm of the industry is responsible for supplying prints of films to the thousands of theaters located across the United States and around the globe. In recent years distribution companies have also supplied films to TV networks and to makers of DVDs. Distribution companies maintain close contact with theater owners all over the world and also provide a transportation and delivery system that ensures that a film will arrive at a theater before its scheduled play date. In addition to booking the film at local movie houses, the distribution company is responsible for making the multiple prints of a film that are necessary when the film goes into general release. They also take care of advertising and promotion for the film. Most of the distribution of motion pictures is handled by the large studios, which are firmly entrenched in both the production and distribution aspects of the business.

The nature of film distribution ensures that the large companies will control a large portion of the business. First, it is too expensive for an independent producer or a small distribution company to contact theaters and theater chains spread all over the globe. The big studios already have this communication network set up and can afford to maintain it. Second, the large studios can offer theater owners a steady stream of films that consistently feature big-name stars. A small company could not withstand that competition for long.

Distribution companies also serve as a source of financing for independent producers. These companies lend money to a film's producer to cover all or most of the estimated cost of a film. In this way the major studios acquire an interest in films that they did not directly produce. This arrangement will be discussed further in the section on film economics.

▲ Exhibition

The exhibition side of the industry went on a building boom in the late 1990s, constructing new multiscreen theaters with stadium seating and surround sound. By 2000 there were about 37,400 movies screens in the United States, an all-time high. As it turned out, however, theater owners had overextended themselves and did not have the cash to pay for this expansion. As a result several big theater chains, including Carmike, Regal, and Loews, filed for bankruptcy and shut down theaters that were losing money. By 2007 the total number of movie screens had dropped to about 37,000.

Multiplex theaters, featuring 12 or 18 screens clustered around a central concession stand, are still the rule. Most new theaters seat 200–400 patrons. The massive movie palaces of the 1920s and 1930s have not reemerged, but there are noticeable changes inside the motion picture theater as exhibitors go after a slightly older demographic. Soundproofing to prevent spill from adjoining theaters is now common, and concession stands are putting real butter on popcorn, with a few even offering mineral water, cappuccino, and valet parking.

OWNERSHIP IN THE FILM INDUSTRY

Big conglomerates, many of them mentioned in earlier chapters, dominate the film industry. As of 2007 the top six were as follows:

1. *The Walt Disney Company:* Headquartered in California, Disney has two movie enterprises: Touchstone, for mature-audience films, and Buena Vista, for general films. Disney has holdings in television, cable, and publishing in addition to its interests

The trend in movie exhibition is big 18- and 24-screen multiplexes. Increased competition and declining profits forced some movie theaters to close during 2004 and 2005.

in theme parks, hotels, music, real estate, golf courses, and cruise ships. Disney also makes money licensing Disney characters for use by other companies.

2. *Time Warner:* Warner Brothers is the motion picture arm of this huge conglomerate, which has interests in the Internet, book and magazine publishing, recorded music, motion picture theaters, and cable TV, among other media.

3. *Paramount (Viacom):* In addition to owning and making motion pictures, Viacom owns cable TV networks, motion picture theaters, and music publishing companies.

4. *Sony/MGM:* In 2004 Sony added MGM to its list of properties that include movie theaters, TV production facilities, consumer electronics, and video games.

5. *NBC Universal:* NBC acquired Universal from Vivendi, a French company, in 2003. GE, the parent of NBC, now has interests in cable and broadcast TV, a motion picture studio, and a recording company.

6. *News Corporation:* Rupert Murdoch's Australian-based company owns 20th Century Fox. The company is also involved in satellite broadcasting and publishing and owns a TV network and a cable news channel.

PRODUCING MOTION PICTURES

▲ Preproduction

How does a film get to be a film? The three distinct phases in moviemaking are (1) preproduction, (2) production, and (3) postproduction.

All films begin with an idea. The idea can be sketchy, such as a two-paragraph outline of the plot, or detailed, such as a novel or a Broadway play.

The next step of the preproduction process is writing the screenplay. In general, the route to a finished motion picture script consists of several steps:

- *Step 1: treatment.* This is a narrative statement of the plot and descriptions of the main characters and locations; it might even contain sample dialogue.

- *Step 2: first-draft script.* This version contains all the dialogue and camera setups and a description of action sequences.

- *Step 3: revised script.* This incorporates changes suggested by the producer, director, actors, and others.

- *Step 4: script polish.* This process involves adding or subtracting scenes, revising dialogue, and making other minor changes.

While all this is going on, the producer tries to find actors (in the film industry, people who act in films are described by the generic term "talent," whether they have any or not) who will appear in the film. The contracts and deals that are worked out vary from astronomical to modest. One common arrangement is for the actor to receive a flat fee. These fees have been rising in the past few years and are one of the reasons films cost so much to produce. For example, Jim Carrey gets about $20 million per picture, and Nicole Kidman receives about $15 million. At the other end of the scale, the Screen Actors Guild has a contract that spells out the minimum salary that must be paid to talent in minor roles and walk-on parts.

Meanwhile, the producer is also trying to secure financial backing for the picture. We will say more about the monetary arrangements in film in the section on economics. For now, it is important to remember that the financial arrangements have to be worked out early in the preproduction process.

At the same time, the producer is busy lining up skilled personnel to work behind the camera. Of these people the film's director is central. When all the elements have been put together, the director will determine what scenes get photographed from what angle and how they will be assembled in the final product. Working closely with the director is the cinematographer (the person responsible for the lighting and filming of the scenes) and the film editor (the person who will cut the film and assemble the scenes in the proper order).

The budget for *Spiderman 3* was reportedly somewhere north of $250 million.

A movie crew contains dozens of other skilled people: set designers, makeup specialists, electricians, audio engineers, crane operators, painters, plumbers, carpenters, property masters, set dressers, caterers, first-aid people, and many others.

Shortly after the director has been signed for the project, he or she and the producer scout possible locations for shooting the film. Some sequences may be shot in the sound studio, but others may need the authenticity that only location shooting can provide. As soon as the locations have been chosen, the producer makes the necessary arrangements to secure these sites for filming. Sometimes this entails renting the studios of a major motion picture production company or obtaining permits to shoot in city streets or other locales. The producer must also draw up plans to make sure that the filming equipment, talent, and technical crew are all at the same place at the same time.

▲ Production

Once all these items have been attended to, the film moves into the actual production phase. Cast and crew assemble at the chosen location, and each scene is shot and reshot until the director is satisfied. The actors and crew then move to another location, and the process starts all over again. Overriding the entire production is the knowledge that all this is costing a great deal of money. Shooting even a moderate-budget film can cost $400,000–500,000 *per day*. Therefore, the director tries to plan everything so that each dollar is used efficiently.

The average shooting schedule for the typical film is about 70 days. Each day's shooting (and some days can be 16 hours long) results in an average of fewer than 2 minutes of usable film.

▲ Postproduction

The postproduction phase begins after the filming has been completed. A film editor, working with the director, decides where close-ups should be placed, what angles scenes should be shown from, and how long each scene should last. The elaborate special effects that some films require are also added during postproduction. Once the scenes have been edited into an acceptable form, postproduction sound can be added. This might include narration, music, sound effects, and original dialogue that, for one reason or another, has to be redone. (About 10–15 percent of outside dialogue has to be

Most of the top 10 films listed on page 208 are from the past couple of decades. This is because tickets have become more expensive over the years. The following list compiled by *The Movie Times* is adjusted for inflation.

Film	Year	Adjusted Box Office (millions)
Gone with the Wind	1939	$1,333
Star Wars IV: A New Hope	1977	1,152
The Sound of Music	1965	925
E.T.: The Extraterrestrial	1982	914
The Ten Commandments	1956	851
Titanic	1997	839
Jaws	1975	832
Doctor Zhivago	1965	787
The Jungle Book	1967	704
Snow White	1937	691

rerecorded because of interfering noises.) Finally, the edited film, complete with final sound track and special effects, is sent to the laboratory where a release print of the film is made.

THE ECONOMICS OF MOTION PICTURES

There are several revenue streams for the motion picture industry: (1) money taken in at the U.S. box office, (2) revenue from the international box office, (3) sales and rentals of DVDs and tapes, and (4) miscellaneous video sources such as pay-per-view and video-on-demand.

As far as the U.S. box office is concerned, revenue dipped from 2004 to 2005 but recovered in 2006 to $9.49 billion. On a less optimistic note movie attendance actually declined over that same period. Also troubling the industry is the fact that revenue from the sales and rentals of DVDs was essentially flat from 2004 to 2006, hovering around the $24-billion mark (note that revenue from DVDs far exceeds box office income). Movie executives are hoping that new high-definition DVDs will stimulate sales. Foreign box office has also shown little growth. In short, Hollywood is not yet experiencing the revenue declines seen in other media, but its future fortunes are hard to predict.

Movies are an expensive medium. In 2007 the cost of producing and marketing the typical film was nearly $100 million, up about 28 percent from 2002. And some films cost much more. *Superman Returns* and *Spiderman 3* both topped the $250-million mark. If you've been to the movies lately, you're also aware that movies are getting expensive for consumers. The average ticket price in 2005 was $6.41, and in many cities a ticket to an evening performance costs more than $10. Add in another $5 for a medium popcorn (about 90 percent of that is profit for the movie theater) and $4 for a soft drink, and a night at the movies can be an expensive proposition.

▲ Financing a Film

Where do producers get the enormous sums of money necessary to make a film? Let us take a look at some common financing methods. If a producer has a good track record and a film looks promising, the distributor might lend the producer the entire amount needed to make the film. In return the distributor gains distribution rights to the film. Moreover, if the distributor also has studio facilities, the producer might agree to rent those facilities from the distributor.

A second method is to arrange for a **pickup.** Under this arrangement a distributor agrees to "pick up" the cost of a finished picture at a later date for a set price. Although this agreement does a producer little immediate good, he or she can take the pickup to a bank to help secure a loan for the cost of the film.

A third method is a **limited partnership,** an arrangement whereby the film is financed through outside investors. Each limited partner puts up a set amount, and his or her personal liability is limited by the amount invested; that is, a partner cannot lose any more money than he or she put up even if the film goes over budget.

A fourth method is a **joint venture.** Under this setup several companies involved in film production and distribution pool their resources and agree to finance one or more films. Given the increasing cost of motion pictures, this arrangement is becoming more common as several companies share the risk and potential rewards of a movie. *Titanic*, for example, was financed by a joint venture.

The producer and distributor also agree on how to divide the distributor's gross receipts from the film (the money the distributor gets from the theater owners, TV networks, pay-TV operations, and DVD revenues). Since the distributor takes the greatest risk in the venture, the distributor is the first to be paid from the receipts of the film. Distribution companies charge a distribution fee for their efforts. In addition, there are distribution expenses (cost of making multiple prints of the film, advertising, necessary taxes, insurance). Lastly, the actual production cost of the film must be repaid. If the distributor or a bank lent the producer $50 million to make the film, that loan has to be paid off (plus interest). Because of all these expenses, it is estimated that a film must earn two and one-half to three times its production cost before it starts to show a profit for the producers. Hollywood accounting tends to be complicated, however, and sometimes it is hard to determine when a film is profitable.

▲ Dealing with the Exhibitor

The distributor is also involved in other financial dealings, specifically with the exhibitors. An exhibition license sets the terms under which the showing of the film will occur. The license specifies the run of the film (the number of weeks the theater must agree to play the picture), holdover rights, the date the picture will be available for showing, and the clearance (the amount of time that must elapse before the film can be shown at a competing theater).

The license also contains the financial terms for the film's showing. There are several common arrangements. The simplest involves a specified percentage split of the money taken in at the box office. The exhibitor agrees to split the money with the distributor according to an agreed-upon formula—perhaps 50/50 the first week, 60/40 the second, 70/30 the third, and so on—with the exhibitor keeping more money the longer the run of the film. Another alternative is the **sliding scale.** Under this setup as the box office revenue increases, so does the amount of money the exhibitor must pay the distributor. For example, if a week's

The videocassette and the DVD have transformed the economic structure of the movie business. With consumers spending more than $24 billion on the sales and rentals of discs and tapes, you might think everybody in the movie business would be happy. Well, some aren't. The creative people of the business—actors, directors, and writers—claim that they are being shut out of the massive profits that come from the sales and rentals of prerecorded movies.

The Writers' Guild, for example, points out that the formula now used to compensate actors, writers, and directors was first devised in the 1980s when home video was in its infancy and the DVD had yet to be invented. Under that arrangement a screenwriter gets about a nickel on the sale of a $20 DVD. Actors share about 15 cents. The Writers' Guild claims that the studios get more than $10 from the sale. The guild also notes that when the original agreement was signed, when manufacturing cassettes was a new and expensive process, it cost the studios about $14 to make a videocassette. Now studios can produce DVDs for less than $2 a disc. The creative community wants to rewrite the formula so that it gets a bigger share.

The producers, on the other hand, argue that making movies is riskier than ever and that the majority do not make a profit. The DVD sales help cover their losses. Further, producers need the additional revenue to cover the increased costs of making and marketing the average film. Lastly, the producers point out that writers, actors, and directors get revenue from the sales of all DVDs and tapes, even if the movie is a flop and the studio never makes a profit.

The people on the creative side of moviemaking counter that the cost of making a film is under the direct control of the studios. If the studio wanted to cut costs, it could. A spokesperson for the Writers' Guild maintains that when the movie studios spend more than $100 million on a movie, it's because they can make it back with DVD sales and rentals.

During the last round of contract negotiations with the actors, directors, and writers in 2004, the movie studios held firm, and the original 1980s formula remained the standard. Nonetheless, with high-definition DVDs coming to the market, this issue is far from settled.

Why should consumers be concerned about this internecine squabbling? A settlement might mean that movie fans will be paying more for their DVDs.

---

revenue was more than $30,000, the exhibitor would pay the distributor 60 percent; if the revenue was between $25,000 and $29,999, the distributor would receive 50 percent; and so on. Another common approach is the 90/10 deal. Under this method the movie theater owner first deducts the house allowance (called the *nut*) from the box office take. The house allowance includes all the operating expenses of the theater (heating, cooling, water, lights, salaries, maintenance, and so on), plus a sum that is pure profit for the theater (this sum is called *air*). From the revenues (if any) that remain, the distributor gets 90 percent and the house 10 percent.

As suggested earlier, concession stand sales are a significant source of income for movie theater owners. If the average moviegoer spends $10 on popcorn, candy, soft drinks, nachos, and other munchies, and a billion or so tickets are sold every year, that works out to about $10 billion in annual revenue.

Movie theaters now have an additional revenue stream from on-screen advertising (see the boxed insert "Advertising in Movie Theaters"). Theaters love this since the cost involved in this process is minimal. In order to clear time to show in-theater commercials, however, the exhibitor often cuts back on the time devoted to showing movie previews, a move that doesn't sit well with the studios.

▲ Promoting a Film

A well-known film executive once said that a film is like a parachute: If it doesn't open, you're dead. The first week that a film is in release is crucial; in fact, since most films open on a weekend, the first 3 days are even more crucial. Films that open badly seldom do well.

Consequently, a good deal of promotion, marketing, and advertising is targeted to getting people into theaters for that opening weekend. The most common strategy is to launch a media blitz that touts the film weeks before it opens. These campaigns are not inexpensive. For instance, Columbia TriStar spent nearly $50 million promoting *Spider-Man 2*.

Maybe this has happened to you. The movie you really want to see is scheduled to start at 7 P.M. You know that you will have to hurry to make it. You rush to the theater, buy an $8 ticket, spend another $8 at the concession stand for a small popcorn and a small drink, and get to your seat just before 7. The house lights go down and pretty soon you are watching . . . commercials. (Note that we are not talking about previews of coming attractions; we are talking about ads for AT&T, Colgate, the U.S. Army . . . real commercials.) This is what you dashed around and paid $16 to see? You could have seen commercials at home on TV for free.

Now showing on more than two-thirds of all movie theater screens, premovie ads are becoming increasingly common, and you should only expect to see more of them along with other in-theater marketing techniques in the future.

There are several reasons why movie theater ads are increasing in number. First, many movie theaters are in financial difficulty, and several big chains, including Regal and Loews, have filed for bankruptcy. In-theater advertising brings in extra dollars to the theater owners, about $520 million in 2005. Second, advertisers know that they have a captive audience. You cannot zap a commercial on the movie screen. Short of leaving the theater, there is no way to avoid them. Third, the moviegoing audience is young and has disposable income—just the target audience that most advertisers are looking for. Finally, they work. A market research survey disclosed that viewer recall of the ads was an amazing 80 percent, much higher than recall for TV spots.

Not everybody is happy with premovie ads. Many feel that ads are simply uninvited guests and argue that they paid their money to see a movie and not commercials. In fact, longtime consumer advocate Ralph Nader has gotten into the act. He is the founder of Commercial Alert, an organization that is pressuring Congress to enact laws to force movie theaters to advertise the time the movie actually begins instead of the time the commercials start. (Such a system is currently used in Europe.) In addition, Commercial Alert is asking audiences to yell, "No commercials!" when the premovie ads come on. Anticommercial Web sites instruct moviegoers to stand up during the ads to block the view. A high school teacher from Chicago was so angry over being subjected to the ads that she filed a lawsuit asking that theater owners compensate her and other moviegoers with $75 in damages for their wasted time.

Nonetheless, theater owners continue to make deals with advertisers. Regal Cinemas partnered with NBC to produce a 20-minute premovie block that consists of a mix of entertainment and ads. The program uses unseen footage from NBC programs such as *The Tonight Show with Jay Leno*. Ads are targeted to local audiences.

Look for more off-screen marketing as well. Motorola sent salespeople dressed in 1970s clothing to theater lobbies during the showing of *Austin Powers in Goldmember* to demonstrate the company's new mobile phone. The Department of Defense rents space in many theaters for kiosks that encourage enlistment. Monster.com struck a deal with theater owners that allowed them to park green-colored vehicles outside movie theaters at which patrons could search for new jobs. Target Department Stores bought space on popcorn bags at more than 100 theaters to advertise its 2003 line of back-to-college supplies. All of these deals meant more money for theater owners.

Will movie audiences rebel against this increasing invasion of commercialism? Probably not. People have become used to seeing ads almost everywhere they go, and theater owners want to keep the added revenue. Draw your own conclusion.

FEEDBACK FOR MOTION PICTURES

▲ Box Office

Feedback in the movie industry revolves around the weekly box office figures compiled and reported in various trade publications including *Variety*. Each week *Variety* reports the top-grossing films in the American and foreign markets. An example of this listing is reproduced in Figure 9-1.

To compile these data, *Variety*, in cooperation with Nielsen Entertainment Data Incorporated, collects box office results from 50,000 movie screens in 14 countries, including the United States, Canada, Mexico, and several countries in South America, Europe, and Asia. Most of the column headings in *Variety*'s chart are self-explanatory. Each film's title is listed, followed by the distributor. The remaining columns show box office revenue, number of screens showing the picture, average revenue per screen, and domestic and foreign revenue estimates. Note that this chart reports only a film's gross earnings; it does not show how much profit, if any, a film has made.

The economic feedback contained in *Variety* is extremely important in the movie industry. One or two blockbuster films can improve the financial position of an entire company. In addition, a film successful at the box office is apt to inspire one or more sequels and several imitators.

FIGURE 9-1 *Variety* Box Office Revenue Chart

, 2007   *VARIETY*   FILM ▪ 9

BOX OFFICE REPORT

Visit Variety.com/boxoffice for a searchable, sortable and international B.O. archive

TITLE/DISTRIBUTOR	Reported Box Office 6/15-6/17 (weekend)	Percent Change in Box Office	Number of Theaters This Week	Number of Theaters Last Week	Weeks Avg $ Per Theater	No. Weeks Release	Domestic Box Office Cumulative	Foreign Box Office Cumulative	Worldwide Box Office Cumulative
Fantastic Four: Rise of the Silver Surfer (20th)	$58,051,684	—	3959	—	$14663	1	$58,051,684	$25,194,730	$83,246,414
Ocean's Thirteen (WB)	19,724,405	-45%	3565	3565	5533	2	70,429,741	67,400,000	137,829,741
Knocked Up (U)	14,069,880	-28%	2907	2876	4840	3	90,016,695	—	90,016,695
Pirates of the Caribbean: At World's End (BV)	12,411,786	-41%	3329	4002	3728	4	274,145,510	549,380,000	823,525,510
Surf's Up (Sony)	9,254,793	-48%	3531	3528	2621	2	34,625,490	4,390,729	39,016,219
Shrek the Third (Par)	9,003,044	-41%	3505	3925	2569	5	297,245,100	108,265,697	405,510,797
Nancy Drew (WB)	6,832,318	—	2612	—	2616	1	6,832,318	—	6,832,318
Hostel: Part II (Lionsgate)	3,026,131	-63%	2350	2350	1288	2	14,208,497	2,660,503	16,869,000
Mr. Brooks (MGM)	2,902,024	-41%	1923	2453	1509	3	23,523,243	1,164,819	24,688,062
Spider-Man 3 (Sony)	2,505,151	-42%	1822	2570	1375	7	330,021,137	543,754,164	873,775,301
Waitress (Fox Searchlight)	1,250,470	-21%	615	707	2046	7	14,071,871	—	14,071,871
La Vie en rose (Picturehouse-TVA)	660,278	+267%	77	8	8575	14	2,806,173	59,292,516	62,098,689
Once (Fox Searchlight)	543,334	+10%	120	95	4528	5	2,503,419	—	2,503,419
Wild Hogs (BV)	502,325	+17%	378	228	1329	16	165,788,226	80,712,000	246,500,226
Paris, Je t'aime (First Look)	487,780	+11%	200	136	2439	7	2,783,486	6,925,667	9,709,153

▲ Market Research

Audience research has become more influential in the movie business because of the tremendous cost of motion pictures. At most studios the first step is concept testing to find promising plotlines. The next step is an analysis of the script. If the script seems promising, the studio will go ahead and film it and make a rough cut. The rough cut is then used by movie researchers in a series of test screenings. In addition, **focus group** sessions are held. A focus group is a small sample (usually about 10–15 people) of the target audience that is asked detailed questions about what the viewers liked and did not like. With this information the studio can add or drop a scene, modify the ending, change the musical score, or make other alterations. Once these changes are completed, the movie is released for a sneak preview. Audience members fill out preview cards that summarize their reactions to a film, its characters, and its stars. It is possible for the director to make limited changes in the film in response to this feedback, but it is usually too late to make wholesale changes.

SOUNDBYTE

Suppose They Made a Movie and Nobody Came . . .

Zyzzyx Road, a film starring Tom Sizemore and Katherine Heigl (from *Grey's Anatomy*), made a whopping $30 at U.S. theaters.

▲ Motion Picture Audiences

Average weekly attendance had been slowly rising from 1980 to 2002, but admissions fell from 2003 to 2005. As shown in Figure 9-2, attendance is nowhere near the levels of the 1930s and 1940s when film was in its heyday.

The movie audience tends to be young. About 60 percent of filmgoers are under 40. Frequent moviegoers (those who see at least 12 films a year) account for about three-quarters of all film admissions. They tend to be young, single (going to movies continues to be a popular dating activity),

FIGURE 9-2

Average Weekly Film
Attendance in the
United States

Source: Motion Picture
Association of America.
Used by permission

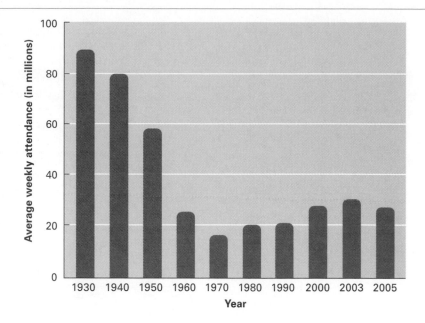

from middle-class families, and from urban areas. The average person in the United States attends about five films a year.

The audience for movies is largest in July and August and smallest in May. The worst 2 weeks of the year for moviegoing are the first 2 weeks in December, when attendance drops 30–50 percent.

MOVIES AT HOME

Home video has become Hollywood's biggest revenue source. In 2006 combined income from the sales and rentals of DVDs topped the $24-billion mark, more than double the amount taken in at the box office. DVD revenue, however, has shown little expansion over

DVDs have reshaped the home video industry. Movie fans bought more than 5 million copies of *Happy Feet.*

the past few years, suggesting to many in the industry that the DVD market has matured and that there is little room left for growth. Hollywood is hoping that new high-definition DVD players and discs will reinvigorate the DVD market. These DVDs, however, have been slow to catch on because of high prices for high-definition playback units and two incompatible high-definition DVD formats: BluRay and HD DVD.

The home video market, like the theatrical market, is driven by big hits. Movies that were popular on the big screen are almost invariably popular on the home screen. *Happy Feet,* for example, sold 4 million DVDs in its first week. At the other end of the spectrum, some films that are box office bombs do significantly better in the home market. *Lords of War* took in only $24 million at the box office but more than $65 million from DVD sales and rentals.

Moreover, the DVD is shrinking the amount of time between the release of a movie in theaters and its appearance on disc. Historically, there was a 6-month gap between theatrical release and entry into the home video market. That interval has shrunk to just 3 months thanks to better duplication and distribution facilities that make DVDs easier to manufacture and deliver to retail shelves. In addition, more films are opening on larger numbers of screens, saturating the market much more quickly than before. The shorter interval helps movie studios take advantage of the movie advertising campaigns that are still fresh in consumers' minds.

Pay-per-view (PPV) television provides another revenue stream for movie companies. More than 30 million homes are equipped with PPV, and the number is growing steadily. In addition, the number of channels available on cable and satellite systems is increasing, and many of these new channels are devoted to PPV. Finally, Hollywood gets income from licensing its movies to premium cable channels, such as HBO and Showtime, in addition to receiving money from selling the rights to movies to traditional over-the-air broadcasters. Given these numerous video aftermarkets, it is no surprise that TV generates more revenue for the movie industry than does the box office. Chapter 10 contains more information on home video.

CAREER >>
OUTLOOK

THE FILM INDUSTRY

A young person who has actual experience in films and filmmaking will probably enjoy more success in finding a job. How do you get this experience? In general, there are two ways: (1) taking college courses that deal with film and (2) making your own films.

About 750 colleges and universities now offer courses in film, 227 offer bachelor's degrees, and many offer graduate degrees. The advantages of a university major in film are substantial. First, it provides students with an opportunity to practice with technical equipment: lights, meters, editing machines, cameras, and so forth. Second, students can take courses in film aesthetics and film history, learning how to make their own films by observing how others have made films. Third, students can take courses in other areas that relate to film, such as art, literature, history, music, and photography. Finally, during the course of his or her studies, a student may have the opportunity to make a film as a final classroom project. This finished film can be shown to potential employers as a sample of the student's capability.

The other approach to gaining experience is to become an independent filmmaker. This method is valuable because it allows a person to gain knowledge of every aspect of filmmaking. Of course, this approach requires that an individual have some money to invest in basic film equipment and the time necessary to devote to the film.

▲ Entry-Level Positions

Once a person has some experience, the next step is to find an entry-level job. This requires securing a job interview—not an easy task. The common technique of mailing a résumé to a potential employer seldom works in the film industry.

There are three ways to overcome this hurdle. The first is to know somebody. As is the case in most industries, if you have a friend or a friend of a friend in the industry, getting a job interview is less difficult.

The second way is to get yourself noticed. A newcomer accomplishes this by seeking out internships or training programs with production companies. The American Film Institute's *Guide to College Courses in Film and Television* lists such opportunities. Many times, help in finding out about and applying for internships can be secured from instructors or campus placement offices. Once you have gained entry into an organization, you will have better success in arranging an interview. Another way to get yourself noticed is to enter the many student film festivals. A newcomer who wins one or more awards at these festivals may find getting through the door into the film industry a little easier.

The third way is to be persistent. This is also the hardest way. Make a list of those companies where you wish to work, and call on them personally. Take to them a one-page summary of your education and special skills. If you have a completed film that is available for viewing, indicate so in your summary. Do not be discouraged if your first visit is fruitless. Keep checking back. As is the case in television, a film newcomer should be prepared to take practically any job as a starter. Once you are inside the company, your path to more creative and challenging positions is easier to follow.

▲ Upward Mobility

Select your first job with an eye toward future advancement. Some routes are best if your ultimate goal is producing and directing. Other avenues are better if top management is your ultimate goal. One early choice an aspiring filmmaker must make is the choice between editing and directing. Although there are some exceptions, most people who start in the editing room stay there, advancing ultimately to the post of supervising film editor. Those interested in producing and directing should begin as production assistants and progress to assistant directors, director, and perhaps producer. To reach high-level management, a person might consider breaking in with the distribution or sales division.

MAIN POINTS

- The motion picture developed in the late 19th century. After being a main attraction in nickelodeons, films moved into bigger theaters, and movie stars quickly became the most important part of the new industry. Sound came to the movies in the mid-1920s.

- Big movie studios dominated the industry until the late 1940s, when a court decision weakened their power. Television captured much of the film audience in the 1950s. By the end of the 1960s, however, Hollywood had adapted to television and was an active producer of TV shows. A major trend in modern movies is the rise of big-budget movies.

- The transition to digital moviemaking may transform the film industry.

- The movie industry consists of production, distribution, and exhibition facets. Large conglomerates control the business. Producing a motion picture starts from a concept, proceeds to the production stage, and ends with the postproduction stage.

- Movie revenues have shown small but steady growth over the past 10 years. DVD sales and rentals and foreign box office receipts are important sources of movie income.

- Movie audiences are getting older, but a significant part of the audience is still the 30-and-under age group.

QUESTIONS FOR REVIEW

1. What are the defining features of motion pictures?

2. What caused the rise and fall of the Motion Picture Patents Company?

3. How did the film industry react to TV?

4. What are the three main segments of the motion picture industry?

5. What are the various ways films are financed?

QUESTIONS FOR CRITICAL THINKING

1. Suppose the movie industry had never moved to Hollywood, staying instead on the East Coast. How might films be different?

2. What are the potential advantages and disadvantages of big corporations controlling motion picture production?

3. Do filmmakers have an obligation to be socially responsible for what they present on the screen? Why or why not?

4. Will any of the antipiracy tactics adopted by the film industry be effective in stopping the illegal copying and distribution of films? Why or why not?

5. Someone once said that Hollywood producers don't make films; they make deals. Comment on the validity of this statement and its implications.

KEY TERMS

Apple TV (p. 199)
phi phenomenon (p. 200)
persistence of vision (p. 200)
Kinetoscope (p. 200)
Motion Picture Patents Company
   (MPPC) (p. 202)

block booking (p. 204)
pickup (p. 218)
limited partnership (p. 218)
joint venture (p. 218)
sliding scale (p. 218)
Variety (p. 220)

focus group (p. 221)
pay-per-view
   (PPV) (p. 223)

INTERNET RESOURCES

Online Learning Center

At the Online Learning Center home page, www.mhhe.com/dominick10, *select* Student Center *and then* Chapter 9.

1. Use the Learning Objectives, Chapter Outline, Main Points, and Time Line sections to review this chapter.

2. Test your knowledge of the chapter using the multiple choice, crossword puzzle, and flashcard features of the site.

3. Expand your knowledge of concepts and topics discussed in the chapter by going to Suggestions for Further Reading and Internet Exercises.

Surfing the Internet

These represent a variety of movie theme sites.

www.imdb.com
The Internet Movie Database. Contains everything you ever wanted to know about movies. Has information about stars, cast, plot, and box office performance for just about every movie.

www.mpaa.org
The official Web site of the Motion Picture Association of America. Contains industry statistics and the latest news releases. Has an extensive section that deals with copyright issues.

www.mrcranky.com
An offbeat review page featuring a reviewer who has high standards and a caustic style. Mr. Cranky rates movies by assigning a number of bombs. For example, four bombs means "As good as a poke in the eye with a sharp stick."

www.variety.com
The Web site of the trade paper that is the bible of the entertainment industry. Includes the latest industry news, global box office charts, film reviews, and a section called a "slanguage dictionary," which translates *Variety's* showbiz language into English. For example, "to ankle" means to walk away from a job; a "sprocket opera" is a film festival.

www.videobusiness.com
Find out the latest trends in home video, satellites, and video-on-demand. Access is free, but you have to register.

www.Warnerbros.com
The Warner Brothers Web site. Check out new releases, view movie trailers, and see which Warner products are available on DVD.

CHAPTER 10

BROADCAST TELEVISION

This chapter will prepare you to:

- trace the development of television

- describe the evolution of the networks

- explain the impact of the Telecommunications Act of 1996

- detail the implications of the digital age for broadcast television

- explain how television ratings are formulated

- describe the departments of the television industry and how programs are produced

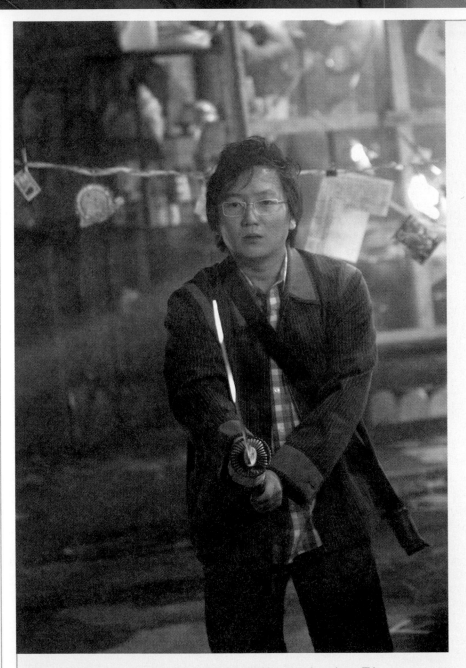

Although competition from the Internet is formidable, some broadcast TV shows such as *Heroes* still draw about 15 million viewers.

For much of its early history, television came into the home via electromagnetic signals broadcast over the airwaves to rooftop antennas. Then in the 1970s consumers had the option of taking down their antennas and getting their TV from signals carried by coaxial cables. A few years later, another possibility opened up when Earth-orbiting satellites began to beam microwave signals to receiving dishes. And, of course, the most recent addition to this list is the Internet.

Granted, most people couldn't care less how their television signal gets to them. Rooftop antenna, cable, satellite, Internet—it doesn't make any difference as long as the picture is clear. Television is television. There are, however, some areas where the channel of distribution does make a difference.

Traditional over-the-air broadcast TV, for instance, is regulated differently from cable, satellite, and Internet. Cable, satellite, and the Internet TV operations have revenue streams different from those of broadcast TV, and their particular means of transmission influences the types of programming that each carries. More importantly, broadcast, cable, satellite, and Internet TV are all coping in different ways with the digital revolution.

Recognizing those facts, we will examine the television industry in two separate chapters. The current chapter examines traditional broadcast TV; the next chapter will look at the newer forms of transmission: cable, satellite, and Internet.

A BRIEF HISTORY

The two men who developed television in the United States could not have been more different. At the age of 16, Philo Farnsworth diagrammed his idea for a television system on the chalkboard in front of his somewhat amazed high school teacher. Farnsworth, an individualistic and lone-wolf inventor, worked at developing his new device, which he called an *image dissector,* and eventually patented it in 1930. In contrast, Vladimir Zworykin was an organization man, working first for Westinghouse and then for RCA. By 1928 he had perfected a primitive camera tube, the iconoscope.

Picture quality of the early television systems was poor, but technical developments during the 1930s improved performance. RCA, with Zworykin's help and with a patent arrangement that permitted it to use Farnsworth's invention, set out to develop TV's commercial potential. NBC, owned by RCA, gave the first public demonstration of broadcast commercial television at the 1939 World's Fair.[1]

The initial public response to TV was lukewarm. Sets were expensive, and there were not many programs for people to watch. Even early TV actors were somewhat skeptical about the future of the new medium. They had to wear green makeup to look normal for the TV camera and swallow salt tablets because the intense heat of the lights necessary for TV made them perspire constantly.

World War II interrupted TV's development. When peace returned in 1945, new technology that had been perfected during the war greatly improved both TV reception and working conditions for the performers. New TV cameras required much less light. TV screens were bigger. There were more programs available, and stations were being linked into networks. All the signs pointed to big things for TV. In 1945 there were only eight TV stations and 8,000 homes with TV in the entire United States. Ten years later, there were nearly a hundred stations, and 35 million households (about 67 percent of the country) had TV.

TV's rapid success caught the industry and the Federal Communications Commission (FCC) off guard. Unless technical standards were worked out, the TV spectrum was in danger of becoming overcrowded and riddled with interference, just as had happened with radio 30 years earlier. To guard against this possibility, the FCC imposed a freeze on all new applications for TV stations. The freeze, which went into effect in 1948, would last for 4 years while the FCC gathered information from engineers and technical experts. When the freeze was lifted in 1952, the FCC had established that 12 VHF and 70 UHF channels (see page 240) were to be devoted to TV. In addition, the commission drew up a list that allocated television channels to the various communities in the United States and specified other rules to minimize interference. Also, thanks largely to the efforts of Frieda Hennock, the first woman to serve on the commission, TV channels were set aside for educational use.

▲ The 1950s: Television Takes Off

Networks, Tape, UHF, and Color   The early television industry was modeled after radio. Local stations served their communities and, in turn, might be affiliated with networks. There were four TV networks during this period: CBS, NBC, ABC, and DuMont, a smaller network that went out of business in 1956. Also much like early radio networks, TV networks quickly became the primary programming sources for their affiliates. NBC and CBS were usually the most popular networks, with ABC trailing behind. Most early network programs were game shows, sports events, and interviews, with a few comedies and dramas interspersed throughout the schedule.

In the early days of TV, most network prime-time programs were produced by advertising agencies that retained control over their content. The agencies also decided on the length and placement of the commercials. After the 1959 scandal that followed the discovery that some quiz shows had been "fixed," the networks reasserted their control over

---

[1]In fairness to Farnsworth, the inventor demonstrated his system in 1934 using what today would be called a *closed-circuit telecast.*

Mr. Television, Milton Berle, dressed in one of the costumes that were his trademark on *Texaco Star Theater.*

programming. Most programs were produced by independent production companies, with much of the financing provided by the networks, an arrangement that would be in place for the next several decades.

Most programs were broadcast live from New York or were filmed in California. Live programs, of course, could not be repeated and often had to be performed again for the West Coast. In 1956 the Ampex Corporation developed videotape, a cheap and efficient way of storing TV programs. By the beginning of the 1960s, most of TV's live programming had switched to tape.

After the FCC-imposed freeze ended, TV stations and TV sets multiplied rapidly. The new UHF channels, however, did not do so well. Few sets equipped with UHF receivers were made during the 1950s. The UHF stations had smaller coverage areas than the VHF stations, and most advertising dollars went to VHF stations. As a result, UHF TV, much like FM radio, started off at a disadvantage.

Color television was introduced during the 1950s. Led by NBC (RCA, the parent company, was manufacturing color TV sets), the networks were broadcasting 2–3 hours of color programming per day by 1960.

The Golden Age of Television   Many broadcast historians refer to the 1950s as the golden age of TV. Many shows that aired during the decade became extremely popular. *Toast of the Town,* hosted by Ed Sullivan, is still regarded as the examplar of the variety series. *Texaco Star Theater,* starring ex-vaudevillian Milton Berle, prompted many people to buy TV sets just to see what wacky stunts Berle would pull off on his next program.

Live prestige dramas were also run in prime time. Programs such as *Studio One* featured plays by Rod Serling, Gore Vidal, and Reginald Rose. Broadway stars such as Rex Harrison

The Beverly Hillbillies was the most popular of the "bucolic" situation comedies. It was the number-one show during the 1961–1962 TV season and spent 9 years on the air.

and Tallulah Bankhead performed in live TV drama. The growing popularity of videotape, however, put an end to these live productions.

By the end of the 1950s, a new genre, the adult Western, in which character and motivation overshadowed gunfights, dominated TV. By 1959, there were 26 Westerns in prime time, including *Gunsmoke, The Life and Legend of Wyatt Earp,* and *Wagon Train.*

▲ Coming of Age: Television in the 1960s

By the early 1960s TV had lost its novelty and become just another part of everyday life. The number of TV stations continued to increase, and by the close of the decade, more than 95 percent of all American households owned at least one TV.

Television journalism came of age during the 1960s. NBC and CBS expanded their nightly newscasts from 15 to 30 minutes in 1963, and ABC followed suit shortly thereafter. In November of that year, TV journalism earned praise for its professionalism during its coverage of the assassination and funeral of President John F. Kennedy. The networks also covered the civil rights movement and the growing social unrest across the country. Perhaps the most exciting moment for television news came in 1969 with its live coverage of Neil Armstrong's historic walk on the moon.

Noncommercial broadcasting also evolved during the 1960s. About 69 educational stations were broadcasting by 1965. A report issued by the Carnegie Commission proposed that Congress establish a Corporation for Public Broadcasting. The commission's recommendations were incorporated into the **Public Broadcasting Act of 1967,** which set up the Public Broadcasting Service.

Another segment of the video industry was also experiencing growth during this time period—cable television. We will discuss the history of cable TV in the next chapter.

Television programs popular in the early 1960s included a number of rural comedies, such as *The Beverly Hillbillies* and *Green Acres.* After the Kennedy assassination, however, fantasy and escapist programs dominated prime time. In 1964, for example, some of the shows that premiered included *Bewitched* (about a friendly witch), *My Favorite Martian* (about a friendly Martian), and *My Mother the Car* (self-explanatory).

▲ The 1970s: Growing Public Concern

As the 1970s began, public concern over the impact of television programming was growing. A panel of scientists set up by the Surgeon General's office to investigate the impact of exposure to TV violence suggested that TV violence was related in a modest way to aggressive behavior in some young children. We'll explore this topic further in Chapter 19.

The early 1970s were also characterized by the growth of citizen group involvement in FCC decisions. Groups such as Action for Children's Television and the Office of Communication of the United Church of Christ and coalitions of minority groups became influential in shaping broadcasting policy.

The three networks continued to dominate the industry during the early-to-mid-1970s, but by the end of the decade, they were beginning to feel the competition from the growing cable industry. Friction between the traditional over-the-air broadcasters and the cable companies continues today.

The biggest trend in television programming during the early 1970s was the growth of law-and-order programs, such as *The FBI, Charlie's Angels,* and *Mannix.* By the middle of

Live TV coverage of the first man landing on the moon in 1969 reached hundreds of millions of viewers.

the decade, these shows were replaced by a number of adult situation comedies, shows that dealt with more mature themes. *All in the Family*, *M*A*S*H*, and *Sanford and Son* typified this trend. By the end of the decade, prime-time soap operas such as *Dallas* and *Dynasty* topped the ratings.

▲ The 1980s and 1990s: Increased Competition

The biggest trends in the TV industry in the 1980s and 1990s were the continuing erosion of the three big networks' audiences and the increased competition from new networks and cable channels. In the early 1970s the three networks routinely pulled down about 90 percent of the prime-time audience. By the late 1990s their share had dropped to less than 60 percent. In addition, a fourth network, the Fox Broadcasting Company, owned by Rupert Murdoch's News Corporation, started broadcasting in 1987. In the early 1990s two other networks started up: the United Paramount Network (UPN) and the Warner Broadcasting Network (the WB). Both began with limited schedules but had plans to expand their offerings. (In 2006, the WB and UPN would merge to form a single network, CW.)

In 1995 the world of network broadcasting was shaken by two megadeals. First, the Walt Disney Company acquired CapCities/ABC for $19 billion. Then, with the ink barely dry on that deal, Westinghouse disclosed that it was buying CBS for $5.4 billion.

▲ Cable's Continued Growth

Cable reached more than 68 percent of the population by 2000. As cable systems increased their capacity, new cable programming services rushed to fill the new channels. By 2000 there were six national pay-per-view services; six premium services, including HBO and Showtime; and more than 75 cable networks, including the Sci Fi Channel, Animal Planet, and the Outdoor Channel. Many cable systems were providing more than 100 channels of television to their subscribers. Some new cable networks were having trouble because there was no room left on local systems to carry them. The growing popularity of cable channels further eroded the audiences of the traditional TV networks.

Advertising revenue also grew, topping the $11-billion mark in 1999. By the turn of the century, it was obvious that the cable industry was a full-fledged competitor of traditional broadcasting.

R. E. "Ted" Turner inherited his family's outdoor advertising company in 1963, when he was 24. The Atlanta-based business was in poor economic shape, but the young Turner managed to turn it around. Six years later, Turner learned that a financially troubled UHF television station was for sale. Disregarding the fact that the station's signal was so weak that he could not pick it up on his own TV set, Turner bought the station, renamed it WTCG, and began to advertise it on his unused billboards around Atlanta. With a skillful programming mix of TV reruns and old movies, the station eventually became one of the few UHF stations in the country at the time to turn a profit. Turner, however, was not content with merely turning the station around. He had much bigger plans for it.

One day in 1976, at a meeting of the station's managers, Turner placed a beat-up model of the RCA Satcom I satellite on the table and proclaimed that WTCG would soon be competing with CBS, NBC, and ABC. Turner had decided that he would use the new communication satellites to beam WTCG to cable systems all over the country, making it a national network. Not surprisingly, his managers were incredulous. Almost everybody dismissed Turner's idea as totally impractical.

There were many reasons to think this bold move would not work. First, cable TV had not yet caught on; it was available in only 16 percent of the country, mostly in rural areas. Second, cable systems relied on terrestrial microwave signals; not many were equipped to receive satellite feeds. Third, the FCC had a rule against leapfrogging that prohibited cable systems from importing signals from distant cities unless they also took the signals of stations closer to their market. Additionally, FCC regulations permitted cable systems to use only expensive 10-meter satellite dishes, which most systems could not afford. Undaunted, Turner pitched his idea to big cable operators. They were not impressed.

As fate would have it, however, 2 weeks later, the FCC dropped its leapfrogging rules and permitted stations to use smaller and cheaper satellite dishes. All of a sudden, Turner's idea did not seem so far-fetched. In December, Turner renamed his station WTBS and started distributing it by satellite, thus creating the first superstation.

WTBS caught on slowly. When it first went on the satellite, the station was received by a grand total of four cable systems. Turner helped its fortunes by purchasing the Atlanta Braves baseball team and making their games available on WTBS. The new superstation continued to grow in popularity, eventually reaching 74 million homes. The success of WTBS inspired the creation of other cable networks and totally changed the cable TV industry. Turner proved that people would subscribe to cable not just to get good reception but also to get programming.

Turner had other ideas. He had encouraged cable systems to carry WTBS by promising them that he would also provide them with additional cable networks. In 1980 he launched the first of those networks—CNN. Cable operators were lukewarm toward the new project. Most refused to provide money to cover start-up costs. Turner invested $21 million in the new venture, which was immediately derided by competitors for its bargain-basement approach to news. Critics labeled CNN the *Chicken Noodle Network*.

CNN started off losing money, but Turner kept the network alive with the profits from WTBS. Finally, CNN went into the black in 1985. Six years later, during the Gulf War, CNN scooped the other networks by having reporters on the scene in Baghdad when the war broke out. CNN's success spawned several 24-hour news service competitors, including MSNBC and Fox News Channel.

Several other Turner decisions have also paid off. In 1986 he paid more than a billion dollars for the MGM/United Artists film library. Turner used the films to help launch two other cable networks—Turner Network Television and Turner Classic Movies. Turner also bought the Hanna-Barbera animation studio and started the Cartoon Network.

However, some of Turner's ventures did not work out so well. After Time Warner merged with AOL, Turner became a vice chair of the new company. The merger was a disappointment, and AOL Time Warner's stock suffered a huge drop in value. Turner lost millions as a result. In 2003 he resigned his position with the company.

Turner also has an interest in philanthropy. His United Nations Foundation grants money to organizations that are interested in population control and the environment. His Turner Foundation concentrates on improving life in the United States. The decline in AOL Time Warner's stock, unfortunately, has meant a cutback in funding for both organizations.

Turner has made some good decisions and some that have not been successful. Regardless, his decisions have had an enormous impact on television and have been key contributors to the design of the modern TV industry landscape.

▲ Zapping, Zipping, Grazing, and DBS

A development that had a significant impact on both traditional TV and the cable industry was the spectacular growth of videocassette recorders (VCRs). Fewer than 5 percent of households had VCRs in 1982. By 2000 that figure was 90 percent. In fact, the VCR was adopted faster than any other appliance except television. The effects of the VCR were many.

First, the renting of movies on cassettes became a multibillion-dollar business, with motion picture studios depending on cassettes for a large part of their revenue.

Second, the VCR encouraged **time shifting,** playing back programs at times other than when they aired. Although this increased total audience by allowing people who might not otherwise have viewed a program to do so, it caused some new problems for advertisers. Some viewers had special machines that *zap* commercials: The VCR paused while the commercial aired and then started up again when the program was on. Also, when viewers played back programs, many fast-forwarded, or *zipped,* their way through the ads.

Finally, the proliferation of the handheld remote-control device has also caused problems for advertisers and programmers. Remote units have encouraged the tendency toward *grazing,* rapidly scanning all the channels during a commercial or dull spot in a program in search of greener pastures.

Low-power television (LPTV), an innovation that allowed a new class of TV stations with a small service area, grew slowly, hampered at first by an avalanche of applications that overwhelmed the FCC. Despite the huge initial interest, LPTV stations did not live up to expectations. LPTV stations are still in operation today, but most are marginal operations at best.

After a slow start, direct broadcast by satellite (DBS) got a big boost in 1994 when two companies, DirecTV and United States Satellite Broadcasting (USSB), offered subscribers about 150 channels of programming beamed directly to their homes via a small (18-inch diameter) receiver.

On the legal side the biggest development was the Telecommunications Act of 1996 (discussed in Chapter 17), which introduced program ratings and the V-chip while encouraging competition between cable and phone companies and easing ownership restrictions on TV stations.

TV programming during the mid-1980s marked the return of warm, family-oriented comedies, such as *The Cosby Show* and *Family Ties.* One reason for the popularity of these shows was economic. Family sitcoms did well in the syndication aftermarket (more on syndication later). The biggest programming trend of the early-to-mid-1990s was the growth of prime-time newsmagazines, such as *60 Minutes, 20/20,* and *Dateline NBC.* At the turn of the century, the success of reality programs, such as *Survivor* and *Big Brother,* surprised many television executives. HBO also enjoyed success with dramatic series such as *The Sopranos* and *Sex and the City.*

CONTEMPORARY BROADCAST TELEVISION

The traditional broadcast television industry is in a state of change. Network and local audiences continue to shrink, and advertising dollars are finding their way to the Web. The Big Four broadcast networks—ABC, CBS, NBC, and FOX—have all moved into new distribution channels. CBS, for example, now offers its programs on iTunes and on its Web site and delivers content to PDAs and cell phones. News Corp., the parent of Fox, purchased MySpace in 2005 and makes some of its TV programs available there. ABC offers free downloads of its hit programs a few hours after they are broadcast. In fact, because viewers can record a show on TiVo or stream it from a Web site, or download it from iTunes and watch it when they prefer, the traditional notion of tuning into a channel at a specific time to watch a program is slowly becoming obsolete. Speaking of TiVo, digital video recorders (DVRs) are becoming more prevalent. As of 2006, more than 20 percent of U.S. homes were equipped with TiVo or other kinds of DVRs, and that number is expected to grow significantly in the future. In addition to allowing viewers to watch programs at more convenient times, the DVR makes it easy for them to fast-forward through commercials, a development that advertisers find troubling.

On the technology front, DVD players have replaced VCRs as the medium of choice for home video. At the beginning of 2007, 8 out of every 10 U.S. households were equipped with a DVD player. And those DVD players are increasingly connected to a big-screen, high-definition TV. A 2006 survey found that about one in three homes were watching programs in high-def. The broadcast networks are offering more of their programs in high-def (more than 60 hours per week in prime time in 2006), and sporting events such as the Super Bowl and the NCAA basketball playoffs are now broadcast in high-def.

By 2008 about 40 percent of all American homes will have an HDTV set, enabling them to see a television picture more than five times sharper than traditional analog TV. This trend has set off some alarms among older television performers because with HDTV every skin imperfection is clearly visible. As Diane Sawyer, one of the mainstays of ABC's *Good Morning America,* put it in a recent article in *AARP The Magazine,* viewers will clearly know if she stayed up late the night before because they will be able to see the puffiness under her eyes.

At local stations many veteran news anchors are concerned that viewers with HDTV might be shocked at how the anchors really look. Good lighting and expert makeup are beneficial (most stations that switch to HDTV bring in makeup specialists to help anchors ease the shock of transition), but sometimes this is not enough. Some older broadcasters have opted for more drastic solutions, including Botox and facelifts. In fact, one TV station that was switching to HDTV requested extra funds in its budget for plastic surgery. Regrettably, that's not always a solution since HDTV also makes it easy to see the results of cosmetic surgery.

One small consolation: Even younger people have trouble with the clarity of HDTV. Many viewers have been surprised to see that many big stars also have skin flaws. The sharp glare of HDTV causes problems for both young and old.

With regard to programming, the broadcast networks are relying more on reality shows and less on scripted programs. Reality shows usually cost much less than a traditional scripted program. The 2006–2007 season contained 14 hours in prime time devoted to reality programs such as *American Idol, Survivor, Dancing with the Stars,* and *Deal or No Deal.* In late 2006 NBC announced that it would no longer schedule scripted programs during the first hour of prime time most nights of the week. Further, the networks seldom offer original programming on Saturday nights, relying instead on reruns. This trend has caused concern among many in the creative community who see their potential market narrowing.

On a more positive note for the broadcast industry, even with the competition from the Internet and other media, the American people continue to watch a lot of TV. In 2006, in the average household, the set was on for 8 hours and 14 minutes per day, an increase of 1 hour from 1996. And even though their audiences are declining, the broadcast networks are still the best means for advertisers to reach a large audience in a hurry. Finally, the networks still own the content that most Americans want to watch. Much of the popularity of the many video-sharing sites, such as YouTube, is due to the fact that they contain clips from popular network shows.

TELEVISION IN THE DIGITAL AGE

Television will officially enter the digital age on February 17, 2009. That is the day that Congress has set for analog broadcasting to end and digital broadcasting to begin. **Digital TV (DTV)** offers many advantages. Digital pictures are clearer; sound quality is better. The screen size is more rectangular (16:9 aspect ration) and less like the traditional "squarish" (4:3 aspect ratio) TV. There are other advantages as well. Digital TV makes super-resolution **high-definition TV (HDTV)** possible. HDTV has about five times the clarity of standard TV. A broadcaster can also subdivide the digital channel and offer several different standard-definition programs in the same space. During the afternoon a local station might, for example, offer a network program on one subchannel, local news on another, and weather on a third. During prime time the station might carry a single HDTV program.

▲ Broadcasters and the Web

As described earlier in the chapter, the broadcast networks and local stations are making more of their programs available on the Internet. NBC Universal, for example, posts episodes of its series *Heroes* on its Web site 4 hours after it is broadcast. CBS also has deals with AOL and MSN that allow them to distribute CBS programs. In mid-2007 CBS announced plans to form the Interactive Audience Network, an advertiser-supported venture that will put CBS content on a number of distribution channels including Yahoo! and the CNet Networks. Local stations owned by Fox make the latest episodes of *24* and *Prison Break* available for downloading on their Web site. All of the major networks provide program episodes for downloading on iTunes. Many local stations in large markets provide streaming news video on their sites. Clearly, much of broadcast video has migrated to the Web.

Broadcasters are also becoming savvier about their own Web sites. ABC's site, for example, offers full-screen, high-resolution streaming video of its programs. ABC and CBS offer original content on their sites while NBC's site has a social networking option. The Fox network created MySpace pages (MySpace is owned by Fox's parent company) for 18 characters on its series *Bones*. Fans can peruse the pages for clues about upcoming episodes. In addition to creating revenue by selling ad space on their sites, the networks offer advertisers the option of inserting ads into the streaming video of their programs.

Broadcasters have not overlooked the podcast as another digital channel by which to reach audiences. All of the major networks offer podcasts of selected programs. ABC, for example, podcasts *Nightline, 20/20,* and some original content. NBC offers podcasts of its news programs.

Local broadcast stations are also realizing that they need to increase their Web presence. When it comes to local online advertising, newspaper Web sites generate more than twice the revenue of local TV station sites. In response, local stations, such as WRAL in Raleigh, North Carolina, have added a social networking component to its site and increased the number of Web-only news stories. Other stations are beefing up their Web coverage of local news events and features. Some have even started video-sharing sites while others now offer original entertainment programs such as local talent shows.

▲ Broadcasters and Broadband

Broadband is a term used to describe high-speed Internet connections, such as those with a cable modem or digital subscriber line (DSL). A broadband connection makes it possible to send video over the Web. Broadcasters take advantage of this when they offer streaming versions of their popular shows online, but broadband has an even greater potential: Broadcasters can create specialized channels that are distributed over a broadband connection.

The big networks are using their broadband channels to offer special-interest programming that would never be successful on their broadcast channels. NBC, for instance, produces OutZone.com, a Web site that appeals to gay men, and DotComedy.com, with content designed for (what else?) comedy enthusiasts. CBS offers ShowBuzz.com, a site that specializes in entertainment news. Another CBS property, CSTV.com, illustrates the capability of broadband by offering subscribers a hundred broadband channels devoted to college sports.

The broadband channels have yet to generate a profit for broadcasters, but they do represent a place where the networks (and even some local stations) can experiment with new programming forms without risking a large amount of money. The networks also recognize that their audience is growing older, and broadband channels provide a way to reach a younger demographic.

▲ Mobile TV

Like other content providers, traditional television broadcasters are increasingly supplying their programming to cell phones. The number of subscribers to mobile video is still relatively small, about 6 million in 2006, but it is growing. A company called MobiTV works with the major cell phone companies to provide subscribers with content from broadcast and cable networks. Cell phone users can also receive content from the individual networks, such as CBS's *Sportsline*, which keeps subscribers up-to-date on all the latest scores and sports news. Fox created a special 1-minute cell phone episode connected to its hit series *24*. Phone maker Samsung is working with local TV stations to create a mobile service that carries weather and traffic news. A new technology, mobile pedestrian handheld, that makes it possible for local broadcasters to send their signals directly to cell phones, was announced in 2007.

Contributed by Kevin Williams
Assistant Professor, Mississippi State University

The concept of interactive television seems always to be just around the corner and out of reach, but in reality this new technology may be closer than we think. The first problem that we must grapple with is how to form a true definition of interactive television. Most researchers in this field agree that there is no easy definition and have spent small parts of their careers conceptualizing an encompassing definition. That being said, I would attempt to define it as a form of television that takes advantage of the digital transmission of content (via digital cable or digital satellite, or even over the air) by allowing the viewer to gain extra information from or "interact" with the current programming.

In short, what do you want television to do for you? Advertisers might argue that interactive television should allow the viewer to push a button and instantly order whatever product is being pitched on the television at that particular moment. Perhaps while watching *Desperate Housewives*, a viewer could click on a button on a remote and order the necklace that Bree is wearing. Television producers may argue that the viewer should be able to access extra information, much like that now offered on DVDs, when viewing favorite programs. Network programmers might want you to be able to search for programs by key word, such as *actor/actress, director, title,* or *genre*.

Some technologies that have been deployed or are currently being developed will serve as a foundation on which to build future interactive capabilities. Perhaps the most overlooked prerequisite to interactive television is the electronic programming guide (EPG). Not long ago, viewers had to read *TV Guide* or newspaper "television books" to find out what was showing on TV throughout the week. On screen, viewers may have been able to consult a guide that constantly scrolled, telling what was on television in the next hour or two. Unfortunately, if the scroll was currently showing what was on channel 2 and you were interested in channel 130, you would have to wait to get your information. EPGs are provided with most digital and cable services today so that the viewer can instantly access programming information.

One of the most promising technologies so far deployed is the digital video recorder (DVR), such as TiVo. Some satellite and cable providers have included DVR capabilities in their receiver and converter boxes. DVRs give the user the ability to pause, rewind, and even slow motion or repeat live television. Nearly all of these machines also act as digital VCRs, using their own EPGs to search for and record upcoming shows that the viewer has chosen. Some DVRs go one step further and suggest programs that a viewer may want to record, based on previous recording preferences. One may ask how this device differs from a VCR; both manufacturers and users proclaim that the DVR interface is much more user-friendly.

Media forecasters believe the use of these current technologies could drastically change the way we watch television. With a DVR, a viewer may watch programs whenever he or she chooses. With the multitude of channels available and the ease of searching for shows via EPGs, some forecasters speculate that viewers will not be as loyal to specific channels and will instead jump among channels more frequently to catch different shows (in essence, a highly informed version of channel surfing). Advertisers worry that viewers will use a DVR to fast-forward through commercials. One effect might be product placement or sponsorship of shows as a replacement for the typical 30-second commercial. With the ever-expanding convergence of media, it is not ridiculous to think that the television and computer will soon be fused into an "all-encompassing" box. Soon we may see the dreams of thousands of college students realized when they can order a pizza via their television.

▲ User-Generated Content

Broadcasters were the first to realize the potential of user-generated content. *America's Funniest Home Videos* premiered in 1989 and, as of this writing, is still on the air. The growth of video on the Internet, however, has opened up new possibilities for the industry, and broadcasters are experimenting with other ways to capitalize on the do-it-yourself video boom. (A lot of broadcast content is used by amateurs to make "mash-ups," where video from several sources is edited together to make a new video.) The biggest problem facing broadcasters (as well as cablecasters) with regard to user-generated content is how to relate to video-sharing giant YouTube. All are trying different strategies. CBS has a deal with YouTube to post news, entertainment, and sports videos on the site. On the other hand, Viacom, owner of several cable channels, sued YouTube for $1 billion and removed more than 100,000 clips from the site, claiming copyright violations. Disney, parent of ABC, has also voiced concern about illegal uploading of their content on YouTube. On the other other hand, News Corp., parent of Fox, and NBC Universal have started their own video-sharing site with content from most of their hit programs. Although the future is always murky, most professionally produced content may wind up on Web sites owned by the copyright holders while the amateur stuff stays with YouTube.

DEFINING FEATURES OF BROADCAST TELEVISION

Like radio, TV is a universal medium. About 99 percent of the homes in the United States have at least one working TV set. In fact, most homes have more than one. Although not quite as portable as radios, miniature TV sets make it possible to take TV anywhere.

Television has become the dominant medium for news and entertainment for Americans. Surveys have consistently revealed that most people choose television as their main source of news. In addition, in the average American household, the TV set is on for about 8 hours every day. Prime-time television series may draw an audience of 20 million households. In short, TV has become an important part of our society.

Further, TV, especially network television, is an expensive business. It costs the production company more than $2 million to produce one episode of a typical one-hour prime-time series. Most series produce about 20–22 original episodes a year. A little math reveals that the total cost for one season of one prime-time hour for one network is about $44 million. Some more math discloses that the total tab for prime-time programming for the four major networks is more than $2 billion. Added to that is the cost of daytime programs and newscasts. TV advertising is also costly, averaging more than $200,000 for a 30-second spot in network prime time.

Finally, over the past several decades, the television industry has watched its audience fragment. Back in 1970, the major networks' share of the audience was about 90 percent. Today, the increase in cable networks, DVD usage, video games, and home video has cut that share in half. The fragmenting audience is most apparent in the cable industry, in which new cable channels are increasingly geared to a small, well-defined audience niche. And even those niche audiences are being divided up. There are two cable networks devoted to health programming, four specializing in women's programs, and five devoted to home and lifestyle topics.

ORGANIZATION OF THE BROADCAST TELEVISION INDUSTRY

The **commercial television** system consists of all those local stations whose income is derived from selling time on their facilities to advertisers. **Noncommercial television** consists of those stations whose income is derived from sources other than the sale of advertising time.

A local TV station is licensed by the FCC to provide TV service to a particular community. In the industry these communities are customarily referred to as *markets*. There are 210 markets in the United States, ranging from the number-one market, New York City, with about 7.4 million homes, to number 210, Glendive, Montana, with about 5,000 homes. Some of these local TV stations enter into contractual agreements with TV networks. As of 2007, six commercial networks in the United States supplied programs to local stations: the American Broadcasting Company (ABC), the Columbia Broadcasting System (CBS), the National Broadcasting Company (NBC), the Fox Broadcasting Company (FBC), the CW, and My Network TV. The Public Broadcasting Service (PBS) serves as a network for noncommercial stations. A local station that signs a contract with one of the networks is an affiliate. ABC, CBS, and NBC have about 200 affiliates scattered across the country; Fox has slightly fewer; and the CW and My Network TV have still fewer. Local stations that do not have network affiliation are independents.

Much like the film industry, the TV industry is divided into three segments: (1) production, (2) distribution, and (3) exhibition. The production element is responsible for providing the programming that is ultimately viewed by the TV audience. The distribution function is handled by the TV networks and cable and syndication companies. The exhibition of television programs—the element in the system that most people are most familiar with—is the responsibility of local TV stations.

▲ Production

Pretend for a moment that you are the manager of a local TV station in your hometown. Your station must provide 24 hours of programming every day, or approximately

A local TV news program. News is the most common form of production at a local station and also produces the most revenue.

8,800 hours of programming each year. Where does one get all this programming? There are three basic sources: (1) local production, (2) syndicated programming, and (3) for some stations, network programs.

Local production consists of those programs that are produced in the local station's own studio or on location with the use of the station's equipment. The most common local productions are the station's daily newscasts, typically broadcast at noon, in the early evening, and in the late evening. These newscasts attract large audiences, which in turn attract advertisers. As a result the local news accounts for a major proportion of the ad revenue that is generated by a local station. Not surprisingly, local stations devote a major share of their production budgets to their news shows. Other locally produced programming might consist of local sporting events, early-morning interview programs, and public affairs discussion shows. It would be difficult, however, for a local station to fill its entire schedule with locally produced programming. As a result most stations turn to programming produced by other sources.

If the station is affiliated with a network (and most stations are), much of its programming problem is solved. Networks typically supply about 65–70 percent of the programming carried by their affiliates. Many of the programs supplied by the networks are produced by the networks themselves. News, sports, early-morning talk shows, and an increasing number of prime-time dramas and sitcoms are network productions. Independent production companies or the TV divisions of major motion picture studios supply other programs. Table 10-1 lists some programs and their production companies.

Many independent production companies sell their shows to syndication firms. For instance, King World Productions handles *Wheel of Fortune, Jeopardy, The Oprah Winfrey Show,* and *Inside Edition.* Programs that have already played on the networks (called *off-net series*) are also distributed by syndication companies. These programs usually air during the late afternoon or early evening, not in prime time. In addition, packages of movies, made up from some of the 23,000 films that have been released for TV, can be leased from syndication companies.

▲ Distribution

The three main elements in the distribution segment of television are the broadcast networks, cable and satellite networks, and syndication companies. The network distributes programs to its affiliates by transmitting them via satellite. The station then transmits them to its viewers as they are received, or it records them and airs them at a later time. The

TABLE 10-1	Production Company	Programs
Examples of Production Companies and Their Programs for the 2006–2007 Season	Networks	
	ABC	*20/20, Primetime Live*
	CBS	*60 Minutes, 48 Hours Mystery*
	NBC	*Las Vegas, The Office*
	Fox	*Cops*
	Independents	
	Mark Burnett Prods.	*The Apprentice, The Contender*
	Endemol	*Deal or No Deal, Extreme Makeover, Home Edition*
	TV Divisions of Film Companies	
	Warner Bros.	*Two and a Half Men, Gilmore Girls*
	Touchstone	*Grey's Anatomy, Lost*

affiliation contract between a local station and the network is a complicated document. In simplified terms the station agrees to carry the network's programs, and in return the network agrees to pay the station a certain amount of money for clearing its time so that the network programs can be seen. (Although it may seem contradictory that the network actually pays the station to carry the network's programming, remember that the network is using the local station's facilities to show the network's commercials.) The amount of money paid by the network varies by market size and is influenced by the competition. (The networks continue to examine their compensation arrangements, and it is likely that affiliates will be receiving less or maybe nothing in the future.) The network then sells time in its programs to advertisers seeking a national audience.

Syndication companies provide another kind of program distribution. These organizations lease taped or filmed programs to local television stations in each local market. Sometimes, as mentioned, the syndication company also produces the program, but more often it distributes programs produced by other firms. Local stations that purchase a syndicated program receive exclusive rights to show that program in their market (a situation complicated by cable TV systems that bring in distant stations). Usually, a station buys a package of programs—perhaps as many as 120 episodes or more—and the contract specifies how many times each program can be repeated.

Inside a TV control room: The director scans the bank of monitors before deciding what to put on the air.

Syndication companies try to sell their shows in as many TV markets as possible. The greater the coverage of the show, the more appealing it is to national advertisers. Top-rated syndicated shows, such as *Wheel of Fortune* and *Jeopardy,* are seen in nearly all TV markets.

Syndication functions as an important aftermarket for prime-time TV shows. In fact, some prime-time series are produced at a deficit, sometimes $200,000 or more for each one-hour episode. Production companies gamble that they can make back this money in the syndication market. It is a risk, but if a show hits it big in syndication, it might earn half a billion dollars or more. To be attractive in the syndication market, however, a prime-time show must have enough back episodes stockpiled so that stations can run episodes for a long time without showing repeats. Since 100 seems to be the magic number, series usually have a big party to commemorate the production of their hundredth episode. Since only 22 or 24 new shows are produced each season, it is obvious that those series that last 4 or 5 years are the best bets for syndication success.

▲ Exhibition

At the start of 2006, there were approximately 1,300 commercial TV stations and 380 non-commercial stations in the United States. Some TV stations are licensed to broadcast in the very-high-frequency (**VHF**) band of the electromagnetic spectrum; these stations occupy channels 2–13 on the TV set. Other stations broadcast in the ultra-high-frequency (**UHF**) part of the spectrum; these stations are found on channels 14–69. As noted earlier, VHF stations have a signal that covers greater distances than UHF stations. Consequently, VHF stations tend to be more desirable to own and operate. These differences will not be as important after the move to digital TV.

As suggested earlier, another important difference among stations concerns their affiliation with national networks. As of 2006, more than 90 percent of all commercial stations were affiliated with CBS, NBC, ABC, or Fox. Of the remaining 10 percent, many are affiliates of the CW or My Network TV.

Those stations not affiliated with networks are called **independents.** For many years independents were hampered because most were UHF stations and had less coverage area than VHFs. The emergence of cable, however, gave UHF independents more of a competitive advantage, since unlike the situation with over-the-air signals, with cable both UHF and VHF stations have the same audience reach. Recently, most independent stations signed on with either the CW or My Network TV. "Pure" independents are now hard to find.

OWNERSHIP IN THE TELEVISION INDUSTRY

As of 2007, all the major networks were under the control of large conglomerates:

- NBC Universal is owned by General Electric. In addition to its holdings in nonmedia areas, such as aerospace, aircraft engines, consumer products, and financial properties, GE has interests in TV stations; cable/satellite networks, including CNBC, MSNBC, and Court TV; and a movie studio.
- ABC is owned by the Walt Disney Company, which also owns theme parks, a cruise line, retail stores, and media holdings that include daily newspapers, magazines, film production companies, radio networks, record companies, cable networks, and TV stations.
- Fox is controlled by Rupert Murdoch's News Corporation, which owns a major film and TV production company, more than 20 TV stations, cable networks, satellite networks, a record company, newspapers, magazines, and a book publishing company.
- CBS is part of CBS Corporation, a company that was spun off from media conglomerate Viacom in 2005. In addition to the network, the CBS Corporation includes the CBS-owned TV and radio stations, a TV production company, and book publisher Simon & Schuster.

	Percentage of U.S. Households Reached (as calculated by the FCC)
Group	
CBS Corp.	38.5
Fox TV Stations	38.0
Ion Media Networks (Paxson)	31.3
Tribune	30.0
NBC Universal	29.8

TABLE 10-2

Top Five Owners of TV Stations, 2006

The two newest networks, the CW and My Network TV, are also part of large organizations. The CW is a joint venture between the CBS Corporation and media giant Time Warner. My Network TV is owned by the News Corporation, parent of Fox.

At the station level the Telecommunications Act of 1996 (see Chapter 17) allowed a person or organization to own an unlimited number of TV stations as long as the combined reach of the stations did not exceed 35 percent of the U.S. population (later amended to 39 percent). By the end of 2005, big groups controlled most of the TV stations in the top 100 markets. Table 10-2 lists the top five group owners.

PRODUCING TELEVISION PROGRAMS

▲ Departments and Staff

There are many different staffing arrangements in television stations. Some big city stations employ 300–400 people and may be divided into a dozen different departments. Small town stations may have 20–30 employees and only a few departments.

In one common arrangement, a station manager is ultimately responsible for all station activities. The rest of the station is organized into five departments:

1. *Sales:* Is responsible for selling time to local and national advertisers, scheduling ads, and billing clients.
2. *Engineering:* Maintains technical equipment.
3. *Production/Programming:* Puts together locally produced programming; also acquires programming from outside sources and is responsible for scheduling.
4. *News:* Is in charge of producing the station's regularly scheduled news programs.
5. *Administration:* Consists of clerical, accounting, and personnel segments that help in the day-to-day running of the station.

At the network level the divisions are somewhat more complicated. Although the major networks differ in their setups, all seem to have departments that perform the following functions:

1. *Sales:* Handles the sale of network commercials and works with advertising agencies.
2. *Entertainment:* Works with producers to develop new programs for the network.
3. *Owned and operated stations:* Administers those stations owned by the networks.
4. *Affiliate relations:* Supervises all contracts with stations affiliated with the network (and generally tries to keep the affiliates happy).
5. *News:* Is responsible for all network news and public affairs programs.
6. *Sports:* Is responsible for all sports programming.
7. *Standards:* Checks all network programs to make sure they do not violate the law or the network's own guidelines for appropriate content.
8. *Operations:* Handles the technical aspects of actually sending programs to affiliates.

▲ Getting TV Programs on the Air

At the local level the biggest effort at a TV station goes into the newscast. Almost every station has a studio that contains a set for one or two anchorpeople, a weather forecaster, and a sportscaster. The station's news director assigns stories to reporters and camera crews, who travel to the scene of a story and videotape a report. Back at the station, the newscast producer and news director are planning what stories to air and allotting time to each. In the meantime the camera crews and reporters return; the reporters write copy and editors prepare videotape segments. When the final script is finished (this may be only a few minutes before airtime), it is given to a director, who is responsible for pulling everything together and putting the newscast on the air.

In addition to the news, the local station might produce one or two interview programs. Some stations also produce a "magazine" program consisting of segments videotaped on location and later edited into final form. Aside from these kinds of shows, most local stations do little other production.

Because they are responsible for filling the hours when the biggest audience is watching (called *prime time*, 8–11 P.M., Eastern Standard Time), the networks must pay special attention to cultivating new shows. For the moment we will concentrate on how a prime-time series is produced.

Everything starts with an idea. Network executives receive hundreds of ideas every year; some come from independent producers, some from TV departments of motion picture companies, some from network employees, and a good many from amateurs hoping for a break. From this mass of ideas, the networks select perhaps 50–75, usually submitted by established producers or companies, for further attention. After examining plot outlines and background sketches of the leading characters for these 50–75 potential series, the networks trim the list once again. For those ideas that survive, the networks request a sample script and a list of possible stories that could be turned into scripts. If the idea still looks promising, the network and producer enter into a contract for a **pilot,** the first episode of a series. In a typical year perhaps 25 pilots are ordered by each network. If the pilot show gains a respectable audience, the network may order five or six episodes produced and may place the program on its fall schedule. From the hundreds of ideas that are sent to the network, only a few ever make it to prime time.

The process does not stop with the fall season. If a program does well in the ratings, the network will order enough episodes for the rest of the season. If the show does not do well, it will be canceled and replaced with another show. Meanwhile, network executives are sifting through the hundreds of program ideas for the next season, and the cycle begins once again.

THE ECONOMICS OF BROADCAST TELEVISION

The television industry has been profitable since 1950, and its total income has increased every year since 1971. In 2006, television advertising revenue amounted to $67 billion. The changing structure of the television industry, however, has had a significant economic impact on both local stations and the networks. We will explore more about this after we look at the traditional sources of television advertising revenue.

▲ Commercial Time

Where did the $67 billion in revenue come from? It came from the sale of commercial time by networks, local stations, and cable systems to advertisers. A station, network, or cable system makes available a specified number of minutes per hour that will be offered for sale to advertisers. There are three different types of advertisers who buy time on TV: (1) national advertisers, (2) national spot advertisers, and (3) local advertisers.

National advertisers are those that sell general-consumption items: soda pop, automobiles, deodorant, hair spray, and so on. These advertisers try to reach the biggest possible audience for their messages and usually purchase commercial time on broadcast network programs or cable networks.

In contrast, other advertisers have products that are used mainly in one region or locale. For example, a manufacturer of snowmobiles would gain little by having his or her ad seen

Kweisi Mfume, president of the NAACP, speaking at his organization's national convention, criticized the four major TV networks for the lack of diversity in the new shows planned for the 1999–2000 season. He noted that none of the 26 series had a minority person in a leading or starring role. Mfume's criticism marked another chapter in the continuing controversy over the portrayals of minorities in prime time.

During the early years of TV, African American performers were difficult to find. And when they did appear, it was usually in a menial or subservient role. In 1965, however, a young Bill Cosby costarred with Robert Culp in *I Spy* and paved the way for more substantial roles for African American performers. By the 1970s several shows that featured black casts appeared in prime time—most were situation comedies, such as *The Jeffersons*. The number of African American performers increased slowly but steadily during the 1980s. For most of the 1990s, the proportion of black characters seen in prime-time TV was about the same as the percentage of African Americans in the general population. This increase, however, was due in part to the emergence of UPN and WB, two networks that targeted several of their series to African American viewers.

The apparent lack of diversity in the 1999–2000 season was especially troubling to Mfume. The NAACP noted that minorities were hard to find behind the camera as well. Of all the writers who worked on TV sitcoms and dramas, only 6 percent were black. FCC data show that minorities own about 2.8 percent of all broadcast stations.

Mfume threatened a boycott of the networks and their sponsors unless something was done. The networks responded by adding some minority characters to the casts of existing shows. CBS aired *City of Angels*, a drama set in an inner-city hospital, that featured a predominantly black cast and creative team. The networks also planned to increase minority hiring and to appoint executives in charge of their diversity efforts. These moves apparently satisfied Mfume, who called off plans for the boycott.

The 2000–2001 TV season did not spark similar protests. In addition to *City of Angels*, there were several new series with African Americans in major roles, such as *Boston Public*. The situation behind the camera and in minority ownership, however, was unchanged. Things improved a bit in the 2002 season when there were 43 series featuring multiethnic characters. Back in 1995, there were only 13 such shows on the air.

The diversity issues surfaced again in 2003, but this time the focus was on cable. Members of the Congressional Black Caucus sent a letter to the cable TV industry asking for more minority-themed programs and more minority-owned cable networks. It resurfaced when the NAACP noted that none of the situation comedies scheduled by the major networks for the 2006 season starred an African American actor or actress.

Why should the networks present a diverse view of society? Many would argue that the networks have a social obligation to present an accurate view of society so that members of minority groups do not feel marginalized or disenfranchised from society. Others would suggest that TV should present role models for all groups. These high-minded reasons aside, it also makes economic sense for the networks to present a diverse menu of programs. The 2000 census showed that minorities constitute more than 35 percent of the U.S. population, and their buying power is increasing each year. Presenting shows that appeal to these groups is simply good business.

Further, some critics suggest that paying large amounts of attention to the way the broadcast networks portray minorities overlooks the gains minorities have made in cable. For instance, Black Entertainment Television draws a significant audience. Two Spanish-language networks, Galavision and Univision, are aimed at Hispanics.

Finally, consider the opinion of commentator Earl Ofari Hutchinson, who suggests that prime-time TV is not worth fighting for. He charges that the networks have oversaturated the airways with silly sitcoms and action shows designed to appeal to young, affluent whites. These types of programs, he argues, have no relevance for African Americans, who should focus their attention elsewhere. In a similar vein Cynthia Tucker, the African American editor of the editorial page of the *Atlanta Constitution*, suggests that the NAACP is misplacing its efforts by concentrating on network TV programs. Instead, she argues, the organization should encourage young African Americans to stop watching TV. "Let prime-time TV keep its bland cast of characters," says Tucker. "There are plenty of good books in which black youngsters can find themselves reflected."[1]

---

[1] Quoted in Richard Breyer, "Color TV," *Word and I,* March 2000, 84.

in Miami or New Orleans. Likewise, a manufacturer of farm equipment would probably not find many customers in New York City. These companies turn to national spot buying. The snowmobile manufacturer would buy spots in several northern markets, such as Minneapolis, Minnesota; Fargo, North Dakota; and Butte, Montana. The farm equipment company would place ads in primarily rural markets.

Finally, many local businesses buy advertising time from TV stations. They purchase time on one or more TV stations located in a single market. Network spots (national advertising) account for 36 percent of the total amount of advertising dollars, and the remainder is divided about equally between national spot and local advertising.

A 30-second spot on *American Idol* during the 2006–2007 season cost more than $600,000.

Revenues depend upon the amount of money a station charges for its commercial time. The larger the audience, the more money a station can charge. The prices for 30- and 60-second commercials are listed on the station's rate card. The cost of an ad will vary tremendously from station to station. A 30-second ad might cost only $100–200 in a small market, but the same ad would cost thousands in a major market.

The same general pricing principles apply at the network level. Shows with high ratings have higher advertising charges than shows with low ratings. For example, in 2006, the average network 30-second spot in prime time cost about $200,000. On top-rated shows, spots were going for about $600,000; on lower-rated shows, the cost was about $100,000. To gain some perspective on how expensive it can get, consider that for the 2007 Super Bowl, a 30-second spot was going for about $2.6 million.

Some television shows are finding novel ways to generate income. Product placement, for example, is prominent in *American Idol*. *The Apprentice* routinely gives exposure to top brands such as Levi's and Mattel. NBC's *Deal or No Deal* runs a Lucky Case Game where viewers can send text messages selecting which of six cases contains a $10,000 or $20,000 prize. A winner is selected at random from those who chose the right case. A 2006 press release from NBC noted that to date there had been about 57 million entries to the game. At 99 cents per entry, that's about $56 million in revenue. Subtract from that the $1 million given out as prize money, and that leaves $55 million to be divided between the show and the wireless phone company. The voting on *American Idol* generates income in the same way.

▲ Where Did the Money Go?

At the network level one of the biggest expenses is programming. For example, a typical half-hour sitcom costs about $1 million. Hit shows cost much more. An hour-long show might have a price tag approaching $3 million. Quiz and reality shows are much cheaper to produce, and it's not a surprise to find that networks are relying on them more and more.

At the local level, the costs are broken down differently, but the heavy cost of programming is evident there as well. Programming costs account for about 35–40 percent of the local station expense dollar, followed by administrative costs and expenses for news.

PUBLIC BROADCASTING

▲ A Brief History

Public broadcasting in the United States has been in existence for more than 40 years. Over that time its achievements have been considerable, but its evolution has been hampered by political infighting, a lack of a clear purpose, and, most of all, insufficient funding.

Until 1967 noncommercial TV was known as educational television. In 1967, following the recommendations of the Carnegie Commission, Congress passed the Public Broadcasting Act, which authorized money for the construction of new facilities and established the Corporation for Public Broadcasting (CPB) to oversee noncommercial TV and distribute funds for programs. The government also created the Public Broadcasting Service (PBS), whose duties resemble those of commercial networks. Although this arrangement seemed

In 2006 the CBS reality series *Survivor* started its 13th competition faced with declining ratings and tough competition from rival networks. The format for the new season was familiar: Contestants were divided into various tribes and were to compete against each other and one another for a $1-million prize until only one person was left. One thing, however, was different. The 20 contestants were to be split into four tribes based on their ethnicity: Hispanic, African American, Asian American, and Caucasian.

Controversy erupted as soon as this new wrinkle was announced. A Hispanic citizens' group called the arrangement an offensive and cheap trick to boost ratings. An African studies expert accused the program of resurrecting old stereotypes. There was a rally in New York City urging CBS to drop the show. General Motors, which had sponsored Survivor since 2000, decided to end its sponsorship. (GM said its decision had nothing to do with the show's new arrangement.)

Throughout its broadcast history, *Survivor* has often reflected social and cultural divisions. Past episodes have featured tribes divided by age and gender, but did this new version cross the line? Critics wondered where the trend might stop. *Survivor* tribes based on religion? Christians versus Muslims versus Jews?

Host Jeff Probst defended the decision, noting that the idea stemmed from criticism that the show was not ethnically diverse enough. He also argued that the show simply reflects reality and that the ethnicity experiment takes the program's social experiment to a new level. Mark Burnett, the show's creator, noted that all of these various denunciations were premature since critics had not even seen the first episode of the new season. In addition, since Caucasians would be voting off Caucasians, Asians voting off Asians, and so on, the show would not be racist. Finally, Burnett hoped that the show might actually help loosen the ethnic boundaries in America by dispelling some stereotypes.

The ethical issues at the basis of this controversy are easy to see. First, trying to improve diversity and dispelling stereotypes, may be worthwhile goals, but are there other ways that the program might have achieved them? Does dividing the contestants by ethnicity do more harm than good?

Second, is it proper to exploit cultural or ethnic differences for economic gain? Despite the claims of the show's executives and host, *Survivor* is a television series; it is not a social experiment. After 6 years on the air, the show needed a publicity boost. Dividing the contestants by ethnic background got *Survivor* exactly what it needed to survive in its ratings battle: plenty of free promotion and media hype.

---

to work well at first, internal disputes soon surfaced concerning which of these two organizations had final control over programming.

In addition, several cable channels began to offer programs that competed for public TV's audience. Many experts felt that much of the traditional programming on public TV would eventually move to cable or to videocassette. On top of this came further reductions in federal funds for public broadcasting.

Then things started to change. Somewhat surprisingly, cable turned out to be more of a friend than a foe to public TV. Since two-thirds of all public stations are in the UHF band, carriage by local cable systems increased their coverage area and helped public TV double its audience from 1980 to 1984. Public TV wound up as the primary cultural channel in the nation, with 90 million viewers every week.

In the mid-1980s, however, the Reagan administration cut funds for public broadcasting and proposed to freeze future funding at current levels. Congress restored some of the cuts, but in 1987 the system was struggling to get along on about the same amount of money it had in 1982. PBS funding became a major political issue again in the early 1990s. Faced with this financial uncertainty, public TV looked to other sources for funding: corporate underwriting, auctions, viewer donations, and sales of program guides.

Public television's problems continued into the new century. PBS's average prime-time ratings are down 25 percent over the past 10 years. More people now watch the cable network TNT than watch PBS. To make matters worse, PBS's loyal audience is getting older (the average viewer is in his or her mid-50s), and younger viewers are not flocking to public TV. Any attempt to attract younger viewers risks alienating public TV's core audience of mature Americans.

Money is still a problem as well. Public stations are moving to digital transmission, a conversion that will cost millions. Dwindling revenues have meant layoffs at local stations and at the network level. Congressional funding continues to be tight. The 2007 budget for the Corporation for Public Broadcasting totaled $400 million. That is about what ESPN collects every 2 months in subscriber fees. In short, public TV faces significant challenges if it is to remain a viable alternative for television viewers.

▲ Programming and Financing

In 1990 PBS presented an 11-hour documentary titled *The Civil War,* which became the highest-rated program in the history of PBS. Although it might be a bit of an exaggeration, much of the history of PBS programming can be described as a civil war between the local public stations and the centralized PBS organization. Each side has scored significant victories in this fray over the years, but most recently, the tide has turned in favor of the centralized authority. Let us quickly review how the system used to work and how it has changed.

Prior to 1990 PBS used a mechanism called the Station Program Cooperative (SPC) to determine which programs were carried by its member stations. The SPC system represented a decentralized decision-making process. Member stations were given a ballot that contained the descriptions of possible programs, and they voted for those they wished to broadcast. After several rounds the initial list was pared down and stations voted again, but this time each station had to promise that it would help pay for the programs it voted for.

This system encouraged the broadcast of programs that already had some funding or series that could be acquired cheaply. Innovative or daring series that were expensive and had no prior funding commitments were seldom produced. The system also leaned heavily on a few big public TV stations that did the bulk of the production work. Finally, PBS had no cohesive national scheduling system.

In 1990, faced with declining funds and viewers, PBS suspended the SPC and moved toward more centralized programming. An executive vice president for national programming was appointed with the power to develop and schedule new programs. By any measure the first PBS season under the new centralized system was a success, exemplified by the fact that the *Civil War* series was watched by millions.

Successive seasons, however, were not as successful. For the entire decade of the 1990s, despite being one of the most established TV networks, PBS got an average prime-time rating of 2.0 (of all the TV homes in America, about 2 percent watched PBS in prime time. PBS's average rating dropped even farther during the first half of the new decade. In addition, PBS occasionally lands in political hot water. In the late 1990s, Congress grilled PBS executives when it was learned that PBS stations, which are supposed to be politically neutral, were providing Democratic and Republican groups with their donor lists. Political parties could then use these lists to solicit donations. In 2005 a congressional subcommittee chastised PBS for producing a children's program in which a cartoon rabbit visited real-life children whose parents were lesbians.

PBS programs have earned numerous awards and substantial praise from critics. *Sesame Street* revolutionized children's TV by presenting educational content in an entertaining format. *Nova* and *Cosmos* introduced millions to the wonders of science. However, PBS programs have also come in for their share of criticism. Many critics have charged that PBS displays a liberal bias, and they have complained about the size of the salaries PBS pays to some of its performers.

Like commercial stations, public TV stations receive licenses from the FCC. As of 2007, there

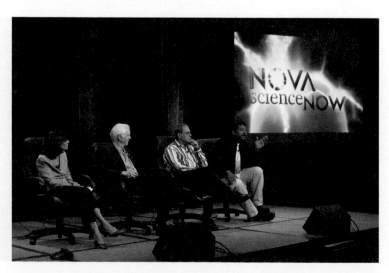

Educational programs, such as *Nova,* make up a significant part of the PBS schedule.

were 354 PBS stations operated by 168 licensees. About half of these licensees are community organizations, another one-third are colleges and universities, about 12 percent are state-operated networks, and the remainder belong to local educational or municipal authorities.

The audience for public TV is substantial. In 2007, more than half the homes in America watched public TV at least once a week. Viewing times, however, are far lower than those for commercial TV. Average household daily viewing time for public TV is about 25 minutes, compared with more than 4 hours for commercial TV.

Unlike commercial TV, public television is funded by a number of sources. About one-third of the support for public television comes from federal, state, and local governments; about one-fourth comes from member contributions; another 15 percent comes from corporations; and the rest comes from foundation grants, auctions, and other miscellaneous sources.

Public broadcasting is inching slowly into the digital age. In order to generate more revenue, the organization has tested selling ads on its PBS Kids Web site as well as on its main site, pbs.org. The move generated controversy among watchdog groups afraid that commercialism would spoil the essence of what PBS stands for.

Previews of upcoming programs are streamed from the PBS site. PBS also makes portions of its popular *News Hour* available on iTunes, and the network is considering a video-on-demand service. One of the problems that PBS will have to solve is that much of its programming is long-form, an hour in length, a format that doesn't easily download to laptops and cell phones.

HOME VIDEO

The home video industry came into existence because of the tremendous growth of VCR sales. By 2005 about 92 percent of homes in the United States were equipped with the device. Recently, the VCR was joined by DVD (digital videodisc) players. DVD offers better pictures and sound than videotape; can contain additional video material, such as outtakes and interviews with a director; and can feature multiple-language soundtracks. DVD sales have skyrocketed; it is estimated that there are now more than 85 million in U.S. homes.

DVD players are used to play back prerecorded discs that can be purchased or rented from video stores such as Blockbuster. There are more than 40,000 prerecorded titles on the market, and many more are introduced each month.

Personal video recorders, such as TiVo, have been slow to catch on, but many experts predict they will change the future of TV viewing.

A new entry in the home video market is the **digital video recorder (DVR),** such as TiVo, which allows viewers to record television programs on a hard drive. Sales of DVRs were slow in the early years of the new century, but experts predict that these new devices will become popular once more people are aware of what they can do.

Like most other businesses, home video can be divided into three segments: production, distribution, and retail. The production side of the industry consists of those companies that produce prerecorded discs. Since much of the home video market consists of movies, many of the large motion picture studios also dominate the DVD business.

These companies sell to distributors, who form the bridge between production and retail. Currently, some 90 distributors in the United States handle DVDs. Major companies include Disney, Fox,

Columbia, and Paramount. Moreover, the DVD distribution business now resembles record distribution as a new breed of rack jobber is making it easy for many retail and department stores to get into the video-renting business.

The DVD has opened up a new aftermarket for television. Boxed sets of an entire season of such contemporary series as *Sex in the City, The Simpsons,* and *24* have generated increased revenue for production companies. Moreover, classic TV series also do well. *I Love Lucy—The First Year* and *The Dick Van Dyke Show—Season One* were among the best sellers in 2004. Even shows that didn't do all that well when they first aired, such as *Sports Night* and *The Family Guy,* have found new life on DVDs. Financial analysts estimate that DVD collections of TV shows will bring in more than $2 billion in 2008.

Sales and rentals are big business. Consumers spent about $23 billion on DVDs in 2006. Retailers are concerned about the competition posed by video on demand and the growing number of premium movies available through direct-broadcast satellites.

FEEDBACK FOR BROADCAST TELEVISION

▲ Measuring TV Viewing

Let us examine how the ratings for both network programs and local stations are determined.

Network Ratings   Nielsen Media Research, serving the United States and Canada, provides the networks with audience data through its Nielsen Television Index (NTI). To compile these ratings, Nielsen uses a device called a *People Meter,* introduced in the late 1980s. The People Meter consists of an apparatus about the size of a clock radio that sits on top of a TV set and a handheld device that resembles a TV remote-control unit. Demographic data are gathered from each household member, and then each is assigned a number. While watching TV, each family member is supposed to periodically punch in his or her number on the handheld device to indicate viewing. People Meters can be used to tabulate all viewing—network, syndicated shows, and cable—and can even tabulate DVD or DVR playbacks. There are more than 10,000 households in the Nielsen People Meter sample, and usable data are obtained from more than 90 percent of the meters. The sample is replaced every 2 years. The People Meter service is not cheap. Networks pay millions of dollars annually for the service.

Nielsen is also testing other systems. The **Portable People Meter (PPM)** is a device about the size of a pager that detects inaudible signals that are encoded into radio and television programs. It requires little effort on the part of the respondent (a person simply clips the PPM to an article of clothing), and there are no buttons to push. The PPM can measure viewing or listening both in and out of the home. Preliminary tests of the device are being carried out in several U.S. cities.

Local-Market TV Ratings   Nielsen surveys more than 200 markets in the United States at least four times a year, using a combination of diary and electronic meter techniques. A computer selects phone numbers at random from all telephone directories in the area. The households selected into the sample are asked to keep a diary record of their television viewing.

Households that agree to participate receive one diary for every working TV in the household. The diary provides a space for entering the viewing of the head of the household as well as that of other family members or visitors. Participants are asked to record their viewing every quarter-hour. In addition, the respondents are asked to record the sex and age of all those who are watching. At the back of the diary are questions concerning how big the family is, where the household is located, and whether the family subscribes to cable. Diaries are kept for 7 days and then returned to the ratings company. Nielsen reports that it is able to use approximately 40–50 percent of all the diaries it sends out.

In about 50 markets, Nielsen has electronic meters that record any time a sample household's TV is turned on or off and the channel being viewed. The meters also record DVR usage. Data from this sample are compiled overnight and sent to subscribers early the next morning. These local meter data are augmented by information from the diary sample.

Nielsen's long-term plans call for the phasing out of paper diaries. The company will use local People Meters in the top 25 markets while the remaining markets will use electronic meters or Internet diaries. Nielsen's ultimate goal is to measure media usage on all media platforms: MP3 players, cell phones, and Internet video.

▲ Ratings Reporting

Television viewing data are reported essentially the same way as for radio. The following formula is used to calculate the **rating** for a TV program in a local market:

$$\text{Rating} = \frac{\text{Number of households watching a program}}{\text{Number of TV HH}}$$

where "TV HH" equals the number of households in a given market equipped with television.

Similarly, the **share of the audience** is found by using the following formula:

$$\text{Share of audience} = \frac{\text{Number of households watching a program}}{\text{Number of HUT}}$$

where "HUT" equals the number of households using (watching) television at a particular time.

Figure 10-1 reproduces a sample page from a local Nielsen ratings book. As can be seen, Nielsen reports shares, ratings, and estimates of the number of people in the audience in various demographic categories for different areas in the market.

Four times every year (February, May, July, and November), Nielsen conducts a "sweep" period during which every local television market in the entire country is

FIGURE 10-1   Sample Page from a Nielsen TV Ratings Book measured. Local stations rely on these ratings to set their advertising rates. Naturally, affiliated stations pressure the networks for special programming that will attract large audiences. And the networks generally go along with the affiliates' desires. As a result, blockbuster movies and specials are scheduled in competing time slots, leaving many viewers to wonder why all the good programs on TV always come at the same time. As Nielsen moves away from diaries to local-market People Meters, demographic audience data will be available year round, thus making the traditional sweep periods less meaningful.

Determining the Accuracy of Ratings   Because the numbers in the rating books are the basis for spending vast amounts of money, it is important that they be as accurate and reliable as possible. During the early 1960s, in the wake of quiz show and payola scandals, Congress took a close look at the broadcasting industry. In response to one congressional committee's criticism of audience measurement techniques, advertising and broadcasting leaders founded the Electronic Media Ratings Council, subsequently renamed the Media Ratings Council (MRC). The task of the MRC is threefold: It monitors, audits, and accredits broadcast measurement services. The council monitors performance of ratings companies by making sure that reported results meet the minimum standards of performance set by the MRC. Audits are performed on a continuing basis. If the ratings company passes the audit, it is accredited and is allowed to display the MRC's seal of approval on its ratings reports.

Despite the MRC's work, broadcast ratings are still subject to widespread criticism. One common complaint, voiced by many who evidently do not understand the statistical theory that underlies sampling, is directed at Nielsen's national survey. How can a sample of only 10,000 homes, these critics ask, accurately reflect the viewing of more than 100 million television households? In actuality, this sample size will generate tolerably accurate results within a specified margin of error. Other criticisms, however, deserve closer attention.

First, it is possible that the type of person who agrees to participate may have viewing habits different from those of the viewer who declines to participate. Second, in the case of the Nielsen reports (based on about 55 percent of the diaries sent out), it is possible that "returners" behave differently from "nonreturners." Third, people who know that their viewing is being measured may change their behavior. Fourth, ratings companies admit that they have a problem measuring the viewing of certain groups. For example, minorities—particularly blacks and Hispanics—may be underrepresented in the ratings companies' samples. Finally, the stations that are being measured can distort the measurement process by engaging in contests and special promotions or by running unusual or sensational programs in an attempt to "hype" the ratings. The distinction between hype and legitimate programming, however, is somewhat fuzzy. Clearly, the ratings are not perfect. Nonetheless, despite all their flaws, they present useful information at an affordable price to advertisers and to the television industry. As long as the United States has a commercial broadcasting system, some form of the ratings will be around.

▲ Questionnaires, Concept Testing, and Pilot Testing

In addition to ratings, the TV networks gather three special types of feedback from the audience to help them predict what television shows will be popular with viewers. The first kind of research consists of questionnaires that attempt to measure audience tastes, opinions, and beliefs. Perhaps as many as 100,000 people per year are questioned in person or over the phone as the networks try to identify what situations and topics might be acceptable for programs.

A second form is called **concept testing.** In concept testing, a one- or two-paragraph description of an idea for a new series is presented to a sample of viewers who are asked for their reactions. Show ideas that do well in concept testing have an increased chance of getting on the air.

CRITICAL / CULTURAL ISSUES

The Bachelor

One of the interesting things about the critical/cultural approach is the range of items that can serve as texts for analysis. From popular mail-order catalogues to mass-marketed toys, critical/cultural scholars have mined all sources for insights on our society. Popular TV shows have also come under scrutiny. For example, a doctoral dissertation by Dr. Amanda Hall about ABC's *The Bachelor* illustrates how audiences use this program to construct meaning.

Hall looked at both the program and its audience. She performed a textual analysis of the program. She interviewed viewers about their impressions of the program and what it meant to them, and she observed groups of viewers as they watched the programs.

What did she discover about the program? She argued that *The Bachelor* is a modern fairy tale. The man is Prince Charming. The competition itself, with the lavish trimmings and carefree lifestyle, is the Big Ball. All of the women are vying to be Cinderella. Moreover, like many fairy tales, there is an element of melodrama (a melodrama has a simplified plot, stereotypical characters, exaggerated emotion, and a happy ending) in *The Bachelor*.

The audience apparently recognized and embraced both the fairy tale and melodramatic dimensions of the program. Hall's research revealed that viewers vicariously helped Prince Charming by participating in discussions with other viewers about whom the bachelor should choose.

She also found evidence of patriarchy in the program. The man was active and dominant and had a voice. The women were passive and subservient and were given a voice only when they were talking about the bachelor and their chances to be the chosen one. Further, the whole program was told from the masculine point of view. The words of the bachelor gave direction and a story line to the program.

The patriarchy was evident on other levels as well. The bachelor was controlled and rational. The women were portrayed as emotional and frequently teary. The competition among them became fierce and resulted in catfights and "bitchy" behavior. As Hall concluded, the program "sends a strong patriarchal message about heterosexual relationships—a woman's place is to serve in a subordinate (and emotional) position to her husband."

Finally, the theme of domestication was vividly present. The ideal wife, the choice of Prince Charming, had to be a mate and potential mother who knew how to behave. Women who did not fit this characterization were often removed early in the competition. Women who understood this requirement and acted accordingly generally lasted longer.

Young women who viewed *The Bachelor* used the program as an aid in understanding themselves and their own relationships. Messages from the program serve to illustrate socially prescribed expectations of gender roles. Viewers enjoyed the show even while recognizing the patriarchal elements. Indeed, many seemed to reject the dominant theme of the program and instead chose to focus on ways that they could reject the patriarchal interpretations and substitute more liberating ones of their own.

In sum, Hall's research underscored a key point in the critical/cultural approach. As she concluded, "A central argument for this study is that text and audience are both powerful—one does not overpower the other. As such, it is necessary to study both in order to effectively engage with issues of consumption and representation."

The third form is **pilot testing,** which consists of placing a group of viewers in a special test theater and showing them an entire program. The audience usually sits in chairs equipped with dials or buttons that are used to indicate the degree to which audience members like or dislike what is shown. For example, the audience might be told to press a green button when they see something on screen that they like and a red button when they see something they dislike.

The networks currently test pilots on cable TV systems since that is the closest thing to real TV viewing. In a cable test several hundred cable subscribers in a certain community are telephoned and asked to participate in the test. They watch the show on an unused channel of their cable system and then respond by telephone to a questionnaire that asks them about plot, character, relationships, and so on.

▲ Television Audiences

The TV set has become firmly entrenched in the life of Americans. As of 2007, some 99 percent of all homes in the country had at least one working television set. About 75 percent had more than one.

FIGURE 10-2

Household Viewing of Television at Various Times of the Day

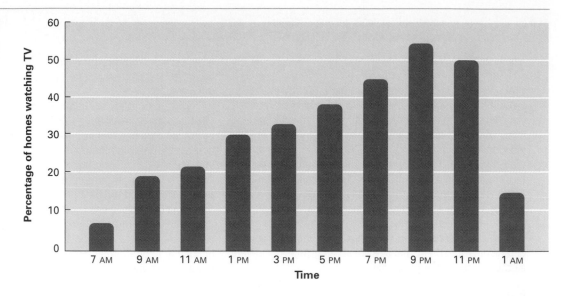

The set in the average household is on for about 8 hours a day, with each individual watching an average of more than 3 hours daily. The TV audience changes throughout the day, steadily growing from 7 A.M. until it reaches a peak from 8 to 11 P.M., Eastern Standard Time. After 11 P.M., the audience drops off dramatically. Figure 10-2 details this pattern of audience viewing.

Not surprisingly, the television audience is largest during the winter months and smallest during July and August, when people spend more time outdoors. The composition of the television audience changes during the day. Preschool and female viewers tend to predominate during the daytime hours from Monday to Friday. On Saturday mornings most of the audience is under 13. Prime time is dominated by those in the 18- to 49-year-old age group.

Various demographic factors, such as age, sex, social class, and education, affect viewership. For example, teenagers watch the least. People in low-income homes generally watch more television than their middle-income counterparts. People with more education tend to watch less, and women watch more often than men.

THE BROADCAST TELEVISION INDUSTRY

Someone hunting for a job in TV quickly discovers that it is a relatively small industry. According to recent figures provided by the FCC, about 110,000 people are employed in commercial TV, 10,000 in noncommercial television, and about 16,000 at TV networks.

▲ Entry-Level Positions

Here are some general hints on job hunting in TV:

1. *Think small.* As in radio, TV small-market stations offer more employment potential than larger-market stations. Moreover, at a small station you have a chance to do more and learn more than you might at a larger station.

2. *Do not be afraid to start at the bottom.* Once you get in, it is easier to move upward into a position that might be more to your liking. Many successful people in TV started in the mailroom, secretarial pool, or shipping department.

3. *Be prepared to move.* Your first job will probably not be a lifetime commitment. Frequently, the road to advancement in TV consists of moving about and up—from a small station to a large station, from an independent station to a network affiliate, from the station to the network.

Select the television media tour (Track 4) on the DVD that accompanies this text.

CBS Affiliate 35WSEE-TV provides programming to Erie, Pennsylvania. The Erie market ranks 143rd out of 210 markets with about 158,000 television households. As such, it is probably typical of a smaller-market TV station. The first part of the video introduces you to key members of the station staff.

The next segment raises some issues for you to consider:

1. Most of the discussion focuses on the news operation. Why? How important is news to a local station?

2. What challenges do these professionals face in practicing quality journalism?

3. How is technology affecting the station? Could the lack of a "human element" hurt or help newscasting? What are the arguments on each side?

4. Would stations in bigger markets face the same issues?

▲ Upward Mobility

Those interested in producing TV shows might consider looking for a job as a camera operator, floor manager (the person who gives cues to the talent and makes sure everything in the studio goes smoothly during the telecast), or production assistant (the person who handles all the odd jobs that need to be done during a show). From there a person might progress upward to become an assistant director or assistant producer or perhaps a writer. Eventually, he or she would hope to become a full-fledged director or producer.

If you are interested in being an on-camera news reporter, your best bet might be to find a general reporting job at a small station. If your interests lie behind the camera, you can start out as a newswriter or news researcher or even a cameraperson or tape editor. Most people interested in performing before the camera generally stay in that capacity. Upward mobility for general-assignment reporters consists of moving into the anchor position. For anchors it consists of moving to bigger and more lucrative markets. For those behind the scenes, the first move up will probably be to the assistant news director slot and then on to the news director position.

Sales is the division that offers the most upward mobility. Most stations prefer people who have had some experience in selling (many move from radio sales to TV sales). Once a salesperson is established, however, his or her monetary rewards can be substantial. Salespeople advance their careers by moving to larger markets or by moving up to the sales manager position.

The highest level a person can reach at the local level is the general manager's position. In the past most general managers came from the sales department. This trend is likely to continue, but it is also probable that more people who start off in the news departments will move into management, since news is becoming more of a moneymaker.

MAIN POINTS

- Electronic television developed during the 1930s. After World War II it quickly grew in popularity and replaced radio as the main information and entertainment medium.

- Three networks—NBC, CBS, and ABC—dominated early TV. Live drama, variety, and quiz and game shows were popular during the 1950s.

- Television matured in the 1960s, and its content became more professional. The public television network began in 1967. Cable TV grew slowly during this decade.

- The 1970s saw TV programs criticized for excessive violence.

- In the 1980s and 1990s, the three traditional TV networks lost viewers to cable and to VCRs. The Fox network became a major competitor.

- The Telecommunications Act of 1996 had a significant impact on TV station ownership and also introduced program content ratings. Rules for the eventual conversion to digital TV were announced in 1997.

- Changing from analog to digital signals will mean better pictures and sound. Consumers will have to buy a new TV set or a converter to receive the new signals. TV stations may use the digital signal to broadcast high-definition television or lower-definition programs among which viewers may choose.

- TV is universal, dominant, and expensive. Its audience is currently fragmenting into smaller segments.

- The broadcast TV industry consists of program suppliers, distributors, and local stations.

- Big conglomerates own the major TV networks, and large group owners control most of the stations in large markets.

- Public broadcasting relies less on tax revenues and more on private sources of funding.

- The Nielsen Company compiles both network and local-station television ratings.

QUESTIONS FOR REVIEW

1. What are the defining features of the TV medium?
2. What are some of the advantages of being an affiliate of a major TV network?
3. Who owns the TV networks?
4. Trace the evolution of U.S. noncommercial TV programming.
5. Compare and contrast Nielsen's method of measuring network TV viewers with its technique for measuring local-market TV viewing.

QUESTIONS FOR CRITICAL THINKING

1. What should be the goal of public television? Should the government support public broadcasting?
2. Large companies control the broadcast television industry. What are some of the good points and bad points of large corporate ownership?
3. The major broadcast networks have been losing viewers for the past two decades or so. Will they still be around 10–15 years from now? Why or why not?
4. In addition to the Nielsen People Meter, what are some ways that television viewing can be measured?
5. Review the boxed insert "The Bachelor," on page 251. Next, consider the following. *The Bachelor* has a female counterpart in *The Bachelorette*. Ratings for *The Bachelorette* have not been as good. Can you think of any reasons why? Are there other reality programs that utilize a fairy tale theme?

KEY TERMS

Public Broadcasting Act of 1967 (p. 230)
time shifting (p. 232)
low-power television (LPTV) (p. 233)
digital television (DTV) (p. 234)
HDTV (p. 234)
commercial television (p. 237)

noncommercial television (p. 237)
VHF (p. 240)
UHF (p. 240)
independents (p. 240)
pilot (p. 242)
digital video recorder (DVR) (p. 247)

Portable People Meter (p. 248)
rating (p. 249)
share of the audience (p. 249)
concept testing (p. 250)
pilot testing (p. 251)

INTERNET RESOURCES

Online Learning Center

At the Online Learning Center home page, www.mhhe.com/dominick10, *select* Student Center *and then* Chapter 10.

1. Use the Learning Objectives, Chapter Outline, Main Points, and Time Line sections to review this chapter.
2. Test your knowledge of the chapter using the multiple choice, crossword puzzle, and flashcard features of the site.
3. Expand your knowledge of concepts and topics discussed in the chapter by going to Suggestions for Further Reading and Internet Exercises.

Surfing the Internet

www.abc.com
Watch hit ABC shows in full screen and high resolution—along with a few commercials.

www.mtr.org
The home page of the Museum of Television and Radio. Contains a guided tour of the museum's New York and Los Angeles locations.

www.wnbc.com
The Web site of the local NBC affiliate in New York City. Note the large number of choices for the user, ranging from news headlines to chances to win tickets to a Broadway play.

www.turnoffyourtv.com
If you do not like TV, this is the site for you. Includes a page that suggests things to do instead of watching TV.

www.nielsenmedia.com
Information about Nielsen Media Research, the firm that rates TV programs. Check out the Ratings 101 link for a basic description of how the TV audience is measured.

CHAPTER 11

CABLE, SATELLITE, AND INTERNET TELEVISION

This chapter will prepare you to:

- trace the development of cable, satellite, and Internet television

- describe the implications of the digital age for these media

- understand the structure, content, and finances of cable, satellite, and Internet TV

- appreciate the potential of user-generated content

- explain the audience measurement techniques used for these media

"I'm in and I'm in to win." Hillary Clinton chose to announce her candidacy for president over the Internet. Her site has attracted more than 400,000 unique visitors a month.

I n 1976, when Jimmy Carter announced that he was running for the Democratic presidential nomination, he did it with a speech before the National Press Club in Washington, D.C. Present were figures from the nation's leading newspapers and correspondents and commentators from the three major broadcast networks. In 1984, when Walter Mondale announced his candidacy, he did it with a speech in his home state of Minnesota that was covered by all the major networks as well as new cable news networks, CNN and CNN Headline News.

When Al Gore announced his candidacy for the Democratic presidential nomination in 2000, he did it with a speech in his home state of Tennessee before cameras from all the major broadcast networks news organizations and reporters from cable networks, CNN, CNN Headline News, Fox News, MSNBC, CNBC, and MTV.

In 2007, when Senator Hillary Rodham Clinton announced her candidacy for the presidency, she did it via an online video clip posted on her Web site. The clip also wound up on video-sharing site YouTube where it was viewed thousands of times. Other candidates followed suit.

This brief chronology of political announcements is just one illustration of how television has changed over the past 35 years. The broadcast networks and local stations are no longer the only players in the game. They have been joined by cable and satellite networks and, more recently, by Internet video. This chapter will examine the history, economics, structure, and potential of these newer forms of television. We'll start with a look at how they came to be.

A BRIEF HISTORY

Cable TV began modestly in the 1950s as a device used to bring conventional television signals to areas that could not otherwise receive them. As cable grew, some systems imported signals from distant stations into markets that were already served by one or two local stations. The local stations, as you might imagine, were not pleased, since their audiences were being siphoned off by the imported signals. This situation caused some political maneuverings as stations affected by cable appealed to the FCC and to Congress for help. The FCC vacillated over the question of cable regulation before issuing, in 1965, a set of rules that retarded the growth of cable in large markets. In 1972 the FCC enacted a new set of less restrictive rules for cable. By 1980, in a move toward deregulation, the FCC had dropped virtually all rules governing cable.

This deregulation move helped systems grow as cable companies scrambled to acquire exclusive franchises in communities across the nation (see Figure 11-1). Some companies made extravagant promises to win these contracts: a hundred or more channels, local-access channels, community channels, shopping and banking at home, two-way services—and all at bargain prices. After the smoke cleared, the industry recognized the economic reality dictating that its performance would fall short of promises.

While all this was going on, the United States and the Soviet Union were competing in the "space race" that culminated with the lunar landing in 1969. One of the by-products of the space race was the development of rockets that could launch communication satellites into Earth orbit. The first satellite TV transmission occurred in 1962 using *Telstar I* (this satellite has the distinction of being the only satellite commemorated by a rock song). In the early 1970s more communication satellites circled the Earth.

Satellite TV transmission came of age in 1976 when a little-known pay-TV cable service, HBO, used a satellite to transmit the "Thrilla in Manila" heavyweight championship fight between Muhammad Ali and Joe Frazier to cable systems across the United States. That

FIGURE 11-1

Growth Within the U.S. Cable TV Industry

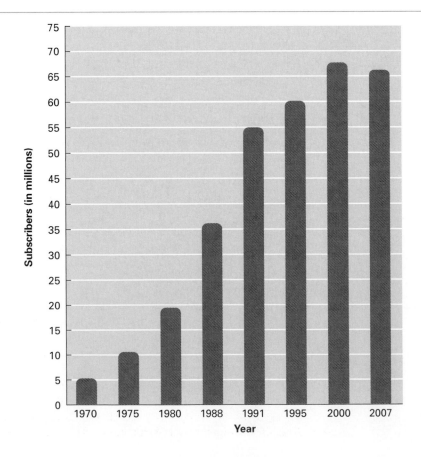

same year, media entrepreneur Ted Turner started transmitting "superstation" WTBS to cable systems. Other satellite-distributed channels quickly followed, and cable subscribers could now receive a host of new programming, including CNN, MTV, and ESPN. This gave people in urban and suburban areas a compelling new reason to subscribe to cable, and the industry grew quickly during the 1970s and 1980s. For example, the percentage of homes with cable increased from about 14 percent in 1975 to more than 50 percent in 1987. By the end of the 1980s, the cable industry was dominated by large **MSOs (multiple system operators)** such as TCI. Locally owned cable systems were quickly disappearing.

As of 1991, 7,500 cable systems served about 55 million households. Keep in mind that this growth occurred despite the fact that cable companies generally avoided expensive urban installations. The growth rate slowed somewhat during the mid-1990s, but by 2007 about 66 million households subscribed to cable.

Cable also scored several programming coups. ESPN signed a contract with the National Football League to carry prime-time pro football games. CNN's coverage of the Gulf War, the O. J. Simpson trial, and 9/11 attacks demonstrated that it could be a formidable competitor to network news. Big-ticket network series bypassed the traditional syndication route and premiered first on cable.

Cable got a competitor in the mid-1990s thanks to the development of high-powered **direct-broadcast satellites (DBS)** that could send a signal directly to a small home satellite dish, bypassing the cable system altogether. Two companies, Echo Star (Dish Network) and DirecTV, eventually dominated the industry. The number of households subscribing to satellite companies increased from about 2 million in 1995 to more than 20 million in 2006.

On the economic side cable advertising revenues exceeded $2 billion in 1990 and rose to about $27 billion by 2007. Although still small in comparison with the ad revenues generated by traditional television, the 2007 figure represents an increase of almost 42 percent over that of 2004.

The most significant developments in the cable industry in the past three decades have been legal ones. In 1984 Congress deregulated the rates cable systems could charge consumers. Eight years later, in response to subscriber complaints, Congress reregulated the industry by passing the Cable Television Consumer Protection and Competition Act, which caused about a 17 percent reduction in rates and mandated that broadcasters choose between *must carry* (the local cable system had to carry the station's signal) and *retransmission consent* (the local station had the right to negotiate compensation for carriage of their signal). Most broadcasters opted for consent and were compensated with promotional time on the system or were granted space for their own existing or planned cable networks. But this situation changed in the mid-2000s when broadcasters, facing declining ad revenues and looking for new sources of revenue, began demanding payment from cable companies in order to carry their programs. Satellite systems and phone companies that offer video already pay a fee to the broadcasters. It is likely that cable will eventually follow suit, a move that would mean increased monthly bills for subscribers.

The next major piece of legislation was the Telecommunications Act of 1996 (discussed in more detail in Chapter 16). The new law gave telephone companies the right to enter the cable business and gave cable companies the right to provide telephone services. In addition, both telephone and cable companies could own competing systems in the same community. Finally, the act allowed most cable companies to once again set their own rates. Significant competition between phone companies and cable companies did not materialize for several years, but by the middle of the decade, the situation was changing. Thanks to a new technology, **voice-over-Internet protocol (VOIP),** cable companies were able to offer an alternative to the traditional phone lines. Comcast, for example, planned to have VOIP service in place for its 40 million household subscribers by 2006. All the other large cable companies are following suit. For their part the telephone companies are moving into the television business. In cooperation with EchoStar, phone giant SBC launched a satellite TV service in 2004. Verizon is experimenting with a fiber optic system that would allow it to carry hundreds of video channels. If the trend continues, all these companies may be providing the same services. After being deregulated by the 1996 act, cable television

For many of you reading this, Judy McGrath would seem to have the ultimate dream job: She is the president of the MTV Networks Music Group and is responsible for MTV, MTV2, VH1, CMT, and all of the company's digital media services. Under her direction MTV has grown from a small niche cable network to an international brand that symbolizes a unique attitude and lifestyle.

Always a music fan, McGrath first tried to get a job writing for *Rolling Stone*. When her efforts proved unsuccessful, she turned to writing advertising copy and then went to work for *Mademoiselle* and *Glamour*. In 1981 she heard about a new cable channel launched by Warner Entertainment that would be devoted to rock music. Despite the fact that she could not even get the channel on her home TV, McGrath joined the newly created MTV as a copywriter and on-air promotion person. (She was one of the ones responsible for using all the space film footage to promote the channel.) To the surprise of many people, MTV was successful in attracting 16- to 24-year-olds, an audience coveted by advertisers. MTV became part of the huge Viacom conglomerate, and McGrath quickly moved up the ranks to creative director, executive vice president, and eventually chair and chief executive at MTV Networks. Under her direction MTV expanded all over the world.

When the music video novelty began to wear off in the mid-1980s and ratings started to sag, McGrath introduced programs that became popular culture icons: *Beavis and Butt-Head, The Real World, The MTV Music Awards, MTV Unplugged,* and *Total Request Live*. She also introduced political coverage to MTV and was instrumental in the development of the 1992 *Choose or Lose* get-out-the-vote campaign. More recently, McGrath has led MTV into other media: movies, books, and the Internet.

What does she see in MTV's future? Since a high proportion of MTV viewers are also Web surfers and spend a good deal of time on MTV.com, look for more integration of the music on MTV and MTV2 with the Web site. MTV.com will be used to highlight some of the artists or genres featured on the cable channels. In addition, plans are underway for more international expansion, particularly in Asia. Finally, it is likely McGrath will continue to provide special programming that deals with important social issues, such as the 17 hours the channel devoted to hate crimes. And, of course, there will always be music videos.

subscription fees increased. As of 2007, there were indications that Congress was considering a review of the 1996 legislation.

Cable was experiencing problems resulting from its own growth. There were more cable networks around than available space on local systems. In addition, like the broadcast networks, cable TV was becoming a victim of audience fragmentation.

Despite these difficulties, the long-range outlook seems positive. Cable continues to draw viewers away from the broadcast TV networks. In addition, thanks to their existing coaxial cable and fiber optic cables, cable companies can offer subscribers high-speed Internet connections.

The late 1990s saw the development of a different way to distribute TV signals: **Internet TV** or Webcasting. The key to this process was an innovation called *streaming,* in which a computer stores video signals—a process known as **buffering**—and plays them back while at the same time storing new, incoming signals. In short, the head end of the video is playing while the tail is being extended.

Video on the Web grew slowly, primarily because most people had slow, dial-up connections, and it took a long time to play even a short clip. But the increasing popularity of high-speed broadband connections and the ease with which video could be uploaded on the Web helped fuel an explosion of user-generated content. By mid-decade, sites such as YouTube, Grouper, and Blinkx, where audience members upload and share their videos, became the hip places to visit. Experts predict that by 2010 more than half of the video content on the Web will be user-generated. The broadcast networks and cable companies started their own broadband channels, as did many private companies and individual entrepreneurs.

The huge success of Apple's iPod sparked another channel for Web video—the **podcast.** A podcast is a media program that is downloaded from a Web site and played back at an individual's convenience over a computer or an MP3 player such as an iPod. By 2007 thousands of video podcasts were available on the Internet.

The phone companies were also moving with more enthusiasm into the video business. AT&T, for example, announced U-Verse TV, a new Internet-based system that would provide 200 channels of video and music.

The biggest use that consumers made of the VCR and later the DVR was "time-shifting"—recording and watching a program at a more convenient time. Now a new device will allow consumers to do "place-shifting"—watching a TV program wherever they want to. The device is called Slingbox, and it may be as revolutionary as the VCR/DVR.

Here's how it works: A consumer connects Slingbox to the video output of the cable box or satellite receiver. Next, Slingbox is connected to broadband Internet, and the appropriate software is downloaded onto a laptop or mobile phone. Slingbox is now ready to send live and recorded TV programs and DVDs via an Internet connection to the laptop or Windows-enabled mobile phone or PDA. With Slingbox's on-screen remote control, a viewer can control all of the functions of his or her TV: changing channels, playing back a recording, fast-forwarding through commercials, turning up the volume, and so on.

Slingbox opens up new possibilities for viewers. Travelers can keep up with their local newscasts. Instead of paying for in-room movies at a hotel, a person could simply watch one that was recorded on his or her DVR. One Slingbox owner took his laptop up on the roof and checked the picture quality while he adjusted his satellite dish. A few consumers have plugged a security TV camera into their Slingbox in order to monitor their homes while on vacation. When on the road, sports teams use Slingbox to watch their competition.

As far as the television industry is concerned, Slingbox seems to be a mixed blessing. On the one hand, it increases the number of screens where programs are available and thus might increase a program's audience. On the other hand, it directly competes with the new downloading or streaming video services that some networks are offering. It makes little sense, for example, to pay $1.99 to download last night's episode of *Lost* when Slingbox can record it and play it back for free.

CABLE, SATELLITE, AND INTERNET TV IN THE DIGITAL AGE

All three of these delivery systems are firmly established in the digital age. Cable and satellite systems now use digital techniques to distribute their programming. Internet TV has always been digital.

For cable and satellite systems, digital signals make possible video-on-demand, interactive program guides, high-definition TV, and digital video recorders (DVRs). Digital signals create sharper and crisper video and can be compressed, increasing the number of channels that can be transmitted over a single system.

In addition to television programs, cable systems use digital technology to provide telephone service to their customers as well as Internet access. Telephone companies are doing the same. This makes it possible for telephone and cable companies to offer a "bundle" of services Internet, TV, phone—for a lower price. Satellite systems have trouble matching this feature.

▲ Mobile Media

Networks carried by cable and satellite have also made their way onto mobile media. MobiTV, for example, sends ESPN, MSNBC, Fox News, and C-SPAN, among others, to cell phones, PDAs, and laptop computers. User-generated content is showing up on cell phones as well. A company called Movidity plans to start a mobile video sharing site. As of mid-2007, wireless provider Verizon and YouTube were talking about a partnership that would give Verizon subscribers the ability to view clips on the video-sharing site.

▲ User-Generated Content

Like the broadcast industry, networks carried by cable and satellite are increasingly turning to user-generated video. CNN has a feature called I-Report that lets individuals send video to the news channel, where it might make it on the air. The cell phone video recorded by a student while the Virginia Tech shootings were in progress was played on CNN dozens of times. MSNBC features FirstPerson, where users can submit news video. ESPN has something similar called Sports Center Home Video.

The biggest place, of course, to find user-generated video is the Internet. Thanks to the success of YouTube (see the boxed insert "The Guys Behind YouTube"), user-generated content has exploded on the web. There were at least 150 video-sharing sites on the Web in mid-2007. YouTube, the most popular, has more than 6 million videos that take a up about

Talk about striking it rich. In the digital age one good idea can be worth money—an awful lot of money.

Chad Hurley was raised in Birdsboro, Pennsylvania. He attended Indiana University of Pennsylvania where he first majored in computer science and later switched to graphic design. After graduating in 1999, he took a job with a new company based in California called PayPal. Steve Chen was born in Taiwan but moved to the United States when he was 15. He majored in computer science at the University of Illinois—Champaign-Urbana. He too wound up working at PayPal in the late 1990s. Jawed Karim also attended the University of Illinois but dropped out to move to Silicon Valley where he too took a job at PayPal.

At a dinner party one night in 2004, the three were talking about how easy it was to share photographs on the Internet but how hard it was to share video clips. They decided to work on that problem and started meeting at Karim's apartment and in Hurley's garage. Karim was impressed by a site called HotorNot.com that let users post pictures of potential dates and rate them on a 1–10 scale. This site was unique because up to this point only the people who owned the site could post content whereas with HotorNot anybody could post photos for everybody else to see.

The three young men managed to cobble together a simple routine that allowed users to post their own videos in any format and play them back using any Web browser. In addition, they built in a search function and allowed people to rate and tag other people's videos. They also incorporated a feature that let people insert a video directly to a Web page. They came up with a name for the site—YouTube—and a slogan—"Broadcast Yourself."

As is sometimes the case with breakthrough technologies, the creators had no idea about the ultimate use of their invention. They thought that people would use it to illustrate items for sale on eBay or to show travel videos. What happened next was totally unexpected: The audience took over the site. They posted karaoke sessions, snowboarding wipe-outs, amateur stand-up comedy routines, stupid pet tricks, and introspective soliloquies. Some posted news footage, such as the aftermath of Hurricane Katrina and rocket attacks in Afghanistan. Others lifted clips from *The Daily Show* and the Cartoon Network and posted them (raising an issue with copyright holders that would become a continuing problem for YouTube). A couple of clips—one featuring Diet Coke and Mentos and another a skit from *Saturday Night Live*—were viewed by millions. Many used YouTube to post videos on their MySpace pages. Less than a year after it was launched, YouTube became a media phenomenon. It now airs more than 100 million videos, and about 70,000 are added every day.

YouTube was lucky to capitalize on two developments that fed on each other. The first was the revolution in digital video made possible by cheap cameras and simple editing software. The second was the rise of the Internet as an interactive social network where users generated and shared information. It was not coincidental that YouTube grew at the same time as Wikipedia, Facebook, MySpace, Flickr, and other, similar sites.

What about the three guys who made YouTube happen? They're a lot richer now. In 2006 Google bought YouTube for $1.65 billion.

---

45 terabytes of computer memory (1 terabyte equals 1,024 gigabytes or about 1 trillion bytes—that's a "1" followed by 12 zeros). YouTube also has what media gurus call "stickiness," the amount of time a person spends visiting a site. Visitors to the video-sharing site spend an average of nearly 15 minutes per session. Most sites are lucky if their stickiness number gets above 5 minutes.

YouTube has become so popular that it is used by politicians (as noted in the chapter opener), advertisers, recording hopefuls (remember Esmee Denters from Chapter 8), aspiring actresses (lonelygirl15), comedians, and others hoping for their 15 minutes of fame. MySpace, the social networking site, contains a tutorial on how users can post a YouTube video into their profile. Many apparently do, as a significant number of visitors to YouTube are MySpace subscribers embedding video on their MySpace site.

DEFINING FEATURES OF CABLE, SATELLITE, AND INTERNET TV

Obviously, a person needs at least one extra piece of equipment in order to receive video from these sources. Cable subscribers rent set-top boxes or use cable "smart cards" to receive their programs. Satellite viewers need a receiver and a satellite dish. Internet TV viewers have to have a computer and a modem.

A second obvious feature is that the consumer has to pay extra to receive these services. Unlike broadcast TV, where a rabbit-ears antenna connected to the set is enough to bring in their programs, cable and satellite subscribers must pay a monthly fee to receive their programs. On the Internet viewers can watch some programs for free but must pay to receive others (such as the $1.99 on iTunes). All, however, have to pay extra for Internet access.

A third feature is that these services carry many channels that appeal to niche or highly differentiated audiences. Unlike broadcasters, who still try to aggregate the biggest possible general audience, cable/satellite systems carry such specialized channels as the History Channel, the Weather Channel, and the Documentary Channel. And even the niche audiences are being divided up. There are two cable networks devoted to health programming, for example, and five devoted to home and lifestyle topics.

Although some mass-appeal TV shows and movies are available via the Internet, broadcasters and movie distributors don't expect them to draw a mass audience. Relatively speaking, only a small number of people download this content. A quick tour of the many Internet video sites will reveal that most of the available content is geared to those who share some special interest—music, comedy, sports, celebrities, pets and animals, and so on.

ORGANIZATION OF THE CABLE AND SATELLITE INDUSTRIES

We'll first focus on the organization of the cable and satellite industries and then take a look at Internet television.

▲ Structure: Cable TV

Cable systems are structured differently from those of conventional TV. There are three main components in a cable system: (1) the head end, (2) the distribution system, and (3) the house drop, (see Figure 11-2).

The **head end** consists of the antenna and related equipment that receive signals from distant TV stations or other programming services and process these signals so that they may be sent to subscribers' homes. Some cable systems also originate their own programming, ranging from local newscasts to weather dials, and their studios may also be located at the head end.

The **distribution system** consists of the actual cables that deliver the signals to subscribers. The cables can be buried or hung on telephone poles. In most systems the main cable (called the *trunk*) has several feeder cables, which travel down side streets or to other outlying areas. Finally, special amplifiers installed along the distribution system boost the strength of the signal as it comes from the head end.

The **house drop** is that section of the cable that connects the feeder cable to the subscriber's TV set. Drops can be one way (the signal travels in only one direction—from the

---

FIGURE 11-2

Diagram of the Transmission of HBO Programming from Studios, via Satellite, to the Pay Subscriber's Television Set.

At the head end the signal is assigned to a cable TV channel before being sent on its way to the subscriber's home.

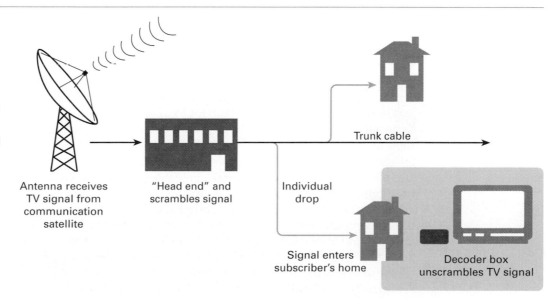

Antenna receives TV signal from communication satellite

"Head end" and scrambles signal

Trunk cable

Individual drop

Signal enters subscriber's home

Decoder box unscrambles TV signal

head end to the house) or two-way (the signal can also be sent back to the head end by the subscriber). Fiber optic cables make it possible to carry 500 or more channels.

▲ Programming and Financing: Cable TV

We will examine these topics from two perspectives: (1) that of a local cable system operator and (2) that of a national cable network.

Local Operators   There are six basic sources of programming for a local system:

1. *Local origination:* This programming might include local news, high school football, and discussions. A local government channel may carry city council meetings or zoning board hearings. Some systems have set aside public access channels for anyone to use for a modest fee.

2. *Local broadcast television stations:* Some cable systems carry signals from nearby cities in addition to local channels.

3. *Superstations:* These are local stations whose signals are carried by many systems nationwide. Major superstations include WGN, Chicago; KTLA, Los Angeles; and WPIX and WWOR, New York. The original superstation, WTBS, Atlanta, changed its status in 1998 to that of a cable network.

4. *Special cable networks:* These are services distributed by satellite to cable systems. Most of these networks are advertiser supported. Examples include MTV, The Weather Channel, USA Network, Black Entertainment Television, and the noncommercial C-SPAN (which covers Congress).

5. *Pay services:* These are commercial-free channels that typically provide theatrical movies and original programming. HBO, Showtime, The Movie Channel, and Cinemax are examples.

6. *Pay-per-view:* These are channels set aside for the showing of recently released theatrical films and special sports and entertainment events. Subscribers receive the programs for a specified price. Movies, for example, might cost $4.95; special events, such as Wrestlemania, might run $20–30.

A local cable system has two basic sources of income: (1) subscription fees from consumers and (2) local advertising. Most systems charge a fee for local stations, superstations, and special cable networks. In addition, consumers might pay an additional fee to receive one or more pay channels. Cable is a capital-intensive industry: It takes a lot of money to start a system. The operating costs of a typical system are more reasonable. A good part of the basic cable monthly subscription fee goes to cover construction and maintenance costs.

Cable systems must also pay for their programming. In the case of pay services, the consumer fee is split between the cable system and the cable network. There has been a recent shift in the composition of cable system revenue. Pay-cable and pay-per-view receipts now account for more than half of cable operators' income. Local advertising on cable represents another source of income for operators. This sum is growing, but it still represents less than 20 percent of total income for local systems. In addition, cable systems that carry home shopping networks generally receive a percentage of the sales revenue generated in their market.

National Operators   At the national level cable networks draw upon three major sources for their programming: (1) original production, (2) movies, and (3) syndicated programs. The all-news channel CNN relies upon original production for virtually all its content. Most of ESPN's programming is also original, as is C-SPAN's. Movies make up most of the content on HBO and Showtime. Superstations program a mix of all three sources, while channels such as USA Network and Lifetime depend heavily on syndicated programs.

There are three main revenue sources for national cable services: (1) advertising, (2) carriage fees, and (3) subscription fees. Pay-TV channels such as Showtime and HBO

Speaker of the House Nancy Pelosi appears on C-SPAN. Special-interest channels such as C-SPAN have fragmented the cable TV audience.

make their money from subscription fees paid by consumers. Some cable networks, such as MTV and ESPN, charge local operators a **carriage fee.** As of 2005, for example, ESPN charged $2.60 per subscriber, Fox Sports about $1.68, and CNN about 45 cents. Cable companies pass these charges along to their customers. Some channels, such as C-SPAN, support themselves entirely from this money. Other networks sell advertising in addition to the carriage fee, and still others, such as TNN, support themselves almost entirely through ads. As mentioned earlier, advertising revenues for cable are growing, but cable still accounts for only a small percentage of the total TV ad dollars. Table 11-1 lists the top cable channels.

▲ Pay-per-View (PPV)

PPV makes most of its money from sporting events (mainly high-profile boxing matches), movies, concerts, and adult content. Subscribers pay fees ranging from $5 to $50 to see these events. After racking up impressive revenue figures during the late 1990s, PPV has fallen on difficult times. Increasing competition from video-on-demand and digital cable channels has forced many cable system operators to reexamine the long-range future of this service. Still, the potential for big money exists. The 2002 Lennox Lewis–Mike Tyson boxing match brought in $106 million and was the biggest money-maker in PPV history.

▲ Video-on-Demand (VOD)

Cable and satellite operators are hoping that **video-on-demand (VOD)** will provide a big boost to their bottom lines. VOD works like this: A cable or satellite company stores movies or TV shows on a huge server. A searchable index contains a list of everything that is available. A subscriber scans the list and selects the program that he or she wants to watch; the selection is sent immediately to the person's TV set. A special set-top box lets the viewer pause, fast-forward, or rewind. In short, you get to watch whatever you want to watch whenever you want to watch it. Most cable/satellite services offer a per-program fee.

VOD has been around for a number of years but was slow to catch on because of a lack of content and a complicated user interface. Its fortunes have improved a bit recently as cable/satellite companies have simplified the ordering process and added more movies and TV shows to VOD libraries. In 2006 cable giant Comcast delivered 1.9 billion VOD sessions, up about 33 percent from the previous year. Movies are still popular, but TV show episodes are the fastest-growing genre.

In the past few years, however, VOD has been less of a priority for cable and satellite companies as they turn their attention to the Web. VOD does not create the same kind of "buzz" as a popular video on YouTube. Further, cable and satellite services are facing

TABLE 11-1	Network	Number of Subscriber Households (in millions)
Top Cable Services, 2006	Discovery	92.3
	ESPN	92.2
	CNN	92.0
	USA	92.0
	TNT	91.9

competition from other companies that now offer VOD. Apple sells TV shows and other content on its iTunes Web site. AOL launched its VOD service with a library of about 5,000 episodes of classic TV series.

▲ Structure: Satellite TV

A satellite system consists of five elements (see Figure 11-3):

1. Content providers, such as ESPN, Nickelodeon, or local broadcast stations, who send their signals to

2. A broadcast center, which takes the programming and transmits it to

3. Geosynchronous communication satellites (a **geosynchronous satellite** is one whose orbit keeps it over the same spot on Earth), which receive the programs from the broadcast center and send them back down to

4. A small satellite receiving dish, which picks up the signal and transmits it to

5. A satellite receiver, which transforms the signal so that it can be viewed on a conventional TV set.

Satellite signals are compressed in order to allow a greater number of channels to be transmitted to and from an orbiting satellite. To prevent people from receiving the signals without a subscription, the signals are **encrypted** (scrambled so that only those with a proper decoder can view them). The satellite receiver decrypts the signals and distributes them to one or more TV sets.

FIGURE 11-3

Diagram of a Satellite Broadcasting System

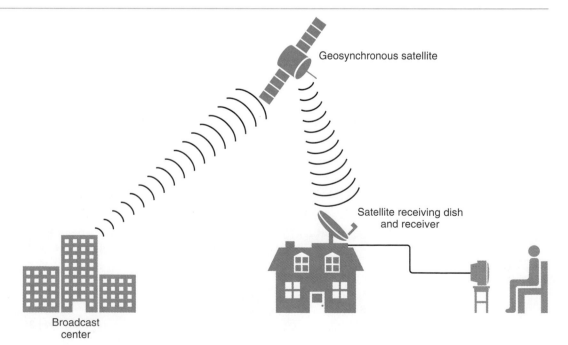

Geosynchronous satellite

Satellite receiving dish and receiver

Broadcast center

▲ Programming and Financing: Satellite TV

The same programming is carried by the major cable companies is also distributed by satellite, including local broadcast stations; superstations; nonbroadcast networks such as MTV, USA, and CNN; pay services such as HBO; and pay-per-view. Unlike cable, satellite networks are national in focus; there is no local origination of programs.

Similar to cable, the biggest source of revenue for satellite companies is the monthly subscription fees paid by their customers. In addition, DirecTV and Dish charge extra for DVRs, HDTV, and additional receivers. Unlike cable, local advertising is not a significant revenue stream.

Also similar to cable, satellite providers' biggest expenses are related to hardware. It costs a lot of money to launch, maintain, and eventually replace a communication satellite. Installing, servicing, and replacing dishes and receivers constitute another significant expense. DirecTV and Dish also pay content producers for the right to carry their programs.

As mentioned above, DirecTV and the Dish Network are having trouble competing against the cable industry's ability to bundle voice, video, and high-speed Internet access. In response, the satellite providers have explored alliances with other companies. The Dish Network, for example, joined AT&T in its Homezone package, providing the television part of a video, phone, and Internet bundle. It is unclear how long this relationship might last, as the phone companies are moving more heavily into providing TV themselves.

▲ Ownership of Cable and Satellite TV

The ownership trend in cable, as in other media, has been toward consolidation. Comcast acquired the assets of AT&T Broadband in 2002 to become the nation's largest cable provider. Comcast and number-two Time Warner serve more than half of all cable customers. The five largest cable companies are listed in Table 11-2.

There are two major companies that dominate the U.S. satellite TV market: DirecTV and Dish Network. DirecTV, with about 15 million subscribers, is controlled by Rupert Murdoch's News Corporation. The Dish Network is owned by EchoStar and has about 12 million customers.

INTERNET VIDEO

Compared to starting a cable or satellite TV channel, starting an Internet TV channel is relatively easy. No expensive studios and pricey equipment are needed. All it takes is a camera, a computer, some software, and a Web site, and you're in business. It's no wonder that this is a hot area.

Further, the explosion of video on the Internet in the recent years is another indication that the convergence between television set and computer is well on its way. Of course, an explosion is a difficult thing to analyze. Internet video is still expanding, and its final configuration is up in the air. This section will try to make some sense out of this rapidly changing area by examining its structure and finances.

▲ Structure: Sources and Content

One way to analyze Web video is to classify it by its source—amateur or professional—and by its content—original or repurposed. Let's first look at professionally produced content.

TABLE 11-2	Company	Number of Subscribers (in millions)
Five Largest Cable System Operators, 2006	Comcast	24.1
	Time Warner	13.5
	Charter Communications	5.5
	Cox Communications	5.4
	Cablevision Systems	3.1

Professionally Produced Content   Professional video can be either original to the Web or produced initially for some other purpose and then posted on the Web. The current TV programs that appear on the broadcast or cable networks' Web sites or that can be downloaded from iTunes are examples of this latter category. Other examples are AOL TV, with its archive of old Warner Brothers–produced TV shows, and Joost, a service that carries Comedy Central and the National Geographic channel, among others. These programs reach (or reached) the majority of their viewers through traditional TV, and the Internet provides a supplemental channel that attracts additional viewers. Parts or sometimes all of these programs might also be available on video-sharing Web sites where their presence can cause copyright issues.

There are numerous examples of professionally produced original online content. These usually use the Internet's broadband capability to carry video. Like their broadcast counterparts, cable networks have discovered broadband channels. In 2006 the Scripps Company, owner of the Food Network and Home and Garden Television, announced plans for as many as 10 broadband channels examining topics such as woodworking and kitchen design. MTV Overdrive has channels devoted to style, movies, and backstage interviews. Oxygen Network produces a broadband channel called Oh Baby that is aimed at new parents. The broadband channels are carving out niches within niches, appealing to even smaller audience segments.

Advertisers and marketers are another source of professionally produced, original Web video. Budweiser, for example, offers Bud.TV, a site that contains programs featuring Hollywood celebrities and an original game show. Land Rover debuted Go Beyond TV in 2006 with six different channels of original programming. French Maid TV offers "how to" instructions on various topics (geared to the needs of marketers) starring a trio of French maids (who else?). Broadband brings additional refinement to target marketing.

Then there are the Web sites that specialize in new programs. Blip.tv, for instance, offers about a dozen broadband channels with comedy and entertainment clips. LX.TV, with channels devoted to food, nightlife, style, and the arts, is designed for affluent young people. Forbes.com caters to those with an interest in business with programs such as *Street Talk* and *Sports Money*.

French Maid TV might look like one of the many X-rated sites on the Web, but it's really a site used to advertise various products and services. Marketers pay about $50,000 for one episode.

Videos on YouTube have been viewed nearly 2 billion times. It has been estimated that the total amount of time people have spent watching YouTube since it first started is more than 9,000 years.

The political announcements mentioned at the opening of the chapter represent another example. Moreover, Democratic presidential candidate Barack Obama's site included BarackTV, with clips of his speeches and campaign appearances. On the Republican side, candidate Mitt Romney's site featured MittTV with similar content. These Web video efforts are another example of the audience-building function mentioned in Chapter 2.

Amateur-Produced Content   Some amateur-produced video might be repurposed, such as posting a homemade wedding video on YouTube, but most amateur-produced content is original. The subject matter of these amateur clips is so diverse that it defies categorization. A quick scan of some of the more popular video-sharing sites reveals clips that range from serious to funny, from mundane to bizarre, and from intriguing to absolutely boring. In addition, they are almost always short clips, seldom more than 5 minutes long—"bite size entertainment," as suggest by a recent issue of *Wired*.

Homemade video, of course, is the ultimate example of user-generated content, and it has spawned a whole new Web industry—video sharing. Why is video sharing so popular? Three possible reasons: (1) We are inherently nosey and want to find out what's happening in other peoples' lives, (2) we have lots of free time, and (3) we all want our 15 minutes of fame.

YouTube, of course, is the best example of what can be done with user-generated content, but it has numerous competitors. Revver, for example, promises to share advertising revenue with its contributors. Google Video requires a verification process to make sure user-generated videos meet its legal and technical requirements. MySpace makes it easy to add a video to a person's profile. Jumpcut offers extensive video editing tools; Vimeo lets subscribers upload 250 megabytes of video every week. No matter how many video-sharing sites appear, there always seem to be videos to fill them up. No wonder *Time* magazine named the user-generating audience its 2006 Person of the Year. Not everybody, however, wants to post his or her videos along with everybody else's on these sites; some prefer a more limited approach. Porsche encourages its customers to post their homemade videos to its Porsche.magnify site. Even the New York Hamster

House, a haven for homeless hamsters in New York City, has user-generated videos on its Web site.

Internet video can also be used for microcasting.

▲ Microcasting

When the Brookwood High School Marching Bronco Band of Snellville, Georgia, spent a few days at band camp in South Carolina, parents back in Georgia could check up on their progress thanks to a Web cam that sent video of their practices over the Internet. Newlyweds Dusty and Fernando of Austin, Texas, put streaming video of their wedding on their Web site so that people who could not attend in person could see the ceremony. At the other end of the spectrum, more than 60 funeral parlors nationwide offer Webcasts of funerals.

The word *broadcasting,* as first used with early radio and then TV, meant sending a message to a large, heterogeneous group of people. When format radio and cable TV networks came into being, the word *narrowcasting* was coined for targeting your message to appeal to a small, well-defined subsegment of the total audience. Top 40 radio stations, for example, narrowcast to 12- to 22-year-olds; ESPN, primarily to male sports fans; and C-SPAN, to aficionados of politics. Video sent over the Internet takes this process one step further by making possible **microcasting,** sending a message to a small group of interested people. This is another example of the "few-to-few" model of communication mentioned in Chapter 1.

Although many experts think that the Internet will ultimately become a mass communication medium and that audiences will watch TV shows and Hollywood movies over their broadband connections, the Internet is also evolving in the other direction. The most

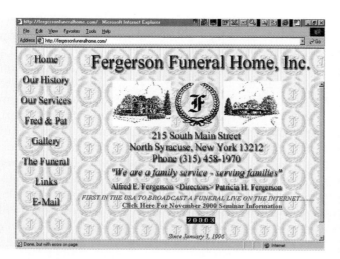

Fergerson Funeral Home microcasts funerals on the Web.

successful applications, such as instant messaging, online auctions, and peer-to-peer file sharing, have been inspired by the end users and not by big mass communication conglomerates. Microcasting is yet another example of this trend.

Before long, Internet-capable cell phones will be equipped with video cameras. When that happens, the possibilities for Web microcasts will become endless. Dad could microcast Scott's and Buffy's soccer games or band recitals to the grandparents in another state. High schools could microcast the

There's good news for those of you who are thinking about television as a career. There are signs that the Internet and the broadband revolution have made it much easier, for some at least, to become a media star.

For instance, consider the case of Andrew Mathas, a college student who posted an online parody of a Fall Out Boy music video, "Sugar We're Going Down" (a song whose slurred lyrics are open to interpretation, to say the least). Mathas's spoof consisted mainly of crudely drawn stick figures and text, but its rudimentary nature didn't put people off; more than a million people watched it on Google TV and other Web sites. One of the people who saw it was an executive for MTV, who offered Mathas a job at Overdrive, MTV's broadband video site.

Then there's Brooke Brodack, a 20-something whose comedy videos brought her to the attention of Carson Daly, who signed her to a production contract with his company.

Finally, how about Andy Milonakis? Comedian Jimmy Kimmel liked his online videos so much that he got Milonakis his own show on MTV2.

For the first time in several years, would-be TV producers and creators have new outlets for their efforts. As of 2006, Comedy Central, for example, was developing 20 series for broadband video and considering 40 more. Court TV has plans to air 30 mini-documentaries on its broadband site.

All of these new channels demand content, and as the above three examples show, the TV industry is using the Internet as a testing ground for new talent. At MTV executives are encouraged to surf online video sites such as YouTube to look for creative people. Finding new talent on the Web entails little risk. A typical broadband production costs only a few thousand dollars, and it takes only a few weeks online to see if the new program attracts an audience. If it does, then its creator can move on to more mainstream and more lucrative projects.

---

prom to interested parents. How about video of the local Little League games? Microcasting, of course, will raise all sorts of questions about privacy that will have to be resolved in the near future.

FEEDBACK FOR CABLE, SATELLITE, AND INTERNET TV

Networks distributed by cable and satellite are measured by Nielsen Media Research. The techniques are the same as reported for broadcast TV in Chapter 10. A national sample using People Meters provides viewing data that are reported in terms of ratings and shares. Ratings for cable/satellite-distributed networks tend to be smaller than for broadcast networks. Nielsen also publishes a *Cable Network Audiences Composition Report* that provides more detailed information about audience demographics.

Gathering feedback on Internet video is a new and difficult area. One company, comScore Media Metrix (see Chapter 12), released its first *Online Video Ratings Report* in 2005. The data are collected from a sample of about 2 million people worldwide who agree to install comScore Media Metrix tracking software on their computers. Nielsen's online division, Nielsen/NetRatings, announced its online video measurement service, VideoCensus, in 2007.

▲ Audience

About 85 percent of American households get their television from either a cable or a satellite provider. Those who subscribe tend to be younger, have more children, and be more affluent than those who are not subscribers. Cable/satellite networks are more specialized than over-the-air networks, and their demographic makeup varies according to their target market. ESPN, for example, attracts a male audience; Oxygen, a female one. Nickelodeon aims for youngsters while CNN and MSNBC try for a more mature audience.

Some preliminary data about the audience for online videos gathered by the Online Publishers Association revealed that about 1 in 4 Internet users watched online video at least once a week, and about 1 in 20 watched every day. A visitor to an online video site, such as YouTube, spends about 15–25 minutes on the site (compare this to the 4+ hours that the average person spends watching conventional TV). Other data suggest that those who share video tend to be male and young, with about half under 20 years of age.

THE CABLE/SATELLITE AND INTERNET INDUSTRIES

The cable/satellite industry is relatively small, employing about 90,000 people, far fewer than the number who work in traditional broadcasting. Nonetheless, the career outlook appears more positive in this area than in some of the traditional media that we have discussed. There are hundreds of cable/satellite networks now in operation and probably more to come. The industry will need more people in production, performance, publicity, marketing, and community relations.

As with the broadcast industry, newcomers should not be afraid to start at the bottom and work their way up the organization. Likewise, your first job in this area may not last long. Be prepared to move on to other opportunities as they become available.

Moreover, the explosion of broadband channels has opened up new career opportunities, especially for those with a creative bent (see the boxed insert "Breaking into TV Has Never Been Easier"). Finally, the online video surge has produced a number of jobs that didn't exist a few years ago. After all, somebody has to decide what videos to feature on the site's home page; somebody has to sell advertising; somebody has make sure the system works correctly; and so on.

MAIN POINTS

- Cable TV began in the 1950s as a way of bringing TV signals to places that could not otherwise receive them.

- Cable TV reached maturity by the turn of the century and was facing competition from DBS satellite systems.

- The Telecommunications Act of 1996 permitted cable and telephone companies to compete with one another.

- Internet TV developed in the late 1990s and became more popular with the growth of broadband.

- Cable and satellite systems are structured differently from those of conventional TV.

- Cable television is dominated by large multiple system operators. Two companies, DirecTV and the Dish Network, are the leading DBS providers.

- Internet video can be categorized by source (professional or amateur) and content (original or repurposed).

- User-generated video, such as those on YouTube, has become extremely popular.

- Internet video sites make money by charging a fee for their content or by selling advertising.

- Nielsen provides rating data for cable/satellite networks. Ratings for online video sharing sites are provided by companies that measure Internet usage.

QUESTIONS FOR REVIEW

1. What are the defining features of cable/satellite TV? Of Internet TV?

2. Who are the major owners of cable and DBS systems?

3. How does cable/satellite programming compare to traditional broadcast network programming?

4. Trace the structure of a cable system from head end to home.

5. How can online video sites make money?

QUESTIONS FOR CRITICAL THINKING

1. How, if at all, will VOD change the cable TV industry?

2. Have you ever posted a video online? Why? Have you ever looked at online videos? Why?

3. Google paid $1.65 billion for YouTube. Do you think Google will get its money back?

4. Why do you think many presidential candidates opted to make their announcements using online video as opposed to a press conference?

KEY TERMS

multiple system operators
  (MSOs) (p. 259)
direct-broadcast satellites
  (DBS) (p. 259)
voice-over-Internet protocol
  (VOIP) (p. 259)

Internet TV (p. 260)
buffering (p. 260)
podcast (p. 260)
head end (p. 263)
distribution system (p. 263)
house drop (p. 263)

carriage fee (p. 265)
video-on-demand (VOD) (p. 265)
geosynchronous satellite (p. 266)
encrypted (p. 266)
microcasting (p. 270)

INTERNET RESOURCES

Online Learning Center

At the Online Learning Center home page, www.mhhe.com/dominick10, *select* Student Center *and then* Chapter 11.

1. Use the Learning Objectives, Chapter Outline, Main Points, and Time Line sections to review this chapter.

2. Test your knowledge of the chapter using the multiple choice, crossword puzzle, and flashcard features of the site.

3. Expand your knowledge of concepts and topics discussed in the chapter by going to Suggestions for Further Reading and Internet Exercises.

Surfing the Internet

http://wedcast.istreamplanet.com/lwc/whitechapel.asp
The Little White Wedding Chapel in Las Vegas has live and on-demand videos of their weddings.

www.blinx.tv
Example of a video-sharing site that mixes professional and amateur content.

www.historychannel.com
Has more about history than it does about the cable network, but contains good examples of streaming video and interactivity.

www.multichannel.com
Multichannel News is the leading trade publication covering cable, satellite, and wireless companies.

www.ncta.com
Web site of the National Cable Television Association. Contains information about the latest issues facing the industry.

CHAPTER 12

THE INTERNET AND THE WORLD WIDE WEB

This chapter will prepare you to:

- describe how computers were invented

- explain how the Internet and the World Wide Web were developed

- understand the advantages of broadband Internet access

- realize the potential impact of Web 2.0

- recognize the economic impact of the Internet

- discuss the social concerns raised by the Internet

Get yourself an avatar and buy an island, build a castle, become a rock star. . . . Almost everything is virtually possible in Second Life.

s there anything that the Internet can't do for us? It entertains us, keeps us informed, helps us keep tabs on our friends, lets us buy and sell used textbooks, gives us an opportunity to share our thoughts with the world, lets us express our personalities, and enables us to find old classmates.

That should be enough, but there's more. The Internet now gives us a second chance at life. Not a real chance, of course, but a virtual chance. It's a Web site called Second Life, and a brief examination of it can tell us a lot about where the Internet is headed.

Developed by San Francisco's Linden Lab in 2003, Second Life is technically an MMORPG (massive multiplayer online role-playing game), but it's not really a game since there aren't any winners or losers. It's more of a life simulation utilizing what's called in Internet-speak a *metaverse*—a 3-D space where people travel about, interact, and build things. As of mid-2007, Second Life had about 3 million registered users. Many of them pay $15 a month for the privilege of buying virtual real estate. Linden Labs also attracts private investors; it recently raised $11 million in private funding.

When you first visit Second Life, you choose an avatar, a virtual representation of a person who will become the virtual person who will lead your second life. Your avatar can have your ideal body, as handsome and as beautiful as you desire. Clothing is up to you. It can range from urban cool to goth (although a large number of avatars seem to look like fuzzy squirrels). You can explore the metaverse by flying or teleporting from place to place.

What can you do in Second Life? You can shop in virtual stores. American Apparel, Reebok, Circuit City, and many others have set up virtual stores in Second Life. Toyota sells a virtual version of its Scion. Second Life has its own economy based on Linden dollars, which can be exchanged for real dollars. You can buy land and build your dream house. Other residents have constructed castles, nightclubs, jungles, skyscrapers, and spaceships. The Swedish government has opened a virtual embassy. You can also find entertainment. MTV sponsors virtual rock concerts, Showtime has built a virtual meeting place for fans of its series *The L Word,* where they can watch episodes and chat with the stars. You can hook up with other avatars (a lot of virtual real estate in Second Life is for adults only). In short, you can do pretty much what you want. You have a whole new life.

In addition to being a mildly addicting game, Second Life holds some lessons about the present-day Internet. First, it illustrates the concept of Web 2.0, an interactive environment where people form collaborative communities (more on Web 2.0 later). Second, it is a world that is constructed by users. Linden Lab provides the basic framework, but the users generate the content. One of the hallmarks of Web 2.0, user-generated content has become increasingly popular on the Web. Third, advertising and marketing are creeping into many popular Web sites as the Internet becomes increasingly commercialized. Finally, like several other Web sites, Second Life has become an opportunity for investors who hope to strike it rich if Second Life is bought by a big company with deep pockets.

A BRIEF HISTORY OF THE COMPUTER

The earliest versions of the computer were basically adding machines designed to take the drudgery out of repetitive arithmetical calculations. In the 17th century, French mathematician and philosopher Blaise Pascal (a modern computer language was named for him) created the *arithmatique*, a machine the size of a shoebox filled with interconnected 10-toothed wheels that could add numbers up to one million. A few decades later, the German mathematician Gottfried Wilhelm von Leibniz explored the subject of binary arithmetic, a system with just two possible values, 0 and 1. The binary system is the one used by modern computers.

During the 19th century, English inventor Charles Babbage, working with Augusta Ada Byron, the daughter of Lord Byron, the English poet, worked out plans for an "analytical engine," a steam-powered device about the size of a football field, that would quickly perform complicated mathematical operations. The existing technology, however, was not sufficient to build this machine, and after 19 years of trying, Babbage and Byron gave up.

In America, Herman Hollerith developed a tabulating machine to help process data collected in the census of 1880. His machine used punched cards and electrical circuits to do calculations, and it worked so well that businesses all over the country clamored for it, prompting him to start his own company, International Business Machines (IBM).

In 1940 a Harvard University mathematician, Howard Aiken, made the next major breakthrough when he created a digital computer—one that worked with binary numbers, 0 and 1, or in Aiken's case, switch closed or switch open. Aiken's computer, the Mark I, was 50 feet long and 8 feet tall and had 750,000 parts. When it was running, it sounded like thousands of knitting needles clicking together. A few years later, researchers at the University of Pennsylvania constructed the first all-electronic computer, ENIAC. Although ENIAC was much faster than any previous mechanical computer, its size was a drawback—it stood two stories tall, weighed 30 tons, and used about 18,000 vacuum tubes.

SOUNDBYTE

How Many Are Elves?

Massive multiplayer online role-playing games (MMPORGs) are massively popular. Consider:

- Population of Denmark (2006): 5.5 Million

- Subscribers to MMPORG
  "World of Warcraft" (2006): 6.0 Million

ENIAC, completed in the late 1940s, was the world's first general-purpose, digital, all-electronic computer. The device took up most of the space in a good-sized room. ENIAC is a far cry from today's laptop computers.

The term *generation gap* refers to the difficulty of one generation understanding another because of different experiences, culture, habits, and behavior. It was first used in the 1960s to describe the growing differences between parents and the "baby boom" generation with regard to fashion, music, and politics. It now seems that the new digital media might be widening that gap.

A 2006 study by ad agency Universal McCann notes that digital media are more apt to be used by the younger generation. For example, twice as many 16- to 34-year-olds belong to a social network site (such as Facebook or MySpace) as 35- to 49-year-olds. In addition, 16- to 34-year-olds are 25 percent more likely to use instant messaging than the older group, three times more likely to write a blog, and nearly three times more likely to have used a peer-to-peer file-sharing service.

The invention of the transistor in the 1950s led to new electronic computers that were smaller, cheaper, and easier to maintain. Integrated circuits made it possible for many transistors to be embedded in a tiny silicon chip, which paved the way for the microprocessor. These advances opened up new markets for computer manufacturers. In the late 1970s, personal computers (PCs), using packaged software, appeared in stores. Designed for home use, these computers were used primarily for word processing, financial management, and game playing.

A few years later, developments in hardware and software expanded the communication function of the computer. The **modem,** from *mod*ulate and *dem*odulate, enabled PCs to converse with one another and with larger computers located in other places over telephone lines. New communications software facilitated the development of local area networks (LANs), which linked several computers into a network. As miniaturization continued, laptop computers and wireless modems became more common.

The next major development in the continuing evolution of the computer will be a move from the office to the living room. Most families keep their computer in an office or den where they use it to read the latest news, check e-mail, manage their money, and do word processing. Computer companies, however, are creating new machines that will make the computer the centerpiece for home entertainment. These new entertainment PCs will allow consumers to record and play back TV shows, look at digital photos, play CDs and DVDs, and participate in online video games all on a large digital display that can double as a TV set. The initial price tag for this new generation of computers will be steep, but experts predict that sales will grow over time.

The 1990s saw an explosion in computer communication that continues today. Every day, billions of pieces of electronic mail (e-mail) are carried over the Internet. Every night millions of individuals log on to social networking sites, check bulletin boards, shop, read the news, share video, download music, and maybe even live a second life.

THE INTERNET

The Internet is a network of computer networks. Think of it as a system that combines computers from all over the world into one big computer that you can operate from your own PC. Some computers are run by government agencies (like the National Aeronautics and Space Administration), some by universities, some by libraries, some by school systems, some by businesses, and so on. The connections among these networks can be ordinary phone lines, microwaves, fiber optic cables, or wires built specially for this purpose. A related example might be the phone system. When you call somebody in Cleveland, the call is routed through several different phone networks in different parts of the country. You really do not care what route it takes or what companies handle it as long as your call gets there. So, too, with the Internet. When you search for information, send e-mail, or chat online, several different networks may handle your messages. Just as there is no one phone company, there is also no one Internet company.

The Internet's seemingly chaotic structure arose from its somewhat fractured history. A little background will help to clarify.

▲ From ARPANET to Internet

Back in the early 1970s, when the cold war was still raging, the U.S. Department of Defense was concerned about the vulnerability of its computer network to nuclear attack. The Pentagon did not want to lose all its computing and communication ability to one well-placed atomic bomb. Consequently, defense computer experts decentralized the whole system by creating an interconnected web of computer networks. The net was designed so that every computer could talk to every other computer. Information was bundled in a packet, called an Internet Protocol packet, which contained the destination address of the target computer. The computers themselves then figured out how to send the packet. Thus, if one portion of the network happened to be disabled, the rest of the network could still function normally. The system that the Pentagon eventually developed was called ARPANET.

At about the same time, companies developed software that enabled computers to be linked to local area networks (LANs) that also contained the Internet Protocol programs. Not surprisingly, many of these LANs were also connected to ARPANET, causing the network to grow even more.

The users of this early network were primarily scientists and computer experts, and most observers thought that it would continue to be of interest only to high-tech types. (The network was once uncharitably labeled a "Disneyland for geeks.") In the late 1980s, however, the National Science Foundation, whose own network was already connected to the Net, created supercomputing centers at U.S. universities. Since they were so expensive, only five could be built. This meant that they had to be shared and interconnected. The ARPANET seemed like the obvious choice for interconnection, but there were too many problems involved. Instead, the National Science Foundation built its own system using the Internet Protocol and hooked together chains of regional networks that were eventually linked to a supercomputer. Thus, the Internet, or Net, was born.

Now that students, scientists, government workers, and others had access to supercomputers, the amount of information at their disposal increased tremendously. The Internet also served as a communications link that enabled scientists from all over the country to share data. Doctors, lawyers, journalists, authors, and business owners recognized the potential of the Net, and traffic increased.

The Internet was still used by only a small fraction of computer owners. Three developments, however, contributed to a meteoric rise in the Internet's popularity.

The first was the development of the World Wide Web (WWW, or Web) in 1990. Engineers working at a physics laboratory in Switzerland created an interconnected set of computers on the Net that all used the same communications program. This program took advantage of **hypertext,** a navigational tool that linked one electronic document, either text or graphics, with another, thus creating a virtual web of pages. The Web started off as an electronic information resource for scientists but was quickly discovered and utilized by the entire Internet community. Any organization or individual could create a page on the Web as long as the person or organization used the communication rules developed in Switzerland. It was not long before conventional media companies, businesses, organizations, and individuals got involved with the Web. By 1998 it was estimated that there were more than a million Web sites in operation.

The second development made it easier for consumers to find what they were looking for on the Web. This happened in 1993 with the creation of user-friendly navigation tools that helped further spur the growth of the Web. The first of these **browsers,** called Mosaic, was able to retrieve data, determine what they were, and configure the data for display. Mosaic created a graphical display for users that simplified navigating the Internet. In 1994 one of the developers of Mosaic formed a commercial company that was eventually named Netscape. Software giant Microsoft introduced its own browser, Internet Explorer, a few years later.

The third development was the **search engine,** a utility that scans the Internet for terms selected by the user and displays the results according to some predetermined criterion, such as relevance. Some well-known search engines are Google and Yahoo! These advances helped users make sense of the Internet and turned it into a useful information tool.

The mid-2000s saw the development of easy-to-use software programs that made it simple to upload content to the Internet. This encouraged the growth of blogs (see below), social networking sites, and video-sharing sites, all of which combined to make the Internet more popular than ever. In 2005 more than 17 million new sites were added to the Web, and there were more than 400 million host computers connected to the Internet. Obviously, the Internet has grown into a powerful mass communication medium.

STRUCTURE AND FEATURES OF THE INTERNET

As mentioned earlier, the Internet is a global network of computer networks. In more technical terms, this means that a group of two or more networks is electronically connected and able to communicate with one another. Together, they act as a single network. For this to work, however, the computers have to speak a common language. The common language, called a **protocol** by computer programmers, that was developed for the Internet is called the Transmission Control Protocol/Internet Protocol (TCP/IP). It is actually a set of protocols that govern how data travel from one machine to another over networks. IP is sort of like the address on an envelope. It tells a computer where to send a particular message. TCP breaks up the information into packets that can be transmitted efficiently and then reassembles them at their destination.

Individuals gain access to the Internet in one of two ways:

1. Through an Internet service provider (ISP), a company that connects a subscriber to the Net and usually charges a fee (many companies, including some local phone companies, function as ISPs)

2. Through an online service provider (OSP) such as America Online or MSN

Technically speaking, the difference between an ISP and an OSP is that OSPs typically offer exclusive content or services to their subscribers, and ISPs simply connect the user directly to the Internet. Many ISPs, however, offer exclusive browser software and other features, so that the distinction between these two services is becoming blurred.

Once connected to the Internet, an individual can make use of a variety of tools for information, entertainment, and communication. Three of the more popular applications are (1) e-mail, (2) newsgroups, and (3) the World Wide Web.

▲ E-Mail

Millions of people are connected to the Internet, and you can send mail to one of them or to many of them. **E-mail** works on the client/server arrangement. To send and read e-mail, users (clients) must access another computer (the server), where their mailbox resides. E-mail messages are not limited to text. Attachments, such as graphics or spreadsheets, can also be sent.

E-mail is usually fast, cheap, and reliable. It is the most widely used Internet resource. In 2006, more than 10 trillion e-mail messages moved through the Net.

E-mail is helpful, but it also has some drawbacks. First, it is not as formal as a printed letter, so there may be some tasks for which it is inappropriate (like telling someone he or she has been fired). Second, e-mail is not as private as a letter in an envelope. Your message

It is not surprising that the computer and the Internet have raised many new ethical questions. Computer experts at the Computer Ethics Institute have developed the Ten Commandments for Computer Ethics. The commandments are rather general and noncontroversial, such as "Thou shalt not use a computer to steal" and "Thou shalt not use a computer program for which you have not paid." There are other areas, however, where the issues are not so clear.

One such area involves anonymity. In the offline world a person has to make an extra effort to remain anonymous. Hiding your true identity might require an unlisted phone number, a fake ID, and a disguise. On the Internet, however, anonymity is the default condition. User names generally are generic and say little about the true identity of the user. A person has to make an extra effort to establish his or her *real* identity.

Anonymity is not necessarily bad. For example, it disguises differences in race, sex, age, and physical appearance. To the extent that these items interfere with fairness, anonymity may serve as an equalizer. Further, people may be encouraged to reveal their true feelings if they know their identity will not be revealed. Battered spouses, for instance, might be better able to ask for help.

Conversely, anonymity can create problems. People are more apt to behave in undesirable ways when they act anonymously. They may send inflammatory or racist messages, post offensive material, and snoop into the affairs of others. It is also easy for a person to claim to be someone he or she is not or to become multiple persons with multiple identities. The best illustration of this is the case of a man who pretended to be a woman and participated in an online discussion group that dealt with women's issues. Is such behavior ethical? What if the man used his online female persona to arrange a date between his true self and a woman in the group?

Anonymity can undermine trust. In the offline world people establish a history of dealing with other people and can decide whether a person is to be trusted. This is far more difficult in the online world, where the same person might have multiple identities, or the same identity might be used by more than one person. You have trouble developing a history because you are never sure whom you are dealing with.

Are there ethical principles (see Chapter 17) that can be applied to anonymity on the Net? One possibility is situational ethics. There may be some situations in which no one expects others to reveal their true identities. Adult-oriented chat rooms, for example, might call for a high level of anonymity (in which everybody assumes that everybody else is not who they purport to be). On the other hand, it would be unethical to participate in a discussion group about the consequences of child abuse by falsely claiming to be an abuse victim. As the popularity of the Net continues to grow, much more attention will be paid to issues such as these.

may travel through several computers where others might have access to it. At some companies employee e-mail might also be available to management. Third, e-mail comes with the ever-present nuisance called **spam.** Spam, the cyber equivalent of junk mail, includes unsolicited messages touting low mortgage rates, porno sites, and miracle cures; clogs up people's mailboxes; and takes time to delete. Spam is on the increase; the Internet carries more spam messages than legitimate e-mail. If that were not bad enough, about one in every 200 spam messages contains a virus. Fourth, there is the problem of information overload. In many businesses memos that used to go to a small group of people now get sent to everybody, and every decision—no matter how small—gets circulated via e-mail. As a result, the average worker at a Fortune 500 company sends and receives nearly 200 messages every day, taking up a big chunk of the workday.

▲ Newsgroups

Newsgroups are collections of electronic bulletin boards, arranged according to topic, where people can read and post messages. Some newsgroups are devoted to current events, but the *news* in *newsgroups* refers to topical discussion groups, not news in the traditional sense. The information or "articles" that make up the news are written by people interested in the topic. Others can read the articles and comment on them. The newsgroups exist on a special network called Usenet, one component of the Internet. There are more than 40,000 different newsgroups, with topics ranging from the highly intellectual to the downright weird.

▲ World Wide Web

As mentioned earlier, the **World Wide Web (WWW)** is a network of information sources incorporating hypertext that allows the user to link one piece of information to another. Note that the Web is *part* of the Internet; the two terms are not synonymous. The Web is nonlinear. This means that the user does not have to follow a hierarchical path from one piece of information to another. The user can jump from the middle of one document into the middle of another. In addition, the Web incorporates text, graphics, sound, and motion.

Some terminology might be useful at this point. The structure of the Web is based on the Web server, a computer connected to the Internet that facilitates the transfer of hypertext pages. One server can hold thousands of hypertext pages. A **Web site** is a complete set of hypertext pages linked to each other that contains information about a common topic. A **Web page** is a hypertext page that is contained within a Web site. The home page of a Web site is the entry or doorway to the site that might contain links to other pages or to various sections of the site.

The protocols for navigating the Web assign each Web page a uniform resource locator (URL) and an Internet address. URLs are structured as follows:

protocol://server.subdomain.top-level domain/directory/filename

For example, the URL for this book is:

http://www.mhhe.com/dominick10

This means that the page is in the hypertext transfer protocol, the server is linked to the WWW, the subdomain name is *mhhe,* the top-level domain is *com,* and the directory name is dominick 10.

The tremendous variety of sites and the motives behind them make it difficult to describe Web sites in general terms. There are sites maintained by big media companies, such as the *New York Times* and the Walt Disney Company, that are used to promote their traditional media products and to build an audience for the online content as well. Other companies, such as Nissan and the Miller Brewing Company, use their Web sites to advertise their product lines. Government agencies, such as the IRS and the Department of Agriculture, have designed Web sites to serve their constituents and to promote good public relations. Professional organizations, such as the Association for Education in Journalism and Mass Communication, use their sites to share information among their members. Groups with special interests, such as the American Diabetes Association, use their sites to disseminate information. Professors set up pages where they post syllabi, readings, and other resources for their classes. Some sites are on the Web to make a profit; they sell advertising or charge a subscription fee. Some sites are simply search engines that enable the user to search other sites.

Many Web sites function as **portals.** A portal, as the name suggests, is an entryway, the first page a person looks at before zooming off into the Web. The strategy behind a successful portal is to offer visitors useful information, such as news headlines, weather, stock information, and bargains, so that they do not go looking for these items at some other site. The longer a person stays at the portal, the greater the chance that she or he might see some of the advertising on the site. Some of the best-known portals are those provided by Yahoo!, Excite, MSNBC, and Netscape.

Finally, some Web pages are published by individuals. Many of you reading this may already have your own Web page or blog.

How big is the World Wide Web? The answer is hard to come by because the Web grows every day. As of 2006, the search engine Google estimated that there were more than 3.3 billion unique pages on the Web. However, although it is called the *World Wide Web*, it is primarily a Web for industrialized nations. About 85 percent of the pages on the Web are in English, Japanese, French, or German.

▲ Online Service Providers

Started back in the 1980s, online service providers (OSPs) were the main ways to access the Internet during its formative years when most consumers had slow dial-up access. Their fortunes waned, however, as other companies provided Internet access and high-speed connections. AOL was the biggest OSP, once having more than 29 million customers. After a disappointing merger with Time Warner and continuing loss of subscribers, AOL changed its business model in 2005 and became a free service. The Microsoft Network (MSN), the second largest OSP, offers chat rooms, bulletin boards, e-mail, security options, and instant messaging. It makes most of its money from advertising, but consumers can subscribe to premium services, such as enhanced e-mail and music channels.

THE EVOLVING INTERNET

The Internet changes so fast that it is hard to predict its future. Nonetheless, here are several trends that most experts agree will significantly affect the Net in the next few years.

▲ Broadband

Broadband refers to any of the several ways to connect to the Internet that carry information many times faster than conventional dial-up modems. The tremendous gain in speed makes it possible to send huge files in much less time. Downloading a typical music file might take more than half an hour with a dial-up modem but only a minute or so with a broadband connection. In addition, broadband makes it practical to send video over the Internet.

Consumers can access broadband through a satellite modem, a cable modem, or a digital subscriber line (DSL) through their telephone. All three methods are more costly than a dial-up connection, averaging anywhere from $50 to $100 per month.

Technology experts have touted broadband for many years as the wave of the Internet future. In addition to facilitating high-speed Internet access, broadband makes possible many other desirable things, including video-on-demand, interactive television, live streaming video, and downloadable movies.

Thanks to increased marketing efforts and special pricing plans, the number of broadband subscribers has increased over the past few years. At the beginning of 2007, about 50 percent of U.S. households had a broadband connection. Nonetheless, the United States lags behind 24 other countries in broadband penetration. South Korea, for example, has 89 percent of its subscribers connected to broadband, Iceland 75 percent, and the Netherlands about 70 percent.

Those who do subscribe to broadband like it. A 2004 study by Forrester Research found that broadband users are online about 11 hours per week, compared to about 6 hours for dial-up users.

▲ Going Mobile: The Wireless Web

As described earlier, wireless technology will become more and more common during the next decade. Not surprisingly, the Internet will reflect this growing trend. There were about 15 million laptop computers with wireless Net access in use in 2005 along with about 30 million cell phone subscribers and PDA users who reported using their devices to connect to the Net. Improved color screens and easier-to-use interfaces will probably increase this number in the near future. Fairly soon, the Internet will be available everywhere.

What makes all of this possible is the development of **wireless fidelity,** or **WiFi,** technology. WiFi uses low-power radio signals to connect devices to one another and to the Internet. A base station serves as a transmitter, and PDAs, computers, and cell phone customers can use special hardware and software to hook into the system.

Many WiFi public access locations or "hot spots" have sprung up all over the country—in airport waiting rooms, cafes, and even parks. People who frequent these hot spots can link up with the Internet at no cost. Experts estimate that there are tens of thousands of WiFi public locations in the United States. (For more information on WiFi, see the boxed insert "The Internet Unleashed.")

As mentioned in Chapter 1, mobility is one of the emerging characteristics of modern mass communication. WiFi was the first step in that direction for the Internet. The next step will be **WiMax,** a technology that will bring wireless Internet access to entire metropolitan areas. WiMax works a lot like WiFi, but instead of a short 200 feet or so range, WiMax permits access across a range of approximately 10 miles. This means an individual

Contributed by Dr. Scott Shamp
Director, New Media Institute, University of Georgia

The Internet gave us our first true taste of on-demand information. With our connected computer we can access information from around the world at any time of the day or night. But any information at any time is not enough. Now we want that information anywhere we are—in the car, at the coffee shop, in the classroom.

Wireless technologies now allow untethered access to the Internet. All wireless systems utilize basic radio technology. And, although there are many different types of systems, two have emerged as the leading wireless options.

The first system, 3G, is an evolution of cellular telephone service. "3G" stands for the third generation of cellular technology. 1G was voice, 2G was data, 3G enables high-speed data transmission. Like other cellular telephone service, 3G divides geographic areas into cells (or zones). Towers equipped with transmitting antennas are strategically placed to provide connectivity to all areas of the cell. The size of the cell differs according to the topology of the land and man-made features such as buildings. Cells are typically measured in kilometers.

Today 3G networks are more a goal than a mature service. High-speed 3G will allow all-new types of data transmission, such as for music and video. Major cellular providers see 3G as a key factor in their continued growth. Consumers already buy more voice minutes than they can use. Data services offer additional revenue opportunities for providers. Each cellular provider is rolling out its own version of 3G, but the costs of refitting towers and buying spectrum space is slowing down 3G implementation.

WiFi (wireless fidelity) provides a very different approach to wireless data transmission. WiFi was originally developed as a wireless local area network for laptop and desktop computers. But today WiFi is being used to deliver connectivity to a range of other types of devices in a variety of settings. In a WiFi network a small, low-powered device called an *access point* (AP), about the size of this textbook, handles transmission to and from computers. The AP then relays the data to the Internet, typically through a broadband wired connection. WiFi is a short-range technology with a typical coverage area of about a city block. It operates in a portion of the electromagnetic spectrum that governments have set aside for amateur use. Therefore, no license is required to operate a WiFi network. The result has been a proliferation of public WiFi networks where users can connect for a small fee or even for free. Businesses and some large cities are offering WiFi connectivity to attract customers and visitors.

The primary advantage of WiFi is higher speed. Currently, there are several different types of WiFi, each with differing transmission speeds. Even the slowest version (802.11b) is at least 10 times faster than existing 3G networks. The latest WiFi iterations could be hundreds of times faster, with much better coverage areas.

Today, 3G and WiFi are distinct and incompatible. 3G networks send data over larger areas at slower speeds, typically to increasingly smaller handheld phones. WiFi networks offer higher bandwidth but in smaller areas, mainly for laptop computers. But the future could look very different. Currently, handset manufacturers are producing cell phones with built-in WiFi that seek and seamlessly connect to highest bandwidth option without any user intervention. With voice, data, music, and even video, the device carried in our pockets, palms, packs, or purses could be our new connection to a world of information.

could log onto the Net while riding on a commuter train or in the back seat of a car. Wireless companies hope that eventually the WiMax network will be as pervasive as today's cell phone net.

▲ Web 2.0

The growing pervasiveness of broadband made Web 2.0 possible. **Web 2.0** is a label given to the developing Internet and the new, interactive ways that people are putting it to use. It's an inchoate term, capable of many interpretations, but generally referring to a second generation of Web services, characterized by collaboration and sharing, such as social networking sites (like Facebook), user-generated sites (such as YouTube), and group effort sites (such as Wikipedia).

As mentioned in Chapter 1, whereas the first-generation Web was a place where users generally consumed content, Web 2.0 is a place where users generate and share content. Whereas Web 1.0 was static, Web 2.0 is dynamic. With Web 1.0 the audience went to Web pages and looked at content provided by the Web site owner. For example, way back in the late 1990s, eons ago in Internet time, people constructed personal pages on the web. Visitors could read something about the person who built the site and maybe even look at a few photos, but that was it. Today, people are more likely to have a page on Facebook or MySpace where they can still post basic information, but now they can join groups, send messages back and forth, check on each others' whereabouts and moods, submit and share videos, sell stuff, and link to other sites.

Web 2.0 has also acquired a more pecuniary aspect. Among investors and entrepreneurs, the term refers to a site that requires little risk and could bring huge rewards. Take Flickr.com, for example. With only 10 people on the payroll and the users providing the content, the site attracted millions of visitors. Not surprisingly, it was acquired by Yahoo! for around $40 million. Social networking site dodgeball.com, started by a couple of NYU students, was snapped up by Google. The growth of Web 2.0 has stimulated investment in Internet properties to such an extent that many fear it is creating another Internet "bubble," similar to the one that burst at the end of the 1990s during Web 1.0 and wiped out billions of dollars.

▲ Monetizing the Web

There is no necessary connection between popularity and financial success. As new Web 2.0 sites attract big numbers of visitors, investors and Web site operators are interested in converting all of these visitors into some form of monetary reward. Hence the emergence of the rather clumsy term *monetizing,* the process of converting something to money. Some solutions are novel. My Second Life sells virtual real estate to real companies so that they can market their products in a virtual world. Shutterfly offers subscribers a chance to upload, edit, and share their photos and charges a small fee for prints. Others are more conventional. Facebook sells display advertising on its pages. Google sells sponsored links next to its search results (see the boxed insert, "Counterfeit Clicks").

No matter what the technique, one thing is certain: Commercialization will continue to increase on the Internet. First, as big companies snap up promising Web 2.0 sites, they will be looking for ways to find a return on their investment. The folks at Yahoo! didn't pay $40 million for Flickr simply because they like to look at pictures. Second, as the traditional media continue to lose audience, advertisers and marketers are looking to the Net to increase the reach of their ads. Heinz, for example, sponsored a contest on YouTube with a $57,000 prize to the person who made the best TV commercial for their catsup.

Even the mainstream media recognize the marketing potential of Web 2.0. The producers of the CBS series *How I Met Your Mother* posted a fake video on MySpace to promote an upcoming episode. The tactic worked as viewership among young adults increased by about a million.

Marketing and advertising are even creeping into the blog world (see below). Authors of influential blogs in a certain area might get special treatment from marketers in return for a couple of favorable mentions about their product in the blog. Record companies give advance copies of new releases to music bloggers hoping for some positive comments. The producers of the CBS sitcom *The New Adventures of Old Christine,* a program that features motherhood as a theme, invited the authors of leading "mommy" blogs to the set of the program, where they visited with the stars and received free DVDs. It probably won't come as a surprise that the show got some positive mentions in the blogs.

▲ Blogs

Blog is short for "web log." Blogs are journals in which people write about whatever they want: news, politics, sports, music, movies, quilting, and so on. Blogs are another manifestation of Web 2.0. Readers can post comments and engage in virtual conversations with the blog author. Blogs often contain links to other blogs, news reports, music clips, and video-sharing sites. The book you are reading has its own blog site. Check out http://dynamicsmasscomm.blogspot.com for updates, examples, and discussions of topics covered in this text.

The Power Line blog was one of many blogs that questioned the authenticity of the documents involved in a CBS report about President George W. Bush's National Guard service.

Blogs got their start in the late 1990s but didn't become popular until free software programs made it easy for anybody to put a blog online. And a lot of people did. Technorati, a Web site that tracks these things, reports there were about 70 million blogs in 2007, and the "blogosphere" has been doubling every 6 months or so. Soon there will be more people writing blogs than reading them.

Blogs are a vivid example of how the Internet can make anybody a mass communicator (see Chapter 1). Bloggers can become instant reporters, sharing text and pictures from anywhere in the world. Some of the most dramatic accounts of the Virginia Tech shooting were posted by bloggers.

Blogs have made their influence felt on the traditional media (bloggers generally refer to traditional media as MSM, or main stream media). When CBS broadcast a report that raised questions about President George W. Bush's military service during the Viet Nam era, bloggers questioned the authenticity of the documents that were at the heart of the story. CBS eventually conceded that it could not authenticate the documents and apologized for the report. Ironically, many of the MSM have started their own blogs.

Blogs are cropping up in other areas as well. At the University of Buffalo, students in a communication course blog their assignments and comments as part of the course requirements. Photographers blog their photos. Literary scholars blog about novels. Hundred of topic areas are represented.

The Internet and the blog have given a voice to those who would not otherwise be heard. As Dan Gillmor puts it in his book *We, the Media:*

> *What . . . matters is the fact that people are having their say. This is one of the healthiest media developments in a long time. We are hearing new voices—not necessarily the voices of people who want to make a living by speaking out, but who want to say what they think. (p. 139)*

▲ Voice-over-Internet Protocol (VoIP)

As mentioned in Chapter 11, VoIP lets individuals make telephone calls using a broadband Internet connection rather than a traditional phone line. In simplified terms, here's how it works: When a person speaks into a telephone, VoIP converts the voice signal into packets of digital data and sends them over the Internet. At the other end the signal is then converted back into voice. Depending upon the VoIP provider, some consumers may only call other subscribers to the service, while others may call anybody with a phone number anywhere in the world.

The number of people using VoIP is increasing—about 16 million as of the start of 2007. This number will grow as cable systems and Internet providers continue promoting the service. AOL, for example, rolled out its VoIP plan in April 2005. Additionally, the FCC has ruled that it and not each individual state had the right to regulate VoIP providers. This ruling makes it easier for companies to expand their service over wide areas.

The big advantage of VoIP is that it is cheaper than traditional wire or wireless phone service. A service plan that offers unlimited local and long-distance calls in the United States and Canada costs around $20 per month. Calls to Europe and Asia cost about 3 or 4 cents per minute.

On the downside, the quality and reliability of individual calls may not be as high as with the traditional phone services, and as with anything over the Internet, VoIP is vulnerable to spam, viruses, and hackers.

THE ECONOMICS OF THE INTERNET AND THE WEB

We will now look at the general impact of the Internet on the national economy, examine the impact of e-commerce, and then focus on the finances of individual Web sites.

▲ The Internet and the National Economy

After a boom period from 1998 to mid-2000, Internet-related businesses hit hard times in the new century. At the beginning of 2001, it was estimated that stocks of Internet companies had lost more than $1.7 trillion in value. Many dot-com companies folded, and thousands of jobs were lost.

The bust, however, may have a silver lining. The dot-com companies that survived the fallout are those that have sound business plans and good cash flow. At the end of 2004, about 40 percent of publicly traded Internet companies were profitable, including such familiar companies as eBay, Expedia, and Yahoo!. As noted above, Web 2.0 has sparked a new wave of investments and speculation. More than $1.6 billion was invested in Web 2.0 Internet firms in 2006, and as an article in *Fortune* magazine proclaimed, "The Boom Is Back." How long it lasts, of course, is another matter.

More traditional brick-and-mortar stores, such as Wal-Mart and Home Depot, use the Internet as an additional revenue stream. Other corporations are turning to the Net as a business tool, using it to buy parts, handle customer relations, and facilitate worker teamwork. In short, the final economic impact of the Net is yet to be determined, but the long-term outlook seems positive.

▲ E-Commerce

E-commerce is the term used to describe the selling of goods, products, and services online. There are two kinds of e-commerce: (1) the better-known type in which companies sell directly to consumers and (2) a less-visible kind called *B2B* or *e-business* in which companies sell to each other. We will look at consumer e-commerce first.

Statistics reveal the scope of e-commerce. From being nonexistent in the early 1990s, global e-commerce came to account for approximately $240 billion in online spending in 2007. About 10 million consumers purchase something online every week. The products and services that account for most of e-commerce are travel, computer hardware and software, apparel, books, and music.

Impressive as these numbers might be, they pale in comparison to B2B e-commerce. In 2006, according to market research firm IDC, the B2B online market accounted for about $2 trillion worldwide in sales. The Internet enables businesses to deal directly with one another, sometimes eliminating the middleperson (another example of disintermediation), making the process more efficient. PerfectCommerce, for example, is a B2B site that helps buyers connect with sellers in industries ranging from auto parts sales to soft-drink bottling. Experts predict that B2B will save American businesses billions of dollars in the years to come.

One way to make money with a Web site is to sell merchandise online as does ecost.com.

Now let us take a more specific look at the financial side of individual Web sites.

▲ Web Site Economics

The tremendous variation in the kinds of people and organizations found on the Internet makes it hard to summarize its economic arrangements. Suffice it to say that the profit motive matters more to some than to others. A company that sells merchandise over the Internet is probably much more concerned with generating revenue than is a government agency or university that maintains a site as a service to its clients. Likewise, Uncle Max is probably not worried whether his blog ever generates a profit.

The rest of this section examines those online operations for which making money is an important consideration. There are three basic ways to make a profit over the Internet.

The first is to create a site with content so compelling that people will pay to see it. One type of company that follows this model offers specialized information that has value for a large number of customers. The *Wall Street Journal*, one such example, charges a subscription fee to access its online edition. *Consumer Reports* offers access to its product evaluations for $26 a year. Web portals, such as Yahoo!, have also instituted charges for such services as game playing and Web hosting.

The other type of business that uses this pay-for-content model is pornography. At last count there were thousands of these sites, and some were among the most profitable on the Web. Sex sells, even on the Internet.

The second way to make money on the Net is to sell merchandise or services online. Amazon.com, the site that sells everything from laptops to lawn mowers, is the best example of this business model. Although many online retailers went bust in the early years of the new century, many of those that remain are profitable. For example, eBay had a profit of about $1 billion in 2006.

The third moneymaking method is for the site to sell advertising. Advertisers spent more than $16 billion in 2006 for online exposure. Online advertising can be broken down into three main categories: (1) paid search ads, (2) display ads, and (3) classified ads. Of these three, paid search ads (such as those sponsored links that show up on the right side of a Google search) account for the most revenue, followed by display ads (banner ads, pop-ups) and classifieds.

Display ads are becoming more sophisticated and harder to avoid. Most now employ some form of "rich media," using color, motion, and clever layouts to attract attention. Video display ads are becoming more common, and many are displayed as soon as a user visits a Web site.

Well-known Web companies with Web sites that attract lots of visitors dominate online advertising revenue. Google, for example, accounted for about 36 percent of gross online revenue in 2006 while Yahoo! accounted for about 28 percent. The top three companies that spent the most on online ads in that same year were Vonage, AT&T, and Dell.

Of course, some Web sites use some combination of one or more of these techniques. For instance, eBay charges for its services, sells advertising, and markets its own customized merchandise.

FEEDBACK FOR THE INTERNET

As with the other industries mentioned in Part II, independent companies provide information about the Internet audience. Reliable data about audience size are important for advertisers who want to place banner ads on Web sites. The two companies that dominate the audience measurement field are ComScore and Nielsen/NetRatings. Both organizations

Ethical Issues   Black Hats Versus White Hats

Suppose you sell shoelaces. Suppose further that you want to sell a lot of your shoelaces online. Suppose even further that you design an attractive, informative, and easy-to-use Web site that shows off your product in the best way possible. It's only a matter of time before people from all over the world are visiting your Web site and buying your shoelaces, right? Not exactly. Even the best-designed Web site is useless if people can't find it.

And how do people find it? Most use search engines like Google and Yahoo!. And the cold fact of the matter is, your site needs to show up near the top of a shoelace shopper's search results page if you expect to make any money.

Just to illustrate: A search for "shoelaces" on Google returned 2.37 million hits. If your Web site was number 678,095 in Google's results, it's unlikely that many people would find it. On the other hand, if you were number 1 (as was lacesforless.com in this example), you would probably do much better. (Statistics show that the first screen of a search results page accounts for 70 percent of all user clicks.) But what does it take to get a Web site into the top ranks? The answer to that question takes us into the rather arcane world of "search engine optimization" and a consideration of "white hat" versus "black hat" techniques raise ethical questions about online marketing and advertising.

Search engines such as Google and Yahoo! use an algorithm (a set of specific instructions) that determines how their results are ranked. "Spider Bots" follow these complex and secret algorithms as they race around the Web at dizzying speed compiling their results for individual searches. If a person knew something about how these algorithms worked, it would be possible to design a Web page that would score high in the ultimate results. Enter a new professional: the search engine optimizer (SEO).

SEOs know that the factors that Google and other search engines use in their algorithms include the number of times search terms turn up in the content of the site, whether the search terms match the key words that describe the site, the number of links to the site, and the "credibility" of those linking sites. Armed with this knowledge, the SEOs redesign the site using "white hat" or legitimate methods, such as making everything on a page visible to the search engine. Product listings, for instance, are moved from an unsearched database to the site itself. Another white-hat technique is participating in a Web ring with other high-quality sites, thus increasing the number of links to the site. A third is making sure that each page has plenty of text that includes relevant terms (search engines don't pay much attention to pictures or graphics).

On the other hand, black-hat techniques are generally considered unethical. These might include "cloaking," creating two versions of a site, one that people see and a bogus site that is visible only to search engines that includes popular search terms, such as "sex." Another is using text containing popular search terms, such as "sex," that users can't see (the background and the foreground colors are the same) but that are visible to spider bots. Yet another is "link farming," using software that automatically generates a huge number of pages with links back to the original site. There are even illegal software programs that can forcibly inject links into sites that search engines score as more credible (such as universities).

Naturally, Google, Yahoo!, and the other search engines are well aware of these scams and do their best to minimize the rigged rankings that result from black-hat techniques. Companies that get caught can have their sites delisted from search results. In 2006, for example, Google accused auto-maker BMW of using the cloaking technique to enhance its search rankings and dropped the company from its results until the offending procedure was removed. Nonetheless, as revenues from Internet search marketing continue to increase, the struggle between the black hats and the white hats will no doubt continue.

---

use a panel of consumers to generate their data. ComScore samples about 1 million people in the United States, using software that works with a computer's operating system to monitor Internet activity at home and at work. Nielsen uses a similar setup with a sample of about 68,000 people. Both services issue periodic reports that list the most popular Web sites. For example, in February 2007, ComScore reported that Yahoo!, Time Warner, Google, Microsoft, and eBay were the parent companies of the top five Web sites.

▲ Audiences

The Pew Foundation has sponsored a number of surveys that have focused on the Internet and the people who use it. As one of its reports put it, "At the infant stage, the Internet's user population was dominated by young, white men who had high incomes and plenty of education. As it passed into its childhood years in 1999 and 2000, the population went mainstream; women reached parity with men online, lots more minority families joined the party and more people with modest levels of income and education came online." In short, by 2007 the Internet population resembled the general population.

The Pew report calls the Internet the "new normal" in the American way of life. About two out of three adults use the Internet. On a typical day more than 80 million adults go online to use e-mail, get their news and weather, search for specific information, and simply browse for fun. Teenagers use the Internet even more, with about 8 out of

Back in the good old days, when your author was in college, if a professor assigned a term paper it meant that students would spend a lot of time in the library, searching for sources, finding relevant information, evaluating its credibility, summarizing it on index cards, and finally organizing the information into a coherent paper. These days, alas, when a research paper is assigned, few students venture into the library. Why go, they ask, when everything you need is available on the Internet?

Most professors will probably agree that when it comes to higher education, the Internet has been a mixed blessing. On the plus side, the Net has made huge amounts of information readily accessible to students. Further, today's students are highly skilled in using the Net quickly to track down facts and figures. Web search engines also help students find many disparate sources of information and encourage them to make connections that were not easily seen before the advent of the Internet.

But there is a downside. My colleagues and I have had the following experience many times. After a research paper is assigned, one or two students will come to us and complain that they cannot find any information on the topic. When asked where they searched, they reply, "Online." When asked if they considered searching in the library, they almost always say no. For many students, if information is not online, it does not exist. Some students are amazed to discover that information

specialists report that only about 15 percent of all information can be found online.

Then there is the problem of students cutting and pasting material from the Web into their own research papers. This situation was more severe a few years ago when many students simply downloaded huge chunks of information and pasted it verbatim into papers. Most now realize that professors have antiplagiarism software that can detect this wholesale borrowing. More common today is the practice of lifting a few sentences, changing a word here, cutting a word there, adding a couple of words at the end, and passing off the result as an original thought.

Perhaps most disturbing is the hopscotch nature of information gathering on the Web. So many possible sources show up that students simply jump from one to another, seldom spending much time digesting the contents of one article before going to the next. As a result, students have trouble constructing a valid argument from premise to conclusion and presenting a logical, coherent framework of supporting evidence. The facts are there, but there is not much of an indication that students have thought much about them.

Well, enough ranting. In closing, I would urge all who read this to go to the library and actually touch books. You might be surprised by how much you enjoy and get from the experience.

Nielsen/NetRatings measures what Internet sites are most popular.

10 reporting that they go online on a regular basis. Moreover, the first "Internet generation" has come of age, and many of them can't recall what things were like before the Web became a reality.

When people go online, here are the top five things that they do: (1) use e-mail, (2) obtain the latest news, (3) buy things, (4) pay bills, and (5) send instant messages. People also multitask. About 40 percent watch TV while online, another 23 percent listen to the radio.

Web 2.0 has opened up new possibilities. Blogging, sharing videos, social networking, rating products and services, playing online games, and similar activities will doubtless become more popular in the future.

THE SOCIAL IMPLICATIONS OF THE INTERNET

Now that you know some of the details about the Internet, let's examine some of the social implications. Keep in mind, however, that the Internet is still evolving, and much has yet to be discovered about its impact on society. Nonetheless, a few consequences are already apparent.

▲ A New Model for News

To begin, the Internet supplements the traditional surveillance function of the mass media. As we have seen, when a news event happens, involved or interested parties can post blogs for others to read. Bloggers posted first-hand accounts of the 2005 terrorist bombings in London. In the aftermath of Operation Iraqi Freedom, bloggers provided details about life in Baghdad. This represents a shift in traditional journalism in which decisions are made by editors and flow from the top down. Now the news can start at the source and go "sideways," to all who are interested. As some experts have put it, traditional news used to be a lecture; now it's a conversation.

Blogs have questioned the accuracy of news stories in the traditional media and have exposed several instances of sloppy or inaccurate reporting. In response, the news media have attempted to make their techniques more transparent. In short, the Internet provides additional checks and balances to the traditional news media and makes them more accountable to the public.

The Internet has also expanded the interpretation function. Blogs, in particular, have made it possible for everyone to chime in with his or her opinion on news topics and controversial issues. Moreover, many politicians and prominent policymakers read blogs, magnifying their influence even more.

▲ Lack of Gatekeepers

As mentioned in Chapter 1, traditional mass media have a number of gatekeepers. On the Internet, however, there are none. This situation has several implications.

First, the risk of overloading the system with unwanted, trivial, worthless, or inconsequential messages is increased. Do we really need 70 million blogs? Suppose I posted this chapter on every active message board on the Internet and e-mailed it to everybody on every mailing list I could get. Suppose everybody did that with everything they thought was important. The system would get bogged down by all the excess traffic.

Second, gatekeepers also function as evaluators of information. Newspaper editors and television news directors consider the authenticity and credibility of potential news sources. Gatekeepers, however, are not infallible. As detailed in Chapter 13, many mistakes can slip through the gates of even the most established TV networks, newspapers, and magazines. Nevertheless, if the system works properly, bogus news tips, unsubstantiated rumors, and false information are filtered out before they are published or broadcast. Information obtained on the Internet, however, comes without a guarantee. Some of it might be accurate; some of it you must use at your own risk. For example, the UFO-related newsgroups contain several accounts of UFO sightings and abductions by aliens. How credible these reports are is anybody's guess.

Third, having no gatekeepers means having no censorship. The Internet is like a huge city. There are some streets where the whole family feels comfortable and other streets where you probably would not want to take your children.

Of course, there are some potential positive benefits from a lack of gatekeepers. Take blogs, for example. Topics that might be considered too controversial or unfavorable to the economic interests of traditional media can be publicized by bloggers. Further, blogs are not bound by the traditions of mainstream journalism. They can be partisan, in questionable taste, and totally individualistic. This makes for lively and exciting content.

▲ Information Overload

The Internet represents an information retrieval tool that is unparalleled—provided a person knows how to use and understand it. In the days before the Net, students doing research would have to look things up in a text, reference book, or encyclopedia—sources that had some recognized authority. Today, students can post a request for information with a relevant newsgroup or use a search engine to look for the topic. The credibility of responses on a newsgroup, however, is open to debate. A Web search indiscriminately displays a list of "sources," which may number in the millions. Every source on the screen seems to have the same credibility, even though some may be scientific documents and others comic books.

For example, while doing research, I used Google to look for references to "virtual reality." My search turned up 77,500,000 matches, including some that were about virtual reality games, quite a few that were XXX-rated, a large number from multimedia companies that produce virtual reality software, some that described technical background, and one about the use of virtual reality techniques for law enforcement and explosive ordinance training. (Of course, I might have narrowed my search using some advanced techniques, but the fact remains: There is so much on the Web that it is sometimes more overwhelming than useful.) Further, other than making a reasoned guess from the titles, I had no clue as to which sources were more authoritative than the others. (Students doing a conventional search would also have to assess the credibility of their sources, but the profuseness of information and the sheer size of the Net make this extremely difficult to do.)

▲ Privacy Concerns

The Internet also raises a number of privacy concerns. Maintaining a person's privacy in the electronic age is not a new problem, but before the advent of the Internet, compiling a detailed dossier on someone required days or even weeks of searching through records scattered in dozens of places. Today, computerized databases enable a person to accomplish the same things with only a couple of clicks of a mouse. What follows are some illustrations of this growing problem:

- In 2007 department store owner TJX, parent company of T. J. Maxx and Marshall's, reported that hackers stole financial and personal information from at least 45.7 million credit and debit cards, data that could be used to steal the identities of customers.

- Some states have put the names and addresses of sex offenders on Web sites. Although the motives behind this practice may be understandable, the potential for harm due to incorrect or outdated information is substantial. In North Carolina a family was harassed because their address was listed online as the home of a known sex offender. The sex offender had actually moved away many months earlier, but the entry was never removed from the database. Many companies now charge as much as $150 to do online searches that will disclose someone's current address, Social Security number, bank account number, criminal record, and work history.

- Another growing concern is identity theft. A person can obtain someone's name, Social Security number, and date of birth from the Internet and can then apply for credit cards, get loans, and even commit crimes under another name. Even more unsettling is the fact that the victim may not even know what has been done in his or her name. In California a young man could not figure out why he was always turned down when he applied for retail jobs. He finally learned that someone had stolen his identity using the Internet and had been convicted of shoplifting. Whenever a potential employer ran a background check on the young man, the shoplifting conviction wrongly appeared on his record.

For the past few years, the government has wrestled with this privacy problem, and several bills have been introduced in state legislatures as well as the U.S. Congress that would restrict the availability of personal information. The issue is complicated because many are concerned that government regulation would be so rigid that legitimate searches for information would be difficult. Many prefer voluntary guidelines to laws.

▲ Escapism and Isolation

Finally, does the Internet detach people from other people? Many individuals already spend lots of time engaging in sending e-mail, instant messaging, online chatting, game playing, online shopping, and maybe even cybersex. As more and more attractions go online, will we spend even more of our lives staring at computer screens? Some psychologists have identified a condition known as *Internet addiction,* similar to drug or alcohol addiction. Early studies of Internet users revealed that those who spent many hours online also showed signs of isolation and depression. Subsequent studies, however, have not found such a link.

THE FUTURE: THE EVERNET

Computers and computer chips keep shrinking. Before long, tiny computers will be part of our household appliances and maybe even our clothes. These devices will be so small that we probably will not even realize they are there. Moreover, experts predict that in the next 10 years advances in technology will enable these microcomputers to carry Web addresses and be connected constantly to the Internet. Imagine a furnace that automatically orders new filters over the Internet whenever it senses that the old ones are dirty. Imagine wearing a tiny computer that automatically unlocks your car, opens your garage door, pays your toll and parking fees, and reminds you that your tires need to be rotated. If you can imagine all of this, you have some idea what the **Evernet,** the successor to the Internet, will be like.

The Evernet (also called the Supranet or Internet II) will mark the convergence of wireless, broadband, and other devices, resulting in a person being connected continuously to the Internet anywhere using any information device. You will no longer have to "log on" to the Net; you and all of the other devices that have computer chips will be automatically "online" all the time and all connected to one another. The Evernet will merge the virtual world with the physical world.

The implications of the Evernet are staggering. A person could send or access information instantly from anywhere in the world. What does that mean for consumers? You could order anything from anywhere at any time. Impulse buying would take on a whole new meaning. Further, shoppers could access price comparison search engines and find out if there was a better deal across the street. What about the implications for business?

A manufacturer's assembly lines could be connected to cash registers all over the country. When sales go up, the assembly line works overtime.

What about daily living? "Smart houses" that run themselves would be possible. A smart house would inform you about your daily appointments and chores, monitor security systems, schedule maintenance and repairs, order food when supplies were low, regulate temperature and lighting, start the coffee brewing, and even run a hot bath.

What about health? People wearing pacemakers could have their heart rate and other medical data transmitted continuously to their physicians. If something were amiss, a person would get a call from his or her doctor's computer: "Your blood pressure is too high. Are you taking your pills?"

Granted, all of this sounds a bit like science fiction, and there is always the possibility that new technology will not impress consumers. Nonetheless, just 30 years ago, the Internet also sounded a lot like science fiction.

THE INTERNET AND THE WEB

The Internet and the Web are so new that it is difficult to define career paths in these areas. Some careers that involve the Internet have been mentioned earlier, such as online journalism, and others, such as online advertising, will be discussed in subsequent chapters. The rest of this section examines general career opportunities for those interested in the online area.

One typical entry-level job would be a Web developer (also called a *Web designer* or *Web publisher*). Web developers are responsible for the actual creation of a Web site. They consult with the appropriate people about the content of the site and put together the content that will appear. Once the content has been assembled, the Web developer converts the documents into hypertext and scans the text, graphics, and pictures into the server. Since many sites now incorporate multimedia, the developer might also include prerecorded or live audio and video. Developers also upgrade sites and make sure that the sites are easy to use.

The next step up from a Web developer is a Web master. This is a managerial position that involves working closely with Web developers and members of the organization that sponsors the site. Web masters consult with staff members from departments such as engineering, customer support, and public relations. Web masters are responsible for all aspects of a Web site. They design the overall look of the site and approve all materials that are published on the site. Web masters make sure the site is performing as expected and is meeting the needs of users and the sponsoring organization.

Many colleges now offer courses in Web page design or related topics. In addition to these, you should probably take courses in computer science, graphic design, journalism, public relations, and English and be on the lookout for those jobs that have not yet been invented.

MAIN POINTS

- The computer's ancestors were machines that performed mathematical calculations.
- By the 1970s personal computers using packaged software were on the market.
- The Internet is a network of computer networks. It was started by the U.S. Department of Defense and in its early years was used primarily by scientists. The current Internet started in the 1980s thanks to the efforts of the National Science Foundation.
- The main features of the Internet are e-mail, newsgroups, and the World Wide Web.

- The introduction of broadband Internet connections will encourage the growth of streaming video and microcasting.
- The Internet has had a beneficial impact on the national economy, and e-commerce continues to grow.
- Web 2.0 refers to the contemporary Internet and the new, interactive ways that people are using it.
- The Internet has created social concerns about lack of gatekeepers, information overload, lack of privacy, and isolation.
- The Evernet may be the successor to the Internet.

QUESTIONS FOR REVIEW

1. How did the Internet come into being?
2. Distinguish between a Web site, a Web page, and a portal.
3. What is Web 2.0? How will it affect your life?

4. What's the difference between e-commerce and B2B e-commerce?
5. What are some of the social implications of the Internet?

QUESTIONS FOR CRITICAL THINKING

1. Check out some of the blogs available on the Net. How many did you find useful?
2. Do a Web search for your name. See how much personal information you can find out about yourself on the Web. How easy was it for you to find the information? Could others have found it as well?
3. Do you read blogs? How influential are they among your friends?

4. Some critics (Roger Ebert among them) have suggested that the era of free information on the Internet is almost over and that ultimately we will pay for most of the content we get over the Net. Do you agree? Would you pay to access a search engine? Or a Web site such as CNN.com?
5. Speculate on some of the implications of the Evernet.

KEY TERMS

modem (p. 277)
hypertext (p. 278)
browsers (p. 278)
search engine (p. 279)
protocol (p. 279)
e-mail (p. 279)

spam (p. 280)
newsgroups (p. 280)
World Wide Web (WWW) (p. 280)
Web site (p. 281)
Web page (p. 281)
portals (p. 281)

broadband (p. 282)
wireless fidelity (WiFi) (p. 282)
WiMax (p. 282)
Web 2.0 (p. 283)
Evernet (p. 293)

INTERNET RESOURCES

Online Learning Center

At the Online Learning Center home page, www.mhhe.com/dominick10, *select* Student Center *and then* Chapter 12.

1. Use the Learning Objectives, Chapter Outline, Main Points, and Time Line sections to review this chapter.
2. Test your knowledge of the chapter using the multiple choice, crossword puzzle, and flashcard features of the site.

3. Expand your knowledge of concepts and topics discussed in the chapter by going to Suggestions for Further Reading and Internet Exercises.

Surfing the Internet

http://news.bbc.co.uk/1/hi/technology/5243862
An interactive history of the Internet provided by the BBC.

http://www.yahoo.com
The address of one of the many popular Web portals.

www.digitaltrends.com
A site that lists the basics of Web 2.0.

www.powerlineblog.com
One of the more influential politically oriented blogs on the Web.

www.secondlife.com
Get yourself an avatar and see what all the fuss is about.

www.technorati.com
Want to read a blog? Want to read 70 million? This is the site that tries to track them all.

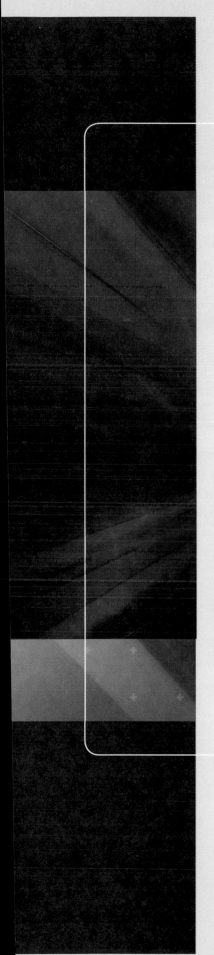

PART III

SPECIFIC MEDIA PROFESSIONS

CHAPTER 13

NEWS GATHERING AND REPORTING

This chapter will prepare you to:

- describe the qualities that characterize news

- identify the three main types of news stories

- understand how the digital revolution has affected news gathering and reporting

- recognize the wire services that provide national and international news

- discuss the strengths and weaknesses of broadcast, print, and online journalism

- describe the changes in the news audience over the past several years

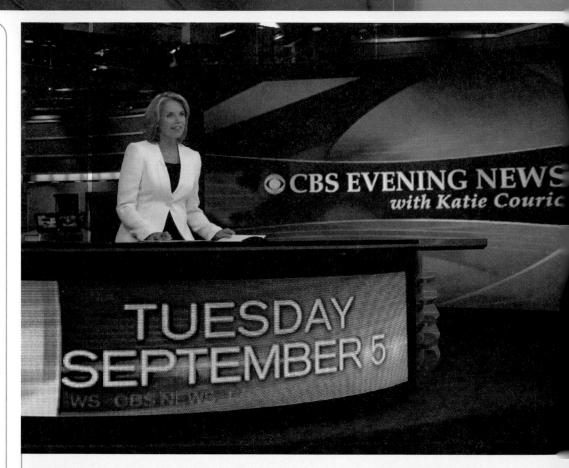

Despite some high-profile moves, such as Katie Couric's debut as anchor of the *CBS Evening News,* the audience for network news continues to decline.

13

As stated on its Web site, the Project for Excellence in Journalism is "a research organization that specializes in using empirical methods to evaluate and study the performance of the press. It is non partisan, non ideological and non political." It is also a highly respected and authoritative source. In short, when this organization says something, people listen.

Here's an excerpt from the Project's report, "The State of the News Media, 2007": "This is the fourth edition of our annual report on the state of the news media—the status and health of journalism in America. The broad context outlined in earlier editions remains the same: the transformation facing journalism is epochal, *as momentous as the invention of the television or telegraph, perhaps on the order of the printing press itself*" (emphasis added).

This is heady stuff. At the basis of this transformation are the digital revolution and the Internet. These twin forces have rocked the foundation of the business model that has supported journalism for the last 180 years or so, given audiences more control over what information they consume and how and where they consume it, and made everybody a potential reporter.

This chapter looks at how this epochal transformation has influenced the basic principles of journalism, the main types of news stories that exist, the technology of news gathering and reporting and how stories are reported.

Senate majority leader Harry Reid meets the press.

DECIDING WHAT IS NEWS

From the millions of events that happen every day, journalists decide which few are worth reporting. Deciding what is newsworthy is not an exact science. News values are formed by tradition, organizational policy, and economics, and, more recently, by the digital revolution. Nonetheless, most journalists still agree that there are five core elements that characterize newsworthy events.

1. **Timeliness:** Put glibly, news is new. Yesterday's news is old news. A consumer who picks up the evening paper or turns on the afternoon news expects to be told what happened earlier that same day. News is perishable, and stale news is not interesting. The digital revolution has put an additional premium on timeliness. With Web sites that operate 24/7 and bloggers who provide first-hand information about an event minutes after it happens, news no longer has to wait for the morning edition or the evening newscast. As a result, the "shelf life" of news has become shorter.

2. **Proximity:** News happens close by. Readers and viewers want to learn about their neighborhood, town, or country. A train derailment in France, for example, is less likely to be reported than a similar derailment in the local train yard. News media are placing additional emphasis on this factor as they examine the potential of hyperlocal news (see below). Proximity, however, means more than a simple measure of distance. Psychological proximity is also important. Subway riders in San Francisco might show interest in a story about rising vigilantism on the New York subways, even though the story is happening 3,000 miles away.

3. **Prominence:** The more important a person, the more valuable he or she is as a news source. Thus, activities of the president, other heads of state, and sports and entertainment figures attract tremendous media attention. Americans apparently love celebrities and seldom tire of news about them. As an example, consider the coverage of the death of model Anna Nicole Smith. About 22 percent of the total news time on the cable TV networks in the week following her demise was devoted to stories about her, about twice the amount of coverage given to the 2008 election campaign. Even the infamous have news value. The past lives and recent exploits of many criminals are frequently given media coverage.

4. **Consequence:** Events that affect a great many people have built-in news value. The reason that an increase in the price of gas is a big story is because it affects nearly everybody in the country.

5. **Human interest:** These are stories that arouse some emotion in the audience—stories that are ironic, bizarre, uplifting, or dramatic. Typically, these items concern ordinary people who find themselves in circumstances with which the audience can identify. Thus, when a poor young mother finds a $10 bill and uses the money to buy a $1-million-winning lottery ticket, the story becomes newsworthy.

In addition to these five traditional elements of news value, economics plays a large role. First, some stories cost more to cover than others. It is cheaper to send a reporter or a camera crew to the city council meeting than to assign a team of reporters to investigate city council corruption. Some news operations might not be willing to pay the price for such a story. Conversely, after spending a large sum of money pursuing a story, the news organization might run it, even if it has little traditional news value, simply to justify its cost to management.

By the same token, the cost of new technology is reflected in the types of stories that are covered. When TV stations went to electronic news gathering (ENG), stories that could be covered live became more important. In fact, many organizations, conscious of the scheduling of TV news programs, planned their meetings and/or demonstrations during newscasts to enhance their chances of receiving TV coverage. Further, after helicopters became an expensive investment at many large TV stations, traffic jams, fires, beautiful sunsets, and other stories that lent themselves to airborne journalism suddenly became newsworthy.

Newspapers are not immune to the pervasive influence of the bottom line. As more corporations and large newspaper chains dominate the business, more businesspeople than journalists are becoming newspaper executives. The topics of greatest interest to this new breed of manager are marketing surveys, budget plans, organizational goals, and strategic planning—not the news-gathering process. This new orientation usually shows up in the newspaper's pages. The paper's "look" improves—more color, better graphics, an appealing design—and there are more features—food sections, personal finance columns, entertainment guides, and reviews. The paper becomes a slickly packaged product. At the same time, however, the amount of space devoted to local news decreases, reporters are discouraged from going after expensive investigative stories, and aggressive pieces about the local business community tend to disappear.

As discussed in more detail below, the audience for news has been dwindling in recent years, a development that poses additional challenges for the news media. Some have questioned whether the traditional business model of advertising-supported news is still viable. Many media companies are publicly owned, and shareholders want to see profits and stock prices increase. One way to do that is to cut back on costs by closing foreign bureaus, laying off reporters, and relying on news prepared by others. Moreover, news organizations hope to increase revenue by putting more emphasis on their Web sites to increase traffic and generate more advertising income.

Speaking of Web sites, this seems a logical place to examine how news reporting has been affected by the digital age.

NEWS REPORTING IN THE DIGITAL AGE

To say that the digital revolution has prompted significant changes in news reporting is an understatement. As the chapter opener suggests, the changes have been epochal. We will discuss six: (1) increasing number of news sources, (2) blogs, (3) citizen journalism, (4) hyperlocal news, (5) converged journalists, and (6) news reporting tools.

▲ More Sources of News

The Internet has increased in the number of a available news sources. Audience members can examine (1) general news sites, such as CNN.com or usatoday.com, that offer video, text, and pictures in broad topic areas like world news, national news, technology, entertainment, and politics; (2) news aggregators, such as Google or Yahoo!, that offer a digest of news from other sources; (3) specialized news sites that offer content with a tight focus, such as ESPN for sports news and the *Wall Street Journal*'s Web site for financial news; and (4) blogs.

▲ Blogs

As mentioned above, first and foremost, blogs represent another source of news, one that is free from economic, corporate, political, or advertising considerations. Morsels of news of interest to a small number of people that would otherwise go unreported go into blogs. There are blogs devoted to political news, technology news, entertainment news, and countless other topics. In countries where the government exercises tight control over the media, blogs offer an alternative version of events.

On October 18, 2006, the CNN program *Anderson Cooper 360* aired video footage of insurgent sniper attacks on U.S. soldiers in Iraq. The video was shot by the insurgents and included audio of the insurgents selecting their targets and praising Allah as they escaped. CNN edited the tapes so that they did not show the actual impact of the shots.

CNN's decision to air the tapes set off another round in the ethical debate over the proper way to cover a war. Critics quickly pointed out that these tapes could cause suffering and anguish for those who have had loved ones killed in the Iraq conflict. In addition, some charged that by airing the tapes CNN was giving a public relations boost to the enemy and might even encourage more sniper attacks. Several bloggers pointed out that the footage was shown only weeks before an important midterm election and accused CNN of using these tapes to influence the results. Some even criticized CNN for not showing the impact of the shots and for sanitizing the gory effects of war.

CNN's decision to air the tape was the subject of a long post in Anderson Cooper's 360 blog by David Doss, the program's executive producer. Doss acknowledged that the footage would be disturbing and that it might prove beneficial to the insurgents in their recruiting efforts. Despite this, he argued, the tape met CNN's criteria for newsworthiness. American deaths in October, 2006, had shown a significant increase, and many of them were due to sniper attacks. The tapes were a vivid reminder of the horrors of war. He also noted that CNN had tried to put the piece in context by interviewing military experts and that the network had aired a warning to viewers before showing the tape. Doss concluded that it was always CNN's goal to present "the unvarnished truth."

Doss's explanations did little to quiet the controversy. A number of bloggers noted that there were times when CNN had no problems shying away from the unvarnished truth. The network refrained from showing people leaping from the World Trade Center during the 9/11 terrorist attacks, nor did it show some of the atrocities during the regime of Saddam Hussein for fear of losing access to stories from Iraq. Others questioned whether it was necessary to show graphic video in order to remind people that war is horrible. As one blogger put it, "It serves no purpose. . . . Do you really need to see some kid get shot to be informed [that war is horrible]?"

The role that economics played in this controversy is unknown. At the time that this story aired, rival Fox had more than 1.5 times the prime-time audience of CNN. Airing a sensational exclusive story would undoubtedly reduce that margin. One would hope, however, that such considerations would not enter into the journalism decision-making process.

Second, blogs have an agenda-setting effect. They can concentrate the attention of the traditional media on selected events and keep those events in the news cycle. CNN has a special reporter who monitors blogs to see what current issues are being discussed. In 2005 blogs called attention to a bribery scandal at the United Nations and kept it in the news for several weeks.

Third, blogs provide a check on the traditional media. For example, during the 2004 election campaign, bloggers called into question documents that CBS has publicized in a story about President George W. Bush's National Guard service. CBS ultimately admitted that it could not authenticate the documents. The established media are not used to this level of scrutiny (particularly from people the media regard as amateurs), and this generates a certain amount of friction between bloggers and traditional journalists.

Fourth, blogs represent an additional outlet for reporters to explain why they reported a story the way they did. Why did the reporter frame a story in a certain way? Why were some sources quoted and not others? Why did the reporter use an anonymous source? As Bill Kovach and Tim Rostentiel, the authors of *The Elements of Journalism,* put it, the audience should be "given a chance to judge the principles by which journalists do their work." Some reporters have started blogs as a first step in this direction. CNN's Anderson Cooper, for example, authors the 360 blog, where he provides background about stories he is working on (see the boxed insert, "Covering a War").

Finally, blogs have made it possible for everybody to be a newsperson and have opened the way for what's being labeled *citizen journalism.*

▲ Citizen Journalism

When a freak October blizzard hit Buffalo, New York, in 2006, local residents posted 100 storm-related videos on YouTube and about 800 still images on the photo-sharing site Flickr. These efforts are all part of a growing trend toward citizen journalism, whereby ordinary citizens become amateur reporters.

The trend was made possible by the development of easy-to-use digital and cell phone video cameras and high-speed Internet access. Its potential was first demonstrated in 2005 when cell phone images of the London Underground bombings and the Asian tsunami were prominently featured on television and in newspapers. More recently, the racist rant by comedian Michael Richards and the video of the Virginia Tech shootings were captured by cell phone cameras and shown numerous times.

It's a trend that's also encouraged by the traditional news media; CNN ("I-Reports"), MSNBC ("First Person"), Reuters/Yahoo! ("You Witness News"), and many newspapers and TV stations ask audience members to submit their photos and video clips.

Of course, one of the reasons that citizen journalism is popular among the mainstream news media is because it is free. In an industry faced with declining audiences and shrinking revenues, citizen input can be a way to cut costs and perhaps eliminate some personnel. Professional journalists, not surprisingly, look upon this trend with some concern. Some argue that these citizen reporters are not journalists at all, but merely witnesses who happen to be in the right place when news breaks out. Legitimate journalism requires balance, fairness, and a sense of ethics, traits that are not necessarily present in amateur reporters.

On the other hand, citizen journalism does empower the audience. News organizations no longer have a monopoly on what gets reported or how it's reported. For example, the official version of the execution of Saddam Hussein was contradicted by a cell phone video shot by someone on the scene.

Citizen journalists often report on news items of interest to a relatively small number of people, a trend labeled *hyperlocal news*.

▲ Hyperlocal News

There's an old maxim in journalism that says "all news is local," but these days it might better be rephrased as "a lot of news is hyperlocal." **Hyperlocal** is another one of those emerging terms that has a wide range of use. Generally, hyperlocal coverage concentrates on the stories, no matter how small, of a particular community or zip code or interest group in a defined geographic area. Most, but not all, hyperlocal coverage can be found on Web sites.

In Naples, Florida, for example, the Web site of the local paper carries detailed news about local real estate prices, restaurant critiques, and extensive information on high school athletics. Other sites might contain coverage of the neighborhood's Little League or soccer teams, rezoning proposals, business start-ups, local crime statistics, and yard sales. The publishers of hyperlocal news hope that the focus on topics that the traditional news media ignore will help them attract the audience that generally does not consume news. MySpace and Facebook are probably the ultimate examples of hyperlocal news. Visitors to these sites can find out news that is of interest to them and their friends.

Making money from hyperlocal coverage presents a challenge. Most Web sites obtain revenue by selling inexpensive ads to local merchants and entrepreneurs who can't afford to buy newspaper space or TV and radio time. A brief tour of some hyperlocal sites revealed ads for neighborhood kids who will work as pet sitters, after-school gymnastics programs, and magicians who perform at local birthday parties. Obviously, these ads may not represent a huge revenue stream, but the cost of hyperlocal news coverage tends to be small. Web sites are simple, without a lot of costly graphics, and much of the content on the site is generated by users.

The journalists who report hyperlocal news have to be skilled in several areas: writing, video, audio and photography. In short, they provide yet another example of convergence.

▲ The Converged Journalist

As mentioned in Chapter 4, the converged reporter is one who can write stories for a print medium or a Web site, shoot and post photos online, and do video reports as well. In short, the print journalist and the video journalist have converged to produce the 21st-century version of the news correspondent. In fact, a couple of new terms have been coined to describe this new type of reporter. The **backpack journalist** is a "do-it-all" reporter who carries around a small digital camera, a laptop, and a satellite phone (presumably in a backpack) that enables her or him to produce stories for print, television, and online media. Next-generation reporters who eschew backpacks in favor of the automobile are called **mobile journalists** or **mojos.** These are staff reporters or freelancers who work out of their cars, covering local news that is usually posted to a Web site or appears in a newspaper print edition.

Whether a traditional reporter or a mojo, journalists in the digital age have a powerful new tool in the Internet.

▲ New Tools

As pointed out by Randy Reddick and Elliot King in *The Online Journ@list,* in the past elite media organizations would send reporters to power centers and other locations where news usually happened to cover events. Today's reporter can sit at his or her desk and instantly access documents, databases, government records, and expert sources. In short, journalists can now bring to their desks information they previously went out to look for.

In order to make the most efficient use of this new tool, however, reporters must learn new skills. The 21st-century journalist must be able to perform Web searches, download data files and analyze them with spreadsheets, set up listsservs, and use geographic mapping software. These skills are generally lumped under the term **computer-assisted reporting.**

Although the changes brought about by the move to digital media are extensive, there are still some constants, and we will examine them next.

CATEGORIES OF NEWS AND REPORTING

Generally, news can be broken down into three broad categories: (1) hard news, (2) features, or soft news, and (3) investigative reports.

▲ Hard News

Hard news stories make up the bulk of news reporting. They typically embody the first four of the five traditional news values discussed. Hard news consists of basic facts: who, what, when, where, how. It is news of important public events, such as government actions, international happenings, social conditions, the economy, crime, the environment, and science. Hard news has significance for large numbers of people. The front sections of a newspaper or newsmagazine and the lead stories of a radio or TV newscast are usually filled with hard news.

Print Media   There is a standard technique used to report hard news. In the print media it is the traditional inverted pyramid form. The main facts of the story are delivered in the first sentence (called the *lead*) in an unvarnished, no-nonsense style. Less important facts

Katie Couric's debut as the anchor of the *CBS Evening News* demonstrated a recent trend in broadcast news. When TV news first started it was a male-dominated profession. Female reporters were rare, and female anchors even rarer. All that has changed. Starting in the 1980s, the number of female anchors steadily increased. By the 1990s the number of female anchors equaled the number of male anchors. In 2006 female anchors outnumbered male anchors 57 to 43 percent. The male-female pairing is the typical coanchor arrangement, but female-female teams are more common, as are solo female anchors. What is rare these days is what was typical a few decades ago: a male-male anchor team or a solo male. (Remember Ron Burgundy in *Anchorman*?)

Women have become more numerous in other positions as well. About 60 percent of all field reporters are female. Behind the camera more than half of newscast producers and writers are female. And the trend looks like it will continue into the future. A recent survey conducted by the University of Georgia noted that about two-thirds of bachelor's degrees in journalism and mass communication were granted to women.

Several reasons are behind this shift. Equal-opportunity employment laws and the journalism profession's promotion of diversity have certainly helped. Additionally, news directors realized that half their potential audience was female and might welcome a women's perspective on news events.

Some observers find the dwindling percentage of males in video journalism a disturbing trend that might lead to the "feminization" of TV news, and the alienation of the male viewers in the audience. Others note that today's male audience is more accustomed to seeing females in powerful roles (senators, secretaries of state, CEOs of large corporations), and the growing journalistic gender disparity should be of little consequence. At any rate, it's highly probable that the TV newsroom will continue to be a place populated by a majority of females.

SOUNDBYTE

Fake News Versus Real News

Here's something that should make those of you whose main source of news is Comedy Central's *The Daily Show* feel better. Researchers at Indiana University did a second-by-second comparison of *The Daily Show* and the traditional network evening newscasts during the early part of the 2004 presidential election campaign. The conclusion as stated by the researchers: "[T]he average amounts of video and audio substance in the broadcast network news stories were not significantly different from the average amounts of visual and audio substance in *The Daily Show*." And that's no joke.

come next, with the least important and most expendable facts at the end. This structure aids the reporter (who uses it to compose facts quickly), the editor (who can lop off the last few paragraphs of a story to make it fit the page without doing wholesale damage to the sense of the story), and the reader (who can tell at a glance if he or she is interested in all, some, or none of the story). This format has been criticized for being predictable and old-fashioned. More literary writing styles have been suggested as alternatives, but the inverted pyramid has survived.

Broadcast Media In the broadcast media, with the added considerations of limited time, sound, and video, broadcast reporting follows a square format. The information level stays about the same throughout the story. There is usually no time for the less important facts that would come in the last paragraphs of a newspaper story. TV and radio news stories use either a "hard" or a "soft" lead. A hard lead contains the most important information, the basic facts of the story—for example, "The city council has rejected a plan to build the Fifth Street overpass." A soft lead is used to get the viewers' attention; it may not convey much information: "That proposed Fifth Street overpass is in the news again." The lead is then supported by the body of the story, which introduces new information and amplifies the lead. The summation, the final few sentences in the report, can be used to personalize the main point ("This means that the price you pay for gasoline is likely to go up"), introduce another fact, or discuss future developments.

The writing style of broadcast news is completely different from that of print news: It is more informal, conversational, and simple. In addition, it is designed to complement sound bites (recorded comments of the newsmaker) or videotape segments.

Online Media The writing style for online media is highly variable. Some newspaper sites may simply post the print version of the story with minor editing. Other sites might post the headline and a couple of sentences highlighting the main points of the story with a link that will take readers to the rest of the story. The newspaper inverted-pyramid style is generally used, and photos and video are integrated into the text. Links to other sites that contain supplemental information are often included. Television network and local station Web sites generally have shorter stories written in the broadcast news style, with video clips that are related to the story.

▲ Soft News

Soft news, or features, covers a wide territory. The one thing that all soft news has in common is that it interests the audience. Features typically rely on human interest for their news value. They appeal to people's curiosity, sympathy, skepticism, or amazement. They can be about places, people, animals, topics, events, or products. Some stories that would be classified as soft news are the birth of a kangaroo at the local zoo, a personality sketch of a local resident who has a small part in an upcoming movie, a cook who moonlights as a stand-up comedian, and a teenager who mistakenly gets a tax refund check for $400,000 instead of $40.

Features are entertaining, and the audience likes them. Many television and print vehicles are based primarily on soft content (*Entertainment Tonight; E!*, the cable entertainment network; *People; Life Styles of the Rich and Famous; Us* magazine; the "Life" section of *USA Today*). Even prime-time newsmagazines such as *60 Minutes* and *20/20* have substantial amounts of soft news. Likewise, the fiercely competitive early-morning network TV shows are turning more to soft news.

The techniques for reporting features are as varied as the features themselves. In the print media, features seldom follow the inverted-pyramid pattern. The main point of the feature is often withheld until the end, much like the punch line to a joke. Some features are written in chronological order. Others start with a shocking statement, such as "Your secrets just might kill you," and then proceed with an explanation: "If you have a medical problem, you should wear a Medic-Alert bracelet." Still other features are structured in the question-and-answer format.

ABC News Chief Investigative Correspondent Brian Ross reports for the *World News with Charles Gibson, Nightline, 20/20,* and other ABC news programs.

TV features are more common than radio features. In some large TV markets, one or more reporters cover nothing but features. Almost all stations have a feature file where story ideas are catalogued. If a local station does not have the resources to produce local features, it can look to syndication companies that provide general-interest features for a fee. Broadcast features also use a variety of formats. Using humorous leads and delaying the main point until the end sometimes work well, a technique often used by Andy Rooney in his features for *60 Minutes.* Other times a simple narrative structure, used in everyday storytelling, is quite effective. The interview format is also popular, particularly when the feature is about a well-known personality.

There are dozens of Web sites, such as *Entertainment Weekly* and *E!* online, that specialize in soft news, particularly celebrity news. Other Web sites may concentrate on a specific topic, such as food (www .food411.com), fashion (www.zoozoom.com), or pets (www.dogster .com).

▲ Investigative Reports

Investigative reports unearth significant information about matters of public importance through the use of nonroutine information-gathering methods. Since the Watergate affair was uncovered by a pair of Washington, D.C., newspaper reporters, investigative reporting has been perceived as primarily concerned with exposing corruption in high places. This connotation is somewhat unfortunate for at least two reasons. In the first place, it encouraged a few short-sighted reporters to look upon themselves as self-appointed guardians of the public good and to indiscriminately pursue all public officials, sometimes using questionable techniques in the hope of uncovering some indiscretion. Much of this investigative journalism turned out to be insignificant. In the second place, this emphasis on exposing political corruption distracted attention from the fact that investigative reporting can concentrate on other topics and perform a valuable public service.

Investigative reports require a good deal of time and money. Because of this heavy investment, they are generally longer than the typical print or broadcast news item. Broadcast investigative reports are usually packaged in documentaries, or in 10- to 15-minute segments of a newsmagazine program (such as *Dateline NBC* or *60 Minutes*). Print investigative pieces are usually run as a series of articles.

The mechanics of investigative reporting are similar in the print and broadcasting media. First, a reporter gets a tip or a lead on a story from one of his or her sources. The next phase consists of gathering facts and cultivating news sources. Eventually, a thick file of information on the topic is developed. These facts are then organized into a coherent piece that is easily digested by the audience. Here the differences between print and broadcast reporting techniques become apparent. The print journalist can spend a good deal of time providing background and relating past events to the topic. Additionally, the print investigative reporter can draw heavily upon published documents and public records. In television and radio, the investigative reporter usually has less time to explore background issues. Documents and records are hard to portray on TV, so less emphasis is placed on them. Instead, the TV reporter must come up with interviews and other visual material that will illustrate the story. Moreover, the length of the TV report will sometimes dictate its form.

Bloggers have also entered the realm of investigative journalism. Bloggers examined a photograph of an Israeli attack on Lebanon published by the Reuters news agency and found evidence that it had been doctored. Conservative blogger Michele Malkin published an investigative report about the financing of Air America radio.

Some noteworthy examples of recent investigative reports include a 2006 Peabody Award–winning 21-part series by KMOV-TV, St. Louis, about problems in the local school system and a Pulitzer Prize–winning report by the *Washington Post* on the activities of Washington lobbyists.

THE NEWS FLOW

As mentioned in Chapter 1, one of the characteristics of traditional mass communication is the presence of a large number of gatekeepers. This fact is seen in the gathering and reporting of news for conventional print and broadcast media. Reporting is a team effort, and quite a few members of the team serve as gatekeepers. Online reporting, in contrast, may have only one or a few gatekeepers. This section will first examine the news flow in the traditional print and broadcast media and then look at online media.

▲ Print Media

There are two main sources of news for a newspaper: staff reports and the wire services. Other, less important sources include feature syndicates and handouts and releases from various sources.

Let us first examine how news is gathered by newspaper personnel. The city editor is the captain of the news reporting team. He or she assigns stories to reporters and supervises their work. There are two types of reporters: (1) Beat reporters cover some topics on a regular basis, such as the police beat or the city hall beat; and (2) general-assignment reporters cover whatever assignments come up. A typical day for the general-assignment reporter might consist of covering an auto accident, a speech by a visiting politician, and a rock concert. Stories from the reporters are passed along to the city editor, where they are approved and sent to the copy desk for further editing. The managing editor and assistant managing editor are also part of the news team. They are responsible for the overall daily preparation of the paper.

Let us review the news flow and the various gatekeepers in the process. The city editor can decide not to cover a story in the first place or not to run a story even if the event is covered. The reporter has a wide latitude of judgment over what he or she chooses to include in the story. The copy editor can change the story as needed, and the managing editor has the power to emphasize or deemphasize the story to fit the day's needs.

▲ Broadcast Media

The sources of news for the broadcast media are similar to those for the newspaper. Special wire services cater to TV and radio stations, and local reporters are assigned to cover nearby events. In addition, many broadcast newsrooms subscribe to syndicated news services or, if affiliated with a network, have access to the network's news feeds.

The broadcast newsroom is organized along different lines from its print counterpart. At the local station the news director is in charge of the overall news operation. In large stations most news directors spend their time on administrative work—personnel, budgets, equipment, and so on. In smaller stations most news directors perform other functions (such as being the anchorperson) as well. Next in command is the executive producer. This person supervises all the producers in the newsroom. Typically, producers are assigned to the early-morning, noon, evening, or late-night newscasts. In addition to looking after the other producers, the executive producer might produce the evening news, typically the station's most important program. Here are some of the things that an executive producer does:

1. Decide which stories are covered, who covers them, and how they are covered.
2. Decide the order in which stories appear in the newscast.
3. Determine the amount of time each story is given.
4. Write copy for some stories.
5. Integrate live reports into the newscasts.

The assignment editor, who assigns and monitors the activities of reporters, camera crews, and other people in the field, works closely with the news producer. Since speed is important in broadcast news, there is great pressure on the assignment editor to get the crews to the story in the shortest amount of time.

Then, of course, there are the "glamour" jobs—on-air reporters and anchors. Most reporters in broadcast news function as general-assignment reporters, although the large-market stations might have one or two regularly assigned to a beat, such as the entertainment scene. In many stations anchors occasionally do field reports, but most of the time they perform their work in the studio, preparing for the upcoming newscast. In addition to the people seen on camera, there are quite a few workers whom no one ever sees or hears. Photographers accompany reporters to shoot the video. Tape editors trim the footage into segments that fit within the time allotted to the story. Big stations also have newswriters and production assistants who pull slides and arrange other visuals needed during the newscast.

Obviously, the chain of gatekeepers in broadcast news is a long and complicated one. Starting with the assignment editor and ending with the anchor, usually more than a half-dozen people have some say-so over the final shape of the newscast. Sometimes, the way a story ends up might be drastically different from the way it started at the beginning of the gatekeeper chain. It is not unusual for a reporter to work all day on a story and then be told by a producer that the story will get only 40 seconds of airtime.

▲ Online Media

The news flow in an online news department is similar to that in the traditional media. Top executives decide how the site will be structured and how many specialty areas (such as sports, finance, weather, and entertainment) it will contain. Editors decide what content will be used on the Web site, which stories will have additional audio and video files, where the stories will be placed, and how often they will be updated. Reporters revise and update their stories when appropriate. Online news departments that are affiliated with a broadcast or cable network, such as CNN or MSNBC, will use the audio and video that appeared on the parent network but may edit it differently. Other stories may be rewritten from wire copy or from copy that has appeared in print or on the air. Not all online news, however, is recycled. Some online news staffs also employ reporters who do original reporting for the Web site.

THE WIRE SERVICES

The next time you read your local newspaper, notice how many stories have the initials AP or UPI in the datelines. *AP* stands for Associated Press, and *UPI* for United Press International. These two organizations are called *wire services,* and together they provide you with much of the news about what is going on outside your local community.

In simplified form, here is how the wire services work: A correspondent covers a local news event, such as a fire. He or she reports the event to the bureau chief of the local wire service. If the bureau chief thinks the story is newsworthy enough, the chief will send it on to the state bureau to go out on the state or regional wire. The state bureau chief then decides whether to send it on for inclusion on the national wire. All in all, the wire services are the eyes and ears for local papers and broadcasting stations that cannot afford to have people stationed all over the country.

The AP has about 240 bureaus around the world. Members of the association pay for this service according to their size and circulation. A large paper, such as the *New York Times,* will pay more than a small-town paper. UPI also has dozens of domestic bureaus and a large number of foreign offices. As with the AP, member payment is based on the subscriber's size and audience.

In 2007 the AP had about 16,000 customers worldwide, including about 1,700 member newspapers. It serves about 5,000 radio and TV stations, plus more than 500 international broadcasters. The AP offers a wide range of services to its clients, encompassing a weather wire, a sports wire, and a financial wire along with a broadcast wire used by TV and radio stations.

In the past few years, UPI has been plagued by financial difficulties. The company was bailed out of bankruptcy in 1992 when it was bought by the Middle Eastern Broadcasting Company, which, in turn, sold it to News World Communications (the publisher of the *Washington Times*) in 2000. As a result of its economic troubles, UPI restructured itself in 2003 to concentrate on two main products: (1) news commentary and analysis and (2) brief news stories tailored for wireless devices, such as PDAs and cell phones, or for Web sites.

AP and UPI are not without competition. Major newspapers, such as the *New York Times*, the *Los Angeles Times*, and the *Washington Post*, offer supplemental news stories generally not covered by other services. Some newspaper groups, such as Gannett, have their own wire services. There is competition overseas as well. The British-based Reuters agency has about 30 bureaus in North America. Agence-France-Press is another formidable worldwide service.

MEDIA DIFFERENCES IN NEWS COVERAGE

It does not take a genius to see that broadcast journalism is different from print journalism and that both are different from Web journalism. Over the years these differences have led many people to argue about which type of journalism is "best." Proponents of print journalism correctly point out that the script of a typical network evening newscast would fill up less than one page of a typical newspaper. They argue that the print media have the potential to conduct in-depth reporting and lengthy analysis, elements that are usually missing from broadcast news because of time constraints. Moreover, some critics have taken to disparaging broadcast journalism as showbiz and commenting on its shallowness. The supporters of broadcast news answer that measuring a network newscast by comparing its word count with that of a newspaper is using the wrong yardstick. They suggest that it is more appropriate to ask how many pages of a newspaper it would take to print the thousands of different visuals that regularly accompany a TV newscast. The emergence of 24-hour news channels, say these proponents, now makes it possible to cover news in depth. Print journalism is criticized for being slow, old-fashioned, and dull.

Critics of online journalism suggest that many Web journalists are too quick to post stories and do not check their facts as thoroughly as do traditional journalists. They also note that many online news sites are slow to post corrections. Moreover, critics point out that the line between reporting and commerce is blurry at many online sites. For example, online music and book reviews include links to sites where readers can buy the music and books online, with part of the profits going to the online news site. Such an arrangement can increase pressure for good reviews. Finally, many people have a problem with how easy it is for someone to become an "online journalist." All that is needed is a Web site; no professional training or credentials are required.

And so the debate goes. Unfortunately, the argument obscures an essential fact: Print, online, and broadcast journalism have their own unique strengths and weaknesses. One should not be considered better than another. All play an important role in informing the public.

▲ Words and Pictures

The inherent characteristics of all three media have an impact on what news gets covered and how it gets covered. In the first place, print and online journalism are organized in space; TV journalism is organized in time. Hence, the newspaper or online site can contain far more stories than the typical TV newscast and can provide more details for any one story. Given the time constraints of broadcasting (even on all-news channels), it is hard for television to provide more than headline and a brief look at a few stories. Even if a topic is treated in depth, the amount of information and detail included is typically much less than what is contained in the newspaper or online. Some observers have said that TV is better at transmitting experience or impressions, while newspapers and online sites are better at providing facts and information. In any case, lengthy analysis and complicated interpretation tend to be better suited to the print or online media.

Second, print and online news have more permanence than broadcast news. A reader can go back and reread difficult parts as many times as necessary for comprehension. Viewers

---

S O U N D B Y T E

We Needed a Study to Tell Us That?

According to an experiment done by the European Society of Psychoanalysis and Psychodynamics, male viewers have trouble paying attention to the news when a pretty female anchor is on the screen. About 75 percent of the men couldn't remember a thing that was said during the first minute of the newscast because they were paying more attention to the anchor's good looks.

of broadcast news do not have this luxury. TV newscasts are written to be understood with a single exposure. This means that complex stories are sometimes difficult to cover in the electronic media.

Third, television news has the advantage of the visual dimension. TV news directors ask if a story has action, visual appeal, something that can be seen. Faced with a choice between two events that are of equal importance, the television news organization will cover the one that has better pictures available. Obviously, the visual dimension is important and represents a powerful weapon in the arsenal of TV reporting. Some of the visuals carried by TV news are deeply ingrained in the national memory: the destruction of the World Trade Center and people fleeing the Indian Ocean tsunami. Nonetheless, it is easy for TV news to needlessly cater to the visual and run news items that have little news value other than their potential for dramatic pictures. There have been many examples of a small, relatively insignificant fire

The aftermath of the I-35 bridge collapse in Minneapolis, Minnesota. Some images of devastation are replayed so often that it's impossible to forget them.

leading a local newscast simply because good pictures were available. This is not to say that print and online reporters do not like a visual story. Quite the opposite. The advent of good color reproduction in newspapers and magazines and the ability of online sites to feature streaming video mean that good visuals can accompany print and online stories.

▲ Print, Online, and Broadcast Journalists

Another key difference among types of media has to do with the fact that in TV news the appearance and personality of the reporter are an important part of the process. This situation is in direct contrast to print and online journalism, in which the reporter stays relatively anonymous, with perhaps only a byline for identification. (Bob Woodward and Carl Bernstein, the newspaper reporters who broke the Watergate story, and Matt Drudge, the online reporter who broke the Lewinsky-Clinton scandal, are exceptions.) In TV the person reading or reporting the news is part of the story. Repeated exposure of newscasters at the local and network levels has turned many of them into celebrities. Some viewers evidently develop what amounts to a personal relationship or a sense of empathy with reporters and anchors. *Today Show* host Matt Lauer probably received more comments about his new haircut than about any of the stories he covered.

▲ Similarities Among the News Media

Although there are significant differences among print, online, and broadcast journalism, there are many similarities as well. All journalists share the same basic values and journalistic principles.

Honesty in news reporting is crucial for television, online, and newspaper reporters. Stories must be as truthful as possible. The print or online journalist should not invent fictional characters or make up quotations and attribute them to news makers. Broadcast journalists should not stage news events or rearrange the questions and answers in a taped interview.

Another shared value is accuracy. Checking facts takes time, but it is something that a professional reporter must do for every story.

A third common value is balance. Every story has two or more sides. All journalists must make sure that they do not publicize or promote just one of them. Information should be offered on all sides of a story.

Print, online, and broadcast reporters also share the value of objectivity. Objectivity means that the reporter tries to transmit the news untainted by conscious bias and without personal comment or coloration. Of course, complete and total objectivity is not possible because the process of reporting itself requires countless judgments, each influenced in some way by the reporter's value system. Nonetheless, journalists have traditionally respected the truth, refused to distort facts deliberately, and consciously detached themselves as much as possible from what they were reporting.

Finally, online, print, and broadcast reporters must maintain credibility with their audiences. The news media periodically undergo crises of confidence, during which people begin to doubt the integrity of journalists. Sometimes these crises occur because of excesses in reporting, as happened during the coverage of the death of Anna Nicole Smith in 2007. They may arise following disclosure of violations of journalistic values. Whenever public opinion polls reveal that the news media have slipped another notch or two in credibility, journalists try to regain the lost confidence. After much soul-searching, the crisis usually passes. Credibility, however, is not something that should be examined only during journalistic crises. If a reader or a viewer loses trust or stops believing what is being reported, the fundamental contract between audience and reporter is undermined, and the news organization cannot survive. It matters little if the news organization is a newspaper, magazine, radio, online site, or TV station; its credibility is paramount to its viability.

READERSHIP AND VIEWERSHIP

Table 13-1 does not paint a positive picture for the news media. The audience for network news, newspapers, and newsmagazines has been shrinking for the past 30 years. The same trend holds true for local TV news. The audience for cable news fluctuates significantly depending

TABLE 13-1

News Audiences,
1980–2006

Year	Network Evening News (total ratings of ABC, NBC, CBS)	Newspapers' Total Weekday Circulation (millions)	Total Readership of Three Major Newsmagazines (millions)
1980	42	62	10.1
1990	30	62	9.8
2000	24	56	9.3
2006	18	53	9.2

on the occurrence of major news events, but, on average, it too has declined. Further, the audience is getting older. The average age of the typical TV newscast viewer is around 60.

Where is the audience going? Some have dropped out entirely; many people report no interest in following the news. Others go online: on a typical day about 30 percent report visiting a traditional online news site such as MSNBC. Quite a few are looking for news on nontraditional sites, such as YouTube. Still others may get their news via cell phone or PDA.

The smaller the audience, of course, the smaller the revenue received from advertising and the smaller the bottom line. This occurrence has already had great impact on those who report the news. Newspapers and TV networks have cut personnel, closed bureaus, and cut back news-gathering costs.

Table 13-2 contains data from two recent Gallup polls about how Americans get their news. An examination of this table reinforces and extends the conclusions of Table 13-1: With the exception of the Internet, there has been a noticeable decline in the degree of exposure to all news sources.

The audience is also becoming less likely to trust the news media. Surveys done by the Pew Research Center for the People and the Press revealed that credibility ratings for local TV news, broadcast news, and cable news had all declined from 2000 to 2006. The same trend showed up for local newspapers, national newspapers, and newsmagazines. All in all, the above data are not encouraging to those in the news-reporting profession.

NEWS GATHERING AND REPORTING

Job prospects for aspiring journalists are somewhat bleak. As the chapter pointed out, many news organizations are cutting back staff and reducing hiring. With convergence and consolidation, the number of people needed to cover stories will decrease. There are, however, some bright spots. Specialized news sources, such as Bloomberg News, have increased their number of employees in the past few years. Likewise, online news sites may need more people as news reporting continues to shift to the Web. Hyperlocal reporting will require correspondents who are familiar with their local communities.

Despite this pessimistic assessment, recent journalism grads continue to be optimistic. A 2005 survey found that about 60 percent were able to find work in a communication-related industry within 6–8 months after graduation. Job satisfaction rating was at its highest level in 10 years.

TABLE 13-2

Sources of News,
2002–2006

Source: Excerpted from Gallup polls, December 2006 and December 2002. Question was, "How often did you get your news from the following sources?" Numbers in the table are the percentages who answered, "Every day."

Site	2002	2006
Local TV news	57%	55%
Local newspapers	47	44
Cable news networks	41	34
Nightly network news	43	35
Morning network news	29	28
Public TV news	35	28
Radio talk shows	22	20
Internet	15	22
National Public Radio	22	19
National newspapers	11	7

A news council is an independent body composed of journalists and private citizens that unofficially hears and adjudicates disputes over press conduct. People and organizations who feel that they have been wronged by news coverage but lack the time, energy, and money to pursue a libel case turn to news councils to help set the record straight. Those who bring complaints before a news council waive the right to file a lawsuit. Staff members look into complaints, and the council holds hearings on those cases that raise significant issues. The council then votes on whether it thinks the complaint should be upheld. Councils have no legal power to enforce their decisions or to impose penalties. Their power stems from the publicity they bring to the case.

News councils are not a new idea. Wisconsin and Colorado had them; Minnesota and Hawaii still do. There was even a National News Council that operated from 1973 to 1984, but it was discontinued because of lack of money and lack of cooperation from influential media organizations. The idea of news councils resurfaced in 1997 when *60 Minutes* correspondent Mike Wallace suggested that the creation of a news council would help counter public skepticism and the negative feelings that members of the public have about the press. After the program was broadcast, residents from a number of states called the Minnesota News Council to ask how they could start their own councils. In mid-2000 a news council started operation in the state of Washington, and another was being planned in Oregon.

Most members of the news media do not share Wallace's enthusiasm for news councils. They make several arguments to support their view. The argument heard most often is that news councils are the first step toward government regulation. One of the reasons the *New York Times* refused to cooperate with the National News Council was its belief that the council would encourage an atmosphere of regulation in which government intervention might gain public support. Many journalists think that lawmakers would use the public complaints to justify more regulation of the press. A second argument is that news councils would discourage hard-hitting stories. Journalists might be fearful of being unfairly targeted and forced to defend their decisions in controversial stories. If a council decision goes against

a reporter, he or she might be afraid of doing any more such stories. Another argument contends that news councils substitute the judgments of people who do not know much about journalism for the judgments of professionals. How, ask the critics, can laypeople question the merits of a story when they do not know what went into producing it? In short, journalism should be left to the journalists. As one longtime journalist put it, "They have no damn business meddling in our business."

Supporters of the council idea first note that councils can prevent long and costly lawsuits. For example, they could give the principals in a defamation suit another forum in which to present their cases. Proponents also note that councils promote media fairness by making news outlets publicly accountable. Moreover, the councils give news media the chance to explain the reasons behind the choices they made and why they believe their decisions were proper. Such a discussion helps educate the public about some of the problems involved in the everyday practice of journalism and may give the public a greater appreciation for the profession.

Supporters also contend that the press sees no problems in holding up other professions to public scrutiny but is unwilling to subject itself to the same treatment. They note as well that there is wide public support for such an idea. Public opinion polls show that 85 percent of the general public likes the idea.

All things considered, the notion of a news council will be a hard sell to members of the news-gathering profession. Many media outlets are adamantly opposed to the notion. Journalists have never been leading supporters of self-criticism. As Edward R. Murrow once said, when it comes to criticism, "The press is not thin-skinned. It is no-skinned."

There are signs, however, that things may be changing. Although the *New York Times* is still not backing the idea of a news council, the *Times* did agree to appoint a "public editor," who will monitor performance at the paper and look into reader complaints. In 2006, the Knight Foundation sponsored a competition for two $75,000 grants that would establish two news councils. Moreover, blogs represent an open-to-all form of a news council that scrutinizes media stories and is quick to point out mistakes.

For the time being, the traditional advice given to those seeking a career in this area still applies. Newcomers should look for their first jobs at small-market newspapers or TV stations and then work their way into larger markets. Wherever a person starts, he or she should be prepared to report the news across several media: print, video, audio, and online.

MAIN POINTS

- The qualities that characterize news are timeliness, proximity, prominence, consequence, and human interest. Economics is also important.

- There are three main types of news stories: hard, soft, and investigative.

- The digital revolution has increased the number of available news sources, encouraged the growth of blogs, contributed to the rise of citizen journalism and hyperlocal news, and supplied new tools to reporters.

- The Associated Press and United Press International are two wire services that provide stories to print and broadcast journalists.

- Print, broadcast, and online journalism have their unique strengths and weaknesses.
- All forms of news media strive for credibility.
- Online news enables audience members to select from more news sources and customize their news.
- The audience for news has been declining across all media.

QUESTIONS FOR REVIEW

1. What are the characteristics that determine newsworthiness? Should others be added to the list?
2. What is the difference between hard and soft news? Is it possible to do a hard-news report on a soft-news topic, such as entertainment?
3. How does blogging differ from traditional print and broadcast reporting?
4. How is blogging similar to traditional print and broadcast reporting?
5. What is hyperlocal news?

QUESTIONS FOR CRITICAL THINKING

1. Should news be what the audience wants to know or what the audience needs to know? Who should decide?
2. Where do you get most of your news about what is going on in the world? Why?
3. What news medium is most believable? Print? TV? Online? Why?
4. Why is the audience for news getting smaller?

KEY TERMS

timeliness (p. 300)
proximity (p. 300)
prominence (p. 300)
consequence (p. 300)
human interest (p. 300)

hyperlocal (p. 303)
backpack journalist (p. 303)
mobile journalist (mojo) (p. 304)
computer-assisted reporting (CAR) (p. 304)

hard news (p. 304)
soft news (p. 306)
investigative reports (p. 306)

INTERNET RESOURCES
Online Learning Center

At the Online Learning Center home page, www.mhhe.com/dominick10, *select* Student Center *and then* Chapter 13.

1. Use the Learning Objectives, Chapter Outline, Main Points, and Time Line sections to review this chapter.
2. Test your knowledge of the chapter using the multiple choice, crossword puzzle, and flashcard features of the site.
3. Expand your knowledge of concepts and topics discussed in the chapter by going to Suggestions for Further Reading and Internet Exercises.

Surfing the Internet

There are hundreds of sites that have a connection to journalism. Only a few are listed here.

www.aim.org
Site of the media watchdog group Accuracy in Media, which critiques the operation of the news media.

www.backfence.com
An example of a hyperlocal news site. Check out what's going on in 14 different communities.

www.cnn.com
CNN Interactive's site. A good example of an online news service. Contains international and national spot news plus links for political, scientific, health, travel, financial, and entertainment news.

www.freedomforum.org
The Freedom Forum is an organization dedicated to exploring and improving journalism.

www.mediachannel.org
A nonprofit site that offers criticism, interviews with journalists, and a discussion forum devoted to news reporting.

www.newslink.org
Has links to other media sources as well as research tools.

www.ojr.org
Home of the *Online Journalism Review,* at the Annenberg School of Communications at the University of Southern California. The single best resource for information concerning online journalism.

www.powerlineblog.com
One of the better-known political blogs.

CHAPTER 14

PUBLIC RELATIONS

This chapter will prepare you to:

- distinguish among *public relations, publicity, press agentry*, and *advertising*

- understand the background of modern public relations

- recognize the impact of the Internet on public relations

- discuss the major areas in which public relations is practiced

- explain the steps involved in developing a public relations campaign

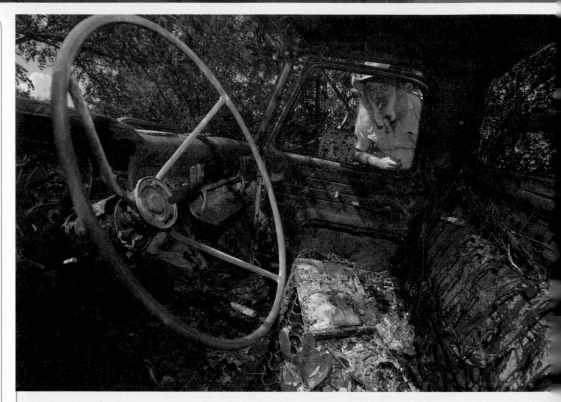

A Dell Inspiron notebook computer was blamed for this fire that totally destroyed a Ford 250 truck.

Dell Computers had a rough introduction to the digital age. In 2005 a disgruntled consumer ranted about his customer service problems with the company in a blog with the title "Dell Hell." Dell did little to assuage his problems. In the days before the Internet and blogging, one unhappy customer might have dissed Dell to family members and a few friends, and that would have been the end of it. With the Internet, however, one person's complaints can be heard by thousands or even millions. Others apparently shared the dissatisfied customer's frustration with Dell, and soon his blog was getting more than 10,000 visits a day, and hundreds of other blogs posted entries with titles such as "I Hate Dell" and "Dell Sucks."

If that wasn't bad enough, in 2006 someone took pictures of a Dell laptop computer self-destructing at a conference in Osaka, Japan. The photos showed the keyboard engulfed in flames, with smoke billowing and conference attendees fleeing the scene. Again, in the days before the Internet, this might have been an isolated incident with limited impact on Dell. As it turned out, the photos were posted on many Web sites and added to Dell's woes. (A 2006 Google search for "Dell Hell" returned 1.77 million hits.)

At first, the company was slow to respond. A Dell spokesperson played down the Osaka fire (or "thermal incident," as he termed it), suggesting that it was a freak accident. Then other reports surfaced on the Internet. One man in Arizona watched as his truck burned after his new Dell computer ignited on the front seat. Others claimed that their Dells incinerated their desks. The *New York Times* carried a story about Dell's problem. Sales fell, as did the stock price.

Clearly, Dell faced a public relations problem.

Under mounting pressure Dell finally took action. It announced that it was recalling 4.1 million notebook computer batteries, the biggest safety recall in the history of the electronics industry. It also announced a thorough investigation into the cause of the trouble. When it was discovered that the problem was lithium batteries made by Sony, rather than blaming one another, Dell and Sony shared the costs of the replacements. Dell also started its own blog. After a rough start the blog, "Direct2Dell," became a key channel of feedback for the company and a means to respond directly to consumer problems. The company also started a social networking site, "IdeaStorm," where users made suggestions about what they would like Dell to do in the future. The efforts paid off. Fewer hostile blog postings appeared, customer satisfaction increased and Dell even made peace with the original disgruntled blogger from 2005. Although Dell still faced problems, its public relations had definitely improved.

We can learn several lessons about public relations in the digital age from Dell's experience. First, the Internet magnifies the influence of a single voice. Companies ignore consumer complaints at their own risk. Second, the Internet makes it crucial for companies to respond quickly to a crisis. Once bloggers get hold of the story, it is difficult to stay on top of the situation. Or, as blogger Teresa Valdez Klein put it, "The blogosphere latches onto a story and runs with it—drowning out anything good or redeeming that the company might say." Finally, companies should not ignore the potential of the Internet as a channel for public relations efforts. At first, Dell evidently didn't think that bloggers carried much influence in the marketplace. After realizing that their initial assessment was incorrect, Dell made effective use of its own blog and social networking site.

Of course, Dell's problems with exploding laptops may not be typical of those faced by public relations agencies and corporate public relations departments, but they do indicate the tremendous importance that public relations can play in the corporate and consumer arenas. The rest of this chapter examines the history and structure of public relations and how it is changing in the digital age.

DEFINING PUBLIC RELATIONS

Before we investigate what public relations is, it may be helpful to compare it with other facets of mass communication. There are, for example, similarities between advertising and public relations. Both are attempts at persuasion, and both involve using the mass media. Public relations, however, is a management function; advertising is a marketing function. Another difference is that advertising uses the mass media and machine-assisted communication settings; unlike PR it does not involve interpersonal communications. A third difference is seen in the fact that advertising is normally sponsored. Public relations messages appear as features, news stories, or editorials, and the space or time involved is not paid for. In many instances, advertising, particularly corporate advertising, is used to help further a public relations program. As we shall see in the next chapter, however, the line between advertising and public relations is becoming blurred as advertisers turn to nontraditional ways of getting their messages to consumers and more businesses adapt the integrated marketing communications perspective. (See the boxed insert "IMC on page 322.")

A concept that is sometimes confused with public relations is promotion. Promotion involves staging events or planning enterprises that attract media or public attention to a person, product, organization, or cause. Although promotion is useful in some PR campaigns, public relations encompasses a much broader area and involves more than just attracting attention.

Another concept that is sometimes confused with public relations is **publicity,** the placing of stories in the mass media. Publicity is a tool in the public relations process, but it is not equivalent to PR. For example, it is perfectly possible for a firm to have extensive publicity and bad public relations. Further, publicity is primarily one-way communication; public relations is two-way.

Having examined what public relations is *not*, we may now turn to what it *is*. The term *public relations* has many interpretations and meanings. One PR veteran has compiled 500 different ones, ranging from the concise "PR is doing good and getting credit for it" to the 100-word definition in the *Encyclopaedia Britannica*. Most of the leading textbooks on PR usually lead off with a chapter that attempts to define exactly what public relations is or is not. Rather than catalogue these many definitions, we may find it more useful to define PR by examining what PR people do:

1. *Public relations involves working with public opinion.* On the one hand, PR professionals attempt to influence public opinion in a way that is positive to the client. For example, in the Dell episode, the public relations campaign was designed to improve Americans' attitudes toward the company.
2. *Public relations is concerned with communication.* Most people are interested in what a given organization is doing to meet their concerns and interests. It is the function of the public relations professional to explain the organization's actions to various **publics** involved with the organization. As noted previously, public relations communication is two-way communication. The PR professional also pays close attention to the thoughts and feelings of the organization's publics. Some experts refer to public relations as a two-way conduit between an organization and its publics.

Note that the word *publics* in the preceding section is plural. This is because an organization typically deals with many different publics in its day-to-day operations. Several PR scholars divide these groups into internal and external publics. *Internal* publics include employees, managers, labor unions, and stockholders. *External* publics consist of consumers, the government, dealers, suppliers, community members, and the mass media. Public relations serves as the link for all these publics.

SOUNDBYTE

Telling Them Apart

The difference between advertising, promotion, publicity, and public relations is illustrated by the following classic example that first appeared some years ago in the *Reader's Digest:* "If the circus is coming to town and you paint a sign saying 'Circus Coming to the Fairground Saturday,' that's advertising. If you put the sign on the back of an elephant and walk it into town, that's promotion. If the elephant walks through the mayor's flower bed and the newspaper reports it, that's publicity. And if you get the mayor to laugh about it and forgive you, that's public relations."

Imagine that your PR firm has been offered a sizable fee to represent Seven-Eleven Limited, a big conglomerate that owns gambling casinos in several states. A state referendum legalizing casino gambling is planned in your state. The casino group wants you to organize a grassroots citizens' group called Citizens for Economic Growth that will campaign in favor of legalizing casino gambling. Seven-Eleven Limited has conducted economic studies that have indeed shown that your state's treasury would benefit from legal gambling. They have ample funds available to set up and finance the operations of the citizens' group. There is one condition, however. The casino group does not want to be connected with Citizens for Economic Growth. They think that revealing the connection would hurt their chances in the referendum. Do you accept the assignment? Is it ethical to conceal information that might have an impact on the results of a public relations campaign?

On the one hand, there would be positive results if your firm took the assignment. Your firm would make a profit, and employees would be happy. Moreover, as the research suggests, casino gambling might in fact benefit the residents of your state. More jobs would be created and more tax revenue generated.

On the other hand, a deception is involved. If a reporter subsequently discovered the casino group's involvement in the campaign, it would hurt the credibility of your firm and maybe hurt the overall credibility of the public relations profession. In addition, the public would be voting on an issue without having all of the relevant facts before them.

The deception may never be uncovered, and the deception might serve a good cause. Is it worth doing?

The Code of Ethics of the Public Relations Association of America offers some guidance. It states, in part, that open communication is necessary for informed decision making. All information that might influence a decision should be revealed: "Be accurate and honest in all communications. . . . Avoid deceptive practices."

3. *Public relations is a management function.* It is designed to help a company set its goals and adapt to a changing environment. Public relations practitioners regularly counsel top management. Inherent in the specification of public relations is a planned activity. It is organized and directed toward specific goals and objectives.

Of course, public relations involves much more than just the three functions mentioned. Perhaps it would be easier, for our purposes, to use the following definition approved by the World Assembly of Public Relations:

> *Public relations is the art and social science of analyzing trends, predicting their consequences, counseling organization leaders, and implementing planned programs of action that serve both the organization's and the public's interest.*

A BRIEF HISTORY

If the term *public relations* is interpreted broadly enough, its practice can be traced back to ancient times. The military reports and commentaries prepared by Julius Caesar can be viewed as a triumph in personal and political public relations. During medieval times both the church and the guilds practiced rudimentary forms of public relations.

It was not until the American Revolution that more recognizable public relations activities became evident. The early patriots were aware that public opinion would play an important role in the struggle with England, and they planned their activities accordingly. For example, they staged events, such as the Boston Tea Party, to gain public attention. They also used symbols, such as the Liberty Tree and the Minutemen, that were easily recognized and helped portray their cause in a positive light. Skillful writers such as Samuel Adams, Thomas Paine, Abigail Adams, and Benjamin Franklin used political propaganda to swing public opinion to their side. As a case in point, note that the altercation between an angry mob and British soldiers became known as the "Boston Massacre," an interpretation well suited to the rebel cause.

Later, the Industrial Revolution and the resulting growth of mass production and mass consumption led to the emergence of big business. Giant monopolies were formed in the railroad, steel, and oil businesses. Many big corporations tended to disregard

The Boston Tea Party was a PR move calculated to gain support for the colonists' cause. Such an event today would be done in daylight so that TV news crews would have an easier time covering it.

the interests of the consumer in their quest for more profits. In fact, many executives felt that the less the public knew about their practices and operations, the better. Around the turn of the 20th century, however, public hostility was aroused against unscrupulous business practices. Muckrakers (see Chapter 5) filled the nation's magazines with exposés of industrial corruption and ruthless business tactics. In response, corporations hired communications experts, many of them former newspaper writers, to counteract the effect of these stories. These specialists tried to combat negative publicity by making sure the industry's side of the issue was also presented. These practitioners were the prototypes of what we might call *press agents* or *publicists.*

The debut of modern public relations techniques dates back to the first decade of the 1900s. Most historians agree that the first real public relations pioneer was a man named Ivy Lee. In 1903 Lee and George Parker opened a publicity office. A few years later, Lee became the press representative for the anthracite coal operators and the Pennsylvania Railroad. When these industries were confronted with a strike in the coal industry, Lee issued a "Declaration of Principles." This statement endorsed the concepts of openness and honesty in dealing with the public; it also marked the shift from 19th-century press agentry to 20th-century public relations. Lee went on to have a successful career counseling people such as John D. Rockefeller Jr. Among other achievements Lee is credited with humanizing business and demonstrating that public relations is most effective when it affects employees, customers, and community members. Moreover, Lee would not carry out a public relations program unless it was endorsed and supported by top management.

The government got involved in public relations during World War I when President Woodrow Wilson set up the Creel Committee (named for its chair, journalist George Creel). Creel enlisted the top figures in the public relations field to mount a campaign that persuaded newspapers and magazines to donate space for ads that urged Americans to save food and to buy war bonds. Creel advised Wilson on communication strategies and was instrumental in publicizing Wilson's war goal "to make the world safe for democracy." The work of the Creel Committee was significant because it demonstrated the power of a well-planned and well-executed public relations campaign. In addition, it helped legitimize the field of public relations.

Public relations pioneer Ivy Lee.

Following World War I, two more public relations pioneers, Carl Byoir and Edward L. Bernays, appeared on the scene. Bernays is credited with writing the first book on public relations, *Crystallizing Public Opinion,* published in 1923. In 1930 Byoir organized a public relations firm that became one of the world's largest.

The Depression caused many Americans to look upon business with suspicion and distrust. In an attempt to regain public favor, many large corporations established their own public relations departments. The federal government, in its attempt to cope with the bad economic climate, also used good public relations practices to its advantage. President Franklin Roosevelt

Ethical Issues   When Is the News Not the News?

It certainly looked like a news story. There was a scene of President George W. Bush signing the new Medicare prescription drug plan into law. There were scenes of senior citizens getting their blood pressure measured and talking to pharmacists. A narrator explained, "It's the same Medicare you've always counted on plus more benefits." The segment ended with "In Washington, I'm Karen Ryan reporting."

The story ran on more than 40 television stations in 33 markets in early 2004. The trouble was that Karen Ryan was not a reporter for a news network or for any of the 40 stations that aired the report. She was a public relations professional, and the story was a video news release prepared by the U.S. Department of Health and Human Services.

The episode once again drew attention to the ethical problems surrounding the use of video news releases. First, some background. Video news releases (VNRs) have been around for decades. They are the video equivalent of the traditional printed press release. VNRs are produced by public relations organizations on behalf of private industry and government organizations and are distributed to television networks and stations across the country by services such as CNN's NewsSource. They are sometimes used in full, but most of the time the video is used as a "B-roll" to illustrate a story produced by the local station. Organizations like VNRs because they're free publicity, and their inclusion on a newscast gives them credibility. Local stations like VNRs because they are a cheap way of filling time on their newscasts. But the Medicare VNR episode raised many ethical issues. Let's take a look at a few of them.

First, what are the obligations of the government when it comes to informing the public? Should the government be using VNRs at all? Critics charged the Bush administration with producing secret propaganda and manufacturing news. Opponents asked the Government Accounting Office (GAO) to investigate. The GAO's study concluded that VNRs that don't include an on-air disclosure (such as "Karen Ryan reporting for the Department of Health and Human Services" rather than "Karen Ryan reporting.") that they were produced by the government were an illegal use of taxpayer dollars. Supporters argued that this issue was simply an attack by political opponents on the Bush administration. VNRs were necessary since the mainstream media did a poor job of informing the public about government programs. In addition, a spokesperson for the Bush administration maintained that as long as the VNRs were accurate and did not advocate just one position, there was no ethical problem. As far as the disclosure of their source was concerned, administration supporters contended that the piece was clearly labeled as a VNR produced by the government when it was sent to distribution services such as

NewsSource. CNN should have alerted newsrooms about the source, and local news editors could have then made the decision to use or not use the story.

What about the obligations of NewsSource? CNN claimed that the story was clearly identified as a VNR when it was fed to the local stations. Local stations did have the option of not running the piece. If there was an ethical lapse, it was on the part of the local stations.

How did the locals respond? They argued that the CNN feed contained both genuine news stories and VNRs mixed together. It was easy to miss the fact that the Medicare story was a VNR. Moreover, many VNRs contain useful information that might be of help to viewers. If there was an ethical problem, it was created by the owners of local TV stations who demand high earnings and who have pressed stations to fill more airtime with fewer resources. As a result, many local stations are running more VNRs in an attempt to fill their news time with inexpensive prepackaged programs.

How would the owners respond? Many would probably argue that the ethical problems were created in the first place by the government's use of VNRs. The issue has come full circle with everybody avoiding ethical responsibility by blaming somebody else. Is there a solution to this dilemma? One possibility invokes an ethical principle called the categorical imperative, described in more detail in Chapter 17. In short, the categorical imperative suggests that certain practices are wrong no matter the circumstances. If news professionals think VNRs are inherently deceptive, they should not be carried, no matter if they are from the government or private industry. For their part, public relations professionals might pay more attention to the Public Relations Society of America's guidelines about VNRs. In part they state, "Organizations that prepare VNRs should not use the world 'reporting' if the narrator is not a reporter," and "Organizations that produce VNRs should clearly identify the VNR as such and fully disclose who produced and paid for it." It also calls for media outlets to clearly label the source of the VNR when aired.

The VNR debate continued into 2006 with the Center for Media and Democracy, an activist group that maintains the Web site PRWatch.org, calling for stronger regulations covering the use of VNRs, including a demand that every frame of a VNR contain a graphic disclosing the source of the content. The PR industry countered by forming the National Association of Broadcast Communicators in order to lead the fight against any proposed legislation.

In the meantime, the news audience should pay careful attention to the stories on the local news. Not all of them might qualify as news.

introduced his New Deal reform program complete with promotional campaigns to win public acceptance. Roosevelt also recognized the tremendous potential of radio in shaping public opinion, and his radio-broadcasted fireside chats were memorable examples of personal public relations. The government intensified its public relations efforts during World War II with the creation of the Office of War Information.

Where does PR fit in the organization? Traditional thinking, as mentioned in the chapter, treats PR as a management function. Another philosophy (which emerged during the mid-1990s), called *integrated marketing communications,* or *IMC,* argues that PR should really be part of the marketing function. This distinction involves more than just an organizational war for turf; it holds significant implications for the future of the field. If PR is subsumed within marketing, it loses much of its management component.

Those who advocate IMC point out that, in addition to product and price, public and social issues influence marketing. An integrated approach ensures that a company responds to all these concerns with a single voice. Additionally, proponents of IMC note that clients want their advertising, PR, and marketing activities coordinated and unified. Further, IMC saves a company money since a single IMC department can operate more efficiently than separate departments of advertising, marketing, and PR. Finally, proponents argue that everything that a PR department does—employee communication, crisis management, promotion—boils down to marketing functions.

Opponents of IMC argue that the credibility of PR efforts will be hurt if they are seen as simply another marketing tool. It is already difficult for PR practitioners to maintain perceptions of honesty and believability on the part of the audience, and lumping the PR department with marketing will make the problem even worse. Another argument suggests that IMC hurts the diversity of opinion available to management. A separate PR department makes it more likely that different suggestions and alternative courses of action will be advanced. Finally, opponents argue that PR involves two-way communication that takes into account the needs of various publics, whereas IMC treats everybody as a customer and places top priority on sales.

One of the struggles for the industry in the years to come will be the development of a structure that recognizes the unique contributions of each of the departments that make up the modern organization.

During the second half of the 20th century, changes in American society created an atmosphere in which public relations grew tremendously in importance. What are some of the reasons behind the recent surge in this area?

- Many corporations recognized that they had a social responsibility to serve the public. Finding the means of fulfilling this responsibility was the task of the public relations department.
- A growing tide of consumerism caused many corporations and government agencies to be more responsive to and communicative with their customers or clients, a function served by the public relations department.
- The growing complexity of modern corporations and government agencies made it difficult for them to get their messages to the public without a department that was specifically assigned that task.
- Increasing population growth along with more specialization and job mobility made it necessary for companies to employ communication specialists whose task it was to interpret the needs of the audience for the organization.

All these trends have combined to make the past 50 or so years the "era of public relations." The profession grew from about 19,000 members in 1950 to more than 200,000 in the United States and 300,000 worldwide in 2006. Along with this growth has come increased professionalization among public relations practitioners. The Public Relations Society of America, founded in 1947, adopted a code of standards in 1954. Public relations education has also made great strides. Recent estimates suggest that about 400 colleges across the country offer courses in public relations. In 1967 the Public Relations Student Society of America was founded. It now has 270 chapters and 8,500 members.

The past decade has seen public relations become even more important. Spin doctors, specialists in political public relations, have assumed prominence in political campaigns and government activities. The Bush administration used public relations extensively to gather public support for Operation Iraqi Freedom in 2003. One facet of this program was the "embedding" of more than 500 journalists with military units to provide firsthand accounts of the action. In the business sector the accounting scandals at major corporations such as Enron, Global Crossing, and Arthur Andersen increased the need for better public relations in order to restore confidence in a company's financial reports and to make top executives more responsible to their employees and shareholders. Despite lost revenue from the dot-com bust, according to the Bureau of Labor Statistics the PR industry is still one of the fastest-growing professions in the United States.

PUBLIC RELATIONS IN THE DIGITAL AGE

The Internet has added several new dimensions to public relations. It has opened up new channels of communication between organizations and the public and between public relations practitioners and the media. It has also become a major channel of feedback for organizations interested in their public image.

▲ Communicating with the Audience

Corporate Web sites have become more than just flashy sites that try to sell a product or service. They have become the first line of communication for organizations, consumers, and shareholders. As illustrated in the Dell example in the chapter opening, Web sites can be used to help an organization react quickly to a crisis or controversy.

Many public relations firms are counseling their clients to integrate the interactive features of Web 2.0 into their site. The Budweiser site, for example, had a feature called Bud-2Bud that allowed visitors (over the age of 21, of course) to invite a friend for a Bud. For those under 21, Pepsi gave consumers a chance to design a new Pepsi can. Most large companies also have pages in Wikipedia. Some agencies place videos for their clients on YouTube. One public relations company has even set up virtual shop in Second Life (see Chapter 12).

Several corporations have adopted the podcast as an additional way to get their message out. McDonald's posted a series of podcasts on its Web site with topics ranging from food safety to diversity. Peterson's, the company that publishes information about colleges, offers podcasts on how to prepare for the new SAT.

Other companies have embraced blogging. A corporate blog can be internal, used for communication with employees and shareholders, or external, used as an outlet to respond to online comments and opinions. Companies are using blogs to resolve consumer complaints before they escalate into real problems (a lesson Dell learned the hard way). As of 2006, more than 50 percent of major companies were engaged in some form of blogging, and that number is likely to increase.

Of course, all of these new channels present new challenges. Web sites require people to design and maintain them. Blogs have to be written, and podcasts have to be produced and posted. Interactive sites need to be monitored and updated. Wikis have to be checked periodically to make sure they haven't been maliciously altered. Despite the added cost and labor burden, the Web will likely continue to be a major public relations tool for the foreseeable future.

▲ Communicating with the Media

It didn't take long for public relations practitioners to start using the Internet to streamline their media efforts. E-mail press releases have replaced the traditional paper-mail releases, and e-mail rather than the telephone has become the preferred means of communication between journalists and public relations professionals. Further, the Web has become an important channel in distributing information to the media. PR Newswire's Web site, for example, collects information from agencies and public relations departments and makes this information available to newsrooms across the country. Practitioners can also distribute photos and video clips via the Internet.

The Internet has made it easier for professionals to target their story proposals and press releases to the appropriate sources. A search engine makes it simple to research a given journalist's recent articles to see what kinds of topics he or she might be interested in. Some online Web sites track journalist's job movements. A reporter just starting a new assignment might be particularly interested in story ideas. Finally, database software and e-mail merge programs make it possible for practitioners to efficiently target possible outlets for stories.

▲ New Channels of Feedback

It's not surprising that public relations agencies use the Web for feedback on companies, products, and issues. PR Newswire offers eWatch, a service that monitors online news media and related sites for mentions of specific organizations. Technorati can be used to search the blogosphere. Agencies commonly examine customer review sites such as Epinions or Bizrate for their clients to spot positive and negative comments. And, of course, the Web can be used for traditional research, such as surveys and online focus groups, to shape public relations decisions.

ORGANIZATION OF THE PUBLIC RELATIONS INDUSTRY

Public relations activities are generally handled in two ways. Many organizations have their own public relations departments that work with the managers of all other departments. About 85 percent of the 1,500 largest U.S. companies have such departments. In many companies these departments are part of top management, and the PR director is responsible to the president of the company. For example, General Motors and General Electric both employ about a hundred people in their U.S. PR departments. Other organizations hire an external public relations counsel to give advice on press, government, and consumer relations. In business and industry, about one-third of the PR activity is handled by outside counseling firms. Many major corporations retain an outside agency in addition to their own internal public relations department.

This billboard is an example of a public-service PR campaign with a tie-in to a grocery chain.

Each of these arrangements has its particular advantages and disadvantages. An in-house department can be at work on short notice and has in-depth knowledge about the company; in addition, its operations tend to be less costly. On the other hand, it is hard for a corporate PR team to take an objective view of the company. Further, internal PR departments tend to have trouble coming up with fresh ideas unless new personnel are frequently added. An outside agency offers more services to its clients than does an internal department. Additionally, external counselors have the advantage of being objective observers, and many firms like the prestige associated with being a client of a respected PR firm. On the other side of the coin, outside agencies are expensive, it takes time for them to learn the inner workings of their client's operations, and their involvement may cause resentment and morale problems among the staff of the client's organization.

Internal or external, public relations professionals perform a wide range of services. These include counseling management, preparing annual reports, handling news releases and other forms of media coverage, supervising employee and other internal communications, managing promotions and special events, fund-raising, lobbying, handling community relations, publishing blogs, creating Web sites, and writing speeches.

Public relations is practiced in a variety of settings. Although the general principles are the same, the actual duties of the PR practitioner will vary according to the setting. Following are brief descriptions of a dozen areas in which public relations is practiced:

1. *Business:* Public relations helps the marketing process by instilling in consumers a positive attitude toward the company. Public relations also helps promote healthy employee-management relations and serves as a major liaison between the firm and government regulators. Further, all businesses have to be located somewhere, and the PR department makes sure the company is a good citizen in its community.

2. *Government and politics:* Many government agencies hire PR specialists to help them explain their activities to citizens and to assist the news media in their coverage of the different agencies. These same specialists also communicate the opinions of the public back to the agency. Government PR is big business; its total expenditures on public information rival the budgets of the four major TV networks. The Department of Defense, for instance, produces thousands of films and TV programs every year. The Department of Agriculture sends out thousands of news releases annually. Political public relations is another growing field. A growing number of candidates for public office hire PR experts to help them get their message across to voters.

3. *Education*: PR personnel work in both elementary and higher education. The most visible area of practice in elementary and high school concerns facilitating communication between educators and parents. Other tasks, however, are no less important. In many school systems the PR person also handles relations with the school board, local and state legislative bodies, and the news media. Public relations at the college and university level, although less concerned with parental relations, has its own set of tasks. Fund-raising, legislative relations, community relations, and internal relations with faculty and students would be concerns of most college PR departments.

4. *Hospitals:* The rising cost of health care and greater public expectations of the medical profession have given increased visibility to the PR departments in our nation's hospitals. Some of the publics that hospital PR staffs have to deal with are patients, patients' families, consumers, state insurance commissions, physicians, nurses, and other staff members. Despite the increasing importance of hospital public relations, many hospitals do not have a full-time PR staff. Consequently, this is one area that should see significant growth in the future.

5. *Nonprofit organizations:* The United Way, the Girl Scouts, the American Red Cross, and the Salvation Army are just a few of the organizations that need PR professionals. Probably the biggest PR goal in organizations such as these is fund-raising. Other objectives include encouraging volunteer participation, informing

contributors how their money is spent, and working with the individuals served by an organization.

6. *Professional associations*: Organizations such as the American Medical Association, the American Dairy Association, and the American Bar Association employ PR practitioners. In addition to providing news and information to the association's members, other duties of the PR staff are recruiting new members, planning national conferences, influencing government decisions, and working with the news media.

7. *Entertainment and sports:* A significant number of PR experts work for established and would-be celebrities in the entertainment and sports worlds. A practitioner handling this type of client has two major responsibilities: Get the client favorable media coverage, and protect the client from bad publicity. Additionally, many sports and entertainment events (such as the Super Bowl, or a motion picture premiere) have PR campaigns associated with them.

8. *International PR:* Corporations with branches throughout the world, global news media such as CNN, an interrelated world economy, the shifting political scene in Europe—all these factors have combined to make this area one of the fastest growing in public relations. International PR specialists help businesses operating in other countries with local customs, language problems, cultural difficulties, and legal dilemmas.

9. *Investor relations:* This area (called *IR* for convenience) entails building a favorable image for a company and keeping shareholders happy. A public company needs to communicate information, both positive and negative, that might have an impact on its stock price to the financial community in general and shareholders in particular. To do this effectively, IR professionals must know the workings of the financial press and the various channels used to communicate with shareholders, such as annual reports, quarterly reports, and annual meetings. As more and more Americans invest in the stock and bond markets and as financial markets become more global, the importance of IR will surely increase.

10. *Politics:* The importance of PR in political campaigns increases with every election. Building the right personal image, putting the proper spin on the interpretation of events, and responding to the charges of other candidates are all part of the job of a political PR specialist. Many PR firms specialize in political campaigns.

11. *Environment:* Global warming, water conservation, recycling, energy conservation, and other environmental issues have made this area extremely visible in recent years. Practitioners represent both advocacy groups and industries.

12. *Crisis management:* Probably the ultimate test for the PR practitioner is dealing with a crisis. Such crises arise infrequently, but poor handling of a crisis can have long-term negative effects that might cripple a company and/or ruin the reputation of a PR firm. In a crisis the public seeks more information, and the organization involved in the crisis is subjected to increased scrutiny by both the media and the public. Experts in crisis management PR generally counsel their clients to accomplish three goals: terminate the crisis, limit damage, and restore credibility.

As this list suggests, the profession requires PR specialists as well as generalists. In the next section, we will see how the PR function is typically organized and what jobs PR professionals perform.

PR DEPARTMENTS AND STAFF

At the outset, remember that no two companies have the same exact departmental structure. In one common arrangement for an internal corporate PR department, the director of public relations reports directly to the president of the company. Since PR affects every department, its supervision by the person who runs the entire organization makes sense. Nonetheless, some organizations endorse integrated marketing communications, which puts the PR department in the marketing division. A recent survey noted that about 40 percent of PR departments report to the CEO while 32 percent report to the head of the marketing department. The PR department is further subdivided into three main divisions that are designed to communicate with both internal and external publics: (1) corporate communications, (2) community relations, and (3) press relations. The corporate communications division handles communication with internal publics (workers, shareholders, unions), and the community relations division deals with external publics (community residents, customers, the government). As its name suggests, the press relations division deals with the news media.

The organization of an external PR agency is more complex. One possible arrangement consists of five departments:

1. *Creative services:* Is responsible for ideas and the production of press releases and audio/video media.
2. *Research:* Supervises survey research, focus groups, and data collection.
3. *Publicity and marketing:* Takes charge of merchandising and sales promotions.
4. *Accounts:* Oversees and coordinates relations with clients.
5. *Administration:* Is responsible for the day-to-day personnel, clerical, legal, and financial tasks that keep a business running.

THE PUBLIC RELATIONS PROGRAM

Imagine that you are the public relations director for a leading automaker. The company is entering into an agreement with a foreign car manufacturer to produce a foreign model in the United States. Unfortunately, to increase efficiency and centralize its operations, the company will have to close one of its plants located in a midwestern city. About a thousand employees will have to be transferred or find new jobs, and the community will face a significant economic blow. It will be the job of the public relations department to communicate this decision to the community.

The thorny problem just outlined is a typical one for the public relations professional. Handling it requires a planned, organized, and efficient public relations program. This section will trace the four main steps involved in developing a typical PR campaign: (1) information gathering, (2) planning, (3) communication, and (4) evaluation.

▲ Information Gathering

The information-gathering stage is an important one because what is learned from it will influence the remaining stages. **Information gathering** can be achieved through several means. Organizational records, trade journals, public records, and reference books serve as valuable sources of data. Personal contacts, mail to the company, advisory committees, and personnel reports represent other sources of information. If more formal research methods are required, they might be carried out by the PR department or by an outside agency that specializes in public opinion polling or survey research. Return to our example. The PR director at the auto company will need to gather a great deal of information. How much will the company save by its reorganization? Exactly how many workers will be transferred? Will the company help find new jobs for the workers who will be unemployed? What will be the precise economic impact on the community? What will become of the empty buildings that will be left behind? Will the employees believe what the company tells them? What do people expect from the company? Will the company's image be hurt in other areas of the United States?

▲ Planning

Phase 2 is the planning stage. There are two general types of planning: **strategic** and **tactical**. Strategic plans involve long-range, general goals that the organization wishes to achieve. Top management usually formulates an organization's strategic plans. Tactical plans are more specific. They detail the tasks that must be accomplished by every department in the organization to achieve the strategic goals. Some plans that are drawn up might be used only once; others might serve as standing plans that set general organizational policy.

Planning is a vital part of the PR program. Some of the items involved in a PR campaign are framing the objectives, considering the alternatives, assessing the risks and benefits involved in each alternative, deciding on a course of action, figuring out the budget, and securing the necessary approvals from within the organization. In recent years many PR practitioners have endorsed a technique known as **management by objectives (MBO).** Simply put, MBO means that the organization sets observable and measurable goals for itself and allocates its resources to meet those objectives. For example, a corporation might set as a goal increasing sales by 25 percent over the next 2 years. When the time had elapsed, it would be easy to see if the goal had been achieved. This approach is becoming more popular in PR because top management typically thinks in these terms, and if PR practitioners speak the same language as chief executives, they can communicate more effectively with them. It also keeps the department on target in solving PR problems, and it provides concrete feedback about the efficiency of the PR process. In our hypothetical example, some objectives might be informing more than 50 percent of the community about the reasons for the move and making sure community and national attitudes about the company are not adversely affected.

▲ Communication

Phase 3 is the communication phase. After gathering facts and making plans, the organization assumes the role of the source of communication. Several key decisions are made at this stage concerning the nature of the messages and the types of media to be used. Because mass communication media are usually important channels in a PR program, it is necessary for public relations practitioners to have a thorough knowledge of the various media and their strengths and weaknesses. Moreover, PR professionals should know the various production techniques for the print and broadcast media. Some common ways of publicizing a message through the mass media are press releases, video news releases, press kits, photographs, paid advertising, films, videotapes, press conferences, and interviews.

Public relations also makes use of other channels to get messages to its publics. These include both the interpersonal and the machine-assisted settings. House publications, brochures, faxes, letters, bulletins, posters, Web sites, blogs, e-mail, billboards, and bulletin boards are communication channels used by a company to reach its own employees. On a more personal level, public meetings, speeches, demonstrations, staged events, open houses, and tours are other possibilities.

In our hypothetical example, the PR director would probably use a variety of messages and media. News conferences, ads, press releases, and public meetings would be appropriate vehicles for explaining the company's position to its external public. Meanwhile, house publications, bulletin boards, speeches, and letters could be used to reach its internal public.

▲ Evaluation

The last phase concerns **evaluation** of the PR program. How well did it work? The importance of evaluation in public relations is increasing through the use of MBO techniques. If a measurable goal was proposed for the PR program, then an evaluation technique should be able to measure success in reaching that goal. Several different aspects might be measured. One easy method is simply to gauge the volume of coverage that the campaign generated. The number of press releases sent out, letters mailed, speeches made, and so on are simple to compute. In like manner, press clippings and mentions in TV and radio news can be tabulated. It is important to remember, however, that volume does not equal results. A million press clippings mean nothing if they are not read by the audience. Measuring the impact of a campaign on the audience requires more sophisticated techniques of analysis. Some common techniques are questionnaires distributed to random samples of the audience, telephone and Web surveys, panels, reader-interest studies, and experimental campaigns. It is likely that our hypothetical PR director would use many of these techniques.

Before closing, we should note that we have been talking about these four steps as though they were distinct stages. In actuality the PR program is a continuous process, and one phase blends into the next. The results learned in the evaluation stage, for example, are also part of the information-gathering phase of the next cycle of the PR program. In our car company example, the PR department would use the results of surveys and focus groups to determine whether the company's image had suffered, how much credibility the company had with consumers, and if there were any change in customer loyalty. These findings would help in planning the goals of the next PR campaign.

THE ECONOMICS OF PUBLIC RELATIONS

It Sounded like a Good Idea at the Time

Some promotions don't quite go as planned. In an attempt to get into the *Guinness Book of World Records,* the Snapple Company tried to erect a 17.5-ton, 25-foot-tall frozen kiwi-strawberry ice pop in downtown Manhattan on the first day of summer. The day was unseasonably warm, and the whole thing turned to slush before it was set in place. Pedestrians had to flee the sticky sludge, and police had to close several streets while workers cleaned up the mess.

The total amount of money spent on corporate public relations activity is hard to measure, but some information is available about the revenues of PR agencies. In 2006 the top 50 independent PR firms in the United States collected about $1.1 billion, up 14 percent from 2005.

The industry is dominated by giant PR firms owned by ad agencies. As of 2007, the biggest PR firms with ad agency parent companies were Porter-Novelli and Fleischman-Hillard (part of the Omnicom Group) and Hill & Knowlton and Burson-Marsteller (part of the WPP Group). The two largest independent PR firms were Edelman and Ruder Finn. The PR business can be volatile, especially for smaller agencies, whose fee income might vary by 40–80 percent from year to year.

The online home of PR Newswire. More than 100,000 journalists can access press releases through this Web site.

PR agencies earn their fees in a variety of ways. Some perform specific projects for specific fees. An annual report, for example, might cost $10,000. Some charge their clients a retainer every month, which might range from a few hundred dollars to considerably more. Hill & Knowlton, for example, charged one client a retainer of more than $20,000 per month in 2006. Other firms keep track of time spent on various projects and charge clients an hourly rate. Still others bill for time plus for extra services and materials.

PUBLIC RELATIONS

The Web site of the Public Relations Student Society of America (PRSSA) has a list of skills that are important for those planning a career in public relations. The top two: (1) effective written communication and (2) persuasive speaking and presentational ability. Note the emphasis on communication. Most entry-level jobs entail writing and editing news releases, reports, employee publications, and speeches as well as making presentations to existing and potential clients. Other qualifications that are desirable are knowledge of public relations research techniques, business practices, the law, the social sciences, and computers. The PRSSA also recommends that students create a professional portfolio of their work that can be sent to employers or left with interviewers.

The U.S. Department of Labor cautions: "Keen competition likely will continue for entry-level public relations jobs, as the number of qualified applicants is expected to exceed the number of job openings. Many people are attracted to this profession because of the high-profile nature of the work." Nonetheless, the Department of labor forecasts that employment in this area is likely to increase faster than average for the next 5 years or so thanks to an increasingly competitive business environment.

New employees in the PR department are expected to perform a wide range of duties. More specifically, a newcomer is expected to write news releases; update mailing lists;

Public relations professionals all agree that the best PR comes from having good word of mouth, or, in the jargon of the trade, a positive buzz—having people say nice things about a product or company. But how do you get the buzz started? How about paying people?

That's the business model behind a Boston company called BzzAgent. The company has recruited a force of about 75,000 worker bees that it describes as "product evangelists" who will go into the streets and tout the virtues of a product to other people, usually without the other people knowing that they've been buzzed. A buzz campaign for the book *The Frog King* illustrates how the process works. Dozens of buzz agents were given free copies of the book and advised to read it on subways, trains, and buses with the cover plainly displayed. Some passages from the book were highlighted to be used as talking points when recommending the book to family and friends. It was also suggested that the agents call local bookstores and ask if the clerk had heard about the book and how many copies were in stock. In 3 months the book sold more than what the publisher thought it would sell in a year.

The buzz is not cheap. For about $90,000, BzzAgent will provide a client with a thousand specially chosen product evangelists who will spread the word in a 12-week campaign. The agents provide written reports of their activities that are transmitted back to the client. The worker bees get free sample of the product, and they earn points that can be redeemed for books, CDs, and other items.

BzzAgent isn't the only company that commercializes ordinary conversation. Sony Ericsson hired 600 actors to ask passersby to take pictures with its new camera phone. The actors then praised the phone to those who cooperated. Procter & Gamble has more than 200,000 teenagers in its "Tremor" word-of-mouth unit who advocate various products to their peers.

What are some of the ethical questions raised by buzz marketing? Most obviously, there's the issue of deception. BzzAgent suggests that its workers tell others that they are being compensated for their recommendations. There is no way, of course, to know how many, if any, do this. When that key fact is not disclosed, the honesty and integrity of human communication is compromised. Is it possible to have a truthful conversation with someone who has a hidden agenda? The next time someone you know tells you that Sony's new Play Station is great and you should buy one, do you believe it? Those who favor the technique point out that those who participate are not asked to spread the buzz about products that they dislike. People naturally talk about products they use and enjoy. Buzz marketing simply encourages a natural tendency.

A second issue involves privacy. Marketing has invaded almost every facet of American life; consumers are bombarded by hundreds of advertisements every day. Shouldn't there be some circumstances that are marketing-proof? Should a talk with a friend become a paid promotional event? How about the family breakfast table? Should teenagers become paid shills to hawk a breakfast cereal to parents? Is it ethical to take up the time of clerks and salespersons as part of a marketing campaign?

Lastly, as detailed in Chapter 17, there is an ethical philosophy called the *principle of self-determination*. In brief, it maintains that you should not use people as objects or as means to an end. It seems that buzz marketing violates this principle. It values people not for their unique humanness but for the fact that they can be turned into stealth salespeople. The fact that the people involved are willing participants does not change the situation.

Despite these concerns, it's probable that buzz marketing will grow in popularity. It's effective and relatively cheap. There's even a professional organization for those involved: the Word of Mouth Marketing Association (WOMMA).

The WOMMA recently drafted a code of ethics for its members. As noted on WOMMA's Web site, the code can be distilled into three propositions:

- *Honesty of relationship*: You say who you're speaking for.
- *Honesty of opinion:* You say what you believe.
- *Honesty of identity*: You never obscure your identity.

Adherence to the code is voluntary.

research materials for speeches; provide material for an organization's Web site; edit company publications; arrange special events; produce special reports; and give public speeches.

One way to gain initial entry into the profession is to secure an internship with a public relations firm while you are still in college. A survey of recent graduates now working in public relations revealed that undergraduate internships turned into full-time jobs for about one-fifth of those surveyed. Internships may carry a modest salary, or they may involve no pay at all; some internships carry college credit, others do not. In any event, all internships can be valuable training experience.

As in other media-related work, the job applicant should not be too choosy about his or her first job. Most counselors recommend taking any job that is available, even if it lacks the glamour and the salary that the applicant was hoping for. Once you are inside the firm, it is much easier to move to those positions that are more attractive.

MAIN POINTS

- *Public relations* is difficult to define, but most practitioners agree that PR involves counseling management about communication strategies that can improve public opinion about an organization.

- Modern public relations began around the turn of the 20th century and has steadily increased in importance.

- The Internet is an important part of PR. It is used to provide information to the public and to obtain background information for PR professionals.

- PR is practiced in numerous settings, including business, government, and the nonprofit sector.

- A PR campaign consists of the following stages: information gathering, planning, communication, and evaluation.

QUESTIONS FOR REVIEW

1. Define *public relations.*
2. What are some of the major areas that make use of public relations?

3. What are the stages in a public relations campaign?
4. How has the Internet changed the practice of public relations?

QUESTIONS FOR CRITICAL THINKING

1. Can you think of any examples of your using PR in your personal life (like putting the best spin on a bad grade in a course)?
2. Why is the term *public relations* so hard to define? Is it important to have a definition that everybody agrees on?

3. Why does the public have little faith in the credibility of PR professionals?
4. Many journalists look with disfavor on the field of public relations. What might account for this attitude?

KEY TERMS

publicity (p. 318)
publics (p. 318)
information gathering (p. 327)

strategic (planning) (p. 328)
tactical (planning) (p. 328)
management by objectives (MBO) (p. 328)

evaluation (p. 329)

INTERNET RESOURCES

Online Learning Center

At the Online Learning Center home page, www.mhhe.com/dominick10, *select* Student Center *and then* Chapter 14.

1. Use the Learning Objectives, Chapter Outline, Main Points, and Time Line sections to review this chapter.

2. Test your knowledge of the chapter using the multiple choice, crossword puzzle, and flashcard features of the site.

3. Expand your knowledge of concepts and topics discussed in the chapter by going to Suggestions for Further Reading and Internet Exercises.

Surfing the Internet

Some of these sites are mentioned in the text. Others appear first on this list. Remember that the Web is always changing. Some sites move, some change their focus, and others simply evaporate.

www.ewatch.com
The Internet monitoring service. As it states on the site, "The fast, easy and cost effective way to track what the media, investors, consumers and the competition are saying about your organization."

www.ketchum.com
The home page of Ketchum Public Relations Worldwide. Includes a description of the company, and a list of the worldwide offices and podcasts.

www.prnewswire.com

A source of news about corporations for reporters and investors. Lists the day's top business stories and offers links to specialized news about entertainment, autos, finance, and leisure activities.

www.prmuseum.com

A museum of public relations. Contains extensive information on the pioneers of PR.

www.prsa.org

The home page of the Public Relations Society of America. Includes general information about the society, a list of relevant publications, and a link to the PR student society. A recently added feature enables members to post their résumés in cyberspace.

CHAPTER 15

ADVERTISING

This chapter will prepare you to:

- define *advertising* and explain how it is classified

- explain how advertising developed

- recognize the impact the Internet has had on advertising

- distinguish among the three main components of the advertising industry

- discuss the components of an advertising campaign

One of the electronic light boxes that caused a panic in Boston.

15

Around eight in the morning on the last day of January 2007, a person coming out of the Sullivan Square transit station in Boston noticed something odd attached to one of the pillars that support an elevated section of Interstate 93. It looked like a circuit board with lights, electrical tape, and wiring. Concerned that the device might be a bomb, the person informed the police, who in turn alerted the bomb squad. Taking no chances, the police shut down northbound I-93 and closed part of the city's public transportation system, causing a huge nightmare for morning commuters. The bomb squad blew up the device with a small explosive charge.

But that was not the end of the story. A couple of hours later, similar devices were reported under bridges and at a busy intersection. Police closed the bridges and a main Boston street, making the traffic problems monumental. Media reports contained speculation that the devices might be the work of terrorists.

As it turned out, it wasn't terrorism but an example of advertising in the digital age. The devices were planted by two men who worked for Interference Inc., a self-styled "guerilla" marketing firm that had been hired to promote a program on the Cartoon Network called *Aqua Teen Hunger Force*. The devices were similar to Lite-Brites, electronic light boxes with light-emitting diodes (LEDs) arranged in the shape of "mooninites," characters from the program. A battery pack provided power to the LEDs, which were particularly noticeable at night. (Interestingly, the Lite-Brites were also placed in nine other cities without incident.)

The Boston authorities were not amused. They condemned Turner Broadcasting, parent company of the Cartoon Network, for not alerting law enforcement officials about what they were doing. Turner issued an apology to the people of Boston and paid the city $2 million to cover expenses. The general manager of the Cartoon Network resigned, and the two men who actually planted the devices agreed to do community service work in return for having the city drop criminal charges against them.

What does this have to do with modern advertising? First, consumers are bombarded with advertising every day, and advertisers are continuously looking for new ways to break through the clutter. Their attempts are likely to get more and more brash. Second, Turner and other companies have realized that audiences for the traditional media are declining and that print and electronic ads are becoming less effective—hence the move toward nontraditional guerilla advertising. Third, the promotion was cheap. The devices cost little to manufacture, and the two men who placed them were paid $300 each. Advertisers are becoming more cost conscious and are relying on inexpensive techniques such as user-generated content, viral advertising (where consumers spread the message; see below), and stunts like the one in Boston.

This chapter examines the history, structure, operation, and social effects of the ever-changing advertising enterprise as it digests the implications of the digital age.

DEFINING ADVERTISING

Simply defined, *advertising* is any form of nonpersonal presentation and promotion of ideas, goods, and services usually paid for by an identified sponsor. Note three key terms in this definition. First, advertising is "nonpersonal"; it is directed toward a large group of anonymous people. Even direct-mail advertising, which may be addressed to a specific person, is prepared by a computer and signed by a machine. Second, advertising typically is "paid for." This fact differentiates advertising from publicity, which is not usually purchased. Sponsors such as Coke and Delta pay for the time and the space they use to get their message across. (Nonprofit organizations, such as the Red Cross or the United Way, advertise but do not pay for time or space. Broadcast stations, newspapers, and magazines run these ads free as a public service.) Third, for obvious reasons, the sponsor of the ad is "identified." In fact, in most instances, identifying the sponsor is the prime purpose behind the ad—otherwise, why advertise? Perhaps the only type of advertising in which the identity of the advertiser may not be self-evident is political advertising. Because of this, broadcasters and publishers will not accept a political ad without a statement identifying those responsible for it.

Before we leave this topic, it should be noted that in the 21st century this definition of advertising has gotten a little blurry around the edges. Many practitioners consider advertising part of the overall marketing mix, along with promotion, branding, word of mouth, and public relations. (Note how this approach is consistent with the integrated marketing communication (IMC) philosophy mentioned in the previous chapter.) Taking that view, differentiating advertising from other forms of marketing is not particularly useful. Note that in the Boston example of guerilla marketing, the "sponsor" of the advertising was not identified. When a company engages in viral advertising, once the message starts to spread, the cost to the advertiser is zero. Although these two cases run counter to the traditional definition, some would consider both to be forms of advertising.

▲ Functions of Advertising

Advertising fulfills five basic functions in society. First, it serves a marketing function by helping companies that provide products or services sell their products. Personal selling, sales promotions, and advertising work together to help market the product. Second, advertising is educational. People learn about new products and services, or improvements in existing ones, through advertising. Third, advertising plays an economic role. The ability to advertise enables new competitors to enter the business arena. Competition, in turn, encourages product improvements and can lead to lower prices. Fourth, advertising reaches a mass audience, thus greatly reducing the cost of personal selling and distribution. Finally, advertising performs a definite social function. By vividly displaying the material and cultural opportunities available in a free-enterprise society, advertising helps increase productivity and raises the standard of living.

▲ Types of Advertising

Advertising can be classified in several ways. One useful approach is to distinguish the **target audience**—the specific segment of the population for whom the product or service has a definite appeal. Many target audiences can be defined; the most general are consumers and businesses. **Consumer advertising,** as the name suggests, is targeted at the people who buy goods and services for personal use. For example, Campbell's (known for its soups) uses consumer advertising to direct its ads to the adults and children most likely to buy soup at the grocery store. Most of the advertising that people are exposed to falls into this category. **Business-to-business advertising** is aimed at people who buy products for business use. Industrial, trade, and professional—as well as agricultural—advertising are all part of this category. Consumer advertising is the focus of most of this chapter, but we will also take a brief look at business-to-business advertising.

Geographic focus is another way to classify advertising. International advertising is employed for products and services that are used all over the globe. Coca-Cola and

An example of a primary demand ad. The "got milk?" campaign was designed to promote milk drinking, not the purchase of a particular brand of milk.

McDonald's, for example, advertise in dozens of countries and in many different languages. National advertising is advertising in many different regions of the same country. Delta, Wal-Mart, and Sprint, for example, run ads on TV networks and in national magazines to reach customers in many different markets across the United States. International advertisers, of course, also use national ads. Retail or local advertising is done within one specific market. The neighborhood restaurant or car dealership typically relies on local ads.

Yet a third way to categorize advertising is by purpose. Some ads are for distinct products or services, such as frozen pizzas or muffler repairs, while others try to improve a company's image or influence public opinion on an issue, such as the ads run by oil companies describing their efforts to keep down fuel costs. Another distinction involves primary demand and selective demand ads. A **primary demand ad** has as its purpose the promotion of a particular product category rather than a specific brand. The campaign to encourage milk drinking that shows various celebrities with milk moustaches is an example of this type. A **selective demand ad** is used by an individual company to sell its particular brand, such as a certain brand of milk. Finally, ads can be classified as direct action and indirect action. A **direct action ad** usually contains a toll-free number, coupon, e-mail or Web address, or some similar device to enable the advertiser to see results quickly. In contrast, an **indirect action ad** works over the long run to build a company's image and increase consumer awareness.

A BRIEF HISTORY

An ad from the 1900s for Coca-Cola. Included at the bottom is a coupon for a free Coke.

Advertising's beginnings are impossible to pinpoint, but several examples date back thousands of years. Clay tablets traced to ancient Babylon have been found with messages that touted an ointment dealer and a shoemaker. The town crier was an important advertising medium throughout England and other countries in Europe during the medieval period.

In more recent times, the history of advertising is inextricably entwined with changing social conditions and advances in media technology. For instance, Gutenberg's invention of printing using movable type made possible several new advertising media: posters, handbills, and newspaper ads. The first printed advertisement in English, produced about 1480, was a handbill that announced a prayer book for sale. Its author, evidently wise in the ways of outdoor advertising, tacked his ad to church doors all over England. By the late 1600s, ads were common sights in London newspapers.

The most outspoken critics of advertising charge that it stimulates greed, envy, and avarice—three of the seven deadly sins—a claim that can be made by no other industry. Specifically, foes of advertising claim that it causes people to buy things that they otherwise would not. Flashy ads for new-model cars prompt people to trade in perfectly good older models simply for the prestige and status of owning new ones. Even though the old DVD player works fine, run out and buy the latest version with new bells and whistles. Still wearing last year's clothes? Shame on you. Go out and buy the latest fashions as seen in print and TV ads. In short, advertising *creates* needs and makes people buy things they do not *really* need or want.

In reply to this criticism, advertising practitioners point out that humans have a variety of needs; some are biological (the need for food) and basic (the need for a safe place to live). Others are more complicated (the need for self-esteem and self-actualization). Advertising, say its supporters, caters to a wide variety of needs, not just basic ones. There is nothing wrong with buying a new car every year if it helps a person's self-esteem. Buying the latest fashions can help a person on a quest for self-actualization. Advertising is directed at many forms of need fulfillment, some of them subtle and personal. It is presumptuous of critics to tell consumers what they need or do not need. In this argument advertising is pictured as catering to a variety of needs that are already present in consumers; it does little to create new ones. As further support for this argument, advertisers point out that many heavily advertised products fail, and there is no evidence to suggest that advertising compels people to purchase things they do not want.

A second line of criticism holds that advertising promotes materialistic values and lifestyles. Advertising persuades us to evaluate others not by who they are, but by what they possess. Material objects are portrayed as desirable goals. The people whom advertising presents as models to be emulated are not those who possess admirable personal qualities. Instead, consumers are compelled to emulate people who drive fancy or powerful cars, wear expensive jewelry, write with the best pen, wear the trendiest clothes, or watch TV on the biggest set. Advertising encourages people to spend and acquire and makes consumption the most important activity in life. Critics go on to point out that this aspect of advertising is particularly disruptive for those with low incomes who do not have the means to attain the material goals portrayed in ads.

In response to this argument, supporters of advertising point out that advertising did not create the emphasis on materialism in American life. Writings about rampant materialism in American culture were present as early as 1830. Major holidays in the United States celebrate consumption and materialism. Christmas, for example, encourages gift giving; Thanksgiving, eating. Our basic economic system of capitalism stresses the production and consumption of goods. Advertising simply reflects the larger values of U.S. society and should not be blamed for portraying them.

Finally, advertising is criticized for its intrusiveness. The typical American is the most advertised-to person in the world. U.S. companies spend more than $500 per person on advertising, more than companies in any other country. According to *Business Week*, we are exposed to about 3,000 commercial messages a day. In addition to the ubiquitous commercials on radio, on TV, on the Internet, and in print, advertising is now piped into supermarkets, airports, and doctors' offices; plastered on bathroom walls; splashed on the sides of race cars; snuck into the plots of feature films; displayed on blimps; and printed on the sides of hot dogs. Plans are even in the works to put ads in outer space. The avalanche of ads has made it difficult for advertisers to get consumers to notice their ads, let alone remember them. This leads to additional pressure to find new channels and new attention-getting techniques and results in even more intrusiveness.

Even advertising's supporters agree that advertising is hard to avoid. But they go on to point out that this is a small price to pay for the social and economic benefits that it provides for society. Without advertising, television and radio would not be free, and magazines and newspapers would cost at least twice as much. Advertising that appears on the sides of buses helps keep fares down. The uniforms worn by Little League teams are often given for free in return for plastering the advertiser's name on the back. Would you mind seeing ads for Coke in this textbook if it meant the price was $10 cheaper?

Obviously, these are complicated issues, made even more difficult because there is no simple way to sort out the effects of advertising from the effects of all the other factors in modern life. Nonetheless, because of its high visibility and its role in the well-being of consumers, advertising will continue to be subjected to intense social scrutiny.

Advertising made its way to the American colonies along with the early settlers from England. Ben Franklin, a pioneer of early advertising, made his ads more attractive by using large headlines and considerable white space. From Franklin's time to the early 19th century, newspaper ads resembled what today are called *classified ads*.

The Industrial Revolution caused major changes in American society and in American advertising. Manufacturers, with the aid of newly invented machines, were able to mass-produce their products. Mass production, however, also required mass consumption and a mass market. Advertising was a tremendous aid in reaching this new mass audience.

The impact of increasing industrialization was most apparent in the period from the end of the Civil War to the beginning of the 20th century. In little more than three decades, the following occurred:

- The railroad linked all parts of the country, making it possible for Eastern manufacturers to distribute their goods to the growing Western markets.
- The population of the United States doubled. More people meant larger markets for manufacturers.
- The invention of new communication media—telephone, typewriter, high-speed printing press, phonograph, motion pictures, photography, rural mail delivery—made it easier for people to communicate with one another.
- Economic production increased dramatically, and people had more disposable income to spend on new products.

This improved economic and communication climate helped advertising thrive. Magazines were distributed from coast to coast and made possible truly national advertising. The development of the halftone method for reproducing photographs meant that magazine advertisers could portray their products more vividly. By 1900 it was not unusual for the leading magazines of the period (*Harper's, Cosmopolitan, McClure's*) to run 75–100 pages of ads in a typical issue.

It is not surprising that the increased importance of advertising in the marketing process led to the birth of the **advertising agency,** an organization that specializes in providing advertising services to its clients. The roots of the modern-day agency can be traced to Volney B. Palmer of Philadelphia. In 1842 Palmer bought large amounts of space in various newspapers at a discount and then resold the space at higher rates to advertisers. The actual ad—the copy, layout, and artwork—was still prepared by the company wishing to advertise; in effect, Palmer was a space broker. That situation changed in the late 19th century when the advertising agency of N. W. Ayer & Son was founded. Ayer & Son offered to plan, create, and execute complete advertising campaigns for its customers. By 1900 the advertising agency had become the focal point of creative planning, and advertising was firmly established as a profession.

SOUNDBYTE

It's Everywhere! It's Everywhere!

In case you haven't already noticed, it's hard to escape advertising. Eventually, we may get to the point where there is no blank space anywhere. Some of the novel techniques that advertisers are using include the following:

- TV monitors are embedded in the tables at mall food courts and run continuous ads.
- Custom postage stamps bear the logo of a company.
- Ads are stamped on the nozzles of gas pumps.
- In some airports electrical outlets where commuters plug in laptops contain commercial messages (a plug on a plug?).
- In the Netherlands sheep grazing by the roadside wear blankets that display ads. (It's called "Lease-a-Sheep.")
- Many companies print advertising on bathroom tissue. (Insert your own joke here.)

The 1920s saw the beginning of radio as an advertising medium (see Chapter 7). Network broadcasting made radio an attractive vehicle for national advertisers; by 1930 about $27 million was being spent annually on network advertising, and many of the most popular shows of the day were produced by advertising agencies. However, the stock market crash of 1929 had a disastrous effect on the U.S. economy, and total dollars spent on advertising dropped from $2.8 billion in 1929 to $1.7 billion in 1935. It would take a decade for the industry to recover. During World War II many civilian firms cut back on their advertising budgets. Others simply changed the content of their ads and, instead of selling their products, instructed consumers on how to make their products last until after the war.

World War II was followed by the Cold War, when Americans were concerned about the rise of communism. Despite growth in mass consumption and economic prosperity, the prevailing mood of the country was one of apprehension as many people were afraid that communists were secretly taking over the government and subverting the American way of life. This mood also had an impact on public opinion about advertising. After the Korean War many stories surfaced about brainwashing and mind control of American prisoners. It was not long before advertising was indicted as a form of mind

CRITICAL / CULTURAL ISSUES

Cultural Meaning and Trade Characters

Tony the Tiger, Mr. Clean, the Maytag repairman, Ronald McDonald, the Jolly Green Giant, Betty Crocker, the Keebler Elves—these are examples of trade characters, fictional beings, played by actors or animated, created to help sell a product, service, or idea. Like slogans, trade characters are popular because they are an effective way of linking the product and its advertising so that consumers can easily remember the message. But trade characters do more than slogans; they give a product personality, style, and depth by creating an image with a clear cultural meaning with which the audience can identify.

Created by the Leo Burnett Agency, the Jolly Green Giant has been ho-ho-ho-ing for more than 40 years.

An article by Barbara Phillips in a 1996 issue of the *Journal of Popular Culture* examines the role of trade characters in American culture. Phillips notes that mass-produced products have little cultural meaning. A Duracell battery is hard to distinguish from an Eveready battery, and neither is likely to arouse any emotional response. Trade characters, however, give meaning and significance to otherwise indistinguishable products by linking a product to an image that has a cultural meaning. One way that trade characters create this meaning is by employing commonly accepted mythical symbols—images that convey cultural meaning. Take the Jolly Green Giant, for example. The giant is a common mythical figure whose size connotes strength, power, and authority. His green color is associated with freshness, while his hearty "ho-ho-ho" imparts warmth and humor. The giant's image on a can of peas makes the product less remote and more friendly.

The use of mythical symbols gives trade characters another quality: They communicate messages without having explicitly to state them. Mr. Clean, for example, immaculate in his all-white costume, symbolizes cleanliness and purity. His image suggests that using his product will produce these results, but he never actually says so. In contrast, an ad that proclaims, "Our cleaner will leave your countertop spotless and pure," might be met with some degree of doubt. Since trade characters do not directly state that a product has specific attributes, their "claims" are less likely to be rejected.

There are, of course, some drawbacks to the use of trade characters. Cultural meanings shift over time, and advertisers must be careful to monitor changing attitudes in society. Perhaps the best example of this potential is Aunt Jemima. The Quaker Oats Company started using this trade character in 1889. Over the years, however, the image became an unacceptable stereotype. In 1968, during the civil rights movement, her image changed: She lost 100 pounds and became younger; her red bandana was replaced by a headband. In 1990 she was made over again into an image that was the black equivalent of Betty Crocker, an image the company hoped was more positive. Some trade characters may be entirely inappropriate. Joe Camel, for example, was the subject of much criticism because the cartoon character seemed designed to encourage children to smoke. Camel eventually phased him out.

Trade characters have become an established part of American culture. Their ranks will undoubtedly increase in the future.

control that seduced people by subtle appeals to subconscious urges. A best-seller called *The Hidden Persuaders* explained how advertisers used psychological research and motivational analysis to sell consumers things they really did not need or want. It was during this time that the concept of subliminal advertising was introduced, which further deepened the suspicions about the advertising industry.

This paranoia gradually subsided during the 1960s, which were characterized by the growth of the creative side of advertising as art directors, copywriters, and TV directors had more input into the way advertising was presented. This trend weakened during the 1970s when a bad economic climate prompted a return to a more direct selling technique and a focus on efficient media planning.

The 1980s and 1990s saw the social and media environment for advertising change drastically. Cable television opened up dozens of new and specialized channels that siphoned

Those sponsored links at the right side of the results page of a typical Google search brought the search engine company more than $6 billion in ad revenue in 2006.

advertising dollars away from the major TV networks. New video forms of marketing emerged, such as the infomercial and home shopping. Moreover, improved transportation and communication gave birth to the mega–ad agency with branches throughout the world. Political changes in Europe created new opportunities for global marketing. Changes in society also had an impact. Advertisers were facing a more culturally diverse marketplace that required more selective ads. Consumer attitudes toward products were changing, and new regulations promised to forever alter tobacco advertising. Liquor ads also drew criticism.

Contemporary advertising finds itself coping with technological and social change. As mentioned in Chapter 1, consumers are taking more and more control over their media choices. The Internet, TiVo, the iPod, cell phones, and other technologies have given consumers the power to choose when, where and how they look for news and entertainment. The traditional advertising model, whereby advertisers interrupt a program or place ads around print articles in the hope that someone sees them, is becoming harder to justify. Couple that trend with the fact that many young people are no longer getting their news and entertainment from traditional media, and it's easy to understand why a lot of advertising money is shifting from the established media to more nontraditional forms, such as text message ads on cell phones or NASCAR race cars, or Internet advertising, or even guerilla marketing.

Speaking of Internet advertising, the industry is exploring ways to use this new medium effectively. When it first appeared in the early 1990s, Internet advertising was hailed as the next great advance in advertising reach. As it turned out, however, these hopes were exaggerated. Banner advertising on Internet sites generated little traffic, pop-up blockers screened out pop-up ads, and spam filters quarantined much of e-mail advertising. As a result, advertising professionals had to rethink their Internet strategies. Contemporary Internet advertising is more targeted. Google, for example, lets advertisers buy space on a Web page that displays the results of an individual's Web search. Second, Web ads are becoming more interactive and more engaging. Proctor & Gamble's Club Olay Web site encourages women to sign up for special offers and free samples and to receive monthly e-mail from the company.

The amount spent on online advertising has risen from about $6 billion in 2002 to $9.75 billion in 2006. This number will doubtlessly increase as advertisers become more skilled at using the Internet. Among the top Internet advertisers in 2006 were Vonage, Time Warner, and Dell.

ADVERTISING IN THE DIGITAL AGE

Online advertising began in 1994 when HotWired, the digital counterpart to the hip *Wired* magazine, started a Web site with about a dozen sponsors who paid to have advertising banners embedded throughout the site. Since that time, advertising as well as the Internet have undergone a number of changes.

▲ Audience Control

As mentioned in Chapter 1, consumers are taking more and more control over their media choices. TiVo, the iPod, video-on-demand, the Internet, and other technologies have given individuals the power to choose when, where, and how they look for news and entertainment. As far as advertising is concerned, consumers are increasingly making media choices that involve avoiding advertising. In a recent survey about half the respondents said that ads spoil their reading or viewing experience. About 8 million people have opted for commercial-free music on satellite radio. Digital video recorders, such as TiVo, are in more than 20 percent of U.S. homes, and the number is increasing daily. As you might expect, about two-thirds of DVR owners fast-forward through the ads. Thousands of commercial-free episodes of TV shows have been downloaded from iTunes. Most people have ad- and spam-blocking software installed on their computers.

These developments have forced advertisers to look for other means to reach the audience. Product placement has become common in movies, TV shows, and even video games. **Viral advertising,** a technique by which companies try to create messages that are so compelling, interesting, funny, or suggestive that consumers willingly and spontaneously share them with others, usually via e-mail, social networking sites, or cell phones, is a hot area. If the technique is successful, word spreads rapidly to a large number of people, much like a virus. For instance, Dove Evolution, a short film posted on YouTube, got more than 1.7 million views thanks to good consumer reaction.

Targeted search advertising, paying for links to a product or service on search results pages, accounted for about $6.5 billion in revenue in 2006. Finally, some advertisers have turned to "buzz marketing" or tactics like those used in the Boston affair to generate word of mouth.

▲ New Channels

The digital revolution has opened up additional avenues for advertising. Bloggers represent a segment of the population that wields significant influence. Advertisers can use networks such as Blogads to target specific blogs whose readers would be likely customers for their product or service.

Podcasts are another emerging channel. Podtrac, for example, offers advertisers access to 1,500 podcasts, ranging from "This Week in Tech" to "Mugglecast" for Harry Potter fans. Advertisers select the demographics and interests of their target market, and Podtrac selects the most appropriate podcasts. Companies typically sponsor an entire podcast and pay on the basis of how many times the podcast was downloaded.

Not surprisingly, advertising is becoming more common on cell phones. Most high school and college students have one, and young people are the audience segment that many advertisers want to reach. Cell phone companies and advertisers are currently exploring various arrangements.

One alternative would let subscribers opt in for ads, agreeing to receive ads on their phones in return for a reduced monthly fee. Another takes advantage of the fact that some phones have global positioning systems. Theoretically at least, a consumer might get a cell phone text message ad when he or she is in the vicinity of a certain store. Consumers who use their phone to access the Internet are already exposed to some advertising. ESPN, for example, includes short video ads along with their video highlights. Advertisers are proceeding cautiously, however, since they fear that cell phone ads might have a boomerang effect and make consumers hostile to the advertised products.

Finally, advertisers are finding creative ways to use their Web sites. One emerging theme is that consumers are more attuned to information and less receptive to overt sales pitches. Consequently, the "soft sell" approach is gaining popularity. Royal Caribbean, the cruise ship line, for example, hosted a video newsletter that highlighted travel destinations, facts about sea creatures, and behind-the-scenes information about cruises. A small banner at the bottom of the screen provided for online reservations. The Toyota Yaris Web site not only let viewers see technical information about the car and its features but also gave them a chance to take a virtual test drive down the main thoroughfares of several American cities, complete with information on local landmarks.

▲ User-Generated Content

As it has in other media areas, user-generated content has become popular with advertisers. Companies such as MasterCard, GM, and Converse have encouraged users to submit homemade commercials. Doritos ran a user-generated ad contest for which the winning entry was shown during the 2007 Super Bowl.

The advantages to advertisers are obvious. Amateur ads cost almost nothing, get consumers to "engage" with the product, and can create word-of-mouth buzz. Companies usually give participants some sort of general theme, simple rules, and a suggested length. Of course, there's a downside. When GM asked users to come up with an ad for their Chevy Tahoe, it got several entries from people who criticized the vehicle for harming the environment.

ORGANIZATION OF THE CONSUMER ADVERTISING INDUSTRY

There are three main components of the advertising industry: (1) advertisers, (2) advertising agencies, and (3) the media. We will discuss each of these in turn.

▲ Advertisers

Advertising is an important part of the overall marketing plan of almost every organization that provides a product or a service to the public. Advertisers can range from the small bicycle shop on the corner that spends $4 on an ad in the local weekly paper to huge international corporations such as General Motors, which spends more than $2 billion annually for ads.

At a basic level we can distinguish two different types of advertisers: national and retail. **National advertisers** sell their product or service to customers all across the country. The emphasis in national advertising is on the product or service and not so much on the place where the product or service is sold. For example, the Coca-Cola Company is interested in selling soft drinks. It does not matter to the company if you buy its product at the local supermarket, at a small convenience store, or from a vending machine. **Retail advertisers** (also called *local advertisers*) are companies such as local restaurants, car dealerships, TV repair shops, and other merchants and service organizations that have customers in only one city or trading area. The retail advertiser wants to attract customers to a specific store or place of business. Some companies are both national and local advertisers. Sears and Target, for example, advertise all over the country, but their individual stores use local advertising to highlight their specific sales and promotions. Franchises, such as McDonald's and Burger King, keep up their national image by advertising on network TV, while

The boss as spokesperson. Papa John's founder John Schnatter frequently appears in his company's commercials.

their local outlets put ads in the paper to attract customers from the local community.

Naturally, the way organizations handle their advertising depends on their size. Some companies have their own advertising departments; a small retail store might have one person who is responsible for advertising and marketing and who may also have other job functions. Whether large or small, all advertisers must attend to several basic functions. These include planning the ads and deciding where they will appear, setting aside a certain amount of money for the advertising budget, coordinating the advertising with other departments in the organization, and, if necessary, supervising the work of an outside agency or company that produces the ad. In addition, some large advertisers have departments that can create and prepare all the advertising materials, purchase the space and airtime for the ads, and check to see if the ads were effective in achieving their goals.

▲ Agencies

According to the American Association of Advertising Agencies, an **agency** is an independent business organization composed of creative people and businesspeople who develop, prepare, and place advertising for sellers seeking to find customers for their goods and services. In the past, advertising agencies were located in a few big cities, such as New York, Chicago, and Los Angeles. That trend has changed, however, and many of the more memorable ad campaigns of recent years have been put together by agencies located far from Madison Avenue. When it comes to total income, however, the big-city agencies still dominate.

The past few years in the agency business have seen the spawning of superagencies, or mega-agencies, resulting from the merger and consolidation of several large ad agencies. In addition, the business has been globalized, since these new mega-agencies have branches all over the world. The five mega-agencies listed in Table 15-1 dominated the industry at the close of 2006.

The global reach of advertising is apparent in the agency business as in many other media. Three of the megagroups in Table 15-1 are foreign-owned.

Agencies can be classified by the range of services they offer. In general terms there are three main types: (1) full-service agencies, (2) media buying services, and (3) creative boutiques.

As the name implies, a **full-service agency** handles all phases of the advertising process for its clients; it plans, creates, produces, and places ads. In addition, it might provide other marketing services, such as sales promotions, trade show exhibits, newsletters, and annual reports. In theory, at least, there is no need for the client to deal with any other company for help promoting its product.

A **media buying service** specializes in buying radio and TV time and reselling it to advertisers and advertising agencies. The service sells time to the advertiser, orders the spots on the various stations, and monitors the stations to see if the ads actually run.

TABLE 15-1	Company	Headquarters	2006 Revenue (in billion U.S. dollars)
Top Five Advertising Agencies, 2006	Omnicom	New York	$11.4
	WPP Group	London	10.8
	Interpublic	New York	6.2
	Publicis	Paris	5.9
	Dentsu	Tokyo	2.9

A **creative boutique** (the name was coined during the 1960s and has hung on to the present) is an organization that specializes in the actual creation of ads. In general, boutiques create imaginative and distinctive advertising themes and produce innovative and original ads. A company that uses a creative boutique would have to employ another agency to perform the planning, buying, and administrative functions connected with advertising.

What does a full-service ad agency do for a client? To begin with, the agency studies the product or service and determines what its marketable characteristics are and how it relates to the competition. At the same time, the agency studies the potential market, possible distribution plans, and likely advertising media. The agency then makes a formal presentation to the client detailing its findings and its recommended advertising strategy. If the client agrees, the agency launches the execution phase. This phase entails writing and producing the ads, buying space and time in various media, delivering the ads to the appropriate media, and verifying that all ads actually appear. Finally, the agency works closely with the client's salespeople to make sure they get the greatest possible benefit from the ads.

As advertising continues to move online, several new advertising agencies specializing in creating and delivering ads to Web sites have emerged. These digital ad agencies work with ad networks, organizations that buy Web space from different sites and resell it to advertisers. Once the Web sites have been lined up by the ad network, the ads themselves are distributed by ad-serving firms, such as DoubleClick.

▲ Media

The final part of the advertising industry consists of the mass media. The media serve as the connection between a company and its customers. The media that are available for advertising include some obvious ones—radio, TV, newspapers, magazines, the Internet—and others that are not so obvious, such as direct mail, billboards, transit cards (bus and car cards), stadium scoreboard ads, point-of-purchase ads, e-mail, chat rooms, and even iPods. Chapters 4, 5, 7, and 10–12 presented an overview of the mainstream mass media and discussed their dependence on various kinds of advertising. This section examines these media from the perspective of an advertiser.

Even the slickest and most imaginative advertising message will fail if it is delivered to the wrong people. To make sure that this does not happen, advertisers employ highly skilled media planners to help them place and schedule their ads.

Advertising specialists evaluate media along four dimensions:

1. *Reach:* How many people can get the message?
2. *Frequency:* How often will the message be received?
3. *Selectivity:* Does the medium actually reach potential customers?
4. *Efficiency:* How much does it cost to reach a certain number of people? (This is usually expressed as cost per thousand people.)

Table 15-2 summarizes how the various media rate on these dimensions.

TABLE 15-2	**CHARACTERISTICS**		**MEDIUM**					
Characteristics of Various Media		**Newspapers**	**Magazines**	**Radio**	**TV**	**Outdoor**	**Direct Mail**	**Internet**
	Reach	High	Low	High	High	High	High	Medium
	Frequency	High	Low	High	High	High	Medium	Medium
	Selectivity	Low	High	High	Medium	Low	High	High
	Efficiency	Medium	Medium	Low	High	High	High	Medium

In addition to considering these factors, advertisers have to take into account many others before deciding on which medium to use. An important part of any decision involves considering the creative limitations imposed by the physical properties of each medium. Television, for example, enables the advertiser to show the product in action. On the other hand, TV ads are short and cannot be used to present a great deal of technical information. A magazine ad can be in full color and can present a large amount of data, but it might not have the same impact as a TV ad. All in all, choosing which media to use in the final advertising mix is a difficult decision.

PRODUCING ADVERTISING

▲ Departments and Staff

There are typically four major departments in a big advertising agency: (1) creative services, (2) account services, (3) marketing services, and (4) administration.

The creative department, as the name implies, actually produces the ad. The people in this department write the advertising **copy** (the headline and message of the ad), choose the illustrations, prepare artwork, and/or supervise the scripting and production of radio, TV, and Web ads.

The account services department is responsible for the relationship between the agency and the client. Because the advertising agency is an organization outside the firm doing the advertising, it is necessary to appoint someone, usually called an *account executive* (AE),

NetFlix is just one of many companies who use pop-up ads. Pop-ups are economical and advertisers think they are effective.

to promote communication and understanding between client and agency. The AE must represent the viewpoint of the agency to the client but at the same time keep abreast of the needs of the advertiser. Since the AE tends to be the person in the middle, his or her job is obviously an important one in the agency.

The marketing services department is responsible for advising the client as to what media to use for his or her messages. Typically, this department makes extensive use of the data collected by the Audit Bureau of Circulations, Arbitron, Nielsen, MediaMetrix, and the other audience research services mentioned in earlier chapters. This department is also in charge of any sales promotions that are done in connection with the advertising. These may include such things as coupons, premiums, and other aids to dealers.

Finally, like any other business, the advertising agency needs a department to take care of the day-to-day administration of the agency. This department is in charge of office management, clerical functions, accounting, personnel, and the training of new employees.

▲ The Advertising Campaign

The best way to illustrate how ads get produced is to present a general discussion of an advertising campaign for a national product. A **campaign** consists of a large number of advertisements, all stressing the same major theme or appeal, that appear in a number of media over a specified time. Following is a discussion, greatly simplified, of the six phases of a typical campaign:

1. Choosing the marketing strategy
2. Selecting the main appeal or theme
3. Translating the theme into the various media
4. Producing the ads
5. Buying space and time
6. Executing and evaluating the campaign

In the first phase, a great deal of research is done to determine the target audience, the marketing objective, the appropriate price for the product or service, and the advertising budget. It is during this phase that the word **positioning** is often heard. Positioning has many interpretations, but in general it means fitting a product or service to one or more segments of the broad market in such a way as to set it apart from the competition without making any change in the product.

For several decades Timex, for example, sold its watches based on their reliability and precision ("Takes a licking but keeps on ticking"), but as more young people use PDA and cell phones to keep track of time, the watch has become more of a personalized fashion accessory. To appeal to today's consumer, Timex attempted to reposition itself as a stylish addition to the modern wardrobe with its "The new faces of Timex" theme to accompany its Color Indiglo lineup of watches.

Similarly, for as long as it had been sold in the United States, Sapporo beer has been associated with sushi bars, and the vast majority of its sales have occurred in Asian-themed restaurants. In 2007 Sapporo tried to reposition itself as a trendy, upscale beer by sponsoring fashion events featuring top urban designers.

Sometimes positioning does not work. Minute Maid orange juice failed in its attempt to reposition its product from simply a breakfast drink to an all-purpose beverage. Despite an $18-million campaign that featured the slogan "Not just for breakfast anymore," sales of orange juice remained flat as customers failed to respond.

Many advertisers like to use well-known celebrities in their ad campaigns. Christina Aguilera, for example, appears in TV commercials for Pepsi and other products.

Media Probe   Ads in Brief

Advertisers must think today's generation has a serious case of attention deficit disorder. In an attempt to fit in with the modern, fast-paced lifestyle, ads on radio and television are getting shorter.

Much shorter.

In fact, some new ads last as long as it took you to read that one-sentence paragraph above this one—about 1 second. That's the length of a "blink" ad being sold by Clear Channel Communication, the largest radio company in the United States. Who would want a 1-second spot? Mini Cooper for one. Its "blink" ad consisted of the toot of a Mini's horn and an announcer saying "Mini."

Compared to a "blink," the 5-second TV minispot put together for Honda must seem like an eternity. The ad quickly shows the features of Honda's new Fit hatchback while a voice says, "The Fit is go." AOL has also created a 5-second spot to tout its new features.

Why the rush? Several reasons. First, the Honda and AOL TV ads are TiVo-proof. The 5-second ads are placed right at the end of a commercial break. To account for viewer reaction time, TiVo and other DVRs have a "jump back" feature that kicks in after the user stops fast-forwarding and backs up the playback a few seconds. With any luck the jump back should put the viewer right into the 5-second spot.

But what about radio? TiVo's not a problem there. What is a problem, however, is that listeners push the button for another station whenever they hear the start of a commercial. With a 1-second ad, you've already heard it before your finger can change the station.

Second, advertisers are looking for ways to break through all of the ad clutter that is found on radio and TV. 1- or 5-second ads stand out because of the novelty effect, and people might even talk about them the next day. Finally, short ads cost less and might be more cost-efficient than longer ads.

On the downside mini-ads can only be used by companies who have well-established brands and memorable tag lines or logos. It would be difficult to cram enough meaningful information in 1 second (or even 5) to help launch a new and unfamiliar product. More seriously, mini-ads may simply increase the commercial clutter. Consumers like TiVo and DVRs because they allow them to skip commercials. These mini-ads might irritate them even more.

(PS: In the time it took you to read this boxed insert, you could have been exposed to approximately 150 blink commercials.)

After the product or service has been positioned, an overall theme for the campaign is developed. Microsoft, for example, settled on the overall theme of "Wow" when it introduced its new Vista operating system in 2007. A consumer competition titled "Show Us Your Wow" gave winners a trip around the world. "Wow" webisodes premiered on Web sites. Several TV spots were created, all with the same ending: A man opens a laptop in a darkened office, as a voice-over says, "Every so often you experience something so new, so delightfully unexpected, there's only one word for it. Wow."

The next phase involves translating the theme into print and broadcast ads. Advertisers try to achieve variety in their ads but with a consistency of approach that will help consumers remember and recognize their product. For example, GEICO, the insurance company, came up with this slogan for its Web site: "So easy a caveman could do it." Its print and TV ads featured a couple of Neanderthalish cavemen registering their dissatisfaction with the slogan and trying to defend themselves against the stereotype of a stupid brute. The Web site even gave people a look at a caveman's rather upscale apartment. The cavemen were so popular that they starred in a sitcom in 2007 on ABC.

The actual production of the ad is done in much the same way that other media content is produced. In the print media the copy, the headline, subheads, any accompanying illustrations, and the layout are first prepared in rough form. The initial step is usually just a thumbnail sketch that can be used to experiment with different arrangements within the ad. The headline might be moved down, the copy moved from right to left, and so on. Next, a **rough layout**—a drawing that is the actual size of the ad—is constructed. Usually, several layouts are prepared, and the best are used to produce the **comprehensive layout,** the one that will be used to produce the ad. Many agencies use outside art studios and printers to help them put together print ads and billboards.

Radio commercials are written and created in much the same way that early radio drama shows were produced. A script is prepared in which dialogue, sound effects, and music are combined to produce whatever effect is desired. The commercial is then either produced in

This may happen to you in the near future. You're standing in line at a movie theater when all of a sudden your cell phone rings with a message that suggests a Coke and some popcorn would help you enjoy your moviegoing experience. Or you could be at the mall when you get a text message alerting you to Old Navy's big sale.

With advertisers finding it increasingly difficult to reach young people through the traditional mass media, it was only a matter of time before they explored the potential of the nearly ubiquitous cell phone as an advertising medium. The industry calls it "mobile marketing," and it takes various forms: text messages and voice, video, and Web ads on Internet-enabled phones.

The efforts in this area are just beginning. Snapple recently sent 25,000 text messages to selected consumers alerting them to a contest that would reward them with prizes if they found lucky bottle caps from Snapple products. Trans World Entertainment (TWE) is testing a system in which consumers with Bluetooth-capable phones are sent text messages about movie trailers and music downloads as soon as they walk into an f.y.e. or Coconuts store. A 2006 survey revealed that almost 90 percent of major advertisers were considering using the cell phone as an advertising tool. Projections suggest that mobile marketing will be a billion-dollar business by 2009.

But what do consumers think about this trend? Most people are irritated when telemarketers interrupt their privacy at home. How will they respond to this possible new intrusion? Not positively, if early indications are typical. One survey disclosed that about 70 percent didn't want ads on their phones. Most were afraid that their cell phones would become as cluttered with ads as their e-mail was with spam.

Faced with this potential resistance, advertisers are looking for ways to make the advertising more attractive. One ad agency is touting the "opt-in" approach—ads will be sent only to those individuals who want them. Another plan offers incentives: Accept ads for a credit on a user's cell phone bill. Consumer groups are also concerned about issues of privacy and intrusiveness raised by cell phone advertising. The Wireless Advertising Industry Association was recently formed to recommend industry guidelines.

As in other areas, advertisers must tread carefully and balance the need to reach consumers with the problems associated with intruding into someone's personal space.

---

the sound studio or recorded live on location. In either case postproduction editing adds any desired special effects, and eventually, a master disc is prepared for duplication and distribution.

The beginning step in the preparation of a television commercial is a **storyboard,** a series of drawings depicting the key scenes of the planned ad. Storyboards are usually shown to the client before production begins. If the client has any objections or suggestions, changes can be made to the script before production. Once the storyboards are approved, the commercial is ready to go into production. Most TV commercials are shot on film (although some are now switching to videotape). Television commercials are the most expensive ads to produce. A 30-second spot can easily cost $350,000. Special effects, particularly animation, can drive the costs even higher. In an effort to keep costs down, much of the time spent producing TV commercials consists of planning and rehearsing. As with the print media, many agencies hire outside production specialists to produce their commercials.

While all this is going on, other members of the creative team are preparing Web ads. Banner ads, pop-ups, and pop-unders are still the most common types of online ads, but other configurations are becoming popular. Splash pages are Web pages that appear before a Web page loads and then disappear a short time later. Skyscraper ads are elongated vertical banners that border one or both sides of a Web page. Floating ads move up, down, or across a page as the user scrolls through a Web site. A wallpaper ad changes the background of the page being viewed. Shorter versions of a TV ad might also be prepared to run on the advertiser's Web site or posted on YouTube.

While the creative department is putting together print, Web, and broadcast ads, the marketing department is buying time in those media judged to be appropriate for the campaign. If the product is seasonal (suntan lotion, snowmobiles), the ads are scheduled to reflect the calendar, appearing slightly before and during the time people might begin buying such items. Other products and services might call for a program of steady advertising throughout the year.

The last phase of the campaign consists of the running of the ads. Testing is done during and after this phase to see if consumers saw and remembered the ads. In addition, sales data are carefully monitored to determine if the campaign had the desired effect on sales.

▲ Advertising Research

Advertising research, which takes place during all phases of the campaign, helps agencies and their clients make informed decisions about their strategy and tactics. **Formative research** is done before the campaign begins to help guide the creative effort. It can take several forms. One is audience definition—identifying the target market, such as "females 18–34" or "all adults." After this is accomplished, audience profiling is done to discover as much as possible about how the target market lives—what they think, what their attitudes are, and how they decide to buy.

The next phase, **message research,** involves pretesting the messages that have been developed for the campaign. At its most basic level, pretesting determines if the audience can actually understand the ads. This type of testing guards against possible double meanings or overlooked sexual connotations that might have eluded the creative staff. In a second type of pretest, researchers show mock-ups of magazines that contain the prototype of the print ad and rough cuts of TV ads to test audiences. Consumers are tested to see whether they recall the main points of the ad and whether their attitude toward the product has shown any change. Some advertising campaigns go through pilot tests in actual markets. A split-cable transmission can show one version of an ad to one group of people and a second version to another group. The ads are compared to see which did a better job. A split-run of a magazine uses the same strategy.

Tracking studies examine how the ads perform during or after the actual campaign. Samples of consumers are studied to see if they recall the ads, if their attitudes about the product have changed, and if they have bought the product or used the service advertised.

THE ECONOMICS OF ADVERTISING

In this section we will examine the economics of advertising on two levels. First, we will look at the total industry and trace expenditures in various media. Second, we will narrow our focus and examine how an advertising agency makes money.

▲ Advertising Volume in Various Media

About $280 billion was spent on advertising in the United States in 2006. Figure 15-1 shows how this money was divided among the various media. Since 1960, newspapers have seen a decrease in their relative share of advertising volumes, as have magazines. Television has shown a significant increase, while radio, outdoor advertising, and direct mail have shown modest growth. The Internet will probably account for more of the pie in the future.

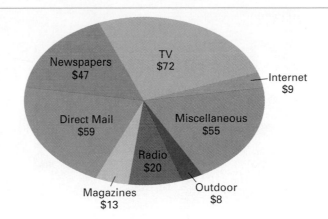

▲ Agency Compensation

Historically, the major mass media have allowed advertising agencies a 15 percent commission on the time and space they purchase. Recently, however, the commission system has been declining in popularity. Many advertisers have struck pay-for-performance deals with ad agencies. Payments to ad agencies are based on sales or some other measure of performance. If sales go up, the ad agency gets more money. Other companies pay agencies a fixed fee, and still others use a combination of a flat fee plus performance-based incentives.

BUSINESS-TO-BUSINESS ADVERTISING

As its name suggests, business-to-business advertising is designed to sell products and services not to general consumers but to other businesses, typically via specialized trade publications, direct mail, e-mail, Web sites, professional journals, and display advertising at trade shows. There are four main categories of business-to-business advertising:

1. *Trade:* Advertising goods and services to wholesalers and retailers who, in turn, resell these items to a more general audience.
2. *Industrial:* Advertising those items that are used in the further production of goods and services, such as copy machines, forklifts, and drill presses.
3. *Professional:* Advertising aimed at doctors, lawyers, architects, nurses, and others who might influence the buying process or use the product in their profession.
4. *Agricultural:* Advertising aimed at farmers and possibly including products such as feed, fertilizer, seed, and chemicals.

Although its visibility might not be high, business-to-business advertising is a multibillion-dollar industry. Some people overlook the potential for a career in business-to-business advertising because they feel it is not as glamorous as consumer advertising. There may be some truth to this: Ads for a chemical solvent, bench-top fermenter, or blast furnace usually are not as flashy as campaigns for sleek new sports cars. In its own way, though, business advertising poses greater creative challenges. Coming up with a theme to sell the sports car is probably much easier than coming up with a winning idea for the chemical solvent.

▲ Consumer Versus Business-to-Business Advertising

There are some obvious differences between advertising directed at consumers and business advertising. In this section we will consider four.

First, the target audience in business advertising is much smaller. In some industries the audience may number in the hundreds. Companies that manufacture storage tanks for

The medium of outdoor advertising has grown rapidly over the past decade. Modern billboards use striking new designs and graphics.

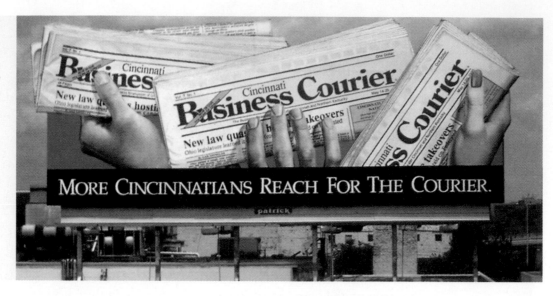

petroleum products, for example, have determined that there are only 400 people in the United States authorized to purchase their product. In other areas, the audience may be in the thousands. This means, of course, that the media used to reach the target market must be selected carefully. In the nuclear reactor business, for instance, everyone in the market may read one or two publications.

Second, most of the products that are advertised tend to be technical, complicated, and high-priced. For the advertiser this means that the ads will probably contain a great deal of technical information and will stress accuracy.

Third, the buyers are professionals—purchasing agents whose only job is to acquire products and services for their company. Generally, the decisions of the purchasing agent are based on reason and research. An error of a penny or two on a large purchase might cost a company thousands of dollars. Consequently, business advertising typically uses the rational approach. Additionally, it is important for advertisers to know exactly who makes buying decisions, since most purchases in large business are generally made in consultation with others in a company.

Fourth, personal selling plays a greater role in the business arena, and advertising is frequently used to support the sales staff in the field. As a result, ad budgets in the business sector may not be as high as those of their consumer counterparts.

▲ Media

The media mix for business advertising is also different from that of consumer advertising. Since the target audience tends to be small, personalized media are best. Business publications tend to be the mainstay of campaigns. One study suggested that about 60 percent of industrial advertising dollars went to business and trade publications. Trade publications can be horizontal, dealing with a job function without regard to industry (such as *Purchasing Agent*), or vertical, covering all job types in an entire industry (such as *LP/Gas*).

Direct mail and e-mail are valuable business advertising tools. Highly differentiated mailing lists can be prepared and ads sent to the most likely prospects. Research has shown that mail is perhaps more effective among businesspeople than among consumers. Whereas a large percentage of direct-mail material is thrown out unopened by the general public, most businesspeople read or at least scan their e-mail and direct-mail ads.

Advertising in trade catalogues is particularly important to companies that sell through distributors rather than via their own sales staff. Since a catalogue is a direct reflection of a company, extra care is taken to make sure it is up-to-date, accurate, and visually appealing.

There is no doubt that advertisers have zeroed in on the child audience. The last few years have seen the growth of kid-specific media: Nickelodeon, Web sites, kid-oriented magazines, movie tie-ins, and even hamburger wrappers. In 2005, about $10 billion was spent on advertising aimed at children.

Part of the reason behind this increase is the fact that kids have become important factors in family buying decisions. First, they have more money to spend. The under-14 set gets allowances, earns money, and receives gifts to the tune of about $20 billion per year. In addition, kids probably influence another $200 billion worth of shopping decisions. Second, the increase in single-parent families and dual-career families means that kids are now making some of the purchasing decisions that were once left to Mom and Dad.

It is not surprising, then, to find that companies are intensifying their efforts to reach this market segment. And it is not just traditional toymakers, cereal companies, and fast-food restaurants that are in the mix. General Motors, for example, placed ads for its new minivan in *Sports Illustrated for Kids* and sent prototype vans to shopping malls where they showed previews of Disney's *Hercules* on a VCR inside the van. GM does not expect many 6-year-olds to go out and buy a van, but the company knows through its research that kids can play an influential role in the decision about which van to buy. In that connection United Air Lines kept its younger travelers happy by serving McDonald's Happy Meals.

Market research that examines children's psychology has been used to help sell goods. Researchers know that 7- and 8-year-olds like to collect things. This urge used to be satisfied by bottle caps, seashells, and baseball cards. More recently, the maker of Beanie Babies cashed in on this urge by creating a large number of different animals to collect, limiting production and discontinuing models to create artificial scarcity.

The marketing even extends into schools. Companies donate money, equipment, and educational materials to schools in return for the opportunity to advertise their products. It all started with Channel One, a news program for students. In return for a donation of electronic equipment, schools agreed to show a newscast that contained commercials. Other companies did not take long to follow Channel One. Nike, for example, mailed out shoe assembly kits to schools. Teachers were supposed to help kids make the sneakers while teaching a lesson on environmentally safe manufacturing (presumably

by companies like Nike). McDonald's sponsored a 7-week curriculum on how to build a McDonald's restaurant and how to interview for a job there. Some school districts, hard up for cash, have sold advertising space on the sides of school buses and in school hallways.

There are many who feel that all this selling to children is not right. They argue that children are an unsophisticated audience and are vulnerable to the flashy, persuasive techniques of the advertising industry. Not many parents would allow a salesperson to come into their home and talk to their kids; why, then, should they allow TV to target their children? Additionally, critics contend that advertising teaches values that are undesirable. Advertising focuses on the superficial and the material, and it glorifies consumption. Finally, critics contend that advertising creates conflicts between parents and children by encouraging kids to pester their parents for all the products they see advertised. Parents must continually say no and run the risk of possible strife. There is some evidence to support these positions (as discussed in Chapter 19). Even without this support, however, many people feel that advertising to kids is just plain wrong.

The advertisers reply that these critics do not give kids enough credit. They feel that kids are more sophisticated consumers than people realize and learn very quickly to see through the hype and manipulation that may be found in some ads. Additionally, the marketing community points out that kids are going to live in a world saturated by advertising. Coming into contact with it at an early age may help them learn how to deal with it when they become adults. Finally, they argue that kids get valuable information about new products and services from advertising, information that improves their lives.

The issue, of course, has legal as well as ethical overtones. To date, the government has weighed in on the side of kids. The Children's Television Act limits the amount of commercial minutes in TV shows that can be directed at children. The government and the tobacco industry worked out an agreement that prohibited the Camel cigarette company from using the cartoon character Joe Camel in its ads because the character appealed to children. There have been proposals to ban or limit beer, wine, and liquor advertising. Despite these efforts it is clear that parents will be the ones to confront this issue head-on.

Business-to-business advertising in the mass media used to be rare, but some large companies, such as FedEx, UPS, and Xerox, have used it to great effect. FedEx, for example, found that its business increased more than 40 percent after it started to advertise in consumer media. Purchasing time and space in the mass media must be done skillfully because of the expense and the chance of wasted coverage if the right decision makers are not in the audience. Specialized cable channels have made it possible for many business-to-business advertisers to use more general media with reduced chances of wasted coverage. CNN's *MoneyLine* and several shows on CNBC, for example, attract an audience that contains many business decision makers. General newsmagazines, such as *Time* and *Newsweek*,

Exceeding Your Expectations

**Cat® 315/315 L:
The New Size in Power
and Efficiency**

To get the highest return on your
machine investment you need an
excavator that will do the job efficiently
and move on to the next job site quickly.
The new Cat 315 is designed to do just
that. With all the performance features
of the Cat 300 Family and a design
which allows it to be hauled on a tag-
along trailer, the new 315 can increase
your productivity. Here are some of
the benefits:

• 300 Family advanced hydraulics with
three Power Mode Settings, three Work
Mode Settings, Automatic Engine Control
and self-diagnostic capabilities for
improved productivity, increased fuel
efficiency and lower maintenance costs.

© 1994 Caterpillar

• 99 FWHP, turbocharged Cat 3046
Engine designed for more efficient,
responsive power and fuel efficiency,
plus reduced sound levels.

• Two undercarriage options, standard
and long (L), both with a maximum
shipping width of less than 9'0" for
hassle-free movement from job to job.

• Three stick options to match your
job needs: 10'2"   8'6"   7'5"

• Standard auxiliary hydraulic valve for
attachment flexibility to do a wider range
of jobs more efficiently.

• New control features, including light-
touch joysticks…automatic low-to-high-
speed travel selection…and winged foot
pedals for easier operation.

• Comfortable, efficient cab with
large windows for excellent visibility…
fully adjustable seat…and sliding
joystick consoles.

All these 300 Family advantages…along
with your Cat Dealer's unsurpassed
service, support and industry-leading
parts network…work together to Exceed
Your Expectations in every way. Stop
in and see the new Cat 315 today!

	315/315 L
Power:	99 FWHP
Operating Weight Up To:	36,000 lb
Ground Level Reach:	30'0"
Maximum Digging Depth:	21'6"
Bucket Capacity Range:	0.68 - 0.97 yd³
Shipping Width, 24" Shoes:	8'6"

CATERPILLAR®

An example of business-to-business advertising. This ad for Caterpillar
industrial equipment contains far more technical information than would be
found in a consumer ad.

along with *Forbes, BusinessWeek*, and *Fortune*, are rather obvious choices for this
type of advertising.

Business advertisers have also increased their use of the Internet. Business-
to-business sites can include large
amounts of technical data, product
descriptions, search engines that allow
customers to find the exact product they
are interested in, and other information
useful to potential purchasers.

▲ Appeals

Close attention is paid to the copy in
business-to-business advertising. Many
consumer ads depend on impression
and style to carry their messages. The
copy tends to be brief and can cater to
the emotions. Business copy tends to
be longer, more detailed, and more factual. A premium is placed on accuracy
and completeness. If the ad contains
technical inaccuracies or exaggerations,
the credibility of the product is compromised. Some of the most-used formats
in business advertising are testimonials,
case histories, new-product news, and
demonstrations.

This is not to say, however, that all
industrial ads must be stodgy and dull.
In recent years several ad agencies specializing in business ads have introduced
warmth, humor, and creativity into their
messages. The philosophy behind this
movement is that businesspeople are
also consumers and that they respond as
consumers to business and trade ads.

ADVERTISING

After a few hard years, the advertising business showed signs of recovery in 2007 as the
general economy improved and the Internet opened up new marketing channels. Employment at U.S. advertising agencies increased about 6 percent from 2006 to 2007, with the
biggest increase coming in jobs related to Web advertising.

▲ Entry-Level Positions

A job applicant must make some basic decisions early in his or her professional training.
Probably the first decision is whether to concentrate on the creative or the business side of
the industry.

The creative side, as mentioned earlier, consists of the copywriters, art directors, graphic
artists, photographers, and broadcast and Web production specialists who put the ads
together. Entry-level jobs include junior copywriter, creative trainee, junior art director,
and production assistant. In most of these positions, a college degree in advertising or the
visual arts is helpful, with a secondary concentration in marketing, English, sociology, or
psychology also a benefit. Good Web skills are also a plus.

The business side of the industry offers careers as account executives, media planners, market researchers, and business managers. Proper preparation for these careers includes extensive course work in both advertising and business, with particular emphasis on marketing. Common entry-level positions in these fields are assistant media buyer, research assistant, junior account executive, and account service trainee.

▲ Upward Mobility

Opportunities for advancement in advertising are excellent. Outstanding performance is rewarded quickly, and many young people progress swiftly through the ranks. Beginning creative people typically become senior copywriters or senior art directors. Eventually, some may progress to creative director, the person in charge of all creative services. On the business side, research assistants and assistant buyers can hope to become research directors and media directors. Account trainees, if they perform according to expectations, move up to account executives and later may become management supervisors. The climb to success can occur rapidly; many agencies are run by people who achieved top status before they reached age 40.

MAIN POINTS

- Advertising is any form of nonpersonal presentation and promotion of ideas, goods, and services paid for by an identified sponsor.

- Advertising can be classified by target audience, geographic focus, and purpose.

- Modern advertising began in the late 19th century and grew during the early 20th century as magazines and radio became mass advertising media.

- After World War II, advertising grew at a fast rate, particularly when TV came on the scene.

- The past two decades have seen the start of new channels for advertising, including cable TV and the Internet. Online advertising has grown in the past few years. It consists of banner ads, pop-ups, and Web sites.

- The three main components of the advertising industry are advertisers, agencies, and the media.

- Advertising agencies put together large-scale campaigns for clients, consisting of a market strategy, theme, ads, media time/space, and evaluation.

- Although not as visible as consumer advertising, business-to-business advertising makes up a significant portion of the industry.

QUESTIONS FOR REVIEW

1. What are the three defining characteristics of advertising?

2. Briefly describe the three main components of the advertising industry.

3. Describe the main types of online advertising.

4. What is positioning? Why is it important to advertisers?

5. How does consumer advertising differ from business-to-business advertising?

QUESTIONS FOR CRITICAL THINKING

1. What would society be like without advertising?

2. Is it right to advertise to children? If you think it is appropriate to advertise to children, what special considerations, if any, should be applied to such ads?

3. Check the national media for ongoing advertising campaigns. What are some themes that are currently running?

4. How can you tell if an advertising campaign has been effective?

5. Will "viral marketing" be around 5 years from now? Why or why not?

6. Review the boxed insert "Cultural Meaning and Trade Characters," and then consider the following. Why do

marketers want us to have emotional connections to mass-produced products? Does the AFLAC duck make you feel more positive toward insurance? In addition to the Aunt Jemima example, how are expectations for and stereotypes of race and gender reflected in trade characters?

KEY TERMS

target audience (p. 336)
consumer advertising (p. 336)
business-to-business advertising (p. 336)
primary demand ad (p. 337)
selective demand ad (p. 337)
direct action ad (p. 337)
indirect action ad (p. 337)
advertising agency (p. 339)

viral advertising (p. 342)
national advertisers (p. 343)
retail advertisers (p. 343)
agency (p. 344)
full-service agency (p. 344)
media buying service (p. 344)
creative boutique (p. 345)
copy (p. 346)
campaign (p. 347)

positioning (p. 347)
rough layout (p. 348)
comprehensive layout (p. 348)
storyboard (p. 349)
formative research (p. 350)
message research (p. 350)
tracking studies (p. 350)

INTERNET RESOURCES

Online Learning Center

At the Online Learning Center home page, www.mhhe.com/dominick10, *select* Student Center *and then* Chapter 15.

1. Use the Learning Objectives, Chapter Outline, Main Points, and Time Line sections to review this chapter.

2. Test your knowledge of the chapter using the multiple choice, crossword puzzle, and flashcard features of the site.

3. Expand your knowledge of concepts and topics discussed in the chapter by going to Suggestions for Further Reading and Internet Exercises.

Surfing the Internet

The following sites represent just a small sample of the hundreds and hundreds of sites that are relevant to this chapter. All were current as of late 2007. Keep in mind, however, that ad sites change rapidly.

www.aaaa.org
Home of the American Association of Advertising Agencies. Contains agency news, career information, and awards programs.

www.adage.com
Advertising Age is the leading trade publication for the industry. Its Web page has current news, useful statistics, and critiques of Web site advertising.

www.cavemanscrib.com
See how the other half (the Neanderthal half) lives, courtesy of GEICO.

www.ddb.com
DDB is an ad agency that handles Bud Light and Volkswagen. At first glance the site does not look like that of an ad agency, but do not let it fool you. A sampling of the agency's current and past award-winning work is available.

www.clioawards.com
The Clios are advertising's counterparts to the Oscars. This site has a listing of winners and a searchable archive.

www.royalcaribbean.com
The cruise line's Web site emphasizes information rather than a hard sell.

PART IV

REGULATION OF THE MASS MEDIA

CHAPTER 16

FORMAL CONTROLS: LAWS, RULES, REGULATIONS

This chapter will prepare you to:

- define *prior restraint*

- understand the special protective privileges of reporters

- distinguish among *libel, slander, libel per se,* and *libel per quod*

- explain how invasion of privacy can occur

- describe copyright law

- recognize the impact of media regulation of the Internet

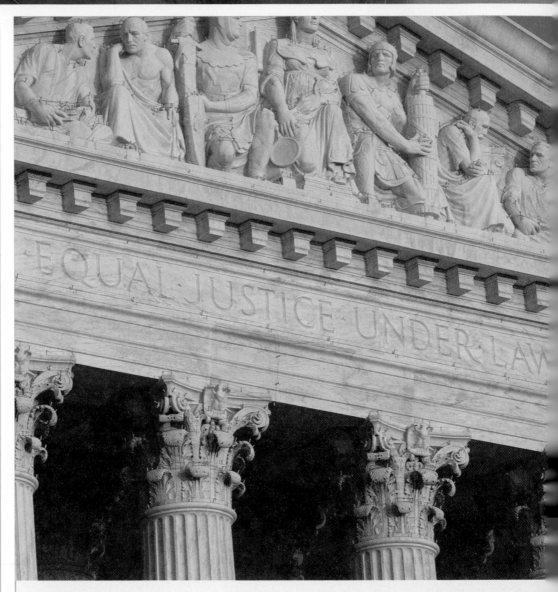

Over the years court decisions have had a major impact on the operations of mass media.

For purposes of this chapter, formal controls over the media include laws, court decisions that refine those laws, and rules and regulations administered by government agencies. We will discuss six different areas in which these formal controls are important: (1) the controversy over a free system of mass communication, (2) copyright, (3) restrictions on obscenity and pornography, (4) regulation of radio and television, (5) regulation of the Internet, and (6) regulation of advertising. Unfortunately, many students have the idea that the field of mass communication law and regulations is dull and boring. Nothing could be further from the truth. In what other academic field could you read about raunchy magazines, the CIA, mass murderers, women in men's locker rooms, four-letter words, juicy divorces, and a man who owned a submarine?

THE PRESS, THE LAW, AND THE COURTS

▲ A Free Press

As noted in Chapter 4, the idea of a free press did not catch on at first in America. The early colonial papers had problems if they were not "published by authority"—that is, if they were not open to censorship by the Crown. Through the Stamp Act the British government attempted to suppress dissent by taxing printed matter. Recognizing these dangers to a free press, the framers of the Constitution added an amendment (the **First Amendment**) that stated in part that "Congress shall make no law . . . abridging the freedom of speech, or of the press." The precise meaning and interpretation of these words, however, have been open to some debate. Let us examine some key instances in which press and government have come into conflict.

▲ Prior Restraint

When the government censors the press by restraining it from publishing or broadcasting material, that act is called **prior restraint.** Attempts at prior restraint have been relatively rare. Nonetheless, this area does illustrate that the provisions in the First Amendment are not absolute. The Supreme Court has ruled that under certain circumstances prior restraint or censorship of the press is permitted, but the government faces a difficult task in proving that the restraint is justified. There are some obvious examples of legal censorship. During wartime a newspaper could be prevented from publishing the sailing schedules of troop transports, and a radio station could be prohibited from broadcasting the location and numbers of soldiers on the front lines. Other attempts at prior restraint have not been particularly successful; the Supreme Court has generally upheld the right of freedom of the press. There are two seminal cases in this area that are beneficial for us to examine. One is not widely known; the other made the front pages.

The Near Case   During the 1920s the Minnesota legislature passed a law under which newspapers that were considered public nuisances could be curtailed by means of an **injunction** (an order from a court that requires somebody to do something or refrain from doing something). The motives behind this law may have been praiseworthy because it appears to have been designed to prevent abusive attacks on minority groups. Using this public nuisance law, a county attorney sought an injunction against the *Saturday Press* and the paper's manager, J. M. Near, on the grounds that the paper had printed malicious statements about city officials in connection with gangland activities allegedly controlled by minority groups. In 1931 the Supreme Court ruled that the Minnesota law was unconstitutional. Said the Court,

> *The fact that for approximately 150 years there has been almost an entire absence of attempts to impose previous restraints upon publications relating to the malfeasance of public officers is significant of the deep-seated conviction that such restraints would violate constitutional rights.*

This issue would not be raised again for 40 years.

The Pentagon Papers   U.S. Attorney General John Mitchell was eager to see the Sunday, June 13, 1971, edition of the *New York Times*. Mitchell had attended the wedding of President Richard Nixon's daughter Tricia the day before, and he wanted to see how the *Times* had covered it. On the left side of page 1, Mitchell saw a flattering picture of the president with his daughter on his arm. Next to the wedding picture, another story caught Mitchell's eyes: "Vietnam Archive: Pentagon Study Traces 3 Decades of Growing U.S. Involvement." As Mitchell read further, he realized that the *Times* article was sure to cause problems.

The basis for the story in the *Times* began 3 years earlier when Secretary of Defense Robert McNamara became disillusioned with the Vietnam War and ordered a massive study of its origins. This study, known eventually as the Pentagon Papers, was put together by 36 different people and ran to more than 7,000 pages. The final report was classified

The first installment of the Pentagon Papers appeared in the *New York Times*. Attempts by the government to halt further publication ended when the Supreme Court ruled in favor of the *Times*.

Source: © 1971 by the New York Times Company.

"Top Secret—Sensitive." During April 1971, one of those Pentagon staff members who compiled the report leaked a copy to a reporter for the *New York Times*. After much study and secrecy, the paper was ready to publish the story in nine installments. The U.S. Justice Department, under John Mitchell's direction, asked a U.S. district court judge to halt publication of the stories on the grounds that they would "cause irreparable injury to the defense interests of the United States." The order was granted, and for the first time in history, a U.S. paper was ordered by the courts to suppress a specific story. By then, however, other newspapers had obtained copies of some or all of the Pentagon documents and started publishing them. The Justice Department sought more restraining orders, but as soon as one paper was ordered to stop publishing, another newspaper in another part of the country would pick up the series. It was obvious that the Supreme Court would eventually have to intervene.

The Court did intervene and with uncharacteristic haste. On June 30, 1971, only 17 days after the story first appeared and only 4 days after hearing oral arguments on the case, the Court decided in favor of the newspapers' right to publish the information. Naturally, the staff at the *New York Times* was delighted. The paper called the decision a "ringing victory for freedom under law." Upon closer examination, however, the victory was not quite as ringing as it was made out to be. The Court did not state that prior restraint could never be invoked against the press. Instead, it pointed out that the government "carries a heavy burden of showing justification" for imposing restraint. The government, in the opinion of the Court, had not shown sufficient grounds for doing this. The government was free, if it wished, to bring other prior restraint cases to the courts to establish exactly how much justification it needed to stifle publication. In addition, each of the nine judges wrote a separate opinion that highlighted the ambiguities and complexities surrounding this topic.

More Recent Cases   After the release of the Pentagon Papers, the prior restraint issue cropped up several times in cases involving ex–CIA agents. In one case the CIA was successful in having portions of a book deleted because they revealed classified information.

In 1983 a principal in Hazelwood, Missouri, deleted from a high school paper an article that dealt with teenage pregnancy and another article about divorce, on the grounds that they were inappropriate. Three student journalists, with the help of the American Civil Liberties Union, filed suit claiming that their First Amendment rights had been violated. The Supreme Court eventually decided the case in favor of the school system. The Court held that since the paper was part of the high school's journalism curriculum and used school supplies and its staff was restricted to journalism students, it was not a public forum and not entitled to First Amendment protection.

Until recently, it appeared that the college press merited more protection. In the fall of 2002, the dean of student affairs and services at Governors State University in Illinois informed the printer of the college's newspaper that prior approval by a university official was required before the paper was printed. The student editors of the paper filed a lawsuit and won a victory when a three-judge panel ruled that the decision in the Hazelwood case did not apply to college newspapers. In 2005, however, the U.S. Court of Appeals reversed that decision declaring that since the newspaper was subsidized by funds from the university, it did not qualify as a public forum. The Supreme Court refused to grant an appeal in the case. Although some states have passed laws providing some degree of protection to student journalists, it appears that high school and college press is entitled to less than the full protection of the First Amendment.

In 1999 a ruling by a district court judge held that the prohibition against prior restraint also included Web sites. The creator of a Web site devoted to news about the Ford Motor Company had posted documents obtained from Ford employees. The company had obtained a ruling that prevented the documents from being posted, but the ruling by the district court judge overturned that prohibition.

Prior restraint received some judicial support in the wake of the rape trial of basketball star Kobe Bryant in 2004. A court reporter mistakenly sent transcripts of confidential proceedings to several media outlets. Upon learning of the error, a judge ordered all copies destroyed and threatened to hold anyone who published the contents in contempt of court. Reporters asked the Colorado Supreme Court to invalidate the order, but the court upheld the restraint, saying that the state's interest in keeping the material secret justified the prior restraint. Further legal action was halted when the judge made public most of the information contained in the transcripts.

More recently, in 2004 an Alabama district court turned down a government request for prior restraint against a Web site that published the names of investigators for the Drug Enforcement Agency. The court ruled that although the site might make some people uncomfortable it did not present a threat so serious as to justify prior restraint. In 2005 an appeals court ruled that a judge could not prevent the press from publishing the names of potential jurors who were identified in open court.

In sum, there is a strong constitutional case against prior restraint, but gray areas exist in which censorship might be legal. These areas will probably remain ambiguous until further court cases help define the limits of government authority. It is likely, however, that the barriers against prior restraint will remain formidable.

PROTECTING NEWS SOURCES

Before we begin an examination of this topic, it is important to consider that the issues are fairly complicated. Conflicting interests are involved. Reporters argue that if they are forced to disclose confidential sources those sources will dry up and the public's right to know will be adversely affected. Government arguments cite the need for the administration of justice and the rights of an individual to a fair trial.

Perhaps a hypothetical example will help bring these issues into focus. Suppose you are a reporter for a campus newspaper. One of your sources calls you late one night and informs you that several students are running a drug ring that has monopolized the sale of illegal drugs on campus. To check the accuracy of this report, you call another one of your sources, one who in the past has given you reliable information on campus drug dealing. This second source confirms what your caller told you and adds more details. For obvious reasons both of your sources ask not to be identified, and you agree. On the basis of these reports and some additional research, you publish a lengthy article in the campus newspaper about the drug ring. A few days later you are summoned before a grand jury that is investigating criminal drug dealings. You are asked to reveal your sources. If you refuse, you will be charged with contempt and possibly fined or sent to jail. What do you do?

▲ The Reporter's Privilege

Other reporters have found themselves in the same fix. One was Paul Branzburg. In 1969 Branzburg wrote a story for the *Louisville Courier-Journal* in which he described how two local residents were synthesizing hashish from marijuana. His article stated that he had promised not to reveal their identities. Shortly thereafter, Branzburg was subpoenaed (ordered to appear) by the county grand jury. He refused to answer questions about his sources, claiming, in part, that to do so would violate the First Amendment provision for freedom of the press. The case ultimately reached the Supreme Court, which ruled that the First Amendment did not protect reporters from the obligation to testify before grand juries to answer questions concerning a criminal investigation.

Initially, this ruling was viewed as a setback for reporters' rights. However, the Court did suggest some situations in which the reporter's claim to privilege would be valid. These included harassment of news reporters, instances in which grand juries do not operate in good faith, and situations in which there is only a remote connection between the investigation and the information sought. Additionally, the Court suggested that Congress and the states could further define the rights of a reporter to protect sources by enacting legislation (called **shield laws**) to that effect.

After the Branzburg decision, state courts were somewhat inconsistent in their rulings. On the one hand, several cases upheld the reporter's right to keep her or his sources secret. In Florida, Lucy Ware Morgan, a reporter for the *St. Petersburg Times*, refused to disclose her source for a story about a grand jury report on corruption in city government. She was promptly convicted of contempt of court and received a 90-day jail sentence. In 1976, however, the Florida Supreme Court overturned the conviction. Using the Branzburg decision as a guideline, the court concluded that the name of her source was not relevant to the investigation of a crime and that the contempt charge was designed to harass her.

Other decisions have narrowly defined the test of relevancy between the case at hand and the reporter's sources. In Virginia a newspaper reporter refused to identify a source during testimony at a 1978 murder trial. The lawyer for the accused argued that the source was needed to question the credibility of a prosecution witness. The Virginia Supreme Court ruled in favor of the reporter and stated that a reporter's privilege must yield only when the defendant's need for the information is essential. To be essential, said the court, the information had to (1) relate directly to the defendant's guilt or innocence, (2) bear on the reduction of an offense, or (3) concern the mitigation of a sentence.

Just because these cases are taken from the 1970s, do not get the idea that reporters no longer go to jail or get fined. From 1999 to 2000, three reporters in California, a state with what many experts consider the strongest shield law in the country, got into legal trouble when they failed to reveal confidential sources of information. One journalist went to jail for 5 days, and another was fined $1,000 a day for every day he refused to testify. Fortunately for the reporters, either the sanctions were overturned on appeal or the original requests were dropped. Finally, there is the complicated case of Judith Miller of the *New York Times* and Matthew Cooper of *Time*. The two were subpoenaed and ordered to reveal their confidential sources during an investigation by the Justice Department probing who leaked the name of a covert CIA operative to a newspaper columnist. The reporters declined to cooperate and turned to the legal system for protection. Two federal courts ruled against them, and in mid-2005 the Supreme Court declined to review the case, raising the possibility that the two could serve up to 18 months in prison. In the wake of the Court's action, Cooper's source released him from his promise of confidentiality. Miller, however, began serving a jail term. Miller was eventually released from jail when she was satisfied that her source had granted permission to reveal his name.

Reporters for the *San Francisco Chronicle* published information leaked from grand jury testimony during investigations concerning the use of performance-enhancing drugs by athletes. In 2006 a new grand jury ordered the reporters to reveal their sources. The reporters appealed the order, but a district court judge ruled that they had to comply with the grand jury's instructions or face a lengthy jail term. The source of the story eventually came forward, and the matter came to a close.

The above examples suggest that the nation's courts are taking a more skeptical view of the media's claim to privilege when it comes to revealing sources. In that connection media organizations are counseling reporters to be careful when making promises of confidentiality.

As of 2007, 32 states and the District of Columbia had shield laws. Journalists generally recognize these laws as helpful, but most realize that they are not the powerful protectors of the press that many had hoped for. In addition, the laws themselves represent a bewildering collection of provisions, qualifications, and exceptions. Some states protect only confidential material; some protect the reporter from revealing the name of a source but do not protect the information obtained from sources. Other state laws confer less protection if the reporter is involved in a libel case. In some states shield laws do not apply to reporters subpoenaed by a grand jury. Further, many courts are interpreting the shield laws on a case-by-case basis and ignoring or limiting the interpretation of judgments contained in the law. A federal shield law was introduced in Congress in 2007, but prospects for its passage were dim.

▲ Search and Seizure

Finally, there is the troublesome question of protecting notes and other records that might disclose sources or other information relevant to an investigation. In this regard the courts have offered little protection. Three particular cases have disturbed the news media.

In the first case, in 1971, four police officers entered the offices of the *Stanford Daily*, the campus newspaper of Stanford University, and produced a warrant authorizing them to search for photographs of a clash between demonstrators and police that the *Daily* had covered the day before. The newspaper brought suit against the authorities, charging that its First Amendment rights had been violated. In 1978 the Supreme Court ruled that the search was legal. (In 1980, however, Congress extended some protection to newsrooms by passing a bill that would require the government to secure a subpoena to obtain records held by reporters. The scope of a subpoena is somewhat more limited than that of a search warrant. In addition, a subpoena can be challenged.)

In the second case, the U.S. Court of Appeals in the District of Columbia decided another case that further eroded reporters' rights to protect sources. In 1974 the Reporters Committee for Freedom of the Press filed suit against AT&T because the company would not pledge to keep records of reporters' toll calls safe from government scrutiny. (An analysis of these calls might help locate a reporter's source of information.) The court of appeals ruled that it was legal for the government to examine such records without a reporter's knowledge or consent. Another court of appeals ruling in 2006 reinforced this viewpoint when it ruled that the phone records of two *New York Times* reporters who refused to cooperate with a grand jury investigation were not protected by privilege. The court declared that the government's need for the records took precedence over First Amendment concerns.

The third case involved *New York Times* reporter Myron Farber. During 1976 Farber had been reporting on the investigation into mysterious deaths at a New Jersey hospital. The stories led to the indictment of a prominent physician on charges of poisoning five patients. Defense lawyers ultimately subpoenaed notes and documents pertaining to the case that were held by Farber and the *Times*. Both Farber and the paper refused to provide the documents, and both were convicted of contempt of court. Farber was sentenced to 6 months in jail and a $1,000 fine; the *Times* was slapped with a $100,000 fine and was ordered to pay $5,000 every day until it complied with the court's order. The *Times* ultimately turned over its files, but a judge ruled that the paper had "sanitized" them by removing some relevant material, so it reinstated the fine. Farber, meanwhile, had spent 27 days in jail. Eventually,

Farber wound up spending 40 days in jail, and the *Times* paid $285,000 in fines. All penalties finally ended with the jury's verdict that the physician was innocent.

In 2005 a freelance journalist/blogger was ordered by a grand jury to turn over to authorities outtakes from videos that he had shot of a violent demonstration in which a police officer was injured. The blogger refused and eventually served 7½ months in federal prison before his lawyer worked out a compromise with prosecutors.

The privacy of computer-stored messages and e-mail received protection from the Electronic Communication Privacy Act, which requires the government to obtain a search warrant before examining online or stored messages intended to be private.

Perhaps the safest conclusion that we can draw is that a reporter's privilege in protecting sources and notes is not absolute. Even those decisions that have favored journalists have been qualified. It also appears that further developments in this area will be put together on a piece-by-piece basis by lower courts unless the Supreme Court issues a precise decision or Congress passes a comprehensive law. As for reporters, they must carefully consider these issues when they promise confidentiality to a news source.

COVERING THE COURTS

On the one hand, the Sixth Amendment guarantees a defendant the right to a trial before an impartial jury; on the other, the First Amendment guarantees freedom of the press. Trial judges are responsible for the administration of justice; reporters are responsible for informing the public about the workings of the legal system. Sometimes these responsibilities clash.

▲ Publicity Before and During a Trial

If a potential jury member has read, seen, or heard stories in the news media about a defendant that appear to indicate that person's guilt, it is possible that the defendant will not receive a fair trial. Although research has not produced definitive evidence linking pretrial publicity to prejudice, this concern has been at the heart of several court decisions that have castigated the news media for trying cases in the newspaper or on television instead of in the courtroom.

The 1960s saw a flurry of cases suggesting that the Supreme Court was taking a close look at pretrial publicity. In 1961 the Court for the first time reversed a criminal conviction entirely because pretrial publicity had made it impossible to select an impartial jury. The case concerned Leslie Irvin, a rather unsavory character who was arrested and charged with six murders. Newspapers carried police-issued press releases that said "Mad Dog" Irvin had confessed to all six killings. The local media seized upon this story with a vengeance, and many stories referred to Irvin as the "confessed slayer of six." Of the 430 potential jurors examined by attorneys, 90 percent had formed opinions about Irvin's guilt—

High-profile criminal cases can illustrate the tension between the First and Sixth Amendments. Jurors in the Phil Spector murder trial were instructed not to read or to watch reports about the trial.

opinions that ranged from suspicion to absolute certainty that he was guilty. Irvin was convicted—hardly a surprise—and sentenced to death. After six years of complicated legal maneuvers, made even more complicated by Irvin's escape from prison, the case went before the Supreme Court. The Court ruled that the pretrial publicity had ruined the defendant's chances for a fair trial and sent the case back to be retried. (Irvin, who had been recaptured, was again found guilty, but this time was sentenced to life imprisonment.)

Perhaps the most famous case of pretrial publicity concerned an Ohio physician. On July 4, 1954, the wife of Cleveland-area osteopath Dr. Sam Sheppard was found slain in the couple's home. Sheppard became a prime suspect, and the news media, especially the Cleveland newspapers, were impatient for his arrest. "Why Isn't Sam Sheppard in Jail?" and "Why Don't Police Quiz Top Suspect?" were headlines that appeared over page-one editorials. News reports carried the results of alleged scientific tests that cast doubt on Sheppard's version of the crime (these tests were never brought up at the trial). Articles stressed Sheppard's extramarital affairs as a possible motive for the crime. After his arrest the news stories and editorials continued. There were enough of them with headlines such as "Dr. Sam Faces Quiz at Jail on Marilyn's Fear of Him" and "Blood Is Found in Garage" to fill five scrapbooks. Every juror but one admitted to reading about the story in the newspapers. The sensationalized coverage continued during the trial itself, which produced a guilty verdict. Twelve years later the Supreme Court reversed Sheppard's conviction because of the extremely prejudicial publicity. This case assumed added importance because the Court listed six safeguards that judges might invoke to prevent undue influence from publicity. These safeguards included sequestering the jury (that is, moving them into seclusion), moving the case to another county, and placing restrictions on statements made by lawyers, witnesses, or others who might have damaging information.

▲ Gag Rules

Some judges have issued restrictive orders, or **gag rules,** that restrain the participants in a trial (attorneys, witnesses, defendants) from giving information to the media or that limit media coverage of events that occur in court. For example, a superior court judge in a Washington murder trial ordered reporters to report only on events that occurred in front of a jury. Two reporters violated this rule by writing about events that took place in the courtroom while the jury was not present; they were subsequently charged with contempt. The Washington State Supreme Court refused to review this ruling.

The whole question of gag rules reached the Supreme Court in 1976. A Nebraska judge had prohibited reporters from revealing certain information about a mass murder case. The Nebraska Press Association appealed the order to the Supreme Court. The Court ruled on the side of the association and held that reporting of judicial proceedings in open court cannot be prohibited. Once again, upon first examination, this rule appeared to be a significant victory for the press. As time passed, however, it became apparent that the Nebraska decision had left the way open for court-ordered restrictions on what the trial participants could say to the press. It seemed to indicate that some legal proceedings, primarily those that take place before the actual trial begins, might be legitimately closed to the public. By the early 1980s this was exactly what was happening. Although the press was left free to report what it chose, its news sources were muzzled by judicial order. During the late 1970s judges began holding pretrial hearings in private to limit pretrial publicity. A 1979 Supreme Court decision held this practice to be constitutional. In 1980 the Court went on record as stating that the press did, in fact, have a constitutional right to attend criminal trials. *Pretrial* events, however, might still be closed. Because many criminal cases are settled out of court, these pretrial hearings are often the only public hearings held.

In the 1980s the press gained wider access to court proceedings. In 1984 the Supreme Court ruled that the jury selection process should be open to the press except in extreme circumstances, and it established standards that judges must meet before they can close a pretrial hearing. A 1986 Supreme Court decision, however, gave the press a major victory in its efforts to secure access to pretrial proceedings. The Court held that preliminary trial proceedings must be open to the press unless the judge could demonstrate a "substantial probability that the defendant's right to a fair trial would be violated." Additionally, lower courts have held that the First Amendment right of access to trials extends to documents used as evidence. Also in 1986, the Supreme Court ruled that the jury selection process, as well as the trial itself, must ordinarily be open to the public. The Court provided a set of strict guidelines that would justify a private selection of a jury.

In summary, Supreme Court decisions do not give the press an absolute right of access to all court proceedings. Some parts of trials and pretrial hearings may still be closed if the judge can fulfill the Court's guidelines regarding closure. Further, the recent Court decisions

In 1935, nearly 3 years after the crime, Bruno Hauptmann was tried for the kidnapping and murder of the 19-month-old son of national hero Charles Lindbergh. The trial was held in the small town of Flemington, New Jersey. When it opened, more than 150 reporters were packed into a small area reserved for the press. During the trial this number swelled to about 700, and members of the press corps prowled the corridors and surrounding rooms of the courthouse in an attempt to cover every aspect of the trial. Photography during the trial was forbidden, but photographers were allowed in the courthouse, and some were even allowed in the courtroom itself to take pictures when the trial was not in session.

As the trial progressed, the overcrowding worsened, and it became obvious that the trial had turned into a media event. The ban against photography during court sessions was broken, but nothing was done about it. A newsreel motion picture camera was placed in the balcony of the courtroom, and despite a promise from the newsreel people that they would not take films during the trial, footage was taken of the testimony of Lindbergh, Hauptmann, and others. The film was shown in movie theaters throughout the country. Photographers, many of them freelancers, became more aggressive as the trial progressed and contributed to a general lack of courtroom decorum. The crush of reporters also aggravated the already severe overcrowding in the courtroom.

The crowds got so bad that the attorneys for both sides subpoenaed their friends in order to make sure that they got into the courtroom. One radio reporter, Gabriel Heatter, had no problem getting a seat. The judge's wife enjoyed his broadcasts so much that she prevailed on the judge to give Heatter a place in the front row. In an attempt to scoop the opposition, an Associated Press employee rigged a secret radio transmitter inside the courtroom.

Out of this confusion and carnival-like atmosphere came Canon 35, a rule adopted by the American Bar Association that limited courtroom reporting by photographers and radio and TV reporters. Controversies that started in that overcrowded courtroom in Flemington are still debated today.

---

have not changed the legal status surrounding the privacy of grand jury hearings—they continue to have the right to secrecy. All in all, it might be safe to conclude that the press has been given a green light to report on matters that occur in open court with little fear of reprisal. But gag orders on news sources and the closing of various legal proceedings threaten to be areas of tension between the press and the judiciary for some time to come.

▲ Cameras and Microphones in the Courtroom

For many years the legal profession looked with disfavor on the idea of cameras and microphones in the courtroom. There was a time when this attitude may have been entirely justified. The whole problem seems to have begun in 1935 when Bruno Hauptmann was put on trial for the kidnapping and murder of the son of national hero Charles Lindbergh. Remember that news photography and radio journalism were still young in 1935, and this fact may have contributed to some of the abuses that occurred during this trial (see the boxed insert "Canon 35 and the Hauptmann Trial"). After the trial the American Bar Association added Canon 35 to its Canons of Professional Ethics. This provision stated that the taking of photographs in the courtroom and the broadcasting (later amended to include telecasting) of court proceedings should not be permitted. Although Canon 35 was not law, its language or some variation of it was adopted as law by every state except Colorado and Texas.

In 1965 the Supreme Court entered the picture when it ruled on the Billie Sol Estes case. Estes was on trial in Texas for allegedly swindling several farmers. The trial judge, over Estes's objections, had allowed the televising of the trial. Estes was found guilty, but he soon appealed that decision to the Supreme Court on the grounds that the presence of television had deprived him of a fair trial. The high court agreed with Estes and argued for the prohibition of television cameras in the courtroom. The Court said that broadcasting a trial would have a prejudicial impact on jurors, would distract witnesses, and would burden the trial judge with new responsibilities. However, the Court went on, there might come a day when broadcast technology would become portable and unobtrusive and television coverage so commonplace that trials might be broadcast. Thus, the decision in the Estes case was not a blanket provision against the televising of trials.

Since 1965 the trend has been toward a general relaxation of the tension between the legal profession and the electronic press. In 1972 the American Bar Association adopted a new code of professional responsibility. Canon 3A(7) of this document superseded the old

Canon 35. Canon 3A(7) maintained the ban on taking photographs and broadcasting in the courtroom, but it did allow the judge the discretion to permit televising a trial to a pressroom or to another courtroom to accommodate an overflow crowd. In 1981 the Supreme Court ruled that broadcast coverage of a criminal trial is not inherently prejudicial, thereby clearing the way for the presence of radio and TV in the courtroom. The Court left it up to the states to devise their own systems for implementing such coverage.

As of 2007, all 50 states allowed some form of coverage. The rules for coverage vary state by state. In Georgia, for example, the judge may permit one television camera in the courtroom. In Ohio trial courts, coverage of nonconsenting victims and witnesses is prohibited. Cameras are not allowed in federal district courts or at Supreme Court proceedings.

REPORTERS' ACCESS TO INFORMATION

▲ Government Information

Reporting the doings of the government can be a frustrating task if the government insists that information about its activities be kept secret. After World War II many members of the press complained that government secrecy was becoming a major problem. Reporters were being restricted from meetings, and access to many government documents was difficult to obtain. Under continuing pressure from journalists and consumer groups, Congress passed the **Freedom of Information Act (FOIA)** in 1966. This law gave the public the right to discover what the federal government was up to—with certain exceptions. The law states that every federal executive-branch agency must publish instructions on what methods a member of the public should follow to get information. If information is improperly withheld, a court can force the agency to disclose what is sought. There are nine areas of exemptions covering material that does not have to be made public, including trade secrets, files of law enforcement investigations, and maps of oil wells. In 2007 a bill was introduced in Congress to streamline the FOIA and make it easier for the public to access government records.

In 1996 the Electronic Freedom of Information Act (EFOIA) was passed to make more information available on the Internet. Currently, many government agency Web sites contain a variety of information, ranging from statistics to press releases, that can be accessed online rather than through an FOIA request. Nonetheless, many agencies have been slow to fully implement the requirements of the EFOIA.

A "Sunshine Act" ensures that regular meetings of approximately 50 federal government agencies will be open to the public. There are, however, 10 different situations that might permit an agency to meet behind closed doors, so the right of access to meetings is far from absolute. In addition, many states have their own versions of laws pertaining to information access and open meetings. The degree of compliance with these laws varies widely from state to state.

In the aftermath of the September 11 terrorist attacks, concerns about safety and security came into conflict with guarantees of press freedom. The **USA Patriot Act,** passed in October 2001, gave the government more power to access e-mail and telephone records. This increased monitoring power can be used not only to track terrorists but also to eavesdrop on journalists. In addition, the new law makes it easier for the government to restrict access to official records, and another provision prevents the press from finding out about FBI searches of books bought in bookstores or borrowed from libraries by those suspected of terrorist activities.

▲ Access to News Scenes

We have already examined the issue of access in our discussion of the right of the press to attend certain judicial proceedings. But what about the reporters' right of access to news settings outside the courtroom? The law here appears to be in the developmental stage. In the few decisions that have been handed down, the courts have given little support to the notion that the First Amendment guarantees a right of access. In separate rulings the courts have declared that journalists may be sued for invasion of privacy, for trespassing on private property, and for disobeying a police officer's legitimate command to clear the way at the scene of a serious automobile accident. Three of the most relevant Supreme Court opinions have focused on the question of access to prisons and prisoners. In these cases the courts have ruled that reporters do not have the right to visit specific parts of a prison, to speak to specific prisoners, or to bring cameras inside. In general, the Court seems to be saying that the access rights of the press are not different from the access rights of the general public. When the public is not admitted, neither is the press.

Some rulings, however, have recognized a limited right of access. A Florida court said that journalists who are customarily invited by police onto private property to view a news scene cannot be prosecuted for trespassing. The courts have also allowed access to news settings in order to halt discrimination among journalists. For example, in one case it was ruled that a female journalist could not be barred from entering a baseball team's locker room if male reporters had been admitted. In sum, the final words on this topic have yet to be written by the courts. A case as influential as the Branzburg or Estes decision has yet to be adjudicated in the area of press access. It is a good bet, however, that such a test will not be long in surfacing.

DEFAMATION

As the preceding discussion makes clear, in its news-gathering activities the press often collides with the government. In addition, the right of free speech and the rights of a free press sometimes come into conflict with the right of an individual to protect his or her reputation. Protection for a person's reputation is found under the laws that deal with **defamation.**

To understand this somewhat complicated area, let us start with some general definitions:

- **Libel:** Libel is written defamation that tends to injure a person's reputation or good name or that diminishes the esteem, respect, or goodwill due a person.
- **Slander:** This is spoken defamation. (In many states, if a defamatory statement is broadcast, it is considered libel even though technically the words are not written. Libel is considered more harmful and usually carries more serious penalties than does slander.)
- **Libel per se:** Some words are always libelous. Falsely written accusations, such as labeling a person a "thief" or a "swindler," automatically constitute libel.
- **Libel per quod:** Words that seem perfectly innocent in themselves can become libelous under certain circumstances. For instance, erroneously reporting that Joe Smith was seen eating a steak dinner last night may seem harmless unless Smith happens to be the president of the Worldwide Vegetarian Society.

For someone to win a libel suit brought against the media, that person must prove five things: (1) that he or she has actually been defamed and harmed by the statements, (2) that he or she has been identified (although not necessarily by name), (3) that the defamatory statements have been published, (4) that the media were at fault, and (5) in most instances that what was published or broadcast was false.

Not every mistake that finds its way into publication is libelous. To report that James Arthur will lead the Fourth of July parade when in fact Arthur James will lead it is probably not libelous because it is improbable that leading a parade will cause harm to a person's reputation. (Courts have even ruled that it is not necessarily libelous to report incorrectly that a person died. Death, said the courts, is no disgrace.) Actual harm might be substantiated by showing that defamatory remarks led to physical discomfort (such as sleepless nights) or loss of income or increased difficulty in performing a job.

Identification need not be by name. If a paper erroneously reports that the professor who teaches Psych 101 at 10 A.M. in Quadrangle Hall is taking bribes from his students, that would be sufficient.

Suppose you were watching a TV news story, and all of a sudden your picture showed up on screen with the words "Convicted Sex Offender" on a banner below your image. Could you sue the TV station for defamation (assuming, of course, that you were not a convicted sex offender)? Here's what happened to a person actually in that situation.

A Catholic diocese in Michigan hired a convicted sex offender to work in the diocese's department of social work. When a spokesperson for the diocese explained the decision, the story was covered by a local TV station. When the story was broadcast, the words "Convicted Sex Offender" appeared beneath the image of the diocesan spokesperson while he has speaking. The spokesperson brought a defamation suit against the TV station claiming he was a victim of libel per se, being erroneously cast as a criminal.

In its review of the case, the Michigan court noted that although the spokesperson was on screen for only a few seconds, the words "Convicted Sex Offender" stayed on screen for the entire report while the scene shifted to show the convicted person. In addition, the spokesperson appeared later in the broadcast without the erroneous label present. The court reasoned that most viewers would probably conclude that the label appeared in error or that it applied to the person who was the focus of the report and not to the spokesperson. Thus, the report did not constitute defamation.

Publication, for our purposes, pertains to a statement's appearance in a mass medium and is self-explanatory.

Fault is a little more complicated. To win a libel suit, some degree of fault or carelessness on the part of the media organization must be shown. As we shall see, the degree of fault that must be established depends on several things: (1) the person who is suing, (2) the subject matter of the suit, and (3) the particular state's laws that are being applied.

A 1986 Supreme Court decision held that private persons (as opposed to public figures) suing for libel must prove that the statements at issue are false, at least when the statements involve matters of public concern. For all practical purposes, however, proving that the media were at fault also involves proving the falsity of what was broadcast or published, so that virtually everyone who brings a libel suit must show the wrongfulness of what was published.

It should be emphasized that a mass medium is responsible for what it carries. It usually cannot hide behind the fact that it only repeated what someone else said. For example, in most situations a magazine could not defend itself against a libel suit by claiming that it simply quoted a hospital worker who said a colleague was stealing drugs. If, in fact, the hospital worker's colleague was not stealing drugs, the magazine would have to look to some other defense against libel. A 2004 decision by the Pennsylvania Supreme Court further clarified this situation when it ruled that the First Amendment does not create a "neutral report privilege" for media when they report newsworthy statements made by one public official about another that might be defamatory. The case stemmed from a story in a local newspaper that quoted one city official calling two other city officials "child molesters." The Pennsylvania court ruled that even though the newspaper reported the story accurately, it could still be sued for defamation if the plaintiff could establish that the paper acted with actual malice.

▲ Defenses Against Libel Suits

What are some of the defenses that can be used? There are three.

The first is truth. If what was reported is proved to be true, there is no libel. This defense, however, is rarely used since it is extremely difficult to prove the truth of a statement. In addition,

Media Probe   What Is Actual Malice?

Many people are confused by the meaning of the phrase *actual malice* as it applies to defamation. Some individuals mistakenly think that a person who is defamed has to prove evil motives, spite, or ill will on the part of the person or medium that allegedly committed the defamation. Not so. In the famous *New York Times* v. *Sullivan* case, the Supreme Court defined *actual malice* as (1) publishing something that is known to be false ("I know what I'm publishing is not true but I'm going to publish it anyway") or (2) publishing something with reckless disregard for whether it is true or not ("I have good reason to doubt that what I'm publishing is true, but I'm going to publish it anyway").

A libel case involving CBS, Inc., and Walter Jacobson, a news anchor and commentator at WBBM-TV (the CBS affiliate) in Chicago, illustrates this definition. The Brown & Williamson Tobacco Corporation (maker of Viceroy cigarettes) claimed that Jacobson libeled their company when he charged during a TV commentary that Viceroy was using an ad campaign to persuade children to smoke. Viceroy, said Jacobson, was equating cigarette smoking with "wine, beer, shaving, or wearing a bra . . . a declaration of independence and striving for self-identity . . . a basic symbol of the growing-up process." The commentary cited as evidence a Federal Trade Commission report that claimed the company had been advised by its advertising agency to launch such a campaign.

Brown & Williamson, forced to prove actual malice on the part of Jacobson because of the company's position as a public figure, denied ever having launched such a campaign. In fact, company lawyers argued that Brown & Williamson was so outraged by its ad agency's advice that it fired the advertising firm. Further, Brown & Williamson argued that Jacobson knew this fact before he broadcast his commentary. In court one of the officials for the tobacco company testified that a researcher for Jacobson had been told that the ad agency had been fired and that the campaign was not used. During the trial Jacobson said that he had rejected a suggestion from this researcher that a disclaimer should be included in the commentary stating that Brown & Williamson had not used the campaign. Evidently, this fact was enough to convince the jury that Jacobson knew that what he was saying was false—thus establishing actual malice. The jury found in favor of the tobacco company and awarded Brown & Williamson more than $5 million in damages.

For their part Jacobson and CBS maintain that the commentary was an accurate summary of the FTC report and that Brown & Williamson had a strategy directed toward children, even if the company did not fully implement it. In late 1985, CBS announced plans to appeal the decision. The appeal was decided in 1988 in favor of the tobacco company. CBS was ordered to pay $3.05 million in damages.

---

since the Supreme Court's decision placed the burden of proving the falsity of a statement on the person bringing the libel suit, the truth defense has become even less attractive.

A second defense is privilege. There are certain situations in which the courts have held that the public's right to know comes before a person's right to preserve a reputation. Judicial proceedings, arrest warrants, grand jury indictments, legislative proceedings, and city council sessions are examples of situations that are generally acknowledged to be privileged. If a reporter gives a fair and accurate report of these events, no lawsuits can result, even if what is reported contains a libelous statement.

The third defense is fair comment and criticism. Any person who thrusts him- or herself into the public eye or is at the center of public attention is open to fair criticism. This means that public officials, professional sports figures, cartoonists, artists, columnists, playwrights, and all those who invite public attention are fair game for comment. This defense applies only to opinion and criticism, not to misrepresentations of fact. You can report that a certain director's new movie stank to high heaven without fear of a lawsuit, but you could not report falsely that the director embezzled funds from the company and expect protection under fair criticism. However, criticism can be quite severe and caustic and still be protected from lawsuit. In 1990 the Supreme Court ruled that expressions of opinion are not automatically exempt from charges of libel. Opinions that contain an assertion of fact that can be proved false might trigger a defamation suit.

In 1964 the Supreme Court, in the *New York Times* v. *Sullivan* case, significantly expanded the opportunity for comments on the actions of public officials and also changed the nature of the law governing defamation. The case involved the *Times* and an official of the Montgomery, Alabama, police department, L. B. Sullivan, and took place during the civil rights struggle of the early 1960s. A civil rights group published an ad in the *Times* concerning a protest in Montgomery that Sullivan claimed libeled him. Testimony in the case revealed that, indeed, several statements in the ad were false. An Alabama court awarded Sullivan $500,000, but the *Times* appealed the case to the Supreme Court.

The Court reversed the Alabama decision and enumerated three major principles that would affect future decisions concerning defamation:

1. Editorial advertising is protected by the First Amendment.
2. Even statements that are false might qualify for First Amendment protection if they concern the public conduct of public officials.
3. To win a libel suit, public officials must prove that false and defamatory statements were made with actual malice.

The Court also clarified what is meant by *actual malice*—publishing a statement with the knowledge that it is false or publishing a statement in "reckless disregard" of whether it is true or not. A few years later, the Court expanded this protection to include statements made about public figures as well as public officials. In 1971 it appeared that the Supreme Court would even require private individuals who become involved in events of public concern to prove actual malice before collecting for a libel suit. Three years later, the Court seemed to retreat a little from this position when it held that a lawyer involved in a civil lawsuit was not a public figure, that he was not involved in an event of public interest, and that he did not have to prove actual malice.

Even more protection was extended to the private citizen in 1976 in a case concerning the divorce of Mary Alice Firestone and tire heir Russell Firestone Jr. The trial lasted 17 months and received large amounts of media coverage. Ms. Firestone even called several press conferences while the trial was taking place. When *Time* magazine erroneously reported that the divorce had been granted on the grounds of extreme cruelty and adultery, Ms. Firestone sued for libel. (Her husband had charged her with adultery, but adultery was not cited as grounds for the divorce.) *Time* argued that she was a public figure and contended that she had to show not only that the magazine was inaccurate but also that it acted with malice. The Supreme Court ruled that she was not a public figure, despite all the attendant press coverage, and drew a distinction between legitimate public controversies and those controversies that merely interest the public. The latter, said the Court, are not protected, and actual malice need not be proved.

The Court affirmed this distinction in 1979 by noting that the fact that someone is involved in a "newsworthy" event does not make the person a public figure. When a U.S. senator presented a scientist with a satirical award used to denote wasteful spending of government funds, the scientist sued for defamation. The Court ruled that even though the scientist became the subject of media attention, his public prominence before receiving the satirical award did not merit labeling him a public figure. Therefore, he did not have to meet the actual malice standard. Private citizens, however, do have to show some degree of fault or negligence by the media. In many states this means showing that the media did not exercise ordinary care in publishing a story. Establishing this allows a private citizen to collect compensation for any actual damages that stem from the libel. The big bucks, however, come from punitive damages assessed against the media. These awards are designed to punish the media for their past transgressions and serve as a reminder not to misbehave again. To collect punitive damages, even private citizens must show actual malice.

The amount of money that juries award to the winners of libel cases can be substantial. Awards of $1 million or more have become common. Singer Wayne Newton, for example, received a $20-million judgment against NBC. On the other hand, most libel cases are appealed, and about 75 percent either are reversed or have the monetary awards substantially reduced. For example, the Wayne Newton verdict was eventually reversed.

The difficulty that public figures face in successfully bringing a libel suit against the media has prompted some news subjects to look for other remedies. In the past decade several subjects of news stories sued the news media for the way they gathered the news rather than based on the content of the story. Lawsuits concerning trespass and invasion of privacy by the media have become more common.

▲ Defamation and the Internet

The Internet has created new problems with regard to defamation. One problem involves who can be sued for defamation. Suppose you post a defamatory message on an AOL

For a private citizen to prevail in a defamation case, he or she must prove some degree of negligence on the part of the media. The standards for determining what constitutes negligence vary from state to state, and as with the actual malice standard, negligence is determined on a case-by-case basis. Nonetheless, some general statements can be made.

A common legal definition of *negligence* states that it is conduct that creates an unreasonable risk of harm. The standard of conduct that the possible negligence is measured against is whether a reasonable person under the same circumstances would behave in the same way. As far as the media are concerned, employees are to be judged against the appropriate practices and customs for their profession. Thus, in many cases the issue of negligence boils down to whether the reporter or editor exercised reasonable care and followed the accepted practices of the profession in determining whether a story was true or false.

Some specific factors might also be taken into account. First, was the story prepared under deadline? If sufficient time and opportunity were available, then reasonable care might require more checking of facts. Second, what was the interest being promoted by the story? Stories covering heated political debates have greater merit than gossip, but gossip can be extremely harmful. Hence, greater care should be exercised in the latter situation.

A concrete example might help illustrate negligence and show how it differs from actual malice. In a 1975 case in Massachusetts, a rookie reporter had been covering a drug trial. The reporter was unaware that a table in the front of the courtroom was reserved for the press. Consequently, he sat in the back, where he had trouble hearing the testimony. One of the defendants was the 20-year-old son of a man named John Stone, who ran the lunchrooms in a public school. When the prosecutor asked a marshal the question of who had the drugs, the reporter thought he heard the marshal say, "Mr. Stone" and assumed he meant John Stone, the only "Mr. Stone" the reporter was aware of. He wrote in his story that John Stone had possession of the drugs. When questioned by his editor, who knew John Stone personally and had a hard time believing that he could have possessed illegal drugs, the reporter said he had heard the name in court. In fact, the marshal was talking about Jeffrey Stone, the son of John Stone. John Stone, naturally enough, sued for libel.

The court found that the reporter was guilty of negligence because he did not sit where he could properly hear and did not check with another source to confirm who the "Mr. Stone" was—two practices that were in keeping with the accepted procedures of journalism. However, the reporter's conduct did not constitute actual malice since he was new in town and did not have reason to doubt that the Stone mentioned in court was the only Stone he knew.

But what about the editor, who knew Mr. Stone personally and had trouble believing the story? The editor had reason to doubt the story but did not even make a phone call to check its accuracy. The court ruled that he had acted with reckless disregard for the truth of the report, which was enough to constitute actual malice.

message board. Can someone sue both you and AOL? Congress addressed this issue in the Communications Decency Act of 1996. The law states that Internet service providers such as AOL are not liable for the content that they carry unless they (the providers) are the actual authors of the content. A 2006 decision by a Pennsylvania court seemed to broaden this protection. The court ruled that a person who republished on a Web site a potentially defamatory story written by someone else was also entitled to protection under the act.

A second vexing question involves jurisdiction. Since the online versions of newspapers, magazines, and newsletters are available all over the world at the click of the mouse, where should a lawsuit be filed? This is an important question because laws governing defamation vary by state. In one recent case, online newspapers in Connecticut published a story about prison conditions in Virginia. A court ruled that the warden of a Virginia prison could sue the newspapers for libel in Virginia because the publications were accessible in that state. This decision, however, was reversed by the court of appeals on the grounds that the newspaper's Web site was not aimed at a Virginia audience. The international situation is muddier. A court in Australia ruled that the Dow Jones Company, based in New Jersey, could be sued for defamation in Australia because the online version of one of its magazines was available for downloading in Australia. Dow Jones eventually lost the case and had to pay out about a half-million dollars in damages. On the other hand, a British appeals courts ruled that a Dow Jones publication that was available online could not be sued in England when it was shown that only five people had clicked on the Web site. The courts said that there had to be evidence of substantial publication in England before a publication could be sued there. This obviously troublesome issue is the subject of an American Law Institute project titled "Recognition and Enforcement of Foreign Judgments"; the group is attempting to draft a federal statute that would make procedures uniform across the states.

INVASION OF PRIVACY

▲ The Right to Privacy

Closely related to libel is the issue of privacy. In fact, a single publication will often prompt both types of suits. The big difference between the two is that libel protects a person's reputation, but the right to privacy protects a person's peace of mind and feelings. A second difference is that libel involves the publication of false information; invasion of privacy might be triggered by disclosing the truth.

There are four different ways that the mass media can invade someone's right to privacy.

Intrusion upon Solitude   The first is intruding upon a person's solitude or seclusion. This generally occurs when reporters wrongfully use microphones, surveillance cameras, and other forms of eavesdropping to record someone's private activities. A TV news crew hiding in a van outside your room and secretly taping your activities while you are inside would probably constitute intrusion.

The use of tiny, hidden cameras and microphones by reporters in their quest for news has raised special problems in this area. In a 1999 decision the California Supreme Court ruled that an ABC reporter committed an invasion of privacy when she went to work for a psychic hot line and secretly videotaped a conversation with a coworker. Even though the conversation took place in an open office and was overheard by others, the court ruled that the coworker had a reasonable expectation that a reporter would not secretly videotape his conversations. This decision suggests that reporters should give extra thought to the use of hidden recordings in their news-gathering activities.

Unauthorized Release of Private Information   The second occasion is the unauthorized release of private information. A newspaper's publishing private medical records that reveal that a person has a dread disease is an example in this area. The courts allowed a suit claiming invasion of privacy to be filed when a newspaper published information about a person's sex-change operation without the person's consent.

Creation of a False Impression   A third method is publicizing people in a false light or creating a false impression of them. This invasion is most closely related to libel because falsity is also involved. Some TV stations get into trouble in this area through the practice of putting new narration over some stock tape footage, which sometimes creates a false impression. For example, a Chicago TV station was sued when it ran stock footage taken 3 years earlier of a doctor performing a gynecological exam with a story describing how another doctor allegedly used an AIDS-infected swab during a similar exam. The face of the doctor in the stock footage was readily identifiable, and she sued the station, claiming the story made it appear that she had performed the allegedly negligent procedure. (The station settled the suit out of court and paid the doctor an undisclosed amount of money.)

Appropriation of Identity   The last means of invading privacy is through appropriation of a person's name or likeness for commercial purposes. This commonly involves stars and celebrities who find their names or images used without their permission in some business or promotional activity. Model Christy Brinkley, for example, successfully filed suit to stop poster stores from selling her picture without her permission. The not-so-famous are also protected against appropriation. One man sued because he found that a camera company had used his picture without permission in its instruction manual.

▲ Trespass

Trespass, defined as unauthorized entry into someone else's territory, is a concept that is closely related to invasion of privacy. The close of the 20th century saw a significant increase in the number of trespass cases brought against the news media. These cases highlighted a fundamental question for news reporting: Do journalists have a special First Amendment privilege to break the law in pursuit of a legitimate news story that will advance the public interest? Several recent court decisions suggest that the answer to this question is no.

In one case a Wisconsin court found that a TV photojournalist who had entered private property with permission of a police officer responding to a call was guilty of trespassing. Similarly, a 1999 circuit court ruling found that journalists who enter a private home with law enforcement officers but without consent of the homeowner could be sued for trespass. In another case reporters who followed antinuclear demonstrators through a fence onto the property of a utility company were found guilty of trespassing. A related 1999 Supreme Court case found that law enforcement officers who permitted the news media to accompany them across the threshold of a home when serving a search warrant were violating the Fourth Amendment's provisions against unreasonable searches.

Finally, consider the 1996 case of *Food Lion* v. *ABC*. Reporters for the newsmagazine *Prime Time Live* faked résumés to get jobs at a Food Lion supermarket and used hidden cameras to shoot video to document their story. After the program aired, Food Lion brought suit against the network not for defamation, but for fraud and trespass. Outside the courtroom, lawyers for Food Lion explained that they thought the story was libelous, but they thought they had a better chance of winning on the basis of the trespass and fraud charges. A jury found in favor of Food Lion and awarded the supermarket chain a whopping $5.5 million in damages. A district court judge reduced this amount to $350,000. Eventually, the circuit court of appeals dismissed most of the case, but it did uphold the trespass decision. The original jury awarded Food Lion only $1 in damages for the trespass, but now that the precedent has been set, it is possible that future lawsuits will seek far greater sums for trespass violations.

COPYRIGHT

Copyright protects an author against unfair appropriation of his or her work. Although its roots go back to English common law, the basic copyright law of the United States was first enacted in 1909. In 1976, faced with copyright problems raised by the new communications technologies, Congress passed legislation covering literary, dramatic, and musical works, as well as motion pictures, television programs, and sound recordings. The law also states what is not covered. For example, an idea cannot be copyrighted, nor can a news event, a discovery, or a procedure.

For works created on or after January 1, 1978, copyright protection lasts for the life of the author plus 70 years. Works published before that date are eligible for copyright protection for a total of 95 years. To obtain full copyright protection, it is necessary to send a special form, copies of the work, and a small fee to the Register of Copyrights. The owner of a copyrighted work can then reproduce, sell, display, or perform the property.

It is important to note that copyright protection extends only to copying the work in question. If a person independently creates a similar work, there is no copyright violation. As a result, one of the things that a person who brings a copyright suit must prove is that the other person had access to the work under consideration. Thus, if you contend that a hit Hollywood movie was actually based on a pirated script that you had submitted to the company, you must show that the people responsible for the movie had access to your work. (To guard against copyright suits, most production companies will not open the envelopes of what look like unsolicited scripts.) Note, however, that you do not have to prove that someone intentionally or even consciously copied your work.

In addition, the law provides that people can make fair use of copyrighted materials without violating the provisions of the Copyright Act. *Fair use* means that copies of a protected work can be made for such legitimate activities as teaching, research, news reporting, and criticism without penalty. Four factors are taken into consideration in determining fair use:

1. The purpose of the use (whether for profit or for nonprofit education)
2. The nature of the copyrighted work

The headline in *Billboard* magazine summed it up: "Grokster Bad; Music Industry Good." The trade press hailed the Supreme Court's 2005 decision in the *MGM* v. *Grokster* case as a monumental victory for the entertainment industry. The Recording Industry Association of America said the court addressed a significant threat to the U.S. economy and protected "the livelihoods of more than 11 million Americans employed by the copyright industries." Another record executive proclaimed that the Supreme Court drove a stake through "the heart of services that rely on theft as a key competitive advantage." Upon closer examination, however, the decision may not have been the last word about the issue.

At the core of the Court's decision was the manner in which the peer-to-peer systems promoted their services. If a system actively encouraged copyright infringement, as shown by clear expression or other actions and inactions, then the service is liable for the resulting acts of infringement by its users. As far as Grokster was concerned, there was ample evidence that the service touted itself to former Napster users who were looking for another source from which to download copyrighted material. Plus Grokster made no effort to develop a filtering system to diminish infringing material.

But what exactly constitutes encouragement to violate copyright? What if a new file-sharing service emerges exactly like Grokster but tells its users not to copy and share copyrighted works? Is it still responsible for the actions of people who disobey its instruction? What if the service develops filtering software and sends messages to copyright infringers to stop what they are doing? Is the service still responsible for those who ignore its warnings? Those who illegally download, of course, would still be liable for copyright infringement, but they would be in the same situation they were in before the Supreme Court decision. These questions are currently being asked concerning video-sharing sites.

3. The amount reproduced in proportion to the copyrighted work as a whole
4. The effect of the use on the potential market value of the copyrighted work

Thus, a teacher who reproduces a passage from a long novel to illustrate writing style to an English class will probably not have to worry about copyright. On the other hand, if a commercial magazine reproduces verbatim a series of articles published in a not-for-profit magazine, it is likely that the copyright statute will be determined to have been violated.

Recent cases involving copyright law have dealt with the new communication media. In what is popularly known as the "Betamax case," the Supreme Court ruled in 1984 that viewers who owned videocassette recorders could copy programs off the air for later personal viewing without violating the Copyright Act. Such taping, ruled the court, was a fair use of the material. In 1991 a federal court ruled that commercial copying companies, such as Kinko's, had to get permission from the publishers before copying and selling copyrighted articles and book excerpts used for college courses.

The 1998 Digital Millennium Copyright Act (DMCA) makes it unlawful to create services that are used to circumvent measures that control access to copyrighted works. In general, service providers, search engines, and Web hosts are immune from copyright infringement liability for simply transmitting information over the Internet. This provision was included to protect companies from having to monitor the activities of everybody who uses the Internet, a practical impossibility. Service providers, search engines, and Web sites do have a responsibility to remove material that appears to constitute copyright infringement when such an infringement is brought to their attention. When that occurs, companies must "expeditiously" remove or block access to the material. However, the DMCA does not provide guidelines on what constitutes an "expeditious" reaction.

The Napster case vividly highlighted some of the copyright problems caused by the Internet. In 1999 the recording industry filed suit against the file-sharing service. Napster argued that its activities were protected by the "fair use" provision of copyright law: Making copies of a song for noncommercial, personal use was the same as videotaping a TV program for personal use. The recording industry argued that Napster was knowingly facilitating the illegal distribution of copyrighted material.

The courts sided with the recording industry and ordered that Napster remove all copyrighted material from its system. The decision spelled the end for Napster, and the service filed for bankruptcy in 2002. Napster's demise, however, did not put an end to file sharing. New, harder-to-shut-down services, such as Kazaa and Grokster, took its place. By 2004 more people were downloading and sharing music than during Napster's heyday.

The recording industry responded in two ways. First, it filed copyright infringement suits against several hundred individuals for sharing music files on the Internet. Those targeted first were those who had more than a thousand songs stored on their hard drives. Some of those who were sued wound up settling their cases by paying thousands of dollars to the recording companies. Second, the recording industry joined the movie industry in attempting to sue not just the individuals who illegally downloaded copyrighted material but also the peer-to-peer services, such as Grokster and Streamcast, that made file sharing possible. In mid-2005 the Supreme Court noted that there was substantial evidence that the file-sharing services had promoted their systems as a way in which users could illegally share protected material and thus induced and encouraged their subscribers to violate the law. The Court then ruled that file-sharing services can be sued for the copyright infringement of their customers. The entertainment industry hailed the decision as a great victory, but the ruling failed to address some key questions (see the boxed insert *MGM* v. *Grokster*). It remains to be seen what effect the Court's decision has on file sharing.

Video-sharing sites are the next battleground for copyright issues. In 2007 Viacom and NBC sued YouTube for $1 billion, claiming that the site hosted videos that infringed upon Viacom's and NBC's copyrights. Google, YouTube's parent company, argued that YouTube had complied with the provisions of the DMCA. NBC and Viacom countered that the site should be more proactive about removing copyrighted material and not shift the burden of enforcement to the victims of infringement. They also argued that YouTube had not done enough to stop copyright infringements and that YouTube's lack of zeal in this area actually promoted copyright violations. If NBC and Viacom are successful in showing that YouTube actually promotes the infringement of copyrights by its users, then, under the Supreme Court's *Grokster* ruling, YouTube could face some drastic consequences.

OBSCENITY AND PORNOGRAPHY

Obscenity is not protected by the First Amendment; that much is clear. Unfortunately, nobody has yet come up with a definition of *obscenity* that satisfies everybody. Let us take a brief look at how the definition of this term has changed over the years. (If, when we are done, you are a little confused about this whole issue, do not feel bad. You are not alone.)

For many years the test of whether something was obscene was the **Hicklin Rule,** a standard that judged a book (or any other item) by whether isolated passages had a tendency to deprave or corrupt the mind of the most susceptible person. Thus, if one paragraph of a 500-page book tended to deprave or corrupt the mind of the most susceptible person (a 12-year-old child, a dirty old man), then the entire book was obscene. The standard was written in the 1860s and widely used for the next 80 years.

In a 1957 case, *Roth* v. *United States*, the Supreme Court tried its hand at writing a new definition. The new test for detecting obscenity would be the following: whether to the average person, applying contemporary standards, the dominant theme of the material taken as a whole appealed to prurient interests. (*Prurient* means 'lewd' or "tending to incite lust.") The Roth test differed from the earlier rule in two significant ways. Not only did the entire work, rather than a single passage, have to be taken into consideration, but the material had to offend the average person, not simply anyone who saw it. Obviously, this standard was less restrictive than the Hicklin rule, but gray areas remained. Should the community standards be local or national? How exactly would prurient interest be measured?

The next few years produced more obscenity cases to plague the high court. According to other decisions the material had to be "patently offensive" and "utterly without redeeming social value" to be obscene. During the 1960s the Supreme Court began considering the conduct of the seller or distributor in addition to the character of the material in question. For example, even if material was not considered hard-core pornography, it could be banned if sold to minors, thrust upon an unwilling audience, or advertised as erotic to titillate customers. A 1969 ruling introduced the concept of "variable obscenity" when it stated that certain magazines were obscene when sold to minors but not obscene when sold to adults.

By 1973 so many legal problems were cropping up under the Roth guidelines that something had to be done. Consequently, the Supreme Court attempted to close up loopholes in the case of *Miller* v. *California*. This decision did away with the "utterly without redeeming social value" test and stated that the "community standards" used in defining obscenity could be local standards, which, presumably, would be determined by local juries. The new test of obscenity included three principles:

1. Whether the average person, applying contemporary community standards, would find that the work as a whole appealed to prurient interests
2. Whether the work depicted or described in a patently offensive way certain sexual conduct that was specifically spelled out by a state law
3. Whether the whole work lacked serious literary, artistic, political, or scientific value

Despite this new attempt, problems were not long in coming. The language of the decision appeared to permit a certain amount of local discretion in determining what was obscene. The question of how far a local community can go in setting standards continues to be troublesome. The Supreme Court has since ruled that the motion picture *Carnal Knowledge* is not obscene, even though a state court said that it was. The Court has also said that *Screw* magazine and the *Illustrated Presidential Report of the Commission on Obscenity and Pornography* are obscene no matter what community's standards are invoked. The Court further clarified the third of the *Miller* guidelines in a 1987 case when it ruled that judges and juries must assess the literary, artistic, political, or scientific value of allegedly obscene material from the viewpoint of a "reasonable person" rather than applying community standards. These issues could be decided with the help of experts who would testify about the value of a work. The first two guidelines, however, would still be decided with reference to contemporary community standards.

Over the years the Court has taken a somewhat more lenient view as to what constitutes obscenity. The Miller case suggested that the Court was encouraging the states to deal with the problem at the local level. Given the long history of controversy that surrounded this topic, however, it was unlikely that this predicament would end soon. In fact, the whole issue surfaced again in 1986 when the Justice Department released a report on pornography. The report, which had strong political overtones, called for more stringent laws concerning pornography. One such law, the Child Protection and Obscenity Enforcement Act, took effect in 1988.

More recent problems have concerned the Internet. Child pornography is illegal on the Internet just as it is in other media. The 1988 act specifically mentions computers as one of the channels through which this illegal material might be circulated. Sexual "stalking" over the Net is also prohibited. In an effort to keep pornographic material from children, Congress passed the Communications Decency Act in 1996. Part of the act made it illegal to use a computer to create, solicit, or transmit any obscene, lewd, lascivious, filthy, or indecent communication. The Supreme Court eventually found the act to be unconstitutional and ruled that the Internet should be given the highest level of First Amendment protection, similar to that given to books and newspapers, rather than the more limited rights of broadcasting and cable, where regulation is more common. The Court noted that even though the government has a legitimate interest in trying to protect children from harmful content, this interest does not justify broad suppression of materials directed at adults.

A second attempt at protecting children from pornography also ran into legal difficulty. The Child Online Protection Act required commercial Web sites to demand proof of age before delivering material that might be harmful to minors. In 2000 an appeals court upheld an injunction that blocked implementation of the act, ruling that the act raised serious First Amendment problems. As a result, the act has never been enforced.

A similar measure, the Children's Internet Protection Act, required libraries that receive federal funds to use filters to block access to pornographic images on their computers. The American Library Association challenged the act, but in 2003 the Supreme Court ruled that the act was constitutional.

As is probably apparent by now, the Internet brings new challenges along with its benefits.

REGULATING BROADCASTING

The formal controls surrounding broadcasting represent a special case. Not only are broadcasters affected by the laws and rulings previously discussed, but they are also subject to additional controls because of broadcasting's unique position and character. When broadcasting was first developed in the early 20th century, it became clear that more people wanted to operate a broadcasting station than there were suitable frequencies available. As a result, the early broadcasters asked the U.S. Congress to step into the picture. Congress passed the Radio Act of 1927, which held that the airwaves belonged to the public and that broadcasters who wished to use this resource had to be licensed to serve in the public interest. A regulatory body, called the Federal Radio Commission (later known as the Federal Communications Commission), was set up to determine who should get a license and whether those who had a license should keep it. Because of this licensing provision, radio and television are subject to more regulations than are newspapers, magazines, films, and sound recording.

▲ The Federal Communications Commission

The Federal Communications Commission (FCC) does not make law; it interprets the law. One of its big jobs is to interpret the meaning of the phrase "public interest." For example, the FCC may write rules and regulations to implement the Communications Act of 1934 if these rules serve the public interest. Moreover, the FCC awards and renews licenses if the award or renewal is in the public interest. Over the years several significant FCC rulings have shed some light on this rather ambiguous concept. One of the first things the commission established was that it would examine programming and determine whether the

The home page of the FCC. In addition to television and radio, the FCC regulates telephone, telegraph and personal communication devices.

public interest was being served. It was not enough for a station to adhere to the technical operating requirements of its license. It would also have to provide a "well-rounded" program structure. In its 1929 Great Lakes decision, the commission also put broadcasters on notice that the broadcasting of programs that tended to injure the public—fraudulent advertising, attacks on ethnic groups, attacks on religions—would not be in the public interest.

What can the FCC do to stations that do not operate in the public interest? It can take several official actions. At the mildest level, it can fine a station up to $325,000. The next level of severity is to renew a station's license only for a probationary period (usually a year). This action typically puts the station on notice that it has to improve its performance or face even more serious consequences. The most severe form of official action is the revoking or nonrenewal of a license. Revocation/nonrenewal is more of a threat, however, than a reality. From 1934 to 1978, the FCC took away the licenses of only 142 stations. This figure should be weighed against the thousands of renewals that the commission granted each of those years. In fact, it has been calculated that 99.8 percent of all licenses are renewed. Nonetheless, the threat of revocation is a potent one that is universally feared among broadcasters.

During the 1980s, as was the case in many industries, the prevailing philosophy that governed broadcasting was one of deregulation. The FCC and Congress eliminated literally dozens of rules and regulations, including the controversial Fairness Doctrine (see the section devoted specifically to this doctrine). The rush to deregulation slowed during the 1990s as the FCC and Congress established new rules and regulations for broadcasting and cable.

For instance, Congress passed the Children's Television Act, which required that TV stations present programs designed to meet the educational and informational needs of young persons through the age of 16. The bill also created a $2-million endowment to fund children's educational programs. Additionally, the act limited the amount of commercial time during children's programming to 10½ minutes per hour on weekends and 12 minutes per hour on weekdays, a limit that applies to both broadcasters and cable operators. Stations and systems that violate these standards could be subject to a fine. In response to a provision in the law that instructed the FCC to encourage children's programming, the commission mandated that stations devote 3 hours per week to informational and educational programs for children.

The FCC is also involved in policy making through its Office of Strategic Planning and Policy Analysis. This office acts as economic, business, and market consultant to the FCC in order to identify trends and recommend future courses of action. Recent studies have examined the impact of wireless devices that do not require a license and market conditions that would best stimulate the effective use of the Internet.

The FCC has no regulatory control over the Internet or over Internet service providers. The commission does have some indirect influence, however, because it has some regulatory power over telephone and cable companies and can thus affect how you connect to the Internet. In 2005 the FCC issued a policy statement endorsing **Internet neutrality**—a provision that would block Internet service providers from favoring one Web company over another. How much jurisdiction the FCC has over this topic, however, is still open to debate.

▲ Indecent Content

When it comes to regulating indecent content, the FCC finds itself caught between the wishes of Congress and the rulings of the federal court system. A 1978 Supreme Court ruling gave the FCC the right to regulate indecency because the pervasive presence of broadcasting made it easily accessible to children. In the late 1980s, after many radio stations began to air raunchy content, Congress passed legislation that instructed the FCC to ban indecent programming 24 hours a day. A federal court declared that this ban was unconstitutional and ordered the FCC to establish a "safe harbor," a time when indecent material

MEDIA TALK

The Debate over Free Speech

DVD, Track 28, 5:08 minutes
This clip examines the FCC crackdown on the broadcast of indecent material. Do you agree with Howard Stern when he charges that the government is infringing upon his First Amendment rights? Who should decide what is or is not indecent?

could be aired without much chance of reaching children. The FCC responded by banning indecent content between the hours of 6 A.M. and 8 P.M. This did not satisfy Congress (there is some political benefit to be derived from being against indecency), which passed a law banning indecency before midnight. This law was ruled unconstitutional, and finally, a law that banned indecent content between 6 A.M. and 10 P.M. was approved. As should be clear by now, trying to protect children from indecency while protecting the First Amendment rights of adults is an exasperating task.

Indecent content became a hot topic in 2004 thanks in part to Janet Jackson's wardrobe malfunction during the Super Bowl halftime show that revealed more of Janet than many people felt was appropriate. The incident sparked renewed regulatory fervor at the FCC and Congress. The FCC issued more than $3.6 million in fines for indecency in 2004, the most ever recorded. The biggest fine, of more than a million dollars, was issued to Fox Broadcasting for airing *Married by America*, in which bachelors licked whipped cream off of strippers. Fox also got hit with a $550,000 fine for the Super Bowl overexposure. Moreover, Congress passed stiffer regulations covering indecency. The maximum amount that a station could be fined for airing indecency was raised to $325,000, 10 times the previous maximum amount.

The FCC continued its crackdown on indecency in 2006. The commission fined CBS and its affiliates more than $3 million for an episode of *Without a Trace* that the FCC ruled obscene. The FCC also changed its policy regarding what it calls "fleeting expletives," such as four-letter words that slip out during a live broadcast. For many years the commission had declined to fine stations for such slips. But in response to a couple of celebrities who used what the FCC termed "the f-word" during awards programs, the commission reversed course and declared that any use of forbidden words, fleeting or not, would invite a fine. The new policy, however, was short-lived. A federal appeals court ruled that the new regulations were arbitrary and declared them null and void. As this book went to press, the FCC was contemplating an appeal to the Supreme Court.

In a related matter the FCC was also attempting to crack down on violent programming. In a 2007 report prepared for Congress, the FCC argued that Congress should enact legislation that would give the commission the power to regulate violence just as it regulates indecent content. Such legislation, of course, would immediately trigger First Amendment concerns and would probably lead to vigorous debate.

▲ The Equal Opportunities Rule

The **Equal Opportunities Rule** is contained in Section 315 of the Communications Act and is thus federal law. Section 315 deals with the ability of bona fide candidates for public office to gain access to a broadcast medium during political campaigns. In simple terms, this section states that if a station permits one candidate for a specific office to appear on the air, it must offer the same opportunity to all other candidates for that office. If a station gives a free minute to one candidate, all other legally qualified candidates for that office are also entitled to a free minute. If a station sells a candidate a minute for $100, it must make the same offer to all other candidates. Congress has made some exceptions to this law, the most notable of which are legitimate newscasts and on-the-scene coverage of authentic news events.

▲ The Fairness Doctrine

The **Fairness Doctrine** no longer exists. The FCC repealed it in 1987. That does not mean, however, that it is dead and buried. There were several proposals in Congress to revive it, with the most recent attempt in 2007.

When it was still in force, the Fairness Doctrine provided that broadcasters had to seek out and present contrasting viewpoints on controversial matters of public importance. On any issue broadcasters had to make a good-faith effort to cover all the opposing viewpoints. This did not have to take place in one program, but the broadcaster was expected to achieve balance over time. Note that the Fairness Doctrine never said that opposing views were entitled to equal time. It simply mandated that some reasonable amount of time be granted.

REGULATING CABLE TV

The regulatory philosophy of the FCC and Congress toward cable has shown wide variation over the years. In the 1950s the FCC ruled that it had no jurisdiction over cable. This notion changed in the 1960s when the commission exerted control over the new medium and wrote a series of regulations governing its growth. By 1972 a comprehensive set of rules governing cable was on the FCC's books. The growth of cable during the 1970s led to successful lobbying efforts by the industry to ease many of these restrictions. In the 1980s, in line with the deregulatory philosophy of the Reagan administration, almost all the FCC rules concerning cable were dropped. Moreover, Congress passed the Cable Communications Policy Act in 1984, which gave cable operators great freedom in setting rates and deciding what channels they could carry on their systems. The law also allowed state and local governments the right to grant cable **franchises** (a franchise is an exclusive right to operate in a given territory).

Unlike broadcast stations, cable systems were not licensed by the FCC. Instead, under the 1984 law, the local franchise authority, should it wish to do so, had the power to terminate the franchise at the end of the franchise period. In addition, cable companies were free to set their own rates.

In the years following the passage of this act, many consumers complained that their cable system raised rates and was insensitive to the needs of its customers. Consequently, in 1992 Congress passed the Cable TV Act, which gave the FCC the authority to regulate the rates of most cable systems, required that cable systems carry the signals of any broadcast station with significant viewing in their market, and allowed commercial broadcast stations to waive their right to be carried in exchange for appropriate compensation from the cable system.

Two provisions in this law had important consequences. First, most consumers saw their monthly cable bills go down as the FCC instituted rate reductions of about 17 percent. Second, the provision requiring cable systems to carry the signals of broadcast stations was challenged in federal court as a violation of the First Amendment rights of cable operators. In 1994 the Supreme Court ruled that cable operators deserved more First Amendment protection from government regulation than did broadcasters but not as much as newspapers and magazines. Consequently, the Court declared that it was constitutional for Congress to pass laws to guarantee that the free flow of information not be restricted by a private company that controlled the means of transmission.

The issue of the constitutionality of the specific rules about which stations must be carried by cable systems was decided in 1997 when the Supreme Court ruled in favor of the "must carry" provision.

In 2006–2007, Kevin Martin, the FCC chair, proposed that consumers be given an "a la carte" option when it came to subscribing to cable. Instead of the traditional bundle or tiers of channels that cable systems typically offer, subscribers would be able to choose only those channels that they wanted to receive. Martin argued that the a-la-carte option would enable customers to avoid cable channels that might carry indecent material. Moreover, the FCC study on violence mentioned above argued that Congress had the power to regulate violent programming carried on basic cable channels. Such legislation would presumably give the FCC power to oversee such programming.

THE TELECOMMUNICATIONS ACT OF 1996

The **Telecommunications Act of 1996** was the first major overhaul of communication laws in more than 60 years. The act contained provisions that affected traditional broadcasters, cable companies, and telephone companies. The following are among the key provisions of the law:

- It removed limits on the number of radio stations that can be owned by one person or organization. Up to eight stations may be owned in a single market. (See Chapter 7.)

- It removed limits on the number of television stations that can be owned as long as stations do not reach more than 35 percent (later changed to 39 percent) of the nation's TV homes.
- It extended the term of broadcast licenses to 8 years.
- It allowed telephone companies to enter the cable TV business.
- It allowed cable TV companies to enter the telephone business.
- It deregulated the rates of many cable systems.
- It mandated that newly manufactured TV sets come with the ability to block unwanted programming based on an electronically encoded rating (popularly called the **V-Chip;** see Chapter 17).
- It mandated that the TV industry come up with a voluntary ratings system for violence, sex, and other indecent materials.

Now that the 1996 Telecommunications Act has been in force for several years, we can see evidence of its impact. As mentioned earlier, the removal of the cap on radio station ownership unleashed a wave of consolidation in the industry. The deregulation of cable rates has led to a general increase in cable subscribers' bills. It took a while but competition between phone companies and cable companies has become more vigorous. Phone company AT&T has started U-Verse, a video service with more than 300 channels. Cable giant Cablevision offers telephone service, and many companies are bundling phone, TV, and Internet service into one package.

The rapid changes in the business and technology environment have prompted Congress to reexamine the 1996 act. Some of the issues being examined include network neutrality, a philosophy that prevents Internet service providers from favoring one Web company over another (for example, charging an extra fee so that one video downloading service runs faster than competitors), and ways to encourage the spread of broadband.

REGULATING ADVERTISING

▲ Deceptive Advertising

The problem of deceptive and potentially harmful advertising has been around a long time. The philosophy of *caveat emptor* (let the buyer beware) was dominant until the early 1900s. Exaggerated claims and outright deception characterized many early advertisements, especially those for patent medicines. Spurred on by the muckrakers (see Chapter 5), the government took steps to deal with the problem when it created the Federal Trade Commission (FTC) in 1914. In the early years of its existence, the commission was concerned with encouraging competition through the regulation of questionable business practices, such as bribery, false advertising, and mislabeling of products; protecting the consumer was not the main focus. The consumer started to receive some protection in 1938 with the Wheeler-Lea Act, which gave the FTC the power to prevent deceptive advertising that harmed the public, whether or not the advertising had any bad effects on the competition.

Like the FCC, the FTC has several enforcement techniques available to it. First of all, it can issue trade regulations that suggest guidelines for the industry to follow. In 1965, for example, it ruled that auto ads must contain both the city and highway estimates of gas mileage. The FTC also uses the **consent order.** In a consent order the advertiser agrees to halt a certain advertising practice, but at the same time the advertiser does not admit to any violation of the law; there is only an agreement not to continue. Somewhat stronger is a **cease-and-desist order.** This order follows a hearing by the commission that determines that a certain advertising practice does indeed violate the law. Violation of a consent order and failure to comply with a cease-and-desist order can result in fines being levied against the advertiser.

In the late 1960s and the 1970s, the FTC took a more active role in the regulation of advertising. The rising tide of interest in the rights of the consumer and the emergence of consumer activist groups (such as Ralph Nader's Raiders) were probably behind this new direction. A flurry of activity took place. First, the FTC wanted documentation for claims. If Brand Y claimed to be more effective in relieving pain than Brand X, the advertiser was now required to have proof for that claim. The FTC also ordered "corrective advertising" in which some advertisers were required to clarify some of their past claims.

More recently, the FTC has been concerned about advertising inappropriately directed toward children. In 1997 the FTC issued an unfair advertising complaint against the R. J. Reynolds Tobacco Company. The FTC argued that ads featuring Joe Camel, the company's cartoon character, encouraged children to start smoking. In response, Reynolds announced it would no longer use the controversial camel in its ads.

In 2000 the FTC targeted the film industry for marketing R-rated movies to persons under 17. An FTC report found that marketing plans for 28 R-rated films included strategies for reaching children as young as 10. The report criticized Hollywood for routinely aiming its advertising at children for movies that its own rating system labels inappropriate. In response, eight movie studios announced plans to reform their promotional efforts. More recently, the FTC has cracked down on products that make deceptive health claims. In 2005, for example, the commission instructed Tropicana orange juice to stop claiming that the product reduced the risk of heart disease and strokes. The FTC also filed lawsuits against six companies whose advertising claimed that people who used their products would lose weight without dieting or exercise. In 2007 the FTC stated that companies that engage in word-of-mouth or "buzz" marketing must disclose these relationships to consumers.

▲ Commercial Speech Under the First Amendment

The 1970s marked a change in judicial thinking about the amount of protection that advertising, or *commercial speech*, as it is called, should receive under the First Amendment. Before the 1970s, advertising had little claim to free-speech protection. In the 1940s

In the 1940s and 1950s, much cigarette advertising promoted the health benefits of smoking. This ad for Camels suggests that doctors endorse not only this brand of cigarette but smoking in general.

F. J. Chrestensen found this out the hard way. Chrestensen owned a former U.S. submarine. There is not much that a private individual can do with a submarine, aside from charging admission to view it. This was Chrestensen's idea, and he wanted to distribute handbills advertising the sub. No way, said the New York City police commissioner. The city's sanitation code did not allow the distribution of advertising matter in the streets. However, handbills of information or of public protest were allowed. Inspired, Chrestensen put his submarine advertising message on one side of the handbill, while the other side was printed with a protest against the City Dock Department. Sorry, said the city, the protest message could be handed out, but the advertising on the other side would have to go. Chrestensen appealed, and 2 years later the Supreme Court ruled against him and agreed with the city of New York that advertising merited no First Amendment protection.

A 1996 *CBS News* report contained charges that the Nike Corporation operated sweatshops in Southeast Asia at which its workers were poorly paid, subject to abuse, and exposed to harmful chemicals. In response, Nike launched a public relations campaign designed to counter the accusations. Using news releases, pamphlets, and op-ed columns in newspapers, the company argued that its workers were treated well and paid a reasonable wage.

A consumer activist in San Francisco sued Nike under California's false-advertising law, asserting that Nike's statements were fraudulent. Nike maintained that the comments were not advertising and therefore not subject to California's law. The case eventually found its way to the California Supreme Court, which ruled that the Nike messages were aimed at consumers of their products and not protected by the First Amendment.

This decision set off alarm bells among companies and the public relations companies that represented them. If commercial speech can be defined that broadly, would any corporation dare to speak out on a public issue if every statement it made could be challenged under consumer protection laws? If an opposing group wanted to intimidate a company to make it stop speaking out, it could do so by filing a flurry of lawsuits forcing the company to defend the truth of every statement it made. Opponents could freely level criticism, no matter how inaccurate or frivolous, while the corporation could be put at legal risk if it responded. (One animal rights group in California sued the California Milk Advisory Board because its advertising and public relations messages portrayed happy cows. The group charged that the messages were misleading because the cows in California are not happy.)

Nike appealed the decision to the U.S. Supreme Court, asking it to rule that the First Amendment protected its responses to the charges. Forty newspapers, professional organizations, and media companies filed briefs in support of Nike. The Court, however, declined to review the case on procedural grounds and sent it back to California for further action. Rather than pursue the case further, Nike settled the case out of court and agreed to pay $1.5 million to a workers' rights group.

The core issue still remains: What are the boundaries of commercial speech? If the California decision becomes accepted nationwide, will the public be deprived of vital information? Or as one lawyer put it, should a company be impeded from entering the marketplace of ideas just because it operates in the marketplace of goods?

Speaking of lawyers, even they have had problems with commercial speech. One law firm in Florida ran a TV ad featuring a bulldog in a spiked collar and the phone number 1-800-PIT-BULL that got it into trouble with the Florida Bar Association. The Florida Supreme Court ruled that the ad did not merit First Amendment protection because it didn't provide verifiable factual information and was thus misleading.

Since that time, however, the Supreme Court has retreated from this view. In 1964, in the *New York Times* v. *Sullivan* case, it extended First Amendment protection to ads that dealt with important social matters. Seven years later, the Court further extended this protection when a Virginia newspaper ran an ad for an abortion clinic located in New York and thus violated a Virginia law against such advertising. The Supreme Court ruled that the ad contained material in the public interest and merited constitutional protection. More recent cases suggest that in many instances commercial speech falls under the protection of the First Amendment.

In a 1980 ruling concerning advertising by an electric utility company, commonly called the Central Hudson case, the Supreme Court enunciated a four-part test for determining the constitutional protection of commercial speech. First, commercial speech that involves an unlawful activity or advertising that is false or misleading is not protected. Second, the government must have a substantial interest in regulating the commercial speech. Third, the state's regulation must actually advance the government interest involved. Fourth, the state's regulations may be only as broad as necessary to promote the state's interest.

A 1984 ruling illustrated the use of these principles: The Court upheld a prohibition against posting signs on city property. The Court first noted that, although the advertising was for a lawful activity and not misleading, the government has a substantial interest in reducing "visual blight" and that the ordinance directly advanced that interest and was not overly broad. Further, the Court affirmed that corporations also have the right of free speech and granted lawyers, doctors, and professionals the right to advertise their prices. Although all the questions surrounding this issue have not been answered, it seems safe to conclude that at least some commercial speech is entitled to First Amendment protection. Its status, however, is less than that given to political and other forms of noncommercial expression (see the boxed insert "The Limits of Commercial Speech").

CONCLUSION

The term *half-life* is a useful concept in physics. It refers to the length of time in which one-half of the radioactive atoms present in a substance will decay. We might borrow this term and reshape its meaning so that it is relevant to this book. The half-life of a chapter in this text is the time it takes for half the information contained in the chapter to become obsolete. With that in mind, it is likely that the half-life of this chapter may be among the shortest of any in this book. Laws are constantly changing; new court decisions are frequently handed down, and new rules and regulations are written all the time. All this activity means that what is written in this chapter will need frequent updating. In addition, it means that mass media professionals must continually refresh their understanding of the law. Of course, this also means that there will be a continuing stream of colorful characters, intriguing stories, and high drama as the courts and regulatory agencies further wrestle with the issues and problems involved in mass communication regulation.

MAIN POINTS

- There is a strong constitutional case against prior restraint of the press.
- Reporters have special privileges that protect them in some instances from having to reveal the names of their news sources. These privileges, however, are not absolute.
- Reporters can cover matters that occur in open court with little fear of reprisal. Some pretrial proceedings can still be closed to the press.
- All but two states now allow cameras in the courtroom on a permanent or experimental basis. Cameras and microphones are still barred from federal trial courts and from the Supreme Court.
- Defamation can be either libel or slander. To prevail in a defamation suit, a public figure must show that the published material was false and harmful and that the media acted with actual malice when they published the information. A private citizen must also show that the material was false and harmful and that the media involved acted with negligence.
- Invasion of privacy can occur when the media intrude upon a person's solitude, release private information,

- create a false impression, or wrongfully appropriate a person's name or likeness.
- Copyright law protects authors from unfair use of their work. There are instances, however, when portions of copyrighted material can be reproduced for legitimate purposes.
- Online file-sharing systems have raised serious questions about copyrights in a digital medium.
- Obscenity is not protected by the First Amendment. To be legally obscene, a work must appeal to prurient interests, depict or describe certain sexual conduct spelled out by state law, and lack serious literary, artistic, political, or scientific value.
- Special regulations and laws apply to broadcasting. The FCC is charged with administering the rules and regulations that deal with cable, TV, and radio. The Telecommunications Act of 1996 had a major impact on the electronic media.
- The FTC oversees advertising. Commercial speech has recently been given more First Amendment protection.

QUESTIONS FOR REVIEW

1. Whom do shield laws protect?
2. Whom do gag orders gag?
3. What is the Freedom of Information Act? How have reporters used it?
4. What is the difference between libel and slander?
5. What factors determine fair use?

6. Briefly explain the significance of the following court cases:
   a. The Betamax case
   b. The Pentagon Papers case
   c. *New York Times* v. *Sullivan*
   d. *Miller* v. *California*

QUESTIONS FOR CRITICAL THINKING

1. Why should reporters have special privileges when other professionals, such as architects, nurses, and accountants, have none?

2. Libel suits can be long and expensive for both sides. What are some other methods of conflict resolution that might cut down the time and the cost but still provide satisfaction for both sides?

3. Why are broadcasting and cable not entitled to the same amount of First Amendment protection as newspapers and magazines? Do you agree with this type of differentiation?

4. Do you think the recording industry's efforts to stop illegal file sharing by suing individuals and file-sharing services will be successful?

5. How can children be protected from exposure to adult-oriented content on the Internet?

KEY TERMS

First Amendment (p. 360)
prior restraint (p. 360)
injunction (p. 360)
shield laws (p. 363)
gag rules (p. 366)
Freedom of Information Act (FOIA)
    (p. 368)
USA Patriot Act (p. 368)

defamation (p. 369)
libel (p. 369)
slander (p. 369)
libel per se (p. 369)
libel per quod (p. 369)
trespass (p. 374)
Hicklin Rule (p. 377)
Internet neutrality (p. 380)

Equal Opportunities Rule (p. 381)
Fairness Doctrine (p. 381)
franchises (p. 382)
Telecommunications Act of 1996
    (p. 382)
V-Chip (p. 383)
consent order (p. 383)
cease-and-desist order (p. 383)

INTERNET RESOURCES

Online Learning Center

At the Online Learning Center home page, www.mhhe.com/dominick10, *select* Student Center *and then* Chapter 16.

1. Use the Learning Objectives, Chapter Outline, Main Points, and Time Line sections to review this chapter.

2. Test your knowledge of the chapter using the multiple choice, crossword puzzle, and flashcard features of the site.

3. Expand your knowledge of concepts and topics discussed in the chapter by going to Suggestions for Further Reading and Internet Exercises.

Surfing the Internet

Many Web sites deal with legal matters. The ones listed here seem most helpful for students.

www.fcc.gov
The FCC's home page. Contains an archive of recent speeches, a search engine, and consumer information along with more technical data.

www.freedomforum.org
Contains a summary of recent First Amendment court decisions, relevant law articles, a First Amendment time line, and a full text of relevant Supreme Court rulings.

www.rcfp.org
The Reporters Committee for Freedom of the Press maintains this site, which contains recent court decisions, legal news, and a link to its publication, *The News Media and the Law.*

www.rtnda.org
Home page of the Radio and Television News Directors Association. Contains information about covering the courts, libel, copyright, and other legal issues.

CHAPTER 17

ETHICS AND OTHER INFORMAL CONTROLS

This chapter will prepare you to:

- distinguish among the types of informal controls on the media

- explain the most important ethical principles

- explain what the standards departments and performance codes are

- discuss the relationship between the media and their advertisers vis-à-vis ethical practices

- understand the pros and cons of pressure groups

Like a winding road, the path to an ethical decision needs to be carefully navigated.

Laws and regulations are not the only controls on the mass media. Informal controls, stemming from within the media themselves or shaped by the workings of external forces such as pressure groups, consumers, and advertisers, are also important. The following hypothetical examples illustrate some situations in which these controls might spring up:

- You are the program director for the campus radio station. You get a call one morning from the promotion department of a major record company offering you a free trip to California, a tour of the record company's studios, a ticket to a concert featuring all the company's biggest stars, and an invitation to an exclusive party where you will get to meet all the performers. The company representative explains that this is simply a courtesy to you so that you will better appreciate the quality of her company's products. Do you accept?

- You are a reporter for the local campus newspaper. The star of the football team, who also happens to be the president of the Campus Crusade for Morality, has been involved in a minor traffic accident, and you have been assigned to cover the story. When you get to the accident scene, you examine the football player's car and find a half-dozen pornographic magazines strewn across the backseat. You have a deadline in 30 minutes; what details do you include in your story?

- You are the editor of the campus newspaper. One of your reporters has just written a series of articles describing apparent health-code violations in a popular off-campus restaurant. This particular restaurant regularly buys full-page ads in your paper. After you run the first story in the series, the restaurant owner calls and threatens to cancel all her ads unless you stop printing the series. What do you do?

- You are doing your first story for the campus paper. A local businessperson has promised to donate $5 million to your university so that it can buy new equipment for its mass communication and journalism programs. While putting together a background story on this benefactor, you discover that he was convicted of armed robbery at age 18 and avoided prison only by volunteering for military duty during the closing months of World War II. In the more than 60 years that have passed since then, his record has been spotless. He refuses to talk about the incident, claims his wife and his closest friends do not know about it, and threatens to withdraw his donation if you print the story. Naturally, university officials are concerned and urge you not to mention this fact. Do you go ahead and include the incident as simply one element in your overall profile? Do you take the position that the arrest information is not pertinent and not use it? Do you wait until the university has the money and then print the story?

We could go on listing examples, but by now the point is probably clear. There are many situations in the everyday operation of the mass media in which thorny questions about what to do or not to do have to be faced. Most of these situations do not involve laws or regulations but instead deal with the tougher questions of what is right or what is proper. Informal controls over the media usually assert themselves in these circumstances. In this chapter we will discuss the following examples of informal controls: personal ethics; performance codes; internal controls, such as organizational policies, self-criticism, and professional self-regulation; and outside pressures.

PERSONAL ETHICS

Ethics are rules of conduct or principles of morality that point us toward the right or best way to act in a situation. Over the years philosophers have developed a number of general ethical principles that serve as guidelines for evaluating our behavior. We will briefly examine five principles that have particular relevance to those working in the mass media professions. Before we begin, however, please note that these principles do not contain magic answers to every ethical dilemma. In fact, different ethical principles often suggest different and conflicting courses of action. There is no perfect answer to every problem. Also, these ethical principles are based on Western thought. Other cultures may have developed totally different systems. Nonetheless, these principles can provide a framework for analyzing what is proper in examining choices and justifying our actions.

▲ Ethical Principles

The Principle of the Golden Mean   Moral virtue lies between two extremes. This philosophical position is typically associated with Aristotle, who, as a biologist, noted that too much food as well as too little food spoils health. Moderation is the key. Likewise, in ethical dilemmas the proper way of behaving lies between doing too much and doing too little. For instance, in the restaurant example mentioned earlier, one extreme would be to cancel the story as requested by the restaurant owner. The other extreme would be to run the series as is. Perhaps a compromise between the two would be to run the series but also give the restaurant owner a chance to reply. Or perhaps the story might contain information about how the restaurant has improved conditions or other tempering remarks.

Examples of the **golden mean** are often found in media practices. For example, when news organizations cover civil disorders, they try to exercise moderation. They balance the necessity of informing the public with the need to preserve public safety by not inflaming the audience.

The Categorical Imperative   What is right for one is right for all. German philosopher Immanuel Kant is identified with this ethical guideline. To measure the correctness of our behavior, Kant suggested that we act according to rules that we would want to see universally applied. In Kant's formulation *categorical* means "unconditional"—no extenuating circumstances, no exceptions. Right is right and should be done, no matter what the consequences. The individual's conscience plays a large part in Kant's thinking. A **categorical imperative** is discovered by an examination of conscience; the conscience informs us what is right. If, after performing an act, we feel uneasy or guilty, we have probably violated our conscience. Applied to mass communication, a categorical imperative might be that all forms of deception in news gathering are wrong and must be avoided. No one wants deception to become a universal practice. Therefore, for example, a reporter should not represent him- or herself as anything other than a reporter when gathering information for a story.

The Principle of Utility   **Utility** is defined as the greatest benefit for the greatest number. Modern utilitarian thinking originated with the 19th-century philosophers Jeremy Bentham and John Stuart Mill. The basic tenet in their formulations is that we are to determine what is right or wrong by considering what will yield the best ratio of good to bad for the general society. Utilitarians ask how much good is promoted and how much evil is restrained by different courses of behavior. Utilitarianism provides a clear method for evaluating ethical choices: (1) Calculate all the consequences, both good and bad, that would result from each of our options; then (2) choose the alternative that maximizes value or minimizes loss.

Looking at the mass communication area, we can easily see several examples of utilitarian philosophy. In 1971 the *New York Times* and other papers printed stolen government documents known as the Pentagon Papers (see Chapter 16). Obviously, the newspapers involved thought that the good that would be achieved by printing these papers far outweighed the harm that would be done. (Note that the Kantian perspective would suggest a different course of action. Theft is bad. Newspapers do not want the government stealing their property, so they should not condone or promote the theft of government property.) Or take the case of a small midwestern paper that chose to report the death of a local teenager who had left town, turned to prostitution and drugs, and been murdered. The paper decided that the potential benefits of this story as a warning to other parents outweighed the grief it would cause the murder victim's family.

The Veil of Ignorance   Justice is blind. Philosopher John Rawls argued that justice emerges when everyone is treated without social differentiations. Everybody doing the same job equally well should receive equal pay. Everybody who got an 80 on the test should get the same grade. Rawls advocated that all parties in a problem situation be placed behind a barrier, the **veil of ignorance,** that conceals roles and social differentiations and that each participant be treated as an equal member of society as a whole. Rawls's veil of ignorance suggests that we structure our actions to protect the most vulnerable members of society. It is easy to see the relevance of this principle to the workings of the mass media. If we applied the veil of ignorance to the problem of hammering out the proper relationship between politicians and journalists, the blatant adversarial relationship so often found between the groups would disappear. Behind the veil all newsmakers would be the same. Inherent cynicism and abrasiveness on the part of the press would disappear, as would mistrust and suspicion on the part of the politicians. On a more specific level, consider the case of a financial reporter who frequently gets tips and inside information on deals and mergers that affect the prices of stocks and passes these tips on to friends who use this information for their own profit. The veil of ignorance suggests that the reporter must treat all audience members the same. Personal friends should not benefit from inside information.

The Principle of Self-Determination   This principle, closely associated with the Judeo-Christian ethic and also discussed by Kant, might be summarized as "Love your neighbor as yourself." Human beings have unconditional value apart from any and all circumstances. Their basic right to **self-determination** should not be violated by using them as simply a means to accomplish a goal. A corollary to this principle is that no one should allow him- or herself to be treated as a means to someone else's ends. Suppose that sources inside a government investigation on political corruption leak to the press the names of some people suspected of taking bribes, and the press, in turn, publishes the allegations and the names of the suspects. The principle of self-determination suggests that the press is being used by those who leaked the story as a means to accomplish their goal. Perhaps those involved in the investigation want to turn public opinion against those named or simply to earn some favorable publicity for their efforts. In any case, the press should resist being used in these circumstances. The rights, values, and decisions of others must always be respected.

▲ A Model for Individual Ethical Decisions

In numerous situations personal ethical decisions have to be made about what should or should not be included in media content or what should or should not be done. Every day, reporters, editors, station managers, and other media professionals have to make these decisions. Too often, however, these decisions are made haphazardly, without proper analysis of the ethical dimensions involved. This section presents a model that media professionals can use to evaluate and examine their decisions. This model is adapted from the work of Ralph Potter.[1]

Definitions → Values → Principles → Loyalties → Action

---

[1]Ralph Potter, "The Logic of Moral Argument," in *Toward a Discipline of Social Ethics,* P. Deats ed. (Boston: Boston University Press, 1972).

Covering sensational court proceedings, such as the Anna Nicole Smith custody hearing, can raise serious ethical problems for journalists.

In short, the model asks the individual to consider four aspects of the situation before taking action. First, define the situation. What are the pertinent facts involved? What are the possible actions? Second, determine what values are involved. Which values are more relevant to deciding a course of action? Third, establish what ethical principles apply. We have discussed five that might be involved; there may be others.

Fourth, decide where our loyalties lie. To whom do we owe a moral duty? It is possible that we might owe a duty to ourselves, clients, business organizations, the profession, or society in general. To whom is our obligation most important?

Let us examine how this model would work in a real situation. It's a sad fact of life for the news media, but tragic events often raise crucial ethical questions. The 1999 Columbine High School shootings, the terrorist attacks of 2001, and the ravages of Hurricane Katrina in 2005 all forced media executives to make tough decisions about how to cover the news. The recent tragedy on the campus of Virginia Tech was only the latest event to prompt questions about media ethics.

On April 16, 2007, a deranged gunman killed 32 people at Virginia Tech before turning the gun on himself. Two days later NBC received a package from the gunman containing written text, 29 digital photographs showing the killer holding various weapons, and video clips in which the gunman ranted about his reasons for the killings. NBC faced a difficult decision when it came to reporting this bizarre development in the story. After much internal discussion, NBC decided to air portions of the material on *NBC Nightly News with Brian Williams*. Was this responsible journalism or harmful sensationalism? Let's apply the Potter model and see what we can conclude.

1. *Establish the facts.* The network was certain the tape and the photographs were authentic, and not some twisted hoax. Executives who viewed the material knew that the images and words would be disturbing to the audience and especially distressing to the family and friends of those involved in the tragedy. They were also aware that the motives behind the shooting had yet to be revealed and that the tape gave some insight into the warped psyche of the killer. Moreover, NBC was unsure why the gunman had sent them the material, and the network was also uncertain if the gunman had sent the same or different material to other news outlets. In short, if they chose not to show it, NBC didn't know if the material would soon appear on the Web or on other newscasts.

2. *Clarify values.* Journalists value responsibility. Broadcasting the hateful and inflammatory remarks of the gunman that might inspire others to commit violence would seem to run counter to this value. At the same time, however, journalists have a duty to inform the public, no matter how disturbing the story might be. Choosing not to publicize this material would have meant abdicating this valuable function. Finally, journalists value their credibility. Too much emphasis on the sensational, the shocking, and the lurid aspects of this story at the expense of solid reporting could have had a deleterious impact on credibility.

3. *State principles.* At least three of the ethical principles discussed above are relevant. The first is utilitarianism. Did the benefits of airing the material outweigh the potential harm? NBC executives had to consider the possibility that the material would cause pain to those closely affected by the shootings and perhaps even inspire copycat crimes. At the same time, the photos and videos could have provided some explanation for why the events occurred and might have helped mental health

authorities prevent another such tragedy. The second principle is the golden mean. The network could have chosen to release none, some, or all of the material. The most shocking and disturbing items could have been kept from public view. The third principle is the categorical imperative. If the network believed that it should not give national exposure to the ravings of a deranged individual, no matter what the possible benefit, then the material should not have been aired regardless of what good it might do.

4. *Determine loyalties.* Journalists have a loyalty to their audience to report fully the facts of a story. That loyalty doesn't extend to protecting the audience. Instead, the primary task of a journalist is to tell the audience the truth, no matter how ugly it might be. The network also had a responsibility to operate in the public interest and not turn its facilities into a forum for a deranged individual. Finally, journalists are human beings and have a loyalty to other individuals and a duty not to cause them needless pain.

What actions resulted in this case? First, the president of NBC news evidently used the utilitarian principle and decided that the benefits of airing the material outweighed the potential harm. He stated that he was aware of the pain that the video might cause but added, "This is as close as we will ever come to being inside the mind of a killer." NBC also relied on the principle of the golden mean. The network chose to air only about 2 minutes of video, 7 of the digital photographs, and 37 sentences out of 23 pages of written material. In short, there were far more disturbing images that didn't make it to air. NBC demonstrated restraint in light of what they might have publicized.

Not everybody, however, agreed with NBC and endorsed these principles. The Canadian Broadcasting Corporation decided to use none of the material, stating that it feared the video would spark copycat killings. Others criticized NBC for publicizing the images on their national broadcast rather than posting them on their Web site, with suitable warning messages.

The controversy continued after NBC chose to air the images when other news organizations picked them up and continued to show them over and over again. Public reaction soon turned negative, and critics charged that legitimate news coverage had been eclipsed by sensationalism. Faced with this backlash, all of the television news media cut back on showing the images.

Of course, journalists and other media practitioners seldom face ethical dilemmas as pronounced and as difficult as those posed by the Virginia Tech shootings. Nonetheless, this tragic event underscores the need for media professionals to have a well-developed personal code of ethics that can offer guidance in all situations.

Most of the time, ethical decisions are made in good faith with a sincere desire to serve the public, and the decisions reflect positively on the profession. Sometimes, however, ethical judgments may be adversely affected by other influences.

▲ Acculturation

One of the factors that influence the judgment of some reporters is a phenomenon known as **acculturation.** Simply defined, *acculturation* in a media context means the tendency of reporters or other media professionals to accept the ideas, attitudes, and opinions of the group that they cover or with whom they have a great deal of contact. Many political reporters, for instance, come to share the views of the politicians they cover. So do many police-beat reporters. Publishers and station managers who spend a great deal of time with business leaders might come to adopt the point of view of industry. One study of reporters and legislators in Colorado revealed that political reporters and politicians held quite similar views. The study also revealed that many reporters identified with legislators, felt a sense of kinship with them, and actually considered themselves part of the legislative process. In the Potter model, these individuals have confused their loyalties. They see their duty to the group they are covering as more important than their duty to the profession of journalism.

Acculturation is not necessarily bad; it can cause concern, however, when it begins to affect judgment. Recently, a California newspaper learned that several off-duty police officers had terrorized a bar and had gotten into fistfights with some of its patrons. The disturbance was so serious that the chief of police recommended that three of the officers be dismissed. The paper, however, sat on the story for almost 6 weeks. It turned out that in the past the police and the paper had developed an easy sense of cooperation. Police officers had been given the OK to look at the paper's files; in turn, the officers would give the paper mug shots if the paper needed a picture of a suspect. It is possible that this close and cooperative atmosphere led some journalists to identify with the police officers, which affected their professional judgment in handling this particular story.

Some critics have argued that the reporters embedded with military units during Operation Iraqi Freedom were also influenced by acculturation.

PERFORMANCE CODES

Many ethical decisions have to be made within hours or even minutes, without the luxury of lengthy philosophical reflection. In this regard media professionals are not very different from other professionals, such as doctors and lawyers. In these professions, codes of conduct or of ethics have been standardized to help individuals make decisions. If a doctor or a lawyer violates one of the tenets of these codes, he or she may be barred from practice by a decision of a panel of colleagues who oversee the profession. Here the similarity with the mass media ends. Media professionals, thoroughly committed to the notion of free speech, have no professional review boards that grant and revoke licenses. Media codes of performance and methods of self-regulation are less precise and less stringent than those of other organizations. But many of the ethical principles discussed are incorporated into these codes.

▲ The Print Media

During the colorful and turbulent age of jazz journalism (see Chapter 4), several journalists, apparently reacting against the excesses of some tabloids, founded the American Society of Newspaper Editors. This group voluntarily adopted the Canons of Journalism in 1923 without any public or governmental pressure. There were seven canons: responsibility, freedom of the press, independence, accuracy, impartiality, fair play, and decency. By and large, the canons are prescriptive (telling what ought to be done) rather than proscriptive (telling what ought to be avoided). Some of the canons are general and vague, with a great deal of room for individual interpretation. Under *responsibility*, for example, it is stated that "the use a newspaper makes of the share of public attention it gains serves to determine its sense of responsibility, which it shares with every member of its staff." This is a noble thought, but it is of little help when it comes to deciding if a newspaper should include the detail about the pornographic magazines in the star football player's car. Other statements seem simplistic. Under *accuracy*, for example, one learns that "headlines should be fully warranted by the contents of the article they surmount." Nevertheless, these canons should not be dismissed as mere platitudes and empty rhetoric. They do represent the first concrete attempt by journalists to strive for professionalism in their field.

When the canons were first released, *Time* magazine held out grandiose hopes for the future of the profession: "The American Society of Newspaper Editors (ASNE) aims to be to journalism what the American Bar Association is to the legal fraternity." *Time* was overly optimistic. The legal fraternity, through its powerful bar associations, has the power to revoke a member's license to practice. Journalists have fiercely resisted any idea that resembles licensing as a restriction on their First Amendment rights. The ASNE has never proposed licensing or certifying journalists for this reason. In fact, the ASNE has never expelled a member in its history, even though it has had ample reason to do so.

When I go to Amazon.com, I have the option of visiting my own little store (called, appropriately enough, "Joe's Store") where Amazon.com makes recommendations about things I might like to buy. Amazon.com is able to do this because the site has scrupulously recorded on some computer somewhere my shopping history every time I have visited. Amazon.com, of course, is not the only organization that keeps track of personal information. Thanks to advances in information processing that make it easier to collect, track, and analyze large amounts of data, marketers know far more about us than ever before.

Some personal data are collected directly from a consumer. Many electronics stores routinely ask customers for their phone numbers when they check out. Some businesses offer a free trial subscription to a magazine. In order to get the free copies, a person must provide the company with a name and a mailing address.

Other data collection techniques are more subtle, such as supermarket frequent-shopper cards. In order to save a little money, consumers allow companies to track their purchases. As a result, someone knows how many cans of tuna a person buys each month and what kind of headache remedy is preferred. Branded credit cards (such as the Visa cards issued by Jeep and Dodge) reveal a customer's credit history and the amount of debt they carry. Radio-Frequency IDentification chips (RFIDs) are tiny devices (some smaller than grains of sand) that can be hidden in products or in frequent-shopper cards and used to track their movements. RFIDs can be read at a distance, without a person's knowledge or consent, by anyone with the proper hardware. RFID readers will probably replace the bar codes that are now scanned when a customer checks out at a supermarket or department store. If people pay by credit card, this will enable a company to secretly collect purchase data and link them with individual consumers. Eventually, RFIDs will probably end up on supermarket shelves where they will track people's shopping behavior by reading their frequent-shopper cards.

Have marketers gone too far? Some think so. About one-third of shoppers have rebelled against supermarket frequent-shopper cards. A group called Consumers Against Supermarket Privacy Invasion has come out against RFIDs. Online shoppers are also becoming more cautious. About 40 percent of Internet users say they routinely delete cookies (small files placed on a person's computer by Web sites that make it easier to identify the user's preferences). In the wake of news stories about companies losing data files and the growing prevalence of identity theft, it appears that consumers are becoming more protective of their privacy.

The Society of Professional Journalists (SPJ; formerly Sigma Delta Chi) adopted its code at about the same time as the ASNE. The code was designed to guide journalists working in all media. The SPJ code was unchanged for more than 45 years, but as journalistic ethics became more problematic, the code was revised in 1973, 1984, 1987, and again in 1996. The newly adopted SPJ code is organized around four main principles:

1. *Seek the truth and report it.* Journalists should be honest, fair, and courageous in reporting the news.

2. *Minimize harm.* Journalists should treat sources, subjects, and colleagues as human beings deserving of respect.

3. *Act independently.* Journalists should be free of obligation to any interest other than the public's right to know.

4. *Be accountable.* Journalists should be accountable to their audience and to each other.

In 1975 the Associated Press Managing Editors (APME) association adopted a code that also discussed responsibility, accuracy, integrity, and independence. Revised in 1995, the APME code covers such issues as plagiarism and diversity. As with the ASNE's canons, adherence to the code is voluntary. Neither the SPJ nor the ASNE association has developed procedures to enforce its codes.

In late 1999 the Gannett Company became the first newspaper chain to spell out ethical principles for its papers. Other newspaper chains have companywide guidelines covering general issues, but individual papers can set policy in their own newsrooms. The Gannett guidelines are the first to be newsroom-specific. The decision to establish guidelines stemmed from a growing public distrust of the media and a desire to reassure readers about the fairness and accuracy of newspaper content. The new guidelines forbid, among other things, lying to get a story, fabricating news, and publishing misleading alterations of photographs. The full text of the guidelines can be found at the company Web site (www.gannett.com).

▲ Broadcasting

For many years radio and television broadcasters followed the National Association of Broadcasters (NAB) Code of Good Practice. This code first appeared in 1929 and was revised periodically over the years. It was divided into two parts, one covering advertising and the other covering general program practices. In 1982, however, a court ruled that the code placed undue limitations on advertising, and the NAB suspended the advertising part of its code. The next year, to forestall more legal pressure, the NAB officially dissolved the code in its entirety.

Although the code is gone, its impact lingers. In 1990 the NAB issued voluntary programming principles that addressed four key areas: children's TV, indecency, violence, and drug and substance abuse. The new guidelines were stated in a broad and general way: "Glamorization of drug use and substance abuse should be avoided. . . . Violence . . . should only be portrayed in a responsible manner and should not be used exploitatively." To stay out of trouble with the Justice Department, the NAB declared that there would be no interpretation or enforcement of these provisions and that the standards were not designed to inhibit creativity.

Trying to resurrect a code for broadcasters is a favorite activity among politicians. In 1997 four U.S. senators introduced a bill that would exempt the broadcasting and cable industries from antitrust laws so that they could develop a new code. Other bills that urged broadcasters to develop a voluntary code of conduct were introduced in Congress in 1998 and 1999.

In the broadcast journalism area, the Radio and Television News Directors Association has an 11-part code that covers everything from cameras in the courtroom to invasion of privacy.

The V-Chip and its companion ratings system are an interesting interaction between formal and informal controls. For purposes of this discussion, it is important to point out that the V-Chip represents an example of the government's pressuring the video industry to adopt "voluntary" guidelines that categorize programming. If the industry failed to develop its own program ratings to work with the V-Chip, Congress left the door open for the FCC to do it for them. The threat of government action has been used before to prod broadcasters into reforms that they were reluctant to make on their own. In fact, scholars who have studied the FCC have even given this phenomenon a name: the "raised eyebrow" technique. The V-Chip legislation is a bit stronger than the raised eyebrow, but its end result is the same.

Producers rate program content according to an age-based scale ranging from "TV-G," suitable for a general audience, to "TV-M," for mature audience only. Further, special advisories for specific content are also displayed: "S" for sexual content and "V" for excessive violence. Parents can set the V-Chip to block whatever programming they feel is unacceptable for their children. For example, the V-Chip can be set to block all "TV-M"-rated shows. Interestingly, in its 2007 report on television violence, the FCC declared that the V-Chip, while helpful, was not an effective tool in protecting young people from violent TV content.

▲ Motion Pictures

Codes of conduct in the motion picture industry emerged during the 1920s. Scandals were racking Hollywood at that time (see Chapter 9), and many states had passed or were considering censorship laws that would control the content of movies. In an attempt to save itself from being tarred and feathered as it were, the industry invited Will Hays, a former postmaster general and elder of the Presbyterian Church, to head a new organization that would clean up films. Hays became the president, chairman of the board, and chairman of the executive committee of a new organization, the Motion Picture Producers and Distributors of America (MPPDA). In 1930 the Motion Picture Production Code was adopted by the new group. The code was mainly proscriptive; it described what should be avoided in order for filmmakers to get their movies past existing censorship boards and listed what topics should be handled carefully so as not to rile existing pressure groups. The 1930 code is remarkable for its specificity; it rambles on for nearly 20 printed pages. The following are some excerpts:

> *The presentation of scenes, episodes, plots, etc. which are deliberately meant to excite [sex and passion] on the part of the audience is always wrong, is subversive to the interest of society, and is a peril to the human race.*
>
> *The more intimate parts of the human body are the male and female organs and the breasts of a woman.*
>
> *a. They should never be uncovered.*
> *b. They should not be covered with transparent or translucent material.*
> *c. They should not be clearly and unmistakably outlined by garments. . . .*
>
> *There must be no display at any time of machine guns, sub-machine guns or other weapons generally classified as illegal weapons. . . .*
>
> *Obscene dances are those: which represent sexual actions, whether performed solo or with two or more, which are designed to excite an audience, arouse passion, or cause physical excitement.*

A few years after the Production Code was drafted, a Roman Catholic organization, the Legion of Decency (see the boxed insert "The Legion of Decency"), pressured the industry to put teeth into its code enforcement. The MPPDA ruled that no company belonging to its organization would distribute or release any film unless it bore the Production Code Administration's seal of approval. In addition, a $25,000 fine could be levied against a firm that violated this rule. Because of the hammerlock that the major studios had over the movie industry at this time, it was virtually impossible for an independent producer to make or exhibit a film without the aid of a member company. As a result, the Production Code turned out to be more restrictive than many of the local censorship laws it was designed to avoid.

The Production Code was a meaningful force in the film industry for about 20 years. During the late 1940s, however, changes that would ultimately alter the basic structure of the motion picture industry also led to the code being scuttled. In 1948 the Paramount case ended producer-distributor control of theaters, thus allowing independent producers to market a film without the Production Code seal. In addition, economic competition from television prompted films to tackle more mature subjects. The industry responded during the 1950s by liberalizing the code; despite this easing of restrictions, more and more producers began to ignore them. Nonetheless, the code, outdated and unenforceable, persisted into the 1960s. A 1966 revision that tried to keep pace with changing social attitudes proved to be too little too late.

In 1968 the motion picture industry entered into a new phase of self-regulation when the Production Code seal of approval was dropped and a new motion picture rating system was established. Operated under the auspices of the Motion Picture Association of America (successor to the MPPDA), the National Association of Theater Owners, and the Independent Film Importers and Distributors of America, this new system, commonly referred to as the **MPAA rating system,** places films into one of five categories:

   G: Suitable for general audiences.

  PG: Parental guidance suggested.

PG-13:   Some content may be objectionable for children under 13 (a new category added in 1984).

   R: Restricted to persons over age 17 unless accompanied by parent or adult guardian.

NC-17:   No children under 17 admitted. (This category replaced the X rating in 1990. The MPAA made the change in response to several producers who argued that adult-themed, daring, but nonpornographic films should not be lumped into the same category as porno films.)

Unlike the old Production Code, which regulated film content, the new system leaves producers more or less free to include whatever scenes they like as long as they realize that,

After World War I, during the roaringest part of the Roaring Twenties, the films that grossed the most money had titles like *Red Hot Romance, She Could Not Help It, Her Purchase Price,* and *Plaything of Broadway.* One movie ad of the period boasted breathlessly of "brilliant men, beautiful jazz babies, champagne baths, midnight revels, petting parties in the purple dawn." Before long, public opposition to such sensational movies began to form. The appointment of Will Hays, the creation of the Motion Picture Producers and Distributors of America, and the adoption of the Motion Picture Production Code were designed, in part, to forestall this public criticism.

Much of the code was suggested by a Roman Catholic layman, Martin Quigley, and a Roman Catholic priest, Father Daniel Lord. Despite the existence of the code, however, sensational films still appeared in significant numbers. This trend was disturbing to many segments in society, particularly the Catholic Church. Keep in mind that at this time the United States was in the midst of a severe economic depression. Many individuals, including prominent Catholics, connected the country's economic poverty with the nation's moral bankruptcy as evidenced by the films of the period. Additionally, an Apostolic Delegate from Rome took the film industry to task in a blistering speech before the Catholic Charities Convention in New York.

In April 1934 a committee composed of American bishops responded to the speech and to the general tenor of the period by announcing the organization of a nationwide Legion of Decency, whose members were to fight for better films. The legion threatened to boycott those theaters that exhibited objectionable films, and it sometimes made good on its threats. The Chicago chapter of the legion enrolled a half-million members in a matter of days and was matched by equal enrollment in Brooklyn. Detroit Catholics affixed "We Demand Clean Movies" bumper stickers to their cars. Other religious groups joined the legion—Jewish clergy in New York, Lutherans in Missouri. Pope Pius XI praised the legion as an "excellent experiment" and called upon bishops all over the world to imitate it.

There were 20 million Catholics in the United States in 1934, and naturally, the film industry took this group seriously. The Production Code Administration was set up with the power to slap a $25,000 fine on films released without the administration's seal of approval. The Legion of Decency's boycotts hurt enough at the box office to force many theaters to book only films that the legion approved. In Albuquerque, New Mexico, 17 of 21 theaters agreed not to book a film condemned by the legion. In Albany, New York, Catholics pledged to avoid for 6 months each theater that had screened the condemned film *Baby Doll.* Producers, frightened by this display of economic power, began meeting with legion members to make sure there were no potentially inflammatory elements in their films.

By the 1960s, however, the Legion of Decency was losing most of its clout. The restructuring of the film industry allowed independent producers to market their films without code approval. Many producers did just that and demonstrated that some films could make money even without legion and Production Code approval. The increasingly permissive mood of the country encouraged an avalanche of more mature and controversial films. Moreover, the legion, renamed the National Catholic Office for Motion Pictures, painted itself into a corner when it condemned such artistically worthwhile films as Bergman's *The Silence* and Antonioni's *Blowup,* and endorsed such films as *Godzilla vs. the Thing* and *Goliath and the Sins of Babylon.* By the 1970s this group had effectively lost all its power; it was essentially disbanded in 1980. Nonetheless, during its prime the Legion of Decency was the single most effective private influence on the film industry.

The Motion Picture Association of America's rating is a prominent part of most movie marquees.

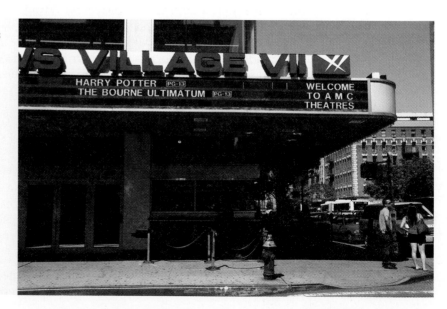

by so doing, they may restrict the size of their potential audience. One possible repercussion of this system may be the steady decline in the number of G-rated films released each year. Producers evidently feel that movies in this category will be perceived as children's films and will not be attractive to a more mature audience. During the first 11 years of the rating system's existence, the percentage of films in the G category dropped, while the percentage of films in the R category increased. X-rated or NC-17-rated films have never accounted for more than 10 percent of the total number of films submitted for review (of course, many low-budget, hard-core pornographic films are never submitted for classification).

In order for the MPAA rating system to work, producers, distributors, theater owners, and parents must all cooperate. There is no governmental involvement in the classification system; there are no fines involved. Moviemakers are not required to submit a film for rating. People evidently think that the system is a good idea. An industry survey done in 2002 disclosed that 74 percent of the adults surveyed considered the ratings "very useful" guides for children's attendance.

▲ The Advertising Industry

In the advertising industry several professional organizations have drafted codes of performance. The American Association of Advertising Agencies first adopted its Standards of Practice in 1924. This code, which covers contracts, credit extension, unfair tactics, and the creative side of advertising, contains provisions prohibiting misleading price claims, offensive statements, and the circulation of harmful rumors about a competitor. The Advertising Code of American Business, developed and distributed by the American Advertising Federation and the Association of Better Business Bureaus International, covers much the same ground. Memberships in these organizations and adherence to the codes are voluntary. In public relations the Public Relations Society of America adopted its first code in 1954 and revised it during the 1980s. As with the other codes, enforcement is essentially voluntary, and the society has no control over a practitioner who is not a member.

INTERNAL CONTROLS

Codes established by professional organizations and individual ethics are not the only informal controls on media behavior. Most media organizations have other internal controls that frequently come into play. Written statements of policy can be found in most newspaper, television, radio, and motion picture organizations. In advertising a professional organization for self-regulation has existed since 1971.

▲ Organizational Policy: Television Networks' Standards and Practices

For many years each major network maintained a large department that was usually labeled "Standards and Practices" or something similar. Staff members in these departments would make literally thousands of decisions each season on the acceptability of dialogue, plotlines, and visual portrayals. During the late 1980s, however, network budget cuts took their toll, and most of these departments were scaled back dramatically. As criticism of television content increased during the 1990s, these departments were enlarged somewhat, but they still have far fewer people working in them than they did in the early 1980s. The departments at Fox, NBC, and ABC review everything their networks air, including commercials. At CBS the standards department reviews children's programs, docudramas, ads, new shows, and about a dozen existing series. The efforts devoted to monitoring standards vary greatly among cable networks. MTV, for example, closely monitors all its programs; the Discovery Channel rarely has problems regarding taste. Pay channels, such as HBO, have more liberal standards.

The broadcast and cable networks are also relying more and more on the judgment of series producers to determine standards of acceptability. Producers, for their part, have a general notion about how far they can go without raising network displeasure. The networks will generally closely monitor the first few episodes of a series that may cause problems. After that they will put more trust in the producers' standards.

It is probably obvious to any casual observer of broadcast television that network standards have become more liberal over the years. For instance, top-rated *CSI* has broadcast episodes dealing with sadomasochism and sexual fetishes. *Brothers and Sisters* has a gay character as a star.

There are several reasons behind these changes. First, society has become more open-minded. Subjects that were once taboo, such as male impotence, are now discussed routinely in commercials. Second, the broadcast networks have to compete with the more permissive cable networks on which shows such as *Sex and the City* have pushed the envelope of acceptability even further. Finally, the sex scandal involving President Bill Clinton and Monica Lewinsky put sexual topics on the evening newscasts and immediately eliminated many taboos.

Despite this liberalization the networks' standards and practices departments still exercise some caution. Offensive stereotypes are not allowed. Networks traditionally have not aired ads for abortion clinics, contraceptives (some local stations have aired contraceptive ads), or massage parlors.

The reality show *Age of Love* raised questions about what was acceptable in prime time.

The Internet can provide an outlet for material that the standards and practices department deems inappropriate for broadcast TV. The unedited versions of comedy skits from network shows such as *Saturday Night Live* sometimes make their way onto YouTube or other video-sharing sites.

In addition to the networks, local stations also exercise self-regulation. Occasionally, a local station will decide that a network show is inappropriate for its audience and decline to show it or broadcast it at a later time. For example, more than 20 local stations refused to air *Maxim's Hot 100*, a one-hour special that featured scantily clad females. In 2006 two NBC stations refused to carry episodes of a controversial series, *The Book of Daniel*.

Local stations also construct a **policy book.** This book typically spells out the station's philosophy and standards of operation and identifies which practices are

Ethical Issues   Is It Real or Is It Photoshop?

The digital revolution in photography has made it possible to alter images with just a couple of mouse clicks. The retouched images are extremely difficult if not impossible to detect. This development has both positive and negative aspects. On the one hand, as most people who have experimented with digital photography are aware, software programs such as Photoshop make it possible to correct for poor lighting conditions, remove the annoying "red eye" effect, and in general tweak an image so that it looks better. On the other hand, digital photography has raised some perplexing issues for photojournalists. How much alteration is ethically acceptable in a news photo?

This dilemma has surfaced several times. Probably the most prominent example occurred during the O. J. Simpson murder trial when *Time* magazine published an altered photo in which his face was darkened and the background was lightened, alterations that made Simpson look more menacing. In the aftermath of this event, all major newsmagazines and newspapers reaffirmed policies that forbade any alteration of news photos.

A more recent example occurred during the 2003 Iraq war when Brian Walski, a photographer for the *Los Angeles Times,* was fired for digitally altering a photo of a British soldier and a group of Iraqi civilians. In order to improve composition and make the crowd of civilians look larger, Walski combined elements of two separate pictures into a composite. A close look at the picture reveals that the images of some Iraqis were copied from one photo and digitally pasted on another.

Walski's behavior raises several issues, not the least of which is why he would do something like this. He was not a novice photojournalist. He had worked for the *Times* for several years and had won several awards from the California Press Photographers Association for his Afghan war photos. Is this a case of a photojournalist working for a major paper being under so much pressure to produce great photos and beat the competition that he overlooks basic journalistic ethics?

Even more puzzling is the fact that the composite photo is not that much different from the originals. Why risk a career over what appears to be a minor improvement in the aesthetics of the picture? Might members of a profession be motivated more by a desire to impress their editors and other photojournalists than they are by ethics?

On a more general level, is it ethically correct to do any kind of alteration to a news photo? What about changing the dark and light tones in a photo to make it more printable in a newspaper or magazine? The content of the photo is the same; it just looks better. What about blurring the foreground and the background in a photo to make the main subject stand out? Again, the content stays the same; it is just that some parts are a little fuzzy. In a technique called *reverse cropping,* a person can lengthen a photo either vertically or horizontally by extending elements of the existing photo. The information in the photo stays basically the same.

Perhaps the results of an audience survey published in a 2001 issue of *Journalism and Communication Monographs* might help journalists establish some cultural norms for these new digital techniques. Almost all of the respondents thought that adjusting the tones in a photo to make it print better was an acceptable practice. Blurring the background and reverse cropping were less acceptable in news photos; only about one in four respondents approved of this process. The digital techniques that almost all respondents felt were unethical were changing the tone of a photograph for dramatic effect, eliminating persons and other distracting items from the background of a photo, and creating composite photos by adding people or objects not in the original.

Most newspaper and magazine editors agree with these respondents, as demonstrated by the existence of many ethics policies, such as the one at the *Los Angeles Times,* that forbid the alteration of news photos. The logic behind such policies is easy to understand. If it is revealed that one news photo is a fake, doubt is cast on all the other photos that have been published. As one contributor to a Web forum for photojournalists put it, "I'll never be able to look at another one of Walski's award-winning photographs without wondering whether or not it is a fake."

---

encouraged or discouraged. For example, most television and radio stations have a policy against newsroom personnel functioning as commercial spokespersons. Radio stations typically have a policy against airing "homemade" tapes and records. Other stations may have rules against playing songs that are drug-oriented or sexually suggestive. Commercials that make extravagant claims or ads for questionable products and services might also be prohibited under local-station policy.

▲ Organizational Policy: Newspapers and Magazines

Newspapers and magazines create policy statements that take two distinct forms. **Operating policies** cover the everyday problems and situations that crop up during the normal functioning of the paper or magazine. **Editorial policies** are guidelines that the newspaper or magazine follows to persuade the public on certain issues or to achieve specific goals.

Operating policies vary from one paper or magazine to another. In general, however, these policies cover such matters as accepting freebies, using deception to gather information, paying newsmakers for a story or exclusive interview (checkbook journalism), taking junkets, conducting electronic surveillance, using stolen documents, accepting advertising for X-rated films, and publishing the names of rape victims. Also covered are outside employment of reporters and editors and conflicts of interest. Here, for example, are excerpts from *Rules and Guidelines* used by the *Milwaukee Journal*:

> *Free tickets or passes to sports events, movies, theatrical productions, circuses, ice shows, or other entertainment may not be accepted or solicited by staff members.*
>
> *A gift that exceeds token value should be returned promptly with an explanation that it is against our policy. If it is impractical to return it, the company will donate it to a charity.*
>
> *Participating in politics at any level is not allowed, either for pay or as a volunteer. Public relations and publicity work in fields outside the Journal should be avoided.*

Some newspapers and magazines are liberal; some are conservative. Some support Democratic candidates; others support Republicans. Some are in favor of nuclear energy; others against. These and other attitudes are generally expressed in the editorial pages of the newspaper. Editorial policy is generally clear at most publications. The *Chicago Tribune* has traditionally expressed a conservative point of view. The *New York Times* has a more liberal policy. The editorial policy of a paper will exert a certain amount of control over the material that is printed on its editorial pages. Of course, the paper has a perfect right to do this. There may be times, however, when the editorial policy of the paper spills over onto its news pages, and this might cause a problem for the paper's reputation for objectivity, responsibility, and integrity.

One problem that crops up periodically is called *boosterism*, a procommunity philosophy that sometimes causes not-so-good news to go unreported. In Flint, Michigan, when the local Fisher Body plant closed, TV networks and newspapers across the country announced the bad news that Flint was about to lose 3,600 jobs. The local Flint paper did not mention the job loss until the 11th paragraph on an inside page. "Good news," however, got prominent play: A story about new shrubs being planted at the local Buick facility earned front-page coverage.

Owners and publishers can exert editorial control over news policy in several ways. They can hire only those people who agree with their editorial views. For example, the *New Orleans Times-Picayune* ran an ad in a trade magazine for a business reporter. One of the qualifications was a "probusiness philosophy." They can also fire people who produce stories that the owner does not like, or they can issue orders to downplay some topics while paying large amounts of attention to others.

What is the significance of these examples for the news-consuming public? For one thing, the sample cases are probably exceptions to the norm rather than the norm itself. Nonetheless, they do illustrate the potential hazards of relying on only one source for news. The intelligent consumer of news and information should rely on several different media to get a more complete picture.

▲ Media Self-Criticism

Some informal control over media content and practices comes from within. Although the amount of internal media criticism has grown in the past few years, it is still small when compared with the amount of investigative reporting and critical analyses that newspapers, magazines, television, and radio conduct about other facets of society. Many newspapers and magazines have media critics and media reporters. The amount of meaningful critical writing done by these journalists, however, is highly variable. Some of the better-known critics in the print media are Ken Auletta of *The New Yorker*, Howard Kurtz of the *Washington Post*, and Tom Shales of *Television Week*.

Several journalism reviews regularly criticize media performance. The *Columbia Journalism Review* is the best known, but its circulation is only about 25,000. Others that are important are the *American Journalism Review* and the *Media Studies Journal*.

The Internet has opened up a new channel for media self-criticism. The Media Channel (www.mediachannel.org), for example, contains news, analysis of issues, and criticism about media across the globe. Journalist Jim Romenesko maintains a similar site at www.poynter.org. The impact of these and similar sites is yet to be determined.

They Obviously Weren't Listening

Thirty-one engineering students enrolled in a course at a Canadian university were recently punished for cheating. The students had downloaded term papers from the Internet and submitted them as original work. What course were they taking? "Introduction to Ethics."

Cable and broadcast television networks usually offer few programs with serious criticism of the media. Newspapers do a bit more in this area; the *Wall Street Journal* has occasionally run an in-depth study of the problems facing the newspaper industry. In film the industry newspaper *Variety* has sometimes published an article critical of the film industry. *Billboard*, the trade publication of the sound-recording industry, has run analytical, if not critical, pieces on the recording industry.

Some newspapers and other media organizations have tried to incorporate an idea from Scandinavia into their operations to provide some internal criticism. An **ombudsperson** is employed by the company to handle complaints from audience members who feel they have gotten a raw deal. The ombudsperson also criticizes in general the performance of the organization's personnel. Although the number of ombudspersons in the United States remains small, interest in the position has grown in recent years, primarily because news organizations are worried that they are losing credibility with their audiences. There are about 40 ombudspersons in the United States, just about all at newspapers. The position is almost nonexistent in TV newsrooms. (One of the reasons may be the difficult-to-pronounce title "ombudsperson." At one newspaper, letters were addressed to the "Omnibus person" or to "Dear Omnipotent.")

▲ Professional Self-Regulation in Advertising

In 1971 the leading advertising professional organizations—the Council of Better Business Bureaus, the American Advertising Federation, the American Association of Advertising Industries, and the Association of National Advertisers—formed the National Advertising Review Council. Its objective is to sustain high standards of truth and accuracy in advertising. The council itself is composed of two divisions: the National Advertising Division (NAD) and the National Advertising Review Board (NARB). When a complaint about an ad is made by a consumer or competitor, the complaint goes first to the NAD, which evaluates it. The NAD can dismiss the complaint as unfounded or trivial, or it can contact the advertiser for an explanation or further substantiation. If the NAD is satisfied that the ad in question is accurate, it will dismiss the complaint. If the NAD is not satisfied with the explanation, it can ask the advertiser to change the ad or discontinue the message.

If the advertiser disagrees, the case goes to the NARB, which functions as a court of appeals. Ultimately, if the case does not result in an acceptable solution, the NARB may call it to the attention of the Federal Trade Commission or other appropriate agencies. Sending a case to the FTC happens rarely. In 1993 the board turned over to the FTC the first fraudulent advertising case in the NARB's 22-year history. Most advertisers generally comply with the NAD's wishes. In 2007, for example, the NAD ruled that Crest toothpaste stop making claims that suggested its Pro-Health toothpaste is recommended by dentists.

Industry groups also exert control over advertising for their products. For example, the Miller Brewing Company and the Anheuser-Busch Company voluntarily agreed to remove their ads from MTV because they did not want to appear to be encouraging underage drinking.

OUTSIDE INFLUENCES

The larger context that surrounds a media organization often contains factors that have an influence on media performance. In this section we will discuss four: (1) economics, (2) pressure groups, (3) press councils, and (4) education.

▲ Economic Pressures

Money is a potent influence on media gatekeepers. In commercial media the loss of revenue can be an important consideration in controlling what gets filmed, published, or broadcast. Economic controls come in many shapes and forms. Pressure can be brought to bear by

As mentioned in the text, an "ombudsman" or "ombudsperson" is a person who listens to complaints and mediates disputes between aggrieved parties. The concept is especially popular in Scandinavia (*ombud* is the Swedish word for "commissioner" or "agent"), where ombudspersons investigate complaints involving citizens and the government.

The ombudsperson model has also been applied to journalism, but the people who hold the position are sometimes called *public editors* or *reader representatives.* Whatever their title, their tasks remain the same: to handle reader and viewer complaints and to explain controversial news decisions. In an era when credibility is a significant issue, one would think that having a public editor would be something that most news organizations would favor. Nonetheless, although there are around 1,500 daily newspapers in the United States, there are only around 30 public editors. Why so few?

For many years the executives at the *New York Times* did not want to appoint a public editor because they feared that such a move might hurt staff morale. Then came the Jayson Blair scandal involving the fabrication of stories, and the *Times* reconsidered. Nonetheless, many reporters and editors don't like the idea of having someone looking over their shoulder and second-guessing their professional judgment.

Some newspapers claim that they don't need a public editor because the publisher and the regular staff editors are the readers' ultimate ombudspersons. Hiring a public editor might encourage other editors to ignore their responsibilities to readers.

Other newspapers cite money as the problem. Public editors tend to come from the senior ranks of newspaper employees and tend to command high salaries (the average salary in 2000 was between $75,000 and $100,000). Many newspapers would argue that their readers are better served by using that money to hire additional reporters.

Despite these objections there are several advantages that come with a public editor. First, it shows that the newspaper considers its readers and their views important. In an era of declining circulation, it's essential for a newspaper not to alienate those concerned readers who take the time to contact the news organization with their complaints and opinions. Public editors can also lessen readers' frustration. Rather than having their calls or e-mails transferred from person to person, readers have a designated person they can contact.

Second, a public editor can function as an educator. The process of journalism may be unfamiliar to many readers, and the public editor can explain the hows and whys behind certain decisions. Why did the paper run a certain controversial photograph? How are headlines written? Why did this topic get so much or so little coverage? The public editor can share insights about decision making and the rationale that guided the newspaper.

Third, having a public editor demonstrates that the newspaper is willing to subject itself to the same scrutiny and analysis that it gives to everybody else. A newspaper should be held accountable for its actions, just like the government or a business. Newspapers have traditionally performed the watchdog function for society; a public editor demonstrates that someone is watching the watchdog.

Finally, are public editors too expensive? Maybe for some smaller papers, but most papers in the top 50 markets could probably afford one. If a full-time editor is too costly, perhaps a part-time editor would be helpful. In any case, there may be costs involved in not having a public editor. Those readers who find that their complaints are ignored or who are not satisfied with an impersonal response might stop subscribing.

In sum, despite all of the advantages, the concept of a public editor is not popular among newspapers and other news organizations. Telephone companies, department stores, credit card issuers, and many other service industries have well-established programs of customer service, but the newspaper industry still lags behind.

---

advertisers, by the medium's own business policy, by the general economic structure of the industry, and by consumer groups.

Pressure from Advertisers   The recording industry gets its revenue from the purchase of individual tracks and discs. Consequently, it earns virtually no money from advertisers and is generally immune to their pressures. The film industry makes most of its money from the sale of individual tickets. Advertisers have some limited influence through what is called *product placement*—an arrangement whereby an advertiser pays a movie studio to include its product in a film. *Casino Royale,* for example, was filled with scenes that featured brands such as Ford, Sony, and Omega. Nonetheless, in relative terms, advertisers have only modest influence over motion picture content. In the print media, on the other hand, newspapers depend on advertising for about 75 percent of their income, while magazines derive 50 percent of their revenues from ads. Radio and television, of course, depend on ads for almost all their income.

It looked like a good story. The video, posted on YouTube, showed what looked like a stock car race victory celebration at Altamont Motorsports Park. Then, out of nowhere, a man crawled through the open window of the winning car and, while everybody else was celebrating, drove off. Security personnel quickly blocked the track with tow trucks, pulled the thief from the vehicle, and threw him to the ground. It was such a good story that more than a hundred TV stations used the YouTube video on their newscasts.

The problem: The event was staged by TaxBrain.com, an online income tax preparation service, to advertise its services. The car and the race car driver were both sponsored by TaxBrain. The apparent thief was an actor, and the event was filmed by three cameras and professionally edited before it was posted on YouTube. Putting the video clip on YouTube was an attempt by TaxBrain to take advantage of online "viral marketing," creating a buzz about a product on the Internet and then capitalizing on the free publicity. In this case, once the prank was revealed, TaxBrain got the publicity it wanted,

but much of it was negative, accusing the company of crossing an ethical line by disguising advertising as news.

Then there's the case of lonelygirl15, an apparent teenager who posted videos on YouTube describing her conflict with her parents and her attempts at romance. Lonelygirl15's video log was hugely popular, generating more than 15 million page views. As it turned out, lonelygirl15 was an aspiring actress, and the videos were a marketing ploy for a planned movie.

Is deceit a legitimate advertising tactic? The Center for Digital Democracy thinks not. The center's position is that all videos that were produced and placed on YouTube and other video-sharing sites for marketing purposes should be labeled as advertising. Some creative executives disagree. They point out that consumers should always be skeptical about the motives and credibility of the people who post videos on the Web.

Finally, there may be a downside to this kind of stealthy promotion. Many of the people who saw the stolen-race-car video recalled absolutely nothing about TaxBrain, the company that put the hoax together in the first place.

The actual amount of control that an advertiser has over media content and behavior is difficult to determine. It is probably fair to say, however, that most news stories and most television and radio programs are put together without much thought as to what advertisers will say about them.

Occasionally, however, you may find examples of pressure:

- In 2000 the USA cable network stopped production of a made-for-TV movie about two Seattle residents who died after taking cyanide-laced Excedrin because of pressure from a leading drug company.
- Executives at the *Boston Herald* suspended a reporter who wrote columns critical of a merger between two big Boston banks. One of the banks was a big advertiser in the newspaper and held the mortgage on the newspaper's building. (Management eventually relented and reinstated the journalist.)

Finally, a 2000 poll conducted by the *Columbia Journalism Review* found that about one in three reporters said they avoided stories that would be detrimental to advertisers.

Business Policies   Economic pressure on media content is sometimes encouraged by the business practices of the media themselves. When the Massachusetts Supreme Court ruled that a creditor could be sued for harassing those who owed money, the Boston newspapers declined to identify the retail store involved in the suit. The store in question was a big newspaper advertiser. In San Francisco a newspaper killed a column that criticized the Nike Company. It so happened that Nike was the sponsor of the paper's popular "Bay to Breakers" race.

Trading news coverage for advertising time or space is a common problem. A TV station in south Florida sent a flyer to its advertisers offering to do a news story on them in return for $5,000. While trying to negotiate a contract to carry live drawings for the New York State Lottery, a TV station promised lottery officials positive news coverage of lottery events. In both instances the stations withdrew the offers when their breach of ethics was revealed.

Then there is the problem of revenue-related reading matter. This issue crops up when a new shopping center or discount store opens in a community and gets heavy news coverage, maybe more than is justified by ordinary journalistic standards, in return for advertising revenue. Recently, in Waco, Texas, the local newspaper devoted half its front page and two inside pages (with seven color photographs) to the opening of a new supermarket. Not surprisingly, supermarkets spend a lot on newspaper ads.

These examples are not meant to criticize or impugn the reputation of any medium or profession. There are probably countless, less-publicized examples of newspapers, magazines, television, and radio stations resisting advertising and economic pressure. What you should learn from this section is the nature of the close relationship that can sometimes exist between advertisers and media and the pressures that can result. Most of the time, this relationship causes few problems. When professional judgment is compromised by dollar signs, however, then perhaps the economic pressures are performing a dysfunction for the media.

▲ Pressure Groups

Various segments of the audience can band together and try to exert control over the operation of mass media organizations. These groups sometimes use the threat of economic pressure (boycotts) or simply rely on the negative effects of bad publicity to achieve their goals. In radio and television, pressure groups (or *citizens' groups*, as they are often called) can resort to applying legal pressure during the license renewal process. Because of broadcasting's unique legal position, it has been the focus of a great deal of pressure group attention. In 1964, for example, a group of black citizens working with the Office of Communication of the United Church of Christ formed a pressure group and attempted to deny the license renewal of a TV station in Jackson, Mississippi, because of alleged discrimination on the part of station management. After a long and complicated legal battle, the citizens' group succeeded in its efforts. This success probably encouraged the formation of other groups. John Banzhaf III headed an organization called ASH (Action for Smoking and Health), for example, which was instrumental in convincing Congress to ban cigarette advertising from radio and television.

At about the same time, perhaps the most influential of all the pressure groups interested in broadcasting was formed: Action for Children's Television (ACT). From a modest start, this group was successful in achieving the following:

- Persuading the networks to appoint a supervisor for children's programming
- Eliminating drug and vitamin ads from kids' shows
- Instituting a ban on the host's selling in children's programs
- Reducing the amount of advertising during Saturday morning programs
- Helping a bill concerning children's TV pass Congress in 1990

ACT disbanded in 1992. In its final press release, the organization said that its major goal had been achieved with the passage of the 1990 Children's Television Act and that people who want better television for kids now "have Congress on their side."

In the mid-1970s other self-interest groups whose primary interest was not broadcasting began to get involved in television programming. The American Medical Association and the National Parent-Teacher Association both criticized TV violence. The National Organization for Women campaigned for more representative portrayals of women in the mass media. The American-Arab Anti-Discrimination Committee protested that Disney's *Aladdin* featured a song whose lyrics contained a slur against Arabs. Protests by gays and lesbians against the 2000 launch of Dr. Laura Schlessinger's TV show prompted many advertisers to back out from sponsoring the show and several stations to drop it altogether. Dr. Laura eventually apologized for some of her antigay remarks.

Pressure groups organized along political lines have also exerted control over media content and practices. One particularly vicious example occurred in the 1950s during the Cold War period, when a massive communist scare ran throughout the country. A self-appointed group called Aware, Inc., tried to point out what it thought were communist influences in the broadcasting industry. Performers whose background was thought to be even the least bit questionable were blacklisted by the organization and were unable to find employment in the industry until they "rehabilitated" themselves by going through a rigid 12-step process. The blacklist went to the heart of the commercial broadcasting system. Its founders threatened to boycott the products of advertisers who sponsored shows with suspected communists. The investigation techniques of Aware, Inc., were slipshod and deficient. Many innocent persons were put on the blacklist and had their careers permanently damaged.

More recent examples of pressure groups are easy to find. In 2007 pressure group Media Matters was instrumental in the firing of radio host Don Imus after he made a racially insensitive remark. CBS canceled plans to show a fictional miniseries about the Ronald Reagan family after pressure from the conservative Media Research Center. (The series eventually aired in 2004 to a much smaller audience on the premium cable network Showtime.) The public interest group Center for a Digital Democracy campaigned in 2003 against a proposed merger of ABC and CNN and threatened legal action if such a move was made. The Center for Media Education is active in monitoring how well local stations follow the FCC's regulations concerning children's broadcasting.

We can sum up by saying that there are both positive and negative aspects to the activities of these citizens' groups. On the one hand, they probably have made some media organizations more responsive to community needs and more sensitive to the problems of minorities and other disadvantaged groups. Citizen group involvement with media organizations probably has also increased the feedback between audience and the media industry. On the other hand, these groups are self-appointed guardians of special interests. They are not elected by anyone, and their wishes may not be at all representative of those of the larger population. In addition, many of these groups have exerted unreasonable power, and some extremist groups, like Aware, Inc., may actually abuse their influence and do more harm than good.

▲ Press Councils

Some of the general issues surrounding press councils, also called *news councils*, were discussed in Chapter 13. The idea of a press council originated in Europe. A press council is an independent agency whose job is to monitor the performance of the media on a day-to-day basis. In Great Britain, for example, the council consists of people with media experience and some laypersons. It examines complaints from the public about erroneous or deficient press coverage. The council has no enforcement powers; if it finds an example of poor performance, it issues a report to that effect. Unfavorable publicity is the only sanction the council can bring to bear.

The idea of a press council has not been popular in the United States. As mentioned in Chapter 13, a National News Council existed in the United States from 1973 to 1984 but was hampered by lack of media cooperation. There are, however, a few local news councils in operation. The most active one is in Minnesota.

▲ Education

Education also exerts informal control over the media. Ethics and professionalism are topics that are gaining more and more attention at colleges and universities. In fact, there has been a recent upsurge of interest in teaching ethics at many schools of journalism and mass communication. About 40 percent of the schools in the United States offer a special ethics course to their students. More than half of the approximately 40 books specifically devoted to mass media ethics have been published since 1980. Most of the experts in this area agreed that instead of teaching specific codes of ethics to students, a systematic way of thinking about ethics should be stressed, so that individuals can consider issues and arrive at decisions rationally.

Even this book can be thought of as a means of informal control. The hope is that, after reading it, you will bring a more advanced level of critical thinking and a more sensitive and informed outlook to your media profession or to your role as media consumer.

MAIN POINTS

- There are several types of informal controls on the mass media, including ethics, performance codes, organizational policies, self-criticism, and outside pressures.

- The most important ethical principles that provide guidance in this area are the golden mean, the categorical imperative, the principle of utility, the veil of ignorance, and the principle of self-determination.

- All the media have performance codes that guide professional behavior.

- Many media organizations have standards departments that monitor the content that is published or broadcast.

- The National Advertising Review Council is the main organization that supervises self-regulation in advertising.

- Outside pressures from advertisers can sometimes influence media conduct.

- Special-interest groups, such as Action for Children's Television, have been successful in modifying the content and practices of the TV industry.

- Although they exist in many foreign countries, only a few press councils operate in the United States.

QUESTIONS FOR REVIEW

1. What are the main ethical principles discussed in the chapter?

2. Why was the NAB Code of Good Practice discontinued?

3. What is the difference between editorial policies and operating policies?

4. What is an ombudsperson? What does he or she do?

5. What are some ways advertisers can influence news content?

QUESTIONS FOR CRITICAL THINKING

1. How would you handle each of the examples mentioned in the introduction to the chapter?

2. What are some of the advantages and disadvantages of written codes of conduct?

3. Do special interest groups exert too much power over the media?

4. Do advertisers have too much power over the media?

5. Consider the case of the Virginia Tech video and photographs delivered to NBC, discussed near the beginning of this chapter. Do you believe NBC handled the matter ethically? Why or why not?

KEY TERMS

golden mean (p. 390)
categorical imperative (p. 390)
utility (p. 390)
veil of ignorance (p. 391)

self-determination (p. 391)
acculturation (p. 393)
MPAA rating system (p. 397)
policy book (p. 400)

operating policies (p. 401)
editorial policies (p. 401)
ombudsperson (p. 403)

INTERNET RESOURCES

Online Learning Center

At the Online Learning Center home page, www.mhhe.com/dominick10, *select* Student Center *and then* Chapter 17.

1. Use the Learning Objectives, Chapter Outline, Main Points, and Time Line sections to review this chapter.

2. Test your knowledge of the chapter using the multiple choice, crossword puzzle, and flashcard features of the site.

3. Expand your knowledge of concepts and topics discussed in the chapter by going to Suggestions for Further Reading and Internet Exercises.

Surfing the Internet

There are few Web sites that deal with the topics discussed in this chapter, but the ones listed here are relevant.

http://jmme.org
The home page of the *Journal of Mass Media Ethics*. Contains scholarly articles regarding issues of mass media and morality.

www.asne.org/ideas/codes/codes.htm
The American Society of Newspaper Editors has collected codes of ethics from about three dozen media organizations.

www.mpaa.org/caramap
Information about the MPAA movie rating system. The MPAA offers Red Carpet Ratings Service—an e-mail update of the ratings of movies about to be released.

www.poynter.org
The Poynter Institute's ethics page. Good for finding out the most current ethical issues.

www.spj.org/ethics.asp
The ethics page of the Society of Professional Journalists. Contains the latest ethics news and an "Ethics Hotline" that you can call for advice.

PART V

IMPACT OF THE MEDIA

CHAPTER 18

INTERNATIONAL AND COMPARATIVE MEDIA SYSTEMS

This chapter will prepare you to:

- recognize the global leaders in newspapers, radio, and television

- distinguish among the four main theories of government-press relationships

- categorize media systems by ownership patterns and degree of government control

- understand how politics, culture, geography, history, and economics affect a country's media system

- explain the media systems in Japan, Mexico, and China

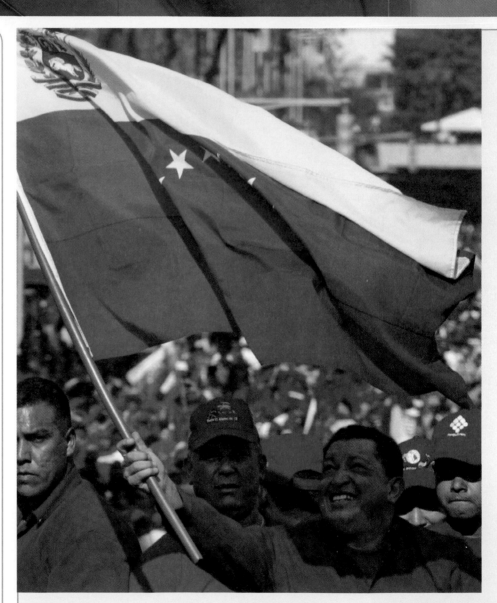

President Hugo Chavez has had his share of problems with some of the mass media in Venezuela.

18

Radio Caracas Television (RCTV) started broadcasting in Venezuela in 1954 and over the years aired thousands of soap operas, telenovelas, and news broadcasts. Of late, RCTV has also been an outspoken critic of Venezuelan president Hugo Chavez and in 2002 cheered on a coup attempt against Chavez that ultimately failed. In 2007, when RCTV's license came up for renewal, Chavez's government refused to extend it and replaced RCTV with a state-run station that broadcast pro-Chavez songs and government-sanctioned programs.

The above is a familiar story in autocratic regimes; many governments have silenced opposition media. Twenty years ago, that would have probably been the end of it, and RCTV would never be heard from again. In the Internet age, however, things are not that simple. Although officially shut down by the government, RCTV found a way to keep broadcasting: It started its own YouTube channel. The station continued to produce three hour-long segments every day and uploaded them to the video-sharing site. The first week it appeared, RCTV's news program, *El Observador*, had more than 9,000 subscribers and 330,000 views, making it YouTube's most subscribed-to channel of the week.

The ultimate fate of RCTV is still unknown. The Chavez administration was widely criticized by other countries in the wake of the shutdown. Protesters have taken to the streets demonstrating in support of the station. Nonetheless, as this book went to press, Chavez had not retreated and had even threatened another station that has been critical of the government with a similar fate. Although such a move would be easier said than done, it's even possible Chavez may try to block Venezuelans from accessing YouTube's Web site.

Whatever the outcome, the Venezuela situation illustrates that in the digital age national borders have become porous and it's becoming increasingly difficult for a government to control what information its citizens see and hear. It also suggests that in the future Internet sites such as YouTube may become another way that individuals and organizations avoid censorship. In sum, the digital age is changing the architecture of international communication.

This chapter examines the vibrant world of international media. We will first look at media that are designed to be distributed to other countries. Then we will examine media systems as they exist in other nations.

INTERNATIONAL MEDIA SYSTEMS

The study of international mass media systems focuses on those media that cross national boundaries. Some media may be deliberately designed for other countries (as is the case with the Voice of Russia, the Voice of America, and the international edition of *Newsweek*); other media simply spill over from one country to its neighbors (as happens between the United States and Canada). Let us look first at those media designed for international consumption.

▲ Global Print Media

Many newspapers provide foreign-language or international editions. The popular ones fall into two categories: general newspapers and financial newspapers. As far as U.S.- and British-based publications are concerned, the following were the leaders at the close of 2006:

■ *The International Herald Tribune,* published by the *New York Times* and headquartered in France, has a worldwide circulation of more than 240,000, most of it in Europe. The paper is printed in 36 sites around the world, including New York, Singapore, and Tokyo.

■ *USA Today International* reaches more than a million readers, mostly in Europe. The Gannett-owned paper is printed in London, Frankfurt, Milan, and Hong Kong. Most of its readers are U.S. citizens traveling abroad.

■ *WorldPaper,* published by the World Times Company in Boston, is distributed as a newspaper supplement primarily in Latin America, Asia, and the Middle East. It is printed in 25 different countries and boasts a circulation of nearly 1 million.

■ *The Financial Times of London,* as its name suggests, specializes in economic news and has a circulation of about 400,000.

■ *The Economist,* also based in London, carries financial news and analysis. Readily available in the United States, the weekly is printed in Virginia, London, and Singapore. It reaches about a million readers.

■ *The Wall Street Journal*'s international editions reach about 1 million people, mainly in Europe, Asia, and South America.

Other papers that enjoy international status are the *New York Times, Le Monde* (France), *El País* (Spain), *The Times* (Great Britain), *The Statesman* (India), and *Al Ahram* (Egypt).

The international flow of news is dominated by global news agencies. Reuters, Associated Press, Agence France-Presse, and ITAR-TASS are the biggest, but in recent years more specialized news organizations, such as the New York Times Syndicate and the Los Angeles Times Syndicate, have also become important.

As far as magazines are concerned, *Reader's Digest* publishes more than 50 international editions read by about 18 million people in nearly 200 countries. Time Warner, in addition to publishing the international edition of *Time,* which is distributed in about 190 countries, also publishes *Asiaweek* and a newsweekly in Chinese. The international edition of *Newsweek* reaches about a half-million readers. Hearst Magazines International oversees the distribution of eight major titles—including *Cosmopolitan, Good Housekeeping,* and *Redbook*—in more than a hundred countries. *Cosmopolitan* alone is sold in about 50 countries, including Japan, Poland, and Russia.

Smaller special-interest magazines are also growing internationally. A Spanish-language version of *Popular Mechanics* is sold throughout Latin America.

On the set of CNN International. During its news broadcasts, CNN International links together anchorpersons from CNN bureaus all over the world.

Men's Health publishes a British edition as well as one for South America (where it is called *Hombre Saludable*). Many business magazines, including *Business Week* and *Fortune,* also have significant foreign readership.

▲ Global Broadcasting

About 150 countries engage in some form of international broadcasting. Many of these services are government run or at least government supervised. Others, like WRMI, Miami, are private operations supported by the sale of commercial time.

In the past, international radio broadcasting was done exclusively in the shortwave part of the radio spectrum (see Chapter 7). Although it goes a long distance, shortwave radio is hard to pick up and prone to interference problems. In an attempt to improve technical quality, major international broadcasters have been striking partnerships with locally operated FM stations. The Voice of America, for instance, has a network of 400 local stations in Latin America that rebroadcast its signal. Further, many international radio services are available in digital form on the Web or carried by satellite.

Listed here are the leading global broadcasters as of 2007:

- The World Service of the British Broadcasting Corporation (BBC) has a worldwide reputation for accurate and impartial newscasts because, in theory at least, it is independent of government ownership. Along with its news, the BBC carries an impressive lineup of music, drama, comedy, sports, and light features. The BBC pioneered the international radio call-in show in which prominent people, such as Prime Minister Tony Blair, answer calls from listeners around the globe. The BBC broadcasts 1,120 hours per week in 33 languages and has about 160 million worldwide listeners. The BBC Web site gets about 32 million visitors a month.

- Voice of America (VOA), now in its sixth decade of operation, broadcasts a thousand weekly hours of news, editorials, and features in more than 40 languages to an audience of about 100 million people, about half of them in Russia and Eastern Europe. The VOA is part of the International Broadcasting Bureau, which also includes Radio Martí, a special AM service aimed at Cuba; its TV counterpart, TV Martí; Arabic-language radio and TV services; Radio Farda, a Persian service; and VOA-TV.

- China Radio International transmits about 1,400 hours of programming weekly in 43 foreign languages. China Radio International carried strident anti-American propaganda until the early 1970s, when improved relations led to a mellowing of its tone. Most of China Radio International's programming consists of news, analysis, commentary, and cultural information about China.

- Deutsche Welle (DW), "German Wave," broadcasts about a thousand hours per week in 30 languages. DW's transmitters are located in Germany, Africa, and Asia. It has a large audience, particularly in Africa.

- Radio France International (RFI) broadcasts more than 300 hours a week to 45 million listeners, many on the African continent, in 20 languages. RFI programming consists of a blend of music, news, commentary, and locally produced features.

The biggest change in international broadcasting in recent years has been the proliferation of global news, sports, and music channels. The pioneer in this area was CNN, which now reaches millions of hotel rooms and numerous cable systems in Europe, Africa, and Asia. CNN International (CNNI), started in 1990, reaches more than 170 million homes in about 200 countries. CNN International is organized into five networks that serve (1) Europe, the Middle East, and Africa, (2) North Asia and the Pacific, (3) South Asia, (4) Latin America, and, (5) North America. CNN International has also started broadcasting newscasts in several local languages as well as in English. CNBC offers 24-hour business news to 147 million households in 70 countries worldwide. In addition, BBC World, a full-time news channel, is available in Europe, Asia, Africa, and some U.S. locations. Russia is also joining the global news business. Russia Today, a 24-hour satellite news channel, began broadcasting in 2005. The new service will have bureaus in Washington, London,

In the aftermath of the 9/11 attacks, many Americans asked why so many people in the world have anti-American attitudes. Several theories were proposed. Some accused the U.S. of cultural insensitivity; others cited U.S. foreign policy in the Middle East. Still others blamed international mass communication. They argued that most people in the world come into contact with U.S. culture through American TV shows and movies that are shown in their home countries. Anybody who watched a steady diet of shows such as *Friends, CSI,* and *Desperate Housewives,* and movies such as *The Departed* and *Grindhouse* and listened to hip-hop music might come away with the notion that Americans are violent and sexually immoral people.

This theory was the subject of a study reported in the April-June 2007 issue of *Mass Communication and Society.*[1] The researchers conducted a survey among college students in Singapore. They measured students' attitudes toward Americans and also tabulated the students' exposure to American media content. They found that these young people were heavily exposed to U.S.-produced material, particularly music, films, and TV shows.

Was there a relationship between consuming U.S. content and attitudes toward Americans? There was, but it was not in the direction that the theory mentioned above would have predicted. Instead, there was a slight positive correlation between exposure to U.S. content and attitudes toward Americans. In short, those who consumed a lot of American media had slightly more positive attitudes toward Americans.

A correlation, of course, does not establish causation (see the next chapter). It may be that students who already have favorable attitudes toward Americans were the ones who saw and heard a lot of U.S. media content while those with negative attitudes avoided the same material. In addition, the sample came from only one country, and the correlation, although statistically significant, was small and did not explain much of the variability in student attitudes. Nonetheless, the study indicates that researchers need to dig more deeply into the effects of exposure to international media.

---

[1] See J. Fullerton, M. Hamilton and A. Kendrick, "U.S.-Produced Entertainment Media and Attitude Toward Americans," *Mass Communication and Society* (2007), Vol. 10, No. 2, pp. 171–188.

Jerusalem, and Brussels. The TV services of Deutsche Welle and China Radio International also show up on many cable and satellite systems.

Sports and music channels also have audiences all over the world. MTV is available almost everywhere, reaching more than 400 million households. ESPN International (ESPNi) is the biggest global provider of sports programming. Launched in 1988, the service is seen in more than 140 countries and territories and reaches about 90 million households. ESPNi serves Canada, Asia, Latin America, the Pacific Rim, Africa, and the Middle East. The News Corporation also operates satellite services that beam news and sports programming to more than 180 million viewers in Europe and Asia. The Cartoon Network, TNT, and Nickelodeon, also have large global audiences.

▲ Film and TV

American films still dominate the box offices of many foreign countries. Exporting films is big business. In 2006, film rentals from foreign countries amounted to more than $9 billion. More than half the revenue for an average film comes from the foreign box office. Some films even do better overseas than they do in the United States. *The Da Vinci Code,* for example, made $272 million in the United States and $532 million overseas.

In addition, a good deal of electronic media traffic consists of films on DVDs that are shipped from one country to another and rented or sold to individuals for home viewing. In 2006 consumers outside the United States spent more than $20 billion on DVDs. This added revenue can add a significant amount to a film's bottom line.

The United States still dominates the international TV program market. After a few down years, the market for U.S. shows picked up in 2006–2007 thanks to the worldwide appeal of *CSI, Lost, Desperate Housewives,* and *Grey's Anatomy.* Locally produced programs give U.S. shows strong competition and dominate prime time in many countries. The international TV business is risky; just because a show is popular in America does not mean that audiences in other countries will like it. *Desperate Housewives* flopped in Spain, *24* bombed in Italy, and *The Sopranos* got whacked no matter where it was shown.

As more countries produce their own TV content, many U.S. production companies, especially those that produce game and reality shows, have concentrated on licensing formats to overseas producers who turn them into local versions. There are dozens of foreign variations of *Wheel of Fortune, Jeopardy, Pimp My Ride,* and *World Poker Tour.* Many reality programs that have been successful on American TV originally came from other countries. *Big Brother* and *Fear Factor* came from the Netherlands, and *Survivor* first aired in Sweden.

Another aspect of international media is the problem of cross-border spillover. TV signals, of course, know no national boundaries, and the programs of one nation can be received easily in another country. The problem has caused some friction between the United States and Canada. Shows on ABC, NBC, and CBS are just as popular in Canada as they are in the United States, and they take away audiences from Canadian channels. Fearful of a cultural invasion of U.S. values and aware of the potential loss of advertising revenue to U.S. stations, the Canadian government has instituted content regulations that specify the minimum amount of Canadian content that must be carried by Canadian stations. Not surprisingly, spillover is also a problem on the crowded European continent. More than a third of TV viewing time in Finland, Ireland, and Belgium involves programs from another country's TV service. In Switzerland 60 percent of viewing is "out of country."

WORLD MEDIA ONLINE

The World Wide Web provides access to worldwide media on a scale never before possible. Radio stations in other countries, for example, are available on the Net. A scan of Web sites in early 2005 found stations in Japan, the Philippines, Hong Kong, Russia, Brazil, Great Britain, and many other countries broadcasting on the Net. Streaming video from other countries is becoming more available on the Web. MediaZone, for example, offers live and on-demand video from China, Trinidad, and Mongolia. Jump TV has a selection of more than 250 channels from 70 countries. Many of the major international and domestic TV systems in many countries have Web sites with streaming video. And, of course, video-sharing sites such as YouTube contain video clips submitted from across the globe.

News from Russia is easily available on the Web. Interfax Russia has subscribers in more than a hundred countries.

Individuals who want to read newspapers or magazines from other countries now have a wide selection at their disposal. In addition to the U.S. papers that have an international readership, such as the *New York Times* and *Wall Street Journal*, papers from France (*Le Monde*), Germany (*Die Welt*), Great Britain (*London Times*), Japan (*Asahi Shimbun*), Australia (*Sydney Morning Herald*), and many other countries make available online versions as well. International magazines that have established Web sites include *Asia Week, Asia Online, New Woman* (Great Britain), *Beat* (Australia), *Der Spiegel* (Germany), *Playmen* (the Italian equivalent of *Playboy*), *Tokyo Journal* (Japan), and *Art Bin* (Sweden).

Furthermore, e-mail has made it possible to send messages across the globe in seconds. Many newsgroups are devoted to news about international events and other cultures, and people all over the world have Web pages that can be visited directly.

We need to keep in mind, however, that although it is called the *World Wide Web*, this new medium is far from globally accessible. In 2006 it was estimated that around a billion people were online. This sounds like a large number, but it represents only about 16 percent of the world's population. The Internet is most accessible to those in the developed countries. More than 225 million are online in North America compared to 24 million in Africa.

COMPARATIVE MEDIA SYSTEMS

Let us now turn our attention to media systems as they exist in individual nations. Before we start, we should note that the media system that exists in a country is directly related to the political system in that country. The political system determines the exact relationship between the media and the government. Over the years several theories have developed concerning this relationship. In the sections that follow are examples of these theories in operation.

▲ Theories of the Press

Since the 16th century, scholars and philosophers have attempted to describe the relationship between the government and the media and its implications with regard to freedom and control. Over the years, as political, economic, and social conditions have changed, various theories of the press have developed to articulate and explain this relationship. All theories, however, fall somewhere between two "isms" that reflect polar opposites in the amount of control the government exerts over the media—authoritarianism and libertarianism (see Figure 18-1). Current theories of the press represent modifications of these two fundamental principles. Let us look at each of them.

The **authoritarian theory** arose in 16th-century England, at about the same time as the introduction of the printing press in that country. Under the authoritarian system the prevailing belief was that the ruling elite should guide the masses, whose intellectual ability was held in low esteem. Public dissent and criticism were considered harmful to both the government and the people and were not tolerated. Authoritarians used various devices to force compliance of the press, including licensing, censorship of material before publication, the granting of exclusive printing rights to favored elements of the press, and the swift, harsh punishment of government critics.

The **libertarian theory** is directly opposed to authoritarianism. Libertarians assume that human beings are rational and capable of making their own decisions and that governments exist to serve the individual. Libertarians believe that the common citizen has a right to hear all sides of an issue to distinguish truth from falsehood. Since any government restriction on

FIGURE 18-1

Theories of Media-
Government
Relationships

"The Repeal, or the Funeral Procession, of Miss-Americ-Stamp." Colonial newspapers operated under an authoritarian philosophy as practiced by the British government. This English cartoon, published in 1766, satirized the repeal of the Stamp Act, an attempt to suppress hostile opinion by placing a tax on the pages of colonial newspapers.

the expression of ideas infringes on the rights of the citizen, the government can best serve the people by not interfering with the media. In short, the press must be free from control.

The libertarian theory fit well with the freewheeling political climate and rugged individualism of early America. By the mid-20th century, however, two world wars and a depression had changed world politics, media industries had become big business, and broadcasting had made it possible to reach millions of people instantaneously. As a result, new theories of the press emerged. In 1956 a book titled *Four Theories of the Press* reexamined the libertarian and authoritarian philosophies and described two more modern approaches. The **social responsibility theory** (also referred to as the *Western concept*) incorporates part of the original libertarian approach but introduces some new elements as well. This approach holds that the press has a right to criticize government and other institutions, but it also has a responsibility to preserve democracy by properly informing the public and by responding to society's needs and interests. The press does not have the freedom to do as it pleases; it is obligated to respond to society's requirements. The government may involve itself in media operations by issuing regulations if the public interest is not being adequately served. The regulation of broadcasting by the Federal Communications Commission is a good example of this latter provision. The United States, Japan, Britain, and many other European countries are examples of countries that subscribe to this theory.

The other theory spelled out in *Four Theories of the Press* is the **communist theory.** This theory is a variant on the authoritarian scheme. The media are "owned" by the people as represented by the state. Their purpose is to support the Marxist system and to achieve the goals of the state as expressed through the Communist Party. Recent history has shown that the communist approach to the press works best in a closed society in which information is tightly controlled by the government. Once information is available from competing sources, people give little credibility to the official media.

This fact was illustrated by events in Russia and Eastern Europe at the end of the 1980s. The British Broadcasting Corporation (BBC), Voice of America, CNN, Radio Liberty, and Radio Free Europe unraveled the Communist Party's media monopoly. TV viewers in Eastern Europe saw Western TV shows beamed from West Germany or sent via satellite. Hollywood movies on videocassette were widely available. The people of Eastern Europe and Russia saw the shortcomings of their political and economic systems and clamored for change. As a result, the communist theory of the press has few proponents today. China, Cuba, and North Korea are about the only places where it can be found, and even in those countries the official version of the theory often bears little resemblance to the actual practices of the media. In short, the communist theory has been rendered obsolete by history.

The blog has opened a new channel of communication for ordinary citizens across the globe. Interestingly, just as mass communication systems are shaped by a country's history, culture, and politics, so are individual blogs.

Take France, for instance. The French have a long tradition of sitting in cafes and coffeehouses and having heated discussions about politics, the arts, and wine. Not surprisingly, this tradition has spilled over to the Internet. The French read more blogs than any other nation. About 60 percent of them visit at least one blog a month, about twice as many as U.S. residents. Moreover, French blogs tend to be longer, more negative, and more confrontational than those from other countries.

What factors account for these characteristics? One explanation is simple numbers. More people read blogs in France because more people in France are connected to the Internet—more than half the population in 2006, and almost all with a broadband connection. Another reason might be technological. The French have a longer history with electronic communication thanks to Minitel, an early version of a computer network that was popular in the 1980s, before the Internet existed. Yet another reason might be political. The French have a history of speaking out and of protesting, dating back to the French Revolution. More recently, bloggers helped spur on the recent demonstrations outside of Paris in 2005 and loudly protested the proposed European constitution in the same year. In addition to the dissenters, mainstream politicians have adopted blogs. Segolene Royal's blog got a half-million visitors during her unsuccessful run for the French presidency in 2007.

China also has millions of bloggers, but their political system does not encourage dissent. A recent government proposal would have required all bloggers to register their real names with authorities before they were permitted to start a blog. The plan was eventually abandoned, but the message was clear: Bloggers should be careful about what they say about their government. Consequently, the number of politically oriented blogs in China is relatively small. Even so, a few still manage to be critical of the government.

The typical blogger in China is a young female who lives in or near a big city. Chinese bloggers tend to focus on themselves and the issues they face. Popular blog topics include celebrity news, problems of everyday life, technology, business, and gossip. In addition to politics, demography may account for the apolitical nature of many Chinese blogs. Those who are able to blog tend to be well off. Many are college students while others have good jobs. This is not the type of person who typically advocates overthrowing the government.

As more researchers become interested in cross-national differences in Internet usage, it is likely that we will learn much more about the global blogosphere and how it differs across nations and ethnic groups.

A more recent formulation is the **developmental theory,** which would fall more toward the authoritarian side of the spectrum. In this ideology the government mobilizes the media to serve national goals in economic and social development. Information is considered a scarce natural resource that must be carefully managed by the government to achieve national goals. Some of the goals the media are expected to help achieve include political integration, literacy, economic self-sufficiency, and the eradication of disease. Until recently, many emerging countries espoused the developmental approach, but changing economic and political conditions have made it less prevalent. Many emerging countries, such as Brazil and Chile, have replaced dictatorships with democracies, and democracies typically look with disfavor upon government control over the media. In addition, even in those countries where democracy has yet to appear, the government has either privatized the formerly state-run media or allowed competition from independent channels. Consequently, the government has less control over the flow of information and is less able to promote the developmental approach. All in all, the growth of democracy and the growing popularity of free-marketplace economics have resulted in more countries endorsing the social responsibility approach.

▲ Control and Ownership of the Media

One helpful way of distinguishing among the various media systems throughout the world is to classify them along the dimensions of (1) ownership and (2) control. Finnish Professor Osmo Wiio has developed a useful analysis scheme, presented in Figure 18-2. As can be seen, ownership can range from private to public (*public ownership* usually means some form of government ownership), and control can range from centralized to decentralized. Note that this typology is an oversimplification. Many countries have mixed media systems in which part of the broadcasting system is owned by the government and part by private interests. In some countries the print media could be placed in one cell of the matrix and the broadcasting system in another. Nonetheless, this model is helpful for displaying some of the major differences among systems.

FIGURE 18-2

Typology of Media
Ownership and Control

Source: From "The
Mass Media Role in the
Western World" by Osmo
A. Wiio, in *Comparative
Mass Media Systems*
by L. John Martin and
Anju Grover Chaudhary.
Copyright © 1983 by
Longman Inc. Reprinted
by permission of Allyn and
Bacon.

In the upper-left cell are type A systems. These represent decentralized control and public ownership, a type best illustrated by the broadcasting systems in European countries such as France, Denmark, and Italy. Some of the broadcasting media are publicly owned, but no single political or special-interest group can control their messages. In Great Britain, for example, the BBC is a government-chartered, publicly owned corporation that is relatively immune to government censorship and interference. Private broadcasting systems also operate in these countries.

In the upper-right cell are type B systems. This arrangement is typical of communist or socialist countries in which the media are publicly owned and controlled by the dominant political party. China is an example.

In the lower-left cell is the decentralized-control, private-ownership model. This is the system that currently operates in the United States and in many European countries. The media are owned by private companies, and there is little, if any, centralized control.

The lower-right cell is the centralized-control, privately owned system. In many countries, particularly the developing countries of Africa and Latin America, the media are owned by private organizations but are firmly controlled by the government. Venezuela would seem to fit in this category.

Far fewer countries today would fall into cell B of the matrix than would have a few years ago. Only a handful of nations still exemplify the communist or socialist media model. (Cuba, China, and North Korea are examples.) In these countries the ruling party exercises control, and freedom of the press belongs to the state, not to the media. Communist countries feel that it is necessary to speak with one voice, and antigovernment or antiparty criticism is forbidden.

Press control is exercised in several ways. First, the government controls the source. Printing and broadcasting equipment are given only to approved organizations. In Cuba, for example, there is a newsprint shortage, and only the government newspaper is supplied with it. Next, journalists are state-trained and state-approved. Finally, news agencies are state-owned, and news sources state-controlled. In China the regime keeps a close eye on the Internet. The government blocks certain Web sites and filters the output from search engines, such as Google, so that a search for certain forbidden terms will yield no results. Blogs, postings on bulletin boards, and Internet chat rooms are also closely monitored.

Those countries that have abandoned the communist philosophy have generally moved into cells A and C of the matrix. The state-run media organizations have seen much of their control taken away, and private media outlets are permitted. Individual media outlets are given much more freedom to criticize the government.

The most significant trend in those countries that fall into cell A of the matrix has been a move toward pluralism in their broadcasting systems. State-owned monopolies in many countries, including France, Italy, Greece, Spain, and some of the Scandinavian countries, have given way to privately owned and commercially sponsored broadcasting systems. In addition, cable promises to bring even more video diversity to these countries.

▲ Role of the Media in Various Countries

The role of a mass media system in a given country will differ according to its place in the typology. For example, as mentioned, in many developing countries where there is strong centralized control over the media, the principal role of mass communication is to help develop and build the nation. Not surprisingly, many less-developed countries are concerned primarily with economic and political development. This concern is translated into a rather focused definition of the role of mass media. In general, the media are expected to help achieve modernization or other national goals. In fact, a new term, *developmental journalism*, has been coined to describe this philosophy. In short, **developmental journalism** means that the role of the media is to support national interests with regard to economic and social development and to support objectives such as national unity, stability, and cultural integrity.

On the one hand, developmental journalism entails finding ways to make abstract stories about commodity pricing, agricultural policies, and educational goals understandable to readers and to highlight the developmental goals achieved by the nation. On the other hand, developmental journalism can also mean that the press refrains from any criticism of the government and prints only what the government deems helpful to its cause. The philosophy of many Asian, Latin American, and African developing nations falls somewhere between these two conceptions of developmental journalism.

The role of the media under the communist theory is straightforward: They are tools of propaganda, persuasion, and education. They function only secondarily as sources of information and entertainment. This philosophy dates back to Lenin, who decreed that the communist press was to help further the revolution.

As we saw in Chapter 2, Western media inform and entertain, but their content is somewhat different from that of communist and less-developed nations' media. Most of the information carried by the media in the Western democracies is geared to the specific political and economic needs of the audience. An examination of the press in the United States and Canada, for example, would reveal a large amount of news about the local and national government, some of it unfavorable and critical. The role of government watchdog, based on the ideas presented in the social responsibility theory, is a function that would be unsettling to many of the countries in cells B and D of the matrix in Figure 18-2. Moreover, a great deal of content in the Western media is consumer oriented, consisting of advertising, news, and entertainment. Further, there is, relatively speaking, little regulation of the content of the entertainment media. Aside from some regulations governing pornography and prohibitions against certain content on the broadcast media, the government takes little interest in entertainment content.

It is the interpretation or editorial function in which the biggest differences are found. The United States and other Western countries have a tradition of press freedom that recognizes the right of the media to present ideas to try to persuade the audience to some point of view. The philosophy of the **free marketplace of ideas** is endorsed by most countries in cells A and C of Figure 18-2. All relevant ideas concerning an issue are examined in the media, and a "self-righting" process occurs. Given the autonomous nature of the Western media, it would be difficult for the government to mobilize the media to support some national goal, as is typically done in developing and communist countries. There is a built-in tension and adversarial relationship between press and government that makes such efforts rare.

▲ Economic Differences in Media Systems

In the United States advertising plays a key role in media support (see Chapter 15). Newspapers, magazines, radio, and television all derive a significant amount of their total income from the sale of advertising time or space. Direct government subsidy or support of the media is minimal, limited to the funds given to public broadcasting. (Of course, the

CRITICAL / CULTURAL ISSUES

Cultural Imperalism?

Cultural domination refers to the process in which national cultures are overwhelmed by the importing of news and entertainment from other countries—mainly from the United States. Residents of many countries are concerned that their national and local heritage will be replaced by one global culture dominated by U.S. values. They point out that American music, books, TV shows, and films are popular around the world. Many are fearful that audiences will become persuaded to adopt the values portrayed in this content—capitalism, materialism, consumption, and so forth. As a result, many countries, including Canada, Spain, and France, have placed quotas on the amount of foreign material that can be carried on their broadcasting systems.

The notion of cultural domination also spills over into the news area. For many years the representatives of many developing nations have been arguing for a New World Information Order. They point out that the existing flow of news is one way: from the industrialized West to the developing nations, sometimes referred to as the *third world*. Under such a system, say the developing countries, news from the third world is scant, and what news there is reflects unfavorably upon the developing nations. For example, what do you know about South America? Most people will mention two things—revolutions and drugs—the two topics that dominate the news coverage. Most know little else about the whole continent. To remedy this imbalance, developing countries have advocated controls over the news and other media content that come across their borders. A resolution reflecting this philosophy was passed by the United Nations Educational, Scientific, and Cultural Organization (UNESCO) in the 1980s. The United States looked with disfavor on this proposal, and it was one of the factors that prompted the United States to withdraw from UNESCO back in the mid-1980s.

Is this charge of cultural imperialism a valid one? One claim of those who urge a New World Information Order has substance. News coverage of third world nations is unbalanced. In response, the Western media have attempted to report more non-Western news and have started programs to train journalists of former third world countries. In addition, several other alternative news agencies have developed—including the Inter Press Third World News

Agency, the South North News Service, and the Pan African News Agency—that supplement and enlarge the coverage of the major Western news organizations.

Any consideration of this debate must also acknowledge that the whole controversy has economic implications. Those who champion the free flow of information across borders also champion their right to profit from the sale of their products across borders. Those who advocate controls in the name of avoiding cultural domination are also assuring themselves of less competition in the marketplace. If a country limits foreign television programs to 30 percent of its schedule, the other 70 percent must be produced locally. How much of the cultural imperialism debate is based on principle and how much on cash is hard to determine.

The cultural imperialism argument seems to assume that people in other countries are weak and simply absorb and accept cultural messages. One of the key things that the critical/cultural analysts point out is that the audience is anything but passive. It is likely that audiences in other cultures pin their own meanings and interpretations on media content. Those in other countries will reinterpret what they receive in light of their own culture and personal experiences.

The changing world political scene and the increasing trend toward market-driven economies and less oppressive governments have increased support for the Western model. The proponents of the New World Information Order received considerable backing from the former communist countries of the Soviet Union and Eastern Europe. Now that these countries have changed governments, there is less support for the notion of increased media control. Consumers the world over seem to welcome the changes.

Those who campaign against cultural imperialism contend that American values are becoming dominant. This raises the question of exactly what American values are. The United States is currently experiencing a wave of multiculturalism, and the heritages of many ethnic and racial groups have influenced the cultural tastes and values of the entire country. In the music area, for example, reggae—which came from Jamaica—found a following among white Americans and went on to influence the development of African American rap music. Is the global popularity of rap a manifestation of Jamaican, African American, or white American values?

government also indirectly helps support the media by buying a lot of advertising.) In Western Europe several countries provide indirect subsidies to the media, such as cheaper mailing privileges and tax concessions. Some Scandinavian countries have a system whereby newspapers controlled by various political parties are given direct financial assistance. Several different systems are used to support broadcasting. In the United Kingdom, for example, the BBC is state-chartered and gets its operating funds from an annual license fee paid by the owners of TV sets. At the same time, the independent TV networks make their money from the sale of advertising time, in much the same way their U.S. counterparts do. Many other Western countries follow this same model.

It is difficult to generalize about the means of economic support for media in less-developed countries. Where the print media are privately owned, money comes from circulation fees and advertising. Publishers are generally free to keep all profits, but in many countries space must be provided free of charge for government announcements. Advertising and license fees are the two major sources of income for broadcasting.

In those few communist countries that still exist, most economic support for the media comes directly from the government. Since the media are state-owned, money for their operation is simply set aside from the government's budget. Because of this subsidy, the single-copy costs of newspapers and magazines tend to be cheap. Advertising used to be a minuscule source of income in communist countries, but recently, these governments have welcomed it as an important revenue stream.

EXAMPLES OF OTHER MEDIA SYSTEMS

Let us now take a more detailed look at the mass media in three different countries: (1) Japan, an industrialized nation, (2) Mexico, a developing nation, and (3) China, a communist country.

▲ Japan

More than 127 million people live on this nation of islands. Japan's geography, culture, history, and economy have shaped its current media system. Education is highly valued in Japan, where the literacy rate is nearly 100 percent. This has helped the country develop a strong print media industry.

There are more than 120 newspapers in Japan with a combined circulation of about 69 million, a total that exceeds that of U.S. papers. Japan has more than 10 newspapers with circulation above the million mark; the United States has only 3. Some of the major national newspapers are *Yomiuri Shimbun, Asahi Shimbun,* and *Mainichi Shimbum.* (As you may have deduced by now, *shimbun* is the Japanese word for "newspaper.") The *Yomiuri Shimbun* has a daily circulation of about 14 million, making it the world leader. By comparison, *USA Today* has a circulation of about 2 million. Along with the national papers, Japan supports many other regional and local dailies. Tokyo alone has a dozen newspapers, several of them in English.

As in other countries, however, newspaper readership is declining, especially among younger readers. Competition from the Internet, video games, cell phones, and television has made it difficult for newspapers to attract a younger audience. Again, much like their counterparts in the United States, the major Japanese newspapers have Web sites that add another revenue stream.

Japan also has several newsmagazines and an influential business magazine. Leisure and lifestyle publications are popular. Asian editions of familiar publications such as *Time, Forbes,* and *Reader's Digest* are widely available. Comic books in Japan sell millions of copies every year. These publications, although they bear a surface resemblance to American comics, are deeply rooted in Japanese culture and are read by young and old. Many Japanese comic books are available in America.

Broadcasting in Japan started in the 1920s when the Japanese government adopted the British model of a noncommercial system headed by a public corporation. Commercial broadcasting started after World War II, a result in part of the influence of the American forces that occupied the country. Japan's economy has helped it become one of the world's leaders in the development of electronic media, and Japan has one of the most technologically advanced broadcasting systems in the world.

The state-run, noncommercial Japan Broadcasting Corporation (*Nippon Hoso Kyokai,* or NHK) is patterned after the BBC. It has an annual budget of more than $5 billion, all of which comes from a license fee imposed on all TV sets in Japan—about $70 a year. Competing with the five NHK channels are five commercial TV networks and two satellite channels. (The most-viewed networks are commercial ones: Fuji Television, Nippon TV,

Media Probe   We All Go to the Movies

A 2005 survey charted film attendance in several countries. People in the United States saw the most films, averaging about five a year. Australia ranked next with an average of four annual cinema visits. Residents of Spain, France, and Britain averaged about three movies a year while Japan came in last with slightly more than one visit a year.

and the Tokyo Broadcasting System, but NHK is not far behind.) TV and radio reach virtually 100 percent of the population as 11,000 transmitters blanket the country. Almost all the programs on Japanese TV are locally produced; American series do not do well in Japan. About 40 percent of all Japanese homes are equipped for cable. At present, however, cable is used to retransmit regular TV into areas that suffer poor TV reception. About 90 percent of all homes have VCRs or DVD players, and the video software business is booming.

Because of its mountainous terrain, Japan pioneered the development of a direct broadcast satellite (DBS) system. NHK has spent about $2 billion in DBS research and now operates three satellite channels that beam entertainment, sports, movies, music, and specials directly from satellite to living room. NHK's system has about 4 million subscribers, but other privately operated satellite systems are struggling to stay in the black. Japan was one of the pioneers of HDTV. However, NHK backed an analog system of HDTV, which has since been surpassed by the digital version (see Chapter 10). In early 1997, NHK finally announced that it too was backing a new digital system. With an eye toward the future, NHK is conducting research on a system of ultrahigh-definition TV, whose picture resolution is 16 times better than the current HDTV system, and is also investigating superthin, flexible display panels.

American films tend to dominate the Japanese box office, but recently, some locally produced movies have provided some unexpected competition. Sony, the huge Japan-based conglomerate, is heavily involved in making Hollywood movies through its Sony Pictures Entertainment unit. *The Da Vinci Code* and *Spider-Man 3* are two of the studio's recent releases.

Japan has been a leader in developing new technologies. As we have already discussed, cell phone use, especially text messaging, is extremely popular in Japan, and many people rely on their cell phones to connect to the Internet. Speaking of the Internet, 73 companies provide Internet service to about 90 million Japanese, about 71 percent of the population. The comparable figure for the United States is about 67 percent.

Clearly, the digital revolution has come to Japan. Newspapers and magazines are searching for new ways to make money from their online versions; TV networks are struggling with the transition from analog to digital; and the influence of the Internet and mobile media is growing. Japan recently launched a service that provides streaming video to cell phones using the electromagnetic spectrum rather than the Internet. In sum, Japan is a media-rich country whose media industries face many of the same problems and challenges found in Great Britain and the United States.

▲ Mexico

The media situation in Mexico is typical of that of many developing countries. It demonstrates some of the myriad challenges faced by nations as they strive to form indigenous systems. The media system in Mexico has been influenced by economics, politics, and geography. A country with 107 million inhabitants and a literacy rate of 92 percent, Mexico has been saddled with massive foreign debt and high inflation. Sharp divisions exist between the rich and the poor. Many urban areas are characterized by relative prosperity, and some rural areas are mired in poverty. Literacy is higher in the cities than in the countryside. Moreover, various governments have taken different attitudes toward the media, vacillating between strict control and relative leniency. Finally, Mexico's media system always operates in the shadow of its neighbor to the north, the United States.

Mexico has approximately 300 daily newspapers. Total daily circulation is about 9 million. For many years the *Excelsior,* published in Mexico City, was the country's leading

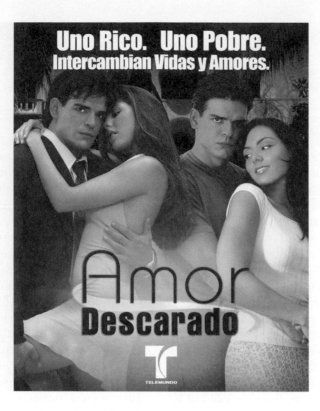

A typical ad for one of the steamy telenovelas popular in Mexico and other Spanish-speaking countries.

newspaper. Ownership and labor problems, however, have plagued the newspaper in recent years. Some provincial newspapers, such as *El Norte* in Monterrey, are also influential. Most large newspapers have their own Web sites.

Mexico publishes more than 200 periodicals. Media conglomerate Televisa is the world's largest publisher of Spanish-language magazines, including many that are aimed at Hispanics living in the United States. Televisa's best-known publication is the women's magazine *Vanidades*.

Freedom of the press has a checkered history in Mexico. For many years the government kept the press in check by controlling the national supply of newsprint. Publications that were critical of the government often found their supply of paper cut off. The government also controlled broadcasting permits and could force radio and TV stations off the air if their reports offended the regime. Finally, the government and ruling political party exerted power by bribing journalists.

In the new century, however, the situation seems to be changing. A new political party came into power and promised press freedoms. A survey by WorldAudit.org, a group that monitors press freedom, gave Mexico a rating of "partly free." Mexico scored 48 out of 100 on WorldAudit's scale of freedom (the lower the score, the more press freedom). By comparison, the United States scored 16. Journalism can be a hazardous profession in Mexico. From 2004 to 2006, 20 journalists were murdered while investigating drug smuggling and corruption.

Radio broadcasting developed in Mexico about the same time as it did in the United States. An official broadcast service signed on in 1923, and the model followed was heavily influenced by the U.S. system. In addition to state-run educational and cultural services, a system of private ownership of stations and commercial support was instituted. During the 1950s the state sold most of its stations to private interests. Today, there are more than 800 commercial radio stations and only 50 noncommercial stations, along with more than a dozen commercial networks.

Television broadcasting was modeled directly on the U.S. system. It began as a commercially supported private enterprise, but a 1960 law dictated that TV had to perform certain social functions, such as promoting moral principles and preserving human dignity. Government became more involved in TV during the 1970s when an agreement with station owners set aside 12.5 percent of the broadcast day for government-produced programs. The government also acquired a Mexico City station as an outlet for its programs.

The private television and radio sector is dominated by Televisa, which controls about 70 of the 120 TV stations in the country. Televisa is the parent company of Univision, a U.S. Spanish TV network, and Televisa produces and exports telenovelas, the Spanish versions of U.S. soap operas, which are tremendously popular throughout Latin America. For most of its existence, Televisa held a virtual monopoly on TV broadcasting, sometimes reaching 95 percent of all Mexican TV homes. In the past few years, however, it has faced competition from TV Azteca, which was government-owned until it was sold to a private firm in the mid-1990s. Broadcasting a program lineup that featured racy telenovelas, TV Azteca attracted about 30 percent of the audience in 2006, and some big advertisers were abandoning Televisa in favor of the younger network. Mexico passed new regulations in 2006 pertaining to the transition from analog to digital broadcasting. One provision of the new law gave Televisa and TV Azteca an advantage over any potential competitors for space in the digital bandwidth. This provision was overturned by Mexico's Supreme Court in 2007, leading to speculation that the Televisa-Azteca duopoly could face meaningful competition.

Some U.S. TV programming is popular in Mexico, but, as in many other countries, the top-rated shows are generally Mexican productions of situation comedies or telenovelas. Some American shows that were carried by Mexican TV in 2007 were *The Simpsons, Bones,* and *Desperate Housewives*. Reality programs came late to Mexico with a local version of *American Idol* premiering in 2003.

VCR and DVD player penetration tops 65 percent, one of the highest figures in Latin America. About 20,000 different video releases are available in video rental stores. Like many developing countries, Mexico has a problem with pirated videotapes and DVDs. One authority calculated that about 25 percent of all videos for rent in Mexico City are pirated copies.

U.S. films do well in Mexico. *Pirates of the Caribbean: At World's End* and *Spider-Man 3* were box office leaders in 2007. Some recent films made in Mexico, such as *El Crimen del Padre Amaro* and *Y Tu Mamá Tambien*, got favorable critical reviews and were also box office successes in the United States. The Televisa conglomerate also has interests in the Mexican film industry through its efforts in financing and producing films. The company also owns a chain of movie theaters.

The growth of new media has been slow in Mexico. About 17 percent of the population has access to the Internet. Cell phones have been adopted more rapidly, but as of 2007, they were in the hands of less than 50 percent of the population. Nonetheless, cell phone use is expected to grow rapidly.

In sum, the media scene in Mexico is changing. More competition is present, and long-time giant Televisa is losing a little of its dominance. In addition, Mexico's proximity to the United States has had many effects. Although a good deal of news and entertainment content flows from the United States to Mexico, there is now a significant flow in the other direction as well. The large Mexican American population in the United States constitutes an enthusiastic audience for Mexico's media. In fact, although hard figures are difficult to find, it is likely that Mexico exports more media content to the United States than does any other nation. This trend is likely to continue.

Newspapers in China are sometimes posted in public places for passersby to read.

▲ China

The media in China have been expanding rapidly, particularly in the past 20–25 years. The past decade or so, with some exceptions, has seen a trend toward less government control and a more diverse media landscape. This trend is due in part to China's move toward a free-market economy and a greater dependence on advertising to support the media. Owners of many print and broadcast outlets are responsive to profit-and-loss considerations and act accordingly. As a result, the marketplace rather than the Communist Party is now the major influence on the content of Chinese media.

The country has about 2,000 newspapers, many started since 1980, with a combined circulation of nearly 200 million. China recently replaced Japan as the country with the largest newspaper circulation and now has 16 newspapers that rank among the top 100 in circulation. For many years China was

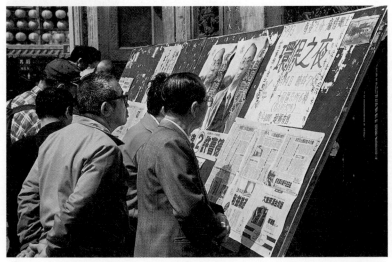

one of the few countries where newspaper circulation and advertising revenue were both increasing. Starting in 2005, however, advertising income started to slip as many readers followed their counterparts in other countries and abandoned the newspaper in favor of the Internet, podcasts, and mobile news services. Newspaper advertising revenue was about $3 billion in 2006, down about 15 percent from 2004.

China has several national newspapers. The party-controlled *People's Daily* once dominated newspaper circulation, but since 1980 its circulation has dropped from 7 million to 2 million. Three other papers—*Xinmin Evening News, Yangcheng Evening News*, and the *Sichuan Ribao*—boast circulations of more than a million. One English-language paper, *China Daily*, is aimed at foreigners living in China and interested foreigners living in America and Europe. Business and sports publications have proliferated, and China now publishes more than a hundred financial newspapers. Xinhua, the Chinese state-run news service, has a hundred overseas bureaus and transmits more than 50,000 words every day to Chinese media.

For decades state-owned newspapers enjoyed a captive audience. People who worked for the Chinese government, a large number of the workforce, were forced to subscribe to government publications. Recent reforms have done away with this practice, and it is expected that the *People's Daily,* the official newspaper of the Communist Party, will see its circulation tumble even more.

The relaxation of government media control has prompted many independent newspapers to start operation. The government's more liberal attitude toward the press was demonstrated during the SARS virus outbreak in 2003. After some initial hesitation, Beijing encouraged newspapers to pursue the story aggressively, and many did just that. This renewed spirit has helped these publications succeed in attracting both readers and advertising revenue.

The total number of magazines published in China is probably somewhere near 10,000. *Look* and *How,* the two most popular magazines, attract significant advertising revenue. In addition, Chinese editions of popular titles, such as *Elle China* and *Business Week China,* are best-sellers.

Most Chinese live in rural areas where literacy rates are lower than in cities. Consequently, many people rely on radio for news and entertainment. The country's 650 radio stations reach more than 95 percent of the population. China National Radio administers three national radio networks that broadcast on the AM, FM, and shortwave bands, and a fourth national network provides an FM-only service. Many local communities also have their own FM stations.

Television in China showed remarkable growth during the 1980s and the 1990s. As of 2007, TV penetration was more than 90 percent, or about 330 million households, making China the largest television market in the world. China Central Television provides 16 channels with 200 hours of programming every day. CCTV-1, the primary service, broadcasts news, entertainment, and special events. The other channels are more specialized, featuring science, children's programming, and music. In addition to CCTV, there are several thousand local and regional TV stations. As of 2007, the hottest show in China was *Super Girl,* sort of a Chinese version of *American Idol.*

The trend toward a free-market economy has encouraged the growth of TV advertising. Commercials are now a common sight on Chinese TV, and experts predict that advertising revenue will continue to grow thanks to China's entry into the World Trade Organization and the Beijing Olympics scheduled for 2008. In 2005 more than $20 billion was spent on advertising in China, making it the world's fifth-largest ad market, behind the United States, Japan, the United Kingdom, and Germany. Marketing experts predict that China could be in second place in another 10 years.

Despite its more liberal attitudes, the Chinese government occasionally takes steps to limit what can be shown in the country. Regulations limit local stations to no more than 25 percent imported programming. The government limits the amount of commercials in prime time to no more than 9 minutes per hour. Many foreign news programs are not allowed to be shown in China.

The students in Iran who demonstrated against the country's government in the summer of 2003 were mobilized by an unlikely source: TV stations in Los Angeles.

Four Iranian TV stations in L.A. beam satellite broadcasts into Iranian homes. The government tightly controls the media in Iran, and the only news that the people receive is filtered through the ruling regime. The authorities do their best to keep out opposing viewpoints. Owning a satellite dish is forbidden in Iran. Many have been arrested for receiving foreign news programs, and the Iranian government has tried repeatedly to jam the signals of the L.A. stations. Nonetheless, it is estimated that about 25 million Iranians, about one of every three people, have access to the outlawed stations. The L.A.-based programming is often recorded on videotape and distributed on the Internet.

The stations offer a wide range of programs. Newscasts that focus on the situation in Iran, not surprisingly, are favorites. But the stations also broadcast music, commentary, and even an occasional comedy skit that makes fun of the mullahs who rule the country. During the uprisings in Tehran, the four stations aired live phone calls from people in Iran describing the demonstrations and urging other Iranians to protest against the government. The L.A. stations also carried pro-democracy and pro-Western messages during the 2004 Iranian parliamentary elections and during the Iranian presidential campaign in 2005. Despite their efforts the elections brought to power a government that was not favorable to the West.

For their part the rulers in Iran see the L.A. stations as subversive and dangerous. They label them tools of the CIA and urge Iranians not to watch. The Iranian minister of information charged that America was waging psychological warfare against Iran.

What should be the official position of the United States toward such activity? The situation in which privately owned broadcast stations in the United States directly encourage subversive activity in another country is unprecedented. U.S. lawmakers have voiced strong support for the democracy movement in Iran. In late 2006 Congress passed the "Iran Freedom Support Act," which authorized the president to provide financial aid to those groups (including broadcasters) that support the spread of democracy in Iran. The United States also supports Radio Farda, a Persian-language station that broadcasts into Iran, but like the VOA, Radio Farda's charter mandates that it be factual and refrain from stirring local unrest. Should the United States channel money to support these stations? Do they serve a national interest? Or do these stations simply make it more difficult for traditional diplomacy to succeed? How would the United States react if a foreign country used the satellite to broadcast programs urging civil unrest to various minority groups in the United States? These are just some of the problems that crop up in the global village.

China has a fairly active motion picture industry, much of it centered in Hong Kong. In 2003 about a hundred movies made in China were released. Competition from foreign films is limited by a quota that allows no more than 20 films to be imported per year. Imported films are also subject to government censorship. *Brokeback Mountain* was not screened in China, and *Pirates of the Caribbean: At World's End* had several scenes deleted before it premiered in Chinese theaters. Despite these restrictions, most of the top Hollywood films are shown in China. An occasional Chinese film, such as *Crouching Tiger, Hidden Dragon*, coproduced with Sony, is successful in the United States.

Internet penetration was about 11 percent in 2006, but this number is deceiving since many Chinese access the Internet not at home but at Internet cafes. Blogging has become popular, with about 16 million Chinese posting blogs with a total readership of about 100 million. Internet advertising revenue is growing, as well, up about 70 percent from 2005 to 2006. The Chinese government is increasingly concerned about the potential power of the Internet. Most Internet users are blocked from accessing Web sites that the government deems inappropriate or harmful. Internet service providers are required to record information that can help track users' Web trails and immediately halt the transmission of subversive material.

Mobile media are also becoming popular. About 33 percent of the population has a cell phone. Cell phones have played an important role in communication. The earliest news of the SARS outbreak in China was not carried by the mainstream media but was spread by individuals sending text messages on their cell phones.

In the years to come, it is likely that the trend toward a free-marketplace economy will continue to have an impact on China's mass media. In turn, the mass media may also influence the country's political climate.

In sum, the media systems in these three countries illustrate the varying influences that economics, culture, geography, and politics have on the development of mass communication systems. Because of these and other factors, each nation will create a media system that is best suited to its own needs.

MAIN POINTS

- Communications across international boundaries have increased in the past two decades.

- Newspapers designed for international consumption include the *International Herald Tribune, USA Today International*, and financial papers. Many magazines also have international editions.

- Global radio broadcasters include the Voice of America, the BBC, China Radio International, Deutsche Welle, and RFI.

- The leaders in global television are CNN, MTV, ESPN, BBC World, and CNBC.

- Comparative analysis of media systems allows us to view alternative ways of structuring the mass media.

- The four main theories of government-media relationships are authoritarian, libertarian, social responsibility, and developmental.

- Media systems can be categorized by examining ownership patterns and degree of government control.

- The development of media systems in various countries is influenced by politics, culture, geography, history, and economics.

- The media systems in Japan, Mexico, and China illustrate how the theories of government-media relationships have operated in other countries and how numerous factors have affected those systems.

QUESTIONS FOR REVIEW

1. Name the major international newspapers and broadcasting services.

2. Compare and contrast the four major theories of the press.

3. Distinguish between public and private ownership of mass media.

4. What is developmental journalism?

5. How has geography shaped the mass communication systems in Japan, Mexico, and China?

QUESTIONS FOR CRITICAL THINKING

1. Why has MTV become such an international phenomenon? What factors influence the international success of a television program?

2. Given the ubiquity of the Internet, is it possible for any nation today to use the authoritarian approach?

3. American media products are easily available in other countries. What media products from other countries are easily available here? Why is there such a difference?

4. As China moves more and more toward a free-market economy, what will happen to the country's media system?

5. Review the "Cultural Imperialism" box on page 423, and consider the following: To what extent do you agree that American media products can influence the traditional values held in other societies? If you were a political leader in another country, would you favor quotes on the amount of foreign material that could be broadcast? Why or why not?

KEY TERMS

authoritarian theory (p. 418)   communist theory (p. 419)   developmental journalism (p. 422)
libertarian theory (p. 418)   developmental theory (p. 420)   free marketplace of ideas (p. 422)
social responsibility theory (p. 419)

INTERNET RESOURCES

Online Learning Center

At the Online Learning Center home page, www.mhhe.com/dominick10, *select* Student Center *and then* Chapter 18.

1. Use the Learning Objectives, Chapter Outline, Main Points, and Time Line sections to review this chapter.

2. Test your knowledge of the chapter using the multiple choice, crossword puzzle, and flashcard features of the site.

3. Expand your knowledge of concepts and topics discussed in the chapter by going to Suggestions for Further Reading and Internet Exercises.

Surfing the Internet

Many sites deal with international mass communication in general, and many others are the home pages of international media. Those listed here are a sampling of both.

www.aib.org.uk
Home page of the Association for International Broadcasting. Contains links to many international broadcasting stations.

www.cctv.com/english
Home page of China Central Television. Includes a program schedule.

www.iht.com
Home of the *International Herald Tribune,* "The World's Daily Newspaper."

www.ipl.org/div/news
The Internet Public Library has links to online papers in every region of the globe.

www.mtv.com/mtvinternational
Check out the various configurations of all the foreign MTV networks. Find out what is the number-one music video in India, and generally keep up to date with this Web site.

www.tvradioworld.com
A directory of Internet radio and TV stations that includes the major international outlets.

CHAPTER 19

SOCIAL EFFECTS OF MASS COMMUNICATION

This chapter will prepare you to:

- explain how scientists use surveys and experiments to study the effects of mass communication

- describe how the media can serve as agents of socialization

- explain why advertisers need to show special consideration for children

- discuss the impact of televised violence

- define the *agenda-setting effect* and *agenda building*

- explain how the media can help crystallize a viewer's political choices

- describe how the Internet may affect social involvement

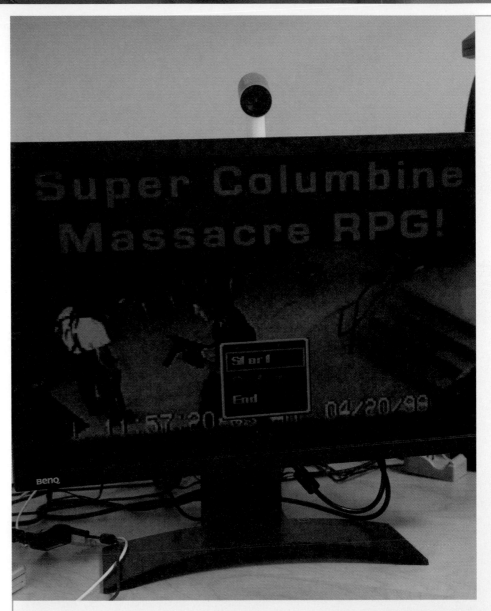

The controversial video game *Super Columbine Massacre RPG* was connected to the shootings at Dawson College in Montreal.

*S*uper Columbine Massacre RPG is a video game based on the shootings that took place at a Colorado high school in 1999. Players assume the role of the two killers and, as the game's directions state, "How many people they kill is ultimately up to you." In the game the two players are dressed in trench coats and carry a duffel bag filled with various weapons that were actually used in the Columbine shootings including shotguns, propane bombs, and TEC-9 semi automatic machine guns. The game then follows the two as they plant bombs in the school and eventually stalk and kill other students. Each time someone is killed, a dialogue box pops up: "Another victory for the Trench Coat Mafia." The game incorporates actual photographs of the crime scene, news coverage of the murders, and actual quotes taken from videotapes or writings of the two killers.

According to newspaper reports, *Super Columbine Massacre RPG* was one of the favorite video games of Kimveer Gill, a 25-year-old resident of Laval, a town near Montreal, Canada. On September 13, 2006, Gill put on a black trench coat; filled a duffel bag with a carbine, a Glock 9mm handgun, and a short-barreled shotgun; drove to Dawson College in downtown Montreal; and started shooting at students outside an entrance to the school. He kept shooting as he headed toward the atrium near the college cafeteria. He managed to get off 60 shots, killing one student and wounding 19 before he was cornered by police and killed himself.

Authorities investigating the crime later came across Gill's personal profile on a Web site called VampireFreaks.com. Gill had written, "Life is like a video game. You gotta die sometime."

Sadly enough, the Dawson College incident was eclipsed in April, 2007, by the horrific killings at Virginia Tech. High school classmates of the gunman in that incident said he was a fan of a video game called *Counterstrike,* in which players try to shoot each other using a variety of weapons.

These, of course, are extreme examples, and we will never know how much of a role, if any, video games played in the motivations for these killings. Not everybody who played *Counterstrike* or *Super Columbine Massacre RPG* went out and committed murder. These examples do, however, highlight the possible connection between media exposure and behavior. Accordingly, this chapter examines the social effects of mass communication. The first part looks at the impact of media on people's attitudes, knowledge, and perceptions. The second part examines how the media affect the way people behave. Before we discuss these effects, however, we need to examine how they have been investigated.

INVESTIGATING MASS COMMUNICATION EFFECTS

There are many ways to investigate what is or is not an effect of mass communication. Some people claim that personal observation is the best way to establish proof. As we noted in Chapter 2, the critical/cultural analysts focus on the various meanings that audience members construct from specific texts. Others rely on expert opinions and evaluations; still others point to common sense when they wish to support their views. All these methods are valuable, but this chapter will focus on the results of scientific studies of the media's impact on individuals. Keep in mind, however, that the scientific approach is only one of many ways to examine this topic.

When it comes to gathering information about media effects, scientists have typically used two main methods:

- A **survey** is carried out in the real world. It usually consists of a large group of individuals answering questions put to them via a questionnaire. Although the survey is usually not sufficient proof of cause and effect, it does help establish associations. A special kind of survey, a **panel study,** enables researchers to be more confident about attributing patterns of cause and effect in survey data. The panel study collects data from the same people at two or more points in time. As a result, it is possible, for example, using sophisticated techniques that control the effects of other variables, to determine if viewing televised violence at an early age is related to aggressive behavior at a later date. Panel studies are expensive and take a long time to complete.

- An **experiment** is performed in a laboratory and usually consists of the controlled manipulation of a single factor to determine its impact on another factor. A special kind of experiment, a **field experiment,** is conducted in a real-life setting. Experiments are useful because they help establish causality.

In the remainder of this chapter, we will focus on scientific findings about the effects of media on knowledge, attitudes, perceptions, and behavior.

EFFECTS OF MASS COMMUNICATION ON KNOWLEDGE AND ATTITUDES

The dividing line between attitudes and behaviors is fuzzy. In many instances we can only infer that an attitude or perception exists by observing relevant behavior. Thus, many of the studies mentioned in this section involve the measurement of *both* behavior and attitudes.

We will examine four topics that have generated the most research interest: (1) the role of the media in socialization, (2) cultivation analysis, (3) the impact of TV advertising on children, and (4) agenda setting.

▲ Media and Socialization

In Chapter 2 we defined *socialization* as the ways in which individuals come to adopt the behavior and values of a group. In this section we will concentrate on the socialization of children. Socialization is a complex process extending over a number of years and involving various people and organizations, called **agencies of socialization,** who contribute in some degree to the socialization process. Figure 19-1 presents a simplified diagram of some of the more common agencies.

FIGURE 19-1

Agencies of
Socialization

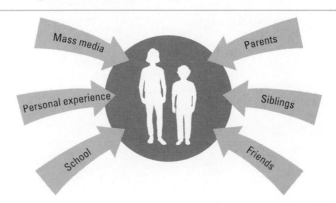

Super Columbine Massacre RPG was posted online in 2005, on the sixth anniversary of the shootings. It was a relatively obscure game until someone working for a popular gaming Web site came across it and gave it some notoriety. It received even more scrutiny after it was connected to Kimveer Gill and the Dawson College shootings.

The game itself is rather primitive. It uses graphical characters that resemble those from early Nintendo games, and much of the game play involves moving a character Pac-Man style around barriers to reach a goal. Surprisingly, there is little portrayal of blood or gore. The most upsetting part of the game is the juxtaposition of real photographs, some taken in the Columbine cafeteria, and the actual words and images of the two killers with the cartoonish action.

The creator of the game, Colorado resident Danny Ledonne, came in for harsh criticism after the Dawson shootings. He defended his creation by saying it was a piece of social commentary and shouldn't be blamed for causing the actions of disturbed individuals. In a published interview he went on to say that he wanted to create something that challenged social taboos and confronted social issues. Ledonne further argued that the game does not glorify killing but instead forces readers to delve deeper into the underlying causes of Columbine. He defended his right to artistic creation with a statement on his Web site: "If one is interested in making something for the public to view—be it a painting, a book, an album, a film, or a video game—should the *possible* harm that may come out of this work be grounds for its suppression from society?"

The game does contain some social commentary. It starts with scenes that show the two killers isolated and marginalized from society. Later on, after the two game characters commit suicide, the game shows the bloody pictures of the real shooters dead on the floor in the school library. The game then starts up again with the two characters in hell and forced to fight a number of demonlike creatures.

Detractors of the game do not temper their criticism. A relative of one of the students wounded at Dawson stated that it was impossible to believe that someone could put a game like *Super Columbine* in the public domain and not expect that no one would be influenced. Other relatives noted that the game trivializes the actions of the murderers and the lives of the victims.

The social responsibilities of artists have been debated many times. Is an artist responsible for any harm caused by her or his creation? Artists are human beings, of course, and it seems desirable that artists, like all human beings, should act in a socially responsible way. Acting in a socially responsible way suggests that "Do no harm" would be the minimum one would expect.

Numbers are hard to pin down, but *Super Columbine Massacre RPG* has probably been downloaded more than 40,000 times.

In many situations the media's contribution to socialization will be slight. Parents might have greater influence ("Eat your spinach; it's good for you"). So might friends

Could a media celebrity, such as Paris Hilton, serve as an agency of socialization for young women? Could she influence their attitudes about what behaviors are appropriate for teens?

("Don't be a tattletale"). So might direct experience ("I'd better not take my sister's stuff because the last time I did, she popped me one").

On the other hand, the media, especially television, may play an important role in socialization when it comes to certain topics. Let us now look at evidence pinpointing some of these areas.

▲ The Media as a Primary Source of Information

Learning is an important part of the socialization process, and the media serve as important sources of information for a wide range of topics, especially politics and public affairs. For example, a survey of sixth and seventh graders found that 80 percent named a mass medium as the source of most information about the president and vice president, 60 percent named a mass medium as the primary source of information about Congress, and half named a mass medium as the chief information source about the Supreme Court.

Other research has shown that the media, primarily TV, serve as primary information sources for many age groups about a wide range of topics. More than 90 percent of Americans cited television as their primary source of information about the September 11 terrorist attacks. Television is the source of most information for local and congressional elections. This phenomenon is not limited to political and public affairs information. There is reason to believe that media presentations, including those in entertainment programs, are important sources of information on topics such as occupations, crime, law enforcement, alcohol and drug usage, the environment, and minorities. One recent study of high school students, for example, found that about 1 in 4 listed rock music as an important source of information about moral values and that 1 in 4 specified it as an important source of information about interpersonal relationships. Another survey found that many young people listed Comedy Central's *The Daily Show* as their main source of news.

▲ Shaping Attitudes, Perceptions, and Beliefs

The mass media also play an important role in the transmission of attitudes, perceptions, and beliefs. Several writers have suggested that under certain conditions the media (especially TV) may become important socialization agencies in determining the attitudes of young people. Specifically, TV will be an influential force when the following factors are operative:

■ The same ideas, people, or behaviors recur consistently from program to program; that is, they are presented in a stereotyped manner.
■ A child is heavily exposed to TV content.
■ A child has limited interaction with parents and other socializing agents and lacks an alternative set of beliefs to serve as a standard against which to assess media portrayals.

All this means that under certain conditions TV will be an influential force in shaping what children think about certain topics. Complicated though the task is, some researchers have identified some of the conditions, the topics, and the children to which this theory applies. Moreover, they have specified some of the effects that may result when television does the socializing.

Stereotypes   In the study of media socialization, it is helpful to identify consistent themes or stereotypes present in media content. For instance, consider how television programs typically portray law enforcement and crime. Programs about crime and law enforcement are a staple of prime-time television; 20–35 percent of all program time consists of shows dealing with cops and criminals. However, the large percentage of law enforcement characters portrayed on TV does not accurately reflect the actual percentage employed in this capacity in real life. Further—on television, at least—crime doesn't pay. One study found that some 90 percent of TV crimes were solved; real-life law enforcement agencies are not nearly as effective.

The September 11 attacks and Operation Iraqi Freedom focused attention on the way Arabs had been portrayed in the mass media. Content analyses of TV revealed that Arab men were typically portrayed via three main negative stereotypes: (1) terrorist, (2) oil sheik, and (3) Bedouin. Arab women were rarely seen and, when they appeared at all, were shown as belly dancers or members of a harem (harems were never common, and none exist today). And how many Arab children have you seen on *Sesame Street*?

In sum evidence suggests that the TV world often presents images that are at odds with reality. Stereotyping has also characterized, in addition to police dramas, gender-role portrayals, the depiction of occupations, methods of problem solving, portrayals of scientists, and the depiction of mental illness.

The Effects of Heavy Viewing   It seems probable that youngsters who are heavy TV viewers would display a pattern of beliefs and perceptions consistent with media portrayals. The earliest research in this area, completed in the 1930s, found that frequent viewing of

Quite a few professors these days have created Facebook pages. Does the content on these pages affect the perceptions and expectations of students who might take their classes? This topic was the subject of an experiment reported in a 2007 issue of *Communication Education.*

The researchers constructed three versions of a Facebook page for a female graduate teaching assistant. One version was labeled "high self-disclosure." It contained photos of her with family and friends in a variety of social situations. Her "Wall" contained messages from other teaching assistants that mentioned her attendance at parties, dances, and weekend get-togethers. She also posted personal information about her favorite movies, books, her relationship status and her membership in several Facebook groups.

A second condition was labeled "medium self-disclosure." In this version photographs were limited to the teaching assistant and her family. There were no comments written on the "Wall," and personal information was limited to favorite books and quotes. The third condition was "low self-disclosure." This version contained only a head shot of the person, with no messages; the only personal information disclosed was about her position at the university.

Students who participated in the experiment were randomly assigned to one of the three conditions above and asked to browse the site in order to form an impression about the person. They were then asked their perceptions about the class that the person taught and whether they would be interested in taking it.

Those exposed to the high-self-disclosure site reported that they would be more motivated in her class than did those who saw the low-self-disclosure version. Those in the high-self-disclosure condition also reported that they thought the classroom climate would be more positive than those in the low condition. And they said they would be more likely to take other courses from this teacher than those who saw the low-self-disclosure version.

These results suggest that the amount or type of information that a teacher reveals on a Facebook page can have an impact on what students expect of the teacher and his or her class. Revealing some personal information might make potential students more comfortable in class and encourage more teacher-student interactions. Of course, the researchers also cautioned that too much self-disclosure might be a bad thing. There are probably things that students really don't want to know about their professors— and vice versa.

crime and gangster movies could change attitudes on topics such as capital punishment and prison reform. More recently, other researchers have noted a connection between heavy viewing of violent TV programs and favorable attitudes toward the use of violence in real life. Further, children who are heavy viewers of cops-and-robbers TV programs are likely to believe that police are more successful in apprehending criminals than are children who are not fans of these shows.

In other areas several studies have linked high levels of television viewing with attitudes favoring traditional gender roles. In other words, children who are heavily exposed to television are more likely to feel, among other things, that men make better doctors and that women make better nurses or that raising children is a job for women rather than men.

Do TV programs such as *The George Lopez Show* represent the most important source of information about Hispanic families for white viewers? Mass media researchers are interested in how television influences attitudes toward minorities.

To be fair, we must again stress that this type of research *assumes* but does not necessarily *prove* that the mass media play a significant part in creating the attitudes held by these youngsters. Surveys can only highlight associations, not prove causality. Although some experimental evidence points to the media as the cause of certain attitudes, we cannot entirely rule out other interpretations. Nevertheless, it is likely that the link between media exposure and certain attitudes demonstrates reciprocal causation. What this means is best shown by an example. Watching violent TV shows might cause a youngster to hold favorable attitudes toward aggression. These favorable attitudes might then prompt him or her to watch more violent TV, which, in turn, might encourage more aggressive attitudes, and so on. The two factors might be said to be mutually causing each other.

The Absence of Alternative Information   Although research evidence is less consistent in this area than in others, it appears that under some circumstances television can affect young people's attitudes about matters for which the environment fails to provide firsthand experience or alternative sources of information. One survey that examined the potential impact of TV on dating behavior found that teenagers are more likely to turn to TV for guidance when they have limited real-life experience with dating.

Where media influence is indirect, it is difficult to pinpoint. This is particularly true when the media operate simultaneously with other agencies of socialization and when interpersonal channels outweigh media channels in forming attitudes and opinions. In the area of politics, for instance, the media probably supply youngsters with information and viewpoints that are subsequently commented on by parents and friends. Political beliefs and attitudes evolve out of this double context. In such cases the socializing impact of parents and other interpersonal sources is more important than that of the media. One study dealing with attitudes toward police found that, although children spend a great deal of time watching TV cop shows, friends and family are the important socializing agents. The point is this: The media play a significant role in socialization. Sometimes this role is easy to detect; sometimes it is indirect and harder to see; at still other times it is apparently slight. Clearly, numerous factors are influential in determining how a child comes to perceive the world. The media (and television, in particular), however, have become important factors in the socialization process.

▲ Cultivation Analysis

Directly related to socialization is an area of research called **cultivation analysis.** Developed by George Gerbner and his colleagues at the University of Pennsylvania, cultivation analysis suggests that heavy TV viewing "cultivates" perceptions of reality consistent with the view of the world presented in television programs. Cultivation analysis concentrates on the long-term effects of exposure—on both adults and children—rather than on the short-term impact on attitudes and opinions.

Methodology   The first stage in cultivation analysis is a careful study of television content to identify predominant themes and messages. Not surprisingly, television portrays a rather idiosyncratic world that is unlike reality along many dimensions. For example, television's world is usually populated by a preponderance of males: Two-thirds to three-quarters of all leading characters are men. Moreover, television overemphasizes the professions of—and, as previously mentioned, overrepresents the proportion of workers engaged in—law enforcement and the detection of crime. Last, the TV world is a violent one—around 50 percent of all programs contain at least one instance of violence.

The second stage involves examining what, if anything, viewers absorb from heavy exposure to the world of television. Respondents are presented with questions concerning social reality and are asked to check one of two possible answers. One of these answers (the "TV answer") is in line with the way things are portrayed on television; the other (the "real-world answer") resembles actual life. Here is an example:

> *What percentage of all males who have jobs work in law enforcement and crime detection? Is it*
>
> _____ *1 percent or* _____ *10 percent?*

On television about 12 percent of all male characters hold such jobs; thus, 10 percent would be the TV answer. In reality about 1 percent are employed in law enforcement; thus, 1 percent is the real-world answer. The responses of a large sample of heavy TV viewers are then compared with those of light TV viewers. If heavy viewers show a definite tendency to choose TV answers, we would have evidence that a cultivation effect is occurring.

Research Findings   Is there evidence to suggest such an effect? Most findings suggest that among some people TV cultivates distorted perceptions of the real world. In one survey of approximately 450 New Jersey schoolchildren, 73 percent of heavy viewers compared with 62 percent of light viewers gave the TV answer to a question about the number of people involved in violence in a typical week. Youngsters who were heavy viewers were also more fearful about walking alone at night in a city. They overestimated how many people

The island nation of Fiji did not get television until 1995, when a local TV station began broadcasting shows such as *ER, Seinfeld,* and *Melrose Place.* In the years that followed, there was an increase in bulimia and other eating disorders among young Fijian girls, disorders that were rare before the arrival of TV. In addition, there was a big jump in the number of females dissatisfied with their body image. A 1998 survey turned up the fact that three of four female teens on the island reported feeling too big or too fat.

An anthropologist who has studied the Fijian culture since 1998 attributed these changes to the influence of television. The traditional Fijian female body type has been described as "robust" and "well muscled." American TV shows, however, portray the ideal body type as thin and wispy. Fijian teen girls apparently believed that this body type was the preferred one in the modern world and tried to emulate it.

The Fiji case illustrates that TV shows do more than just entertain; they also embody the social values of the nation that produces them. As this book went to press, no follow-up anthropological study had been published that updated these research findings. An updated study would be interesting because the following shows were available on Fiji TV in 2006: *Friends, Desperate Housewives,* and *Grey's Anatomy.*

How many doctors are like the acerbic but brilliant Dr. House on the Fox show of the same name? Cultivation analysis suggests that for some heavy viewers, TV portrayals might influence their perceptions of real life.

commit serious crimes, how often police find it necessary to use force, and how frequently police shoot at fleeing suspects.

Other cultivation research has focused specifically on college students. In one study students' exposure to pornography was examined to see if stereotyped perceptions were being cultivated. Among males, those who were heavy users of pornography were more apt to report that they had less confidence in females doing certain jobs (such as mechanic or mayor). They also tended to agree more with stereotypes of sexuality ("Men have stronger sexual urges than women; women say 'no' to sex when they don't really mean it") than did light users. These relationships held even after rigorous statistical controls removed possible influences of other factors. Women showed no such effects from exposure. A 1993 study found that college students who had high exposure to televised portrayals of sexual behavior thought that those behaviors happened more frequently in real life than did students with lower levels of exposure. More recently, a 2007 study looked at the cultivation impact of TV's portrayal of mental health. Content analysis revealed that in prime-time programs the mentally ill were 10 times more likely to be violent criminals than those without mental problems. In line with cultivation, a survey disclosed that heavy television viewers were more fearful of having a mental health facility located in their neighborhood and were less likely to support living next to someone who was mentally ill.

Although the results of cultivation analysis studies are evocative and fascinating, conclusions are clouded by three problems. First, it is difficult to determine cause and effect. For example, does heavy TV viewing cause people to be fearful of walking alone at night, or does being fearful cause them to stay home and watch more TV?

The second problem concerns the fact that people differ in ways other than their TV viewing habits. Consequently, factors other than TV watching might affect the differences in perceptions and attitudes between heavy and light viewers. When certain factors that appear relevant to the cause-and-effect relationship (such as age, sex, and education) are statistically controlled, one factor at a time, the association between TV watching and perceptions is evident but somewhat weakened. When two or more factors are controlled simultaneously (such as examining the relationship between TV viewing and anxiety while simultaneously controlling for effects of both sex and age), some overall relationships disappear. We cannot conclude, however, that a relationship does not exist. In fact, recent research indicates that certain subgroups will show a cultivation effect and others will not.

One group of researchers, for example, detected a phenomenon they labeled **main-streaming,** whereby differences apparently due to cultural and social factors tend to diminish among heavy TV viewers. They have also found evidence for what they call **resonance,** a situation in which the respondent's real-life experiences are congruent with those of the television world, thereby leading to a greater cultivation effect.

Third, technical decisions about the way TV viewing and attitudes are measured can have a significant impact on findings. For example, the precise wording of the questions has been shown to be important. In addition, some researchers argue that exposure to a particular kind of program (such as, violent shows) gives a more accurate picture of cultivation than simply measuring overall TV viewing. Others note that deciding on the number of hours of viewing that differentiates heavy and light viewers has a bearing on the magnitude of cultivation.

Perhaps the most comprehensive summary of cultivation research is a 1997 review of more than 5,600 findings collected over two decades. The authors of this review found evidence of a small but persistent cultivation effect that may have significance for the social, cultural, and political climate. As the authors concluded, "Certainly not all of the [cultivation] issues are resolved, but, taken as a whole, the data show that cultivation theory has amply demonstrated the nature, importance, and resilience of its findings."[1]

To sum up and perhaps oversimplify, we can say that, although not all mass communication scholars are totally convinced by the reasoning underlying cultivation analysis, a growing body of evidence suggests that the cultivation effect is indeed real for many people.

▲ Children and Television Advertising

If you have ever watched Saturday morning television, you are probably familiar with Tony the Tiger, Captain Crunch, Count Chocula, Ronald McDonald, and Snap, Crackle, and Pop. This is not surprising because, by the time you graduated from high school, you had already seen about 350,000 TV commercials. A typical child will see about 20,000 commercials every year, mostly for toys, cereal, candy, and fast-food restaurants. During the 1970s the citizens' group Action for Children's Television brought this issue to the attention of the Federal Communications Commission (FCC) and the Federal Trade Commission (FTC). By the early 1980s, most people had accepted the notion that children deserve special consideration from television advertisers, for the following reasons:

- Children are a vulnerable audience and should not be exploited by TV advertising.
- Children, especially younger children, might be deceived by TV techniques that make products appear more desirable than they really are.
- Long-term of exposure to TV ads might have a negative effect on children's socialization as future consumers.

Using this threefold division, we will examine some of the many research studies that have investigated the effects of TV advertising on children.

Vulnerability of the Audience   Adults can easily distinguish commercials from regular TV programs, but what about children? Research suggests that children from 5 to 8 years of age can separate ads from the rest of a program, but they have little idea as to the purpose of the ads. Older children (from 9 to 12) are better able to identify ads and are aware that their purpose is to persuade people to buy things. Partly as a result of these

---

[1]This review was done by Michael Morgan and James Shanahan and appears on pages 1–46 of *Communication Yearbook*, 1996, edited by Brant Burleson and published by Sage.

The typical child sees up to 20,000 commercials in a year, many for games and toys. The impact of television advertising and its role in consumer socialization is a popular research topic.

findings, in 1974 the FCC concluded that some device was needed to clearly separate commercials from programs. Current programs aimed at children use such signals as "We will return after these messages" or "We now return to [name of show]." Experiments have shown that these program separators are not effective with kids under the age of 5 but are somewhat effective with older children.

Effects of Special Selling Techniques   When you were much younger, you may have had an experience like the following. On Saturday morning, while watching your favorite cartoon, you saw an ad for a toy, perhaps a plastic model truck called "Toughie." In the ad the truck, with headlights flashing and horn blowing, was shown dumping a load of sand in the middle of a miniature construction site, surrounded by miniature construction workers. The truck was then shown close up, practically dwarfing the young child in the background. Excited, you told your parents that Toughie was the one thing you wanted most for Christmas. When Christmas arrived and you were lucky enough to find Toughie under the tree, you were disillusioned to find that the actual truck was much smaller than it had appeared to be on TV. The headlights did not flash and the horn did not blow because batteries were not included with the truck. There was no sand, no miniature construction site, no tiny construction workers. Somehow, it was not the same toy that you remembered.

Obviously, toys and other products designed for children can be made to look more appealing through the use of camera angles, lenses, advertising copy, sound effects, animation, and lighting techniques. The ability of children to distinguish the illusion created by these techniques from the real object has been an area of continuing interest among policy makers and mass communication researchers. Recently, in response to tighter industry guidelines, commercials directed toward children have included disclaimers—messages

441

such as "Some assembly required" or "Batteries not included" or "Accessories sold separately," which are read by an announcer and/or flashed on the screen. Some critics have argued that these disclaimers are not understood by children, and several research studies have examined this area.

Consumer Socialization   Consumer socialization includes all those processes by which children learn behaviors and attitudes relevant to their future behavior as consumers. Research in this area is not clear-cut, but we can make some generalizations. First, as children get older, they tend to distrust commercials and even become cynical about them. One study revealed that the percentage of youngsters who believed commercials declined to only 7 percent by the fifth grade. Second, exposure to TV commercials is not related to consumer skills, such as price comparisons. Watching a lot of commercials on TV does not make a person an intelligent consumer.

We have seen in this brief review that some criticisms voiced by public-interest groups such as Action for Children's Television appear to be supported by research. Some children, especially younger ones, have trouble understanding the basic intent of advertising. As a child matures, repeated exposure to commercials evidently results in disillusionment and cynicism about the merits of advertising. This whole topic raises questions about regulation. Ideally, organizations such as the FTC and the FCC will construct a public policy on advertising for children in the near future.

▲ Agenda Setting

One influence of mass media that has turned up in many studies of mass communication is the **agenda-setting effect.** (An agenda is a list of things to be considered or acted upon.) When we say that the media have an impact on agenda setting, we mean that they have the ability to choose and emphasize certain topics, thereby causing the public to perceive these issues as important. To paraphrase Bernard Cohen in his book *The Press and Foreign Policy*, we can say that the media may not always be successful in telling people what to think, but they are usually successful in telling people what to think about.

Agenda-setting studies typically concern themselves with information media: newsmagazines, newspapers, television, and radio. Much of the research on agenda setting has been carried out during political campaigns. There are two reasons for this. First, messages generated by political campaigns are usually designed to set agendas (politicians call this tactic "emphasizing the issues"). Second, political campaigns have a clear-cut beginning and end, thus making the time period for study unambiguous.

One typical agenda-setting study was an investigation of the 1968 presidential election. The researchers asked a sample of voters to rank what they believed to be the key

TV coverage of news events, such as the violence in postwar Iraq, can help shape the public's agenda.

issues of the campaign. While this was going on, the researchers examined newsmagazines, newspapers, and television newscasts and ranked the campaign issues according to the time and space the media devoted to each issue. When the media's ranking was compared with the voters' ranking, there was a strikingly high degree of correspondence. In other words, the voters perceived as important those issues that the media judged important, as evidenced by the amount of coverage they received. Similar studies of more recent elections have found similar results. Although such studies strongly suggest a relationship between personal agendas and media agendas, they do not address the question of causation, an issue that we have encountered before.

Some studies indicate that there are situations in which the direction of cause and effect is unclear—or will even depend on the medium under consideration. At least two studies report that newspapers exert a greater agenda-setting effect than does television. In fact, one survey found that during a political campaign

How Often Do You Use Your Cell Phone?

A recent study that examined the cell phone habits of 575 high school students in Korea found that heavy cell phone use—more than 90 calls or text messages in a day—was related to feelings of anxiety, depression, and unhappiness, and other emotional hang-ups.

television appeared to alter its coverage to conform to voter interest, and newspapers appeared to shape the voters' agendas.

Recent reviews published in scholarly journals noted two new directions of research interest. The first pertains to the notion of **framing,** the general way a news topic is treated by the media. This line of research posits that not only do the media tell us what to think about, they also tell us how to think about it by the way the story is framed. For example, suppose Congress is considering changes in the food stamp program. One way the media might frame this story is by concentrating on both the increased efficiency that might result from the changes and the savings to taxpayers. Alternatively, the media might choose to emphasize the hardships that might be experienced by people who will no longer qualify for the program. The particular choice of frames will affect the salience of the story and our attitudes toward the revised program.

A second direction concerns **agenda building.** Research on this topic examines how the media build their agenda of newsworthy items. Some factors that seem to have an impact are presidential press conferences, congressional hearings, and public relations efforts. One recent study, for example, found that a public relations effort by the Christian Coalition was influential in shaping the media agenda some 3 months later. Another recent study suggested that a journalist's own personal agenda (the issues that he or she considers important) might also have an impact on the media agenda. A study published in 2005 suggested that entertainment programs that focus on crime and law enforcement are influential in building the audience's personal agenda, which may eventually have an impact on polling data that help shape the media agenda.

Research into the impact of online media on agenda setting is a growing area. There is obvious evidence that bloggers can set the news media agenda, as seen in the controversy over CBS News's airing of questionable documents relating to President George W. Bush's military service during the Viet Nam era. Bloggers first raised questions about the authenticity of the documents, and the story was quickly picked up by the mainstream media. A 2006 study done in Korea noted that online newspapers may also have an agenda-setting effect.

President Franklin D. Roosevelt used radio effectively as a political communications tool during his "fireside chats" with the nation. The increasing importance of radio as a tool prompted several large-scale studies during the 1940s.

MEDIA EFFECTS ON BEHAVIOR: A SHORT HISTORY

The political effects of the mass media, especially radio, prompted much of the early research. Many people feared that a skilled political demagogue might use the new medium of radio to gain political power. As a result, large-scale studies were conducted during the 1940s to gauge the extent of media influence. Somewhat surprisingly, these early surveys found that the media had little direct effect on political decision making. Personal influence was more important, and individuals labeled "opinion leaders" were thought to be more important in transmitting political orientations.

The explosive growth of TV during the 1950s and 1960s shifted the research focus to young people. Early large-scale surveys noted that television could influence children's values and perceptions of the world. In addition, the new medium might adversely affect social relationships and skills necessary for success in school.

The impact of media portrayals of violence was of special concern as evidenced by Senate subcommittee hearings on the topic in 1961 and 1964. In 1967 a national commission concluded that a steady diet of media violence had "an adverse effect on human character and attitudes."

The topic was revisited again in 1970 when the United States Surgeon General issued a report that linked exposure to TV violence with antisocial behavior. A 1982 follow-up study reinforced the conclusions of the original report. Media violence remained the center of attention during the 1990s. As mentioned in previous chapters, the Telecommunications Act of 1996 contained provisions for program ratings and a V-Chip that enabled parents to block violent and other unwanted programming from their TVs. Televised violence came under the spotlight again in 1999 after the Columbine shootings and yet again after the Virginia Tech massacre. In 2007 the FCC urged Congress to draft legislation that would permit the FCC to regulate the presentation of violent material.

We will next examine more closely some of the topics mentioned in the 1970 report summary, beginning with the topic that has generated the most research attention: the effects of TV violence.

THE IMPACT OF TELEVISED VIOLENCE

Does television viewing prompt violent or other antisocial behaviors on the part of the viewer? As we have just seen, this question has been debated for the better part of four decades. It is a complicated issue, and the definitive answer has not yet been found. Nonetheless, enough evidence has been gathered that we can begin to point to some preliminary conclusions. To arrive at these conclusions, we must examine research data from surveys and from experiments.

▲ Survey Results

Table 19-1 contains abbreviated and modified questionnaire items taken from surveys designed to analyze the viewing of TV violence and aggressive behavior.

As you can see, with measures such as the ones in the table (assuming, of course, a questionnaire that was much longer), it would be possible to index a person's viewing of programs that generally contain violence. It would also be possible to measure that same

TABLE 19-1		Almost always	Often	Sometimes	Never
Questionnaire Items	**1. About how often do you watch the following TV programs?**				
	The Sopranos	_____	_____	_____	_____
	Scrubs	_____	_____	_____	_____
	Cold Case	_____	_____	_____	_____
	The Office	_____	_____	_____	_____
	CSI	_____	_____	_____	_____
	Law & Order	_____	_____	_____	_____

2. Next, what would you do if these things happened to you?
   a. Pretend somebody you know took something from you and would not give it back. What would you do?
      _____ Hit the other person and take my property back.
      _____ Call the police.
      _____ Ask the person to return it.
      _____ Nothing.
   b. Pretend somebody was telling lies about you. What would you do?
      _____ Hit the person and make the person stop.
      _____ Ask the person to stop telling lies.
      _____ Nothing.

What makes some children imitate the violent acts they see on TV? Scientists have been studying this question since the early 1950s.

person's tendency to report his or her willingness to use violence in everyday situations. If viewing violent TV does affect behavior, we would expect to find some relationship between reported heavy viewing of violence and an individual's own self-report of aggressive tendencies. If we do not find such a link, we might assume that exposure to media violence has no impact on subsequent aggressive tendencies. If, however, we do find a connection, we might suspect that media violence actually causes aggression. We could not be sure, however, because survey data alone are not sufficient to establish a cause-and-effect relationship. We must also keep in mind that there are different ways of measuring exposure to TV violence and aggressive tendencies.

Viewed as a whole, surveys compiled over the years are difficult to summarize. Perhaps the most concise generalization is one that appeared in a recent summary of television research findings. After carefully analyzing all survey results, the authors of this summary "conclude that the evidence to date indicates that there is a significant correlation between the viewing of violent television programs and aggressive behavior in day-to-day life."

Nevertheless, as already mentioned, a relationship is not necessarily evidence of cause and effect. Remember, however, that the special survey technique known as a *panel study* gives us a little more confidence in making cause-and-effect statements based on survey data. However, since panel studies cost a lot and sometimes take years to complete, not many exist. Further, the results from those that are available are not as clear as we might like them to be. One panel study whose methods might have been stronger was included in the 1970 Surgeon General's report on television and social behavior. It found evidence that viewing violent TV shows at an early age was a cause of aggression in later life.

Additional survey evidence appeared in 1982 with the publication of *Television and Aggression: A Panel Study*. This book reported the results of a 3-year research project sponsored by NBC. Data on aggression, TV viewing, and a large number of sociological variables were collected on six different occasions from children in two midwestern cities. Eventually, about 1,200 boys in grades two through six participated in the main survey.

Lengthy and detailed analysis of the data suggested that there was no relationship between the viewing of TV violence and subsequent aggressive behavior. Later, other researchers were given the opportunity to reanalyze the NBC data. One reexamination did find some partial evidence of a causal relationship between TV violence and aggression, but its impact was tiny. In sum, if a causal relationship was present in the NBC data, it was extremely weak and hard to find.

In 1986 an international team of scientists reported the results of panel studies done in five countries: the United States, Finland, Australia, Israel, and Poland. The U.S. study and the Polish study found that early TV viewing was significantly related to later aggression. The Finnish study reached a similar conclusion for boys but not for girls. In Israel viewing TV violence seemed to be a cause of subsequent aggression among boys and girls who lived in urban areas but not among those who lived in rural areas. The panel study done in Australia was not able to find a causal relationship. Despite these differences the five panels were consistent in at least two findings. First, the relationship between the viewing of violence and aggression tended to be somewhat weak. Second, there was a pattern of circularity in causation. Viewing violent TV caused some children to become more aggressive. Being aggressive, in turn, caused some children to watch more violent TV.

The results of an extensive panel survey reported in 2002 found that teens who watched more than one hour of TV a day were more likely to commit violent acts in later years than were teens who watched less. The survey tracked 707 children for more than 17 years. The researchers interviewed the participants several times and also checked arrest records to document violent behavior. The relationship between TV viewing and aggressive acts was still evident after other factors such as low family income and a prior history of violence were controlled statistically. The results of the study were weakened, however, by the fact that the researchers measured the total amount of TV exposure rather than exposure to violent content. It is difficult to explain why general TV exposure, much of it to nonviolent programs, would be related to aggression.

A study published in 2004 found results consistent with past research. More than 400 third, fourth, and fifth graders were surveyed at the beginning and at the end of the school year. The researchers found that children who were exposed early in the school year to media violence in TV, movies, and video games were more likely to see the world as a hostile place and to behave more aggressively at the end of the year.

What are we to make of all these panel studies? On the whole, they seem to suggest that there is a mutual causal connection between watching TV violence and performing aggressive acts. This connection, however, is small and influenced by individual and cultural factors. At this point, we will turn to the results of laboratory studies to aid us further in forming a conclusion about what causes what.

▲ Experimental Results

Imagine that it is a cold winter night. As part of the requirements of Psychology 100, a course in which you are enrolled, you are required to serve as a subject in 3 hours of research. Tonight is your night to fulfill part of your obligation. Thus, you find yourself trudging across campus to the Psychology Building. Upon arriving, you join several dozen other students in a large auditorium. Before long, an individual enters the room, introduces himself as Professor So-and-So, and tells you that you are about to begin your first experiment of the evening.

Professor So-and-So has a new IQ test that he is trying to develop, and he needs your cooperation. The test booklet is passed out, and you are told to begin. As soon as you start the test, you realize that it is unlike any IQ test you have ever seen before. There are questions about advanced calculus, early Greek architecture, and organic chemistry, which you have no idea how to answer. In a few minutes the professor starts making sarcastic comments: "You'll never finish college if this simple test takes you so long"; "It looks as if this group will certainly flunk out"; "High school students have finished this test by now." Finally, with an air of exasperation, the professor says, "There's no hope for you. Hand in the papers. Since most of you won't be in school after this semester's grades, let me say good-bye to you now." With that the professor storms out of the room.

A few minutes go by, and then another individual enters the room and calls out two lists of names. Each group is assigned to another room down the hall. When you report to your assigned room, you find another professor already there. She tells you that this is the second experiment you will participate in tonight. It is a study to see how much people remember from films. You are going to be shown a brief excerpt from a film, and then you will be asked questions about it. The lights go out, and all of a sudden you are watching an 8-minute fight scene from a Kirk Douglas film called *The Champion*. In the movie Douglas, playing a boxer, gets the stuffing beaten out of him as he competes for the title. (Unknown to you, that other group of students is also seeing a film. At the same time you are watching Douglas get battered, they are viewing a scene from the film *Canal Boats in Venice*.) When the film ends, you are asked several questions about its content.

You are then directed to yet another room. Once in this cubicle, you are told that the third and last experiment is to begin. You are seated in front of a rather strange-looking machine with a dial that can be moved from a setting of 1 to 11. You also notice a button and a light connected to something behind the machine. The researcher explains that you are to be part of an experiment designed to investigate memory. In another room, but wired up to this same machine, is a student who is learning a word-association test. Every time this other student makes a mistake, you are to punish him by giving him a shock. The dial on your panel determines the intensity of the shock; when you press the button, it will be administered. You can choose any level you like; you can hold the button down as long as you like. The experimenter then gives you a level-2 shock to show you what it feels like. You jump and wonder why you did not take poly sci instead of psych. Your thoughts are interrupted,

The old adage that sticks and stones can break your bones but that names will never hurt you may not be accurate. Research has shown that verbal aggression—calling people names, insulting them, and spreading gossip—can do psychological harm to individuals just as much as physical violence can do them bodily harm. To make matters worse, the Internet has made verbal aggression easier and has made its potential effects much more serious.

Bullying has always been a problem for young children. With traditional bullying, however, children had a chance to escape. They could go home and shut the door. With the Internet, however, it's hard to avoid. One study in Australia found that bullies now use postings in chat rooms, instant messages, or text messages on cell phones to extend the range of their harassment. Some even started special Web sites to bully their victims. Another study discovered that 30 percent of the children they surveyed had suffered bullying via the Internet.

Online harassment can be particularly cruel. High school officials in New York recently discovered a Web site that listed names, phone numbers, and the alleged sexual exploits of dozens of female students. Online lists of students considered "most ugly" or "most boring" are common. One seventh grader sent a video of himself singing a song to a girl he liked. The girl posted the video all over the Internet. Another boy received a revealing picture from his girlfriend and promptly sent it to all his friends.

This form of maltreatment is even worse than the face-to-face kind. Cyber-bullying is less noticeable to adults and can be more publicly humiliating. Many victims are mortified when insults, embarrassing pictures, or harmful gossip are easily circulated among all their peers with just a few mouse clicks. Additionally, Internet bullying exaggerates the distance between bully and victim; the bullies can easily inflict pain and not see its immediate effect. There is little that the victim can do in response to these attacks.

Public awareness of this problem is growing. Wired-Safety.org is a nonprofit group whose Web site contains advice to parents and children about cyber-harassment. In the past much of its efforts were devoted to protecting young kids from bad adults. Now it is also concerned with protecting kids from other kids.

---

however, when the little light on the panel flashes on. The other student has made a mistake. It is your job to administer punishment. Your hand reaches for the dial. . . .

▲ The Catharsis Versus Stimulation Debate

This is an abstracted, simplified, and condensed version of the prototype experimental design used in several key studies to investigate the impact of media violence. The idea behind this experiment is to test two rival theories about the effects of watching violence. The first theory is thousands of years old; it is called the **catharsis theory** and can be traced back to Aristotle. This theory holds that viewing scenes of aggression can actually purge the viewer's own aggressive feelings. Thus, a person who sees a violent television program or movie might end up less likely to commit violence. The other theory, called the **stimulation theory,** argues just the opposite: Seeing scenes of violence will actually stimulate an individual to behave more violently afterward.

As you may have understood, in the hypothetical experiment, everybody was first insulted and presumably angered (this part of the experiment gave you some hostility to be purged); one group saw a violent film, and the other saw a nonviolent film. Both groups were then given a turn at the punishment machine. If catharsis was at work, then the group that saw *The Champion* would have given less intense shocks; if stimulation was at work, then *The Champion* group would have given more intense shocks.

The catharsis versus stimulation debate was one of the earliest to surface in the study of mass media's effects. One early study seemed to point to catharsis, but a series of studies carried out by psychologist Leonard Berkowitz and his colleagues at the University of Wisconsin found strong support for the stimulation hypothesis. Since that time, the bulk of the evidence seems consistent: Watching media violence tends to stimulate aggressive behavior on the part of the viewer. There is little evidence for catharsis.

▲ Bandura's Experiment

The catharsis versus stimulation question was only one of several topics that sparked early experimental work in the investigation of the effects of the media. Another controversy arose over the possibility that TV and movies were serving as a school for violence. Would children imitate violent behavior they had just observed in films or TV programs? A series

A series of still photographs of the famous study by Albert Bandura and colleagues. In this experiment children watched adults act aggressively toward a Bobo doll. When allowed to play in the same room, these children imitated the behavior of the adult models.

of experiments conducted by psychologist Albert Bandura and his colleagues during the 1960s indicated that, in fact, films and TV might teach aggressive behaviors.

Preschool children were shown films in which a model reacted violently to a large rubber doll (called a Bobo doll). When children were placed in a play situation similar to the one they had just observed, they mimicked the behaviors they had seen, performing far more aggressively toward the unfortunate Bobo doll than did children who had not seen the film. It was further determined that children would behave more aggressively if they were rewarded for doing so or if they saw the model in the film rewarded. Of course, there is a big difference between hitting an inanimate doll and hitting a human being. To account for this, more recent studies have substituted a human being dressed as a clown for the faithful Bobo doll. Although more children were willing to hit the rubber doll, a large number also physically assaulted the human clown. This reaction did not occur among children who had not seen the violent film.

▲ Complicating Factors

Of course, many complicating factors might influence the results of such experiments. To begin with, many of these studies used specially made films and videotapes. In laboratory situations the experimental "program" may not duplicate the impact of actual TV or films. In those films and tapes produced especially for laboratory use, the violence is concentrated in a short period; there is usually a clear connection between the violence and its motivations and consequences. Films and TV shows are not this direct, and violence is usually embedded in a larger story line. Punishment for violence may not occur until the end of the program. Motives may be mixed or unclear.

Further, it is likely that a person's age, sex, social class, and prior level of aggression influence the ultimate effect of viewing televised violence. Boys, for example, tend to be more affected by TV violence than are girls. Children who come from homes in which there are no explicit guidelines condemning violence also seem to be strongly affected. A similarity between the circumstances surrounding televised violence and the situation in which a person finds him- or herself immediately after viewing it seems to be an important factor as well. The more alike the two settings, the more aggressively the person is likely to behave.

Finally, the reactions of other people directly influence aggression. If children watch an aggressive film in the company of an adult who makes positive comments about the media violence, they act more aggressively than do children who view the aggression with a silent adult. Conversely, children who hear the on-screen aggression condemned commit fewer aggressive acts. It has also been shown that children who view violence in pairs act more aggressively than do children who are alone.

▲ Field Experiments

In field experiments people are studied in their typical environment, where they probably react more naturally than they do in the lab. Field experiments are therefore subject to the contaminating influences of outside events.

At least two field experiments done in the early 1970s revealed no link between TV and aggression. On the other hand, five field experiments have yielded data consistent with the survey and lab data. Their main conclusion is that people who watch a steady diet of violent programs tend to exhibit more antisocial or aggressive behavior.

One of the more elaborate field experiments involved a Canadian town that did not receive a TV signal until 1974. Two similar towns were selected for comparison—one could get only Canadian TV, and the other could get Canadian and U.S. channels. The research team gathered data from all three towns in 1974 and again 2 years later. Children in the town that had recently received access to U.S. TV showed an increase in their rate of aggressive acts that was more than three times higher than that of children living in the other two towns. Taken as a whole, the results from the field experiments tend to support the notion that viewing TV violence fosters aggressive behavior.

▲ What Can We Conclude?

Let us now try to summarize the results of these surveys and experiments. Although no single survey or experiment can provide a conclusive answer, and although every study has certain shortcomings, there appears to be a thread of consistency running throughout these studies. Surveys and panel studies have shown a relationship between the viewing of violent programs and aggressive behavior. Lab and field experiments also have shown that watching violence increases the possibility of behaving aggressively. Taken as a whole, these results encourage a tentative acceptance of the proposition that watching violence on television increases aggressiveness on the part of at least some viewers.

However, viewing TV violence is only one of many factors that might prompt a person to behave aggressively, and in relative terms its influence is not particularly strong. But is a weak relationship an inconsequential relationship? Much of the recent debate about TV violence has centered on this question. In statistical terms researchers gauge the strength of any relationship by the amount of variability in one measure that is accounted for by the other. For example, height and weight are two factors that are related. If I know how tall you are, I can make a better guess about your weight than if I do not know your height. I may not get your weight exactly right, but at least I will be closer to the correct figure. Consequently, height "explains" some of the variability associated with weight. If two factors are perfectly related, one explains 100 percent of the variability of the other. If two factors are not related (for example, weight and IQ), one explains 0 percent of the variability of the other. Exposure to TV violence typically explains from about 2–9 percent of the variability of aggression. In other words, about 91–98 percent of the variability in aggression is due to something else. Given these figures, can we conclude that the impact of TV violence is really that important?

The answer to that question is more political and philosophical than scientific, but research does provide some benchmarks for comparison. In psychology the relationship between undergoing psychotherapy and being "cured" of your mental ailment is only slightly stronger than that between TV violence and aggression. Further, the effect size for TV violence's impact on antisocial behavior is only slightly less than that of the effect size between viewing *Sesame Street* and readiness for school. *Sesame Street*, of course, was regarded as a great success. Lastly, the Food and Drug Administration has released for general use several drugs whose therapeutic effect is about the same as or even less than the effect of TV violence on aggression. Thus, although the effect might be small, it is not necessarily trivial.

ENCOURAGING PROSOCIAL BEHAVIOR

Most early research into the effects of mass communication dealt with the negative or anti-social effects of the media. Toward the end of the 1960s, however, sparked perhaps by the success of public television's *Sesame Street*, researchers recognized that positive behaviors could be promoted by television programs. (These behaviors are generally referred to by the umbrella term **prosocial behavior** and can include actions such as sharing, cooperating, developing self-control, and helping.)

▲ Experiments

Lab experiments have shown that films and TV programs can affect the performance of prosocial behavior, including such things as exercising self-control, cooperating, sharing, and helping. These experiments typically show a brief segment from a television program demonstrating one of these behaviors to one group of children and show a different program or no program at all to another group. After watching the segment, the children are given a chance to exercise self-control (such as by following directions from the experimenter) or to share (such as by winning money in a game and giving some to charity).

▲ Surveys

Surveys measure what TV programs children watch and how often they perform prosocial acts in real life. A wide range of prosocial behaviors have been examined, including altruism, sharing, friendliness, and peaceful conflict resolution. Some surveys ask children how often they have performed the above behaviors while others rely on parents' or teachers' reports of these actions.

▲ Research Results

Do prosocial messages actually influence day-to-day behavior? Generalizing about the results of research in this area is difficult because the term *prosocial behavior* covers so many different areas. The best summary available comes from a 2006 review published in *Media Psychology* that examined the results of 34 studies, both experiments and surveys, conducted between 1970 and 1990. The authors noted that experimental results showed a moderate short-term impact of exposure to prosocial material. Children who were exposed to prosocial programs were slightly more likely to perform prosocial acts in a laboratory setting. Interestingly, surveys that measured voluntary exposure to prosocial programs revealed a moderate positive impact, about as strong as the negative effect that resulted from viewing violent content. The one prosocial behavior that was affected the most by exposure to prosocial media content was altruism, a behavior that was simple and easy to imitate. In sum, as the authors concluded, "Television has the potential to foster positive social interactions . . . and encourage viewers to be more tolerant and helpful."

The lovable Blue from *Blue's Clues*, a program with obvious prosocial messages.

POLITICAL BEHAVIOR EFFECTS

Trying to summarize the many studies that have been conducted about the influences of the media on politics would require far more space than we have available. Consequently, we will restrict our discussion to the more central findings. At the core of our current discussion will be an examination of the individual's most important political behavior, the ultimate payoff in any political campaign—namely, voting behavior.

▲ Negative Advertising

Recent political campaigns have centered attention on negative political advertising. Although there is no standard definition of this term, most political experts interpret it as a personal attack on the opposing candidate or an attack on what the opposing candidate stands for. There was much speculation that negative advertising would turn off voters, make them

CRITICAL / CULTURAL ISSUES

The Question of Technological Determinism and the Kennedy-Nixon Debate Myth

Contributed by Paul Myron Hillier, Ph.D. candidate, University of Georgia

The first-ever televised presidential debate took place on September 26, 1960, between the youthful, "telegenic" Senator John Kennedy of Massachusetts and the makeup-free Vice President Richard Nixon. Erika Tyner Allen of the Museum of Broadcast Communications writes, "Those who heard the first debate on the radio pronounced Nixon the winner. But the 70 million who watched television saw a candidate still sickly and obviously discomforted by Kennedy's smooth delivery and charisma. Those television viewers focused on what they saw, not what they heard. Studies of the audience indicated that, among television viewers, Kennedy was perceived the winner of the first debate by a very large margin."[1]

Kennedy defeated Nixon in their first debate primarily due to the appearance of the presidential candidates and the power of televised images, the story goes. Television exposed Nixon as uncomfortable, and perhaps sinister, while Kennedy came across as articulate and sincere. And to support this argument that television made the difference—some go so far as to say changed the nature of politics itself—many scholars and commentators have suggested that the majority of the audience who listened to the debate on the radio thought Nixon "won" while those who watched the debate on TV declared Kennedy the "winner." Indeed, this claim is made so often and by so many different people that one might get the impression there's something more than anecdotal evidence to support the argument.

"One of the most perplexing legacies of the first Kennedy-Nixon debate is the claim that radio listeners and television viewers came to opposite conclusions about the debate winner," David L. Vancil and Sue D. Pendell wrote in their 1987 article, "The Myth of Viewer-Listener Disagreement in the First Kennedy-Nixon Debate."[2] Vancil and Pendell convincingly and exhaustively demonstrated that none of the empirical research done during the period supports or even reports this viewer-listener disagreement. In fact, as the authors' unpack all of the major polling organizations' surveys, they confirm that the polls "could not have shown Nixon as having 'a clear advantage' among radio listeners" because none of the organizations distinguished between the radio and television audience to begin with.

While questions of audiences' interpretations and political discourse in the age of TV are interesting and important, this myth of a viewer-listener disagreement highlights some key presumptions about the role and function of communication technologies in society. The argument that different communication technologies, like radio and television, have different "effects," and that the Kennedy-Nixon debate is a watershed moment that illustrates the social and cultural consequence of television, for good or ill, is commonplace, even logical to assume. However, it is important to recognize and emphasize that no technology operates—indeed, has no meaning—outside of cultural and social conditions. Television itself does not determine its uses or readings.

Vision is a fundamental element in the Kennedy-Nixon debate myth, but the assumption that Nixon's appearance caused people to look unfavorably upon him, that he "lost" the debate because of the way he looked, is problematic on a number of levels. Addressing this point, Vancil and Pendell sensibly note, "Appearance problems, such as Nixon's perspiring brow, *could* have had a negative impact on viewer perceptions, but it is also possible for viewers to be sympathetic to such problems, or to interpret them as evidence of attractive or desirable qualities."[3] Appearance alone does not lead one to any natural or essential conclusions. One person's "used-car salesman" can be another's "best bud." Reading a person's perspiration as evidence of a dishonest character isn't a natural reaction to a televised image but rather a socially constructed one. An important detail missing from this attention to how a person appears is context.

It is tempting to address those arguments that emphasize visual "effects" at the same level of sense. A whole set of complicating and contrary positions can be imagined. On what basis can one really claim that what we see trumps what we hear? Would this be true in every instance and in all contexts? Someone eloquently advocating criminal behavior on the radio has more of an effect on those who listen as opposed to those who see the person speaking is an obese man in a burlap sack? However, to critique television or any technology in terms of the senses is to miss the larger picture. The championing of a kind of polished image, a blue suit, a youthful complexion, certain types of gestures, and a particular body image did not happen because of *television*, but because of social and cultural goals, desires, and ends, all advanced and chosen by people. Television altered nothing *by itself*.

Forms of technological determinism show up everywhere, from academia to popular culture. They are found in rationalizations and histories of the steam engine, the cotton gin, the automobile, and the computer. Internet video, DVRs, blogs, interactive TV, and video game systems are all said to have changed or will change the world. As Raymond Williams perceived of the ways most people talk about technology, "It is either a self-acting force which creates new ways of life, or it is a self-acting force which provides materials for new ways of life. These positions are so deeply established, in modern social thought, that it is very difficult to think beyond them."[4] But think beyond them we must. Seeing communication technologies as social practices, not in terms of independent objects, effects, problems, or answers alone, is to underscore the material fact that technologies are not independent of people and context.

――――――

[1]Erika Tyner Allen, "The Kennedy-Nixon Presidential Debates, 1960," The Museum of Broadcast Communications, http://www.museum.tv/

archives/etv/K/htmlk/kennedy-nixon/kennedy-nixon.htm (17 April 2007).

[2] David L. Vancil and Sue D. Pendell, "The Myth of Viewer-Listener Disagreement in the First Kennedy-Nixon Debate," in *Central State Speech Journal,* Spring 1987, 38(1), 16–27.

[3] Vancil and Pendell, 17.

[4]Raymond Williams, *Television: Technology and Cultural Form* (London and New York: Routledge Classics, 2003), 2.

distrustful of politics, and make them less inclined to participate in the political process. Both survey and laboratory research suggested that most of these fears were unfounded. When compared with those who did not view negative ads, voters who were exposed to negative ads were just as likely to vote, were just as involved, and showed little difference in the amount of trust they placed in the political system. There was a tendency, however, for negative advertising to be related to more polarized attitudes, but this polarization did not seem to have much impact on political behavior.

More recent surveys indicate that those candidates who use a lot of negative advertising tend to receive a lower proportion of the vote. This does not necessarily mean that negative ads are ineffective; it may be that candidates who are behind in preelection polls turn to negative advertising since they have little to lose. (For a summary of the rather voluminous literature on negative advertising, read Chapter 5 in *Television: What's On, Who's Watching, and What It Means*, by George Comstock and Erica Scharrer.)

▲ Mass Media and Voter Choice

A person's decision to vote for a particular candidate is affected by not only the mass media but also many other factors, both social and psychological. Still, some tentative generalizations can be made.

It would appear that conversion (changing your vote from Republican to Democrat, for example) is unlikely to result from media exposure, because it is difficult for the media to persuade someone whose mind is already made up to change and because most people (roughly two-thirds) have already made up their minds before the campaign begins. Far more common are two effects that have a direct bearing on voter choice: reinforcement and crystallization. **Reinforcement** means the strengthening or support of existing attitudes and opinions. **Crystallization** means the sharpening and elaboration of vaguely held attitudes or predispositions. If a person approaches a campaign undecided or neutral, then crystallization is likely to occur. If the person has already made up his or her mind, then reinforcement will probably take place.

In recent national elections there has been an increase in ticket splitting (supporting one party's candidate for president and another's for governor, for example). This phenomenon may be due to crystallization, which in turn results from exposure to mass media. The flow of information during the campaign evidently crystallizes a voter's vague intention, and in many instances these new choices do not square with party loyalty. On the other hand, when partisan voters are exposed to the media, reinforcement is likely.

These findings do not necessarily mean that the media are not influential. A key factor in winning any election is to keep the party faithful loyal (reinforcement) and to persuade enough of the undecideds to vote for one side or the other (crystallization). Thus, even though widespread conversion is not usually seen, the media are still influential. Even more importantly, the media may have significant indirect influence on the electorate. By serving as important sources of political news, by structuring "political reality," and by creating an image of candidates and issues, the media may have a potent effect on a person's attitudes toward the political system. Furthermore, our discussion has been mainly concerned with the effects of the media in national elections. Local elections present a somewhat different picture. Most research evidence indicates that the media, especially local newspapers, might be highly influential in affecting voter choice in a city, county, or district election.

▲ Televised Debates

The first series of presidential debates between John Kennedy and Richard Nixon during the 1960 election prompted more than 30 different studies. Most concluded that the main effect of the debates was reinforcement, since most people had made up their minds before the debates. There was also evidence of a crystallization effect as independent voters shifted to the Kennedy camp. Although the crystallization effect was small, the 1960 election was decided by a tenth of a percentage point, suggesting that even small effects can have significant results.

The reinforcement effect was found again during the 1984 and 1988 debates. In 1996 the debates between Bill Clinton and Bob Dole seemed to have little impact on voter choice. Any effect of the debates between Al Gore and George W. Bush in the 2000 election was difficult to detect. The audience for these debates was the smallest ever due to competition from sporting events and entertainment programs. Most surveys done about the 2004 debates between Bush and John Kerry indicated that Kerry was perceived the winner in all of them. Nonetheless, Bush still won reelection, suggesting that winning a debate does not necessarily translate into winning an election.

▲ Television and the Political Behavior of Politicians

On a general level, it is clear that the emergence of television has affected the political behavior of politicians and political campaigns. A comparison of pre-TV practices with those occurring after TV's adoption reveals the following:

- Nominating conventions are now planned with television in mind. They are designed not so much to select a candidate as to make a favorable impression on the public.
- Television has increased the cost of campaigning.
- Television has become the medium around which most campaigns are organized.
- Campaign staffs now typically include one or more television consultants whose job it is to advise the candidate on his or her television image.
- The Internet has become an important channel of political communication and a new means of fund-raising. Many influential blogs are concerned with politics.

RESEARCH ABOUT THE SOCIAL EFFECTS OF THE INTERNET

For obvious reasons, research concerning the effects of spending time on the Internet is still in a formative stage. Nonetheless, we can already identify two major trends in Net studies: (1) the impact of Internet use on other media and (2) the relationship between Internet use and social involvement.

The Internet seems to have had the most impact on television usage. This is not surprising since much Internet use takes place during the evening—the same time that most TV viewing generally takes place. Magazine and newspaper reading, radio listening, and moviegoing seem not to have been significantly affected.

As mentioned in Chapter 13, the Internet is becoming more important as a source of news. At the same time, there has been a decline in the number of people who rely on broadcast TV and newspapers as their main sources of news. At the moment, online news sources are no threat to replace traditional TV and print journalism, but their form and function might be altered by online media.

Early studies that looked at the Internet and social involvement suggested that people who were heavy users of the Internet were also those who reported greater feelings of loneliness and social isolation. More recent surveys, however, have discovered just the opposite. One survey found that Internet use was related to more social involvement in the local community; another found that those who spent a great deal of time on the Internet were more politically involved and had more contacts than those who did not spend time online. Yet another found that Internet users were the ones with the most social contacts. Apparently, both the audiences and the Internet have changed over the past few years, and innovations such as instant messaging encourage greater social contact. Not all demographic groups, however, are benefiting from the expanding Internet. One 2004 study revealed that Internet use had no impact on social involvement or psychological well-being among low-income Americans.

All in all, surveys that have studied people's Internet use support the "rich get richer" model. Extroverted people are the ones who gain the most social contacts through the Internet. To them, it is just another channel to use to link up with friends. Conversely, introverted people who go online tend to shy away from social contacts.

COMMUNICATION IN THE FUTURE: THE SOCIAL IMPACT

Let us close this chapter (and this book) with an examination of some of the relevant questions about the impact of the new communications technology on society. Advances in media technology usually have an upside and a downside. The telephone, for example, made communication at a distance much more convenient. It also meant that we could be interrupted, awakened, or bothered at any hour of the day or night. Radio and television brought immediate access to information and entertainment but also encouraged the proliferation of couch potatoes. What might the future bring?

▲ Threats to Privacy

Computers have opened up threats to privacy. Some systems enable supervisors to monitor every keystroke of their employees to observe productivity. E-mail, no matter how personal, can be read by anyone with access to the system. Consumers who subscribe to computerized data services run the risk of having their personal files examined by unauthorized persons or, even worse, having their identities stolen.

Some scary examples: In 2005 Choicepoint, a firm that provides data to insurance companies, financial institutions, and the government, revealed that it had released sensitive information on 163,000 people to scammers who had signed on as bogus customers. The mistake resulted in at least 800 cases of identity theft. The next year two teens stole a laptop from the Department of Veterans Affairs that contained financial data on 25 million veterans and others still on active duty. Luckily, it appeared that the teens never accessed the data. Finally, CardSystems, an organization that handles data processing for MasterCard, admitted that online thieves had pilfered information on more than 40 million customers. Unfortunately, there are plenty of other examples.

In the past, spying on our personal habits was made difficult simply because information was scattered about in different places. Now computers store huge amounts of information about us in one centralized place, the computer's memory, that is easily accessed from anywhere over phone lines. We willingly provide much of this information when we apply for a credit card, buy a car or a house, take out insurance, file a lawsuit, claim unemployment benefits, and so on. What many consumers do not know is that much of this information is sold to other organizations for other purposes. This is one of the reasons many of us are hit with barrages of spam from organizations we have never heard of.

Computer scanning systems used at the checkout counters of supermarkets and drug and discount stores now record your every purchase. Such information is invaluable to marketers. For instance, the makers of Mylanta can offer discounts to people who regularly buy Tums to get them to switch to their product. Bumble Bee tuna can send free samples to Chicken of the Sea buyers. Although this is great for marketing purposes, it is troubling for consumers. If you are like the rest of us, there are some purchases you make that you might like to keep private. Do you want everybody to know what kind of birth control method you use?

▲ Fragmentation and Isolation

The mass media are increasingly serving the needs of more specialized audiences. Magazines, radio stations, satellite radio, cable TV networks, and broadband TV channels, with their highly targeted niche audiences, are the best examples of this trend, but the other media are moving in this direction. Technology is increasingly directing individuals toward more selective content exposure as demonstrated by the iPod, TiVo, and Facebook. If this trend continues, it might result in a generation of consumers fragmented into smaller and smaller interest groups with little in common with the rest of society. If people are overspecialized in their interests, they may run the risk of being ignorant about the rest of the world.

This phenomenon has been labeled the *cocoon effect* by sociologists. From their perspective it refers to the process whereby people surround themselves with only the political and social information that they find comforting, appealing, or acceptable. It is as though people retreat into their informational cocoon to escape some of the uncertainty of modern life and to help reduce the multitude of choices that have to be made in today's society. It seems possible that this cocooning could generalize into cultural and recreational use of knowledge as well, further increasing an individual's isolation from society.

Moreover, as telecommuting becomes more popular, more and more people will stay at home. The computer will enable people to work, bank, shop, and be entertained at home. Books, groceries, flowers, movies, meals, medicines, diapers, and deodorants can be delivered directly to a consumer's door. With worries over personal safety mounting daily, will people decide to just stay at home?

▲ Escape

The issue of escape has been around almost since the time that the mass media were invented. Many parents and educators were worried that young people would much prefer to spend time in the media world instead of the real world. Social critics have painted bleak pictures of mesmerized children attending to various forms of media: radio, movies, TV, video games, and Net surfing. In the future this concern might have more validity since the media realities that are available are becoming more and more like life outside the media. Home theaters that duplicate the theater experience are already on the market. Big-screen HDTV sets with stereo sound and interactive features are also available. Manufacturers of video games are experimenting with ways to make their displays three-dimensional. And who knows what advances will be made in the virtual reality area? What happens when it is far more fun to be in some media-generated reality than in real life? In fact, virtual reality simulations raise the question "What exactly is 'real' life anyway?" Will large numbers of us abandon socially relevant pursuits for a romp in the media world?

Will the home computer increase isolation as more people interact online and not in person?

And what happens farther down the road? In William Gibson's 1984 novel *Neuromancer*, people plug computer chips, called *stims*, directly into their brains. Stims provide experiences for all the senses and are usually preprogrammed, but there is also the possibility of becoming a *rider*, traveling through the world computer matrix (which bears an eerie resemblance to the Internet) or even shifting yourself into another person's reality and experiencing the world as the other person experiences it. Could this be the ultimate media experience? Alternate realities hardwired into the cerebral cortex? You decide.

MAIN POINTS

- Surveys and experiments are the two main quanti-tative techniques used to study the effects of mass communication.

- Media can serve as socialization forces when they are the primary sources of information about a topic and that information is presented in a consistent manner.

- Media can cultivate false perceptions of reality among some heavy users.

- TV ads directed at children can influence attitudes and perceptions about certain products.

- The media can set the priority of certain issues for the public.

- TV violence shows a small but persistent correlation with antisocial behavior among heavy viewers.

- Experiments have shown that TV can produce prosocial behavior, and some evidence of this effect has been found in surveys.

- The media are more effective in reinforcing or crystal-lizing a person's voting choice. TV has had a signifi-cant impact on the conduct of politicians and political campaigns.

- The main topics of research concerning the Internet are its effects on the usage of other media and the relation-ship between social isolation and online media use.

- Other concerns about the effects of mass communi-cations focus on the areas of privacy, isolation, and escape.

QUESTIONS FOR REVIEW

1. What are the two main methods that social scientists use to investigate media effects?

2. What gets cultivated in a cultivation analysis?

3. Summarize the catharsis versus stimulation debate. What viewpoint does research evidence favor?

4. What is the difference between the public's agenda and the media's agenda?

5. How do the media influence the voting choices of the audience?

QUESTIONS FOR CRITICAL THINKING

1. Why is it difficult to establish the effects of mass communication?

2. Young children are not the only ones who go through a socialization period. College students have to be social-ized as well. What were the main socialization agencies that prepared you to fit into college life? How important were the media?

3. How are college students portrayed on prime-time TV? Do these portrayals perpetuate any stereotypes?

4. Why has the debate over media violence gone on so long? Will scientists ever amass enough evidence to satisfy everybody? Why or why not?

5. What sorts of research projects should be developed to study the social impact of the internet?

6. Review the boxed insert on page 451, "The Question of Technological Determinism and the Kennedy-Nixon Debate Myth," and consider the following: Can you think of other forms of technological determinism that surround the Internet? The cell phone? Blogs? What does this analysis suggest about uncritical acceptance of empirical research findings?

KEY TERMS

survey (p. 434)
panel study (p. 434)
experiment (p. 434)
field experiment (p. 434)
agencies of socialization (p. 434)
cultivation analysis (p. 438)

mainstreaming (p. 440)
resonance (p. 440)
agenda-setting effect (p. 442)
framing (p. 443)
agenda building (p. 443)
catharsis theory (p. 447)

stimulation theory (p. 447)
prosocial behavior (p. 450)
reinforcement (p. 452)
crystallization (p. 452)

INTERNET RESOURCES

Online Learning Center

At the Online Learning Center home page, www.mhhe.com/dominick10, *select* Student Center *and then* Chapter 19.

1. Use the Learning Objectives, Chapter Outline, Main Points, and Time Line sections to review this chapter.

2. Test your knowledge of the chapter using the multiple choice, crossword puzzle, and flashcard features of the site.

3. Expand your knowledge of concepts and topics discussed in the chapter by going to Suggestions for Further Reading and Internet Exercises.

Surfing the Internet

In addition to Web sites, several newsgroups and listservs are useful to those interested in mass media effects. The listings that follow represent only a small sample.

www.aber.ac.uk/media/Documents/short.cultiv.html
Contains a thorough description of the history, techniques, and issues connected to cultivation analysis.

www.aejmc.net/mcs
Home page of the Mass Communication and Society division of the Association for Education in Journalism and Mass Communication. Contains a link to various news groups.

www.car.ua.edu
Site devoted to content analysis of communication messages. Contains summaries of studies of media content, some of which deal with violence and stereotyping.

http://tvnews.vanderbilt.edu
Home page of the Vanderbilt University Television News Archive. Researchers can examine abstracts of network news programs dating back to 1968.

>> Glossary

acculturation   In a media context the tendency of reporters or other media professionals to adopt the ideas and attitudes of the groups they cover or with which they have a great deal of contact.

advertising agency   A company that handles both the creative and the business side of an advertising campaign for its clients.

agencies of socialization   The various people or organizations that contribute to the socialization of an individual.

agency   An organization that handles basic needs of advertisers.

agenda building   The ways the media decide what is newsworthy.

agenda-setting effect   The influence of the mass media created by emphasizing certain topics, thus causing people to perceive those same issues as important.

alphabet   A group of letters used to symbolize each of the sounds that make up a word.

AM   Amplitude modulation of radio waves.

Apple TV   A device that streams video content from a computer to a TV set.

Arbitron   The professional research organization that measures radio audiences.

Audit Bureau of Circulations (ABC)   An organization formed by advertisers and publishers in 1914 to establish ground rules for counting circulation data.

authoritarian theory   The prevailing belief that a ruling elite should guide the intellectually inferior masses.

backpack journalist   A reporter who can prepare news stories for print, electronic, and online media.

best-seller lists   The ranking of best-selling books based on retail sales.

beware surveillance   A media function that occurs when the media inform the public of short-term, long-term, or chronic threats.

Billboard   The sound recording industry trade publication that tabulates record popularity.

block booking   A policy of major film studios that required theater owners to show several of a studio's low-quality films before they could receive the same studio's top-quality films.

blog   A personal journal kept on the Web.

broadband   Increased bandwidth for Internet connections, which speeds up downloads.

browsers   A type of software that enables individuals to search for content on the Web.

buffering   Storing video signals for video transmitted via the Internet.

business-to-business advertising   Advertising directed not at the general public but at other businesses.

campaign   In advertising a large number of ads that stress the same theme and appear over a specified length of time.

carriage fee   A fee paid by cable systems to carry a cable network.

categorical imperative   The ethical principle that people should behave as they wish all others would behave.

catharsis   A release of pent-up emotion or energy.

catharsis theory   The theory that viewing aggression will purge the viewer's aggressive feelings.

cease-and-desist order   A Federal Trade Commission order notifying an advertiser that a certain practice violates the law; failure to comply with a cease-and-desist order can result in fines being levied against the advertiser.

channels   Pathways by which a message travels from sender to receiver.

circulation   The total number of copies of a publication delivered to newsstands, vending machines, and subscribers.

clock hour   A radio format that specifies every element of the program.

commercial television   Television programs broadcast by local stations whose income is derived from selling time on their facilities to advertisers.

Communications Act of 1934   An act of Congress creating the Federal Communications Commission.

communist theory   The theory of the press that the media should promote the goals of the ruling political party.

comprehensive layout   The finished model of a print ad.

computer-assisted reporting (CAR)   Skills involved in using the Internet to aid reporting.

concept testing   A type of feedback in which a one- or two-paragraph description for a new series is presented to a sample of viewers for their reactions.

consent order   A Federal Trade Commission order in which the advertiser agrees to halt a certain advertising practice without admitting any violation of the law.

consequence The importance or weightiness of a news story.

consumer advertising Advertising directed at the general public.

controlled circulation A type of circulation in which publications are sent free or distributed to a select readership, such as airline passengers or motel guests.

convergence The blending of communication technologies, operations, or businesses.

conversational currency Topic material presented by the media that provides a common ground for social conversations.

copy The headlines and message in an ad.

corporate convergence The merging of companies with holdings in one medium with companies that have assets in other media.

creative boutique An advertising organization that specializes in the creative side of advertising.

credibility The trust that the audience holds for media that perform surveillance functions.

critical/cultural approach An analytical technique that examines power relationships in society and focuses on meanings people find in texts.

crystallization The sharpening and elaboration of a vaguely held attitude or predisposition.

cultivation analysis An area of research that examines whether television and other media encourage perceptions of reality that are more consistent with media portrayals than with actuality.

culture Common values, behaviors, attitudes, and beliefs that bind a society together.

custom magazines Free magazines published by corporations for current and prospective customers.

cycle In all-news radio, the amount of time that elapses before the program order is repeated.

decoding The activity in the communication process by which physical messages are translated into a form that has eventual meaning for the receiver.

defamation The act of harming the reputation of another by publishing false information.

demo A demonstration tape used to sell a musical performer or group.

developmental journalism A type of journalism, practiced by many less-developed countries, that stresses national goals and economic development.

developmental theory The assumption that government uses media to further national, economic, and social goals.

device convergence The tendency for functions once served by separate machines to be merged into a single device.

Digital Millennium Copyright Act Protects Internet service providers from copyright suits for simply transmitting over the Internet information provided by others.

digital technology A system that encodes information—sound, text, data, video—into a series of on and off pulses that are usually denoted as zeros and ones.

digital television (DTV) Television signals consisting of binary signals that enable improved picture quality.

digital video recorder (DVR) A device, like TiVo, that records television content on a hard disc.

digital videodisc (DVD) A disc that stores audio, movies, video, and graphics in a digital format that is compatible with DVD players and home computers.

direct action ad An ad that contains a direct response item (such as a toll-free number) that enables advertisers to see results quickly.

direct broadcast satellite (DBS) A system in which a home TV set receives a signal directly from an orbiting satellite.

disintermediation The process of delivering a product or service directly to the consumer.

distribution system The cables that deliver the signals to subscribers.

double features The practice started by theaters in the 1930s of showing two feature films on the same bill.

dummy A rough version of a magazine that is used for planning how the final version will look.

dysfunctions Consequences that are undesirable from the point of view of the welfare of society.

e-book A digital version of a book, which can be read by using a computer or a special reader.

editorial policies Guidelines the print media follow to persuade the public on certain issues or to achieve specific goals.

e-mail Electronic messages sent from computer to computer.

encoding The activity in the communication process by which thoughts and ideas from the source are translated into a form that may be perceived by the senses.

encryption Scrambling video signals so that only those with the proper decoding hardware can receive them.

Equal Opportunities rule   Part of the Communications Act of 1934; Section 315 allows bona fide candidates for public office to gain access to a broadcast medium during political campaigns.

evaluation   Research done to measure the effectiveness of an advertising or a public relations campaign.

Evernet   The successor to the Internet; an arrangement by which an individual is constantly connected to the Internet using various information devices.

experiment   A research technique that stresses controlled conditions and manipulates variables.

Fairness Doctrine   A now defunct FCC doctrine that required broadcast stations to provide various points of view on a controversial issue.

Federal Communications Commission (FCC)   A regulatory agency, composed of five individuals appointed by the president, whose responsibilities include broadcast and wire regulation.

feedback   The responses of the receiver that shape and alter subsequent messages from the source.

field experiment   An experiment that is conducted in a natural setting as opposed to a laboratory.

First Amendment   The first amendment of the Bill of Rights, stating that Congress shall make no law abridging the freedom of speech or of the press.

FM   Frequency modulation of radio waves.

focus group   A group of 10–15 people led by a moderator that discusses predetermined topics.

format   Consistent programming designed to appeal to a certain segment of the audience.

format wheel   A visual aid that helps radio programmers plan what events happen during a given time period.

formative research   Advertising research done before developing a campaign.

framing   The general way a news medium treats a topic.

franchises   Exclusive rights to operate a business in a given territory.

Freedom of Information Act (FOIA)   A law stating that every federal executive-branch agency must publish instructions on the methods a member of the public should follow to get information.

free marketplace of ideas   A press philosophy that endorses the free flow of information.

full-service agency   An ad agency that handles all phases of advertising for its clients.

functional approach   A methodology that holds that something is best understood by examining how it is used.

gag rules   Judicial orders that restrict trial participants from giving information to the media or that restrain media coverage of events that occur in court.

gatekeepers   Individuals who decide whether a given message will be distributed by a mass medium.

geosynchronous satellite   A satellite whose orbit keeps it over the same spot on Earth.

golden mean   The ethical principle that moderation is the key to virtue.

gramophone   A "talking machine" patented in 1887 by Emile Berliner that utilized a disk instead of a cylinder.

graphophone   A recording device similar to the phonograph but utilizing a wax cylinder rather than tinfoil.

hard news   Timely stories with significance for many people.

head end   The antenna and related equipment of the cable system that receives and processes distant television signals so that they can be sent to subscribers' homes.

heavy metal   A counterculture musical trend of the 1960s–1970s, characterized by a vaguely threatening style and heavy use of amplification and electronic equipment.

hegemony   The dominance of one entity over another.

Hicklin rule   A long-standing obscenity standard based on whether a book or other item contains isolated passages that might deprave or corrupt the mind of the most susceptible person.

HD Radio   Digital radio service with greatly improved quality.

HDTV   A supersharp television system that delivers about twice the resolution of traditional TV.

house drop   The section of the cable that connects the feeder cable to the subscriber's TV set.

human interest   A news value that emphasizes the emotional, bizarre, offbeat, or uplifting nature of a news story.

hyperlocal   News that concentrates on stories from a small geographic area.

hypertext   A digital navigational tool that links one electronic document to another.

ideology   A particular set of beliefs or ideas.

independents   Radio or TV stations unaffiliated with any network.

indirect action ad   An advertisement that works over the long run to build a company's image.

information gathering   A phase of a public relations campaign in which pertinent data are collected.

injunction   A court order that requires an individual to do something or to stop doing something.

instrumental surveillance   A media function that occurs when the media transmit information that is useful and helpful in everyday life.

Internet neutrality   The idea that Internet service providers cannot favor one company over another.

Internet TV   Sending video signals over the Internet.

interpersonal communication   A method of communication in which one person (or group) interacts with another person (or group) without the aid of a mechanical device.

investigative reports   News reporting that requires extraordinary efforts to gather information about matters of public importance.

jazz   A form of popular music that emerged during the Roaring Twenties and was noted for its spontaneity and disdain of convention.

jazz journalism   Journalism of the Roaring Twenties that was characterized by a lively style and a richly illustrated tabloid format.

joint-operating agreement (JOA)   An agreement, intended to preserve editorial competition, in which two newspapers merge their business and printing operations but maintain separate newsrooms.

joint venture   A method of movie financing in which several companies pool resources to finance films.

Kinetoscope   The first practical motion picture camera and viewing device, developed by William Dickson in 1889.

libel   Written defamation that tends to injure a person's reputation or good name or that diminishes the esteem, respect, or goodwill due a person.

libel per quod   Written material that becomes libelous under certain circumstances.

libel per se   Falsely written accusations (such as labeling a person a "thief" or a "swindler") that automatically constitute libel.

libertarian theory   The assumption that all human beings are rational decision makers and that governments exist to serve the individual.

limited partnership   A method of movie financing in which a number of investors put up a specified amount of money for a film.

linkage   The ability of the mass media to join different elements of society that are not directly connected by interpersonal channels.

low-power television (LPTV)   A TV station that has a small coverage area.

machine-assisted interpersonal communication   A method of communication involving one or more persons and a mechanical device (or devices) with one or more receivers.

macroanalysis   A sociological perspective that considers the functions performed by a system (such as mass media) for the entire society.

magazines   Printed publications that contain an assortment of materials that appear on a regular basis.

mainstreaming   In cultivation analysis the tendency of differences to disappear among heavy-TV-viewing people, apparently because of cultural and social factors.

management by objectives (MBO)   A management technique that sets observable, measurable goals for an organization to achieve.

marketing   Developing, pricing, distributing, and promoting an idea, a good, or a service.

mass communication   The process by which a complex organization, with the aid of one or more machines, produces and transmits public messages that are directed at large, heterogeneous, and scattered audiences.

mass media   The channels and the institutions of mass communication.

meaning   The interpretation an audience makes of text.

media buying service   An organization that specializes in buying media time to resell to advertisers.

Mediamark Research Inc. (MRI)   A company that measures magazine readership.

media vehicle   A single component of a mass medium, such as a newspaper or TV network.

message   The actual physical product in the communication process that the source encodes.

message research   Pretesting messages in an ad campaign.

microanalysis   A sociological perspective that considers the functions performed by a system (such as mass media) for the individual.

microcasting   Sending an audio or video message to a small group of interested people.

mobile journalist (mojo)   Reporters who work out of cars covering local community news.

mobile parenting   An arrangement by which parents keep track of children by using cell phones and pagers.

modem   A device that enables computers to communicate via phone lines.

Motion Picture Patents Company (MPPC)   An organization formed by the nine leading film and film equipment manufacturers in 1908 for the purpose of controlling the motion picture industry.

MPAA rating system   The G, PG, PG-13, R, NC-17 rating system for movies administered by the Motion Picture Association of America.

muckrakers   A term coined by Theodore Roosevelt to describe the reform movement undertaken by leading magazines in the 1890s to expose corrupt practices of business and government to the general public.

national advertisers   Advertisers who sell a product all across the country.

National Public Radio (NPR)   A noncommercial U.S. radio network.

network   An organization composed of interconnecting broadcasting stations that cuts costs by airing the same programs.

newsgroups   A section of the Internet devoted to message boards that are organized according to topic.

newshole   The amount of space available each day in a newspaper for news.

nickelodeons   The popular name for the many penny arcades and amusement centers that emerged around the beginning of the 20th century and specialized in recordings and film.

noise   In communication, anything that interferes with the delivery of a message.

noncommercial television   Television programs broadcast by those stations whose income is derived from sources other than the sale of advertising time.

nonduplication rule   An FCC rule passed in 1965, stating that an AM-FM combination may not duplicate its AM content on its FM channel for more than 50 percent of the time.

ombudsperson   An individual in a media organization assigned to handle complaints from audience members.

one-stops   Individuals who sell records to retail stores and jukebox operators who are not in a position to buy directly from the record company.

operating policies   Guidelines that cover the everyday problems and situations that crop up during the operation of a media organization.

operational convergence   A system used in media organizations whereby one staff produces content for two media.

paid circulation   A type of circulation in which the reader must purchase a magazine through a subscription or at a newsstand.

panel study   A research method in which data are collected from the same individuals at different points in time.

paradigm   A model used for analysis.

parasocial relationship   A situation whereby audience members develop a sense of kinship or friendship with media personalities.

pass-along audience   That portion of a magazine's total audience composed of individuals who pick up copies of a magazine while at the doctor's office, at work, while traveling, and so on.

payola   Bribes of gifts and money paid to DJs by record companies in order to gain favorable airplay for their releases.

pay-per-view (PPV)   A system that enables cable TV subscribers to pay a one-time fee to view one specific program or movie.

penny press   The mass-appeal press of the early 19th century.

persistence of vision   The quality of the human eye that enables it to retain an image for a split second after the image has disappeared.

personal digital assistants (PDAs)   Digital devices that keep track of addresses, schedules, and other useful information.

phi phenomenon   The tendency of the human perceptual system to perceive continuous motion between two stationary points of light that blink on and off; the basis for the illusion of motion in motion pictures.

phonograph   A "talking machine" developed by Thomas Edison in the late 1870s; the hand-cranked device preserved sound on a tinfoil-wrapped cylinder.

photojournalism   Journalism in which written text is secondary to photographs in news stories.

pickup   A technique of financing a motion picture.

pilot   The first episode of a projected television series.

pilot testing   A process that involves showing a sample audience an entire episode of a show and recording their reactions.

pod casting   Prerecorded programs prepared for the iPod that can be downloaded and played at the listener's convenience.

policy book   At radio and TV stations, a book that spells out philosophy and standards of operation and identifies practices that are encouraged or discouraged.

political press   Newspapers and magazines of the 1790–1820 era that specialized in publishing partisan political articles.

polysemic   Having many meanings.

Portable People Meter (PPM)   A small device carried by an individual that automatically records radio and television exposure.

portals   The first pages a person sees when opening an Internet browser.

positioning   In advertising, stressing the unique selling point of a product or service to differentiate it from the competition.

primary audience   That portion of a magazine's total audience made up of subscribers or those who buy it at the newsstand.

primary demand ad   An advertisement that promotes a specific product category, such as milk.

printing on demand   One-at-a-time printing of books that exist in a digital database.

prior restraint   An attempt by the government to censor the press by restraining it from publishing or broadcasting material.

prominence   News value that stresses the importance of the person involved in the event.

protocol   A common language accepted by computer programmers.

proximity   News value based on the location of a news event.

Public Broadcasting Act of 1967   A congressional act that established the Public Broadcasting Service.

publicity   The placing of stories in the mass media.

publics   The various audience served by public relations.

publishers   A segment of the print media industry responsible for the creation of content.

rack jobbers   Individuals who service record racks located in variety and large department stores by choosing the records to be sold in each location.

Radio Act of 1927   A congressional act establishing the Federal Radio Commission, a regulatory body that would issue broadcasting licenses and organize operating times and frequencies.

rate base   The number of buyers guaranteed by a magazine and used to compute advertising rates.

rating   The ratio of listeners to a particular radio station to all people in the market; the ratio of viewers of a particular TV program to the number of households in the market equipped with TV.

receiver   The target of the message in the communication process.

reinforcement   Support of existing attitudes and opinions by certain messages.

resonance   In cultivation analysis the situation in which a respondent's life experiences are reinforced by what is seen on TV, thus reinforcing the effect of TV content.

retail advertisers   Businesses that have customers in only one trading area.

rough layout   An early version of a print ad.

search engine   Software that enables users to search the Internet for specific information.

selective demand ad   An ad that stresses a particular brand.

self-determination   The ethical principle that human beings deserve respect for their decisions.

share of the audience   The ratio of listeners to a particular radio station to the total number of listeners in the market; the ratio of the number of households watching a particular TV program to the number of households watching TV at that time.

shield laws   Legislation that defines the rights of a reporter to protect sources.

slander   Spoken defamation; in many states, if a defamatory statement is broadcast, it is considered libel, even though technically the words are not written; libel is considered more harmful and usually carries more serious penalties than does slander.

sliding scale   An arrangement between a motion picture exhibitor and a distributor that details how much box office revenue will be kept by the movie theater.

social responsibility theory   The belief that the press has a responsibility to preserve democracy by properly informing the public and by responding to society's needs.

social utility   The media function that addresses an individual's need to affiliate with family, friends, and others in society.

socialization   The ways an individual comes to adopt the behavior and values of a group.

soft news   Features that rely on human interest for their news value.

source   A person who initiates communication.

spam The electronic equivalent of junk mail.

status conferral A process by which media attention bestows a degree of prominence on certain issues or individuals.

stimulation theory A theory that suggests viewing violence will actually stimulate an individual to behave more violently.

storyboard A series of drawings depicting the key scenes in a TV ad.

strategic planning A management technique that sets long-range, general goals.

subsidiary rights Rights given by a publisher to others, allowing them to reproduce certain content.

surveillance The news and information function of the mass media.

survey A technique of gathering data that typically uses a questionnaire.

tabloids Heavily illustrated publications usually half the size of a normal newspaper page.

tactical planning A management technique that sets short-range, specific goals.

target audience In advertising the segment of the population for whom the product or service has an appeal.

technological determinism The theory that contends technology drives historical change.

Telecommunications Act of 1996 A major revision of U.S. communication laws that affected broadcasting, cable, and telephone industries.

text The object of analysis in the critical/cultural approach.

timeliness News value that stresses when an event occurred.

time shifting Recording programs and playing them back at times other than when they are aired.

time softening Tendency of cell phone users to treat appointed times with more flexibility.

tracking studies Studies that examine how ads perform during or after a campaign.

trespass Illegal entry onto another's property.

UHF The ultra-high-frequency band of the electro-magnetic spectrum; channels 14–69 on the TV set.

underground press A type of specialized reporting that emerged in the mid-to-late 1960s, with emphasis on politically liberal news and opinion and cultural topics such as music, art, and film.

USA Patriot Act A law that gave the government increased powers of surveillance.

uses-and-gratifications model A model proposing that audience members have certain needs or drives that are satisfied by using both nonmedia and media sources.

utility The ethical principle that stresses the greatest good for the greatest number.

Variety The entertainment industry trade publication.

V-Chip A device installed in a TV set that restricts the reception of violent or objectionable material.

veil of ignorance The ethical principle that everyone should be treated equally.

VHF The very-high-frequency band of the electromagnetic spectrum; channels 2–13 on the TV set.

video on demand A system by which a cable TV system can provide movies to customers at times of the customers' choosing.

viral advertising Technique of creating messages so interesting that consumers spontaneously share them.

voice-over-Internet protocol (VoIP) Method for sending a phone call over the Internet.

voice tracking A technique in radio in which a disc jockey prerecords the voice portion of a shift that is later broadcast on several stations.

Web 2.0 The label given to the current version of Web that emphasizes interactivity and sharing.

Web page A hypertext page contained within a Web site.

Web site A set of hypertext pages linked to each other that contain information about a common topic.

WiMax Technology that allows wireless Internet access over a wide area.

wireless fidelity (WiFi) A system by which personal computers and other information devices connect to the Internet without wires.

World Wide Web (WWW) A network of information sources that uses hypertext to link one piece of information to another.

yellow journalism Sensationalized journalism, appearing during the 1890s, noted for its emphasis on sex, murder, popularized medicine, pseudoscience, self-promotion, and human-interest stories.

zoned editions Newspapers that have special sections for specific geographic areas.

>> Photo Credits

Chapter 1

p. 2, © Rick Wilking/Reuters/Corbis; p. 6, © AP/ Wide World Photos; p. 8, © Raymond Reuter/Corbis Sygma; p. 12, © Warner Bros./Courtesy Everett Collection; p. 13, Photo: ABC/Danny Feld, © ABC/ Courtesy Everett Collection; p. 23, © Karen Bleier/ AFP/Getty Images

Chapter 2

p. 26, © Frank Micelotta/American/Getty Images; p. 29, © Tony Freeman/PhotoEdit; p. 32, © AP/Wide World Photos; p. 38, © Spencer Platt/Getty Images; p. 41, © AP/Wide World Photos; p. 43, © Paramount/ Courtesy Everett Collection; p. 44, Everett Collection

Chapter 3

pp. 50, 54, © Robert Brenner/PhotoEdit; p. 56, © Brown Brotherspp. 60, 61, 62, 63, © The Granger Collection, New York; p. 67, © TLC/Courtesy Everett Collection; p. 73, © Creatas/PunchStock

Chapter 4

p. 82, © Brown Brothers; p. 83, © General Research and Reference Division. Schomberg Center for Research in Black Culture. The New York Public Library. Astor, Lenox and Tilden Foundations; p. 84, © Collection of The New York Historical Society, #54956; p. 86, © Brown Brothers; p. 96, © Cynthia Johnson/Getty Images; p. 97T, © Syracuse Newspapers/Dennis Nett/The Image Works; p. 97B, © The McGraw-Hill Companies, Inc./Erica S. Leeds, photographer; p. 103, Courtesy FMC Corporation

Chapter 5

p. 108, © Steve Granitz/WireImage/Getty Images; p. 111, © The Granger Collection, New York; p. 112T, © Timepix/Getty Images; p. 112B, © Margaret Bourke-White/Getty Images/Timepix; p. 117, © Michael Dwyer/Stock Boston; p. 121, © Mark Zemnick; p. 122, Courtesy Johnson Publishing Company, Inc.

Chapter 6

p. 130, © The McGraw-Hill Companies, Inc./Keith Eng, photographer; p. 132, © PhotoEdit; p. 133, © Eric Sander/Getty Images; p. 138, Courtesy of Carole Dominick; p. 144, © Brad Barket/Getty Images

Chapter 7

p. 148, Courtesy ibiquity Digital Corporation; p. 150, National Archives; p. 152, Stock Montage; p. 153, © Culver Pictures; p. 157, © 2003 ABC News/ABC Photography Archives; p. 158, © AP/Wide World Photos; p. 160, Courtesy Carole Dominick; p. 162, © AP/Wide World Photos; p. 164, © Scott Olson/ Getty Images

Chapter 8

p. 174, © The McGraw-Hill Companies, Inc./Keith Eng, photographer; p. 176, © Brown Brothers; p. 178T, © Nina Leer/Getty Images/Timepix; p. 178B, © Getty Images; p. 180T, © Russ Einhorn/Getty Images; p. 180B, Everett Collection; p. 181L, Everett Collection; p. 181R, © Getty Images; pp. 182, 188, © AP/Wide World Photos; p. 192, Mitch Leigh Studio, Walters/ Storyk Design Group. Photo by Robert Wolsh Designs

Chapter 9

p. 198, © AP/Wide World Photos; p. 200, © Bettmann/ Corbis; pp. 204, 205, 206, Photofest; p. 207, © J.R. Eyerman/Getty Images/Timepix; p. 211, © Warner Bros./Courtesy Everett Collection; p. 212, Photofest; p. 214, © Michele Burgess/Stock Boston; p. 216, © Sony Pictures/Courtesy Everett Collection; p. 222, © The McGraw-Hill Companies, Inc./Keith Eng, photographer

Chapter 10

p. 226, Photo: Paul Drinkwater /© NBC/Courtesy Everett Collection; p. 229T, © Bettmann/Corbis; p. 229B, Everett Collection; p. 231, © Ed Carlin/Index Stock Imagery; p. 238, ©David Frazier/The Image Works; p. 239, © Frances Roberts/Alamy; p. 244, Photo: Michael Becker/TM and Copyright © 20th Century Fox Film Corp. All rights reserved, Courtesy: Everett Collection; p. 246, © Frederick M. Brown/ Getty Images; p. 247, © AP/Wide World Photos

Chapter 11

p. 256, © Nicholas Kamm/AFP/Getty Images; p. 265, © AP/Wide World Photos

Chapter 12

p. 276, Courtesy University of Pennsylvania's School of Engineering and Applied Science

Chapter 13

p. 298, © John P. Filo/CBS/Landov; p. 300, © AP/ Wide World Photos; p. 306, © Brad Barket/Getty Images; p. 311, © AP/Wide World Photos

Chapter 14

p. 316, © John Gurzinski/The New York Times/ Redux; p. 320, © Bettmann/Corbis; p. 324, © Bob Daemmrich/The Image Works

Chapter 15

p. 334, © AP/Wide World Photos; p. 337T, Serena and Venus Williams © 1999 National Fluid Milk Processor Promotion Board; p. 337B, © Culver Pictures; p. 340, © Tony Freeman/PhotoEdit; p. 344, Courtesy Papa John's International; p. 347, © Clive Brunskill/Getty Images; p. 352, Institute of Outdoor Advertising; p. 354, Courtesy Caterpillar

Chapter 16

p. 358, © Royalty-Free/Corbis; p. 361, © 2008 by The New York Times Co. Reprinted by permission; p. 365, © Getty Images; p. 384, PAR Archive

Chapter 17

p. 388, © Royalty-Free/Corbis; p. 392, © Getty Images; p. 398, © The McGraw-Hill Companies, Inc./Erica S. Leeds, photographer; p. 400, Photo: Mitchell Haaseth/© NBC/Courtesy: Everett Collection

Chapter 18

p. 412, © Pedro Rey/AFP/Getty Images; p. 414, © The CNN Inc.; p. 419, © The Granger Collection, New York; p. 426, Courtesy Telemundo; p. 427, © Dave Saunders/Stone/Getty Images

Chapter 19

p. 432, © The McGraw-Hill Companies, Inc./Keith Eng, photographer; p. 435, © AP/Wide World Photos; p. 437, Photo: Justin Lubin/© ABC/Courtesy Everett Collection; p. 439, © 20th Century Fox Film Corp. All rights reserved./Courtesy Everett Collection; p. 441, © B.Grover/Index Stock Imagery; p. 442, © AP/Wide World Photos; p. 443, © Bettmann/Corbis; p. 445, © Edouard Berne/Getty Images/Stone; p. 448, © Albert Bandura; p. 450, © Ted Thai/Getty Images/Timepix; p. 455, © Mark Richards/PhotoEdit

» Text & Illustration Credits

P. 11: IBM Lotus Notes Screen Capture Copyright 2005. IBM Corporation. Used with permission of IBM Corporation. IBM, Lotus and Notes are trademarks of IBM Corporation, in the United States, other countries, or both.

P. 16: Screen capture used by permission of Milos Radakovich.

P. 35: Screen capture used by permission of craigslist inc.

P. 80: Star Tribune home page. Reprinted with permission of Tribune Media Services.

P. 91: Screen capture used by permission of Spokesman-Review.

P. 115: Zinio.com home page, www.zinio.com. Reprinted with permission.

P. 118, Table 5.1: © 2006 Magazine Publishers of America. Used by permission.

P. 143: Quotation from Jon Bekken, Albright College. Used by permission.

P. 195, Fig 8.4: © 2007 VNU Business Media, Inc. Used with permission from Billboard.

P. 221, Fig 9.1: "Box Office Report" from *Variety*. Copyright © 2007 by Reed Business Information. Reprinted by permission.

P. 249, Fig 10.3: Excerpt from *Nielsen Station Index, Viewers in Profile* (February 2003). Copyright 2003 by Nielsen Media Research. Reprinted with permission of Nielsen Media Research.

P. 268: Screen capture used by permission of French Maid TV.

P. 269: Screen capture used by permission of YouTube.

P. 270: Screen capture used by permission of Fergerson Funeral Home Inc.

P. 274: Screen capture used by permission of Second Life.

P. 285: Screen capture used by permission of powerlineblog.com.

P. 287: Screen capture used by permission of eCOST.com.

P. 290: Nielsen//NetRatings, screen capture of Net View Usage Metrics screen, www.netratings.com/news.jsp?section=dat_to. Copyright © 2004 by NetRatings, Inc. Reprinted with permission.

P. 330: PR Newswire, screen capture of News & Information screen, www.prnewswire.com/news (November 5, 2003). Reprinted with permission.

P. 341: Screen capture used by permission of Google Inc.

P. 346: Screen capture used by permission of Netflix.com.

P. 379: Screen capture used by permission of the Federal Communications Commission.

P. 417: Screen capture of Interfax homepage (English version), www.interfax.ru/?lang=e Reprinted by permission of Interfax News Agency.

P. 421, Fig 18.2: From "The Mass Media Role in the Western World" by Osmo A. Wiio in *Comparative Mass Media Systems* by L. John Martin and Anju Grover Chaudhary. Published by Allyn and Bacon, Boston, MA. Copyright © 1983 by Pearson Education. Reprinted by permission of the publisher.

>> Index